Polymorphous Linguistics

**Polymorphous Linguistics
Jim McCawley's Legacy**

edited by Salikoko S. Mufwene, Elaine J. Francis, and Rebecca S. Wheeler

A Bradford Book
The MIT Press
Cambridge, Massachusetts
London, England

© 2005 Massachusetts Institute of Technology

All rights reserved. No part of this book may be reproduced in any form by any electronic or mechanical means (including photocopying, recording, or information storage and retrieval) without permission in writing from the publisher.

MIT Press books may be purchased at special quantity discounts for business or sales promotional use. For information, please e-mail special_sales@mitpress.mit.edu or write to Special Sales Department, The MIT Press, 5 Cambridge Center, Cambridge, MA 02142.

This book was set in Times New Roman on 3B2 by Asco Typesetters, Hong Kong.
Printed and bound in the United States of America.

Library of Congress Cataloging-in-Publication Data

Polymorphous linguistics: Jim McCawley's legacy / edited by Salikoko S. Mufwene, Elaine J. Francis, and Rebecca S. Wheeler.
   p. cm.
"A Bradford book."
Includes bibliographical references and index.
ISBN 0-262-06245-3 (alk. paper); 0-262-56209-X (pbk.)
1. McCawley, James D. 2. Linguistics. I. Mufwene, Salikoko S. II. Francis, Elaine J., 1971– III. Wheeler, Rebecca S., 1952–
P85.M38P65   2005
410—dc22   2004059576

10 9 8 7 6 5 4 3 2 1

Contents

Acknowledgments   ix

Jim McCawley: Scholar, Teacher, Inspiration   xi
Salikoko S. Mufwene

Publications by Jim McCawley   xvii

Introduction   1

PART I
Phonology   25

Chapter 1
Sequential Voicing and Lyman's Law in Old Japanese   27 — Timothy J. Vance

PART II
Syntax   45

Chapter 2
NP Gaps in Tamil: Syntactic versus Pragmatic   47 — E. Annamalai

Chapter 3
***Vācya*, *Prayoga*, and Hindi Sentences without Grammatical Subjects**   69 — Michael C. Shapiro

Chapter 4
The Grammaticalization of Aspect in Tamil and Its Semantic Sources   83 — Harold F. Schiffman

Chapter 5
Causation and Tense in Subordinate Clauses: Conjunctive Participles and Conditionals in Bangla and Hindi   109

Tista Bagchi

Chapter 6
Independence in Subordinate Clauses: Analysis of Nonrestrictive Relative Clauses in English and Japanese   135

Etsuyo Yuasa

Chapter 7
Syntactic Mimicry as Evidence for Prototypes in Grammar   161

Elaine J. Francis

Chapter 8
Gerundive Modifiers in English and Korean   183

Geoffrey J. Huck

Chapter 9
Multiple Mechanisms Underlying Morphological Productivity   203

Yoko Sugioka

Chapter 10
How Many *Be*s Are There in English?   225

Salikoko S. Mufwene

PART III
Tense, Aspect, and Mood   247

Chapter 11
On McCawley on Tense   249

Robert I. Binnick

Chapter 12
On the Fuzzy Boundary between Tense and Aspect in Japanese   261

Wesley M. Jacobsen

Chapter 13
Counterfactuality in Burmese   283

Lynn Nichols

Chapter 14
Retrospective Mood in Korean: A Constraint-based Approach   295

Suk-Jin Chang

Contents

PART IV
Semantics and Pragmatics   327

Chapter 15
An *Un-* paper for the Unsyntactician   329   Laurence R. Horn

Chapter 16
Semantic Noun Phrase Typology   367   Donka F. Farkas

Chapter 17
The Paradox of Mass Plurals   389   Almerindo E. Ojeda

Chapter 18
Everything That Linguists Have Always Wanted to Know about Ironic Presuppositions and Implicatures but Were Ashamed to Ask   411   Katharine Beals

PART V
Knowledge of Language   431

Chapter 19
Deficits in Pronoun Interpretation: Clues to a Theory of Competence and Acquisition   433   William O'Grady

Chapter 20
Why Verb Agreement Is Not the Poster Child for Any General Formal Principle   455   Jerry L. Morgan and Georgia M. Green

Chapter 21
A Cognitively Plausible Model of Linguistic Intuition   479   Barbara J. Luka

PART VI
Encyclopedia and Language   503

Chapter 22
Language and Languages in the Eleventh *Britannica*   505   Peter T. Daniels

Abbreviations   531

Contributors   537

Index   545

Acknowledgments

Under the current pressures of academic life, a project like this could not have been completed without the support and assistance of many individuals. First, we are grateful to all the contributors who joined our efforts to produce this memorial to Jim. We would also like to thank all the colleagues listed here for their time, their interest, and the work they invested in reviewing the chapters included here or withdrawn: Barbara Abbott, Chris Barker, Tej Bhatia, Bernard Comrie, Bill Croft, Probal Dasgupta, Alex Francis, Adele Goldberg, Georgia Green, Shoko Hamano, Eric Hamp, Randy Hendrick, Ray Jackendoff, Yamuna Kachru, Chiharu Uda Kikuta, Marcia Linebarger, Brian MacWhinney, Louise McNally, Lynn Murphy, Fritz Newmeyer, Toshiyuki Ogihara, Eric Pederson, Jerry Sadock, Carson Schütze, Peter Sells, Tim Stowell, Elizabeth Traugott, Natsuko Tsujimura, Yoshio Ueno, J. Marshall Unger, Veneeta Dayal, Tom Wasow, Stephen Wechsler, and Etsuyo Yuasa. It is largely thanks to their constructive feedback that this volume can uphold the high standards of scholarship that Jim set and the intellectual eclecticism that his own work reflects.

Our thanks also go to Jerry Sadock and John Goldsmith for allocating part of the Jim McCawley Fund, in the Division of the Humanities, University of Chicago, to the completion of this project, as well as to Chris Catanzarite for her dedication and diligence in attending to the mechanical aspects of readying the manuscript for the publisher. The book itself would not have become available to our readers if MIT Press, through their supportive linguistics editor Tom Stone, had not accepted it for publication, at a time when interest in edited volumes without a strong thematic focus (other than the scholar being celebrated) has waned. Last but not least, this book owes much of its accessible prose and consistency in citation style and presentation of facts to our dedicated copyeditor Anne Mark, whose meticulous work has saved us a few editorial embarrassments.

Jim McCawley: Scholar, Teacher, Inspiration

Salikoko S. Mufwene

Jim was the Andrew MacLeish Distinguished Service Professor of Linguistics and East Asian Languages and Civilizations, at the University of Chicago, when he died—a massive heart attack having brought his life to an abrupt end on 10 April 1999.

He was born 30 March 1938, in Glasgow, Scotland, the son of James Q. McCawley, a journalist, and Monica Maud Bateman McCawley, a physician. He was almost 6 when his family immigrated to the United States and settled in Chicago in 1944. He then bore the birth name James Latrobe Quillan McCawley, "in honor of Benjamin Latrobe, a distinguished architect and engineer in the family and architect of the American White House" (Goldsmith and Sadock 1999, 257). He changed it to *James David McCawley* at the age of 21, when he became a naturalized American citizen.

Jim enrolled as an undergraduate student at the University of Chicago in 1954, earned an MS in mathematics in 1958, and came one course short of a BS in biology in 1961. He spent a year in Münster, Germany (1959–1960), where he attended classes at Westfälische Wilhelms-Universität. In the summer of 1961, he attended the Linguistic Institute (of the Linguistic Society of America) at the University of Texas. The following autumn, he enrolled in the first PhD class in linguistics at the Massachusetts Institute of Technology, where he would earn his PhD in 1965, having studied with Noam Chomsky, Morris Halle, Roman Jakobson, Edward Klima, Hu Matthews, and Paul Postal. His dissertation was titled "The Accentual System of Modern Standard Japanese" (published by Mouton in 1968 as *The Phonological Component of a Grammar of Japanese*; see "Publications by Jim McCawley" in this volume).

This biography is a revised version of Mufwene 2001. I am grateful to Eric Hamp for comments on the draft of that earlier version and to Elaine J. Francis, Larry Horn, and Haj Ross for feedback on the draft of this one. I am alone responsible for any inaccuracies it may contain.

The conditions of his hiring at the University of Chicago in 1964—namely, that he was to teach transformational syntax in addition to generative phonology—led Jim to train himself in syntax, semantics, and pragmatics. In collaboration with fellow MIT graduates George Lakoff and John Robert (Haj) Ross, he developed the Generative Semantics approach (see below), which was very influential in the late 1960s and early 1970s. Although this research program had crested by the late 1970s, its mark on Jim's own brand of syntax and semantics, which he would resist identifying by any name, was embodied in both *Everything That Linguists Have Always Wanted to Know about Logic—but Were Ashamed to Ask* (1981, revised 1993) and *The Syntactic Phenomena of English* (1988, revised 1998). Throughout his career, he distinguished himself as a leading authority in phonology, syntax, semantics, lexicology/lexicography, and other areas, such as philosophy of language and philosophy of science. He was one of the most eclectic and encyclopedic linguists of his time, and indeed of the twentieth century. He was highly regarded even among those who did not practice his brand of linguistics.

Jim argued that semantics played a significant role in determining syntactic structures. According to him, an adequate representation of meaning entails not only breaking the meanings of words into smaller semantic features but also using notions from predicate calculus and intensional logic. He used logical tools such as quantifier scope and possible-world semantics to shed light on a wide range of linguistic facts. Thus, he offered an explanation for why sentences such as *The boys did not like all the girls* and *All the girls were not liked by the boys* are not necessarily synonymous (namely, the quantifier and the negator do not have scope over the same constituents in each sentence). By the same token, he showed that it is possible to derive passive sentences from active deep structures in a transformational framework of syntax, without deriving the above pair from exactly the same deep structure. His wonderfully rich logic book continues to instruct and inspire new generations of semanticists.

When reading Jim's list of publications, one is struck by how many of his papers have been reprinted and translated into other languages, reflecting the extent of his influence on the development of generative linguistics and philosophy of language. Because he published generously, even in places where one wouldn't think to search for linguistics (e.g., *Playboy* and *Liberty* magazines) and in professional anthologies and journals with limited circulation in the West, it is a blessing for historiographers that he republished numerous essays, typically revised and/or annotated, in *Grammar and Meaning* (1973), *Adverbs, Vowels, and Other Objects of Wonder* (1979), and *Thirty Million Theories of Grammar* (1982). Most of these republished papers are classics that shaped not only his approach to syntactic analysis but also the kinds of issues addressed by linguists today: for instance, levels of representation, tests for constituent structure, coordinate structures, deep and surface structure constraints, negation and polarity, presupposition, implicature, illocution, ellipsis, and anaphora.

Jim wrote *Everything That Linguists Have Always Wanted to Know about Logic . . .* largely to liberate linguistics from a philosophical tradition that underrepresented important semantic distinctions so relevant to linguistic analysis, such as distinctions among the various universal quantifiers (e.g., *all*, *every*, *each*, *many*). On the other hand, he used to advantage some distinctions already established in logic (such as possible worlds) that shed light on linguistic representations. Perhaps to avoid the abstractness that was partly responsible for driving Generative Semantics under, Jim shifted to a practice of syntax that showed less and less of the abstract semantic structures and focused instead on many syntactic phenomena that deserve articulating (more) explicitly. He pointed out clearly what then-current approaches to syntax accounted for and what they left unexplained. *The Syntactic Phenomena of English* is the compendium of this keen flair for interesting data and outstanding perception for problematic cases and thorny issues. It is marked by an impressive sense of modesty, which clearly articulates the limits of Jim's own understanding of the facts. The same curiosity about interesting facts is evidenced in *A Linguistic Flea Circus* (first circulated in 1991), a collection of attested linguistic examples that Jim updated annually and shared with colleagues and students. Based mostly on English, but increasingly on Spanish, and drawing richly from broadcasts and journalism, it reflects his commitment to (participant) observation as a data collection technique and his reliance on natural linguistic behavior in addition to elicited data.

When he died, Jim was about to complete a book manuscript on the philosophy of science as it applies to the development of linguistics as a discipline, a subject he had taught for several years. The history of linguistics was also one of his interests, and the work of Otto Jespersen fascinated him. He published numerous discussions on Jespersen's approach to the study of language, and he wrote the introduction to a reprint of Jespersen's *Analytic Syntax* (1984) and an introduction and index for a reprint of his *Philosophy of Grammar* (1992). This fascination with Jespersen's work, especially regarding his attention to details and to perplexing and recalcitrant data, should not be surprising to those familiar with Jim's own scholarship. According to Larry Horn (pers. comm., 2004), "it might be said that Jim's standing with respect to his generation of linguists is comparable to Jespersen's within his."

Overall, Jim spoke and wrote knowledgeably about many other earlier linguists. One can only wish now that he had lived long enough to publish his own history of the development of linguistics, which would surely include comparison with the evolution of other disciplines, on which he was equally well versed. Jim's other interests included music (on which Yoko Sugioka's 1999 obituary is informative) and cuisine. He composed a piece that was performed at a concert of linguist-composers at the

1997 annual meeting of the Linguistic Society of America, held in Chicago. He published *The Eater's Guide to Chinese Characters* (1984), a glossary of characters that helps diners order meals in a more informed way than by just reading the English menu, as they reveal the authentic Chinese descriptions of the dishes. Eric Hamp (pers. comm., 2000) reminds me of his parties: St. Cecilia's Day, at which guests had to perform, sing in chorus, or turn music pages, etc.; Hangul Day, which is, according to Jim, "the only national holiday devoted just to linguistics"; and Bastille Day, which featured potluck cuisine from any country that has thrown off French rule.

Jim's career was marked by several nondegree honors and distinctions. He was invited to teach repeatedly at the institutes of the Linguistic Society of America: at the University of Illinois at Urbana-Champaign (1968), the University of Hawaii (1977), the University of New Mexico (1980), the University of Maryland (1982), Georgetown University (1985), and the University of Arizona (1989). He was scheduled to teach again at the LSA institute at the University of Illinois at Urbana-Champaign in the summer of 1999. He also taught as a visiting professor, typically during the North American summer months, at numerous other universities, including the University of Michigan (1970), the University of California at Santa Cruz (1971), the Australian National University (1973), the University of Illinois at Chicago (1978), the University of Delhi (1985), and National Tsing Hua University (in Taiwan, 1994). He was scheduled to teach at Riga (Latvia) in 1999.

Among the honors that Jim received in his academic life were membership in the American Academy of Arts and Sciences (1983–death), an honorary doctorate from the University of Göteborg (1991), the presidency of the Linguistic Society of America (1996), and two festschrifts celebrating his accomplishments: *Studies out in Left Field: Defamatory Essays Presented to James D. McCawley on the Occasion of His 33rd or 34th Birthday* (Zwicky et al. 1971) and *The Joy of Grammar* (Brentari, Larson, and MacLeod 1992). The essays included in both collections come close to representing the breadth of Jim's intellectual interests. The first volume, which is light-spirited (including titles such as "A Note on One's Privates" and "Well Donne" by pseudonymous authors, respectively P. R. N. Tic Douloureux and Forthcoming Larynx-Horn), captures the ambience of the times when generative semanticists disputed established positions on syntax and semantics. Those were also the times when Jim did not hesitate to contribute an equally formative essay on the semantics of verbs for lovemaking to *Playboy* magazine, nor, as I was reminded by Eric Hamp (pers. comm., 2000) "to include in his serious publications references or linguistic examples alluding to or naming, never with rancor or bad taste but always with wit, matters political or naughty viewed through Jim McCawley's liberated lens."

Politically, Jim was a Libertarian. Under this ticket, he ran twice or so, without success, for a position on the Board of Trustees of the University of Illinois. This

Jim McCawley

experience was in sharp contrast with his academic life, where he served on the Executive Committee of the Linguistic Society of America (1978–80) and in several capacities on the editorial boards of *Language* (1969–72, 1988–90), *Linguistic Inquiry* (1970–75), *Foundations of Language* (1974–76), *Papers in Japanese Semantics* (1972–death), *Linguistics* (1979–92), *Journal of Semantics* (1981–death), *Natural Language and Linguistic Theory* (1983–86), *Revista Argentina de linguística* (1985–death), and *Journal of East Asian Linguistics* (1991–death). His wisdom and expertise were indeed very much in demand. As busy as he was, he spared time to read voraciously, devouring contemporary publications and works in progress and commenting on many of them. According to John Lawler (2003, 616), "Jim was a very gregarious person" even in this respect; "his line was busy half the night, as he talked to people all over the world and in his local community." (Jim operated on a peculiar circadian cycle, going to bed in the early hours of the morning and waking up at midday.) He was indeed very generous in sharing his insights and knowledge on issues in linguistics and science in general. He wrote insightful reviews of many books, especially the most central and/or influential ones in the field. I remain impressed by the length—over 100 pages—of his 1975 review article on Noam Chomsky's *Studies on Semantics in Generative Grammar*.

Jim also distinguished himself by an encyclopedic knowledge of the scholarly history of several topics and could cite wide-ranging and obscure references bearing on them. Rare were the occasions when a colleague was better informed on a current topic in the field. While appreciating the diversity of approaches in syntax and semantics in particular, he did not abandon his own analytical framework but constantly adapted it with an inspiring eclecticism. He learned much from the large number of professional meetings he attended and commented accurately on the contents of presentations he had attended months or years earlier. His elephant-like memory for names of people and places was also unequaled, a capacity that helped him remember restaurant and street names all over the world, not to mention who he had been there with. Jim had a tremendous sense of detail, accuracy, and comprehensiveness, which are well reflected in his publications. Those of us who interacted on a more regular basis with him at the University of Chicago will remember how well he knew the city, being current on the place and time of most cultural events and ready to update his directory of ethnic restaurants every year. This is very impressive for a person who did not own or drive a car and typically got around either on his bicycle (even during the coldest Chicago winters) or by mass transit. Yes, those of us who attended the University of Chicago and/or had him as a colleague will remember him, among other things, not only for his preeminent academic stature, his enthusiasm for new ideas, and the warmth of his personality but also for his preferred mode of transportation and, in the 1960s and 1970s, his very interesting somewhat hippie look. I can't forget his bulging shirt pocket overfilled with a notebook and a row of pencils and pens, which he occasionally pulled out to note down something he did not want to forget from our discussions. Who would not appreciate full-time field research "at home" after working with such an inspiring teacher!

References

Brentari, Diane, Gary N. Larson, and Lynn A. MacLeod, eds. 1992. *The joy of grammar*. Amsterdam: John Benjamins.

Goldsmith, John, and Jerrold M. Sadock. 1999. James D. McCawley (1938–1999). Obituary. *Historiographica Linguistica* 26, 257–61.

Lawler, John. 2003. James D. McCawley. Obituary. *Language* 79, 614–25.

McCawley, James D. 1975. Review article on Noam Chomsky, *Studies on semantics in generative grammar*. *Studies in English Linguistics* 3, 209–311.

Mufwene, Salikoko S. 2001. James D. McCawley. In *American national biography*. New York: Oxford University Press.

Sugioka, Yoko. 1999. James D. McCawley (1938–1999). Obituary. *English Linguistics* 16, 563–67.

Zwicky, Arnold M., Peter H. Salus, Robert I. Binnick, and Anthony L. Vanek, eds. 1971. *Studies out in left field: Defamatory essays presented to James D. McCawley on the occasion of his 33rd or 34th birthday*. Amsterdam: John Benjamins. Reprinted, 1992.

Publications by Jim McCawley

Abbreviations
BLS: *Proceedings of the Berkeley Linguistics Society*
CLSN: *Papers from the Nth Regional Meeting of the Chicago Linguistic Society*
ESCOL: *Proceedings of the Eastern States Conference on Linguistics*
LACUS: *Linguistic Association of Canada and the United States*
NELS: *Proceedings of the North Eastern Linguistic Society*
UCWPL: *University of Chicago Working Papers in Linguistics*

1963a. Finnish noun morphology. In *Quarterly Progress Report 68*, 180–86. Cambridge, MA: MIT, Research Laboratory of Electronics.

1963b. Consonant mutation in Finnish. In *Quarterly Progress Report 70*, 268–73. Cambridge, MA: MIT, Research Laboratory of Electronics.

1963c. Stress and pitch in the Serbo-Croatian verb. In *Quarterly Progress Report 70*, 282–90. Cambridge, MA: MIT, Research Laboratory of Electronics.

1964. Review of *Estonian grammar* by Robert T. Harms. *Word* 19, 114–26.

1965. (with E. Wayles Browne III) Srpskohrvatski akcenat. *Zbornik za Filologiju i Lingvistiku* 8, 147–51. (English original "Serbo-Croatian accent" in *Phonology: Selected readings*, ed. by Erik Fudge, 330–35. Harmondsworth: Penguin, 1973.)

1966a. Review of *Papers of the CIC Far Eastern Language Institute*, ed. by Joseph K. Yamigiwa. *Language* 42, 170–75.

1966b. Review of *Set theory and syntactic description* by William S. Cooper. *Foundations of Language* 2, 408–10.

1967a. Edward Sapir's "Phonologic representation." *International Journal of American Linguistics* 33, 106–11. (Reprinted in McCawley 1979b, 3–9, and in *Edward Sapir: Appraisals of his life and work*, ed. by Konrad Koerner, 153–58. Amsterdam: John Benjamins, 1984.)

1967b. Meaning and the description of language. *Kotoba no Uchu* 2.9, 10–18; 2.10, 38–48; and 2.11, 51–57. (Reprinted in McCawley 1973e, 99–120, and in *Readings in the philosophy of language*, ed. by Jay F. Rosenberg and Charles Travis, 514–33. Englewood Cliffs, NJ: Prentice-Hall, 1970. German translation in *Semantik und generative Grammatik*, ed. by Ferenc Kiefer. Frankfurt: Athenäum, 1972.)

1967c. The phonological theory behind Whitney's *Sanskrit grammar*. In *Languages and areas: Studies presented to George V. Bobrinskoy*, ed. by Howard I. Aronson, 77–85. Chicago: University of Chicago, Humanities Division. (Reprinted in McCawley 1979b, 10–19.)

1967d. (Letter concerning misconceptions about transformational grammar.) *Chicago Daily News*, 13 October.

1968a. Can you count pluses and minuses before you can count? *Chicago Journal of Linguistics* 2, 51–56. (Reprinted with afterword in *The best of CLS*, ed. by Eric Schiller, Barbara Need, Douglas Varley, and William H. Eilfort, 257–61. Chicago: University of Chicago, Chicago Linguistic Society.

1968b. The accentuation of Japanese noun compounds. *Journal-Newsletter of the Association of Teachers of Japanese* 5, 1–11.

1968c. Lexical insertion in a transformational grammar without deep structure. In *CLS 4*, 71–80. Chicago: University of Chicago, Chicago Linguistic Society. (Reprinted in McCawley 1973e, 155–66. German translation in *Probleme des "Lexikons,"* ed. by Steffen Stelzer, 42–56. Frankfurt: Athenäum, 1983. Spanish translation in *Semántica y sintaxis en la lingüística transformatoria*, ed. by Victor Sánchez de Zavala, 259–75. Madrid: Alianza Editorial, 1974.)

1968d. A note on Faroese vowels. *Glossa* 2, 11–16.

1968e. Review of *English syntax: A combined tagmemic-transformational approach* by Dang Liem Nguyen. *American Anthropologist* 70, 427–28.

1968f. Concerning the base component of a transformational grammar. *Foundations of Language* 4, 243–69. (Reprinted in McCawley 1973e, 35–58.)

1968g. *The phonological component of a grammar of Japanese*. The Hague: Mouton.

1968h. The role of semantics in a grammar. In *Universals in linguistic theory*, ed. by Emmon Bach and Robert T. Harms, 124–69. New York: Holt, Rinehart and Winston. (Reprinted in McCawley 1973e, 59–98. Russian translation by Igor A. Mel'cuk in *Novoe v zarybezhnoy lingvistike 10*, 235–301. Moscow: Progress, 1981.)

1968i. Review of *Current trends in linguistics 3* ed. by Thomas Sebeok. *Language* 44, 556–93. (Reprinted in McCawley 1973e, 167–205.)

1968j. The genitive plural in Finnish. *Ural-altaische Jahrbücher* 40, 10–17.

1969. Length and voicing in Tübatulabal. In *CLS 5*, 397–405. Chicago: University of Chicago, Chicago Linguistic Society. (Reprinted in McCawley 1979b, 30–40.)

1970a. On the applicability of *vice-versa*. *Linguistic Inquiry* 1, 278–80. (Reprinted in McCawley 1973e, 237–39.)

1970b. English as a VSO language. *Language* 46, 286–99. (Reprinted in McCawley 1973e, 211–28; in *Semantic syntax*, ed. by Pieter A. M. Seuren, 74–95. Oxford: Clarendon, 1974; and in *The logic of grammar*, ed. by Donald Davidson and Gilbert Harman, 100–13. Encino, CA: Dickenson, 1975. German translation in *Generative Semantik*, ed. by Pieter A. M. Seuren, 150–74. Düsseldorf: Schwann, 1975.)

1970c. Review of *Analytic syntax* by Otto Jespersen. *Language* 46, 442–49. (Reprinted in McCawley 1973e, 229–36.)

1970d. Some tonal systems that come close to being pitch accent systems but don't quite make it. In *CLS 6*, 526–32. Chicago: University of Chicago: Chicago Linguistic Society. (Reprinted in McCawley 1979b, 41–47.)

1970e. Phonology. *Times Literary Supplement*, 23 July, 817–19.

1970f. A note on reflexives. *Journal of Philosophical Linguistics* 1.2, 6–8.

1970g. A note on tone in Tiv conjugation. *Studies in African Linguistics* 1, 123–30. (Reprinted in McCawley 1979b, 48–52.)

1970h. Where do noun phrases come from? In *Readings in English transformational grammar*, ed. by Roderick A. Jacobs and Peter S. Rosenbaum, 166–83. Waltham, MA: Ginn. (Revised version in *Semantics*, ed. by Danny D. Steinberg and Leon A. Jakobovits, 217–31. Cambridge: Cambridge University Press, 1971. Reprinted in McCawley 1973e, 133–54. Spanish translation in *semántica y sintaxis en la lingüística transformatoria*, ed. by Victor Sánchez de Zavala, 232–58, Madrid: Alianza Editorial, 1974. German translation in *Syntax und generative Grammatik*, ed. by Ferenc Kiefer and David Perlmutter, vol. 2, 129–60, Frankfurt: Athenäum, 1974.)

1970i. Semantic representation. In *Cognition: A multiple view*, ed. by Paul L. Garvin, 227–47. New York: Spartan. (Reprinted in McCawley 1973e, 240–56. Czech translation in *Studie z transformacní gramtiky*, ed. by Eva Hajicová, vol. 1, 75–89. Praha: Státní Pedagogické Nakladatelství, 1975. Korean translation in *Yŏnŏ kwahak ilan muŏs inga*, ed. by C. Lee et al., 87–111. Seoul, 1977.)

1970j. Meaningful noises. *Times Literary Supplement*, 23 July, 117–18.

1970k. *Similar in that* S. *Linguistic Inquiry* 1, 556–60.

1971a. Tense and time reference in English. In *Studies in linguistic semantics*, ed. by Charles J. Fillmore and D. Terence Langendoen, 96–113. New York: Holt, Rinehart and Winston. (Reprinted in McCawley 1973e, 257–82. Czech translation in *Studie z transformacní gramtiky*, ed. by Eva Hajicová, vol. 2, 151–65. Praha: Státní Pedagogické Nakladatelství, 1975.)

1971b. Interpretative semantics meets Frankenstein. *Foundations of Language* 7, 285–96. (Reprinted in McCawley 1973e, 333–42.)

1971c. Prelexical syntax. In *Report of the 22nd Georgetown Round Table Meeting on Languages and Linguistics*, ed. by Richard O'Brien, 19–33. Washington, DC: Georgetown University Press. (Reprinted in McCawley 1973e, 343–56; in *Semantic syntax*, ed. by Pieter A. M. Seuren, 29–42. Oxford: Clarendon, 1974. German translation in *Generative Semantik*, ed. by Pieter A. M. Seuren, 98–114. Düsseldorf: Schwann, 1975.)

1972a. A program for logic. In *Semantics of natural language*, ed. by Donald Davidson and Gilbert Harman, 498–544. Dordrecht: Reidel. (Reprinted in McCawley 1973e, 285–319. German translation in *Generative Semantik*, ed. by Werner Abraham and Robert I. Binnick, 157–212. Frankfurt: Athenäum, 1973.)

1972b. Notes on Japanese potential clauses. *Studies in Descriptive and Applied Linguistics* 5, 18–40. (Reprinted in McCawley 1973e, 357–68.)

1972d. An argument for a cycle in Japanese syntax. *Papers in Japanese Linguistics* 1, 69–73.

1972e. On interpreting the theme of this conference. In *Limiting the domain of linguistics*, ed. by David Cohen, vi–xi. Milwaukee: University of Wisconsin, Department of Linguistics. (Reprinted in McCawley 1979b, 217–22.)

1972f. McCawley-hakase o kakonde. (Transcript of question-answer session, translated into Japanese and edited by S. Saito and R. Kobayashi.) *Eigo Kyoiku* 21.8, 33–41; 21.9, 24–29.

1972g. Kac and Shibatani on the grammar of killing. In *Syntax and semantics 1*, ed. by John Kimball, 151–56. New York: Academic Press.

1972h. Translation of "Towards a family tree for accent in Japanese dialects" by Munemasa Tokugawa. *Papers in Japanese Linguistics* 1, 301–20.

1972i. The role of a system of phonological features in a theory of language. In *Phonological theory*, ed. by Valerie B. Makkai, 322–28. New York: Holt, Rinehart and Winston. (Reprinted in McCawley 1979b, 20–29. French translation in *Langages* 8, 112–23, 1973. German translation in *Phonologie und generative Grammatik*, ed. by Ferenc Kiefer, vol. 2, 73–91. Frankfurt: Athenäum, 1975.)

1972j. Japanese relative clauses. In *The Chicago which hunt: Papers from the Relative Clause Festival*, ed. by Paul M. Peranteau, Judith N. Levi, and Gloria C. Phares, 205–14. Chicago: University of Chicago, Chicago Linguistic Society.

1973a. External NPs versus annotated deep structures. *Linguistic Inquiry* 4, 221–40.

1973b. William Dwight Whitney as a syntactician. In *Issues in linguistics: Studies presented to Henry and Renée Kahane*, ed. by Braj Kachru et al., 554–68. Urbana and Chicago: University of Illinois Press. (Reprinted in McCawley 1973e, 320–32.)

1973c. Comments on papers by George Lakoff and Robin Lakoff. *Proceedings of the New York Academy of Sciences* 211, 165–71.

1973d. (Letter concerning Japanese verb morphology and pedagogical glossaries.) *Journal of the Association of Teachers of Japanese* 8.2, 64–65.

1973e. *Grammar and meaning*. Tokyo: Taishukan. Contains an annotated version of 1967b, 1968cfhi, 1970abchi, 1971abc, 1972ab, 1973b, and four previously unpublished papers: "Quantitative and qualitative comparison in English" (1965, 1–14); review of *Transformational grammar and the teaching of English* by Owen Thomas (1966, 15–34); "The annotated *respective*" (1968, 121–32); and "A note on multiple negations" (1970, 206–10).

1973f. The role of notation in generative phonology. In *The formal analysis of natural languages*, ed. by Maurice Gross, Morris Halle, and Marcel-Paul Schützenberger, 51–62. The Hague: Mouton. (Reprinted in McCawley 1979b, 204–16.)

1973g. Tone in Tonga. In *A festschrift for Morris Halle*, ed. by Stephen R. Anderson and Paul Kiparsky, 140–52. New York: Holt, Rinehart and Winston. (Reprinted in McCawley 1979b, 53–67.)

1973h. Fodor on where the action is. *The Monist* 57, 396–407. (Reprinted in McCawley 1979b, 76–83.)

1973i. Syntactic and logical arguments for semantic structures. In *Three dimensions of linguistic theory*, ed. by Osamu Fujimura, 259–376. Tokyo: TEC.

1973j. Global rules and Bangubangu tone. In *Issues in phonological theory*, ed. by Michael Kenstowicz and Charles Kisseberth, 160–68. The Hague: Mouton.

1974a. On identifying the remains of deceased clauses. *Language Research* 9.2, 73–85 (Seoul). (Reprinted in *Linguistics at the crossroads*, ed. by Adam Makkai, Valerie Becker Makkai, and Luigi Heilmann, 131–42. Lake Bluff, IL: Jupiter, 1977; in *Readings in the theory of grammar*, ed. by Diane D. Bornstein, 288–98. Cambridge, MA: Winthrop, 1976; and in McCawley 1979b, 84–95.)

1974b. Review of *The sound pattern of English* by Noam Chomsky and Morris Halle. *International Journal of American Linguistics* 40, 50–88. (Reprinted in *Essays on "The sound pattern of English*," ed. by Didier Goyvaerts and Geoffrey K. Pullum, 145–97. Ghent: Story-Scientia, 1976.)

1974c. (Interview conducted by Herman Parret.) In *Discussing linguistics*, ed. by Herman Parret, 249–77. The Hague: Mouton.

1974d. Review of *Transformational grammar as a theory of language acquisition* by Bruce L. Derwing. *Canadian Journal of Linguistics* 19, 177–88.

1974e. (Letter concerning sexism and English pronouns.) *New York Times Magazine*, 10 November, 103.

1974f. *If* and *only if*. *Linguistic Inquiry* 5, 632–35.

1975a. On what is deep about deep structures. In *Cognition and the symbolic processes*, ed. by Walter B. Weimer and David S. Palermo, 125–28. New York: Halsted Press.

1975b. Review of *Studies on semantics in generative grammar* by Noam Chomsky. *Studies in English Linguistics* 3, 209–311 (Tokyo). (Reprinted in McCawley 1982d, 10–127.)

1975c. (Letter concerning vocabulary and attitudes toward sex.) *Playboy*, June, 52.

1975d. Truth-functionality and natural deduction. In *Proceedings of the International Symposium on Multi-valued Logic*, ed. by George Epstein, 412–18. Long Beach, CA: IEEE Computer Society.

1975e. On the category status of modal auxiliary verbs. *Foundations of Language* 12, 597–601. (Reprinted in McCawley 1979b, 96–100.)

1975f. Comments on "Generative semantic methodology: A Bloomfieldian counterrevolution" by Ray Dougherty. *International Journal of Dravidian Linguistics* 4, 151–58.

1975g. Lexicography and the count-mass distinction. In *BLS 1*, 314–21. Berkeley: University of California, Berkeley Linguistics Society. (Reprinted in McCawley 1979b, 165–73.)

1975h. Verbs of bitching. In *Contemporary research in philosophical logic and linguistic semantics*, ed. by D. Hockney, W. Harper, and B. Freed, 313–32. Dordrecht: Reidel. (Reprinted in McCawley 1979b, 135–50. French translation entitled "Le téléscopage" in *Communications* 20, 1–38, 1973.)

1975i. Review of "McCawley and logic" by T. Y. Pak. *Mathematical Reviews* 50, 846.

1976a. Review of *Spatial and temporal uses of English prepositions: An essay in stratificational semantics* by David C. Bennett. *Times Literary Supplement*, 30 January, 121.

1976b. Madison Avenue, si, Pennsylvania Avenue, no! In *The Second LACUS Forum*, ed. by Peter A. Reich, 17–28. Columbia, SC: Hornbeam. (Reprinted in McCawley 1979b, 223–33.)

1976c. Morphological indeterminacy in underlying syntactic structure. In *Proceedings of the 1975 Mid-America Linguistics Conference*, ed. by Frances Ingemann, 317–26. Lawrence: University of Kansas, Department of Linguistics. (Reprinted in McCawley 1979b, 113–21.)

1976d. Some ideas not to live by. *Die neueren Sprachen* 75, 151–65. (Reprinted in McCawley 1979b, 234–46.)

1976e. Notes on Jackendoff's theory of anaphora. *Linguistic Inquiry* 7, 319–41. (Reprinted under the title "How to get an interpretive theory of anaphora to work" in McCawley 1982d, 128–58.)

1976f. Review of *Language and woman's place* by Robin Lakoff. *Reason*, August, 40–42. (Reprinted in McCawley 1979b, 174–78.)

1976g. Remarks on what can cause what. In *The grammar of causative constructions*, ed. by Masayoshi Shibatani, 117–29. Syntax and Semantics 6. New York: Academic Press. (Reprinted in McCawley 1979b, 101–12.)

1976h. (editor) *Notes from the linguistic underground.* Syntax and Semantics 7. New York: Academic Press.

1976i. Relativization. In *Japanese generative grammar*, ed. by Masayoshi Shibatani, 295–306. New York: Academic Press.

1977a. Evolutionary parallels between Montague Grammar and transformational grammar. In *NELS 7*, 219–32. Amherst: University of Massachusetts, GLSA. Reprinted in McCawley 1979b, 122–32.

1977b. (Letter concerning verbs relating to orgasm.) *Psychology Today* 10.11, 128.

1977c. Accent in Japanese. In *Studies in stress and accent*, ed. by Larry Hyman, 251–302. USC Occasional Papers in Linguistics 4. Los Angeles: University of Southern California, Department of Linguistics.

1977d. Remarks on the lexicography of performative verbs. In *Proceedings of the Texas Conference on Performatives, Presuppositions, and Implicatures*, ed. by Andy Rogers, Bob Wall, and John P. Murphy, 13–25. Arlington, VA: Center for Applied Linguistics. (Reprinted in McCawley 1979b, 151–64.)

1977e. Lexicographic notes on English quantifiers. In *CLS 13*, 372–83. Chicago: University of Chicago, Chicago Linguistic Society. (Reprinted in McCawley 1979b, 179–90.)

1977f. A use-mention fallacy. In *Book of squibs*, ed. by Samuel Ethan Fox, Woodford A. Beach, Shulamith Philosoph, and Gerald Gazdar, 71. Chicago: University of Chicago, Chicago Linguistic Society.

1977g. A propos de "Questions de sémantique" de N. Chomsky. (French translation by Michel Galmiche of excerpts from 1975b.) *Langages* 48, 50–59.

1977h. Acquisition models as models of acquisition. In *Studies in language variation: Semantics, syntax, phonology, pragmatics, social situations, ethnographic approaches*, ed. by Ralph W. Fasold and Roger W. Shuy, 51–64. Washington, DC: Georgetown University Press.

1977i. The nonexistence of syntactic categories. In *Second Annual Metatheory Conference Proceedings*, ed. by James P. Wang, 212–32. East Lansing: Michigan State University. (Substantially revised version in McCawley 1982d, 176–203.)

1977j. (Interview conducted by F. G. A. M. Aerts.) *Forum der Letteren* 18, 213–52.

1977k. Review of *Introduction to contemporary linguistic semantics* by George Dillon. *American Journal of Computational Linguistics* 14, 22–32.

1978a. Restrictive relatives and surface constituent structure. In *NELS 8*, 154–66. Amherst: University of Massachusetts, GLSA.

1978b. Conversational implicature and the lexicon. In *Pragmatics*, ed. by Peter Cole, 245–59. Syntax and Semantics 9. New York: Academic Press. (Reprinted in *Pragmatics: Critical concepts*, ed. by Asa Kasher, vol. 4, 332–46. London: Routledge, 1998.)

1978c. Relative and relative-like clauses. In *Symposium on semantic theory*, ed. by Pieter A. M. Seuren, 149–88. Grammarij 9. Nijmegen: Katholieke Universiteit.

1978d. Jakobsonian ideas in generative grammar. In *Roman Jakobson: Echoes of his scholarship*, ed. by Daniel Armstrong and C. H. van Schooneveld, 269–83. Lisse: Peter de Ridder.

1978e. Notes on Japanese clothing verbs. In *Problems in Japanese syntax and semantics*, ed. by John Hinds and Irwin Howard, 68–78. Tokyo: Kaitakusha.

1978f. Logic and the lexicon. In *Papers from the Parasession on the Lexicon*, ed. by Donka Farkas, Wesley M. Jacobsen, and Karol W. Todrys, 261–77. Chicago: University of Chicago, Chicago Linguistic Society.

1978g. What is a tone language? In *Tone: A linguistic survey*, ed. by Victoria Fromkin, 113–31. New York: Academic Press.

1978h. Foreword to *The syntax and semantics of complex nominals* by Judith N. Levi, xi–xiii. New York: Academic Press.

1978i. Where you can shove infixes. In *Syllables and segments*, ed. by Alan Bell and Joan Bybee Hooper, 213–321. Amsterdam: North Holland.

1978j. Notes on the history of accent in Japanese. In *Recent developments in historical phonology*, ed. by Jacek Fisiak, 287–307. The Hague: Mouton.

1978k. World-creating predicates. *Versus* 19–20, 79–93.

1978l. Review of *Introduction to the principles of transformational grammar* by Adrian Akmajian and Frank W. Heny. *Studies in Language* 2, 385–95.

1979a. Two notes on comparatives. In *Linguistic and literary studies presented to Archibald A. Hill*, ed. by Mohammad Ali Jazayery, Edgar C. Polomé, and Werner Winter, vol. 2, 67–72. Lisse: Peter de Ridder. (Reprinted in McCawley 1979b, 71–75.)

1979b. *Adverbs, vowels, and other objects of wonder*. Chicago: University of Chicago Press. Contains 1967ac, 1969, 1970g, 1972ei, 1973fgh, 1974a, 1975egh, 1976bcdfg, 1977ade, 1979a, and "Statement vs. rule in linguistic description" (previously unpublished); with introduction and notes.

1979c. Comments. In *Current approaches in phonological theory*, ed. by Daniel A. Dinnsen, 294–302. Bloomington: Indiana University Press.

1979d. Concerning a methodological pseudo-exorcism. *Linguistics* 17, 3–20.

1979e. Presupposition and discourse structure. In *Presupposition*, ed. by Choon-Kyu Oh and David A. Dinneen, 371–88. Syntax and Semantics 11. New York: Academic Press. (Spanish translation by Marcos Cánovas in *Textos clásicos de pragmática*, ed. by María Julio and Ricardo Muñoz, 193–214. Madrid: Arco, 1998.)

1979f. (Letter concerning Black English and elementary education.) *Chicago Tribune*, 9 August.

1979g. Creativity and personal freedom. (Review of *Liberty and language* by Geoffrey Sampson.) *Inquiry*, 10 September, 22–24.

1979h. Remarks on Cena's vowel shift experiment. In *The elements: A parasession on linguistic units and levels*, ed. by Paul R. Clyne, William F. Hanks, and Carol L. Hofbauer, 110–18. Chicago: University of Chicago, Chicago Linguistic Society.

1979i. Language universals in linguistic argumentation. *Studies in the Linguistic Sciences* 8.2, 205–19. (Reprinted in McCawley 1982d, 159–75.)

1979j. Helpful hints to the ordinary working Montague grammarian. In *Linguistics, philosophy, and Montague Grammar*, ed. by Steven Davis and Marianne Mithun, 103–25. Austin: University of Texas Press.

1980a. Tabula si, rasa no! *Behavioral and Brain Sciences* 3, 26–27.

1980b. Speaker- and addressee-based sincerity conditions. In *Alvar: A linguistically varied assortment of readings* (studies presented to Alvar Ellegård on the occasion of his 60th birthday), ed. by Jens Allwood and Magnus Ljung, 130–37. Stockholm Papers in English Language and Literature 1. Stockholm: University of Stockholm, Department of English.

1980c. Review of *Liberty and language* by Geoffrey Sampson. *Language* 56, 639–47. (Reprinted in *Noam Chomsky: Critical assessments*, ed. by Carlos P. Otero, vol. 3, 232–44. London: Routledge, 1995.)

1980d. A rejoinder to Larry Horn's comments. In *Current syntactic theories: Discussion papers from the 1979 Milwaukee Syntax Conference*, ed. by Michael B. Kac, 135–40. Bloomington: Indiana University Linguistics Club.

1980e. An un-syntax. In *Current approaches to syntax*, ed. by Edith A. Moravcsik and Jessica R. Wirth, 167–93. Syntax and Semantics 13. New York: Academic Press.

1981a. *Everything that linguists have always wanted to know about logic—but were ashamed to ask*. Chicago: University of Chicago Press, and Oxford: Blackwell.

1981b. Fuzzy logic and restricted quantifiers. In *Philosophy and grammar*, ed. by Stig Kanger and Sven Öhman, 101–18. Dordrecht: Reidel.

1981c. The syntax and semantics of English relative clauses. *Lingua* 53, 99–149.

1981d. Review of *Linguistic theory in America* by Frederick J. Newmeyer. *Linguistics* 18, 911–30.

1981e. Notes on the English present perfect. *Australian Journal of Linguistics* 1, 81–90.

1981f. Newmeyer on what happened to Generative Semantics. *Linguistics* 18, 1099–104.

1982a. Parentheticals and discontinuous constituent structure. *Linguistic Inquiry* 13, 91–106.

1982b. (Letters on miscellaneous topics.) In *What's the good word?*, by William Safire, 141–42, 148–49, 228. New York: Times Books.

1982c. How far can you trust a linguist? In *Language, mind, and brain*, ed. by Thomas W. Simon and Robert J. Scholes, 75–87. Hillsdale, NJ: Ablex.

1982d. *Thirty million theories of grammar*. London: Croom Helm, and Chicago: University of Chicago Press. Contains McCawley 1975b, 1976e, 1979i, and an expanded version of McCawley 1977i, with an introduction and added notes.

1982e. Review of *The logic of common nouns* by Anil Gupta. *Journal of Philosophy* 79, 512–17.

1982f. Comments on Bowerman's paper. *Quaderni di Semantica* 3, 71–75.

1983a. Towards plausibility in theories of language acquisition. *Communication and Cognition* 16, 169–83.

1983b. What's with *with*? *Language* 59, 271–87.

1983c. Review of *Dictionary of logic* by Witold Marciszewski. *Semiotica* 42, 279–83.

1983d. Accent. *Encyclopedia of Japan* 1, 6–8.

1983e. The syntax of some English adverbs. In *CLS 19*, 263–82. Chicago: University of Chicago, Chicago Linguistic Society.

1983f. Review of *Lingua mentalis* by Anna Wierzbicka. *Language* 59, 654–59.

1983g. Execute criminals, not rules of grammar. *Behavioral and Brain Sciences* 6, 410–11.

1984a. *The eater's guide to Chinese characters*. Chicago: University of Chicago Press. (Reprinted 2004.)

1984b. (Letters on miscellaneous topics.) In *I stand corrected*, by William Safire, 16, 109–11. 135–36, 204–5. New York: Times Books.

1984c. Review of *Grammatical theory and language acquisition* by Lydia White. *Language* 60, 431–36.

1984d. Exploitation of the cyclic principle as a research strategy in syntax. In *Sentential complementation: Proceedings of the International Conference held at UFSAL, Brussels, June, 1983*, ed. by Wim de Geest and Yvan Putseys, 165–83. Dordrecht: Foris.

1984e. Introduction to reprint of *Analytic syntax* by Otto Jespersen, xi–xix. Chicago: University of Chicago Press.

1984f. Anaphora and notions of command. In *BLS 10*, 220–32. Berkeley: University of California, Berkeley Linguistics Society.

1984g. Review of *Japanese in action*, 2nd ed., by Jack Seward. *Language* 60, 994–95.

1985a. Speech acts and Goffman's participant roles. In *ESCOL 1*, 260–74. Columbus: Ohio State University, Department of Linguistics.

1985b. Review of *The nature of syntactic representation* ed. by Pauline Jacobson and Geoffrey K. Pullum. *Australian Journal of Linguistics* 5, 85–109.

1985c. Review of *Grammatical theory* by Frederick J. Newmeyer. *Language* 61, 668–79.

1985d. What price the performative analysis? In *UCWPL 1*, 43–64. Chicago: University of Chicago, Department of Linguistics.

1985e. Review of *Linguistic categories: Auxiliaries and related puzzles* by Frank Heny and Barry Richards. *Language* 61, 849–62.

1985f. Kuhnian paradigms as systems of markedness conventions. In *Linguistics and philosophy: Essays in honor of Rulon S. Wells*, ed. by Adam Makkai and Alan K. Melby, 23–43. Amsterdam: John Benjamins.

1986a. (with Katsuhiko Momoi) The constituent structure of *-te* complements in Japanese. In *Working papers from the First SDF Workshop on Japanese Syntax*, ed. by S.-Y. Kuroda, 97–116. La Jolla: University of California at San Diego, Department of Linguistics. (Expanded version in *Papers in Japanese Linguistics* 11, 1–60, 1986.)

1986b. Actions and events despite Bertrand Russell. In *A companion to Davidson's "Essays on actions and events,"* ed. by Ernest Lepore, 177–92. Oxford: Blackwell.

1986c. Today the world, tomorrow phonology. *Phonology Yearbook* 3, 27–43. (Earlier version in *The uses of phonology*, ed. by Geoffrey S. Nathan and Margaret E. Winters, 88–102. SIU Occasional Papers in Linguistics 12. Carbondale, IL: Southern Illinois University, Coyote Press, 1984.)

1986d. What linguists might contribute to dictionary-making if they could get their act together. In *The real-world linguist*, ed. by Peter C. Bjarkman and Victor Raskin, 1–18. Norwood, NJ: Ablex.

1986e. (Transcript of question-answer session held in Trivandrum, India, freely translated into Indian English.) *Newsletter*, International School of Dravidian Linguistics.

1986f. Review of *The native speaker is dead!* by Thomas Paikeday. *Linguistics* 24, 1137–39.

1986g. Competence vs. performance. In *Encyclopedic dictionary of semiotics*, 141–42. Berlin: Mouton de Gruyter.

1986h. Syntax. In *Encyclopedic dictionary of semiotics*, 1061–71. Berlin: Mouton de Gruyter.

1987a. (Garbled version of letter.) *Psychology Today*, March, 6.

1987b. Review of *The vastness of natural languages* by D. Terence Langendoen and Paul M. Postal. *International Journal of American Linguistics* 53, 236–39. (Also in *UCWPL 3*, 177–81. Chicago: University of Chicago, Department of Linguistics.)

1987c. Some further evidence for discontinuity. In *Discontinuous constituency*, ed. by Geoffrey J. Huck and Almerindo E. Ojeda, 185–200. Syntax and Semantics 20. Orlando, FL: Academic Press.

1987d. A case of syntactic mimicry. In *Functionalism in linguistics*, ed. by René Dirven and Vilém Frid, 459–70. Amsterdam: John Benjamins.

1987e. The syntax of English echoes. In *CLS 23*, 246–58. Chicago: University of Chicago, Chicago Linguistic Society.

1987f. Review of *Nihongo: In defence of Japanese* by Roy A. Miller. *Language* 63, 904–6.

1987g. Review of *Discourse semantics* by Pieter A. M. Seuren. *Journal of Semantics* 5, 261–67.

1988a. Comments on Chomsky's "Language and problems of knowledge." In *UCWPL 4*, 148–56. Chicago: University of Chicago, Department of Linguistics.

1988b. Introduction to "Syntax and semantics" section. In *The best of CLS*, ed. by Eric Schiller, Barbara Need, Douglas Varley, and William H. Eilfort, 2–4. Chicago: University of Chicago, Chicago Linguistic Society.

1988c. Review of *Knowledge of language* by Noam Chomsky. *Language* 64, 355–65. (Reprinted in *Noam Chomsky: Critical assessments*, ed. by Carlos P. Otero, vol. 1, 463–79. London: Routledge, 1995.)

1988d. The multi-dimensionality of pragmatics. *Behavioral and Brain Sciences* 10, 723–24.

1988e. Adverbial NP's: Bare or clad in see-through garb? *Language* 64, 583–90. (Preliminary version appears in *Metropolitan Linguistics* 6, 1–13 (Tokyo), 1986.)

1988f. *The syntactic phenomena of English*. Chicago: University of Chicago Press.

1988g. (Letters on miscellaneous topics.) In *You could look it up*, by William Safire, 234, 296–98, 325–26. New York: Times Books.

1988h. The comparative conditional construction in English, German, and Mandarin Chinese. In *BLS 14*, 176–87. Berkeley: University of California, Berkeley Linguistics Society.

1989a. 1978 TINLAP comments. In *UCWPL 5*, 83–89. Chicago: University of Chicago, Department of Linguistics.

1989b. The bleen years. In *UCWPL 5*, 90–91. Chicago: University of Chicago, Department of Linguistics.

1989c. Infl!, Spec, and other fabulous beasts. *Behavioral and Brain Sciences* 11, 350–52. (Expanded version in *UCWPL 5*, 92–95. Chicago: University of Chicago, Department of Linguistics, 1989.)

1989d. Review of *Terminologie zur neueren Linguistik* by Werner Abraham. *Language* 65, 872–73.

1989e. Notes on Charles Li and Sandra Thompson's *Mandarin Chinese. Journal of the Chinese Language Teachers' Association* 24, 19–42.

1989f. On making life easier for users of Chinese-English dictionaries. *Journal of the Chinese Language Teachers' Association* 24, 105–9.

1989g. Individuation in and of syntactic structures. In *Alternative conceptions of phrase structure*, ed. by Mark R. Baltin and Anthony S. Kroch, 117–38. Chicago: University of Chicago Press. (Preliminary version in *UCWPL 3*, 151–76, Chicago: University of Chicago, Department of Linguistics, 1987.)

1990a. (Letter concerning the Sapir-Whorf hypothesis.) *Liberty* 3.5, 8.

1990b. *In, into*, and *enter*. In *Development and diversity: Linguistic variation across space and time*, ed. by Jerold A. Edmondson, Crawford Feagin, and Peter Mühlhäusler, 225–37. Arlington, TX: Summer Institute of Linguistics.

1990c. (Letters on miscellaneous topics.) In *Language maven strikes again*, by William Safire, 87–91, 141–42, 234–35. New York: Doubleday.

1990d. The dark side of reason (review of *Farewell to reason* by Paul Feyerabend). *Critical Review* 4, 277–85.

1990e. Iwakura on discontinuity. *English Linguistics* 7, 188–97.

1991a. Remarks on adverbial constituent structure. In *Interdisciplinary approaches to language: Essays in honor of S.-Y. Kuroda*, ed. by Carol Georgopoulos and Roberta Ishihara, 415–33. Dordrecht: Reidel.

1991b. Natural deduction discourse structure. In *Peter T. Geach: Philosophical encounters*, ed. by Harry A. Lewis, 151–59. Dordrecht: Kluwer. (Earlier version in *UCWPL 2*, 115–22. Chicago: University of Chicago, Department of Linguistics, 1986.)

1991c. Review of *Otto Jespersen: Facets of his life and work* by Arne Juul and Hans Nielson. *Language* 67, 117–20.

1991d. Foreword to *The great Eskimo vocabulary hoax* by Geoffrey K. Pullum, vii–x. Chicago: University of Chicago Press.

1991e. *A linguistic flea circus*. Bloomington: Indiana University Linguistics Club.

1991f. (Letters on various topics.) In *Coming to terms*, by William Safire, 77, 90, 141, 254–55. New York: Doubleday.

1991g. Patients and clients. In *UCWPL 6*, 37–38. Chicago: University of Chicago, Department of Linguistics.

1991h. *Would* and *might* in counterfactual conditional sentences. In *UCWPL 6*, 39–48. Chicago: University of Chicago, Department of Linguistics.

1991i. Negative evidence and the gratuitous leap from principles to parameters. *Behavioral and Brain Sciences* 14, 627–28.

1991j. Contrastive negation and metalinguistic negation. In *CLS 27*, vol. 2, 189–206. Chicago: University of Chicago, Chicago Linguistic Society.

1992a. Foreword to *Japanese street slang* by Peter Constantine. New York: Weatherhill.

1992b. Justifying part-of-speech distinctions in Mandarin Chinese. *Journal of Chinese Linguistics* 20, 211–46.

1992c. Linguistic aspects of musical and mathematical notation. In *The linguistics of literacy*, ed. by Pamela Downing, Susan D. Lima, and Michael Noonan, 169–90. Amsterdam: John Benjamins.

1992d. Review of *Order and constituency in Mandarin Chinese* by Y.-H. Audrey Li. *Language* 68, 596–605.

1992e. Introduction and index to reprint of *The philosophy of grammar* by Otto Jespersen, 1–9, 315–63. Chicago: University of Chicago Press.

1992f. Modifiers hosted by indefinite and interrogative pronouns. *Linguistic Inquiry 23*, 663–67.

1992g. The biological side of Otto Jespersen's linguistic thought. *Historiographia Linguistica* 19, 97–110.

1992h. The cyclic principle as a source of explanation in syntax. In *CLS 28*, vol. 2, 158–80. Chicago: University of Chicago, Chicago Linguistic Society.

1992i. A note on auxiliary verbs and language acquisition. *Journal of Linguistics* 28, 445–51.

1993a. (Letters on miscellaneous topics.) In *Quoth the maven*, by William Safire, 38, 221–22, 235, 295. New York: Random House.

1993b. 2nd edition of *Everything that linguists have always wanted to know about logic—but were ashamed to ask* (= 1981a). Chicago: University of Chicago Press.

1993c. Gapping with shared operators. In *BLS 19*, 245–53. Berkeley: University of California, Berkeley Linguistics Society.

1993d. How to achieve lexicographic virtue through judicious and selective sinning. *Dictionaries* 14, 120–29.

1993e. Introduction to reprint of *Progress in language* by Otto Jespersen, xi–xvii. Amsterdam: John Benjamins.

1993f. A Japanese and Ainu linguistic feast (review article on *The languages of Japan* by Masayoshi Shibatani). *Journal of Linguistics* 29, 469–84.

1994a. Some graphotactic constraints. In *Writing systems and cognition*, ed. by W. C. Watt, 115–27. Dordrecht: Kluwer. (Earlier version in *UCWPL 5*, 96–103. Chicago: University of Chicago, Department of Linguistics, 1989.)

1994b. Remarks on Mandarin Chinese yes-no questions. *Journal of East Asian Linguistics* 3, 179–94.

1994c. (Letters on miscellaneous topics.) In *In love with Norma Loquendi*, ed. by William Safire, 59–60, 209, 221. New York: Random House.

1994d. Linguistics as biology, as psychology, and as linguistics. In *LACUS 20*, 134–50. Linguistic Association of Canada and the United States.

1994e. The cyclic principle. In *Encyclopedia of language & linguistics*, ed. by R. E. Asher, 801–2. Oxford: Pergamon Press.

1994f. Generative Semantics. In *Encyclopedia of language & linguistics*, ed. by R. E. Asher, 1398–403. Oxford: Pergamon Press.

1995a. Otto Jespersen's 1917 monograph on negation. *Word* 46, 29–39.

1995b. Review of *Language, thought, and logic* by John M. Ellis. *Language* 71, 351–59.

1995c. Comparative and comparative-conditional clauses in Mandarin and Cantonese. In *In honor of William S.-Y. Wang: Interdisciplinary studies on language and language change*, ed. by Matthew Chen and Ovid Tzeng, 313–22. Taipei: Pyramid.

1995d. Review of *Grammatical theory in the United States from Bloomfield to Chomsky* by Peter H. Matthews. *Journal of Linguistics* 31, 444–53.

1995e. Review of *The human language* (videotape series) by Gene Searchinger. *Language* 71, 622–29.

1995f. Generative Semantics. In *Handbook of pragmatics*, ed. by Jef Verschueren, Jan-Ola Östman, and Jan Blommaert, 311–19. Philadelphia: John Benjamins.

1995g. English. In *Syntax: An international handbook of contemporary research*, ed. by Joachim Jacobs, Arnim von Stechow, Wolfgang Sternefeld, and Theo Vennemann, vol. 2, 1319–47. Berlin: Mouton de Gruyter.

1996a. Musical notation. In *The writing systems of the world*, ed. by Peter T. Daniels and William Bright, 846–54. Oxford: Oxford University Press.

1996b. An overview of "appositive" constructions in English. In *ESCOL 95*, 95–211. Ithaca, NY: Cornell University, Cornell Linguistics Circle.

1996c. Conversational scorekeeping and the interpretation of conditional sentences. In *Grammatical constructions*, ed. by Masayoshi Shibatani and Sandra Thompson, 77–101. Oxford: Oxford University Press.

1996d. Acceptability judgments in the teaching and doing of syntax. In *CLS 32*, vol. 2, 119–32. Chicago: University of Chicago, Chicago Linguistic Society.

1996e. The focus and scope of *only*. In *Discourse and meaning: Papers in honor of Eva Hajicová*, ed. by Barbara H. Partee and Petr Sgall, 171–93. Amsterdam: John Benjamins. (Earlier version in *UCWPL 2*, 101–13. Chicago: University of Chicago, Department of Linguistics.

1997a. More on Chinese parts of speech. In *Proceedings of 3rd International Symposium on Chinese Language and Linguistics*, 91–101. Taipei: Academia Sinica.

1997b. A note on Japanese passives. In *Speech production and language: In honor of Osamu Fujimura*, ed. by Shigeru Kiritani, Hajime Hirose, and Hiroya Fujisaki, 271–77. Berlin: Mouton de Gruyter.

1997c. Review of *New horizons in Chinese linguistics* by C.-T. James Huang and Y.-H. Audrey Li. *Journal of Chinese Linguistics* 25, 341–56.

1997d. (Letters on various topics.) In *Watching my language*, ed. by William Safire, 36–37, 64–65, 128–29, 211–13, 256–58. New York: Random House.

1997e. The long and short of numbers. *English Language and Linguistics* 1, 177–79.

1997f. Hangul and other writing systems. In *Proceedings of the conference on literacy and Hangul, commemorating the 600th anniversary of King Sejong's birth*, ed. by the International Association for Korean Language Education (IAKLE). Electronic publication at http://www.koreandb.net/sejong600/sejong03.htm.

1998a. 2nd edition of *The syntactic phenomena of English* (= 1988f). Chicago: University of Chicago Press.

1998b. (Letter concerning culinary vocabulary in East Asian languages.) *American Way*, March.

1998c. (Abridged version of letter concerning misrepresentation of Chinese phonology.) *Chicago Tribune*, March.

1998d. Review of *A linguist's life* by Otto Jespersen. *Language* 74, 861–63.

1999a. Review of *Dictionary of linguistics and phonetics*, 4th ed., by David Crystal. *International Journal of Lexicography* 12, 67–75.

1999b. Why surface syntactic structure reflects logical structure as much as it does, but only that much. *Language* 75, 34–62. (Jim gave a version of this article as his presidential address at the annual meeting of the Linguistic Society of America on 4 January 1997.)

1999c. Syntactic concepts and terminology in mid-20th-century American linguistics. *Historiographia Linguistica* 26, 407–20.

1999d. Participant roles, frames, and speech acts. *Linguistics and Philosophy* 22, 595–619.

1999e. Newmeyer's cyclic view of the history of generative grammar. Review article. *Journal of Linguistics* 35, 151–66.

1999f. Some interactions between tense and negation in English. In *The clause in English: In honour of Rodney Huddleston*, ed. by Peter Collins and David Lee, 177–85. Amsterdam: John Benjamins.

1999g. Unconfirmed sightings of an "ordinary language" theory of language. *Synthese* 120, 213–28.

1999h. Conversational scorekeeping and the interpretation of narrative and expository prose. *Journal of Literary Semantics* 28, 46–57.

1999i. Towards a linguistically realistic logic of conditional sentences. In *Papers from the 1997 Mid-America Linguistics Conference*, ed. by Xingzhong Li, Luis López, and Thomas Stroik, 1–13. Columbia: University of Missouri.

Introduction

This book is intended as a monument to a person the editors and contributors consider their teacher: Jim McCawley. Most of us were literally his students, having taken several courses with him at the University of Chicago and in some cases having also written a master's thesis and/or a doctoral dissertation under his supervision. Only Larry Horn may be considered a peripheral member of this category, although he rightfully considers himself a former student of Jim's, having attended his classes at an institute of the Linguistic Society of America.

Jim's legacy to linguistics in the second half of the twentieth century can undoubtedly be characterized as seminal. Rare are aspects of phonology, syntax, semantics, pragmatics, and philosophy of language where he is not (or should not be) credited for contributing to a better understanding of an interesting phenomenon. We are among those who have benefited the most from his thinking, as, through his classes, he molded us into the kinds of scholars we have become. His influence, direct and sometimes indirect, has been pervasive; each of us has heard that familiar voice reminding us of the relevance of potentially embarrassing data—especially from dialects and languages other than the object of our investigation—and of the significance of bridging our research in linguistics with research in other academic disciplines such as anthropology and psychology, or even physics and biology.

In this volume, the authors of chapters on related topics, such as syntax or time reference, do not all use the same analytical framework. Jim seems to have thought of frameworks as varying more or less like natural languages, with their respective idiosyncratic ways of packaging information and conveying particular ideas; and he believed that analysts—rather than the frameworks themselves—are to be credited for specific insights (e.g., McCawley 1977, 1979b). He was far from being dogmatic regarding what framework should be used; he believed that every scholar should use the tools he or she finds most rewarding. As editors, we thought a good way of celebrating how Jim did linguistics would be to produce a book that reflects questions that interested him about language, regardless of whether they fall in phonology (the area of his graduate training at MIT), in syntax and semantics (which he could hardly keep separate), in pragmatics, or in something that he just would have preferred not naming, and regardless of the author's analytical framework.

A book literally true to our goal of celebrating Jim's legacy would have included more diverse essays than are published here. Even if we had commissioned chapters expected to be as complementary as the pieces of a mosaic, there would have been no way for 23 contributors to cover the full range of Jim's interests in, and knowledge of, languages and his theorizing on their different structural and pragmatic aspects. There was no way of balancing the different areas, either, because in training us he never planned to produce a certain number of phonologists, a certain number of syntacticians, and so on. The chapters of this book give only a glimpse of the kinds of linguistic phenomena that he either sought or would have sought to explain. In some cases, they are clarifications or elaborations of issues he probably would have revised himself or been happy to see somebody else address. We regret that some of Jim's other language-related interests—such as logic for linguists and the philosophy of science for the purposes of linguistic historiography—are not represented here.

For convenience' sake, then, we have organized the book into six parts: **Part I: Phonology** (where Jim's career as a linguist began); **Part II: Syntax**; **Part III: Tense, Aspect, and Mood**, which we have kept separate from **Part IV: Semantics and Pragmatics** just to highlight a subarea of semantics and pragmatics in which Jim's work has been seminal beyond theoretical linguistics; **Part V: Knowledge of Language**; and **Part VI: Encyclopedia and Language**. After the abstracts had been selected and the submissions had been reviewed and revised, we simply tried to categorize what we received. Because we initially had no sense of which, or what proportion, of Jim's former students worked in a particular research area, the general call for papers specified no area preferences.

As noted above, Jim started his career as a professional linguist in phonology. He contributed to the development of generative and natural phonologies, and he worked first on Japanese before expressing interest in several other languages (see the list of his publications). **Timothy J. Vance** may be one of the last phonologists trained by Jim, at a time when Jim was more deeply invested in syntax, semantics, pragmatics, and philosophy of science, among many other things. In "Sequential Voicing and Lyman's Law in Old Japanese," Vance explores a phenomenon that fascinated him already during his graduate student days at Chicago: *rendaku*, "a Japanese morphophonemic [sequential voicing] phenomenon found in compounds and in prefix + base combinations." This is a topic that he and Jim must have discussed countless times while he wrote his dissertation, as Jim had approached it in his own dissertation but could not explain how it works. In retrospect, we can speculate that Jim's inability to account for rendaku may partly be due to a then prevalent practice in linguistics that was similar to doing Newtonian physics instead of chaos or complexity theory. That is, linguists often tried to capture significant generalizations (aimed at subsuming the broadest body of data under one rule) in a rectilinear explanation style, shying away from explanations that invoke the interactions of several small-range principles or factors. As Vance observes, "More than 30 years later, there is still no reason to doubt that rendaku is fundamentally irregular, but there are some strong tendencies in the data."

As part of his investigation of constraints on the application of rendaku, Vance conducted a dictionary search for relevant items in Old Japanese. He found that both the "strong" and "weak" versions of Lyman's Law (a process that inhibits the application of rendaku in certain contexts) hold true for Old Japanese with only a couple of exceptions in the case of the "strong" version. However, only the "weak" version holds true of modern Japanese. This is particularly puzzling, Vance argues, because there seems to be no straightforward way of modifying the "weak" version to predict the effects of the "strong" version. Thus, there is still no general account of the effects of Lyman's Law on the application of rendaku. After considering a wide range of diachronic and synchronic data, Vance concludes, "it may well be that the inhibiting effects of following voiced obstruents and preceding voiced obstruents [which constrain the application of rendaku] were separate phenomena in Old Japanese." In other words, it may be the case that the "strong" version of Lyman's Law should be split into two independent processes, only one of which has survived in modern Japanese. In the later stages of his career, Jim often provided similar kinds of explanations. To wit, he split the old Tense-Hopping rule into Attraction to Tense and Tense-Hopping, and he even went so far as to design a Tense Replacement rule that would account for the absence of tense suffixes and for the presence of *have* interpreted as past (rather than as perfect) in English nonfinite clauses (see McCawley 1988/1998).

Half the chapters in **Part II: Syntax** deal with Indic languages, in which Jim had a strong interest, as evinced by his learning Urdu. **E. Annamalai**'s "NP Gaps in Tamil: Syntactic versus Pragmatic" is a convenient starting point. It zeroes in on Jim's notion that acceptability judgments in syntax reflect speakers' sensitivity to, or awareness of, not only purely structural considerations but also semantic and pragmatic factors. One is also reminded here of his (1988/1998) discussion of anaphoric devices, in regard to which he distinguishes between identity of sense and identity of reference, as illustrated in (1).

(1) a. Alice's *car*$_i$ is bigger than Janet's $\emptyset_i$. (identity of sense)
   b. *John*$_i$ called me before *he*$_i$ went home. (identity of reference)
   c. I won't talk to *John*$_i$ until the *bastard*$_i$ apologizes to me. (identity of reference)

Annamalai's discussion of NP gaps articulates a number of structural and pragmatic constraints that govern the interpretation of this linguistic strategy in Tamil.

In particular, he suggests, the referents of NP gaps "are recovered from many sources: from the background world knowledge of the interlocutors, from the discourse context or the speech act by pragmatic rules, from the agreement marker of the finite verb predicate (in the case of a missing subject) by morphological redundancy rules, and from the syntactic context by principles of coindexing with other nouns in the sentence." Annamalai identifies two kinds of gaps: "free/open" and "closed." The closed ones tend to be interpreted differently depending on whether the antecedent is a subject or a nonsubject argument.

Matters are further complicated by the fact that gaps and pronouns (lexical anaphoric devices) are not mutually exclusive in Tamil, although they do have preferred interpretations associated with them. An important question is how to determine (1) which contexts permit a pronoun but not an NP gap, and vice versa, and (2) which contexts privilege one or the other interpretation. Different kinds of clauses seem to impose different kinds of constraints, some of which have to do with animacy-related specifications that determine what kind of item can function as the complement of what kind of predicate. Equally important is the question of how to select the antecedent of an NP gap when more than one NP can be identified as an antecedent. Annamalai concludes with the observation that "any theory about reference of a nominal gap in a sentence should account for [the] interconnection" among syntax, semantics, and pragmatics—a powerful demonstration of Jim's position that speakers' acceptability judgments are influenced by many considerations, not all of them syntactic (see also Luka, this volume).

Annamalai's chapter is well complemented by **Michael C. Shapiro**'s "*Vācya, prayoga*, and Hindi Sentences without Grammatical Subjects." These subjectless sentences have traditionally been treated as passive constructions. Those that Shapiro focuses on "hav[e] to do with agreement, transitivity, voice, and the ways they are expressed in Hindi, for which our understanding can be enhanced by utilizing insights derived from corners of the Hindi grammatical tradition not commonly visited by Western linguists." The conditions for verb agreement alone are quite complex, as such agreement need not be with the subject, and the conditions cannot be stated in a simple way. Considerations of gender also bear on this aspect of Hindi grammar. Contrary to the usual interpretation, these subjectless sentences need not correspond to passive constructions in English. According to Shapiro, "despite all of the inconsistency and internal controversy that exists in the Hindi grammatical tradition, there are areas [including this one] where the tradition offers insights into particular phenomena that have not, as a rule, been well described in other schools and traditions of grammatical investigation.... The insights of some of the best traditional Hindi grammarians can provide a perspective that in many ways is complementary to that seen in Western grammar." As the author concludes, Jim would have undoubtedly appreciated this perspective, which invokes the interaction of diverse factors bearing on well-formedness.

Introduction

No less related to Annamalai's chapter is **Harold F. Schiffman**'s "The Grammaticalization of Aspect in Tamil and Its Semantic Sources." The author observes that aspectual verbs have always posed problems for students of Indic languages, especially because of dialectal and interidiolectal variation in their interpretation. He approaches them from the point of view of grammaticalization, which enables him to consider whether the extent to which a particular item has become grammaticalized can be correlated with its variability. In his own words, "aspect is a *variable* category in Tamil, but this variability is a product of the process of *grammaticalization* (Hopper and Traugott 1993 [see also Heine 1993]), rather than representing or expressing sociolinguistic parameters."

It is not clear either that these aspectual verbs consistently mark aspect, in the sense of specifying whether an action is completed, in process, in its inception, and so on. Some of them express attitudes to the propositional content of a statement. Thus, the data raise an interesting question about the crosslinguistic application of terms such as *aspect*, *tense*, and *mood*, and whether they can be used uncritically. Schiffman argues that some metaphorical extension is involved in the way the meanings of aspectual markers have evolved from those of the basic lexical items from which they have been or are becoming grammaticalized. When the markers have fully grammaticalized, they behave like suffixes rather than like separate verbs. Part of the variability thus seems to follow from what morphosyntactic features a linguist considers significant in identifying a verb as an aspect marker and whether each of the relevant verbs exhibits enough of these features to fit in the proposed grammatical category. Different linguists have reached different conclusions. Jim's notion of prototype category (McCawley 1988/1998; also discussed in Francis, this volume) becomes relevant here; and it is refreshing to see the process of grammaticalization invoked to account for why the members do not equally fit together in the same group.

Schiffman focuses on "those elements of the meanings of lexical verbs recruited to serve as aspectual verbs that have to do with *spatial relations*—in particular, relations perceived by the speaker to express his or her personal space and/or relationship to his or her body." Among his most important observations is this: "Theories of syntax that require categorical rules, or fixed grammaticality cannot capture generalizations about aspect in these languages." Regarding the use of aspectual verbs, he also notes that "pragmatic considerations are involved in the choice of whether aspect can occur or not," suggesting that grammatical systems are not based on one particular kind of principle only.

Equally probing in this group of chapters on Indic languages is **Tista Bagchi**'s "Causation and Tense in Subordinate Clauses: Conjunctive Participles and Conditionals in Bangla and Hindi." Subscribing to Jim's practice of not discussing syntactic phenomena independently of semantic and pragmatic considerations, Bagchi sets out to demonstrate that "causation and temporal dependence play significant roles in the semantics and pragmatics" of conjunctive participles and conditionals in both Bangla and Hindi, despite the influence of unaccusativity phenomena and split ergativity on the constructions, respectively, in the two languages. There are issues that arise from an implicature and tense restrictions associated with both kinds of constructions that render a strictly semantic interpretation of the relevant sentences difficult. Following McCawley (1981/1993), Bagchi argues for a hybrid analysis that can capture "the interaction between the temporal semantics and the causative-implicative pragmatics of conditional and conjunctive participial constructions." She attempts this by drawing upon "McCawley's characterization of tense in terms of time-variable arguments ... and the logicosemantic formalism employed by Sadock (1991) for the relationship between propositions and predicate-argument combinatorics."

Bagchi's chapter thus carries on the kind of eclecticism that marked Jim's teaching, lectures, and publications over the years, as he easily incorporated in his approach to grammar insights of fellow researchers using different frameworks. Although his earliest students could still recognize the generative semanticist who shaped the later, less sectarian linguist he turned out to be by the early 1980s, his scholarship always reflected the enriching complementary influence of diverse approaches (to the extent that he would not even name his brand of syntax and semantics; see Horn, this volume).

Bagchi's combination of insights from both Jim's scholarship and the syntactic work of his colleague Jerry Sadock is not surprising. Both linguists supervised several of the same syntax students and, true to the Chicago Linguistics Department's tradition of collaborative competition and selection for younger minds, students were encouraged to cross-pollinate ideas, rather than become clones of their professors. The hybrid nature of Bagchi's chapter is also found in **Etsuyo Yuasa**'s "Independence in Subordinate Clauses: Analysis of Nonrestrictive Relative Clauses in English and Japanese." The goals of this chapter are threefold. First, Yuasa shows that beyond the arguments that Jim originally adduced in McCawley 1988/1998 to support the view that English nonrestrictive relative clauses (RC) are independent of the main clause, his position can be further supported by the distribution of certain adverbs, bound variable interpretations, and occurrence of E-type pronouns. Second, she argues that Japanese nonrestrictive RCs should also be analyzed as independent of the main clause. Third, she submits that "to explain why the properties of an independent clause occur in these seemingly subordinate constructions, ... a nonrestrictive RC should be considered an instance of mismatch in syntax and semantics." This insight, straight from Jerry Sadock's Autolexical Syntax, is incipient in chapter 10 of McCawley 1988/1998, as those who have done syntax with Jim will recognize.

Yuasa concludes that "the mixed properties of a subordinate clause and of an independent clause manifested by nonrestrictive RCs are due to the fact that nonrestrictive RCs are just like restrictive RCs in syntax, while they are independent clauses in semantics." Nonrestrictive RCs thus fall in the category of nonprototypical constructions, given the apparent incongruity between their representations in the syntactic and the semantic modules, an idea that is also consistent with the way Jim handles syntactic categories (including the clause or sentence) in chapter 7 of McCawley 1988/1998.

The lesson many of Jim's students undoubtedly learned from years of seeing him practice and improve his brand of linguistics is obvious: it is not so much the analytical framework one uses to articulate one's hypotheses that matters, but the insights the analysis sheds on the relevant data (see also Mufwene, this volume). As noted above, much as natural languages vary in the way they package information, analytical frameworks also often vary in the way they convey similar insights about linguistic facts. Analytic shortcomings often lie in the particular analyses rather than in the frameworks themselves. Jim made this point explicitly in McCawley 1977, explaining in fact why he continued to modify his Generative Semantics into an interesting blend of transformational syntax and logic but did not adopt another framework.

Hybridism in syntactic frameworks is also evident in **Elaine J. Francis**'s "Syntactic Mimicry as Evidence for Prototypes in Grammar." The author starts by observing that members of syntactic categories do not fit into them uniformly. Instead, some members display "defective grammatical behavior" compared with other, prototypical members that exhibit the full range of grammatical behavior associated with the relevant category. Heeding Jim's proposals (McCawley 1982, 1987, 1988/1998), she argues that traditional notions of syntactic categories in generative grammar cannot account adequately for the category-internal variation in grammatical behavior typical of graded membership. She therefore advocates an approach in terms of prototype categories. In discussing nouns such as *snap*, *bitch*, and *breeze* in constructions like (2a–c), she adopts Jim's (McCawley 1987, 459) notion of *syntactic mimicry*, according to which, in this case, "surface configurations that admit nouns are used to simulate syntactic constructions typical of adjectives."

(2) a. The problem was a snap/bitch/breeze to solve.
 b. **Finnegan's Wake* and *Ulysses* are a bitch of books to read.
 c. *John solved every bitch of a problem that they asked him to solve.

Adjectival nouns present some puzzling grammaticality patterns whereby sentences that appear to be both syntactically and semantically well formed are nevertheless ungrammatical (McCawley 1987, 464–65). Jim argues that (2b) and (2c) are ill formed because of the explicit way in which these nouns violate the prototypical syntax-semantics mapping (i.e., by being modifiers rather than heads). Francis argues that such data crucially support a prototype theory of syntactic categorization, whereby syntactic categories are prototypically linked to semantic categories.

Contrary to Newmeyer (1998, 2000), she argues that prototypes are significant for grammatical competence because they constitute expectations that speakers and listeners use in sentence processing. While some violations of these expectations are permissible, as in (2a), others are not, as in (2b–c). This approach, also evident in Francis 1999, is multimodular and influenced not only by the Autolexical Syntax notion of cross-modular mismatches (Sadock 1991) but also by cognitive and functional approaches to grammar (e.g., Hopper and Thompson 1984; Lakoff 1987; Croft 1991, 2001; Taylor 1995). In fact, for Francis, a purely modular approach cannot account for the intracategory variation in syntactic behavior discussed in this chapter.

Another hallmark of Jim's approach to syntax is its typological dimension. He encourages articulating an analysis in relation to various alternatives, in the sense of stating the properties of the object language in such a way that one can tell how the strategies it uses differ from those used by languages known to be typologically different. He is quite explicit about this (McCawley 1998, 39–45). For instance, he asks "whether it is possible for a language to be just like English except that the tense-bearing verb of the passive agrees with the underlying subject of the clause rather than with the surface subject" (p. 40). **Geoffrey J. Huck**'s "Gerundive Modifiers in English and Korean" squares clearly with this typological orientation, especially if the reader starts by asking whether, in the first place, Korean has a gerund and how it is marked. Huck's study is intended to show that gerundive modifiers in both English and Korean "form a subtype of the general type of relative modifiers" (similar to adjectives such as *former*, *alleged*, and *near*). He argues that "gerundives in the two languages should be assigned essentially the same semantic structure [and] there is also good reason to assume that this structure is not homomorphic in either language with the syntactic structure with which it is paired." In English, the gerundive is nominal, even though its suffix is homophonous with the participial *-ing*; but it is understood as a deverbal nominal and combines with a head that denotes an instrument, a locative, or a patient. The gerundive can be paraphrased to specify the purpose of the head noun. Huck observes distributional differences between these constructions:

(3) a. car for everyday driving
　　b. ?car for driving
　　c. #driving car (with the meaning of (3a))

He argues that "the source of the deviance [of (3c)] cannot be purely structural," nor is it "a consequence of universal pragmatic or semantic conditions," because the acceptability pattern of the Korean translations does not parallel that of the English constructions.

(4) a. wuncenha-nun cha (lit., 'driving car')
　　b. #ilk-nun ankyeng ('reading glasses')

Introduction 9

As a matter of fact, regarding contrastive focus, Korean gerundives differ from their English counterparts: they "are not inherently loci of contrast and in this respect resemble English infinitival relatives." The situation is complicated by the fact that a Korean clause can have null arguments, so that the gerundive constructions are sometimes indistinguishable from relative clauses with null arguments. And there are still more facts to consider—for example, that English is a prepositional language whereas Korean is postpositional—which lead Huck to the conclusion that "a gerundive modifier is interpreted semantically as containing a variable that is coindexed with the nominal head that it modifies and that [in syntax] language-particular restrictions on this relationship apply." The evidence seems to favor a multimodular approach—again consistent with the way Jim did his syntax, allowing for semantic and pragmatic considerations to bear on acceptability judgments.

Somewhat related to issues arising from Huck's chapter is **Yoko Sugioka**'s "Multiple Mechanisms Underlying Morphological Productivity." A central question in Sugioka's chapter is whether the most productive strategies in word formation produce the most frequent words. In other words, is the frequency of complex forms a function of the productivity of the structural strategies that produced them? Related to this is the question of why words inflected by less frequent strategies, such as suppletion, have not been replaced by those inflected by more regular strategies or produced by more productive word formation strategies.

The topic is quite reminiscent of transderivational constraints over lexicalization of semantic materials in Generative Semantics (Lakoff 1970). Jim invokes conversational implicatures to account for something similar, namely, why '*causing* something *to die*' does not mean the same thing as '*killing* it', or why *pink* does not have the same meaning as *pale red*, the phrase some dictionaries use to define it (McCawley 1977). Approaches have changed but the data still seem to cry out for adequate explanation.

Comparing English and Japanese data, Sugioka distinguishes between rule- and analogy-based formations. Anticipating partly O'Grady's chapter in this volume, she correlates this research question with whether memory-based knowledge can be clearly distinguished from rule-based knowledge. A case in point is irregular past tense and past participle inflections in English: what does a linguist make of the partial verb patterns (e.g., *ring~rang~rung* and *sink~sank~sunk*) and mistakes that speakers commonly make (e.g., *bring~*brang~*brung*, especially in nonstandard dialects)? Sugioka argues that associative memory can be the basis for analogical formations, which suggests that irregular forms are not completely unproductive, especially where suppletive forms are involved.

Another relevant question is whether the coexistence of regular and irregular devices is limited to inflection or also applies to derivation. Sugioka argues that both aspects of morphology provide interesting data that bear on her research questions. Even compounding is subject to the competition between rule- and analogy-based word formation patterns. Sugioka concludes that "multiple mechanisms underlie productivity in word formation."

The last contribution in part II is **Salikoko S. Mufwene**'s "How Many *Be*s Are There in English?" In this revisionist chapter, Mufwene adopts some of Jim's own arguments not to represent the copula in deep structure but to insert it transformationally during the derivation of a sentence (McCawley 1988/1998, chaps. 5–7). He then adduces other evidence involving the absence of *be* from constructions like those in (5) that would require it in finite sentences. On this basis, he argues that all instances of *be* (in progressive, passive, modal, and existential constructions) are copular.

(5) a. Bush Heading for the Middle East (headline or picture caption)
    b. Prince Driven Out of Power (headline or picture caption)
    c. John $\emptyset$ to be with Mary here. (relevant *be* represented by $\emptyset$)
    d. We heard kids (*be) singing louder/more than adults.

Endorsing Dik's (1983) position that the copula is a semantically empty morpheme that is for all intents and purposes an auxiliary verb, Mufwene argues that the position also makes it easier to account for the variable absence of *be* from finite clauses in African-American English. It likewise facilitates accounting for the omission of *be* from certain syntactic environments in some English creoles. For Mufwene, all this follows from the fact that the copula is a semantically empty verb, which in Jim's approach to syntax need not be represented in the deep structure. Typologically, Mufwene distinguishes between V'-oriented languages, which require that every predicate phrase be headed by a V in the surface structure, and PredP-oriented languages, which do not have this requirement. The former category includes most Indo-European languages and the latter Mandarin Chinese and the Kwa languages of West Africa, though the specifics of the environments that allow this orientation do vary. The proposed analysis is made possible by the fact that Jim's syntax accommodates some of the mismatch phenomena by allowing, in the deep structure predicate position, the syntactic category O'—for constituents of unspecified parts of speech—which eventually converts to A' or P' in the surface structure, depending on how semantic information is normally lexicalized in the relevant language. One must perhaps assume that V is the default surface structure category for Predicate. The implications of this innovation in grammatical theory are yet to be explored.

The chapters in **Part III: Tense, Aspect, and Mood** reflect no less of Jim's influence. **Robert I. Binnick**'s "On McCawley on Tense" explores how (far) the theory of tense in formal linguistics would have evolved if McCawley 1971 had been better understood, at least as well as Partee 1973. Binnick compares the two approaches, highlighting their strengths and shortcomings, and favors Jim's on the following counts:

it is able to capture the relational nature of tense and to motivate the treatment of tenses as bound variables essentially by recognizing the reference point and the role of context and by allowing extrasentential antecedents. Partee's failure to recognize the role of the reference point, her approach's identification of deicticity with the lack of an intrasentential antecedent, and its inability to capture the inherently relational nature of tense lay in her purely pragmatic distinction between "temporal deixis and temporal anaphoresis" open to reinterpretations. Her analysis eventually produced artifacts such as the paradox that some tenses are at once anaphoric and deictic (although these seem to have been attended to in Partee 1984).

Jim sought instead "to reconcile the apparent compositionality of verbal expressions, in which auxiliary verbs apparently take verbal complements, with the unitary interpretation of verbal complexes implied by Reichenbach's [(1947)] theory." He also wished "to account for the multitudinous interpretations of the present perfect verbal complex [in English]." He later did this by embedding PAST in the PRESENT and producing the surface structure auxiliary verb *have* by invoking Tense Replacement, a transformation that changes PAST to *have* in nonfinite clauses (McCawley 1988/1998). The proof for this was adduced from the following pair of sentences, in which the past tense and the present perfect have the same meaning of PAST:

(6) a. I believe that John *came*.
  b. I believe John to *have come*.

The explanatory power of Jim's approach can also be tested typologically against data from languages other than English. **Wesley M. Jacobsen**'s "On the Fuzzy Boundary between Tense and Aspect in Japanese" represents precisely such a test. Starting his discussion with a footnote of Jim's (McCawley 1993, 595), he addresses two central questions: (1) Is it true that Japanese has no tense? (2) Are tenses so clearly distinct from aspects? He focuses on "several temporal phenomena in Japanese that appear to involve both tense and aspect in an attempt to better understand how these two realms of meaning are interconnected and whether they should in fact be treated as ultimately distinct from one another." He argues that, in the case of Japanese at least, there is a "latent presence of tense relationships in the very notion of aspectual structure, and vice versa," a view consistent with Jim's philosophy of two-tense deep structure representation for English "present perfect" or "past perfect."

What complicates things in the case of Japanese, which has also been claimed to have relative tenses, is that the tense markers RU and TA appear to have different temporal interpretations depending on the particular kinds of clauses they are used in. Jacobsen derives some of his best support for Jim's analysis of the "perfect" tense from Japanese stative constructions with RU and TA, which he considers strictly "eventive," in the sense of denoting current states resulting from past events or "situations that occur over an interval of time extending from a point of time in the past up to and (crucially) including the time of speech."

Jacobsen also argues that whether time reference markers are treated as tense or aspect morphemes is a matter of how their semantic components are weighted relative to each other. In the case of RU and TA in Japanese, he argues against the received doctrine that they have tenselike, rather than aspectlike, functions, whereas TE-I(ru) should be analyzed just the other way around. He also submits that an analysis that associates surface temporal expressions with combinations of underlying tenses and/or aspects accounts more adequately for Vendler's (1957) notions of accomplishment and achievement, which, we believe, fall out from what Binnick (this volume) characterizes as Jim's compositional analysis of tenses.

In "Counterfactuality in Burmese," **Lynn Nichols** focuses on "the semantic contribution of counterfactual morphology [to] show that the morphology supplies the missing piece; that is, it is the morphology that ultimately contributes the ordering component to counterfactual interpretation." What makes Burmese an interesting case, compared with English, is that its marker of counterfactuality conveys an attitude evaluation of distance, "indicating that some proposition P is true in some world or set of worlds that is far from the actual world." Nichols distinguishes between *normal context* (the real world) and *modal context*, and she also examines two factors invoked by Kratzer (1981) as bearing on the interpretation of the latter: a *modal base*, a "selection function picking out kinds of sets of worlds," and an *ordering source*, which orders the worlds "with respect to how closely they reflect the state of affairs in some world/set of worlds selected as the ideal case or basis of comparison." She argues that they do not play a role in the interpretation of counterfactuals.

On the other hand, at least from the point of view of grammaticalization, it appears that the attitudinal meaning of the Burmese counterfactual marker *khé* is related to the meaning it has in indicative and imperative clauses for temporal and/or geographical distance. She observes that the counterfactual interpretation of a clause "arises from the speaker's assertion that P is true only in a world distant from the actual world." For her, "Burmese counterfactual *khé* evaluates distance with respect to some *context* even in the indicative domain (to convey PAST)." From a typological point of view, Nichols argues that the particular morpheme(s) that a language uses to express counterfactuality depend(s) largely on the basic semantic resources it can draw from, and "an attitude evaluation of distance is simply one strategy." As pointed out by Schiffman (this volume), one can also approach this issue from the point of view of grammaticalization.

The other chapter of related interest is **Suk-Jin Chang**'s "Retrospective Mood in Korean: A Constraint-based Approach." The "retrospective mood" denotes the speaker's recollection of his or her past cognition of a state of affairs. Chang attempts to elucidate "some of its salient speech act constraints in the framework of

Introduction   13

Constraint-based Unified Grammar of Korean," inspired in part by Jim's decompositional approach to meaning, especially the way he identified the constituents of the meaning of a linguistic expression. For the purposes of her analysis, Chang adds two more time distinctions to Reichenbach's (1947) three-way opposition between *utterance time*, *reference time*, and *event time*: *retrospection time* and *observation time*. These are both limited to the retrospective. Retrospection appears to be constrained by several factors, including predicate type, thematic role, and sentence type. Pragmatic considerations are important too, especially regarding emotive verbs, as the speaker must specify the basis of his or her knowledge of the subject's emotions and thus has a choice between the *experience* and the *perception* type of retrospection.

We couldn't help grouping **Semantics** and **Pragmatics** together in **Part IV**, to reflect the intertwining of Jim's work in these areas (see, e.g., McCawley 1978). Part IV begins with **Laurence R. Horn**'s "An *Un-* Paper for the Unsyntactician," whose title is admittedly patterned on the title of a revisionist paper of Jim's, McCawley 1980, in which he recognizes a number of phenomena traditionally associated with syntax that can be explained with morphological or other principles.

In this chapter, Horn uses the coinages *unpaper* and *unsyntactician* in a rich way that both invites reflection on Jim's coinage and symbolizes the subject matter he is discussing. *Un*-prefixed nouns that are neither deadjectival nor deverbal are more common than one would imagine, and they represent a highly productive word formation strategy that traditionally would have been treated as exceptional and marginal, simply because the prefix *un-* in its 'negation' sense is generally assumed to combine with adjectives and related adverbs, whereas *un-* in its 'reverse' sense combines with verbs. Words such as *Uncola*, *unbirthday*, *unworld*, *unthing*, and *unmen* are not nearly as rare or exceptional as one might first imagine. They denote 'privation' of what is denoted by their lexical base morpheme and do not seem to compete with words taking the 'negation' prefixes *iN-* and *non-*, such as *impossible* and *nonstandard*. However, they sometimes help create contrasts like that between *non-Christian* and *un-Christian* (Algeo 1971).

The same prefix *un-* is also attested in some adjectives such as *uncool* 'not hip' (but not *'warm') and *ungreen* 'environmentally incorrect' (but not *'not green'), which call for the kind of detailed semantic and pragmatic analysis that Horn provides for the privative *un*-words. Horn explores a number of semantic factors that bear on the relevant word formations, such as why it is difficult to imagine somebody talking about an *unnuclear physics/bomb* but quite easy to find attestations of *unnuclear family*. What he wants to explain here is germane to the distinction between the meaning of *undead* and that of *alive*, likewise between that of *unalive* and that of *dead*. One of the principles that Horn invokes is that *unX* words and the *X* words from which they are derived have denotations that may be treated as subsets of the same thing, in the same way that *Uncola*, applied to 7-Up, denotes a beverage of basically the same kind as Coca-Cola and Pepsi-Cola. The denotata differ, however, with respect to the feature that is denied. Thus, unvegetarian individuals are bad vegetarians, rather than meat-eaters. Horn brings to light that *un*-words have a wide range of meanings that do not necessarily convey the meaning of 'privation'.

From an evolutionary point of view (in the sense of how this word formation strategy has evolved), one is reminded of prototype categories, according to which analogical extensions from the prototypical case are not necessarily based on one single perceptual or conceptual characteristic of the prototype. Thus, things called *shoe* do not all have the same shape, nor do they all serve the function of covering or protecting some other entity. The same can be said of parts of bodies or of objects called *head*. This evolutionary pattern also shows itself in words such as *un-Martini* and *un-Clinton*, which denote not the 'privation' meaning associated with *Uncola*-like formations but rather the meaning 'almost'. As Horn explains it, such class B *un*-words denote nonprototypical members of the categories identified by the relevant base words. They seem to do the opposite of what "lexical clones" such as *SALAD-salad* and *DOCTOR-doctor* do in identifying prototypical members. But the question of whether all such formations fall in two clear-cut categories remains open. Horn argues also for the need for a "lexical pragmatics," whose origin he associates with McCawley 1978 and which articulates how lexical phenomena also need syntactic, semantic, and pragmatic considerations for more accurate explanations.

Also very much in the tradition of Jim's scholarship, despite differences in analytical framework, is **Donka F. Farkas**'s "Semantic Noun Phrase Typology," in which the author allocates NPs/arguments to different categories depending on what they do in a sentence/proposition. She focuses on these questions: (1) What semantic types of NPs are there crosslinguistically? and (2) How are these types grammatically encoded? Using a modified version of Discourse Representation Theory that she relates to the spirit of McCawley 1970, 1981, Farkas investigates, among other things, the nature of the contribution that an expression makes to semantic representation and how it relates to the rest of that representation. She notes that more questions arise in this regard: "these issues concern whether the nominal introduces a discourse referent or not, how it combines with the rest of the semantic structure, and, in case a discourse referent is introduced, what the nature of the restriction placed on it is." She also distinguishes between "full-fledged NPs," which "introduce a discourse referent and some restrictive condition(s) on it," and "incorporated argumental nominals," which "contribute a predicative condition and no discourse referent."

This is clearly reminiscent of chapter 7 in McCawley 1988/1998, where Jim discusses using prototype categories as a model for syntactic categories (see also Francis, this volume) and explains precisely that not all NPs in a sentence have a referential function. Farkas further subcategorizes full-fledged NPs into quantificational and nonquantificational ones, depending on whether they include a quantifier or not. After proposing some finer distinctions, she argues that McCawley's surface combinatoric constraints "may be sensitive to the semantic structural distinctions" she proposes.

Farkas also extends her approach to the semantics of nominal number, which Jim discussed (see McCawley 1968, 1975) and which is among the phenomena analyzed by Ojeda (1992, 1993, this volume). She proposes a distinction "between semantically number-neutral nominals and nominals with number entailments." It is worth comparing this analysis with Ojeda's, especially since the analytical frameworks differ somewhat, providing an opportunity to verify whether a particular analytical framework can constrain the kinds of data that investigators cover in their analyses and base their conclusions on.

Among several interesting hypotheses, Farkas proposes a three-way number distinction between *singular*, *plural*, and *number neutral*. She suggests a pragmatic approach to morphologically plural NPs that lifts the default atomic interpretation (i.e., individuation, as opposed to group interpretation in this case) associated with them and instead has the relevant discourse and other pragmatic considerations determine the interpretation of the referent. The comparison between Farkas's and Ojeda's analyses is made more compelling by their discussion of morphologically singular NPs that are claimed to be semantically plural and morphologically plural NPs that are claimed to be semantically singular.

Almerindo E. Ojeda's "The Paradox of Mass Plurals" focuses on what he terms the "embarrassing predicament [and] paradox of mass plurals." This is in reference to mass nouns such as *clothes* (as opposed to *clothing*) that "should refer to discrete entities taken in bulk rather than collectively and, at the same time, to discrete entities taken collectively rather than in bulk." Building on some of Mufwene's ideas (1980a,b, 1981, 1984), especially the distinction between morphological and semantic number, Ojeda proposes an opposition between *singular* and *cosingular* and between *plural* and *coplural*. The metaconcept *cosingular* applies to items such as *clothes* (which should not be confused with the plural of morphologically singular mass nouns like *wines* and *beers* that have pluralized count uses), whereas *coplural* applies to items such as *clothing*, which "should refer to entities that are taken individually rather than in bulk and, at the same time, in bulk rather than individually." (The latter case, Ojeda notes, raises the "paradox of mass singulars.")

Ojeda's arguments boil down to the position that at the semantic level the opposition between *singular* and *plural* should be restricted to count nouns only and is not applicable to mass nouns. Adducing morphological evidence especially from Lingala and Zuni, in which both morphologically singular and morphologically plural nouns carry specific class/number markers, he also argues that the singular/plural contrast is equipollent and neither member of the opposition is unmarked. He uses model-theoretic semantics to argue that "the model for the interpretation of mass nouns on a particular occasion of linguistic use is simply the ordered pair formed by the universe of discourse of such an occasion followed by the partitive relation of that occasion." That is, he defends the position that in the case of mass singular nouns talking about entities, partitive/part-of relations are more important than individuation. He proposes 'set of entities taken in bulk' as the meaning of plural mass nouns, and this is what he means by *cosingular*.

This part ends with **Katharine Beals**'s "Everything That Linguists Have Always Wanted to Know about Ironic Presuppositions and Implicatures but Were Ashamed to Ask." As Beals points out, this is a topic that Jim certainly prepared his students well to discuss but on which he himself hardly wrote—a surprising gap, given the encyclopedic breadth of his teaching and publications. Still, Beals's study draws inspiration from one of the exercises in Jim's logic textbook (McCawley 1981/1993), in which an utterance predicted by Grice's theory to be ironic is not easily interpretable as such. Under what conditions, Beals asks, does a listener recognize an implication as ludicrously at odds with the background of an utterance and therefore identify the utterance as ironic? She distinguishes irony from implicature and identifies the latter as part of what makes it possible in many cases to recognize the former. Various kinds of implicature, such as those having to do with quantity, relation, and manner, can produce irony given the appropriate background assumptions. For example, Beals notes that in the exchange in (7), B's utterance carries a relation implicature that allows A to infer that the white Lexus belongs to Bill and that Bill is at Sue's house.

(7) A: Where's Bill?
    B: Well, there's a shiny white Lexus outside Sue's house.

However, if A and B both know that Bill drives a beat-up old Oldsmobile, the same relation implicature gives rise to an ironic interpretation of B's utterance. Beals argues that in order for an implicature to give rise to irony, it must involve some element of linguistic convention. For example, in the exchange in (7), A asks a question, and B's response is assumed to be an answer to the question. This is reinforced by the presence of the word *well*, which is conventionally used to introduce the response to a question. Beals observes that if B utters the same sentence without the word *well*, and not in direct response to any question, but still in a situation in which people who know that Bill drives a beat-up Oldsmobile are wondering about Bill's whereabouts, the irony does not succeed. This is, she argues, because the implicature on which the irony depends, although still present, is not sufficiently obvious.

Part V: Knowledge of Language addresses issues that were implicit in many of Jim's essays. In "Deficits in Pronoun Interpretation: Clues to a Theory of Competence and Acquisition," **William O'Grady** discusses a topic on which Jim only made passing comments here and there but in which he was certainly very much interested (see, e.g., McCawley 1976, 1983, 1995). O'Grady proposes to account for "a set of parallel deficits that are manifested in first language acquisition, in second language learning, and in the agrammatism associated with Broca's aphasia." His arguments are anchored in a view of the language faculty that seeks to explain language acquisition in terms of a more general theory of learning (see also Luka, this volume), including an efficiency requirement on processing, and he claims that "there is no grammar per se." Accordingly, sentence processing involves "a simple combinatorial operation that brings together functors (i.e., argument-taking categories such as verbs) and their arguments" and proceeds incrementally from left to right in the case of English.

O'Grady also conceives of language deficit as reflecting "the operation of an intact but underpowered computational system," which "is like trying to drive an electric car with a weak battery." Like the driver of such a car who is aware of its shortcoming, "language learners and agrammatics avoid unnecessary computations, ... they prefer short, quick computations, and ... they have difficulty with computations that are complicated by external factors." A natural consequence of this is the kinds of mistakes language learners and agrammatics make in interpreting uses of definite pronouns that violate the Efficiency Requirement.

O'Grady also asserts that "there is ... reason to think that no part of the brain is set aside in advance specifically to provide computational space for sentence processing" and that the extent of neural circuitry involved in processing a sentence is proportionate to its structural complexity. He also cites Deacon (1997, 218) as saying that "the relative sizes of the brain's functional divisions are determined in a systematic competition for space." O'Grady adduces evidence for his position from the fact that in children who have suffered brain lesions, some brain regions are reallocated to carry on the functions originally performed by the damaged parts. Accordingly, the underpowering of the computational system in language processing occurs after brain space allocation for language processing is complete. He views grammar as "nothing but an efficiency-driven processor that is available from the beginning of the language acquisition process." It produces a number of routines that can be described as rules or principles, and, at least to one of us (Mufwene), its emergence can be analogized to the emergence of patterns in complex adaptive systems (the notion used in Mufwene 2001 to characterize a linguistic system from an evolutionary point of view). Mufwene also speculates that such a study raises the question of whether *rules*, which have played such a central role in linguistic analysis, are made possible by *analogies*, which actually guide speakers' linguistic behavior (including language acquisition and those communicative activities that cumulatively also lead to language change).

Whether or not readers agree with O'Grady, they will have to ask themselves whether it is accurate to characterize the language faculty or Universal Grammar as an organ. How can a biological organ be a component of the mind, which is responsible for language acquisition and linguistic behavior, while the mind itself is not physical but a state of the brain in activity?

Equally thought-provoking is **Jerry L. Morgan** and **Georgia M. Green**'s "Why Verb Agreement Is Not the Poster Child for Any General Formal Principle." This chapter is about rough edges of verb agreement in English, which individual speakers handle in different ways and which question a UG-based "single, neat, uniform, and coherent account." The authors are concerned with sentences like the following, among others, in connection with what Morgan (1972, 1984) identifies as the "selection problem" (having to do with identifying the constituent that controls agreement):

(8) a. Is/Are there an orchestra or two digital pianos in that room?
    b. Is/Are there two digital pianos or an orchestra in that room?

As originally proposed in Morgan 1985, Morgan and Green argue that cases exist where "there may not be conflict resolution principles" that apply, at least not consistently from one speaker to another. They observe that "the range of variation exhibited in verb agreement choices suggests that individuals' internal grammars for this basic phenomenon of language not only vary idiosyncratically, but may be incomplete or inconsistent." They conclude that "the internal grammars of individuals may be far from elegant and may contain lacunae which occasion a variety of behaviors which result in the apparent chaos of the elicited judgments" on noncanonical cases. (A similar idea whereby grammar consists of coexistent, incomplete systems has been expressed by Labov (1998).) Constructions involving a measure term such as *acre*, *bushel*, or *ton* can command singular or plural agreement depending on whether the speaker interprets the term as individuated or not (see also McCawley 1995). Variation in the case of conjoined constructions such as *pickles and ice cream* depends on whether the speaker views the items he or she is referring to as a collection of objects or a composed object. Things can be muddled when the conjunction is changed to *or*, making it unclear whether reference with *pickles or ice cream* is inclusive or exclusive.

Citing the results from their survey-questionnaire on verb agreement, Morgan and Green question the validity of assuming that normal members of a language community use identical grammars. Those who have read McCawley 1988/1998 are aware of Jim's sensitivity to interidiolectal variation, identified with the % stigmatum. Chomsky (2000) may be headed in the same direction, away from a uniform communal grammar or "public language," in observing:

Successful communication between Peter and Mary does not entail the existence of shared [i.e., identical] meanings or shared pronunciations in a public language.... The only (virtually) "shared structure" among humans generally is the initial state of the language faculty. Beyond that we expect to find no more than approximations, as in the case of other natural objects that grow and develop.... [S]peaking the same language is on a par with being-near or looking-alike [i.e., speaking idiolects that are alike, but not identical]. (pp. 30–31)

Morgan and Green endorse McCawley's (1976) position that speakers' grammars develop gradually, through a sequence of ad hoc adjustments to new data. Two or more speakers who have been exposed to different primary linguistic data from the "same language" can develop different, though similar, grammars. Morgan and Green submit that their findings are consistent with research on child language (e.g., Bates and MacWhinney 1979, 1982).

Barbara J. Luka's "A Cognitively Plausible Model of Linguistic Intuition" is a very apt complement to the preceding chapter, as it focuses on the validity of data about which syntacticians have theorized. Except implicitly, in polemics over particular data used to prove a point, this is a topic that has received much less attention than it should in theoretical linguistics. For instance, introspection and elicitation of intuitions from other speakers (sometimes even from single speakers) have prevailed as data collection practices, but there has been little discussion about whether this is the best way to study how utterances in a language are produced and/or processed. Jim's *Linguistic Flea Circus* (McCawley 1991) stood out as a source of interesting unelicited, nonintrospected data, which often led him to question established tenets about grammatical structure or language acquisition. As major reflections on the data that theoretical linguists have worked with, Cowart 1997 and Schütze 1996 are marginal compared with the vast literature on methodology that is available to social scientists in fields such as sociology and economics.

Luka argues that linguistic intuitions themselves are an interesting research area and "provide a fruitful experimental case in which to test hypotheses about the interaction between conscious and unconscious processing." She shares with Jim, O'Grady (this volume), and Morgan and Green (this volume) the position that "linguistic intuitions are dependent on cognitive processes such as learning, memory, and decision making, and that linguistic judgments are not easily separable from more general (nonlinguistic) cognitive processes." She reports, for instance, that familiarity with particular kinds of structures (owing to frequency or recency of perceiving a structure) accounts partly for the higher ratings that informants assign them, as they are easier to process. Her discussion also raises the question of what to make of discrepancies between informants' acceptability judgments and their own production of constructions that they rate as nonoptimal or ill formed.

Luka reviews a variety of factors that bear on speakers' acceptability judgments, such as their age, their ability to think metacognitively about language, their analytical skills, and their literacy and education. She bridges linguistics and psychology in inviting the reader to think about whether acceptability judgments must be taken at face value or must be contextualized and assessed relative to recency and frequency effects, for example. Frequency itself as a factor raises the question of what to make of common constructions that prescriptive grammarians consider marginally acceptable or ill formed but are widely produced. If theoretical linguists theorize about language, isn't it important to assess the value of the data that inform their theorizing?

We end the volume with **Part VI: Encyclopedia and Language**. In "Language and Languages in the Eleventh *Britannica*," Peter T. Daniels explores "the knowledge about language and languages that was available to the educated layperson in the second decade of the twentieth century," based on the Eleventh Edition of the *Encyclopædia Britannica*. He surveys who wrote on linguistics for the Eleventh Edition, and about what topic, and, implicitly, how that knowledge compares with what is known about languages and linguistics today. He makes comparisons with the Thirteenth Edition and sometimes with the Fifteenth. He assesses the kinds of biases that reflect the colonial atmosphere of the time, especially in terms of what languages are included and how they are discussed. Regarding language representation and detail of explanations, we may want to ask ourselves how much has changed since then in linguistics itself, as we endeavor to articulate language universals and classify languages into structural types. Are we as linguists equally informed about all the languages considered in our generalizations?

Jim McCawley contributed monumentally to our understanding of how language works, reminding the profession of mistaken paths, clarifying which research questions have been (in)adequately addressed, opening new research avenues, refining methodology, directing attention to interesting data that should not be overlooked, and much more. We would have been remiss in not keeping alive the spirit of his contribution to our collective scholarship. May this book reveal how much we have learned from a teacher we will not cease to admire even long after his death. And may the reader join the contributors in pursuing some of the topics they discuss and others they undoubtedly suggest.

References

Algeo, John. 1971. The voguish uses of *non-*. *American Speech* 46, 87–105.

Bates, Elizabeth, and Brian MacWhinney. 1979. The functionalist approach to the acquisition of grammar. In *Developmental pragmatics*, ed. by Elinor Ochs and Bambi Schiefflin, 167–209. New York: Academic Press.

Bates, Elizabeth, and Brian MacWhinney. 1982. Functionalist approaches to grammar. In *Child language: The state of the art*, ed. by Eric Wanner and Lila Gleitman, 173–218. Cambridge, MA: MIT Press.

Chomsky, Noam. 2000. *New horizons in the study of language and mind.* Cambridge: Cambridge University Press.

Cowart, Wayne. 1997. *Experimental syntax: Applying objective methods to sentence judgments.* Thousand Oaks, CA: Sage Publications.

Croft, William. 1991. *Syntactic categories and grammatical relations.* Chicago: University of Chicago Press.

Croft, William. 2001. *Radical Construction Grammar.* Oxford: Oxford University Press.

Deacon, Terrence. 1997. *The symbolic species: The co-evolution of language and the brain.* New York: Norton.

Dik, Simon C. 1983. Auxiliary and copula *be* in a functional grammar of English. In *Linguistic categories: Auxiliaries and related puzzles.* Vol. 2, *The scope, order, and distribution of auxiliary verbs*, ed. by Frank Heny and Barry Richards, 121–43. Dordrecht: Reidel.

Francis, Elaine J. 1999. Variation within lexical categories. Doctoral dissertation, University of Chicago.

Heine, Bernd. 1993. *Auxiliaries: Cognitive forces and grammaticalization.* Oxford: Oxford University Press.

Hopper, Paul J., and Sandra A. Thompson. 1984. The discourse basis for lexical categories in Universal Grammar. *Language* 60, 715–17.

Hopper, Paul J., and Elizabeth Traugott. 1993. *Grammaticalization.* Cambridge: Cambridge University Press.

Kratzer, Angelika. 1981. The notional category of modality. In *Words, worlds and contexts: New approaches to word semantics*, ed. by Hans-Jürgen Eikmeyer and Hannes Rieser, 38–74. Berlin: de Gruyter.

Labov, William. 1998. Co-existent systems in African-American vernacular English. In *African-American English: Structure, history and use*, ed. by Salikoko S. Mufwene, John R. Rickford, Guy Bailey, and John Baugh, 110–53. London: Routledge.

Lakoff, George. 1970. *Irregularity in syntax.* New York: Holt, Rinehart and Winston.

Lakoff, George. 1987. Cognitive models and prototype theory. In *Concepts and conceptual development: Ecological and intellectual factors in categorization*, ed. by Ulric Neisser, 63–100. Cambridge: Cambridge University Press.

McCawley, James D. 1968. Review of *Current trends in linguistics 3. Language* 44, 556–93.

McCawley, James D. 1970. Where do noun phrases come from? In *Readings in English transformational grammar*, ed. by Roderick Jacobs and Peter S. Rosenbaum, 166–83. Waltham, MA: Ginn.

McCawley, James D. 1971. Tense and time reference in English. In *Studies in linguistic semantics*, ed. by Charles Fillmore and D. Terence Langendoen, 96–113. New York: Holt, Rinehart and Winston.

McCawley, James. 1975. Lexicography and the count-mass distinction. In *Proceedings of the First Annual Meeting of the Berkeley Linguistics Society*, 314–321. Berkeley: University of California, Berkeley Linguistics Society. Reprinted in McCawley 1979a, 165–73.

McCawley, James D. 1976. Some ideas not to live by. *Die neueren Sprachen* 75, 151–65. Reprinted in McCawley 1979a, 234–46.

McCawley, James D. 1977. Evolutionary parallels between Montague Grammar and transformational grammar. In *Proceedings of the Seventh Annual Meeting of the North Eastern Linguistic Society*, ed. by Judy Anne Kegl, David Nash, and Annie Zaenen, 219–32. Amherst: University of Massachusetts, GLSA. Reprinted in McCawley 1979a, 122–32.

McCawley, James D. 1978. Conversational implicature and the lexicon. In *Syntax and semantics 9: Pragmatics*, ed. by Peter Cole, 245–59. New York: Academic Press.

McCawley, James D. 1979a. *Adverbs, vowels, and other objects of wonder*. Chicago: University of Chicago Press.

McCawley, James D. 1979b. Helpful hints to the ordinary working Montague grammarian. In *Linguistics, philosophy, and Montague Grammar*, ed. by Steven Davis and Marianne Mithun, 103–25. Austin: University of Texas Press.

McCawley, James D. 1980. An un-syntax. In *Syntax and semantics 13: Current approaches to syntax*, ed. by Edith Moravcsik and Jessica Wirth, 167–93. New York: Academic Press.

McCawley, James. 1981. *Everything that linguists have always wanted to know about logic—but were ashamed to ask*. Chicago: University of Chicago Press. 2nd. ed., 1993.

McCawley, James D. 1982. The nonexistence of syntactic categories. In *Thirty million theories of grammar*, 176–203. Chicago: University of Chicago Press.

McCawley, James D. 1983. Towards plausibility in theories of language acquisition. *Communication and Cognition* 16, 169–83.

McCawley, James D. 1987. A case of syntactic mimicry. In *Functionalism in linguistics*, ed. by René Dirven and Vilém Frid, 459–70. Amsterdam: John Benjamins.

McCawley, James D. 1988. *The syntactic phenomena of English*. Chicago: University of Chicago Press. 2nd. ed., 1998.

McCawley, James D. 1991. *A linguistic flea circus*. Bloomington: Indiana University Linguistics Club.

McCawley, James D. 1995. English. In *Syntax: An international handbook of contemporary research*, ed. by Joachim Jacobs, Arnim von Stechow, Wolfgang Sternefeld, and Theo Vennemann, vol. 2, 1319–47. Berlin: Walter de Gruyter.

Morgan, Jerry L. 1972. Verb agreement as a rule of English. In *Papers from the Eighth Regional Meeting, Chicago Linguistic Society*, ed. by Paul M. Peranteau, Judith N. Levi, and Gloria C. Phares, 278–86. Chicago: University of Chicago, Chicago Linguistic Society.

Morgan, Jerry L. 1984. Some problems of agreement in English and Albanian. In *Proceedings of the Tenth Annual Meeting of the Berkeley Linguistics Society*, ed. by Claudia Brugman and Monica Macaulay, 233–47. Berkeley: University of California, Berkeley Linguistics Society.

Morgan, Jerry L. 1985. Some problems of determination in English number agreement. In *Proceedings of the First Eastern States Conference on Linguistics*, ed. by Gloria Alvarez, Belinda Brodie, and Terry McCoy, 69–78. Columbus: Ohio State University, Department of Linguistics.

Mufwene, Salikoko S. 1980a. Bantu class prefixes: Inflectional or derivational? In *Papers from the Sixteenth Regional Meeting, Chicago Linguistic Society*, ed. by Jody Kreiman and Almerindo Ojeda, 246–58. Chicago: University of Chicago, Chicago Linguistic Society.

Mufwene, Salikoko S. 1980b. Number, countability and markedness in Lingala LI-/MA- noun class. *Linguistics* 18, 1019–52.

Mufwene, Salikoko S. 1981. Non-individuation and the count/mass distinction. In *Papers from the Seventeenth Regional Meeting, Chicago Linguistic Society*, ed. by Roberta A. Hendrick, Carrie S. Masek, and Mary Frances Miller, 221–38. Chicago: University of Chicago, Chicago Linguistic Society.

Mufwene, Salikoko S. 1984. The count/mass distinction in the English lexicon. In *Papers from the Parasession on Lexical Semantics*, ed. by David Testen, Veena Mishra, and Joseph Drogo, 200–21. Chicago: University of Chicago, Chicago Linguistic Society.

Mufwene, Salikoko S. 2001. *The ecology of language evolution*. Cambridge: Cambridge University Press.

Newmeyer, Frederick J. 1998. *Language form and language function*. Cambridge, MA: MIT Press.

Newmeyer, Frederick J. 2000. The discrete nature of syntactic categories: Against a prototype-based account. In *Syntax and semantics 32: The nature and function of syntactic categories*, ed. by Robert D. Borsley, 221–50. San Diego, Calif.: Academic Press.

Ojeda, Almerindo. 1992. The markedness of plurality. In *The joy of grammar*, ed. by Diane Brentari, Gary N. Larson, and Lynn A. MacLeod, 275–89. Amsterdam: John Benjamins.

Ojeda, Almerindo. 1993. *Linguistic individuals*. CSLI Lecture Notes 31. Stanford, CA: CSLI Publications.

Partee, Barbara Hall. 1973. Some structural analogies between tenses and pronouns. *Journal of Philosophy* 70, 601–9.

Partee, Barbara Hall. 1984. Nominal and temporal anaphora. *Linguistics and Philosophy* 7, 243–86.

Reichenbach, Hans. 1947. *Elements of symbolic logic*. London: Macmillan.

Sadock, Jerrold M. 1991. *Autolexical Syntax: A theory of parallel grammatical representations*. Chicago: University of Chicago Press.

Schütze, Carson T. 1996. *The empirical base of linguistics: Grammaticality judgments and linguistic methodology*. Chicago: University of Chicago Press.

Taylor, John R. 1995. *Linguistic categorization*. 2nd ed. Oxford: Clarendon Press.

Vendler, Zeno. 1957. Verbs and times. Reprinted in Zeno Vendler, ed. *Linguistics in philosophy*, 97–121. Ithaca, NY: Cornell University Press, 1967.

PART I
Phonology

Chapter 1
Sequential Voicing and Lyman's Law in Old Japanese

Timothy J. Vance

1.1 Introduction

The term *sequential voicing* is Martin's (1952, 48) translation of the Japanese technical term *rendaku*, which refers to a Japanese morphophonemic phenomenon found in compounds and in prefix + base combinations.[1] Since the Japanese term is not only shorter but also quite commonly used by linguists writing in English, this chapter will adopt it throughout. According to one version of a putative constraint (Lyman's Law), Old Japanese did not allow rendaku if a voiced obstruent either preceded or followed a potential rendaku site within a word. Despite the obvious appeal of a single bidirectional constraint, this chapter argues that two separate phenomena were involved.

1.2 Rendaku

A morpheme that exhibits rendaku has one allomorph beginning with a voiceless obstruent and another allomorph beginning with a voiced obstruent, and the voiced allomorph of such a morpheme appears only when it is a noninitial morph in a word.[2] The examples in (1) illustrate the pairs of phonemes that alternate.

(1) a. /f/~/b/   /fune/ 'boat'
              /kawa+bune/ 'river boat'
    b. /h/~/b/   /hako/ 'case'
              /haši+bako/ 'chopstick case'
    c. /t/~/d/   /tama/ 'ball'
              /me+dama/ 'eyeball'

I am grateful to Shoko Hamano, Kazutoshi Ohno, and Jim Unger for helpful suggestions. Versions of this chapter were presented at the 2000 meeting of the Western Branch of the American Oriental Society in Tempe, Arizona, and to audiences at International Christian University, the University of Illinois at Urbana-Champaign, and UCLA.

d. /k/~/g/ /kami/ 'paper'
/iro+gami/ 'colored paper'
e. /c/~/z/ /cuka/ 'mound'
/ari+zuka/ 'anthill'
f. /s/~/z/ /sora/ 'sky'
/hoši+zora/ 'starry sky'
g. /č/~/ǰ/ /či/ 'blood'
/hana+ǰi/ 'nosebleed'
h. /š/~/ǰ/ /šika/ 'deer'
/ko+ǰika/ 'young deer'

Because of well-known historical changes, some of the alternations in modern Japanese involve more than just a difference in voicing. Notice that /b/ alternates with /f/ ([ɸ]; (1a)) and /h/ (1b), not with /p/.[3] Notice also that /z/ ([dz] or [z]) alternates both with /c/ ([ts]; (1e)) and with /s/ (1f) and that /ǰ/ ([ɟʑ]) alternates both with /č/ ([cɕ]; (1g)) and with /š/ ([ɕ]; (1h)).[4]

1.3 Lyman's Law

Jim McCawley's first book was, of course, a revised version of his dissertation on Japanese phonology, and his characterization of rendaku (McCawley 1968, 87) is refreshingly candid: "I am unable to state the environment in which the 'voicing rule' applies. The relevant data are completely bewildering." More than 30 years later, there is still no reason to doubt that rendaku is fundamentally irregular, but there are some strong tendencies in the data.[5]

The best-known tendency is that a voiced obstruent in a morpheme inhibits rendaku. For example, Okumura (1955) compares /oo+kaze/ 'strong wind' and /oo+zora/ 'open sky', both of which contain the prefix /oo/ 'big'. He says that sequential voicing does not apply to give */oo+gaze/ for 'strong wind' because /kaze/ 'wind', unlike /sora/ 'sky', already contains a voiced obstruent. The first scholar to mention this inhibiting effect was Motoori Norinaga (1730–1801), but the first non-Japanese to write about it was Benjamin Lyman (1894), and it is sometimes called Lyman's Law.[6] There are counterexamples to Lyman's Law in modern Japanese, but they are extremely rare.[7]

The earliest substantial written records of Japanese date from the eighth century and presumably reflect the language of the aristocracy in the capital city of Nara at that time. This language is usually called Old Japanese, and Ramsey and Unger (1972) claim that sequential voicing did not occur in Old Japanese if either the first or the second element of a compound contained a voiced obstruent. Unger (1975, 9) refers to this as the "strong version" of Lyman's Law, and he attributes its original discovery to Ishizuka Tatsumaro (1764–1823).[8] No one has ever suggested that the strong version of Lyman's Law applies to modern Japanese, and counterexamples such as /mado+giwa/ 'window-side' (cf. /kiwa/ 'side') and /de+beso/ 'protruding navel' (cf. /heso/ 'navel') are easy to find.

1.4 Dictionary Search

This chapter reports the results of a systematic dictionary search for Old Japanese lexical items relevant to the two versions of Lyman's Law. The search targeted noun+noun and prefix+noun combinations that appear as headwords in the definitive dictionary of Old Japanese: Jôdaigo Jiten Henshû Iinkai 1967 (hereafter JJHI). The first step was to go through the appendix, which lists each headword and its part of speech. For every monomorphemic noun headword beginning with a voiceless obstruent and consisting of one or two syllables, the entry in the main body of the dictionary was checked. Each entry includes a list of longer items containing the headword, and all the longer words ending with that morpheme were added provisionally to the data set. For example, the appendix lists the two-syllable noun ^{OJ}/kuti/ 'mouth', and the entry under this headword lists 10 longer words and phrases containing it.[9] Of these, 3 are headwords that end with this morpheme for 'mouth': the noun+noun combination ^{OJ}/yama+guti/ 'starting point for climbing a mountain' (with rendaku), the prefix+noun combination ^{OJ}/opo+kuti/ 'large mouth' (without rendaku), and the phrase ^{OJ}/mîti+nö+kuti/ 'road entry point' (without rendaku), in which the genitive particle ^{OJ}/nö/ connects two nouns.[10] Headwords of this last type, that is, two nouns joined by a genitive particle (^{OJ}/nö/, ^{OJ}/ga/, or ^{OJ}/tu/), were excluded from the data set. While such items were undoubtedly set phrases in Old Japanese, their phrasal character presumably made rendaku unlikely, and including them in the data set might confound the assessment of Lyman's Law. Consider the headword ^{OJ}/okî+tu+kadi/ 'offshore oar', with the voiced obstruent ^{OJ}/d/ in the final element ^{OJ}/kadi/ 'oar'. The rendaku form *^{OJ}/okî+tu+gadi/ would certainly violate the weak version of Lyman's Law, but it seems unwise to attribute the lack of rendaku to Lyman's Law in such cases.[11]

Since the great majority of Old Japanese noun morphemes were realized as one or two syllables, the length limitation facilitated the search process enormously while excluding only a very few potentially relevant nouns such as three-syllable ^{OJ}/pîtuzi/ 'sheep'.[12] The length limitation also had the benefit of automatically skipping over many noun headwords derived from verb stems, such as ^{OJ}/kazar-i/ 'decorating' (cf. ^{OJ}/kazar-u/ 'decorate'). The hyphen in these transcriptions represents the boundary between the stem and the inflectional ending according to one influential analysis of Japanese verb inflection, and on this account, a word like ^{OJ}/kazar-i/ is not monomorphemic.[13] A more important consideration for present purposes is that, just like modern Japanese, Old Japanese had compound verbs consisting of a verb stem plus a verb, such as ^{OJ}/kak-î+tor-u/ 'write down' (cf. ^{OJ}/kak-u/ 'write', ^{OJ}/tor-u/ 'take'), and compound nouns consisting of a verb stem plus another verb stem, such as ^{OJ}/sOp-î+tukap-î/ 'second-ranking official' (cf. ^{OJ}/sOp-u/ 'accompany', ^{OJ}/tukap-u/ 'use').[14] It is often unclear whether a compound of this second type (i.e., a verb+verb compound noun) should be understood as a combination of two nouns (each derived from a verb stem) or as a noun derived from the stem of a single compound verb. The problem is that verb+verb compound verbs (i.e., words like ^{OJ}/kak-î+tor-u/) typically do not show rendaku (Vance 1987, 142–44), so a noun derived from the stem of such a verb would not show rendaku either, regardless of whether rendaku would violate either version of Lyman's Law.[15] For this reason, it seemed advisable simply to exclude all words ending with a verb stem from the data set—even the many two-syllable verb stems such as ^{OJ}/kak-î/ 'writing'. On the other hand, words containing a verb stem (or an adjective stem) elsewhere are not problematic. For example, the data set includes ^{OJ}/pakar-i+kötö/ 'plans' (cf. the verb ^{OJ}/pakar-u/ 'plan' and the noun ^{OJ}/kötö/ 'fact').

At this point, the data set consisted of all headwords in JJHI ending with an obstruent-initial noun morph of one or two syllables. Using O to stand for any obstruent, V for any vowel, and C for any consonant (either obstruent or sonorant), it follows from Old Japanese phonotactics that every example in the data set contains a final morph of the form OV (as in ^{OJ}/yödö+se/ 'stagnant shallows') or OVCV (as in ^{OJ}/yupu+dukï/ 'evening moon'; cf. ^{OJ}/tukï/ 'moon').

Several further limitations were then imposed on the data set. First, coordinate compounds such as ^{OJ}/kaze+kumO/ 'wind and clouds' were excluded, since rendaku typically does not occur in coordinate compounds (Vance 1987, 144–45). Second, numeral+counter combinations such as ^{OJ}/puta+tabî/ 'two times' were excluded, since such combinations seem to disfavor rendaku (Vance 1987, 142).[16] Third, items ending in a Sino-Japanese morpheme were excluded, since even today rendaku is much less likely to occur in a Sino-Japanese morph than in a native morph.[17] There are very few headwords of this type in JJHI, but one example is ^{OJ}/kusuri+si/ 'doctor' (cf. native ^{OJ}/kusuri/ 'medicine' and Sino-Japanese ^{OJ}/si/ 'expert'). Fourth, items labeled eastern dialect forms were excluded.[18] Finally, items with final "morphemes" for which the etymology is sheerly speculative were excluded. On the other hand, examples for which the etymology of the final morpheme is merely dubious remained in the data set.[19] The purpose of all these additional limitations (especially the first two) was to eliminate items in which a lack of rendaku might be due to some factor other than either version of Lyman's Law.[20]

1.5 Results

To assess the status of the weak version of Lyman's Law in Old Japanese, items in which rendaku would violate the strong version were removed from the data

Sequential Voicing and Lyman's Law in Old Japanese

Table 1.1
The weak version of Lyman's Law in Old Japanese

Final element type	Number of final elements showing rendaku in at least one word	Total number of words showing rendaku
O⁻ V	14/35 (40%)	50/182 (27%)
O⁻ V S V	50/74 (68%)	137/313 (44%)
O⁻ V O⁻ V	40/73 (55%)	117/333 (35%)
O⁻ V O⁺ V	0/25 (0%)	0/83 (0%)

set. Such items have a nonfinal morpheme containing a voiced obstruent, as in ᴼᴶ/mîdu+töri/ 'water bird'.[21] The resulting subset contains 911 noun+noun and prefix+noun combinations involving 207 different final morphemes. Using O⁻ to stand for any voiceless obstruent, O⁺ for any voiced obstruent, S for any sonorant, and V for any vowel, the forms of these 207 morphemes that appear as independent words can be divided into the following four categories: O⁻ V (e.g., ᴼᴶ/pa/ 'leaf'), O⁻ V S V (e.g., ᴼᴶ/tuna/ 'rope'), O⁻ V O⁻ V (e.g., ᴼᴶ/satô/ 'village'), and O⁻ V O⁺ V (e.g., ᴼᴶ/kazu/ 'number'). The frequency of rendaku in final elements of each type is shown in table 1.1. Rendaku in a word ending with a morpheme in the last category would, of course, violate the weak version of Lyman's Law, but as the last row in table 1.1 shows, there are no such violations in the data set. In other words, the weak version of Lyman's Law seems to have held categorically in Old Japanese.

To assess the status of the strong version of Lyman's Law in Old Japanese, three types of items were removed from the data set. The first type was items in which rendaku would violate the weak version. Such items have a final morpheme containing a noninitial voiced obstruent (e.g., ᴼᴶ/yupu+kagë/ 'evening shadow'). The second type was items ending in a morpheme that never shows rendaku in any headword listed in JJHI. Needless to say, if the rendaku allomorph of a morpheme is unattested, no attested headword ending with that morpheme could violate either version of Lyman's Law. Such a morpheme might simply have been idiosyncratically immune to rendaku, just as some modern morphemes are (e.g., /cuyu/ 'dew' and /himo/ 'string'). One example of a morpheme in this category is ᴼᴶ/posi/ 'star', which appears as the final element in three headwords, all without rendaku.[22] Removing items of this second type guards against inflating the number of examples in which absence of rendaku can be attributed to the strong version of Lyman's Law. The third type removed from the data set was items ending in a morpheme that happens not to occur in any headwords containing an earlier voiced obstruent. For example, ᴼᴶ/kapa/ 'river' occurs as the final morpheme in 12 headwords, 6 with rendaku (as in ᴼᴶ/tani+gapa/ 'valley river') and 6 without (as in ᴼᴶ/isi+kapa/ 'stony river'), but

Table 1.2
The strong version of Lyman's Law in Old Japanese

Location of preceding voiced obstruent	Number of words showing rendaku
0	144/367 (39%)
−1	0/46 (0%)
−2	2/14 (14%)
−3	1/2 (50%)

none of these 12 headwords contains a voiced obstruent in the portion preceding the morph for 'river'. There is no point in looking at final elements that do not occur in headwords of the relevant form.

The resulting subset of the data set contains 429 noun+noun and prefix+noun combinations involving 26 different final morphemes. These 429 items were divided into four categories depending on the location of the voiced obstruent preceding the final morph: 0 meaning nowhere (e.g., ^{OJ}/paru+pana/ 'spring flower'), −1 meaning the syllable immediately preceding the final morph (e.g., ^{OJ}/siba+kakî/ 'brushwood hedge'), −2 meaning the second syllable preceding the final morph (e.g., ^{OJ}/pIdari+te/ 'left hand'), and −3 meaning the third syllable preceding the final morph (e.g., ^{OJ}/saburap-î+pîtö/ 'aristocrat's retainer'; cf. ^{OJ}/saburap-u/ 'serve as a retainer' and ^{OJ}/pîtö/ 'person'). The frequency of rendaku in the items in each category is shown in table 1.2.

As the second row in table 1.2 shows, there are no violations of the strong version of Lyman's Law in items containing a voiced obstruent in the syllable immediately preceding the final morph. The only apparent exception that turned up in the course of the dictionary search was ^{OJ}/mugî+gara/. This item is not listed as a headword in JJHI, but it appears in the lists of compounds under the headwords ^{OJ}/mugî/ 'grain' and ^{OJ}/kara/ 'stem'. The authoritative historical dictionary of Japanese (Nihon Daijiten Kankôkai 1972–76) lists this word as having the modern form /mugi+kara/ (without rendaku), but it gives /mugi+gara/ (with rendaku) as an alternative, and there are three citations. The oldest (ca. 934) implies that the Old Japanese form was ^{OJ}/mugî+kara/ (without rendaku), while the other two (ca. 1100 and 1698) indicate /mugi+gara/. The entry also lists five longer compounds (none with citations), four beginning with /mugikara/ (/mugikara+gusa/, /mugikara+sanada/, /mugikara+bue/, /mugikara+booši/) and one beginning with /mugigara/ (/mugigara+bune/). All of this at least suggests that the modern alternative pronunciation with rendaku, /mugi+gara/, is a later development, and that the Old Japanese form was in fact ^{OJ}/mugî+kara/.

The last two rows in table 1.2 show that there were two violations of the strong version of Lyman's Law in items containing a voiced obstruent in the second syllable preceding the final morph, and one violation in items containing a voiced obstruent in the third syllable preceding the final morph. As it turns out, all three of these violations occur in words consisting of three morphemes: ^{OJ}/tugE+wo+gusi/ 'boxwood small-comb' (cf. ^{OJ}/tugE/ 'boxwood', ^{OJ}/wo/ 'small', ^{OJ}/kusi/ 'comb'), ^{OJ}/kuzu+pa+gata/ 'kudzu-leaf vine' (cf. ^{OJ}/kuzu/ 'kudzu', ^{OJ}/pa/ 'leaf', ^{OJ}/kata/ 'vine'), and ^{OJ}/naga+nak-î+döri/ 'chicken' (lit., 'long-singing bird'; cf. ^{OJ}/naga-si/ 'long', ^{OJ}/nak-u/ 'sing', ^{OJ}/töri/ 'bird'). These three items figure prominently in the discussion in section 1.6.

Incidentally, a fourth apparent violation, ^{OJ}/yob-u+kô+döri/, was discounted as phrasal. The entry in JJHI says that the meaning of this item is uncertain, but it clearly consists of the adnominal form of the verb ^{OJ}/yob-u/ 'call', the noun ^{OJ}/kô/ 'child', and the rendaku allomorph of the noun ^{OJ}/töri/ 'bird'.[23] Since the combination ^{OJ}/yob-u+kô/ has the grammatical form of a phrase meaning 'which calls children', ^{OJ}/yob-u+kô+döri/ is not a simple noun+noun combination, and it is not clear whether the strong version of Lyman's Law should be expected to apply to such an item. The word formation pattern involved is quite interesting, since a two-word phrase is functioning as the first element in a compound. A modern Japanese example with the same kind of structure is /haya-i+mono+gač-i/ 'success to the person who arrives first', which consists of the adjective /haya-i/ 'early', the noun /mono/ 'person', and the rendaku allomorph of the verb stem /kač-i/ 'victory' (cf. the verb /kac-u/). The first element of this compound is the two-word phrase /haya-i mono/ 'early person'.

As table 1.2 shows, only a fairly small number of Old Japanese vocabulary items (a total of 62) contain a voiced obstruent preceding a potential rendaku site. Nonetheless, it seems fair to sum up by saying that the strong version of Lyman's Law comes very close to being a true generalization about the attested vocabulary.

1.6 Kuroda's "Antirendaku"

Kuroda (2002), reviving an idea that he first articulated in a graduate school term paper (Kuroda 1963), suggests thinking of rendaku as word-initial devoicing rather than word-medial voicing.[24] This proposal links rendaku to the well-known ban on word-initial voiced obstruents that is standardly attributed to pre–Old Japanese. As Kuroda notes, there were already a few exceptions in Old Japanese, but even today very few native Japanese words begin with a voiced obstruent.

Inspired by Itô and Mester (1986), Kuroda proposes that an obstruent unspecified for voice is voiceless and that an autosegmental feature ɣ (gamma), which can link only to obstruents, has the effect of converting a default voiceless obstruent to its voiced rendaku counterpart, that is, to the voiced partner listed in (1). Itô and Mester assume that their equivalent of ɣ appears in the process of compounding; Kuroda assumes that ɣ is present underlyingly in all morphemes but is unlinked in a morpheme with no obstruent or in a rendaku-immune morpheme. The examples in (2) illustrate Kuroda's underlying forms.

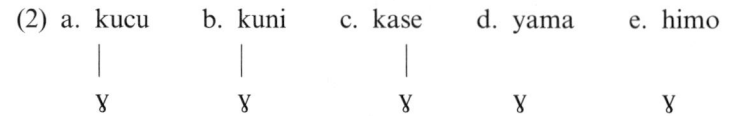

(2) a. kucu   b. kuni   c. kase   d. yama   e. himo
       | | |
       ɣ   ɣ   ɣ   ɣ   ɣ

In the underlying forms of /kucu/ 'shoe' (2a) and /kuni/ 'province' (2b), ɣ is linked to the initial obstruent because these morphemes show rendaku when they occur as final elements, as in /kawa+gucu/ 'leather shoe' and /yama+guni/ 'mountainous province'. In /kaze/ 'wind' (2c), ɣ is linked to the medial obstruent. There is no link in the underlying form of /yama/, which contains no obstruent, or in /himo/, which is rendaku-immune (cf. /kucu+himo/ 'shoelace'). A morpheme like /neko/ 'cat', which always appears with the medial voiceless obstruent /k/, also has no underlying link.

Two constraints are necessary to account for the alternation patterns of these morphemes. The first is that ɣ cannot be linked to a word-initial segment, which means that the underlying link in morphemes like /kucu/ and /kuni/ must be severed when they appear word-initially, as illustrated in (3).

(3) a. kuni   b. yama + kuni
       ǂ |
       ɣ   ɣ   ɣ
    c. himo   d. kucu + himo
                     ǂ
       ɣ   ɣ   ɣ

The severed link in (3a) yields the pronunciation /kuni/, while the intact link in (3b) yields /yama+guni/. The constraint has no effect on (3c), since there is no underlying link, and the severed link in (3d) yields the pronunciation /kucu+himo/. As Kuroda is careful to point out, this analysis cannot handle the many morphemes that sometimes do and sometimes do not undergo rendaku. One example of such a morpheme is /kuči/ 'mouth', which appears with rendaku in /cuge+guči/ 'tattling' (cf. /cuge-ru/ 'tell'), without rendaku in /haya+kuči/ 'fast talking' (cf. /haya-i/ 'fast'), and either way in /waru+guči/~/waru+kuči/ 'bad mouthing' (cf. /waru-i/ 'bad').[25]

The second constraint is that ɣ can be linked only to one segment per morpheme, and the weak version of Lyman's Law is an automatic consequence of this constraint. The examples in (4) illustrate this.

(4) a. yama + kase b. *yama + kase
       | \/
       ɣ   ɣ   ɣ   ɣ

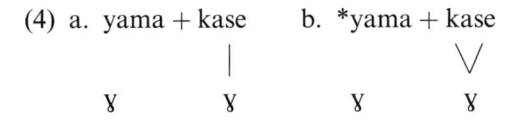

(4a) represents the actually occurring form /yama+kaze/ 'mountain wind'. (4b) represents */yama+gaze/, which violates the weak version of Lyman's Law; but this form cannot arise because it involves linking ɣ to two segments in the same morpheme.

As mentioned above, there are a few native Japanese words that begin with a voiced obstruent, including /gama/ 'toad'.[26] Modern Japanese is also replete with word-initial voiced obstruents in borrowings from Chinese, such as /doku/ 'poison', and in more recent borrowings from other languages, such as /bosu/ 'boss'. As shown in (5), to avoid violating the constraint against ɣ being linked to a word-initial segment, Kuroda treats word-initial voiced obstruents as underlyingly specified for voicing rather than as unspecified obstruents linked to ɣ.

(5) a. gama   b. doku   c. bosu   d. ǰazu
                                     |
     ɣ   ɣ   ɣ   ɣ

Treating morpheme-initial voiced obstruents in this way also makes it possible to have two voiced obstruents in a morpheme without violating the constraint against multiply linked ɣ. Since Kuroda restricts underlying specification for voicing to morpheme-initial position, (5d) represents the borrowing /ǰazu/ 'jazz': the initial /ǰ/ is underlyingly specified for voicing, whereas the medial /z/ is underlyingly unspecified for voicing but linked to ɣ.

1.7 Kuroda's Account and the Strong Version of Lyman's Law

The last question to be considered in this chapter is how Kuroda's account of rendaku could be adjusted to accommodate the strong version of Lyman's Law. The strong version subsumes the weak version and therefore rules out rendaku if the affected morpheme contains a medial voiced obstruent, but the strong version also rules out rendaku if the element preceding the affected morpheme contains a voiced obstruent. As the results in section 1.5 show, the strong version comes very close to being a true generalization about the attested Old Japanese vocabulary.

At first glance, it looks as if the strong version of Lyman's Law would follow as an automatic consequence of a simple adjustment to Kuroda's first constraint, namely, allowing only one gamma link per word rather than only one gamma link per morpheme. This version of the constraint would work as in (6).

(6) a. ^{OJ} pîtö + kötö   b. ^{OJ} akî + kase

    ≠ | |

    ɣ   ɣ   ɣ

c. ^{OJ} mîtu + töri

    | ≠

    ɣ   ɣ

The compound in (6a) surfaces as ^{OJ}/pîtö+götö/ 'another person's words' (cf. ^{OJ}/pîtö/ 'person' and ^{OJ}/kötö/ 'word') because Kuroda's other constraint severs a link between ɣ and a word-initial segment. The initial consonant of the first morpheme must be linked to ɣ underlyingly, since this morpheme shows rendaku in words such as ^{OJ}/uta+bîtö/ 'singer' (cf. ^{OJ}/uta/ 'song').[27] The compound in (6b) surfaces as ^{OJ}/akî+kaze/ 'autumn wind' (cf. ^{OJ}/akî/ 'autumn' and ^{OJ}/kaze/ 'wind'), with its sole underlying link intact. The compound in (6c) surfaces as the attested form ^{OJ}/mîdu+töri/ 'water bird' (cf. ^{OJ}/mîdu/ 'water' and ^{OJ}/töri/ 'bird') on the assumption that the second of two links to ɣ is severed within a word. Notice that the constraint on word-initial segments must have priority, since severing the second link in (6a) would yield *^{OJ}/bîtö+kötö/.

One problem with this adjustment to Kuroda's second constraint is that it cannot account for the apparent counterexamples to the strong version of Lyman's Law that turned up in the dictionary search. As mentioned in section 1.5, the three items in question are all three-morpheme words. In one, ^{OJ}/tugE+wo+gusi/ 'boxwood small-comb', the last two morphemes clearly form a semantic constituent that combines with the first morpheme, as in (7).

(7) [^{OJ}/tugE/ + [^{OJ}/wo/ + ^{OJ}/kusi/]]
['boxwood' + ['small' + 'comb']]

If Lyman's Law is taken to apply to each layer of combination, this item does not violate the strong version. The inner layer is the prefix+noun combination ^{OJ}/wo+gusi/, and neither ^{OJ}/wo/ 'small' nor ^{OJ}/kusi/ 'comb' contains a voiced obstruent. The outer layer is the noun+noun combination ^{OJ}/tugE+wogusi/, and rendaku is inapplicable, since ^{OJ}/wogusi/ does not begin with an obstruent. Interestingly, the noun+noun compound ^{OJ}/tugE+kusi/ 'boxwood comb' also appears as a headword in JJHI, and it does not show rendaku. In this case, of course, rendaku would violate the strong version of Lyman's Law.

In each of the other two apparent counterexamples to the strong version, ^{OJ}/kuzu+pa+gata/ 'kudzu-leaf vine' and ^{OJ}/naga+nak-î+döri/ 'chicken', the first two morphemes clearly form a semantic constituent that combines with the last morpheme, as in (8).

(8) a. [[^{OJ}/kuzu/ + ^{OJ}/pa/] + ^{OJ}/kata/]
[['kudzu' + 'leaf'] + 'vine']
b. [[^{OJ}/naga/ + ^{OJ}/nak-î/] + ^{OJ}/töri/]
[['long' + 'singing'] + 'bird']

In fact, the noun+noun compound ^{OJ}/kuzu+pa/ 'kudzu leaf' (8a) is also listed as a headword in JJHI. The layers of combination in these two three-morpheme words will not let them circumvent Lyman's Law. In both cases, the outer layer is a noun+noun combination in which the first element contains a voiced obstruent: ^{OJ}/kuzupa+gata/ and ^{OJ}/naganakî+döri/.

Another problem with the proposed adjustment to Kuroda's second constraint is that it makes an incorrect prediction about items such as ^{OJ}/mîdu+kagë/ 'water reflection'. The medial obstruent in each morpheme of this word must be linked underlyingly to ɣ, as in (9).

(9) ^{OJ} mîtu + kakë
     | |
     ɣ   ɣ

The proposed adjustment to Kuroda's second constraint prohibits more than one gamma link per word, but severing either of the two links in (9) will yield an incorrect form.

In short, there does not seem to be any obvious way of adjusting Kuroda's account so as to handle the strong version of Lyman's Law in Old Japanese. Perhaps this is because the rendaku-inhibiting effect of a preceding voiced obstruent is not really the same phenomenon as the rendaku-inhibiting effect of a following voiced obstruent. Recall from section 1.5 that the dictionary search turned up no counterexamples to the strong version of Lyman's Law involving a voiced obstruent in the syllable immediately preceding the potential rendaku site. Repeating two of the examples given above, ^{OJ}/tugE+wo+gusi/ shows rendaku while ^{OJ}/tugE+kusi/ 'boxwood comb' does not. At the same time, as (7) and (8) show, the earlier voiced obstruent in all three apparent counterexamples is also not in the morpheme immediately preceding the potential rendaku site. These observations suggest that a preceding voiced obstruent had only a local effect in Old Japanese. One possibility is that the preceding voiced obstruent had to be in the immediately preceding morpheme; another possibility is that it had to be in the immediately preceding syllable. The tiny number of relevant examples are compatible with either of these two alternatives.

Kuroda succeeds in producing the effect of the weak version of Lyman's Law and makes no attempt to handle the strong version. As the preceding discussion has shown, there is no obvious way to extend Kuroda's account to produce the effect of the strong version of Lyman's Law, and this may well be a virtue. After all, the rendaku-inhibiting effect of a preceding voiced obstruent seems to have been a genuine characteristic of Old Japanese, but it has not survived into modern Japanese. On the other hand, the rendaku-inhibiting effect of a following voiced obstruent (i.e., the weak version of Lyman's Law) is almost universally regarded as a genuine characteristic of both Old Japanese and modern Japanese.[28] If the two effects were indeed separate phenomena, then perhaps it is no puzzle that one has disappeared while the other has survived.

There is, however, one last idea that merits brief consideration. Some statements of the weak version of Lyman's Law (e.g., Okumura 1955; Nakagawa 1966) claim that rendaku is inhibited only by a voiced obstruent in the syllable immediately following the potential rendaku site. If so, the weak version of Lyman's Law is a local effect, and rendaku in an item such as /nawa+bašigo/ 'rope ladder' (cf. /hašigo/ 'ladder') does not constitute a violation.[29] This characterization of the weak version of Lyman's Law makes it quite parallel to the local rendaku-inhibiting effect of a preceding voiced obstruent suggested for Old Japanese in the paragraph just above. Given these assumptions, the strong version of Lyman's Law is a bidirectional local constraint that prevents the creation of adjacent syllables containing voiced obstruents. On this account, the diachronic change from the strong version to the weak version was just the restriction of the effect to one direction.

Nonetheless, this characterization of the weak version of Lyman's Law as a local constraint is not very attractive. The drawback is that it makes the third syllable of a three-syllable morpheme irrelevant to rendaku. For example, the absence of rendaku in a noun+noun combination such as /doku+tokage/ 'poisonous lizard' cannot be attributed to this more limited Lyman's Law. As mentioned in section 1.4, the great majority of Old Japanese noun morphemes were realized as one or two syllables, and there are not very many relevant three-syllable noun morphemes like /tokage/ 'lizard' in modern Japanese. The obvious solution is simply to treat /tokage/ as rendaku-immune, since, as noted in section 1.5, rendaku-immune morphemes exist anyway. On the other hand, relevant three-syllable nouns derived from verb stems are not so rare, and the behavior of these items makes it difficult to accept the idea that Lyman's Law is a local constraint. The examples in (10) illustrate this.

(10) a. /hanas-u/ 'speak'
/hanaš-i/ 'speaking'
/mukaši+banaš-i/ 'old legend'
b. /todoke-ru/ 'report'
/todoke/ 'reporting'
/koNiN+todoke/ 'marriage registration'
c. /kaseg-u/ 'make a living'
/kaseg-i/ 'making a living'
/tomo+kaseg-i/ 'joint livelihood'

Verb stems with no voiced obstruents, like /hanaš-i/ (10a), often show rendaku in compounds, but verb stems with a voiced obstruent in the second syllable, like /todoke/ (10b), or in the third syllable, like /kaseg-i/ (10c), never show rendaku in comparable compounds. It seems unlikely that this pattern is just a coincidence; but if the weak version of Lyman's Law is a local constraint, it can account for the absence of rendaku in compounds ending with /todoke/ but not for the absence of rendaku in compounds ending with /kaseg-i/. The verb stem /kaseg-i/, and every other verb stem with a voiced obstruent in the third syllable, would have to be treated as idiosyncratically rendaku-immune.

1.8 Conclusion

The attested vocabulary of Old Japanese is consistent with the claim that a voiced obstruent following a potential rendaku site prevented rendaku. It is also consistent with the claim that a voiced obstruent in the syllable immediately preceding a potential rendaku site prevented rendaku. The inhibiting effect of a following voiced obstruent is known as (the weak version of) Lyman's Law, and it has sometimes been suggested that the two effects are a single phenomenon, referred to jointly as the strong version of Lyman's Law. The weak version still holds with very few exceptions in modern Japanese, but the strong version does not. Kuroda (2002) proposes an analysis of rendaku that, despite its acknowledged shortcomings, seems at first glance to offer a simple diachronic path from the strong version of Lyman's Law to the weak version. On closer scrutiny, however, this elegant account of the diachronic change breaks down, and it may well be that the inhibiting effects of following voiced obstruents and preceding voiced obstruents were separate phenomena in Old Japanese.

Notes

1. For an introduction to rendaku, see Vance 1987, 133–48. For historical details in the context of a more general discussion of voicing distinctions, see Martin 1987, 84–120.
2. There are, however, a few instances of rendaku in phraselike items. See note 11.
3. Many linguists prefer to analyze [h], [ç], and [ɸ] as allophones of a single phoneme except in recent borrowings. I am assuming a uniform phonemic inventory for all vocabulary strata and a split that has resulted in a contrast between [ɸ] and [h]/[ç]. Either way, the rendaku alternation is not simply a matter of voicing. The ancestor of modern /h/ and /f/ was pronounced [p], although there is some controversy about how long the [p] pronunciation persisted in the central dialects (Kiyose 1985).
4. In earlier work (Vance 1987, 24), I said that the two allophones of /z/, [dz] and [z], are distributed as follows: [dz] word-initially or immediately following the mora nasal /N/ and [z] elsewhere. The actual distribution is certainly not this clean, but there is no contrast, and the two are unquestionably allophones of a single phoneme. The modern rendaku pairing of /z/

with /c/ and /s/ reflects the historical merger of a voiced affricate and a voiced fricative, and so does the pairing of /ǰ/ with /č/ and /š/.

5. For an account of why rendaku is irregular, see Vance 1983. For examples and discussion, see Vance 1987, 146–48, and Ohno 2000.

6. According to Miyake (1932, 136), Motoori stated categorically that if the second element of a compound contains a voiced obstruent, its initial consonant does not voice.

7. Counterexamples include /nawa+bašigo/ 'rope ladder' and several other compounds ending with /bašigo/ (cf. /hašigo/ 'ladder'), /šoo+zaburoo/ (a personal name) and several other names ending with /zaburoo/ (cf. /saburoo/ '3rd son'), and /fuN+ǰibar-u/ 'tie up' (cf. /šibar-u/ 'tie'). See Vance 1980 for an attempt to test the psychological status of Lyman's Law experimentally.

8. Miyake (1932, 136) gives the relevant quotation from Ishizuka's *Kogen Seidakukô* (1801).

9. All Old Japanese examples are marked with a superscript *OJ*. The transcription conventions follow Miller's (1986, 198) slightly modified version of the system first adopted by Mathias (1973) and endorsed by Martin (1987, 50). The transcription reflects the fact that many modern standard syllables with one of the vowels /i e o/ correspond to two distinct eighth-century syllables. (For details, see Lange 1973 and Shibatani 1990, 125–39.) For each such eighth-century pair, it is standard practice to label one syllable *type A* (*kô-rui*) and the other *type B* (*otsu-rui*), following Hashimoto (1917/1949, 173–86). Some researchers construe the phonological differences between the type A and type B syllables as vowel quality distinctions; others construe them as distinctions between syllables with and without a glide: CV versus CGV. In any case, the transcription adopted here represents type-A syllables with a circumflex over the vowel /î ê ô/, type-B syllables with a diaresis over the vowel /ï ë ö/, and syllables for which there was no A/B distinction with no diacritic /i e o/. A capitalized vowel /I E O/ indicates a syllable for which there was an A/B distinction but for which the category is unknown.

10. The Old Japanese prefix [OJ]/opo/ 'big' is the ancestor of the modern Japanese prefix /oo/ that appears in the examples /oo+kaze/ 'strong wind' and /oo+zora/ 'open sky' cited above.

11. On the other hand, there are some noun+GENITIVE+noun examples that actually show rendaku, as in [OJ]/ama+nö+gapa/ 'Milky Way' (cf. [OJ]/kapa/ 'river'), although these are unusual.

12. Even though [OJ]/pîtuzi/ 'sheep' appears as a headword in JJHI, the entry lists no compounds, so excluding it from the search had no effect on the eventual data set.

13. The morphemic segmentations of inflectional forms in this chapter follow the widely adopted analysis of Bloch (1946). I use these segmentations as a convenience and not as an endorsement of the analysis on which they are based.

14. As Martin (1987, 93) points out, the second constituent verb in such a compound was treated as a separate accent phrase in Classical Japanese and presumably in Old Japanese as well. In modern Japanese, compound verbs are prosodically unified.

15. For an account of why verb+verb compounds typically do not show rendaku, see Vance 1983.

16. However, combinations in which a large "numeral" such as [OJ]/mOmO/ 'hundred' or [OJ]/ti/ 'thousand' seems to mean just 'many' were kept in the data set. An example of this type is [OJ]/mOmO+kï/, which JJHI defines as 'many trees'.

17. For details on rendaku in Sino-Japanese, see Vance 1996.

18. In the eighth century, the area around what is now Tokyo was the eastern frontier of the Japanese cultural and political sphere.

19. The distinction between "sheerly speculative" and "merely dubious" is, of course, a judgment call. In any case, only a small number of examples were involved.

20. Unger (2000) used the data set to investigate the frequency of rendaku in different proto-Japanese (i.e., reconstructed) accent classes of monosyllabic and disyllabic nouns. His results serve as a step in a complex argument in favor of a genetic link between Japanese and Korean.

21. In some of these items, such as [OJ]/mîdu+kagë/ 'water reflection', rendaku would violate both versions of Lyman's Law and give us no way of separating the two. Items of this type will come up again in section 1.7.

22. The modern descendant of this morpheme shows rendaku quite consistently as a final element, even in /hiko+boši/ 'Altair' (lit., 'boy star'), the ancestor of which appears in JJHI as [OJ]/pîkô+posi/.

23. The modern Japanese descendant of this item, /yob-u+ko+dori/, is a nickname for a cuckoo.

24. I first heard about this term paper in one of Jim McCawley's classes at the University of Chicago in the mid-1970s, and Yuki Kuroda was kind enough to give me a copy in 2000. Kuroda (2002) is careful to point out that the rendaku alternations are not just a matter of the presence or absence of voicing. Aside from the effects of historical changes pointed out in section 1.2 above, voiced obstruents in Old Japanese were almost certainly prenasalized, just as their descendants are in some modern nonstandard Japanese dialects (Vance 1987, 108–9; Martin 1987, 20–25). In some of these same dialects, word-medial nonrendaku stops are actually voiced, although not prenasalized. These complications will be ignored here, since the phonetics of the alternations are not at issue.

25. The "infinitives" of many Japanese verbs, including /cuge-ru/ 'tell', have no overt inflectional ending. I have opted not to clutter the transcriptions of such forms with a zero morph (e.g., /cuge-∅/).

26. According to the entry in the authoritative historical dictionary of Japanese (Nihon Daijiten Kankôkai 1972–76), the word for 'toad' used to begin with a voiceless velar stop, and the earliest citation (720) has [OJ]/k/.

27. Actually, this morpheme meaning 'person' is one of those that sometimes do, and sometimes do not, undergo rendaku. As noted in section 1.6, Kuroda (2002) does not claim that his analysis can handle such morphemes.

28. This is not to say that there is no doubt whatever about the psychological status of the weak version of Lyman's Law in modern Japanese. For an experimental study, see Vance 1980.

29. See note 7. According to Martin (1987, 115), /hašigo/ 'ladder' has an uncertain etymology, but it probably goes back to a diminutive of /haši/ 'bridge' (cf. /ko/ 'child; small').

References

Bloch, Bernard. 1946. Studies in colloquial Japanese I: Inflection. *Journal of the American Oriental Society* 66, 97–109.

Hashimoto, Shinkichi. 1917. Kokugo kanazukai kenkyûshijô no ichihakken. *Teikoku Bungaku* 23, 123–63. Reprinted in *Moji oyobi kanazukai no kenkyû*. Tokyo: Iwanami, 1949. References are to the 1949 edition.

Ishizuka, Tatsumaro. 1801. *Kogen seidakukô*. Cited in Miyake 1932.

Itô, Junko, and Ralf-Armin Mester. 1986. The phonology of voicing in Japanese. *Linguistic Inquiry* 17, 49–73.

Jôdaigo Jiten Henshû Iinkai [JJHI], ed. 1967. *Jidaibetsu kokugo daijiten: Jôdaihen*. Tokyo: Sanseidô.

Kiyose, Gisaburô N. 1985. Heianchô hagyô-shiin p-onron. *Onsei no Kenkyû* 21, 73–87.

Kuroda, S.-Y. 1963. A historical remark on "rendaku," a phenomenon in Japanese morphology. Manuscript, MIT.

Kuroda, S.-Y. 2002. Rendaku. In *Japanese/Korean linguistics 10*, ed. by Noriko M. Akatsuka and Susan Strauss, 337–50. Stanford, CA: CSLI Publications.

Lange, Roland A. 1973. *The phonology of eighth-century Japanese*. Tokyo: Sophia University.

Lyman, Benjamin S. 1894. *Change from surd to sonant in Japanese compounds*. Philadelphia: Oriental Club of Philadelphia.

Martin, Samuel E. 1952. Morphophonemics of standard colloquial Japanese. Supplement to *Language* (Language Dissertation No. 47).

Martin, Samuel E. 1987. *The Japanese language through time*. New Haven, CT: Yale University Press.

Mathias, Gerald B. 1973. On the modification of certain proto-Korean-Japanese reconstructions. *Papers in Japanese Linguistics* 2, 31–47.

McCawley, James D. 1968. *The phonological component of a grammar of Japanese*. The Hague: Mouton.

Miller, Roy Andrew. 1986. *Nihongo: In defence of Japanese*. London: Athlone.

Miyake, Takerô. 1932. Dakuonkô. *Onsei no Kenkyû* 5, 135–90.

Nakagawa, Yoshio. 1966. Rendaku, rensei (kashô) no keifu. *Kokugo Kokubun* 35.6, 302–14.

Nihon Daijiten Kankôkai, ed. 1972–76. *Nihon kokugo daijiten*. Tokyo: Shôgakukan.

Ohno, Kazutoshi. 2000. The lexical nature of *rendaku* in Japanese. In *Japanese/Korean linguistics 9*, ed. by Mineharu Nakayama and Charles J. Quinn, Jr., 151–64. Stanford, CA: CSLI Publications.

Okumura, Mitsuo. 1955. Rendaku. In *Kokugogaku jiten*, ed. by Kokugo Gakkai, 961–62. Tokyo: Tôkyôdô.

Ramsey, S. Robert, and J. Marshall Unger. 1972. Evidence for a consonant shift in 7th century Japanese. *Papers in Japanese Linguistics* 1, 278–95.

Shibatani, Masayoshi. 1990. *The languages of Japan*. Cambridge: Cambridge University Press.

Unger, J. Marshall. 1975. Studies in early Japanese morphophonemics. Doctoral dissertation, Yale University. Published, Bloomington: Indiana University Linguistics Club, 1977.

Unger, J. Marshall. 2000. *Rendaku* and Proto-Japanese accent classes. In *Japanese/Korean linguistics 9*, ed. by Mineharu Nakayama and Charles J. Quinn, Jr., 17–30. Stanford, CA: CSLI Publications.

Vance, Timothy J. 1980. The psychological status of a constraint on Japanese consonant alternation. *Linguistics* 18, 245–67.

Vance, Timothy J. 1983. On the origin of voicing alternation in Japanese consonants. *Journal of the American Oriental Society* 102, 333–41.

Vance, Timothy J. 1987. *An introduction to Japanese phonology*. Albany, NY: SUNY Press.

Vance, Timothy J. 1996. Sequential voicing in Sino-Japanese. *Journal of the Association of Teachers of Japanese* 30, 22–43.

PART II
Syntax

Chapter 2
NP Gaps in Tamil: Syntactic versus Pragmatic
E. Annamalai

2.1 Postulating Two Kinds of Gap

Tamil is an SOV language with free word order and no invariant requirement that the verb be final in a clause (Annamalai 2004). It freely permits absence of nouns, called *NP gaps* in this chapter, in utterances in discourse as well as in sentences (simple and complex) in isolation. The referents of NP gaps are recovered from many sources: from the background world knowledge of the interlocutors, from the discourse context or the speech act by pragmatic rules, from the agreement marker of the finite verb predicate (in the case of a missing subject) by morphological redundancy rules, and from the syntactic context by principles of coindexing with other nouns in the sentence. Of these, the principles of syntactic coindexing are internal to a grammatical theory. Pretheoretically, the coindexing principles for pronouns in Tamil are the following.[1] Of the two kinds of pronouns in Tamil, the general pronoun is coindexed with a noun phrase in the sentence that is not a subject and that precedes or c-commands it. The reflexive pronoun is coindexed with a noun phrase that is a subject and that c-commands it in the same clause or in the embedded clause (for details, see Annamalai 1999).

NP gaps are hypothesized to be of two kinds: open or free, and closed or bounded. A gap is identified when there is formally no noun phrase in a syntactic slot that is the site for a referent. It is *free* if the referent is in principle unconstrained syntactically. It does not have its antecedent in the sentence or is barred by the syntactic

---

A longer version of this chapter was originally written when I was a Visiting Fellow at the Max Planck Institute for Psycholinguistics, in Nijmegen. I am grateful for the material support and intellectual stimulation I received there. I greatly benefited from my hosts' penetrating questions skeptical of syntactic recovery of gaps, when I gave a talk to the Argument Structure Group of the Institute. The critical comments of the editors of this volume and of the two anonymous reviewers helped me describe the problem in a more precise and readable fashion. Any part of the chapter that remains unclear is a residue of my original expansive description of the problem.

configuration from being coindexed with an antecedent in the sentence. In other words, the referent of the free gap is recovered from outside the sentence or from the sentence itself when syntactic conditions do not apply. Any intrasentential referents of the free gap, if recovered at all under syntactic conditions, will be less privileged. They will be a subset of its extrasentential referents. The recovery of the referent of the free gap must be based on pragmatic principles that draw on a theory of inference from background knowledge, a theory of discourse organization, or a theory of speech acts.[2] The pragmatic principles cannot, however, operate without the syntactic principles of argument structure, which posit the gap.

A gap is *bounded* if the referent is governed syntactically; that is, its recovery is made with an antecedent present in the sentence by syntactically defined coindexing principles. That is, the referent of a bounded gap is necessarily intrasentential. Nevertheless, in many syntactic contexts, the bounded gap does not preclude a referent beyond the sentence in discourse. In these contexts, recovery of the intrasentential referent is privileged. The possible extrasentential referent adds to the syntactically coindexed referent, making the sentence multiply ambiguous.

Free gaps are marked by X in the examples below, indicating their free referential value or interpretation; bounded gaps are marked by $\emptyset$, indicating their bounded referential value or interpretation. Each bounded gap is marked with a subscript, which links it with the coindexed antecedent(s) in the sentence. The glosses given for the examples are the only possible or the preferred interpretation(s) of the sentences.

Of the two kinds of pronouns differing in form, the reflexive pronoun is always governed syntactically, and so is the gap that has the subject of its clause or a higher clause as its antecedent, like the reflexive pronoun. The general pronoun may or may not be governed syntactically. When the pronoun is governed syntactically, its referent is recovered intrasententially, and when it is not, it is recovered extrasententially, just as with gaps.[3] These facts suggest that pronouns and gaps have the same properties. This leads to the hypothesis that the gap that alternates with the pronoun whose referent is recovered by applying syntactic conditions is a bounded gap ($\emptyset$). Heuristically, then, the optional absence of a syntactically bound pronoun is an indicator of the site of the bounded gap ($\emptyset$), differentiating it from the free gap (X), which, by the above hypothesis, has the same privilege of occurrence as the syntactically unbounded general pronoun. This chapter examines the validity of this hypothesis, particularly whether the alternation with $\emptyset$ takes place in all or some of the syntactic contexts in which the bounded pronoun occurs.

The test is carried out in different syntactic contexts to find out if the syntactically bound pronoun and $\emptyset$ alternate in them, and if they do not, which of the two is possible in a particular syntactic context. The test shows that they alternate in most syntactic contexts, but they do not alternate in a few, where only one of them occurs. This makes the hypothesis that the pronouns and gaps have the same properties a qualified one. It is nevertheless used as a working hypothesis for the purpose of testing the facts about gaps. To confirm the syntactic nature of ∅, further tests examine whether, in any of the syntactic contexts, the gap does not allow an extrasentential referent (X interpretation), and if it does allow one, whether the intrasentential referent is privileged in recovery (in the sense that one must imagine a pragmatic context to cancel that referent out) in those syntactic contexts.

2.2 Sentential Noun Phrases

We shall first take up gaps in embedded clauses, which are noun phrases either formally ((1), (3)) or positionally (2), being used as sentential direct object and subject.

(1) ∅$_1$/avanukku$_1$ veele keDeccirukradu kumaare$_1$ sandooSappaDuttum
    he-to   job is-available-that Kumar-ACC make-happy-will
    'That he$_1$ has got a job will make Kumar$_1$ happy.'

(2) ∅$_2$/avane$_2$ ∅$_1$/taan$_1$ veelekki vaccikiDreennu kumaar$_1$ raajaaTTe$_2$ sonnaan
    he-ACC   self   job-for keep-PRES.PNG.that Kumar Raja-to said
    vaccukiDradaa
    keep-PRES.NOM.ADV
    'Kumar$_1$ told Raja$_2$ that he$_1$ would give him$_2$ a job.'

(3) ∅$_{1/2}$/tanakku$_1$/avanukku$_2$ veele keDeccirukrade raaja$_1$ innom
    self-to   he-to   job be-available-NOMZ.ACC Raja yet
    kumaarTTe$_2$ keDeccirukkunnu sollale
    Kumar-to   be-available-PRES.that say-not
    'With respect to his$_{1/2}$ having gotten a job, Raja$_1$ has not yet told Kumar$_2$ that he$_{1/2}$ has gotten a job.'

∅ in the embedded clause of (1)–(3) is coindexed with antecedents in the matrix clause, and it alternates with corresponding pronouns. ∅ in all positions (subject, direct object, and indirect object), it should be noted, does not exclude an extrasentential referent (i.e., X interpretation). It may refer to speech act participants (e.g., (1) could also mean 'That I have got a job will make Kumar happy') or a discourse referent in an appropriate discourse context (e.g., 'That Raja has got a job will make Kumar happy') and thus have the properties of X. Intrasentential referents are, however, privileged for recovery in these sentences in isolation.

2.3 Infinitive Clauses

We shall now consider ∅ in sentences with an infinitive clause.

(4) kumaar$_1$ ∅$_1$/taan$_1$ X aDikka kambu keeTTaan
    Kumar   self   hit-INF stick asked
    'Kumar$_1$ asked for a stick to hit with.'

In (4), the subject of the infinitive clause is ∅, as it is coindexed with the subject of the matrix clause and alternates with the reflexive pronoun. Incidentally, note that there is no gap in the subject position of the matrix clause in (4). The subject of the matrix clause has been reordered to the front of the whole S, and no gap is left at the site when a noun phrase is reordered to serve discourse functions. The predicate of the infinitive clause *aDi* 'hit', being a transitive verb, must have a Patient argument, and this missing argument is marked by X, as it does not specify any referent intrasententially. The noun *kambu* 'stick', the direct object of the matrix clause, is unsuitable to be the direct object of *aDi* 'hit' in the infinitive clause because in the argument structure it would be extraordinary for the patient and the instrument to be identical. *Kumar*, the subject of the matrix clause, can be the direct object of the infinitive clause marked X. This direct object can be formally present as the reflexive pronoun *tanne* 'self-ACC' in the infinitive clause to give the meaning 'Kumar$_1$ asked for a stick to hit him$_1$ (by himself$_1$ or someone else)'. This is not, however, a preferred interpretation with the gap in the direct object position of the infinitive. This interpretation requires a special discourse context, or a verbal reflexive in the predicate as in (5a). There is thus a difference between the gaps in subject position and direct object position of the infinitive clause in terms of preferred referential interpretation, which is indicated by designating the gap differently in the two positions.

The subject gap in the infinitive clause in (4) allows an X interpretation also. The extrasentential referent in a discourse context is unspecified (i.e., 'someone'). This unspecified-referent interpretation is more preferred with a variant of the infinitive, namely, the nominalized verb with tense plus dative case (= *for* V-*ing* in English)— that is, when *aDikradukkku* 'for hitting' is used instead of *aDikka* 'to hit'.

The above facts show that although the possible referents of ∅ and X are not mutually exclusive, the two kinds of gaps have different preferred interpretations and required contexts of use. One may conclude from this that any difference between ∅ and X is not categorical. There are, however, syntactic contexts like the one discussed below, where only ∅ occurs, with no extrasentential reference.

The gap in the direct object position of the infinitive can be coindexed only with the subject of the infinitive clause when the predicate of the infinitive clause is inflected for the verbal reflexive by addition of the auxiliary verb *kiDu*, as in (5a). The verbal reflexive stipulates a clausemate (local domain) condition, namely, that the antecedent and the reflexive pronoun be in the same clause (Annamalai 1999). The same gap is not coindexed with the subject of the matrix clause in (5b). Neither of them has a discourse referent and so they are ∅. ∅ alternates with the reflexive pronoun *tanne* 'self-ACC' when the infinitive predicate contains the verbal reflexive. Recall that ∅ in the direct object position of the infinitive is not privileged to be coindexed with the subject in (4), whose infinitive predicate does not contain the verbal reflexive. These show that coindexing of ∅ in direct object position of the infinitive is subject to the clausemate condition of the verbal reflexive, and thus show the gap to be syntactic.

Chapter 1
Sequential Voicing and Lyman's Law in Old Japanese

Timothy J. Vance

1.1 Introduction

The term *sequential voicing* is Martin's (1952, 48) translation of the Japanese technical term *rendaku*, which refers to a Japanese morphophonemic phenomenon found in compounds and in prefix + base combinations.[1] Since the Japanese term is not only shorter but also quite commonly used by linguists writing in English, this chapter will adopt it throughout. According to one version of a putative constraint (Lyman's Law), Old Japanese did not allow rendaku if a voiced obstruent either preceded or followed a potential rendaku site within a word. Despite the obvious appeal of a single bidirectional constraint, this chapter argues that two separate phenomena were involved.

1.2 Rendaku

A morpheme that exhibits rendaku has one allomorph beginning with a voiceless obstruent and another allomorph beginning with a voiced obstruent, and the voiced allomorph of such a morpheme appears only when it is a noninitial morph in a word.[2] The examples in (1) illustrate the pairs of phonemes that alternate.

(1) a. /f/~/b/   /fune/ 'boat'
                 /kawa+bune/ 'river boat'
    b. /h/~/b/   /hako/ 'case'
                 /haši+bako/ 'chopstick case'
    c. /t/~/d/   /tama/ 'ball'
                 /me+dama/ 'eyeball'

I am grateful to Shoko Hamano, Kazutoshi Ohno, and Jim Unger for helpful suggestions. Versions of this chapter were presented at the 2000 meeting of the Western Branch of the American Oriental Society in Tempe, Arizona, and to audiences at International Christian University, the University of Illinois at Urbana-Champaign, and UCLA.

d. /k/~/g/ /kami/ 'paper'
/iro+gami/ 'colored paper'
e. /c/~/z/ /cuka/ 'mound'
/ari+zuka/ 'anthill'
f. /s/~/z/ /sora/ 'sky'
/hoši+zora/ 'starry sky'
g. /č/~/ǰ/ /či/ 'blood'
/hana+ǰi/ 'nosebleed'
h. /š/~/ǰ/ /šika/ 'deer'
/ko+ǰika/ 'young deer'

Because of well-known historical changes, some of the alternations in modern Japanese involve more than just a difference in voicing. Notice that /b/ alternates with /f/ ([ɸ]; (1a)) and /h/ (1b), not with /p/.[3] Notice also that /z/ ([dz] or [z]) alternates both with /c/ ([ts]; (1e)) and with /s/ (1f) and that /ǰ/ ([ɟʑ]) alternates both with /č/ ([cɕ]; (1g)) and with /š/ ([ɕ]; (1h)).[4]

1.3 Lyman's Law

Jim McCawley's first book was, of course, a revised version of his dissertation on Japanese phonology, and his characterization of rendaku (McCawley 1968, 87) is refreshingly candid: "I am unable to state the environment in which the 'voicing rule' applies. The relevant data are completely bewildering." More than 30 years later, there is still no reason to doubt that rendaku is fundamentally irregular, but there are some strong tendencies in the data.[5]

The best-known tendency is that a voiced obstruent in a morpheme inhibits rendaku. For example, Okumura (1955) compares /oo+kaze/ 'strong wind' and /oo+zora/ 'open sky', both of which contain the prefix /oo/ 'big'. He says that sequential voicing does not apply to give */oo+gaze/ for 'strong wind' because /kaze/ 'wind', unlike /sora/ 'sky', already contains a voiced obstruent. The first scholar to mention this inhibiting effect was Motoori Norinaga (1730–1801), but the first non-Japanese to write about it was Benjamin Lyman (1894), and it is sometimes called Lyman's Law.[6] There are counterexamples to Lyman's Law in modern Japanese, but they are extremely rare.[7]

The earliest substantial written records of Japanese date from the eighth century and presumably reflect the language of the aristocracy in the capital city of Nara at that time. This language is usually called Old Japanese, and Ramsey and Unger (1972) claim that sequential voicing did not occur in Old Japanese if either the first or the second element of a compound contained a voiced obstruent. Unger (1975, 9) refers to this as the "strong version" of Lyman's Law, and he attributes its original discovery to Ishizuka Tatsumaro (1764–1823).[8] No one has ever suggested that the strong version of Lyman's Law applies to modern Japanese, and counterexamples such as /mado+giwa/ 'window-side' (cf. /kiwa/ 'side') and /de+beso/ 'protruding navel' (cf. /heso/ 'navel') are easy to find.

1.4 Dictionary Search

This chapter reports the results of a systematic dictionary search for Old Japanese lexical items relevant to the two versions of Lyman's Law. The search targeted noun+noun and prefix+noun combinations that appear as headwords in the definitive dictionary of Old Japanese: Jôdaigo Jiten Henshû Iinkai 1967 (hereafter JJHI). The first step was to go through the appendix, which lists each headword and its part of speech. For every monomorphemic noun headword beginning with a voiceless obstruent and consisting of one or two syllables, the entry in the main body of the dictionary was checked. Each entry includes a list of longer items containing the headword, and all the longer words ending with that morpheme were added provisionally to the data set. For example, the appendix lists the two-syllable noun ^{OJ}/kuti/ 'mouth', and the entry under this headword lists 10 longer words and phrases containing it.[9] Of these, 3 are headwords that end with this morpheme for 'mouth': the noun+noun combination ^{OJ}/yama+guti/ 'starting point for climbing a mountain' (with rendaku), the prefix+noun combination ^{OJ}/opo+kuti/ 'large mouth' (without rendaku), and the phrase ^{OJ}/mîti+nö+kuti/ 'road entry point' (without rendaku), in which the genitive particle ^{OJ}/nö/ connects two nouns.[10] Headwords of this last type, that is, two nouns joined by a genitive particle (^{OJ}/nö/, ^{OJ}/ga/, or ^{OJ}/tu/), were excluded from the data set. While such items were undoubtedly set phrases in Old Japanese, their phrasal character presumably made rendaku unlikely, and including them in the data set might confound the assessment of Lyman's Law. Consider the headword ^{OJ}/okî+tu+kadi/ 'offshore oar', with the voiced obstruent ^{OJ}/d/ in the final element ^{OJ}/kadi/ 'oar'. The rendaku form *^{OJ}/okî+tu+gadi/ would certainly violate the weak version of Lyman's Law, but it seems unwise to attribute the lack of rendaku to Lyman's Law in such cases.[11]

Since the great majority of Old Japanese noun morphemes were realized as one or two syllables, the length limitation facilitated the search process enormously while excluding only a very few potentially relevant nouns such as three-syllable ^{OJ}/pîtuzi/ 'sheep'.[12] The length limitation also had the benefit of automatically skipping over many noun headwords derived from verb stems, such as ^{OJ}/kazar-i/ 'decorating' (cf. ^{OJ}/kazar-u/ 'decorate'). The hyphen in these transcriptions represents the boundary between the stem and the inflectional ending according to one influential analysis of Japanese verb inflection, and on this account, a word like ^{OJ}/kazar-i/ is not monomorphemic.[13] A more important consideration for present purposes is that, just like modern Japanese, Old Japanese had compound verbs consisting of a verb stem plus a verb, such as ^{OJ}/kak-î+tor-u/ 'write down' (cf. ^{OJ}/kak-u/ 'write', ^{OJ}/tor-u/ 'take'),

and compound nouns consisting of a verb stem plus another verb stem, such as
[OJ]/sOp-î+tukap-î/ 'second-ranking official' (cf. [OJ]/sOp-u/ 'accompany', [OJ]/tukap-u/
'use').[14] It is often unclear whether a compound of this second type (i.e., a verb+verb
compound noun) should be understood as a combination of two nouns (each derived
from a verb stem) or as a noun derived from the stem of a single compound verb.
The problem is that verb+verb compound verbs (i.e., words like [OJ]/kak-î+tor-u/)
typically do not show rendaku (Vance 1987, 142–44), so a noun derived from the
stem of such a verb would not show rendaku either, regardless of whether rendaku
would violate either version of Lyman's Law.[15] For this reason, it seemed advisable
simply to exclude all words ending with a verb stem from the data set—even the
many two-syllable verb stems such as [OJ]/kak-î/ 'writing'. On the other hand, words
containing a verb stem (or an adjective stem) elsewhere are not problematic. For example, the data set includes [OJ]/pakar-i+kötö/ 'plans' (cf. the verb [OJ]/pakar-u/ 'plan'
and the noun [OJ]/kötö/ 'fact').

At this point, the data set consisted of all headwords in JJHI ending with
an obstruent-initial noun morph of one or two syllables. Using O to stand for any
obstruent, V for any vowel, and C for any consonant (either obstruent or sonorant),
it follows from Old Japanese phonotactics that every example in the data set contains
a final morph of the form OV (as in [OJ]/yödö+se/ 'stagnant shallows') or OVCV (as
in [OJ]/yupu+dukï/ 'evening moon'; cf. [OJ]/tukï/ 'moon').

Several further limitations were then imposed on the data set. First, coordinate
compounds such as [OJ]/kaze+kumO/ 'wind and clouds' were excluded, since rendaku
typically does not occur in coordinate compounds (Vance 1987, 144–45). Second,
numeral+counter combinations such as [OJ]/puta+tabî/ 'two times' were excluded,
since such combinations seem to disfavor rendaku (Vance 1987, 142).[16] Third, items
ending in a Sino-Japanese morpheme were excluded, since even today rendaku is
much less likely to occur in a Sino-Japanese morph than in a native morph.[17] There
are very few headwords of this type in JJHI, but one example is [OJ]/kusuri+si/ 'doctor' (cf. native [OJ]/kusuri/ 'medicine' and Sino-Japanese [OJ]/si/ 'expert'). Fourth, items
labeled eastern dialect forms were excluded.[18] Finally, items with final "morphemes"
for which the etymology is sheerly speculative were excluded. On the other hand,
examples for which the etymology of the final morpheme is merely dubious remained
in the data set.[19] The purpose of all these additional limitations (especially the first
two) was to eliminate items in which a lack of rendaku might be due to some factor
other than either version of Lyman's Law.[20]

1.5 Results

To assess the status of the weak version of Lyman's Law in Old Japanese, items
in which rendaku would violate the strong version were removed from the data

Table 1.1
The weak version of Lyman's Law in Old Japanese

Final element type	Number of final elements showing rendaku in at least one word	Total number of words showing rendaku
O⁻ V	14/35 (40%)	50/182 (27%)
O⁻ V S V	50/74 (68%)	137/313 (44%)
O⁻ V O⁻ V	40/73 (55%)	117/333 (35%)
O⁻ V O⁺ V	0/25 (0%)	0/83 (0%)

set. Such items have a nonfinal morpheme containing a voiced obstruent, as in ᴼᴶ/mîdu+töri/ 'water bird'.[21] The resulting subset contains 911 noun+noun and prefix+noun combinations involving 207 different final morphemes. Using O⁻ to stand for any voiceless obstruent, O⁺ for any voiced obstruent, S for any sonorant, and V for any vowel, the forms of these 207 morphemes that appear as independent words can be divided into the following four categories: O⁻ V (e.g., ᴼᴶ/pa/ 'leaf'), O⁻ V S V (e.g., ᴼᴶ/tuna/ 'rope'), O⁻ V O⁻ V (e.g., ᴼᴶ/satô/ 'village'), and O⁻ V O⁺ V (e.g., ᴼᴶ/kazu/ 'number'). The frequency of rendaku in final elements of each type is shown in table 1.1. Rendaku in a word ending with a morpheme in the last category would, of course, violate the weak version of Lyman's Law, but as the last row in table 1.1 shows, there are no such violations in the data set. In other words, the weak version of Lyman's Law seems to have held categorically in Old Japanese.

To assess the status of the strong version of Lyman's Law in Old Japanese, three types of items were removed from the data set. The first type was items in which rendaku would violate the weak version. Such items have a final morpheme containing a noninitial voiced obstruent (e.g., ᴼᴶ/yupu+kagë/ 'evening shadow'). The second type was items ending in a morpheme that never shows rendaku in any headword listed in JJHI. Needless to say, if the rendaku allomorph of a morpheme is unattested, no attested headword ending with that morpheme could violate either version of Lyman's Law. Such a morpheme might simply have been idiosyncratically immune to rendaku, just as some modern morphemes are (e.g., /cuyu/ 'dew' and /himo/ 'string'). One example of a morpheme in this category is ᴼᴶ/posi/ 'star', which appears as the final element in three headwords, all without rendaku.[22] Removing items of this second type guards against inflating the number of examples in which absence of rendaku can be attributed to the strong version of Lyman's Law. The third type removed from the data set was items ending in a morpheme that happens not to occur in any headwords containing an earlier voiced obstruent. For example, ᴼᴶ/kapa/ 'river' occurs as the final morpheme in 12 headwords, 6 with rendaku (as in ᴼᴶ/tani+gapa/ 'valley river') and 6 without (as in ᴼᴶ/isi+kapa/ 'stony river'), but

Table 1.2
The strong version of Lyman's Law in Old Japanese

Location of preceding voiced obstruent	Number of words showing rendaku
0	144/367 (39%)
−1	0/46 (0%)
−2	2/14 (14%)
−3	1/2 (50%)

none of these 12 headwords contains a voiced obstruent in the portion preceding the morph for 'river'. There is no point in looking at final elements that do not occur in headwords of the relevant form.

The resulting subset of the data set contains 429 noun+noun and prefix+noun combinations involving 26 different final morphemes. These 429 items were divided into four categories depending on the location of the voiced obstruent preceding the final morph: 0 meaning nowhere (e.g., ^{OJ}/paru+pana/ 'spring flower'), −1 meaning the syllable immediately preceding the final morph (e.g., ^{OJ}/siba+kakî/ 'brushwood hedge'), −2 meaning the second syllable preceding the final morph (e.g., ^{OJ}/pIdari+te/ 'left hand'), and −3 meaning the third syllable preceding the final morph (e.g., ^{OJ}/saburap-î+pîtö/ 'aristocrat's retainer'; cf. ^{OJ}/saburap-u/ 'serve as a retainer' and ^{OJ}/pîtö/ 'person'). The frequency of rendaku in the items in each category is shown in table 1.2.

As the second row in table 1.2 shows, there are no violations of the strong version of Lyman's Law in items containing a voiced obstruent in the syllable immediately preceding the final morph. The only apparent exception that turned up in the course of the dictionary search was ^{OJ}/mugî+gara/. This item is not listed as a headword in JJHI, but it appears in the lists of compounds under the headwords ^{OJ}/mugî/ 'grain' and ^{OJ}/kara/ 'stem'. The authoritative historical dictionary of Japanese (Nihon Daijiten Kankôkai 1972–76) lists this word as having the modern form /mugi+kara/ (without rendaku), but it gives /mugi+gara/ (with rendaku) as an alternative, and there are three citations. The oldest (ca. 934) implies that the Old Japanese form was ^{OJ}/mugî+kara/ (without rendaku), while the other two (ca. 1100 and 1698) indicate /mugi+gara/. The entry also lists five longer compounds (none with citations), four beginning with /mugikara/ (/mugikara+gusa/, /mugikara+sanada/, /mugikara+bue/, /mugikara+booši/) and one beginning with /mugigara/ (/mugigara+bune/). All of this at least suggests that the modern alternative pronunciation with rendaku, /mugi+gara/, is a later development, and that the Old Japanese form was in fact ^{OJ}/mugî+kara/.

The last two rows in table 1.2 show that there were two violations of the strong version of Lyman's Law in items containing a voiced obstruent in the second syllable preceding the final morph, and one violation in items containing a voiced obstruent in the third syllable preceding the final morph. As it turns out, all three of these violations occur in words consisting of three morphemes: ^{OJ}/tugE+wo+gusi/ 'boxwood small-comb' (cf. ^{OJ}/tugE/ 'boxwood', ^{OJ}/wo/ 'small', ^{OJ}/kusi/ 'comb'), ^{OJ}/kuzu+pa+gata/ 'kudzu-leaf vine' (cf. ^{OJ}/kuzu/ 'kudzu', ^{OJ}/pa/ 'leaf', ^{OJ}/kata/ 'vine'), and ^{OJ}/naga+nak-î+döri/ 'chicken' (lit., 'long-singing bird'; cf. ^{OJ}/naga-si/ 'long', ^{OJ}/nak-u/ 'sing', ^{OJ}/töri/ 'bird'). These three items figure prominently in the discussion in section 1.6.

Incidentally, a fourth apparent violation, ^{OJ}/yob-u+kô+döri/, was discounted as phrasal. The entry in JJHI says that the meaning of this item is uncertain, but it clearly consists of the adnominal form of the verb ^{OJ}/yob-u/ 'call', the noun ^{OJ}/kô/ 'child', and the rendaku allomorph of the noun ^{OJ}/töri/ 'bird'.[23] Since the combination ^{OJ}/yob-u+kô/ has the grammatical form of a phrase meaning 'which calls children', ^{OJ}/yob-u+kô+döri/ is not a simple noun+noun combination, and it is not clear whether the strong version of Lyman's Law should be expected to apply to such an item. The word formation pattern involved is quite interesting, since a two-word phrase is functioning as the first element in a compound. A modern Japanese example with the same kind of structure is /haya-i+mono+gač-i/ 'success to the person who arrives first', which consists of the adjective /haya-i/ 'early', the noun /mono/ 'person', and the rendaku allomorph of the verb stem /kač-i/ 'victory' (cf. the verb /kac-u/). The first element of this compound is the two-word phrase /haya-i mono/ 'early person'.

As table 1.2 shows, only a fairly small number of Old Japanese vocabulary items (a total of 62) contain a voiced obstruent preceding a potential rendaku site. Nonetheless, it seems fair to sum up by saying that the strong version of Lyman's Law comes very close to being a true generalization about the attested vocabulary.

1.6 Kuroda's "Antirendaku"

Kuroda (2002), reviving an idea that he first articulated in a graduate school term paper (Kuroda 1963), suggests thinking of rendaku as word-initial devoicing rather than word-medial voicing.[24] This proposal links rendaku to the well-known ban on word-initial voiced obstruents that is standardly attributed to pre–Old Japanese. As Kuroda notes, there were already a few exceptions in Old Japanese, but even today very few native Japanese words begin with a voiced obstruent.

Inspired by Itô and Mester (1986), Kuroda proposes that an obstruent unspecified for voice is voiceless and that an autosegmental feature ɣ (gamma), which can link only to obstruents, has the effect of converting a default voiceless obstruent to its voiced rendaku counterpart, that is, to the voiced partner listed in (1). Itô and Mester assume that their equivalent of ɣ appears in the process of compounding; Kuroda assumes that ɣ is present underlyingly in all morphemes but is unlinked in a morpheme with no obstruent or in a rendaku-immune morpheme. The examples in (2) illustrate Kuroda's underlying forms.

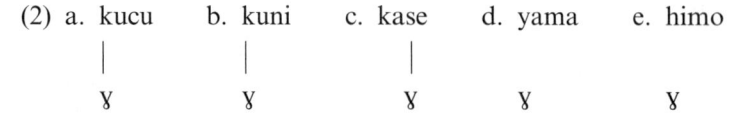

(2) a. kucu   b. kuni   c. kase   d. yama   e. himo
       | | |
       ɣ   ɣ   ɣ   ɣ   ɣ

In the underlying forms of /kucu/ 'shoe' (2a) and /kuni/ 'province' (2b), ɣ is linked to the initial obstruent because these morphemes show rendaku when they occur as final elements, as in /kawa+gucu/ 'leather shoe' and /yama+guni/ 'mountainous province'. In /kaze/ 'wind' (2c), ɣ is linked to the medial obstruent. There is no link in the underlying form of /yama/, which contains no obstruent, or in /himo/, which is rendaku-immune (cf. /kucu+himo/ 'shoelace'). A morpheme like /neko/ 'cat', which always appears with the medial voiceless obstruent /k/, also has no underlying link.

Two constraints are necessary to account for the alternation patterns of these morphemes. The first is that ɣ cannot be linked to a word-initial segment, which means that the underlying link in morphemes like /kucu/ and /kuni/ must be severed when they appear word-initially, as illustrated in (3).

(3) a. kuni   b. yama + kuni
       ╪ |
       ɣ   ɣ   ɣ
    c. himo   d. kucu + himo
                         ╪
       ɣ   ɣ   ɣ

The severed link in (3a) yields the pronunciation /kuni/, while the intact link in (3b) yields /yama+guni/. The constraint has no effect on (3c), since there is no underlying link, and the severed link in (3d) yields the pronunciation /kucu+himo/. As Kuroda is careful to point out, this analysis cannot handle the many morphemes that sometimes do and sometimes do not undergo rendaku. One example of such a morpheme is /kuči/ 'mouth', which appears with rendaku in /cuge+guči/ 'tattling' (cf. /cuge-ru/ 'tell'), without rendaku in /haya+kuči/ 'fast talking' (cf. /haya-i/ 'fast'), and either way in /waru+guči/~/waru+kuči/ 'bad mouthing' (cf. /waru-i/ 'bad').[25]

The second constraint is that ɣ can be linked only to one segment per morpheme, and the weak version of Lyman's Law is an automatic consequence of this constraint. The examples in (4) illustrate this.

Sequential Voicing and Lyman's Law in Old Japanese

(4) a. yama + kase   b. *yama + kase
        | \/
ɣ   ɣ   ɣ   ɣ

(4a) represents the actually occurring form /yama+kaze/ 'mountain wind'. (4b) represents */yama+gaze/, which violates the weak version of Lyman's Law; but this form cannot arise because it involves linking ɣ to two segments in the same morpheme.

As mentioned above, there are a few native Japanese words that begin with a voiced obstruent, including /gama/ 'toad'.[26] Modern Japanese is also replete with word-initial voiced obstruents in borrowings from Chinese, such as /doku/ 'poison', and in more recent borrowings from other languages, such as /bosu/ 'boss'. As shown in (5), to avoid violating the constraint against ɣ being linked to a word-initial segment, Kuroda treats word-initial voiced obstruents as underlyingly specified for voicing rather than as unspecified obstruents linked to ɣ.

(5) a. gama   b. doku   c. bosu   d. ǰazu
                                        |
ɣ   ɣ   ɣ   ɣ

Treating morpheme-initial voiced obstruents in this way also makes it possible to have two voiced obstruents in a morpheme without violating the constraint against multiply linked ɣ. Since Kuroda restricts underlying specification for voicing to morpheme-initial position, (5d) represents the borrowing /ǰazu/ 'jazz': the initial /ǰ/ is underlyingly specified for voicing, whereas the medial /z/ is underlyingly unspecified for voicing but linked to ɣ.

1.7 Kuroda's Account and the Strong Version of Lyman's Law

The last question to be considered in this chapter is how Kuroda's account of rendaku could be adjusted to accommodate the strong version of Lyman's Law. The strong version subsumes the weak version and therefore rules out rendaku if the affected morpheme contains a medial voiced obstruent, but the strong version also rules out rendaku if the element preceding the affected morpheme contains a voiced obstruent. As the results in section 1.5 show, the strong version comes very close to being a true generalization about the attested Old Japanese vocabulary.

At first glance, it looks as if the strong version of Lyman's Law would follow as an automatic consequence of a simple adjustment to Kuroda's first constraint, namely, allowing only one gamma link per word rather than only one gamma link per morpheme. This version of the constraint would work as in (6).

(6) a. ^{OJ}pîtö + kötö   b. ^{OJ}akî + kase

      ≠ | |

      ɣ   ɣ   ɣ

  c. ^{OJ}mîtu + töri

      | ≠

      ɣ   ɣ

The compound in (6a) surfaces as ^{OJ}/pîtö+götö/ 'another person's words' (cf. ^{OJ}/pîtö/ 'person' and ^{OJ}/kötö/ 'word') because Kuroda's other constraint severs a link between ɣ and a word-initial segment. The initial consonant of the first morpheme must be linked to ɣ underlyingly, since this morpheme shows rendaku in words such as ^{OJ}/uta+bîtö/ 'singer' (cf. ^{OJ}/uta/ 'song').[27] The compound in (6b) surfaces as ^{OJ}/akî+kaze/ 'autumn wind' (cf. ^{OJ}/akî/ 'autumn' and ^{OJ}/kaze/ 'wind'), with its sole underlying link intact. The compound in (6c) surfaces as the attested form ^{OJ}/mîdu+töri/ 'water bird' (cf. ^{OJ}/mîdu/ 'water' and ^{OJ}/töri/ 'bird') on the assumption that the second of two links to ɣ is severed within a word. Notice that the constraint on word-initial segments must have priority, since severing the second link in (6a) would yield *^{OJ}/bîtö+kötö/.

One problem with this adjustment to Kuroda's second constraint is that it cannot account for the apparent counterexamples to the strong version of Lyman's Law that turned up in the dictionary search. As mentioned in section 1.5, the three items in question are all three-morpheme words. In one, ^{OJ}/tugE+wo+gusi/ 'boxwood small-comb', the last two morphemes clearly form a semantic constituent that combines with the first morpheme, as in (7).

(7) [^{OJ}/tugE/ + [^{OJ}/wo/ + ^{OJ}/kusi/]]
   ['boxwood' + ['small' + 'comb']]

If Lyman's Law is taken to apply to each layer of combination, this item does not violate the strong version. The inner layer is the prefix+noun combination ^{OJ}/wo+gusi/, and neither ^{OJ}/wo/ 'small' nor ^{OJ}/kusi/ 'comb' contains a voiced obstruent. The outer layer is the noun+noun combination ^{OJ}/tugE+wogusi/, and rendaku is inapplicable, since ^{OJ}/wogusi/ does not begin with an obstruent. Interestingly, the noun+noun compound ^{OJ}/tugE+kusi/ 'boxwood comb' also appears as a headword in JJHI, and it does not show rendaku. In this case, of course, rendaku would violate the strong version of Lyman's Law.

In each of the other two apparent counterexamples to the strong version, ^{OJ}/kuzu+pa+gata/ 'kudzu-leaf vine' and ^{OJ}/naga+nak-î+döri/ 'chicken', the first two morphemes clearly form a semantic constituent that combines with the last morpheme, as in (8).

(8) a. [[^{OJ}/kuzu/ + ^{OJ}/pa/] + ^{OJ}/kata/]
[['kudzu' + 'leaf'] + 'vine']
b. [[^{OJ}/naga/ + ^{OJ}/nak-î/] + ^{OJ}/töri/]
[['long' + 'singing'] + 'bird']

In fact, the noun+noun compound ^{OJ}/kuzu+pa/ 'kudzu leaf' (8a) is also listed as a headword in JJHI. The layers of combination in these two three-morpheme words will not let them circumvent Lyman's Law. In both cases, the outer layer is a noun+noun combination in which the first element contains a voiced obstruent: ^{OJ}/kuzupa+gata/ and ^{OJ}/naganakî+döri/.

Another problem with the proposed adjustment to Kuroda's second constraint is that it makes an incorrect prediction about items such as ^{OJ}/mîdu+kagë/ 'water reflection'. The medial obstruent in each morpheme of this word must be linked underlyingly to ɣ, as in (9).

(9) ^{OJ} mîtu + kakë
　　　　|　　|
　　　　ɣ　　ɣ

The proposed adjustment to Kuroda's second constraint prohibits more than one gamma link per word, but severing either of the two links in (9) will yield an incorrect form.

In short, there does not seem to be any obvious way of adjusting Kuroda's account so as to handle the strong version of Lyman's Law in Old Japanese. Perhaps this is because the rendaku-inhibiting effect of a preceding voiced obstruent is not really the same phenomenon as the rendaku-inhibiting effect of a following voiced obstruent. Recall from section 1.5 that the dictionary search turned up no counterexamples to the strong version of Lyman's Law involving a voiced obstruent in the syllable immediately preceding the potential rendaku site. Repeating two of the examples given above, ^{OJ}/tugE+wo+gusi/ shows rendaku while ^{OJ}/tugE+kusi/ 'boxwood comb' does not. At the same time, as (7) and (8) show, the earlier voiced obstruent in all three apparent counterexamples is also not in the morpheme immediately preceding the potential rendaku site. These observations suggest that a preceding voiced obstruent had only a local effect in Old Japanese. One possibility is that the preceding voiced obstruent had to be in the immediately preceding morpheme; another possibility is that it had to be in the immediately preceding syllable. The tiny number of relevant examples are compatible with either of these two alternatives.

Kuroda succeeds in producing the effect of the weak version of Lyman's Law and makes no attempt to handle the strong version. As the preceding discussion has shown, there is no obvious way to extend Kuroda's account to produce the effect of the strong version of Lyman's Law, and this may well be a virtue. After all, the rendaku-inhibiting effect of a preceding voiced obstruent seems to have been a genuine characteristic of Old Japanese, but it has not survived into modern Japanese. On the other hand, the rendaku-inhibiting effect of a following voiced obstruent (i.e., the weak version of Lyman's Law) is almost universally regarded as a genuine characteristic of both Old Japanese and modern Japanese.[28] If the two effects were indeed separate phenomena, then perhaps it is no puzzle that one has disappeared while the other has survived.

There is, however, one last idea that merits brief consideration. Some statements of the weak version of Lyman's Law (e.g., Okumura 1955; Nakagawa 1966) claim that rendaku is inhibited only by a voiced obstruent in the syllable immediately following the potential rendaku site. If so, the weak version of Lyman's Law is a local effect, and rendaku in an item such as /nawa+bašigo/ 'rope ladder' (cf. /hašigo/ 'ladder') does not constitute a violation.[29] This characterization of the weak version of Lyman's Law makes it quite parallel to the local rendaku-inhibiting effect of a preceding voiced obstruent suggested for Old Japanese in the paragraph just above. Given these assumptions, the strong version of Lyman's Law is a bidirectional local constraint that prevents the creation of adjacent syllables containing voiced obstruents. On this account, the diachronic change from the strong version to the weak version was just the restriction of the effect to one direction.

Nonetheless, this characterization of the weak version of Lyman's Law as a local constraint is not very attractive. The drawback is that it makes the third syllable of a three-syllable morpheme irrelevant to rendaku. For example, the absence of rendaku in a noun+noun combination such as /doku+tokage/ 'poisonous lizard' cannot be attributed to this more limited Lyman's Law. As mentioned in section 1.4, the great majority of Old Japanese noun morphemes were realized as one or two syllables, and there are not very many relevant three-syllable noun morphemes like /tokage/ 'lizard' in modern Japanese. The obvious solution is simply to treat /tokage/ as rendaku-immune, since, as noted in section 1.5, rendaku-immune morphemes exist anyway. On the other hand, relevant three-syllable nouns derived from verb stems are not so rare, and the behavior of these items makes it difficult to accept the idea that Lyman's Law is a local constraint. The examples in (10) illustrate this.

(10) a. /hanas-u/ 'speak'
/hanaš-i/ 'speaking'
/mukaši+banaš-i/ 'old legend'
b. /todoke-ru/ 'report'
/todoke/ 'reporting'
/koNiN+todoke/ 'marriage registration'
c. /kaseg-u/ 'make a living'
/kaseg-i/ 'making a living'
/tomo+kaseg-i/ 'joint livelihood'

Verb stems with no voiced obstruents, like /hanaš-i/ (10a), often show rendaku in compounds, but verb stems with a voiced obstruent in the second syllable, like /todoke/ (10b), or in the third syllable, like /kaseg-i/ (10c), never show rendaku in comparable compounds. It seems unlikely that this pattern is just a coincidence; but if the weak version of Lyman's Law is a local constraint, it can account for the absence of rendaku in compounds ending with /todoke/ but not for the absence of rendaku in compounds ending with /kaseg-i/. The verb stem /kaseg-i/, and every other verb stem with a voiced obstruent in the third syllable, would have to be treated as idiosyncratically rendaku-immune.

1.8 Conclusion

The attested vocabulary of Old Japanese is consistent with the claim that a voiced obstruent following a potential rendaku site prevented rendaku. It is also consistent with the claim that a voiced obstruent in the syllable immediately preceding a potential rendaku site prevented rendaku. The inhibiting effect of a following voiced obstruent is known as (the weak version of) Lyman's Law, and it has sometimes been suggested that the two effects are a single phenomenon, referred to jointly as the strong version of Lyman's Law. The weak version still holds with very few exceptions in modern Japanese, but the strong version does not. Kuroda (2002) proposes an analysis of rendaku that, despite its acknowledged shortcomings, seems at first glance to offer a simple diachronic path from the strong version of Lyman's Law to the weak version. On closer scrutiny, however, this elegant account of the diachronic change breaks down, and it may well be that the inhibiting effects of following voiced obstruents and preceding voiced obstruents were separate phenomena in Old Japanese.

Notes

1. For an introduction to rendaku, see Vance 1987, 133–48. For historical details in the context of a more general discussion of voicing distinctions, see Martin 1987, 84–120.

2. There are, however, a few instances of rendaku in phraselike items. See note 11.

3. Many linguists prefer to analyze [h], [ç], and [ɸ] as allophones of a single phoneme except in recent borrowings. I am assuming a uniform phonemic inventory for all vocabulary strata and a split that has resulted in a contrast between [ɸ] and [h]/[ç]. Either way, the rendaku alternation is not simply a matter of voicing. The ancestor of modern /h/ and /f/ was pronounced [p], although there is some controversy about how long the [p] pronunciation persisted in the central dialects (Kiyose 1985).

4. In earlier work (Vance 1987, 24), I said that the two allophones of /z/, [dz] and [z], are distributed as follows: [dz] word-initially or immediately following the mora nasal /N/ and [z] elsewhere. The actual distribution is certainly not this clean, but there is no contrast, and the two are unquestionably allophones of a single phoneme. The modern rendaku pairing of /z/

with /c/ and /s/ reflects the historical merger of a voiced affricate and a voiced fricative, and so does the pairing of /ǰ/ with /č/ and /š/.

5. For an account of why rendaku is irregular, see Vance 1983. For examples and discussion, see Vance 1987, 146–48, and Ohno 2000.

6. According to Miyake (1932, 136), Motoori stated categorically that if the second element of a compound contains a voiced obstruent, its initial consonant does not voice.

7. Counterexamples include /nawa+bašigo/ 'rope ladder' and several other compounds ending with /bašigo/ (cf. /hašigo/ 'ladder'), /šoo+zaburoo/ (a personal name) and several other names ending with /zaburoo/ (cf. /saburoo/ '3rd son'), and /fuN+ǰibar-u/ 'tie up' (cf. /šibar-u/ 'tie'). See Vance 1980 for an attempt to test the psychological status of Lyman's Law experimentally.

8. Miyake (1932, 136) gives the relevant quotation from Ishizuka's *Kogen Seidakukô* (1801).

9. All Old Japanese examples are marked with a superscript *OJ*. The transcription conventions follow Miller's (1986, 198) slightly modified version of the system first adopted by Mathias (1973) and endorsed by Martin (1987, 50). The transcription reflects the fact that many modern standard syllables with one of the vowels /i e o/ correspond to two distinct eighth-century syllables. (For details, see Lange 1973 and Shibatani 1990, 125–39.) For each such eighth-century pair, it is standard practice to label one syllable *type A* (*kô-rui*) and the other *type B* (*otsu-rui*), following Hashimoto (1917/1949, 173–86). Some researchers construe the phonological differences between the type A and type B syllables as vowel quality distinctions; others construe them as distinctions between syllables with and without a glide: CV versus CGV. In any case, the transcription adopted here represents type-A syllables with a circumflex over the vowel /î ê ô/, type-B syllables with a diaresis over the vowel /ï ë ö/, and syllables for which there was no A/B distinction with no diacritic /i e o/. A capitalized vowel /I E O/ indicates a syllable for which there was an A/B distinction but for which the category is unknown.

10. The Old Japanese prefix [OJ]/opo/ 'big' is the ancestor of the modern Japanese prefix /oo/ that appears in the examples /oo+kaze/ 'strong wind' and /oo+zora/ 'open sky' cited above.

11. On the other hand, there are some noun+GENITIVE+noun examples that actually show rendaku, as in [OJ]/ama+nö+gapa/ 'Milky Way' (cf. [OJ]/kapa/ 'river'), although these are unusual.

12. Even though [OJ]/pîtuzi/ 'sheep' appears as a headword in JJHI, the entry lists no compounds, so excluding it from the search had no effect on the eventual data set.

13. The morphemic segmentations of inflectional forms in this chapter follow the widely adopted analysis of Bloch (1946). I use these segmentations as a convenience and not as an endorsement of the analysis on which they are based.

14. As Martin (1987, 93) points out, the second constituent verb in such a compound was treated as a separate accent phrase in Classical Japanese and presumably in Old Japanese as well. In modern Japanese, compound verbs are prosodically unified.

15. For an account of why verb+verb compounds typically do not show rendaku, see Vance 1983.

16. However, combinations in which a large "numeral" such as [OJ]/mOmO/ 'hundred' or [OJ]/ti/ 'thousand' seems to mean just 'many' were kept in the data set. An example of this type is [OJ]/mOmO+kï/, which JJHI defines as 'many trees'.

17. For details on rendaku in Sino-Japanese, see Vance 1996.

18. In the eighth century, the area around what is now Tokyo was the eastern frontier of the Japanese cultural and political sphere.

19. The distinction between "sheerly speculative" and "merely dubious" is, of course, a judgment call. In any case, only a small number of examples were involved.

20. Unger (2000) used the data set to investigate the frequency of rendaku in different proto-Japanese (i.e., reconstructed) accent classes of monosyllabic and disyllabic nouns. His results serve as a step in a complex argument in favor of a genetic link between Japanese and Korean.

21. In some of these items, such as [OJ]/mîdu+kagë/ 'water reflection', rendaku would violate both versions of Lyman's Law and give us no way of separating the two. Items of this type will come up again in section 1.7.

22. The modern descendant of this morpheme shows rendaku quite consistently as a final element, even in /hiko+boši/ 'Altair' (lit., 'boy star'), the ancestor of which appears in JJHI as [OJ]/pîkô+posi/.

23. The modern Japanese descendant of this item, /yob-u+ko+dori/, is a nickname for a cuckoo.

24. I first heard about this term paper in one of Jim McCawley's classes at the University of Chicago in the mid-1970s, and Yuki Kuroda was kind enough to give me a copy in 2000. Kuroda (2002) is careful to point out that the rendaku alternations are not just a matter of the presence or absence of voicing. Aside from the effects of historical changes pointed out in section 1.2 above, voiced obstruents in Old Japanese were almost certainly prenasalized, just as their descendants are in some modern nonstandard Japanese dialects (Vance 1987, 108–9; Martin 1987, 20–25). In some of these same dialects, word-medial nonrendaku stops are actually voiced, although not prenasalized. These complications will be ignored here, since the phonetics of the alternations are not at issue.

25. The "infinitives" of many Japanese verbs, including /cuge-ru/ 'tell', have no overt inflectional ending. I have opted not to clutter the transcriptions of such forms with a zero morph (e.g., /cuge-∅/).

26. According to the entry in the authoritative historical dictionary of Japanese (Nihon Daijiten Kankôkai 1972–76), the word for 'toad' used to begin with a voiceless velar stop, and the earliest citation (720) has [OJ]/k/.

27. Actually, this morpheme meaning 'person' is one of those that sometimes do, and sometimes do not, undergo rendaku. As noted in section 1.6, Kuroda (2002) does not claim that his analysis can handle such morphemes.

28. This is not to say that there is no doubt whatever about the psychological status of the weak version of Lyman's Law in modern Japanese. For an experimental study, see Vance 1980.

29. See note 7. According to Martin (1987, 115), /hašigo/ 'ladder' has an uncertain etymology, but it probably goes back to a diminutive of /haši/ 'bridge' (cf. /ko/ 'child; small').

References

Bloch, Bernard. 1946. Studies in colloquial Japanese I: Inflection. *Journal of the American Oriental Society* 66, 97–109.

Hashimoto, Shinkichi. 1917. Kokugo kanazukai kenkyûshijô no ichihakken. *Teikoku Bungaku* 23, 123–63. Reprinted in *Moji oyobi kanazukai no kenkyû*. Tokyo: Iwanami, 1949. References are to the 1949 edition.

Ishizuka, Tatsumaro. 1801. *Kogen seidakukô*. Cited in Miyake 1932.

Itô, Junko, and Ralf-Armin Mester. 1986. The phonology of voicing in Japanese. *Linguistic Inquiry* 17, 49–73.

Jôdaigo Jiten Henshû Iinkai [JJHI], ed. 1967. *Jidaibetsu kokugo daijiten: Jôdaihen*. Tokyo: Sanseidô.

Kiyose, Gisaburô N. 1985. Heianchô hagyô-shiin p-onron. *Onsei no Kenkyû* 21, 73–87.

Kuroda, S.-Y. 1963. A historical remark on "rendaku," a phenomenon in Japanese morphology. Manuscript, MIT.

Kuroda, S.-Y. 2002. Rendaku. In *Japanese/Korean linguistics 10*, ed. by Noriko M. Akatsuka and Susan Strauss, 337–50. Stanford, CA: CSLI Publications.

Lange, Roland A. 1973. *The phonology of eighth-century Japanese*. Tokyo: Sophia University.

Lyman, Benjamin S. 1894. *Change from surd to sonant in Japanese compounds*. Philadelphia: Oriental Club of Philadelphia.

Martin, Samuel E. 1952. Morphophonemics of standard colloquial Japanese. Supplement to *Language* (Language Dissertation No. 47).

Martin, Samuel E. 1987. *The Japanese language through time*. New Haven, CT: Yale University Press.

Mathias, Gerald B. 1973. On the modification of certain proto-Korean-Japanese reconstructions. *Papers in Japanese Linguistics* 2, 31–47.

McCawley, James D. 1968. *The phonological component of a grammar of Japanese*. The Hague: Mouton.

Miller, Roy Andrew. 1986. *Nihongo: In defence of Japanese*. London: Athlone.

Miyake, Takerô. 1932. Dakuonkô. *Onsei no Kenkyû* 5, 135–90.

Nakagawa, Yoshio. 1966. Rendaku, rensei (kashô) no keifu. *Kokugo Kokubun* 35.6, 302–14.

Nihon Daijiten Kankôkai, ed. 1972–76. *Nihon kokugo daijiten*. Tokyo: Shôgakukan.

Ohno, Kazutoshi. 2000. The lexical nature of *rendaku* in Japanese. In *Japanese/Korean linguistics 9*, ed. by Mineharu Nakayama and Charles J. Quinn, Jr., 151–64. Stanford, CA: CSLI Publications.

Okumura, Mitsuo. 1955. Rendaku. In *Kokugogaku jiten*, ed. by Kokugo Gakkai, 961–62. Tokyo: Tôkyôdô.

Ramsey, S. Robert, and J. Marshall Unger. 1972. Evidence for a consonant shift in 7th century Japanese. *Papers in Japanese Linguistics* 1, 278–95.

Shibatani, Masayoshi. 1990. *The languages of Japan*. Cambridge: Cambridge University Press.

Unger, J. Marshall. 1975. Studies in early Japanese morphophonemics. Doctoral dissertation, Yale University. Published, Bloomington: Indiana University Linguistics Club, 1977.

Unger, J. Marshall. 2000. *Rendaku* and Proto-Japanese accent classes. In *Japanese/Korean linguistics 9*, ed. by Mineharu Nakayama and Charles J. Quinn, Jr., 17–30. Stanford, CA: CSLI Publications.

Vance, Timothy J. 1980. The psychological status of a constraint on Japanese consonant alternation. *Linguistics* 18, 245–67.

Vance, Timothy J. 1983. On the origin of voicing alternation in Japanese consonants. *Journal of the American Oriental Society* 102, 333–41.

Vance, Timothy J. 1987. *An introduction to Japanese phonology.* Albany, NY: SUNY Press.

Vance, Timothy J. 1996. Sequential voicing in Sino-Japanese. *Journal of the Association of Teachers of Japanese* 30, 22–43.

PART II
Syntax

Chapter 2
NP Gaps in Tamil: Syntactic versus Pragmatic

E. Annamalai

2.1 Postulating Two Kinds of Gap

Tamil is an SOV language with free word order and no invariant requirement that the verb be final in a clause (Annamalai 2004). It freely permits absence of nouns, called *NP gaps* in this chapter, in utterances in discourse as well as in sentences (simple and complex) in isolation. The referents of NP gaps are recovered from many sources: from the background world knowledge of the interlocutors, from the discourse context or the speech act by pragmatic rules, from the agreement marker of the finite verb predicate (in the case of a missing subject) by morphological redundancy rules, and from the syntactic context by principles of coindexing with other nouns in the sentence. Of these, the principles of syntactic coindexing are internal to a grammatical theory. Pretheoretically, the coindexing principles for pronouns in Tamil are the following.[1] Of the two kinds of pronouns in Tamil, the general pronoun is coindexed with a noun phrase in the sentence that is not a subject and that precedes or c-commands it. The reflexive pronoun is coindexed with a noun phrase that is a subject and that c-commands it in the same clause or in the embedded clause (for details, see Annamalai 1999).

NP gaps are hypothesized to be of two kinds: open or free, and closed or bounded. A gap is identified when there is formally no noun phrase in a syntactic slot that is the site for a referent. It is *free* if the referent is in principle unconstrained syntactically. It does not have its antecedent in the sentence or is barred by the syntactic

---

A longer version of this chapter was originally written when I was a Visiting Fellow at the Max Planck Institute for Psycholinguistics, in Nijmegen. I am grateful for the material support and intellectual stimulation I received there. I greatly benefited from my hosts' penetrating questions skeptical of syntactic recovery of gaps, when I gave a talk to the Argument Structure Group of the Institute. The critical comments of the editors of this volume and of the two anonymous reviewers helped me describe the problem in a more precise and readable fashion. Any part of the chapter that remains unclear is a residue of my original expansive description of the problem.

configuration from being coindexed with an antecedent in the sentence. In other words, the referent of the free gap is recovered from outside the sentence or from the sentence itself when syntactic conditions do not apply. Any intrasentential referents of the free gap, if recovered at all under syntactic conditions, will be less privileged. They will be a subset of its extrasentential referents. The recovery of the referent of the free gap must be based on pragmatic principles that draw on a theory of inference from background knowledge, a theory of discourse organization, or a theory of speech acts.[2] The pragmatic principles cannot, however, operate without the syntactic principles of argument structure, which posit the gap.

A gap is *bounded* if the referent is governed syntactically; that is, its recovery is made with an antecedent present in the sentence by syntactically defined coindexing principles. That is, the referent of a bounded gap is necessarily intrasentential. Nevertheless, in many syntactic contexts, the bounded gap does not preclude a referent beyond the sentence in discourse. In these contexts, recovery of the intrasentential referent is privileged. The possible extrasentential referent adds to the syntactically coindexed referent, making the sentence multiply ambiguous.

Free gaps are marked by X in the examples below, indicating their free referential value or interpretation; bounded gaps are marked by $\emptyset$, indicating their bounded referential value or interpretation. Each bounded gap is marked with a subscript, which links it with the coindexed antecedent(s) in the sentence. The glosses given for the examples are the only possible or the preferred interpretation(s) of the sentences.

Of the two kinds of pronouns differing in form, the reflexive pronoun is always governed syntactically, and so is the gap that has the subject of its clause or a higher clause as its antecedent, like the reflexive pronoun. The general pronoun may or may not be governed syntactically. When the pronoun is governed syntactically, its referent is recovered intrasententially, and when it is not, it is recovered extrasententially, just as with gaps.[3] These facts suggest that pronouns and gaps have the same properties. This leads to the hypothesis that the gap that alternates with the pronoun whose referent is recovered by applying syntactic conditions is a bounded gap ($\emptyset$). Heuristically, then, the optional absence of a syntactically bound pronoun is an indicator of the site of the bounded gap ($\emptyset$), differentiating it from the free gap (X), which, by the above hypothesis, has the same privilege of occurrence as the syntactically unbounded general pronoun. This chapter examines the validity of this hypothesis, particularly whether the alternation with $\emptyset$ takes place in all or some of the syntactic contexts in which the bounded pronoun occurs.

The test is carried out in different syntactic contexts to find out if the syntactically bound pronoun and $\emptyset$ alternate in them, and if they do not, which of the two is possible in a particular syntactic context. The test shows that they alternate in most syntactic contexts, but they do not alternate in a few, where only one of them occurs. This makes the hypothesis that the pronouns and gaps have the same properties a qualified one. It is nevertheless used as a working hypothesis for the purpose of test-

NP Gaps in Tamil

ing the facts about gaps. To confirm the syntactic nature of $\emptyset$, further tests examine whether, in any of the syntactic contexts, the gap does not allow an extrasentential referent (X interpretation), and if it does allow one, whether the intrasentential referent is privileged in recovery (in the sense that one must imagine a pragmatic context to cancel that referent out) in those syntactic contexts.

2.2 Sentential Noun Phrases

We shall first take up gaps in embedded clauses, which are noun phrases either formally ((1), (3)) or positionally (2), being used as sentential direct object and subject.

(1) $\emptyset_1$/avanukku$_1$ veele keDeccirukradu kumaare$_1$ sandooSappaDuttum
    he-to   job   is-available-that Kumar-ACC make-happy-will
    'That he$_1$ has got a job will make Kumar$_1$ happy.'

(2) $\emptyset_2$/avane$_2$ $\emptyset_1$/taan$_1$ veelekki vaccikiDreennu kumaar$_1$ raajaaTTe$_2$ sonnaan
    he-ACC   self   job-for   keep-PRES.PNG.that Kumar   Raja-to   said
    vaccukiDradaa
    keep-PRES.NOM.ADV
    'Kumar$_1$ told Raja$_2$ that he$_1$ would give him$_2$ a job.'

(3) $\emptyset_{1/2}$/tanakku$_1$/avanukku$_2$ veele keDeccirukrade   raaja$_1$ innom
    self-to   he-to   job   be-available-NOMZ.ACC Raja   yet
    kumaarTTe$_2$ keDeccirukkunnu   sollale
    Kumar-to   be-available-PRES.that say-not
    'With respect to his$_{1/2}$ having gotten a job, Raja$_1$ has not yet told Kumar$_2$ that he$_{1/2}$ has gotten a job.'

$\emptyset$ in the embedded clause of (1)–(3) is coindexed with antecedents in the matrix clause, and it alternates with corresponding pronouns. $\emptyset$ in all positions (subject, direct object, and indirect object), it should be noted, does not exclude an extrasentential referent (i.e., X interpretation). It may refer to speech act participants (e.g., (1) could also mean 'That I have got a job will make Kumar happy') or a discourse referent in an appropriate discourse context (e.g., 'That Raja has got a job will make Kumar happy') and thus have the properties of X. Intrasentential referents are, however, privileged for recovery in these sentences in isolation.

2.3 Infinitive Clauses

We shall now consider $\emptyset$ in sentences with an infinitive clause.

(4) kumaar$_1$ $\emptyset_1$/taan$_1$ X aDikka kambu keeTTaan
    Kumar   self   hit-INF stick asked
    'Kumar$_1$ asked for a stick to hit with.'

In (4), the subject of the infinitive clause is ∅, as it is coindexed with the subject of the matrix clause and alternates with the reflexive pronoun. Incidentally, note that there is no gap in the subject position of the matrix clause in (4). The subject of the matrix clause has been reordered to the front of the whole S, and no gap is left at the site when a noun phrase is reordered to serve discourse functions. The predicate of the infinitive clause *aDi* 'hit', being a transitive verb, must have a Patient argument, and this missing argument is marked by X, as it does not specify any referent intrasententially. The noun *kambu* 'stick', the direct object of the matrix clause, is unsuitable to be the direct object of *aDi* 'hit' in the infinitive clause because in the argument structure it would be extraordinary for the patient and the instrument to be identical. *Kumar*, the subject of the matrix clause, can be the direct object of the infinitive clause marked *X*. This direct object can be formally present as the reflexive pronoun *tanne* 'self-ACC' in the infinitive clause to give the meaning 'Kumar$_1$ asked for a stick to hit him$_1$ (by himself$_1$ or someone else)'. This is not, however, a preferred interpretation with the gap in the direct object position of the infinitive. This interpretation requires a special discourse context, or a verbal reflexive in the predicate as in (5a). There is thus a difference between the gaps in subject position and direct object position of the infinitive clause in terms of preferred referential interpretation, which is indicated by designating the gap differently in the two positions.

The subject gap in the infinitive clause in (4) allows an X interpretation also. The extrasentential referent in a discourse context is unspecified (i.e., 'someone'). This unspecified-referent interpretation is more preferred with a variant of the infinitive, namely, the nominalized verb with tense plus dative case (= *for* V-*ing* in English)— that is, when *aDikradukkku* 'for hitting' is used instead of *aDikka* 'to hit'.

The above facts show that although the possible referents of ∅ and X are not mutually exclusive, the two kinds of gaps have different preferred interpretations and required contexts of use. One may conclude from this that any difference between ∅ and X is not categorical. There are, however, syntactic contexts like the one discussed below, where only ∅ occurs, with no extrasentential reference.

The gap in the direct object position of the infinitive can be coindexed only with the subject of the infinitive clause when the predicate of the infinitive clause is inflected for the verbal reflexive by addition of the auxiliary verb *kiDu*, as in (5a). The verbal reflexive stipulates a clausemate (local domain) condition, namely, that the antecedent and the reflexive pronoun be in the same clause (Annamalai 1999). The same gap is not coindexed with the subject of the matrix clause in (5b). Neither of them has a discourse referent and so they are ∅. ∅ alternates with the reflexive pronoun *tanne* 'self-ACC' when the infinitive predicate contains the verbal reflexive. Recall that ∅ in the direct object position of the infinitive is not privileged to be coindexed with the subject in (4), whose infinitive predicate does not contain the verbal reflexive. These show that coindexing of ∅ in direct object position of the infinitive is subject to the clausemate condition of the verbal reflexive, and thus show the gap to be syntactic.

NP Gaps in Tamil

(5) a. kumaar₁ Ø₁/taan₁ Ø₁/tanne₁ aDiccukiDa kambu keeTTaan
Kumar self self-ACC hit-PAST.VR.INF stick asked
'Kumar₁ asked for a stick to hit himself₁.'

b. kumaar₁ raajaa₂ Ø*₁/₂/tanne*₁/₂ aDiccukiDa kambu keeTTaan
Kumar Raja self-ACC hit-PAST.VR.INF stick asked
'Kumar₁ asked for a stick for Raja₂ to hit himself₂.'

Certain sentences like (6) allow the preferred interpretation of Ø in the direct object position in the infinitive clause to be coreference with the subject even without the verbal reflexive. This is because of the pragmatic relation between 'see' and 'mirror', which is reflexive. This shows that the syntactic clausemate condition is superfluous when pragmatics dictates coreference. Ø (but not the pronoun *ade* 'it') may also be coindexed with the direct object (*kaNNaaDi* 'mirror') of the matrix clause when a discourse context (like shopping for mirrors) favors it. This coreference with Ø is also possible when the object of the matrix clause bears the accusative case marker and is therefore definite. Note that the object position of the infinitive clause does not allow a general pronoun (*ade* 'it'), whose antecedent is outside the clause because of the clausemate condition.

(6) kumaar₁ Ø₁/taan₁ Ø₁/₂/tanne₁/*ade₂ paakka kaNNaaDi₂ keeTTaan
Kumar self self-ACC it-ACC see-INF mirror asked
'Kumar₁ asked for a mirror₂ to look at himself₁/*it₂.'

That the pronoun cannot occur in the object position of the infinitive clause in (6) is due to an additional condition on coindexing the pronoun: *ade* 'it' in the embedded clause and *kaNNaaDi* 'mirror' in the matrix clause have the same case.[4] This pronoun has only an extrasentential or disjoint reference. Example (7a) is another instance of the condition whereby noun phrases in the embedded and matrix clauses bearing the same case cannot corefer. This condition, which applies to the pronoun, does not apply to Ø, as mentioned above. If the case is different, the pronoun is needed to carry the case marker (as it is needed to carry the emphatic marker). Ø, being a noncarrier of morphological markers, is less constrained syntactically compared with the pronoun. This is an instance where the pronoun does not alternate with Ø under the condition of having the same case as the antecedent. Example (7b) illustrates that the pronoun alternates with Ø when its case is different from that of its antecedent.

(7) a. kumaar₁ Ø₂/*avane₂ aDikka raajaave₂ kuupTaan
Kumar he-ACC hit-to Raja-ACC called
'*Kumar₁ called him₂ to hit Raja₂.'

b. kumaar₁ Ø₂/avane₂ aDikka raajaaTTeyee₂ kambu keeTTaan
Kumar he-ACC hit-to Raja-DAT.EMP stick asked
'Kumar₁ asked Raja₂ for a stick to hit him₂.'

The referent of the gap in the object position of the infinitive clause is not restricted to being intrasentential (i.e., ∅). It may be unspecified as well in (6); the object is interpreted preferentially as 'someone or something' when *kaNNaaDi* means 'eyeglasses'. Example (6) with ∅ in the direct object position of the infinitive clause would mean 'Kumar asked for glasses to look at something'. The referent of ∅ in the same position in (7b) may be unspecified without the emphatic *-ee* on direct object of the matrix clause, and it will be the privileged interpretation: 'Kumar asked Raja for a stick to hit someone'. The above discussion shows that recovery of ∅'s referent in a sentence in isolation depends on syntactic and semantic factors of the predicate, and on definiteness, case status, and emphasis of the noun.

The condition that the pronoun cannot have the same case as its antecedent but can have a different case also holds for the general pronoun in the matrix clause. ∅, as defined, does not occur at all in the matrix clause (except in the genitive position) of the infinitive clause sentence. The gap in the matrix clause is X. The reverse of the sentences in (7) is shown in (8).

(8) a. kumaar₁ raajaave₂ aDikka *∅/*avane₂ kuupTaan
    Kumar Raja-ACC hit-to   him   called
    '*Kumar₁ called him₂ to hit Raja₂.'
   b. kumaar₁ raajaave₂ aDikka *∅₂/avanTeyee kambu keeTTaan
    Kumar Raja   hit-to   he-DAT.EMP stick   asked
    '*Kumar₁ asked him₂ for a stick to hit Raja₂.'

Given these facts, the occurrence and nonoccurrence (marked with *) of the general pronoun and ∅ are schematically presented in (9). ∅ alternates with the reflexive pronoun in all the positions where it can occur (namely, any position other than the subject of the matrix clause). It alternates with the reflexive pronoun alone when the predicate of the clause contains the verbal reflexive. That is, the gap will not have the X interpretation.

(9)	Infinitive clause	Main clause
Same case	*GP/∅	*GP/*∅
Different case	GP/∅	GP/*∅

Where ∅ is not permissible (i.e., in the syntactic contexts of *∅ in (9)), the gap has extrasentential referents (it has the X interpretation). When the general pronoun is permitted but absent in these contexts of nonalternation with ∅ (GP/*∅ in (9)), it amounts to the general pronoun alternating with X. If the general pronoun alternates with X in some syntactic contexts, one could say that in fact, it alternates with X in most contexts because ∅ does not exclude an X interpretation in most syntactic con-

NP Gaps in Tamil 53

texts. It follows that alternation with the pronoun alone is not sufficient to differentiate ∅ from X. This calls into question a categorical distinction between ∅ and X.

There are, however, certain contexts in which ∅ can occur, but X cannot. Certain matrix-clause predicates allow only intrasentential interpretation of the gap in subject position of the infinitive clause. Depending on the predicate, it is coindexed with the subject of the matrix clause, as in (10a–b); with the direct object, as in (10c); or with both, as in (10d). In none of these sentences does ∅ have an extrasentential referent.[5] The predicate *maru* 'decline' in (10a) requires the same subject in the matrix and embedded clauses, but the predicate *asseppaDu* 'desire' in (10b) does not have such a requirement. Even with this predicate, the gap in the subject position of the infinitive is not coindexed with an extrasentential noun phrase (or with the direct object of the infinitive).

(10) a. kumaar₁ ∅₁/taan₁maTTum raajaave₂ viiTTukku kuupDa maruttaan
       Kumar   self-alone   Raja-ACC   house-to   invite-INF refused
       'Kumar₁ refused (*himself₁ alone) to invite Raja home.'
    b. kumaar₁ ∅₁/taan₁maTTum raajaave₂ viiTTukku kuupDa aaseppaTTaan
       Kumar   self-alone   Raja-ACC   house-to   invite-INF desired
       'Kumar₁ wanted to (*himself₁ alone) invite Raja₂ home.'
    c. kumaar₁ raajaave₂ ∅₂/*avan₂maTTum viiTTukku pooga sonnaan
       Kumar   Raja-ACC   he-alone   house-to   go-INF told
       'Kumar₁ told Raja₂ to (*him₂ alone) go home.'
    d. kumaar₁ raajaave₂ ∅₁&₂/taanaga₁&₂maTTum viiTTukku pooga kuupTaan
       Kumar   Raja-ACC   selves-alone   house-to   go-INF invited
       'Kumar₁ invited Raja₂ for themselves₁&₂ to go home.'

In (10a,b,d), the reflexive pronoun occurs, in alternation with ∅, as the subject of the infinitive clause with the emphasis marker *maTTum* 'alone'; it does not occur (and there is a gap) without this marker. The general pronoun coindexed with the matrix-clause direct object does not occur at all as subject of the infinitive clause alternating with ∅.[6] The fact that there are syntactic contexts with specific predicates where the gap excludes an X interpretation suggests that ∅ and X are not the same kind of gap.

2.4 Conditional and Temporal Clauses

We shall now examine ∅ in sentences with conditional and temporal subordinate clauses. Like sentential NPs, conditional and temporal clauses freely permit the gap to have an intrasentential (∅) or extrasentential (X) referent. The gap is marked ∅ because it can alternate with the pronoun whose antecedent is in the sentence. All three gaps in (11)—located in subject position of the embedded clause, genitive position modifying a noun, and direct object position of the matrix clause—are referentially ambiguous: the referent can be determined by the discourse, can be the speaker/hearer, or can correspond to that of an antecedent in the sentence. With no condition that all $\emptyset$s in the same sentence must have the same referent, interpretations multiply. The gloss given is for intrasentential reference. Example (11) may also mean 'Kumar will scold X if X goes to X's house' or 'Kumar will scold X if X goes to Kumar's house'; and X can refer to the speaker ('If I go to my house' Kumar will scold me') or the hearer ('If you go to your house, Kumar will scold you') or can have a discourse referent.

(11) $\emptyset_1$ X viiTTukku poonaa kumaar$_1$ X tiTTuvaan
      GEN-house-to go-if   Kumar   scold-will
     'Kumar$_1$ will scold X if he$_1$ goes to his$_1$ house.'

Sentences (12a–b), where there is only one noun, show that an utterance with many gaps allows many referential interpretations from the discourse. Because other factors intervene, all possible interpretations are not realized, however. In (12a), *Kumar* is the subject of the matrix clause and has been reordered to the front of the sentence. It is coindexed with the direct object of the conditional clause. The subject of the matrix clause is not the antecedent for the subject of the conditional clause, because of the semantics of the verb *kuupDu* 'call': in the ordinary world, the agent and patient of this predicate would not be identical. Instead, its referent ordinarily comes from the discourse or speech act. When it is unspecified, the conditional clause translates in English into passive, as the gloss shows. In (12b), *Kumar* is the subject of the conditional clause and the second X in the subject position of the matrix clause again cannot be coindexed with it, because of the semantics of the verb *kuupDu* 'call' in the conditional clause. Since there is no other antecedent in the sentence, X in both places (the direct object position of the infinitive clause, the first one, and the subject position of the matrix clause, the second one) takes its referent from the discourse. The third person ending of the predicate of the matrix clause rules out reference to speech act participants, speaker and hearer. In (12a), if the conditional verb were *sonnaa* 'if tells, promises', instead of *kuupTaa* 'if called', X could be interpreted as finding its referent in the discourse or as the subject of the matrix clause. In appropriate discourse contexts, the Xs in (12b) may have different referents, though the preferred interpretation is that they have the same referent.

(12) a. kumaar$_1$ X $\emptyset_1$ kuupTaa varuvaan
         Kumar   call-if   come-will
        'Kumar$_1$ will come if called.'
     b. kumaar$_1$ X kuupTaa X varuvaan
         Kumar   call-if   come-will
        'Will come if Kumar$_1$ calls.'

In (12a), the only noun is the antecedent of the gap $\emptyset$ (in the direct object position), and the referents of the other gap (X) come from the discourse; in (12b), the only noun is not the antecedent of any gap, and all referents come from the discourse. The examples in (12) are utterances embedded in a discourse.

When there are many potential antecedents in an autonomous sentence with a conditional or temporal clause, the coindexing of $\emptyset$ is subject to the coindexing principles applicable in Tamil generally. In the subject position of the embedded clause that precedes the main clause, a gap is most preferred; the reflexive pronoun is less preferred and it needs some emphasis; and the general pronoun (when its antecedent is not the subject) is even less preferred and it also needs some emphasis. (In the last situation, the full noun (antecedent) is most preferred in the position in question, with the general pronoun or $\emptyset$ in the matrix clause.) In the subject position of the matrix clause, neither the reflexive pronoun nor $\emptyset$ as its alternate occurs, because it is not in a c-commanded position; $\emptyset$ or the general pronoun may occur, though the latter is less preferred. In other positions, the general pronoun and $\emptyset$ alternate. There is no same-case condition in sentences with conditional and temporal clauses.

(13) a. $\emptyset_1$/taan$_1$maTTum ooTTalukku poonaa kumaar$_1$ iDli saapDuvaan
        self alone   hotel-to   go-if   Kumar idli eat-will
    'Kumar$_1$ will eat *idli* if he$_1$ alone goes to the restaurant.'

b. $\emptyset_1$/taanum$_1$/$\emptyset_2$/avan$_2$maTTum ooTTalukku poonaa kumaar$_1$ raajaave$_2$
       self-also   he-only   hotel-to   go-if   Kumar Raja-ACC
iDli saapDa solluvaan
idli eat-to say-will
'Kumar$_1$ asks Raja$_2$ to eat *idli* if he$_{1/2}$ goes to the restaurant.'

(14) a. $\emptyset_1$/taan$_1$ $\emptyset_2$/avane$_2$ ooTTalukku kuuTTikkiTTupoonaa kumaar$_1$taan
       self   he-ACC hotel-to   take-if   Kumar-EMP
raajaavukkum$_2$ paNam kuDuppaan
Raja$_2$-also-to   money give-will
'Kumar$_1$ will pay for Raja$_2$ also if he$_1$ (*himself$_1$) takes him$_2$ to the restaurant.'

b. $\emptyset_1$/taan$_1$ $\emptyset_2$/avane$_2$ // $\emptyset_2$/avan$_2$ $\emptyset_1$/tanne$_1$ ooTTalukku
       self   he-ACC   he   self-ACC hotel-to
kuuTTikkiTTupoonaa kumaar$_1$ raajaave$_2$ paNam kuDukka solluvaan
take-if   Kumar Raja-ACC money give-to   say-will
'Kumar$_1$ asks Raja$_2$ to pay if he$_1$ takes him$_2$ to the restaurant // Kumar$_1$ asks Raja$_2$ to pay if he$_2$ takes him$_1$ (*himself$_1$) to the restaurant.'

In (13) and (14), $\emptyset$ and alternating pronouns occur in the subordinate clause. When $\emptyset$ occurs, it refers to any of the antecedents in the matrix clause, subject to the coindexing principles. There are two $\emptyset$s in (14b) and both allow coindexing with either of the two antecedents in the matrix clause, making four possibilities. Nevertheless, the interpretation of $\emptyset$ coindexed with the subject of the matrix clause is privileged.

In (15), the general pronoun and $\emptyset$ alternate in the matrix clause.

(15) kumaar$_1$ $\emptyset_1$/taan$_1$ raajaave$_2$ ooTTalukku kuuTTikkiTTupoonaa $\emptyset_2$/avane$_2$
     Kumar   self   Raja-ACC hotel-to   take-if   he-ACC
     iDli saapDa solluvaan
     idli eat-to say-will
     'Kumar$_1$ will ask him$_2$ to eat *idli* if himself$_1$ takes Raja$_2$ to the restaurant.'

The gap in the sentences in (13)–(15) does not have an extrasentential referent because of the pragmatics of the situations these sentences describe. As (11)–(12) show, sentences with conditional and temporal clauses allow discourse referents. In all its occurrences, the gap's alternation with pronouns is possible. In all the examples above, the temporal clause, which is marked by *-appa* instead of *-aa*, may substitute for the conditional clause, and the temporal clauses have the same properties with regard to $\emptyset$ and pronouns as described above.

(16)	Conditional/ temporal clause	Main clause
Same/different case	GP/$\emptyset$	GP/$\emptyset$

2.5 Conjoined Sentences

We shall now examine conjoined sentences in Tamil. In this construction, the verb appears in participial form in all sentences that are conjoined except the final one. The final verb is in finite form, agreeing in person, number, and gender with the subject (or is a modal without agreement). The gap in the subject position in nonfinal clauses alternates with the reflexive pronoun. However, the gap is preferred in this position; the reflexive pronoun occurs when the subject is emphasized. A conjoined sentence is not a coordinate structure creating syntactic islands (Annamalai 1970). The nonfinal or participial clauses of the conjoined sentence have the properties of subordinate clauses. Their subordinate property allows the subject of the participial clauses to be c-commanded by the subject of the main clause and thus to be a reflexive pronoun, according to the coindexing principles mentioned above.

(17) $\emptyset_1$/taanee$_1$ kambe   eDuttu   kumaar$_1$ raajaave$_2$ aDiccaan
      self-EMP stick-ACC take-PAST Kumar Raja   hit
     '*Himself$_1$ took a stick and Kumar$_1$ hit Raja$_2$.'

NP Gaps in Tamil

As in the infinitive-clause construction, the general pronoun does not occur in the participial clause of the conjoined sentence when it has same case as its antecedent, whereas ∅ does occur there (18a). But, unlike in the infinitive-clause construction, the general pronoun occurs in the main clause, bearing the same case as its antecedent in the participial clause, and alternates with ∅ (19a). When the case is different, the conjoined sentence, again like the infinitive-clause sentence, allows the general pronoun (with emphasis) in its participial clause (18b) and does not allow ∅ in its main clause (19b). Nonoccurrence of ∅ means that the intrasentential interpretation of the gap is not the privileged one, though it alternates with the general pronoun. The difference between the infinitive and participial clauses is that the infinitive clause allows ∅ when the case is different (7b), but the participial clause does not (18b).

(18) a. kumaar$_1$ ∅$_1$ ∅$_2$/*avane$_2$ kuupTu raajaave$_2$ aDiccaan
    Kumar   he-ACC call-PAST Raja-ACC hit
    'Kumar$_1$ called *him$_2$ and hit Raja$_2$.'
  b. kumaar$_1$ ∅$_1$ *∅/avanTTeyee$_2$ kambe vaangi raajaave$_2$ aDiccaan
    Kumar   he-from-EMP stick-ACC get-PAST Raja-ACC hit
    'Kumar$_1$ got a stick from him$_2$ and hit Raja$_2$.'

(19) a. kumaar$_1$ ∅$_1$ raajaave$_2$ kuupTu ∅$_2$/avaneyee$_2$ aDiccikiTTurundaan
    Kumar   Raja-ACC call-PAST   he-ACC.EMP as-hitting
    'Kumar$_1$ called Raja$_2$ and was hitting him$_2$ (= Having called$_2$, Kumar$_1$ was hitting him).'
  b. kumaar$_1$ ∅$_1$ raajaaTTe$_2$ kambe vaangi *∅/avaneyee$_2$ aDiccaan
    Kumar   Raja-from stick-ACC get-PAST   he-ACC.EMP hit
    'Kumar$_1$ got a stick from Raja$_2$ and hit him$_2$.'

The distribution of the general pronoun and ∅ in the conjoined sentences is given schematically in (20).

(20)	Participial clause	Main clause
Same case	*GP/∅	GP/∅
Different case	GP/*∅	GP/*∅

When the antecedent and the general pronoun bear different cases, as in (18b) and (19b), ∅ is prohibited in both main and participial clauses (except in the subject position of the participial clause, where ∅ alternates with the reflexive pronoun). These gaps marked for nonoccurrence of ∅ are X. The gap in the main clause of the conjoined sentence does not allow an extrasentential referent (19a). The same is true of the gap in (21). The gap in the subject position of the participial clause does not allow an extrasentential referent, as mentioned above. This is also a same-case context. The gap in the same-case context is only ∅, and not X. This is another instance where the gap is exclusively intrasentential, like the gap in the subject position in the infinitive clause. One might think of a syntactic reason why X is excluded from the subject position, based on the fact that the participial clause must have the same subject as the main clause. Though it is uncommon for participial clause and main clause to have different subjects, it is not prohibited, so this explanation cannot be maintained.

(21) a. kumaar$_1$ ∅$_1$ pustagatte$_2$ eDuttu   ∅$_2$/adeyee$_2$ paattukiTTurundaan[7]
         Kumar   book-ACC   take-PAST   it-ACC.EMP was-looking
         'Kumar$_1$ took the book$_2$ and was looking at it$_2$.'
     b. kumaar$_1$ ∅$_1$ raajaaTTe$_3$ pustagatte$_2$ vaangi   ∅$_{2/*3}$/adeyee$_2$/*avaneyee$_3$
         Kumar   Raja-from   book-ACC   get-PAST   it-ACC.EMP/him-EMP
         paattaan
         saw
         'Kumar$_1$ got the book$_2$ from Raja$_3$ and looked at it$_2$/*him$_3$.'

Sentence (21b) is structurally identical to (19b), but the gap is not X, because its referent is only intrasentential, as in the same-case construction of (19a) and (21a). Further, in (21b), unlike (19b), the gap does not alternate with the general pronoun in a different case from its antecedent. I do not have an explanation for this difference except to speculate that there is a case hierarchy in recovering the referent of the gap in the main clause when both same-case and different-case antecedents are possible referents: the same-case referent preempts the different-case referent. (Though the direct object of the participial clause in (19b) is a possible referent for the gap in the direct object position in the main clause (same case), the semantics of 'hitting the stick', not being commonplace, does not make it the privileged interpretation and therefore the gap is X.) Sentence (22), which is identical to (21a) except for the completive aspect of the participial verb (which translates into English as 'and then' rather than 'and'), appears to be an instance where the gap in the main clause is X. If the completive aspectual marker is taken to mark an event boundary—in other words, there is disjunction between the events represented in the participial clause and in the main clause (as conceptualized by the speaker (Lindholm 1975); see Herring 1988 for treating aspect as a discourse marker), it might be possible to explain why the gap does not have an intrasentential referent. One might say that syntactic coindexing does not cross an event boundary, just as it does not cross a sentence boundary.

(22) kumaar$_1$ ∅$_1$ pustagatte$_2$ eDuttuTTu   *∅/*ade   paattaan
     Kumar   book-ACC   take-PAST.COMPL   it-ACC saw
     'Kumar$_1$ took the book$_2$ and then looked at (something).'

However, this explanation is not borne out in (23), whose participial clause has a completive aspectual marker. Instead, the gap in the main clause allows intrasentential coreference, along with an extrasentential alternative.

(23) a. ammaa₁ ∅₁ piLLekki₂ cooru kuDuttuTTu ∅₂/adukkee₂ paalum kuDuttaa
mother child-to rice give-PAST.COMPL it-EMP milk-also gave
'The mother₁ gave rice to the child₂ and then gave it₂ milk also.'
b. ammaa₁ ∅₁ piLLkki₂ cooru kuDuttuTTu ∅₁/₂/adukku₂ caTTe pooTTaa
mother child-to rice give-PAST.COMPL it₂-to dress put on
'The mother₁ gave rice to the child₂ and then put the dress on it₂.'

The gap in the main clause is coindexed with the dative in the participial clause whether the predicates of both clauses are the same (23a) or different (23b). That is, the gap in (23) allows intrasentential coreference, unlike (22), but like (21). It allows extrasentential coreference also, as ∅s in many syntactic contexts do. ∅ in the main clause in (23a) does not refer to 'mother' because of the semantics of the verb *kuDu* 'to give (to someone)', and it will refer only to 'mother' in (23b) if the predicate includes the verbal reflexive (*pooTTukiTTaa*).

The fact that the gap in (22) does not have an intrasentential referent, unlike the one in (21a), must have an explanation, which cannot simply derive from the presence of the completive aspect marker in (22). The difference between (22) and (23) probably lies in the notion of "contrary to the normal conceptualization of the event." The participial and main clauses in (21) describe an event that is normally conceptualized as a single event with multiple actions. Those in (23) describe two events that are normally conceptualized as disjoint. The completive aspect marker occurs when a conjoined sentence describes two normally disjoint events, as in (23). Sentence (22) without the aspect marker would normally describe a single event, like (21). The contrastive event separation caused by use of the aspect marker in (22) blocks an intrasentential referent for the gap. In other words, the inappropriate event boundary blocks ∅. The gap is X, which in this context suffers the blocking effect and does not allow an intrasentential referent (∅) interpretation that is permitted on syntactic grounds. This is a deviation from the general principle that the pragmatic interpretation does not exclude a permissible syntactic interpretation except when canceled on pragmatic grounds. To sum up, in the conjoined sentence, the general pronoun and the gap do not alternate at all. When the gap does not alternate with the general pronoun, by the initial definition, it is X. The gap (marked as *∅ to indicate nonoccurrence of ∅) in the different-case context either in the main clause or in the participial clause is X ((18b), (19b)). The possibility of an intrasentential referent for this gap shown by the ability of the general pronoun with emphatics to occur in these sentences is permitted by the general principle, mentioned earlier, that X may have an intrasentential referent when the gap meets the syntactic conditions for coreference. The absence of alternation between the gap and the general pronoun in the same-case context in the participial clause (18a) is of a different kind. Here the general pronoun does not occur, but the referent for the gap is only intrasentential. So this gap is $\emptyset$, though it is X when the conjoined sentence describes two disjoint events (23a–b). This is so because coreference crosses an event boundary, which is also true of (22), though there is a crucial difference: the gap does not allow an intrasentential referent nor does the general pronoun alternate with it. This is because the event boundary indicated by the completive aspect marker is contrary to the normal single-event conceptualization of the actions in the participial and main clauses and so is marked.

2.6 Relative Clauses

The last syntactic construction we shall consider is the relative clause. The relativized noun phrase takes the form of a gap in Tamil. It is a special kind of gap because it does not alternate with any pronoun (including the reflexive pronoun) and its antecedent is unique, namely, the head of the relative clause. Complements (i.e., sentential modifiers of nouns) have the form of a relative clause, but they do not contain a gap. For example, (24a) has a gap, but (24b) does not. The difference between the two sentences lies in the presence of a gap that is coreferential with the head of the relative clause in the former and its absence in the latter. (24a) has a corresponding co-relative with the same sense, but (24b) does not.

(24) a. naan $\emptyset$ paDicca   kadeye   sonneen
       I   read-PAST.REL story-ACC said
       'I told the story I read.'
    b. naan paDicca   kadeye   sonneen
       I   study-PAST.REL story-ACC said
       'I told the story of my studies (= I told the story of how I studied).'

There may be more than one gap in a relative clause, one of which is necessarily coindexed with the head of the relative clause. This is the gap of the relativized noun, indicated in the examples by $\emptyset_r$. $\emptyset_r$, having a unique referent, does not allow any extrasentential referent. Other gaps in the relative clause are $\emptyset$s, and they may allow an extrasentential referent. One problem with the gaps in the relative clause is identifying which one of them is $\emptyset_r$. The argument structure of the predicate narrows down the number of possible $\emptyset$s in the clause, but it does not help to specifically identify $\emptyset_r$. Identification is subject to island constraints discussed in Annamalai 1969, as no $\emptyset$ in a syntactic island as S of S + NP can be $\emptyset_r$.

(25) a. naan $\emptyset_r$ paDiccadaa sonna kade yaarukkum piDikkale
I read-PT.NOM.that say-PAST.REL story no-one like-not
'No one liked the story I said I read.'
b. *naan $\emptyset_r$ paDiccade sonna kade yaarukkum piDikkale
I read-PT.it-ACC say-PAST.REL story no-one like-not
'*No one liked the story I said the fact I read.'

$\emptyset_r$ does not carry any case marker, and assigning case to it is another problem. The case of $\emptyset_r$ and its antecedent (i.e., the head of the relative clause) need not be identical, except in the ablative case (Annamalai 1969). Since the order of noun phrases is free within the clause, where $\emptyset_r$ occurs in relation to the predicate (i.e., relative participle) of the participial clause does not help in assigning the case of $\emptyset_r$. Consider the following sentences:

(26) a. $\emptyset_1$/taan$_1$ kooyille $\emptyset_r$ paatta poNNeyee kumaar$_1$
self temple-in see-PAST.REL girl-ACC Kumar
kalyaaNampNNikkiTTaan
married
'Kumar$_1$ married the girl he$_2$ saw in the temple.'
b. $\emptyset_{1/2}$/taan$_1$/avan$_2$ kooyille $\emptyset_r$ paatta poNNeyee kumaarukku$_2$
self he temple-in see-PAST.REL girl-ACC Kumar-to
raajaa$_1$ kalyaaNampaNNivaccaan
Raja marriage-caused
'Raja$_1$ married to Kumar$_2$ the girl he$_{1/2}$ saw in the temple.'

There are two gaps in (26), and either one of them could be $\emptyset_r$ coindexed with the head of the relative clause. Let us arbitrarily designate the direct object position of the predicate of the relative clause as $\emptyset_r$ and its subject position as $\emptyset$. $\emptyset$ is coindexed with possible antecedents in the sentence in accordance with coindexing principles. Coindexing with the subject of the matrix clause, however, is privileged. $\emptyset$ in the relative clause alternates with pronouns (26), where $\emptyset$ is in the subject position of the relative clause. $\emptyset$ does not occur in the direct object position (27).

(27) a. $\emptyset_r$ kooyille *$\emptyset$/tanne$_1$ paatta poNNe kumaar$_1$
temple-in self-ACC see-PAST.REL girl-ACC Kumar
kalyaaNampaNNikkiTTaan
married
'Kumar$_1$ married the girl who saw him$_1$ in the temple.'
b. $\emptyset_r$ kooyille *$\emptyset$/tanne$_1$ / avane$_2$ paatta poNNe raajaa$_1$ kumaarukku$_2$
temple-in self-ACC he-ACC see-PAST.REL girl-ACC Raja Kumar-to
kalyaaNampaNNivaccaan
marriage-caused
'Raja$_1$ married to Kumar$_2$ the girl who saw him$_{1/2}$ in the temple.'

∅ does not occur in the direct object position of the relative clause as the alternate of the general pronoun, because ∅ in the subject position of the relative clause must be coindexed and when this is ∅_r, the remaining gaps are not coindexed syntactically. They are X. The verb *paaru* 'see' is transitive, and it requires semantically a patient argument. Nevertheless, the direct object position is not ∅ but X because coindexing with the subject is privileged, as mentioned above. This means that a missing argument may not be a syntactically coindexed gap (∅) in the relative clause. Given a discourse context like (28), X is interpretable as the direct object and the missing argument is recoverable pragmatically.

(28) a. kooyille   oru poNNu kumaare₁   paattukiTTeeyirundaa
      temple-in a   girl   Kumar-ACC see-DUR.EMP.PNG
      'A girl was looking at Kumar₁ in the temple.'
   b. X₁ paattukiTTurunda poNNeyee X₁ kalyaanampaNNikkiTTanaa?
         see-DUR.PAST.REL   girl-ACC.EMP married
      'Did (he₁) marry the girl who was looking at (him₁)?'

∅ in the relative clause, like the gap in other subordinate clauses, may allow an extrasentential referent (X interpretation). In (26) and (27), the missing subject is allowed to refer to the speaker, the hearer, or both, or to refer to a discourse referent, or to be unspecified. Under the unspecified referent interpretation, the relative clause is the translation equivalent of passive in English: 'Kumar married the girl seen in the temple'.

X interpretation of the gap is possible in the matrix clause also. (29) with a gap, instead of a general pronoun, may mean 'Raja married to someone the girl Kumar saw in the temple'. In an appropriate discourse context, ∅ may refer to the speaker or the hearer or a discourse referent.

(29) kumaar₁ kooyille   paatta   poNNe raajaa₂ ∅₁/avanukkee
     Kumar   temple-in see-PAST.REL girl-ACC Raja   he-to-EMP
     kalyaaNampaNNivaccaan
     marriage-caused
     'Raja₂ married to him₁ the girl Kumar₁ saw in the temple.'

Among the many ∅s in the relative clause, the privileged referent assignment is to the subject of the matrix clause and so the privileged interpretation of (26a–b) with two ∅s is to coindex one ∅ (the first one) with subject of the matrix clause. Since ∅ in the subject position of the relative clause is also privileged to be coindexed, as mentioned earlier, it gets an additional reason to be coindexed with the subject of the matrix clause. This double privilege accruing to the subject forces the remaining ∅ (the second one) in the direct object position of the relative clause to be ∅_r. This explains why (26a) without the reflexive pronoun *taan* 'self' in the subject position of the relative clause does not mean 'Kumar₁ married the girl who saw him₁ in the tem-

NP Gaps in Tamil

63

ple' (the meaning that arises when the reflexive pronoun *tanne* 'self(acc)' appears in place of the second $\emptyset$) and (26b) does not mean 'Raja₁ married to Kumar₂ the girl who saw him$_{1/2}$ in the temple'.

Privileged referent assignment differs, however, depending on pragmatic factors that include discourse context and world knowledge and on semantic factors relating to the predicate. If *paaDu* 'sing' is the relative participle instead of *paaru* 'see' in (26), $\emptyset_r$ in the subject position of the relative clause (not the subject of the matrix clause) gets privilege in referent assignment. This is motivated by the syntactic fact that one gap must be $\emptyset_r$ and by the semantic fact that the animacy of the head *poNNu* 'girl' precludes it from being the direct object of *paaDu* 'sing'. Since there is no inanimate noun in the matrix clause in (26), $\emptyset$ in the direct object position in the relative clause will remain unindexed syntactically when the predicate of the relative clause is *paaDu* 'sing'.

When the pragmatic and semantic facts are neutral (which is not uncommon), more than one $\emptyset$ in the relative clause is eligible to be coindexed with its head, that is, to be $\emptyset_r$, and the sentence is open to multiple interpretations. Since $\emptyset_r$ is not restricted to arguments and can be an adjunct as well, all arguments may be available for coindexing with antecedents other than the head of the relative clause in the sentence when $\emptyset_r$ is an adjunct. This further increases the number of possible interpretations.

To sum up, $\emptyset_r$, unlike other $\emptyset$s, has a unique antecedent, which is the head of the relative clause and has an unambiguous referent. It excludes discourse reference and it does not alternate with pronouns. Compared with other gaps in the relative clause, the gap in the subject position is privileged to be syntactically coindexed, and it is $\emptyset$; the gap in other positions is X. In the matrix clause, the gap is syntactically coindexed within it, but the intrasentential referent is not the privileged one and so the gap is likely X.

2.7 Differentiating the Gaps

The gap marked as $\emptyset$ and defined as having syntactically determined intrasentential referents allows pragmatically determined extrasentential referents in many syntactic contexts (though these are less preferred). The gap marked as X and defined as having extrasentential referents allows intrasentential referents (though these are less preferred) when the syntactic conditions for coreference are met. This raises the question whether the difference between $\emptyset$ and X is not categorical and lies only in what interpretation is preferred. The answer is no because there are syntactic contexts in which the gap allows only intrasentential referents (see below).

The alternation between $\emptyset$ and the syntactically governed general pronoun was taken to mean that the gap is syntactic. But this alternation is absent in certain syntactic contexts. In one case where alternation is absent, the general pronoun occurs, but not ∅. The contexts are the main clause of the infinitive sentence with different case (8b) and the participial and main clauses of the conjoined sentence with different case ((18b), (19b)). The nonoccurrence of ∅ (marked as *∅) means that the gap is X. (The gap was called *∅, and not X, initially on the basis of its alternation with the pronoun.) If this gap is X, then there are syntactic contexts in which X alternates with the pronoun. It follows that the alternation between the pronoun and the gap does not exclusively differentiate ∅ from X.

In simple sentences, not addressed here, the gap is X, except when the predicate has the verbal reflexive, in which case the gap, alternating with the reflexive pronoun, has only an intrasentential referent.[8] The gap in the subject position of simple sentences could be recovered from the agreement marker of the finite verb, which, however, is restricted to the person, number, and gender of the referent. The specific referent is only pragmatically recovered and so this gap is X.

In another case where alternation is absent, ∅ occurs, but not the general pronoun. The contexts are the infinitive clause with same case ((6), (7a)) and the participial clause with same case (18a). The gap in this context of the participial clause of the conjoined sentence crucially differs from the gap in the infinitive clause in that it excludes any extrasentential referent. This nonalternating gap in the participial clause with same case is purely syntactic. The gap in the subject position of the infinitive clause with a certain class of predicates does not allow an extrasentential referent, and this gap is also purely syntactic.

In the following syntactic contexts, the general pronoun and ∅ have the same privilege of occurrence; that is, either is possible, or neither. The only syntactic context where neither ∅ nor the pronoun is possible is the main clause of the infinitive sentence with same case. This gap is X. The initial marking of this gap as *∅, whose preferred interpretation is the extrasentential referent, is unmotivated.

The contexts where either ∅ or the pronoun is possible are the contexts of alternation: sentential NPs ((1)–(3)), conditional and temporal sentences ((13a–b), (14a–b), (15)), infinitive clauses with different case (7b), and main clauses with same case as the conjoined sentence (19a). However, the general pronoun is less preferred and requires emphasis or some such semantic feature in these contexts, except in sentential NPs. In these alternating contexts, the gap in the conjoined sentence is crucially different from the others. It does not allow an extrasentential referent when the conjoined sentence conceptually represents one event. This gap is purely syntactic.

The gap is syntactic in four contexts, one alternating and three nonalternating. The alternating context is the main clause of the conjoined sentence with same case (19a); the nonalternating contexts are the infinitive (10c) and participial (18a) clauses with same case, as well as the relative clause, where the gap at the site of the relativized noun phrase has a unique referent.

The four gaps considered to be syntactic are not purely syntactic, however. The gap in the subject position of the infinitive clause is controlled by the semantics of the main predicate and not by the syntactic position of the antecedent alone. The self-benefactive meaning of the modal bars any extrasentential interpretation of the gap in the direct object position. The pragmatic notion of the relevant event plays a role in the interpretation of the syntactic gap in the conjoined sentence. The case of the gap in the relative clause coreferring with its head is unrecoverable syntactically, as it need not be the same as the case of the head of the clause. Pragmatic factors play a role in assigning case to this gap, in addition to the preference for subject interpretation. All these facts show that even gaps that are likely syntactic depend upon semantic and pragmatic factors for their interpretation. Moreover, the syntactic properties of these gaps are not restricted to the structural configuration (like c-command); instead, they include as well the case status of the gap in relation to its antecedent.

Nor are the nonsyntactic gaps purely pragmatic. To explain the preference for a gap over the pronoun in the contexts where they can alternate, one must draw on the semantics of emphasis and its scope. Grammatical relation makes a difference in privileging the reference of the nonsyntactic gaps. When there is more than one noun in a sentence with which the gap can be coindexed, nouns bearing a certain grammatical relation to the gap are preferred as its antecedent. The antecedent noun in the subject position is privileged for coreference. Nouns in the subordinate clause, whose case is different from that of the gap in the main clause, are the least privileged for coreference. When there is no preferred antecedent noun in the sentence, an extrasentential interpretation is preferred.

Such facts about NP gaps in Tamil show the interconnection among syntax, semantics, and pragmatics. Any theory about reference of a nominal gap in a sentence should account for this interconnection. Any pretheoretical separation of these three areas of meaning, McCawley showed us, would be counterproductive methodologically and counterintuitive theoretically. His work is a testimony against a rigid "compartmentalization of the parts of a linguistic analysis or of a linguistic theory ... among e.g. syntax, semantics and pragmatics" (McCawley 1994, 1399).

Notes

1. The term *pronoun* is used in this chapter in a theory-neutral sense to refer to nominal proforms, which are not fully specified and whose meanings are derived by coindexing them with another noun; it is used as a cover term to include the notions "anaphor" and "pronoun" of the binding theory of Government-Binding (GB) grammar. Two kinds of pronouns, different formally and semantically, are called *general pronoun* (GP: *avan* 'he', etc.) and *reflexive pronoun* (RP: *taan* 'self'). The antecedent of a general pronoun may be a noun phrase in another sentence, but this usage of general pronouns is not discussed in this chapter.

2. It is an open question whether it is necessary at all to have syntactic principles for coindexing gaps to get meaning. If they are necessary, the subsequent question is whether they are sufficient and whether there is any overlap between syntactic and pragmatic principles. Jackendoff (1992, 30) points out that restricting the theory of referential meaning to syntactic principles like Chomsky's (1988) binding principles is a historical artifact of the period before the emergence of explicit theories of meaning, and he argues that "we ought to consider mixed alternatives when the facts push us that way." Pretheoretically, it is not necessary that the syntactic and pragmatic overlap should correlate with the intrasentential-extrasentential boundary. Freely occurring gaps in Tamil blur, if not erase, this boundary. Pragmatic principles may not be homogeneous theoretically; they may be derived from a theory of cooperative communication of a Gricean kind (Levinson 1991) or any other pragmatic theory such as a theory of discourse processing (Kuno 1987) or a theory that uses inference from world knowledge to interpret words and their absence. If the same pragmatic principles will do for both extrasentential and intrasentential coindexing, separate syntactic principles for intrasentential coindexing are not needed. On the other hand, it is possible that pragmatic principles are combined with some (though not all) syntactic principles, such as the binding principles, to distribute the load among syntax, semantics, and pragmatics (Reinhart 1983; Levinson 1987, 1991; Huang 1994). All these options go to show that there's no logical necessity for clam sauce to go only with spaghetti and the combinations are matters of ingrained preference (McCawley 1982).

3. This is a pretheoretical fact about the occurrence of the general pronoun. A theory may differentiate *avan* (and its gender/number variants) into pronouns and referential expressions, as Government-Binding Theory does. In such a case, one will be forced to posit empty referential expressions, since the gaps in Tamil may alternate with the so-called referential expressions.

4. The same-case condition is not as unqualified as stated here. Distance between the general pronoun and its antecedent also must be taken into account. The greater the distance, the more likely the admissibility of the general pronoun. Aside from distance between the antecedent and the pronoun, pragmatic and semantic factors such as the following bear on the acceptability of coreference in this case: plausibility and reasonableness in the real world, the meaning of the predicate, and emphasis on the noun. C-command and the order of the constituents remain relevant syntactic factors.

5. Note that if the subordinate clause is not an infinitive but is a sentential object, $\emptyset$ can have a discourse referent, in addition to having the subject of the matrix clause as its referent.

(i) kumaar₁ viiTTukku poonade maruttaan
    Kumar house-to go-PT.it-ACC denied
    'Kumar₁ denied that he₁ went home.' //
    'Kumar₁ denied that X (someone) went home.'

In the following discourse, (iib) is infelicitous as an answer to question (iia) because $\emptyset$ in it does not refer to Mala. There must be a pronoun coindexed with *Mala* for the sentence to be a felicitous response.

(ii) a. maalaa₁ aDuttu enna seyyappooraa?
        Mala next what do-to-going
        'What is Mala₁ going to do next?'
     b. ava₁ appaa₂ $\emptyset$₂/ava₁ amerikkaavule paDikka aaseppaDraaru
        her father she America-in study-INF desires
        'Her₁ father₂ wants to study/her₁ to study in the U.S.'

Note also that the scope of the emphatic does not include the subject of the matrix clause. For example, (10a) does not mean that Kumar alone refused to invite Raja.

6. The sentence in (i) is possible with the general pronoun in the accusative. This general pronoun is a duplicate needed to carry the parenthetical addition of the emphatic particle.

(i) kumaar₁ raajaave₂ avane₂maTTum viiTTukku pooga sonnaan
 Kumar Raja-ACC he-ACC-alone house-to go-INF told
 'Kumar₁ asked Raja₂—him₂ alone—to go home.'

The optional parenthetical addition of the pronoun as a carrier of emphatic particles is found with nouns in other grammatical relations also, including subject, as in (ii) and (iii). The general pronoun is coindexed with the subject in this plain coreferential function as an alternative to the reflexive pronoun in (iii), where it is a parenthetical addition, and in (iv), where it is an inherent case.

(ii) naan kumaarukku₁—avanukku₁maTTum—iDli vaangikuDutteen
 I Kumar-to he-to-only idli bought
 'I bought *idli* for Kumar₁—for him₁ alone.'

(iii) kumaar₁—taan₁/avan₁maTTum—iDli saapTaan
 Kumar he-alone idli ate
 'Kumar₁—himself₁/he₁ alone—ate *idli*.'

(iv) ?kumaar₁ tanne₁ / avane₁maTTum—aDiccukiTTaan
 Kumar self-ACC he-ACC-alone hit-PT.VR.PNG
 'Kumar₁ hit himself₁/him₁ alone.'

7. The sentence-initial subject is the subject of the matrix clause that has been reordered. The subject of the participial clause is indicated by ∅; it may alternate with the reflexive pronoun with some emphasis like *taanee* 'self-EMP'. To follow the structure of Tamil, the English gloss must have ∅ for the subject of the participial clause, not for the subject of the main clause. The gloss of (21a), for example, must be 'Took the book and Kumar was looking at (it)'.

8. This fact, however, is not tied in a straightforward manner to the morphology of the verb because the meaning of the self-benefaction auxiliary *kiDu* (the verbal reflexive marker) is broader than reflexivity (Annamalai 1985). This semantic feature of the morphological marker makes it possible for the gap to have X interpretation with some predicates having the verbal reflexive.

References

Annamalai, E. 1969. Adjectival clauses in Tamil. Doctoral dissertation, University of Chicago. Publ., Tokyo: Institute for the Study of Languages and Cultures of Asia and Africa, 1997.

Annamalai, E. 1970. On moving from a coordinate structure in Tamil. In *Papers from the Sixth Regional Meeting, Chicago Linguistic Society*, 131–46. Chicago: University of Chicago, Chicago Linguistic Society.

Annamalai, E. 1985. *Dynamics of verbal extension in Tamil*. Thiruvananthapuram, India: Dravidian Linguistics Association of India.

Annamalai, E. 1999. Lexical anaphors and pronouns in Tamil. In *Lexical anaphors and pronouns in selected South Asian languages: A principled typology*, ed. by Barbara Lust, Kashi Wali, K. V. Subbarao, and James Gair, 169–293. Berlin: Mouton de Gruyter.

Annamalai, E. 2004. The constituent structure of Tamil. In *The yearbook of South Asian languages and linguistics, 2003*. The Hague: Mouton de Gruyter.

Chomsky, Noam. 1988. *Language and problems of knowledge: The Managua lectures*. Cambridge, MA: MIT Press.

Herring, Susan. 1988. Aspect as a discourse category in Tamil. In *Proceedings of the Fourteenth Annual Meeting, Berkeley Linguistics Society*, ed. by Shelley Axmaker, Annie Jaisser, and Helen Singmaster, 280–93. Berkeley: University of California, Berkeley Linguistics Society.

Huang, Yan. 1994. *The syntax and pragmatics of anaphora: A study with special reference to Chinese*. Cambridge: Cambridge University Press.

Jackendoff, Ray. 1992. Mme. Tussaud meets the binding theory. *Natural Language and Linguistic Theory* 10, 1–31.

Kuno, Susumu. 1987. *Functional syntax: Anaphora, discourse analysis and empathy*. Chicago: University of Chicago Press.

Levinson, Stephen. 1987. Pragmatics and grammar of anaphora: A partial reduction of binding and control phenomena. *Journal of Linguistics* 2, 379–434.

Levinson, Stephen. 1991. Pragmatic reduction and binding conditions revisited. *Journal of Linguistics* 27, 107–61.

Lindholm, James. 1975. The conceptual basis of the Tamil adverbial participle. Doctoral dissertation, University of Chicago.

McCawley, James D. 1982. *Thirty million theories of grammar*. Chicago: University of Chicago Press.

McCawley, James D. 1994. Generative Semantics. In *Encyclopedia of language & linguistics*, ed. by R. E. Asher, 3:1398–403. New York: Pergamon Press.

Reinhart, Tanya. 1983. *Anaphora and semantic interpretation*. London: Croom Helm.

Chapter 3

Vācya, Prayoga, and Hindi Sentences without Grammatical Subjects

Michael C. Shapiro

Throughout his professional career Jim McCawley displayed a great interest in, and respect for, diverse schools of linguistics and linguistic traditions of different parts of the world. The Indian grammatical tradition, as viewed from both Western and native Indian perspectives, was something about which Jim expressed much curiosity. Although to the best of my knowledge Jim never published on traditional Indian grammar per se, he wrote at least one paper (1967) on the theory of phonology inherent in William Dwight Whitney's *Sanskrit Grammar*. That Jim showed an interest in Indian grammar, in all its various guises, should surprise no one who knew him. Jim's enthusiasm for all corners of linguistic investigation was boundless. It was also contagious. And it is this aspect of his intellectual legacy for which I am personally most grateful. Jim transmitted to his students the belief that it is the duty of a linguist, regardless of his or her doctrinal persuasion, to understand and use the results of linguistic analyses produced by diverse schools of linguistic interpretation. This moral imperative pervaded Jim's writing and his classroom teaching. And it is in the spirit of this sensibility of Jim's that I offer, as an expression of gratitude, a modest study of an aspect of Hindi grammar, one having to do with agreement, transitivity, voice, and the ways they are expressed in Hindi, for which our understanding can be enhanced by utilizing insights derived from corners of the Hindi grammatical tradition not commonly visited by Western linguists.

As is generally known, modern standard Hindi (MSH) has a well-developed set of rules by which a finite verb under some conditions agrees with the "logical subject" of a clause, under other conditions with the logical "direct object," and under others with neither, in which case it appears in an "unmarked" third person masculine singular form. Simplifying greatly, a finite verb in MSH agrees with its logical subject in one or more of number, person, and gender unless that verb is transitive and in

An earlier version of this chapter was delivered at the annual meeting of the American Oriental Society on March 26, 1984.

the perfective aspect, in which case the ergative postposition *ne* is inserted after the logical subject, which is placed in its oblique case form, and the verb agrees with its direct object. However, if the direct object is followed by the dative/accusative postposition *ko*, then the verb automatically shows third person masculine singular terminations. Examples of these three patterns of agreement are illustrated in (1)–(3).

Subject-Verb Agreement
(1) a. laṛkā   skūl   jātā hai
       boy-M.SG.DIR school habitually goes–3M.SG.PRES.HAB.OF *jānā* 'to go'
       'The boy (habitually) goes to school.'
    b. laṛkī   skūl   jātī hai
       girl-F.SG.DIR school habitually goes-3F.SG.PRES.HAB.OF *jānā* 'to go'
       'The girl (habitually) goes to school.'
    c. ajit   ū̃cī   imārat
       Ajit-PROP.M.DIR tall-F building-F.SG.DIR
       dekh rahā thā
       was looking at-3M.SG.PAST.PROG.OF *dekhnā* 'to look at/see'
       'Ajit was looking at a/the tall building.'
    d. mādhurī   ū̃cī   imārat
       Madhuri-PROP.F.DIR tall-F building-F.SG.DIR
       dekh rahī thī
       was looking at-3F.SG.PAST.PROG.OF *dekhnā* 'to look at/see'
       'Madhuri was looking at a/the tall building.'
    e. ye tīn laṛke   kal   mũbaī
       these three boys-M.PL.DIR yesterday Mumbai
       gae
       went-3M.PL.SI.PERF.OF *jānā* 'to go'
       'These three boys went to Mumbai yesterday.'
    f. ye tīn laṛkiyā̃   kal   mũbaī   gaī̃
       these three girls-F.PL.DIR yesterday Mumbai went-3F.PL.SI.PERF.OF *jānā*
       'to go'
       'These three girls went to Mumbai yesterday.'

Object-Verb Agreement
(2) a. rām   ne ū̃cī   imārat
       Ram-PROP.M.OBL ERG tall-F building-F.SG.DIR
       dekhī thī
       had seen-3F.SG.PAST.PERF.OF *dekhnā* 'to look at/see'
       'Ram had seen a/the tall building.'

Hindi Sentences without Grammatical Subjects

    b. kamleś   ne baṛī   imārat
       Kamlesh-PROP.F.OBL ERG large-F building-F.SG.DIR
       dekhī thī
       had seen-3F.SG.PAST.PERF.OF *dekhnā* 'to look at/see'
       'Kamlesh had seen a/the large building.'
    c. kamleś   ne tāj mahal
       Kamlesh-PROP.F.OBL ERG Taj Mahal(PROP.M.DIR)
       dekhā thā
       had seen-3M.SG.PAST.PERF.OF *dekhnā* 'to look at/see'
       'Kamlesh had seen the Taj Mahal.'
    d. laṛkõ   ne ye   kitābẽ
       boys-M.PL.OBL ERG these books-F.PL.DIR
       paṛhī thĩ
       had read-3F.PL.PAST.PERF.OF *paṛhnā* 'to read/study'
       'The boys had read these books.'

Verb Agrees with Neither Subject Nor Object
(3) a. laṛkī   ne us laṛke   ko
       girl-F.SC.OBL ERG that boy-M.SG.OBL DAT/ACC
       dekhā thā
       had seen-3F.SG.PAST.PERF.OF *dekhnā* 'to look at/see'
       'The girl had seen that boy.'
    b. in   laṛkiyõ   ne un   laṛkiyõ   ko
       these girls-F.PL.OBL ERG those girls-F.PL.OBL DAT/ACC
       dekhā hogā
       must have seen-3M.SG.PSMT.PERF.OF *dekhnā* 'to look at/see'
       'These girls must have seen those girls.'

Instances in which the verb agrees with a logical direct object are not limited to the perfective of transitive verbs, however. Such object-verb agreement also occurs among many (although not all) Hindi speakers in constructions of the type X *ko* infinitive + *cāhiye*, X *ko* infinitive + the copula *honā*, and X *ko* infinitive + *paṛnā* 'to fall', all of which indicate some degree of obligation to carry out the action expressed by the infinitive. In instances in which the infinitive element of these construction types has a direct object, the infinitive and any verbal element that follows it can agree in number and gender with that direct object.

(4) a. ham ko   ek dūsre kī   madad   karnī   cāhiye
      us DAT/ACC of each other help-F.DIR to do-INF.F.SG ought to
      'We ought to help each other.'

b. pramilā   ko   kuch   cīzẽ   xarīdnī
   Pramila-PROP.F DAT/ACC some-F.SG things-F.PL.DIR to buy-INF.F
   thī̃
   was-F.PL.PAST.OF COP *honā* 'to be'
   'Pramila had to buy some things.'
c. balvindar   ko   hāl mẽ apne būṛhe   ghoṛe
   Balvindar-PROP.M.OBL DAT/ACC recently own old-M.PL.OBL horses-M.PL.OBL
   becne   paṛe
   to sell-M.PL.INF fell-M.PL.SI.PERF.OF *paṛnā*
   'Balvindar was obligated recently to sell his old horses.'

If, however, the direct object of such an infinitive is itself followed by *ko*, the infinitive and any following verbal elements must appear in their default, that is, third person masculine singular forms. Thus, in sentence (5) the infinitive *le jānā* 'to take' does not agree with its direct object (which would be *bacce* in the direct case), because that direct object is followed by *ko* (thus converting the direct object to its oblique case form *baccõ*). The verbal construct *le jānā thā* 'had to take' (in form an infinitive followed by the past tense of the copula *honā*), which in effect is blocked from agreeing with either a logical subject or a logical object, is in a (third person) masculine singular form by default.

(5) kal   mujhe apne baccõ   ko   ḍākṭar ke pās
    yesterday to me own children-M.PL.OBL DAT/ACC doctor to
    le jānā thā
    had to take-3M.SG.PAST.INF.OF *le jānā* 'to take someone or something somewhere'
    'Yesterday I had to take my children to the doctor.'

Cases such as those illustrated by (5) can, not unreasonably, be considered to constitute a type of sentence that lacks an overt grammatical subject. Hindi sentences lacking overt grammatical subjects are by no means limited to those discussed so far. Certain types of "passive" sentences can also reasonably be deemed subjectless. Under normal circumstances (as in the examples in (6)), the surface grammatical subject of a passive sentence is the logical object of the main verb.

(6) a. uttar prades   mẽ hindī kī kaī   boliyā̃
       Uttar Pradesh in Hindi of several dialects-F.PL.DIR
       bolī jātī haĩ
       are spoken-3F.PL.PRES.HAB.PASS.OF *bolnā* 'to speak'
       'Several dialects of Hindi are spoken in Uttar Pradesh.'
    b. hamāre ghar mẽ tarah tarah ke samācārpatra
       our   home in of all kinds   newspapers-M.PL.DIR
       paṛhe jāte haĩ
       are read-3M.PL.PRES.HAB.PASS.OF *paṛhnā* 'to read/study'
       'All kinds of newspapers are read in our house.'

Hindi Sentences without Grammatical Subjects

This agreement pattern, however, is not observed in certain special cases. If the grammatical subject of a passive sentence is a form that would be followed by *ko* while serving as the direct object of what would be the corresponding active sentence, *ko* is retained in the passive, and the passive verb construction is third person masculine singular—that is, effectively subjectless. Compare (7a) and (7b).

(7) a. sītā   ko   pārk mẽ
Sita-PROP.F.OBL DAT/ACC park in
ghūmte-phirte
strolling-ADV.IMPF.PART.OF *ghūmnā-phirnā* 'to wander/stroll'
dekhā gayā
was seen-3M.SG.SI.PERF.PASS.OF *dekhnā* 'to see'
'Sita was seen strolling in the park.'

   b. ham ne   sītā   ko   pārk mẽ ghūmte-phirte
we ERG Sita-PROP.F.OBL DAT/ACC park in strolling
dekhā
saw-3M.SG.SI.PERF.OF *dekhnā*
'We saw Sita strolling in the park.'

In addition, there also exists in Hindi an impersonal or pseudopassive construction, showing the overt morphological properties of the true passive (e.g., use of *jānā* as an auxiliary following the perfective stem of the main verb). Often this construction, whose verbal elements are always in the third person masculine singular, has negative capabilitive sense.

(8) a. yahā̃ baiṭhā nahī̃ jātā
here 3M.SG.NEG.PRES.HAB.PASS.OF *baiṭhnā* 'to sit'
'One can't sit here.'

   b. dhūp   mẽ calā nahī̃ jātā
heat of sun in 3M.SG.NEG.PRES.HAB.PASS.OF *calnā* 'to move, walk'
'One shouldn't go out in the hot sun.'

   c. kal   rāt ko   mujh se soyā nahī̃ gayā
yesterday at.night me by 3M.SG.NEG.SI.PERF.PASS.OF *sonā* 'to go to sleep'
'I couldn't manage to sleep last night.'

   d. us   se rahā nahī̃ gayā
him/her by 3M.SG.NEG.SI.PERF.PASS.OF *rahnā* 'to remain, abide'
'He/She couldn't take (it any more).'

Furthermore, there are constructions other than "passive" ones in Hindi in which the finite verb lacks either an overt or even an implicit subject. One particularly interesting construction, which has the sense of incapacity to carry out some action, but with the implication that the "subject" wished to perform the action, but could not do so through force of circumstances, has the form X + *se* ('by, by means of'), followed by verb stem + *-te* (i.e., the indeclinable adverbial form of the imperfective participle), followed by *bannā* (literally 'to be/get made').

(9) raśīd se hindī mẽ ek bhī kahānī
Rashid-PROP.M by Hindi in even one story-M.SG
sunāte nahī̃
telling-ADV.IMPF.PART.OF *sunānā* 'to tell' not
bantā
gets made-3M.SG.PRES.HAB.OF *bannā* 'to be/get made'
'Rashid can't manage to tell even a single story in Hindi.'

The analysis of Hindi sentences that, for one reason or another, lack an overt grammatical subject has been a particularly vexing one for grammarians both within and outside of the native Hindi grammatical tradition. Clearly the phenomenon has something to do with the grammatical category of voice. But the problem also clearly goes beyond voice, at least in the sense that the term is generally understood in Western grammar, and intersects with other issues such as transitivity and causality, agreement, and case. All of the major traditional grammarians of Hindi have in one way or another attempted to explain the relationships among data of the sort presented here (although they do so in very different contexts) in terms of various grammatical categories. These categories have often been a mélange of categories directly borrowed from one or another variety of traditional Indian grammar, categories borrowed from Western grammar, and categories created specifically to explain phenomena in New Indo-Aryan languages. For the most part, the solutions advanced concerning these phenomena, and describable in terms of sets of these categories, have been less than satisfactory and have generated much terminological confusion. They have also varied considerably from one another.[1]

It is not my purpose in this brief chapter to undertake the construction of a comprehensive and coherent morphology for a major portion of Hindi's grammatical system. That is a task requiring book-length treatment. My point is rather a much less ambitious one, namely, that despite all of the inconsistency and internal controversy that exists in the Hindi grammatical tradition, there are areas where the tradition offers insights into particular phenomena that have not, as a rule, been well described in other schools and traditions of grammatical investigation. In particular, insight into some of the types of sentences described above, in particular those that can be thought of as lacking overt grammatical subjects, can be achieved by examining two grammatical terms, *vācya* and *prayog*, that have been employed by some Indian grammarians of Hindi. It is my contention that an understanding of what Hindi grammarians understand by these terms and of how they employ them to describe specific morphological and syntactic constructions can sharpen the understanding of linguists of all persuasions concerned with Hindi and perhaps impel their descriptions in new directions.

In describing the understanding of *vācya* and *prayog* within Hindi grammar, it is important to understand that neither of these terms has been used in a single consistent sense throughout the Hindi grammatical tradition. The first of these, *vācya*, has been employed frequently as a translation of the Western grammatical term *voice*, although there is much disagreement among Hindi grammarians about what sort of linguistic phenomena this term refers to. The second of these terms, *prayog* (literally 'usage' or 'application'), is used in the grammatical literature in several different senses. For some, *prayog* is simply a synonym of *vācya*. This is the position taken by the influential lexicographer Bholanāth Tivārī in an extensive dictionary of grammatical terminology (Tivārī 1964, 602). His enumeration of the putative subcategories of voice (i.e., *vācya*) lists synonyms of these subtypes in which the word *prayog* is simply substituted for *vācya*. For some other Hindi writers, however, *prayog* indicates noun-verb agreement, in which sense it is synonymous with *anvaya*, or more properly, with the phrase *anvaya tathā ananvaya* ('agreement and/or the lack of agreement').

Without doubt, the most sophisticated treatment of *vācya* and *prayoga* is to be found in Kāmtā Prasād Guru's landmark *Hindī Vyākaraṇ* [*Hindi Grammar*] (Guru 1920/1962). To my mind, the most interesting and helpful characteristic of Guru's analysis of sentences without overt grammatical subjects is that it considers *vācya* and *prayog* to be independent grammatical categories and classifies various Hindi constructions in terms of their intersection. Guru's definition of *vācya* is somewhat unusual: "*Vācya* is that grammatical category (*rūpāntar*) by which it is known whether the performance (*vidhāna*) of a sentence is apropos the agent (*kartā*), the direct object (*karma*), or only an abstract concept (*bhāva*)" (p. 255). This translation might be rendered more freely as follows: "*Vācya* is the grammatical category used to express whether the focus of a sentence is the agent, the direct object, or the verbal action itself." The three varieties of *vācya* constituted by Guru's definition are referred to as *kartṛvācya*, *karmavācya*, and *bhāvavācya*, respectively. In a lengthy commentary to his definition of *vācya*, Guru notes the difference between his definition and that of other Hindi grammarians, who treat *vācya* as a synonym of *prayog*, a practice Guru asserts to be an unwarranted carryover from Sanskrit grammar (pp. 255–56). From his discussion of the three categories of *vācya*, it is clear that he intends for *vācya* not to correspond to any single overt property (a recurrent inflection, the use of a single postposition, etc.). The differentiation of types of *vācya* is determined, in Guru's system, by the syntactic constituent that serves as the grammatical focus (*uddeśya*) of a sentence. This determination is independent of the morphological markings assigned to the verb and attendant nouns in that sentence. A verb is *karmavācya* not because it occurs in its perfective participial form followed by some form of the auxiliary *jānā* (i.e., showing "passive" morphology), but because the *karma* is the focus of the sentence, regardless of the overt morphosyntax of the sentence and of its various constituents.

Prayog, by contrast, is restricted by Guru to properties of noun-verb agreement. He defines the term as "agreement or lack of agreement between a verb and its agent or object in terms of person, gender, and number" (p. 268). He identifies three *prayog*s in Hindi: (1) *kartariprayog* (literally, 'application (with regard to the) agent'), (2) *karmaṇiprayog* (literally, 'application (with regard to the) object'), and (3) *bhāveprayog* (literally, 'application (with regard to a) *bhāva*'). These three *prayog*s are employed with reference to situations when the verb agrees grammatically with the subject, the direct object, or neither. It is important to reiterate that Guru's use of the term *prayog* does not correspond precisely to the English grammatical term *voice*. Guru intends *prayog* to refer only to the mechanical property of grammatical agreement between noun and verb regardless of the functional uses to which such agreement is put.

By treating *vācya* and *prayog* as independent grammatical categories, Guru, in effect, creates a three-by-three matrix (shown in table 3.1) in which it is possible to distribute various Hindi verbal constructions. Guru actually makes use of only six of the nine combinations in this matrix. He does not discuss the combinations *kartariprayog* + *karmavācya*, *kartariprayog* + *bhāvavācya*, and *karmaṇiprayog* + *bhāvavācya*, presumably because such combinations would be inherently contradictory or because no constructions occur in Hindi that it would make sense to characterize by these combinations of grammatical categories.

The analytic framework offered by Guru has not been entirely satisfactory to all observers. In particular, V. R. Jagannāthan, in his thoughtful Hindi style manual *Prayog aur prayog* (Jagannāthan 1981, 220–21) has criticized Guru for what he believes to be Guru's inadequacies in describing the categories *vācya* and *prayog*. Jagannāthan accepts the need for distinguishing between the two categories—he parenthetically chastises the well-known grammarian Kiśorīdās Vājpeyī (1957) for treating *vācya* and *prayog* as the same category—but he claims that the basis on which Guru differentiates among the three types of *vācya* is unscientific and not supported by overt morphological properties. He further states that there is no need to differentiate between a category of *bhāvavācya* and one of *bhāveprayog*. He thus posits a framework in which there are only two *vācya*s: *kartṛ* and *karma*. But although Jagannāthan's analysis is less differentiated than Guru's in some regards, it is more complicated in others. In particular, Jagannāthan presents an interesting, although extremely subtle, subcategorization of *karmavācya* in terms of different possibilities for the nonexpression of the logical agent (*akartṛtva*, literally 'nonagentness'). Whereas Guru's definition of voice, in its manifestation as *vācya*, centers on which party to a verbal action serves as the focus of a sentence (i.e., whether it is the agent (*kartā*), object (*karma*), or something else (*bhāva*)), Jagannāthan's, when it enters the universe of object-centered constructions, focuses on the possibilities for the non-specification of the agent (*kartā*). Jagannāthan differentiates between what he calls *akartṛtvabodhak* constructions and those he refers to as *akartṛtvasūcak*.[2] Unfortunately, Jagannāthan defines only the first of these terms, and one is forced to deduce the difference in meaning between the two terms from the examples adduced for each of them. The term *akartṛtvabodhak* seems to indicate true passives of the type illustrated in (10a) and (10b).[3]

(10) a. yahā̃ har hafte mẽ ek ek film
       here each week in one one film
       dekhī jātī hai
       is seen-3M.SG.PRES.HAB.PASS.OF *dekhnā* 'to see'
       'One film is seen here per week.'
   b. saṛak par ek ādmī mārā gayā
       street on one man was killed-3M.SG.SI.PERF.PASS.OF *mārnā* 'to strike, kill'
       'A man was killed on the street.'

The most important trait of constructions of this type is that the existence of an agent is implied, even though it is not formally expressed. *Akartṛtvasūcak* sentences differ from *akartṛtvabodhak* ones in that sentences of the former type do not even imply the existence of an agent. They are, in effect, inherently agentless, in contrast to sentences in which the agent is implied but not overtly manifest. Sentences of this type are (11a–c).

(11) a. darvāzā khulā
       door-M.SG.DIR opened-M.SG.SI.PERF.OF *khulnā* 'to open'
       'The door opened.'
   b. peṛ
       tree-M.SG.DIR
       kaṭ gayā
       was cut down-3M.SG.SI.PERF.OF *kaṭ jānā* 'to be cut down, to be felled'
       'A/The tree was cut down.'
   c. sunne mẽ āyā hai ki ...
       hearing in [it] has come that
       'It is heard that ...'

It should also be noted that in Jagannāthan's analysis there is no place for sentences of the sort *rām se pustak paṛhī gaī* (literally 'A/The book has been read by Ram'), permitted by some Hindi grammarians. Jagannāthan considers such constructions, containing a "true" passive of a transitive main verb (here *paṛhnā* 'to read, study') and marking the agent of the verb by means of the postposition *se* 'by' or *ke dvārā*

Table 3.1
Combinations of vācya and prayoga (following Guru 1920/1962)

	Kartariprayog	Karmaṇiprayog	Bhāveprayog
Kartṛvācya	laṛkā caltā hai boy-M.SG.DIR walks-3M.SG.PRES.HAB.OF *calnā* 'to walk/move' 'The boy walks.' laṛkī kapṛā sītī hai girl-F.SG.DIR cloth-M.SG.DIR sews-3F.SG.PRES.HAB.OF *sīnā* 'to sew' 'The girl sews the cloth.'		
Karmavācya		citṭhī bhejī gaī letter-F.SG.DIR was sent-3F.SG.SI.PERF.PASS.OF *bhejnā* 'to send' 'The letter was sent.' laṛkā bulāyā gayā boy-M.SG.DIR was called-3M.SG.SI.PERF.PASS.OF *bulānā* 'to call/summon' 'The boy was called.' mujh se pustak paṛhī gaī me by book-F.SG.DIR was read-3F.SG.SI.PERF.PASS.OF *paṛhnā* 'to read/study' 'The book was read by me.'	use adālat mẽ peś kiyā gayā to him/her court in was brought-3M.SG.SI.PERF.PASS.OF *peś karnā* 'to present, summon to court' 'He/She was brought into court.' naukar ko vahā̃ bhejā jāegā servant-M.SG.DIR DAT/ACC there will be sent-3M.SG.FUT.PASS.OF *bhejnā* 'to send' 'The servant will be sent there.'

Hindi Sentences without Grammatical Subjects

Bhāvavācya

yahā̃ baiṭhā nahī̃ jātā
here 3M.SG.NEG.PRES.PROG.PASS.OF
baiṭhnā 'to sit'
'It isn't permitted to sit here.'

mujh se calā nahī̃ jātā
me by 3M.SG.NEG.PRES.HAB.PASS.OF
calnā 'to walk, move'
'I'm not able to walk.'

'by means of', to be artificial and unnatural. The lack of specification of an agent is thus viewed by Jagannāthan to be an essential and not incidental property of sentences of the type *pustak paṛhī gaī.*

What, then, is one to make of the terminological complexity with regard to aspects of the Hindi verbal system manifested by writers such as Guru and Jagannāthan? More particularly, does the type of morphological analysis carried out by these writers offer insights lacking in the approaches of linguists operating out of other analytic frameworks? To the latter question, my answer is a qualified yes. I certainly do not wish to argue that the many analyses of aspects of Hindi morphology and syntax written from within various schools of Western linguistics do not provide deep insight into such matters as agreement (or its lack), transitivity, ergativity, case marking, and the like. But I would argue that the insights of some of the best traditional Hindi grammarians can provide a perspective that in many ways is complementary to that seen in Western grammar. The phenomena discussed in this chapter provide, I believe, a nice illustration of this point.

From the point of view of many Western approaches to grammatical analysis, structuring a grammar to handle Hindi verbal morphology in terms of a set of maximally productive categories is problematic. If one structures the grammar in terms of overt inflectional and morphological categories, one finds that single construction types can be put to multiple uses. The morphological passive is a case in point. There is a single construction type (i.e., the perfective participle (showing adjectval agreement with a grammatical subject, if there is one) followed by an inflected form of *jānā* 'to go') that characterizes the so-called passive. However, this morphological construction is also used for many functions (e.g., polite requests, negative capacity) that have little in common with the overall set of semantic and features (i.e., turning a logical direct object into the topic of a predication and making it the grammatical subject of a sentence) that collectively constitute what we generally mean by "passive voice." Conversely, single semantic or grammatical functions (although perhaps nuanced with subtle shading of meaning) can be expressed with highly diverse grammatical constructions. The incapacity to carry out some action, for example, can be expressed (in combination with negative markers) in Hindi not only by modal auxiliaries such as *saknā* and *pānā*, but also by various forms of the passive, including so-called impersonal passives, lacking overt grammatical subjects.

The argumentation carried out by linguists such as Guru, Vājpeyī, Jagannāthan, and others serves the useful function of focusing our attention on the distinction between morphological features in and of themselves and the pragmatic or grammatical functions to which those features are put. But the analyses of different traditional Hindi grammarians are hardly identical. Guru's analysis of the two terms under discussion here, *vācya* and *prayog*, has the virtue of differentiating the establishment of a syntactic focus for a sentence (*vācya*) from one of the mechanical means (i.e., grammatical agreement (*prayog*)) by which the establishment of a syntactic focus is formally executed. Thus, as seen in the cells in table 3.1 showing the interaction of *karmaṇiprayog* and *karmavācya*, on the one hand, and the interaction of *bhāveprayog* and *karmavācya*, on the other, Guru is able to differentiate sentences having an object as their focus and in which the agent serves as the grammatical subject from those in which there is, in effect, no grammatical subject, but the verb nevertheless shows overt "passive" morphology. Jagannāthan, I believe, in his criticism of Guru, fails to appreciate fully what Guru is doing in setting up these two distinct grammatical categories the way he does. He also fails to appreciate the reasons for setting up the two distinct categories of *bhāvavācya* and *bhāveprayog*. But Jagannāthan adds something new and insightful to this discourse, namely, the enumeration of the distinct functions to which the morphological passive can be put, along with a description of the subtle shadings of meaning achieved by the lack of specification of agents in certain types of grammatical constructions. Hindi, as is the case with most New Indo-Aryan languages, is rich in grammatical means for according (or failing to accord) prominence to the nouns that serve syntactic functions relative to verbal predicates. These are visible in sets of related sentences such as *maĩ ne laṛkī ko dekhā* 'I saw the girl' (using the ergative construction, with the "subject" marked with *ne* and the direct object with *ko*), *laṛkī dekhī gaī* 'The girl was seen' (morphological passive with verb agreeing with *laṛkī* 'girl'), *laṛkī ko dekhā gayā* 'The girl was seen' (morphological passive, agreement blocked by *ko*), and *laṛkī dikhāī dī* 'The girl was seen' (formed from quasi-passive verb *dikhāī denā* 'to be seen', which lacks passive morphology but agrees with logical object). Selecting a set of morphological parameters in terms of which to describe these sentences is hardly a minor matter in Hindi. On the contrary, selecting such parameters, as a subset of morphological parameters for language as a whole, is one of the most central issues for the grammatical analysis of Hindi.

In concluding this chapter, I would not like to argue that the discussions by Guru and Jagannāthan provide a comprehensive framework for untangling the webs of morphological relations in Hindi. On the contrary, both offer what most linguists would consider to be only partial solutions to the daunting task of positing a complete morphological analysis of Hindi. Nevertheless, both of these works, operating in intellectual frameworks light-years away from those of most Western schools of formal linguistics, offer insights into Hindi grammar that are illuminating, convincing, and in accord with the instincts and judgments of Hindi speakers about their language. Each in its own way, these discussions emphasize the distinction in Hindi between formal morphological categories and the purposes to which those properties are put. In the course of doing so, these studies demonstrate how, within the confines of Hindi grammar, the nonspecification of a particular grammatical category can be as significant as the specification of that category. Jim McCawley, I'm fairly confident, would have appreciated the point.

Notes

1. For a comprehensive overview of the entire Hindi grammatical tradition, both Western and Indian, see Bhatia 1987. Bibliographic references to much research into Hindi morphological and syntactic categories and structures can also be found in Shapiro 1978, 2003.

2. The terms *akartṛtvabodhak* and *akartṛtvasūcak*, in their literal senses, are virtually synonymous and have the sense 'indicating (*-bodhak*/*-sūcak*) nonagentness (*akartṛtva*)'.

3. By "true passive," I refer to constructions showing a passive morphology (i.e., perfective participle + inflected form *jānā*) used as an auxiliary, and in which the logical direct object serves as grammatical subject.

References

Bhatia, Tej K. 1987. *A history of the Hindi grammatical tradition.* Leiden: E. J. Brill.

Guru, Kāmtā Prasād. 1920/1962. *Hindī vyākaraṇ* [Hindi grammar]. Vārāṇasī: Nāgarī Pracāriṇī Sabhā.

Jagannāthan, V. R. 1981. *Prayog aur prayog* [Handbook of Hindi usage]. Delhi: Oxford University Press.

McCawley, James D. 1967. The phonological theory behind Whitney's *Sanskrit grammar.* In *Languages and areas: Studies presented to George V. Bobrinskoy*, ed. by Howard I. Aronson, 77–85. Chicago: University of Chicago, Humanities Division.

Shapiro, Michael C. 1978. Current trends in Hindi syntax: A bibliographic survey. *Studien zur Indologie und Iranistik* 3, 3–53.

Shapiro, Michael C. 2003. Hindi. In *The Indo-Aryan languages*, ed. by George Cardona and Dhanesh Jain, 250–85. London: Routledge.

Tivārī, Bholanāth. 1964. *Bhāṣā vijñān koś* [Dictionary of linguistics]. Vārāṇasī: Jñānmaṇḍal.

Vājpeyī, Kiśorīdās. 1957. *Hindī śabdānuśāsan* [Hindi grammar]. Vārāṇasī: Nāgarī Pracāriṇī Sabhā.

Chapter 4

The Grammaticalization of Aspect in Tamil and Its Semantic Sources

Harold F. Schiffman

4.1 Introduction

Tamil has a number of verbs, sometimes referred to as "aspectual verbs" (or "aspect markers," "aspectual auxiliaries," "verbal extensions," "postverbs," "intensive verbs," etc.), that are added to a main or lexical verb to provide semantic distinctions such as duration, completion, habituality, regularity, continuity, simultaneity, definiteness, expectation of result, remainder of result, current relevance, benefaction, antipathy, and certain other notions.

Researchers have generally found these aspect markers (AM) difficult to describe in a categorical way, and in only a few studies (e.g., Annamalai 1985) has any attempt been made to treat aspect in Tamil (or for that matter, any Dravidian language) as a *variable* component of the grammar, or as a system that is in a state of dynamic evolution (Steever 1983). In this chapter, I will attempt to summarize what is known about the facts of aspect marking in Tamil and to place it in a larger framework, recognizing that a number of different analytic approaches to this difficult topic are necessary. Aspect is a *variable* category in Tamil, but this variability is a product of the process of *grammaticalization* (Hopper and Traugott 1993), rather than representing or expressing sociolinguistic parameters.[1]

Tamil verbal aspect was the subject of my 1969 University of Chicago dissertation, and Jim McCawley was a member of my committee. Dealing with this topic in an *Aspects* model of syntax was daunting, but as Jim was moving away from the "Standard (*Aspects*) Theory" and, along with others, working toward a Generative Semantics model, I finally chose that as a better framework for handling this issue than the "Standard Theory." Without his encouragement, I might never have finished that thesis. Obviously, my ideas about this have changed again, but once Jim encouraged me to take the road "less traveled by," I have never returned to the beaten path.

4.2 Aspect and Commentary

Tamil AMs provide information and commentary about the *manner* in which an action occurred, especially how it began or ended, whether it was intentional or unintentional, whether it had an effect on the speaker or on someone else, whether it preceded another action or was synchronous with it, and so on. Some of these notions are what have been considered aspectual in other languages (having to do with completion or noncompletion, continuity or duration, manner of inception or completion), but some have little or no relation semantically to classical notions of aspect, by which I mean aspect as seen, for example, in the Slavic languages. These "extended" uses of AMs therefore sometimes involve value judgments by the speaker about the actions of others; in other words, they indicate what the speaker's *attitudes* or *expectations* about the verbal action in question are.

Most AMs are derived historically from some lexical verb that is more or less still in use in Tamil but has its own lexical meaning. The "meaning" of AMs is primarily grammatical or syntactic and can usually only vestigially be related to the lexical meaning of the verb from which it is derived. It is here that the role of metaphor comes into play, since it is by *metaphoric* extension of the lexical meaning (especially the spatial meanings) that the grammatical meaning is arrived at.

Syntactically, AMs are added to the adverbial participle (AVP) of the lexical ("main") verb. AMs then are marked for tense and person-number-gender (PNG), since the AVP preceding them cannot be so marked. Morphologically (but not phonologically), they then act identically to the lexical verb from which they are derived; that is, they take the tense and other markers of the class of lexical verb they are identical to. In most analyses of aspect in Tamil, researchers have focused on literary Tamil (LT) and have tried to show that aspect can be considered a syntactic process, since the AMs appear to function independently of morphology. I believe this claim is enabled by the artifact of modern writing, where Tamil AMs are (or can be) written with spaces between them and the AVP of the lexical verb. In spoken Tamil (ST), as I have tried to show, aspect has become (or is becoming) grammaticalized; that is, AMs now function (in many cases) as part of the *morphology* of the language, as evidenced by the phonological processes that apply to them that usually only apply *word-internally* (Schiffman 1993).[2] In this chapter, I will show that Tamil aspect is a category that is variably grammaticalized. I will focus on the role of *metaphor* in the evolution of this system, such that the lexical meanings of the source verb being aspectualized gradually yield or expand to metaphoric extensions of those meanings; as the lexical meanings are leached out, grammaticalization of the verb as an *aspectual* marker takes place. These AMs are thus no longer lexical verbs; nor are they, when completely grammaticalized, independent verbs at all. They lose their syntactic independence and become morphological suffixes attached to main or lexical verbs, as evidenced by their lack of syntactic freedom, which we see from the phonological rules that apply to them but not their lexical analogues.

4.2.1 Types of Lexical Meanings

What is crucial in the role of metaphor is the types of lexical meanings that the source verbs have or had; in almost all cases, we can identify the following semantic elements:

- *Deixis*, having to do with motion, spatial relation, or proximity to(ward) or away from the speaker. This varies, of course, and as we will see, the "meanings" of different directions with regard to the speaker are valued differently (e.g., "up is good, down is bad").
- *Stasis*, having to do with continuity, duration, lack of boundedness, habituality, and so on, of action or state.
- *Antipathy*, in which the value of the action or state is negative (the speaker does not like some action or state; the negative or pejorative notions are what I refer to below as *attitudinal*).
- *Containment*, in particular, abrupt closure, interruption, boundedness, or finiteness of an action, but also *continuity* or *duration*.

In many cases, more than one of these semantic elements is part of the lexical meaning of the source verb, and the metaphoric extension/abstraction of any or all of these meanings moves the verb along the continuum to grammaticalized aspect in different ways. Aspect as a grammatical category is thus derived from the semantic elements of deixis, stasis, antipathy, and/or containment. (Parallels with the evolution of aspect in other languages may suggest themselves, since many languages that have aspectual systems seem to have involved the grammaticalization of semantic elements similar to one or more of these meanings.)[3]

4.2.2 Metaphor and Metonymy

Metaphoric extension, however, is not the only semantic process involved in grammaticalization, and some researchers in fact prefer to emphasize the role of metonymy, or metonymic transfer, instead of metaphor. *Metonymy* of course refers to the transfer of meaning from adjacent material, as in the evolution of French negation involving particles such as *pas*, which originally meant 'pace, step' and was originally used only with verbs of motion. Thus, in a sentence such as *Je ne marche pas* (I NEG walk pace) 'I don't walk', the lexical item *pas* was probably used originally emphatically, and probably only with verbs of motion; but as French came to delete the negative particle *ne* in most modern colloquial speech, *Je ne marche pas* was reduced to *Je marche pas*, and the meaning of 'negation' was transferred metonymically from the no-longer-present *ne* to *pas*. This is now the overall pattern in modern colloquial French; and it is not restricted just to simple negation with *pas*, but is found with other nouns or particles that now function as negative markers, such as *personne*, *guère*, *rien*, and *que*, since *ne* is not present in most informal colloquial speech. Similarly, forms in English like *gonna* '(be) going to', which originally had a directional meaning, as in *He's gonna get married* 'He is proceeding to a place where he will get married', have gradually come to have an 'intentional' or 'future' meaning and the 'directional' meaning has been lost. The 'intentional' or 'future' meanings are in fact derived metonymically from the 'future' meaning that is *implied* by sentences like *He's going to get married*; that is, if he's proceeding to the place to get married, marriage is what *will* take place, and he's *intending* to do so, not just moving in that direction.

Thus, the 'intentional' or 'future' meaning is metonymically transferred to *be going to* and this is then phonologically reduced to *gonna*—but if and only if the meaning is 'future/intentional', not if the meaning is still directional. If the meaning of *He's going to the store* is 'He is proceeding toward the store', it cannot be reduced to **He's gonna the store*. Therefore, while I do not deny the importance of metonymic transfer in the evolution of grammaticalization, I do not see it as the main operative factor in the Tamil material at hand; metaphor still seems to me to be what underlies the evolution of Tamil aspectual verbs, as I will show in what follows.

4.3 The Focus of This Chapter

In this chapter, I will focus on those elements of the meanings of lexical verbs recruited to serve as aspectual verbs that have to do with *spatial relations*—in particular, relations perceived by the speaker to express his or her personal space and/or relationship to his or her body. That is, verbs that express motion away from or toward the speaker, verbs that express static proximity to or distance from the speaker, verbs that express benefit or benefaction to the speaker (e.g., as the result of obtaining some benefit, containing some action or benefit, or something pertaining to the speaker) seem to be those that are recruited as AMs. Furthermore, any action that is antithetical or malefactive to/for the speaker (the speaker perceives the motion, the action, the pertainment to be threatening, annoying, disgusting, invasive, etc.) may also become an aspectual verb, but with this clear element of antipathy or malefaction overtly present, unlike what we find with the benefactive verbs. In other words, malefaction is probably more marked than benefaction, so benefaction is the default unless a clearly malefactive or antipathetic action is involved.

To be a candidate for successful aspectual grammaticalization, a lexical verb must contain at least one of the four elements of motion (or perhaps better, *deixis*), stasis, containment/pertainment/obtainment, and malefaction/antipathy, with the added complexity that these can combine in various ways to yield different surface aspectual verbs, as well as complexities of meaning for individual AMs that are a challenge for my analysis. To illustrate briefly, the location/static verb *iru* 'be (located)' and the containment verb *koL*, when combined, are recruited to form a durative/continuative aspectual marker *kiTTiru*. The metaphoric 'holding' of *koL* (its lexical meaning is 'hold, contain') plus the metaphoric static 'being' of *iru* yield an aspectual marker expressing duration: 'holding the being, or continuing the holding'. This parallels what we find in English, where the verb *hold* has been extended metaphorically. For example, in telephone usage, it has been extended from its original meaning expressing 'holding' the telephone receiver (i.e., not hanging up) while waiting for a line or a connection, so that *Will you hold?* means, not 'Will you hold the receiver and not hang it up?', but 'Will you wait for a connection?' It is then further extended to express the kind of waiting that takes place at airports when planes are in a *holding* pattern: 'waiting for a runway'. The literal meaning of *holding* is no longer present (nothing's actually grasped in anyone's hand), but waiting—in particular, waiting in a pattern that gives priority to those planes that have been there the longest—is the metaphoric meaning. It is no accident that the Tamil verb *koL* 'hold, contain' originally involved holding something in the hand, in proximity to the body (i.e., no further than arm's length). This defines the original perimeter of one's personal space, and things entering or leaving this space, or the action of leaving something, or remaining in proximity to it, and the verbs that express this, are the crucial ones for recruitment as AMs.

Aspectual verbs in Tamil are on a kind of continuum from completely grammaticalized to only-beginning-to-be-grammaticalized. This is evident from the fact that some aspectual verbs (those I call *completely grammaticalized*) have complete freedom of occurrence with other verbs: they can occur with any verb, transitive or intransitive, with all persons, and with all tenses. They can be used with modals, in the negative, in any context. The most completely grammaticalized aspectual verb is *(v)iDu*, which is based on the lexical verb *viDu* 'leave, let'. Furthermore, such completely aspectualized verbs also exhibit phonological peculiarities, another indicator (Hopper and Traugott 1993) of grammaticalization. In this case, the initial [v] of the lexical verb is lost in ST, something that never happens at word boundaries in Tamil but is quite common word-internally.

Less advanced on the scale of grammaticalization are aspectual verbs that can only be used in certain contexts—for example, only with transitive verbs, or only with third person subjects, or only in the past tense—or perhaps have restrictions on use with modal or negative verbs. Moreover, the less grammaticalized an aspectual verb is, the fewer instances of phonological peculiarity it displays, so that the AM *vayyi* 'future utility' (based on the lexical verb *vayyi* 'put (for safekeeping)') does not exhibit *v*-deletion (as does *viDu*) and can only occur with transitive verbs. Fully grammaticalized AMs can even occur with their lexical analogues (e.g., *naan ade viTTu-TTeen* 'I completely left it; I finished it and got it over with'), whereas less completely grammaticalized AMs do not do this as freely.

Verbs that are the least grammaticalized are those that are used only in very limited contexts, or are used only by certain speakers and/or dialects, or are used in a metaphoric sense only some of the time. The verb *kuDu* 'give' is an example; some speakers can use it freely with other verbs, but many can or do not. There is a phrase *sollikuDu* meaning 'teach' ('say and give; give by saying') that expresses this metaphoric usage well and is used by many speakers. But beyond this collocation many do not use it, or would consider this a lexicalization, a "phrasal verb," but not an aspectual usage, so I relegate *kuDu* to "early candidacy" as an AM. If some argue that it is an AM, it is so only in some dialects, or for some speakers.[4]

Note of course that the verb *kuDu* 'give' in its basic meaning involves the use of the hands, and involves motion of an object from the physical space of one person (the giver) into the physical space of the recipient, and perhaps into his or her hands.[5]

The hands are also involved in the verb *taLLu* 'push, shove', which is the source of the AM *taLLu* 'riddance; distributive'. The latter meaning indicates that motion is metaphorically "out of one's hands" and into the hands or possession of "unspecified recipients."

4.4 Aspect and Modality

Lest it be assumed that some of the kinds of meanings carried by AMs are like modal verbs in other languages, or that some of these semantic distinctions are in fact modal, it should be noted that Tamil has a full set of modal verbs that express the kinds of notions that are expressed by English modals such as *can*, *should*, *might*, *want*, and *need*, and that modal verbs in Tamil are syntactically different—they occur after the infinitive (e.g., *naan pooha-Num* (I to-go-want) 'I want to go'). As a result, the term *auxiliary* (as in *aspectual auxiliary*) is one I usually abjure, in order to avoid the confusion with modal auxiliaries. Aspectual verbs, in contrast, occur syntactically after a so-called *verbal (past) participle* (also referred to by some researchers as an "adverbial participle" or AVP). In fact, then, aspect and modality can both be expressed in the same sentence/verb phrase (e.g., *niinga vandukiTTirukka-Num* (you come+DURATIVE+OBLIGATION) 'You **should** have **been** coming').[6] Modal verbs occur as the last element of the verb phrase and are usually unmarked for person, number, and gender. AMs, on the other hand, are "finite" verbs as far as their morphology is concerned, and they occur phrase-finally unless something else, such as a modal, occurs.

4.4.1 What Are the Aspect Markers of Tamil?

As noted above, the verbs that can be treated as aspectual fall on a gradient scale (or cline) of grammaticalization. Those that are more completely grammaticalized (primarily aspectual and minimally attitudinal) are *(v)iDu* 'completive', *kiTTiru* 'durative', *vayyi* 'future utility', *aahu* 'finality, expected result', *vaa* 'iterative', *poo* 'change of state', *koo* 'self-benefactive', *iru*[1] 'perfect', *iru*[2] 'result remains', and *iru*[3] 'epistemic'. The lexical analogues of these AMs are, respectively, *viDu* 'leave, let', *koNDiru* (no lexical analogue, but made up of elements of the lexical verb *koLLu* and *iru* 'be located'),[7] *vayyi* 'put away', *aahu* 'become', *vaa* 'come', *poo* 'go', *koL(Lu)* 'hold, contain', and *iru* 'be located'.

The AMs that are less completely grammaticalized (i.e., primarily express notions about the speaker's *attitude* toward actions or other speakers but nonetheless involve some aspectual notion) are *taLLu* 'distributive', *tole* 'riddance', *pooDu* 'malicious intent', and some others that vary from dialect to dialect, such as *kuDu*, which has a 'benefactive' meaning in some dialects. The lexical analogues (or "source verbs") of these AMs are, respectively, *taLLu* 'push, shove', *tole* '(go to) ruin', *pooDu* 'drop, plunk; put on (clothes)'. The lexical analogue of *kuDu* is, not surprisingly, *kuDu* 'give'.[8]

The notion that attitudes or value judgments might be semantically related to aspect may at first seem problematic. However, as Lakoff and Johnson (1980) show, words that originally expressed spatial or deictic notions are used metaphorically in many languages for positive and negative meanings. In English, for example, things that are "up" are (usually) good, and things that are "down" are (often) bad; but the same prepositions *up* and *down* have evolved (probably also via metaphor) into aspectual notions in English, so that *up* as a verbal extender has the meaning 'completive', as in *eat up, use up, tie up, burn up*, while *down* used with the same or similar verbs has another meaning, perhaps not clearly aspectual, as in *tie down, shut down, pin down, burn down*. Similarly in Russian, the preposition *u* meaning 'in proximity to; in the possession of' (*u m'en'a est'* (near me is) 'I have') is also used as an aspect marker of completion or inchoativeness: *znat'* 'to know' versus *uznat'* 'come to know, realize', *snut'* 'to sleep' versus *usnut'* 'to fall asleep'.

An attempt to schematize these four elements as they semantically characterize the lexical verbs in question is shown in tables 4.1 and 4.2.

4.4.2 Primarily Aspectual Verbs

4.4.2.1 *(v)iDu* **'Completive'** The aspectual verb *(v)iDu* contributes the semantic notion that an action was, is, or will be complete or definite. It is similar to aspectual verbs in other languages (Russian, Hindi, etc.) that impart the notion of 'perfective' (not 'perfect'). Its lexical correlate is *viDu* 'leave, let'. For example:

Table 4.1
Lexical verbs that serve as sources for the primarily aspectual markers in Tamil

	Stasis	Containment	Deixis	Antipathy
viDu 'leave'	−	−	+	−
vayyi 'put, place'		+	+	−
kiTTiru (no lexical analogue)	+	+	−	−
iru 'be (located)'	+		−	
koo 'contain, hold'	+	+ −		+ −
aahu 'become'		+	−	−
poo 'go'	−	−	+	(+?)
vaa 'come' (usually literary Tamil)	−		+	−

Table 4.2
Lexical verbs that serve as sources for the primarily attitudinal aspect markers in Tamil

	Stasis	Containment	Deixis	Antipathy
taLLu 'push'	−	−	+	−
pooDu 'drop, plunk'	−	+	+	+
kuDu 'give'	−	+	+	−
tole '(go to) ruin'	−	−	+	+

(1) avan pooy**TT**aan
    he went-COMPL.PNG
    'He went away; he's definitely gone.'

(2) naan vand-**iD**reen
    I come-COMPL.PRES.PNG
    'I am definitely coming; I'll come for sure.'

(3) avane anuppuccu**Du**
    him send-CAUS.COMPL.IMP
    'Send him away; get rid of him.'

(4) ade saappi**TT**u**TT**een
    it-ACC eat-COMPL.PAST.PNG
    'I ate it all up.'

4.4.2.2 *vayyi* 'Future Utility' The aspectual verb *vayyi*[9] has a lexical analogue *vayyi* 'take, put something somewhere for safekeeping'. It is usually used with transitive main verbs only (since the main verb *vayyi* is definitely transitive), but may occur with some intransitive verbs, such as *siri* 'laugh' (see example (11)). Other aspectual verbs (e.g., *(v)iDu*) may follow *vayyi*; but when present, *vayyi* always immediately follows the AVP of the main verb. The aspectual metaphor conveyed by *vayyi* is the notion that some action is performed because it will have (usually useful or beneficial) future consequences. It is often translatable as 'in reserve' or 'up'; for example, there are verb + *vayyi* combinations with the meanings 'stock up' (on something), 'read up' (on something), 'lay in/up' (a stock of something), which in English also imply that an action is done with an eye to future consequences, or preemptively. In the examples below, the glossed portion within square brackets is not literally present in the Tamil sentence, but is given as one or more of the consequences that the use of *vayyi* implies.

(5) taNNiire kuDiccu **vepp**oom
    water-ACC drink   FUTUTIL.FUT.1PL
    'We will tank **up** on water [We will drink our fill of water so as to avoid future thirst].'

(6) ammaa piLLengaLukku doose suTTu-**vecc**aa
    mother children-DAT   pancake heat-FUTUTIL.PAST.3SG.F
    'The mother made dosas for the children [to eat later].' 'The mother cooked **up** some dosas [to have ready] for the children [to eat later].'

(7) pooliiskiTTe edeyaavadu   oLari-**vekk**aadee
    police-to   something-or-other babble-FUTUTIL.NEG.IMP
    'Don't go blabbing anything to the police [Make sure to take precautions to avoid getting yourself into even more hot water later].'

(8) naan naaye   kaTTi-**vekk**alle
    I   dog-ACC bind-FUTUTIL.NEG
    'I neglected to tie **up** the dog [and keep it from biting people, messing up people's yards, etc.].'

(9) sundaram tan mahaLukku nalla eDattle   kalyaaNam
    Sundaram his daughter-DAT nice place-LOC marriage
    senju-**vecc**aar
    did-FUTUTIL.PAST.3SG.EPIC
    'Sundaram got his daughter married **off** well [i.e., nicely set **up** for the future].'

(10) talevar   kuuTTatte   taLLi-**vecc**aar
    head-person assemblage-ACC push-FUTUTIL.PAST.3SG.EPIC
    'The chairman postponed the meeting [i.e., put **off** the meeting].'

(11) DairekTar oru jook sonnaar; naan siriccu **vecc**een
    director   a   joke said   I   laugh FUTUTIL.PAST.1SG
    'The director told a joke, and I laughed [dutifully, just in case].'

(12) kalyaaNa viiTTle   tummi kimmi   **vecciDaadee**
marriage house-LOC sneeze ECHOREDUP FUTUTIL.COMPL.NEG.IMP
'Don't do anything stupid like sneeze or anything during the wedding ceremony [Take steps to prevent inauspicious behaviors ... avoiding bringing bad omens **later**].'

4.4.2.3 *kiTTiru* **'Durative'**   The AM *kiTTiru* has no single lexical analogue, but it is constructed from the two lexical verbs *koL-* 'hold, contain' and *iru* 'be located'. In LT the combination of the AVP of *koL*, which is *koNDu*, plus *iru* gives *koNDiru*, but in ST this undergoes rather radical phonological reduction and is realized in non-Brahman dialect as *kiTTiru*, and in Brahman dialect as *-NDiru*. In non-Brahman dialect, intervocalic *-k-* is also often deleted by the same process that deletes intervocalic *-v-*, so that in more rapid speech *kiTTiru* is often realized as *-iTTiru*. Since this AM is constructed from *koL* and *iru*, examples are given later (see (44)–(48)).

4.4.2.4 *aahu* **'Expected Result; Finality'**   The aspectual verb *aahu* has the lexical analogue *aahu* 'become'. It is usually found only in the neuter past, that is, in the form *aaccu*. Suffixed to a main verb, it expresses the notion that the action was expected, or occurred after a long wait, or was a regularly expected occurrence.

(13) poosT vand-**aaccu**
mail   came-XPRESLT
'The mail has come [as it **usually** does by this time of day].'

(14) inda kaNakkuhaL-ellaam paatt-**aaccu**
this bills-all   seen-XPRESLT
'These bills have all been checked [as they were **supposed to** have been].'

(15) saappiTT-**aacc**aa?
eat-XPRESLT.Q
'Have you eaten [as you **ought to** have, given the time of day]?'

4.4.2.5 *vaa* **'Iterative; Connected Continuity'**   The aspectual verb *vaa* has a lexical analogue *vaa* that means 'come'. The notion conveyed by aspectual *vaa* is that an occurrence is or was of long-standing duration, but more as a series of connected events (or waves of occurrences) than as uninterrupted continuity.[10] Aspectual *vaa* may often express a kind of "narrative" or "historical" (or perhaps even "mythological") past, describing an action that was common practice in a past time. Since it is only used in LT, example (16) is in LT rather than ST.[11]

(16) anta kaalattil intiyaavil aneeka aracarkaL aaNTu **vant**aarkaL
       those times-in India-in many   kings   rule   ITERAT.PAST.3PL
'In those times, many kings were ruling in India.'

4.4.2.6 *poo* 'Change of State'

The aspectual verb *poo* resembles the lexical verb *poo* 'go' in its morphology. It is used to express the notion that a change of state definitely has taken place (or definitely will take place). It is therefore aspectually completive, but the main verbs to which it is attached always themselves contain some semantic notion of change; the addition of *poo* shows that the change is complete. Usually the net result is also judged to be unfortunate or undesirable, so that it must be (as an aspect marker) marked "+antipathy." Since states are thought of as "bounded entities" (Lakoff and Johnson 1980), it is not surprising that changing states involves "motion" ("across the boundaries") from one to another, which we also find in English in expressions like *go crazy*, *go bananas*, *go nuts*, and *run amuck*.

(17) avan settu **poo**naan
    he   died CHGOFST
    'He died [He is definitely dead, alas].'

(18) adu keTTu **poo**ccu
    it spoiled CHGOFST
    'It got spoiled (i.e., went bad).'

(19) tuNiyellaam kaanju **poo**hum
    clothes-all dry   CHGOFST.NTR.FUT
    'The clothes will all get dry.'

4.4.3 Primarily Attitudinal Aspectual Verbs

4.4.3.1 *taLLu* 'Distributive', 'Riddance', 'Exdeixis'

The lexical verb that the aspectual verb *taLLu* is derived from is *taLLu* 'push, shove'. In addition to its basic aspectual notion implying completion, *taLLu* expresses the notion that an action 'got rid of' something. Its sense may range from the satisfaction of having cleaned up some sort of mess, to that of giving away all of one's wealth to the poor; the thing gotten rid of was thus usually undesirable or no longer wanted. Moreover, the recipients of this distribution are unspecified. That is, a sentence like *raaman pustahangaLe kuDuttu taLLinaan* 'Raman gave away his books' will not have a dative-marked recipient.

(20) naan anda kaDidatte paDiccu **taL**neen
    I   that letter-ACC read   EXDEIX
    'I read that letter [and got the task **out of the way**, over and done with].'

(21) avan aDutta viiTTukkaaran vaangna kaDane eRudi **taL**naan
    he next house-person taken loan-ACC wrote EXDEIX
    'He wrote **off** [as a bad debt] the loan [taken, i.e.] owed [him] by his next-door neighbor.'

(22) raajaa tan paNatte kuDuttu **taLnaan**
    king his money-ACC give EXDEIX
    'The king gave **away** all his money [i.e., to the poor, rather than to his heirs].'

4.4.3.2 *pooDu* 'Malicious Intent' The aspectual verb *pooDu* has an analogous lexical verb *pooDu* that means 'put, drop, plop (down); serve (food)' or 'put on' clothes. It has a connotation of some lack of care, so if deliberate, careful placing or setting is intended, *vayyi* is used instead. (The 'serving food' use of this verb is appropriate, since to avoid contact and ritual pollution, in India food is often "dropped" on the plate, rather than placed carefully.) The aspectual verb *pooDu* varies semantically more than some others; for many speakers, the notion it conveys is bad faith, bad motives, or even malicious intent. Annamalai (1985) calls it "the verb of casualness"; for him, the main notion is that speakers attribute "lack of care, inconsiderateness," and so on, to others when using this aspectual verb. For others, the speaker's use of *pooDu* implies careless disregard for the likes and desires of others, malice, and so on, on the part of someone else. When bad motives are being attributed, the most felicitous English translations for this aspectual verb use expletives, pejorative adjectives, or the like—hence its "+antipathy" marking.

(23) neettu varakkuuDaadu-NNu sonneenee. aanaa, neettu
    yesterday come-NEG.NECESS.QT said-EMP but yesterday
    paattu vandu-**pooTTaanga**
    deliberately came-MALICE.TNS.PNG
    'I told them not to come yesterday, but they deliberately came **anyway** [the jerks!].'

(24) tiruDanga en naaye ko**NNupooTTaanga**
    thieves my dog-ACC kill-MALICE.TNS.PNG
    '[Those (expletive deleted)] thieves [deliberately and **maliciously**] went and killed my dog.'

(25) koRande taaLe kiRiccu **pooTT**adu
    child paper-ACC tear MALICE.TNS.PNG
    'The child [carelessly] tore the paper.'

(26) avan ajaakkradeyaa kadave tirandu **pooTTuTTu** pooyirukkaan
    he carelessly door-ACC opened MALICE go-PERF.PNG
    'He has gone out, inconsiderately leaving the door ajar.'

4.4.3.3 *tole* 'Impatience, Disgust' The aspectual verb *tole* is related to the lexical verbs *tole* (2 intr 'come to an end, die, be ruined') and *tole* (6b tr, 'finish, exhaust, destroy, kill, rout'); as a result, the AM has both a transitive and an intransitive version.[12] The use of the aspectual verb *tole* expresses the speaker's impatience, antipathy, or even disgust with another person's actions, and in some cases, even his or her general personal attributes. In English, this would often be translated by some expletive or by a pejorative adjective (e.g., *the dumb kid, the rotten bastard*).[13] Even though this aspectual verb expresses impatience and disgust, it does not necessarily express lack of respect, since it may be used by wives to husbands, with politeness markers. When so used, the antipathy is toward the event rather than toward the addressee.

(27) tiisas innum muDiccu **tole**kkalleyaa?
     thesis still finish IMPAT.NEG.Q
     'Haven't you finished [that troublesome] thesis yet, [slowpoke]?'

(28) pooy-tole, engeyaavadu pooy-**tole**
     go-IMPAT.IMP somewhere go-IMPAT.IMP
     'Oh all right go on, go, go somewhere, [what the hell].'

(29) ade saappiTTuTTu pooy-**tole**nga!
     it-ACC eat-COMPL go-IMPAT.POLIMP
     'Please eat it and go! [or there'll be even more botheration].'

(30) kaaru tondaravu kuDuttu-kiTTirundadu; ade
     car trouble give-DUR.PAST it-ACC
     viTTu **tole**ccuTTeen
     abandon-IMPAT.COMPL.PAST.PNG
     'My car was giving me trouble; I sold the [dumb] thing [and was rid of it].'

(31) avan sondakkaaranaa veeru irundu **tole**kkraan
     he kinsman-ADV moreover be-IMPAT.PRES.PNG
     'He happens to be a relative of mine [so there's no way to get out of helping the jerk].'

(32) ellaarum biir kuDikka Num-NNaanga. naanum kuDiccu **tole**cceen
     everyone beer drink must they-said I-also drink-IMPAT.PAST.PNG
     'Everyone was [expected to be] drinking beer [which I don't like but] I drank some too [to get it over with and avoid making a fuss].'

(33) avan namma viSayatte DairakTarkiTTe solli-**tole**cciTTaan
     he our matter-ACC director-to say-IMPAT.COMPL.PAST.PNG
     '[Mr. Bigmouth] has blabbed [spilled the beans/let the cat out of the bag] about our [little] caper to the director [and now we're in for it].'

4.4.3.4 The Aspectual Verb *koo* One of the most complex of the Tamil aspectual verbs is *koo*, derived from the lexical verb *koo* (LT *koL-*) 'hold, contain'. In both LT and ST, lexical *koL* occurs usually with neuter subjects only, that is, in sentences in which something is said to hold or contain something, not someone. Lexical *koL* does occur as an AVP with the verbs of motion *poo* 'go' and *vaa* 'come', and the combinations *koNDupoo* and *koNDuvaa* mean 'take (something)' (i.e., 'hold and go') and 'bring (something)' (i.e., 'hold and come'), respectively. Since lexical *koL* is a class 1 verb, with present *koreen*,[14] past *kiTTeen*, and future *koveen*, these are also the forms for aspectual *koo*. Its AVP is *kiTTu*. The phonology of the spoken form of this aspectual verb differs much more from its LT counterpart than could be predicted by regular historical or morphophonemic rules. Moreover, it varies tremendously from dialect to dialect. In some dialects, there is a present form *kiDreen* and infinitive *kiDa* that are back-formations from the past *kiTTu*; in other dialects, the AVP is *-NDu*, from LT *koNDu* with deleted intervocalic *-k-*.[15]

4.4.3.4.1 Aspectual Distinctions The aspectual verb *koo* can provide a sentence with several different aspectual distinctions. Traditionally (Arden 1942, 282ff.), it is referred to as a "reflexive" verb, but this is hardly the best analysis of its meaning. The following are some of the notions provided by aspectual *koo*:

• Self-affective or self-benefactive action.[16]
• Simultaneous action. Here, *koo* indicates that one action is occurring together with another action. Sometimes, these actions are wholly coterminous; at other times, *koo* merely states that some portion of the duration of the two actions overlapped.
• Completive aspect. Here, *koo* indicates that an action is, has been, or will be definite and complete(d); but even when completive aspectual distinctions are provided, the meaning is always more than it would be if the AM *(v)iDu* were used.
• Inchoative versus punctual meaning. Aspectual *koo* is used with a number of stative verbs to indicate that a state has begun or been entered into.
• Lexicalization. Sometimes *koo* has only marginal lexical or aspectual value of its own and is attached to verb stems that no longer occur alone as bare stems. It therefore serves as a lexicalizing suffix for these verbs.
• Purposeful versus accidental meaning. Use of *koo* sometimes indicates that the action was purposeful and volitional; or (paradoxically) the action was accidental, depending on what is considered to be culturally appropriate.

4.4.3.4.2 Self-affective or Self-benefactive Action Self-affective or self-benefactive action is action that affects the subject of the sentence in some way, usually to his or her benefit, but sometimes not in any clearly beneficial way. (This use of *koo* has been called "reflexive" by other grammarians, but that term does not adequately describe many of its uses.) Sometimes the benefit clearly accrues to someone else, as in (40). Beyond its sense of benefaction, *koo* is essentially a completive AM as well,

Grammaticalization of Aspect in Tamil

since whatever else happens, the implication is that the action was definitely accomplished. Compare sentences with and without *koo* such as (34) and (35).

(34) kumaar veele teeDinaan, aanaa keDekkalle
    Kumar work looked-for but available-not
    'Kumar looked for a job, but didn't find one.'

(35) kumaar veele teeDik-**kiTT**aan
    Kumar work looked-for-BENEF-COMPL
    'Kumar looked for a job **and found one**.'

The latter implies completion, so cannot be followed by ... *aanaa keDekkalle* '... but didn't find one' without contradiction. Other examples of uses of the AM *koo* are these:[17]

(36) payyan tanne aDiccu-**kiTT**aan
    boy self-ACC beat-BENEF.PAST.PNG
    'The boy hit himself.'

(37) raaman saTTe pooTTu-**ko**raan
    Raman shirt-ACC put-BENEF.PRES.PNG
    'Raman dresses himself.'

(38) naan paNatte eDuttu-**kiTT**een
    I money-ACC take-BENEF.PAST.PNG
    'I took the money for myself.'

(39) niinga paattu-**koo**nga!
    you see-BENEF.IMP
    'Watch out [for yourself]!'

(40) nii koRandengaLe paattu-**ka**Num
    you children-ACC see-BENEF.MUST
    'You need to take care of [watch] the children.'

(41) kumaar nallaa naDandu-**kiTT**aan
    Kumar well conduct-BENEF.PAST.PNG
    'Kumar behaved well.'

(42) raamasaami muDiye veTTi-**kiTT**aan
    Ramasamy hair cut-BENEF.PAST.PNG
    'Ramasamy cut his hair [on purpose].'

(43) raamasaami kayye veTTi-**kiTT**aan
    Ramasamy hand-ACC cut-BENEF.PAST.PNG
    'Ramasamy cut his hand [by accident].'

If example (38) did not contain aspectual *koo* (i.e., if it were simply *naan paNatte eDutteen*), the meaning would be 'I took the money [but not for myself (i.e., I transported it somewhere for someone else)]'. The accidental and volitional meanings of *koo* are somewhat problematic, since the interpretations of (42) and (43) can also be reversed (i.e., they could mean that Ramasamy cut his hair by accident and that Ramasamy cut his hand on purpose); but since this is not what one usually expects of people, the expected result is the preferred interpretation.[18] The decision whether an action was deliberate or accidental depends on how society values the effect. In this case, South Asian society values deliberate hair-cutting and devalues deliberate mutilation of one's body, unless done for religious reasons.

4.4.3.4.3 *Durative or Continuous Action* Durative or continuous action, similar to the "progressive" construction *V+ing* in English, is expressed in Tamil by combining *koo* in its AVP form *kiTTu* with the "stative" aspectual verb *iru* and affixing the result *kiTTiru* to the AVP of a main verb: *vandu+kiTT-irundeen* 'I was com-ing'. Thus, the 'containment' semanteme combined with the 'stasis' semanteme results in 'continuous, durative action', similar to English *holding* as a metaphor for continuing to wait (on the telephone, above congested airports, etc.).

(44) ellaarum peesi-**kiTTiru**-ndaanga
 all speak-DUR-were
 'Everyone was talking.'

(45) raaman saappiTTu-**kiTTiru**-kkaaru
 Raman eat-DUR.PERF.PNG
 'Raman is eating.'

(46) kamalaa vanda poodu, naan paDiccu-**kiTTiru**-ndeen
 Kamala came when I read-DUR.TNS.PNG
 'When Kamala arrived, I was reading.'

(47) koRande eeRu maNikkuLLee tuungi-**kiTTiru**-kkum
 child seven o'clock-within sleep-DUR-will-be
 'By 7:00, the child will be sleeping.'

(48) engee pooy-**kiTTiru**-kkiinga?
 where go-DUR.PRES.PNG
 'Where are you going?'

(49) en kaaru tondaravu kuDuttu-**kiTTiru**ndadu
 my car trouble give-DUR.PAST
 'My car was giving me a lot of trouble.'

4.4.3.4.4 Inchoative and Punctual Notions

Aspectual *koo* can also serve to mark the beginning of a new state or action. This use of *koo* emphasizes the point of beginning, rather than the duration of the state. For example, with stative verbs that require the dative (e.g., *teri* 'know', *puri* 'understand'), the addition of *koo* emphasizes the point of beginning (in this case, the point of beginning to understand or know). Erstwhile dative-stative verb stems affixed with *koo* become nominative-subject action verbs. The (a) examples in (50)–(52) illustrate verbs without *koo*, and the (b) examples illustrate verbs with *koo*.

(50) a. adu enakku teriyum
     that to-me known
     'I know that.'
  b. naan ade terinju**kiTT**een
     I that-ACC know-INCHOAT.PAST.PNG
     'I realized [came to know; found out] that.'

(51) a. avar solradu ungaLukku puriyumaa?
     he says-thing to-you understand-Q
     'Do you understand what he says?'
  b. avar solradu purinju-**kiTT**iingaLaa?
     he says-thing understand-INCHOAT.PAST.PNG.Q
     'Did you [finally] understand what he is talking about? [Do you *get* it?]'

(52) a. okkaarunga
     sit-IMP.POL
     'Please remain seated.'
  b. okkaandu**koo**nga
     sit-INCHOAT.POL
     'Please be seated; please sit down [Please enter the state of being seated].'

4.5 Getting to Aspect

The crux of the matter is this: How do we get from notions of deixis, stasis, antipathy, and containment to aspect? In particular, how does it happen that so many of the Tamil AMs contain a notion of perfectiveness (also identified as completive or definite in Schiffman 1999)? Moreover, we have not fully specified what types of deixis pertain in the various source verbs, and how these different types are transformed or metaphorized into the various types of semantic values that we are calling aspectual.

Let us take the easy part first: the notion of stasis easily transforms into duration; states of various sorts, or any kind of stative/static element, make sense as a durative

Table 4.3
Motion and Ego

Direction re Ego	Symbol	Meaning
Away from Ego	E▶	lateral exdeixis
Up/Away from Ego	E▲	vertical exdeixis
Down to Ego	E▼	downward addeixis
Toward Ego	E◀	lateral addeixis

or continuous AM. Deixis and containment, however, are more complex. To begin with, deixis has to be specified with respect to whether the motion is *away from* or *toward* Ego, and whether it is *up* or *down*. For convenience, let us use the conventions shown in table 4.3. As noted earlier, many languages have orientational metaphors to the effect that "down is bad/bad is down" (Lakoff and Johnson 1980, 16), so any verb in Tamil that contains any element expressing downward deixis—that is, E▼—will be valued negatively or antipathetically. For example, *tole* and *pooDu* both (as lexical verbs) express notions of downward deixis, and are thus (as AMs) used to express the notion of antipathy. Similarly, lateral exdeixis, or motion away from speaker, is part of the meaning of a number of the lexical source verbs, such as *vayyi* 'put away for safekeeping' and *taLLu* 'push, shove'. These seem to be a subset of the "up is good/good is up" metaphor; that is, *foreseeable future events are up* (and *ahead*). Getting things "put away" for safekeeping, or "pushed away" and gotten rid of, gives Ego control over the future, and *vayyi* and *tallu* therefore seem to be positively valued when used as aspectual markers.

This does not hold for all types of lateral exdeixis, however, since *poo*, which indicates a change of state and has the verb *poo* 'go' as its lexical source, generally is negatively valued, since the changes of state involved may themselves be negatively valued: death, spoilage, breakage, and so on. On the other hand, drying (*kaanju poo*) is usually desirable, as when the expectation is that laundry hung out to dry will indeed dry.

Lateral addeixis, or motion toward Ego (E◀), is problematic. Logically speaking, being the opposite of lateral exdeixis, which is positively valued, it should be negatively valued, but that is not always the case in Tamil. The aspectual verb *vaa*, which has its lexical source in the verb *vaa* 'come', has a meaning of 'iterative or repetitive continuity'—an action that comes "toward" the speaker from the past, as it were. The "benefactive" aspectual verb *kuDu*, however, based on the lexical verb *kuDu* 'give', certainly involves E◀—that is, goods and services flowing toward Ego. It is perhaps worth noting that Lakoff and Johnson do not have a ready metaphor for this kind of time/motion relationship. It is also perhaps useful to remember that though some actions can be perceived as invasive, annoying, threatening, and so on, as personal space is invaded or encroached upon, other approaches or movements into personal space can be pleasant, agreeable, and beneficial, if culturally or personally they are so perceived. It could also be noted that when 'come' is used aspectually in other languages, its meaning is 'immediate past', as in French *Il vient d'arriver* (he come from arrive-INF) 'He has *just* arrived'.

4.6 Summarizing So Far

This summary of what is known about Tamil aspect is not meant to be exhaustive; it may never be possible to encapsulate all that can be said about this issue. But we do seem to be able to make the following generalizations:

• Apparently, a category of aspect must be recognized for Tamil that involves a continuum of grammaticalization from none (i.e., purely lexical or syntactic concatenation) to full-fledged morphologization.
• Most dialects (and LT) recognize a subset of AMs that are clearly aspectual and overlap little or not at all with their lexical analogues. Indeed, the lexical verb can often be followed by its corresponding aspectual verb.
• Most dialects also have a set of aspectual verbs that involve a component of aspect, but also an attitudinal notion of some sort. This set varies from dialect to dialect; nevertheless, language-wide and even family-wide features are shared. For example, the analogue of Tamil *pooDu* 'malicious intent' (lexically 'put') in Kannada is *haaku*; the two verbs have the same aspectual and lexical meanings, even though they are quite different phonologically. This feature of the Indian linguistic area has been noted for many languages. That is, the lexical-aspectual-attitudinal polarity is found in languages as different as Tamil and Bengali; one even notes some carryover into Indian English.
• Theories of syntax that require categorical rules or fixed grammaticality cannot capture generalizations about aspect in these languages.
• Clearly aspectual auxiliaries are often phonologically different from their lexical analogues, having undergone certain phonological rules that do not apply to lexical verbs because the conditions for their application are not met there. Phonological rules that operate across morpheme boundaries of concatenated verbs do not have the same privilege of application when what is concatenated is a verb and an aspectual verb.[19]
• The role of metaphor is clearly visible in the development of aspectual verbs in Tamil. Without it, we can only with difficulty describe what is going on, and with respect to the verbs that we call "attitudinal," the metaphoric extension from the lexical meaning to the "attitudinal" one is the only explanation we have of how the

meaning is changing. When the grammaticalization process is complete, however, metaphor is no longer operative; the new aspectual verb is totally functional grammatically, and it no longer relies on metaphor for its meaning, though the role of metaphor in its development is clear in retrospect.[20]

4.7 Pragmatic Considerations

4.7.1 Pragmatics: Optionality and Other Issues

Another variable feature of Tamil aspectual verbs is that pragmatic considerations are involved in the choice of whether aspect can occur or not. Since aspect is not an obligatory category, it may or may not be present. However, there is a tendency not to mark aspectual distinctions in certain constructions, even if they might be technically grammatical. The reasons for this are pragmatic, having to do with politeness, shared perceptions, the nature of truth propositions, and so on. There is also a tendency to use aspectual marking to add speaker commentary to the sentence, even with the "purely aspectual" AMs, but especially with the attitudinal ones.

• Aspect marking is an optional category; unlike tense or some other obligatory categories, its marking in Tamil is not required. There is a polarity of going and coming, known and unknown, culturally correct and incorrect.
• Aspect marking occurs most often in positive declarative sentences, rarely in negative ones; however, it is common in both positive and negative *imperative* constructions.
• Even in cases of nonattitudinal aspect marking, aspect marking can be used expressively to comment, deprecate, and so on. An example is *kattiru* 'be learning', whose illocutionary force is sarcastic or ironic.[21]
• Aspect may be bipolar and paradoxical, meaning 'intentional' in one context and 'accidental' in another. (Recall examples (42) and (43), 'Ramaswamy cut his finger/ hair'.)

4.7.2 Grammaticalization

I claim that it is the theoretical literature on grammaticalization (e.g., Hopper and Traugott 1993) that sheds light on the verbal category of aspect. Most analyses of verbal aspect marking in languages I am familiar with have dealt with aspectual verbs as if they were simply a special kind of verb with special syntactic properties, rather than a morphological marking of an obligatory or optional category.

This approach has characterized most previous analyses (including my own). But as the result of a study of certain phonological processes that seem to apply only word-internally in Tamil, I had to conclude (Schiffman 1993) that in ST, verbal aspect marking, once explainable as a syntactic process, has become morphological.

Grammaticalization of Aspect in Tamil   103

Since verbal aspect marking is clearly not inflectional in the same way that (say) tense marking is, it almost seems to be more of a derivational process than an inflectional one.[22] The fact that the evidence for this is phonological is problematic, but the very absence of the phonological reduction (e.g., intervocalic *v*- and *k*-deletion) in LT has meant that verbal aspect marking can be handled as a syntactic phenomenon with impunity in LT.[23] And in fact, most syntactic studies of verbal aspect marking (e.g., Steever 1983; Annamalai 1985; Dale 1975) have relied on data from LT, rather than ST. Had these studies used the spoken language for data, they would, I believe, have been forced to draw slightly different conclusions.[24] In the history and structure of a language, a lot can happen in seven centuries; as far as verbal aspect marking is concerned, the difference seems to be that the grammaticalization of this category has made radical progress since the time LT was last codified, in the thirteenth century.

How do studies of grammaticalization in general bear on the analysis of the aspectual system of ST in particular? Let us review some of the characteristics of grammaticalization, the process by which lexical items become grammatical morphemes in various languages.

• Grammaticalization is a common process involving lexical items that are recruited to function as modals or auxiliaries or to express aspectual distinctions in some way.[25]

• Grammaticalization may be more widespread if data from spoken languages are considered, rather than data from their written versions, and especially if diglossia is involved. Newly grammaticalized modals in English like *gonna*, *gotta*, *sposeta*, and *hafta* (derived, of course, from *be going to*, *have got to*, *be supposed to*, and *have to*, respectively) are found with those pronunciations in vernacular English, but tend to be replaced by other items (e.g., *be going to*, *must*, *should*) in written English.

• The process is gradual, lasting perhaps centuries. However, the item retains semantic traces of the lexical past and its history, and it remains polysemous even when fully grammaticalized.

• Phonologically, a newly grammaticalized item operates differently from its lexical analogue: [hæftə] instead of *have to* [hæv tu], [spostə] instead of *supposed to* [səpozd tu], and [gonna] instead of *going to* [goɪŋ tu] except when 'motion toward' is meant. Compare (53a) and (53b).

(53) a. He's gonna go to the store.
     b. *He's gonna the store. [≠ He's going to the store.]

Formal grammatical descriptions of languages in which grammaticalization is ongoing, and not yet codified, tend to ignore the process and give information only about the older norm(s); the existence of newer developments may be used or noted humorously (as in cartoons, jokes, etc.), but is not taken seriously. Or prescriptivism may prevail, and the spoken forms may be treated as "ungrammatical" or "nonstandard."

As we can see, then, the aspectual system of ST exhibits many of the signs of grammaticalization:

• The system shows great variability in syntax, morphology, and phonology. No one set of rules (e.g., phonological, sociolinguistic) can account for all of the kinds of variability. In particular, phonological "reduction" is seen to proceed further in grammaticalized items than in "regular" forms; that is, the "regular" phonological rules cannot explain forms like *kiTTu*.
• There are more aspectual verbs in modern ST than in LT, and aspectually marked verbs are more common in the ST data than in LT.
• Aspectual verbs all have lexical analogues, but those that are more grammaticalized exhibit more phonological deviance (i.e., phonological reduction) from the lexical form.
• ST aspectual verbs display idiolectal, dialectal, and pragmatic variation, but none of these types of variation explains everything. Moreover, there are other differences that arise from the variability of the grammaticalization process itself.
• The most grammaticalized of the AMs (such as *(v)iDu*) are quite uniform in their regularity and freedom of occurrence, and have few if any attitudinal nuances; less fully grammaticalized AMs retain semantic notions that are commentarial and judgmental, and hence highly variable. This is what researchers in grammaticalization refer to as being "speaker-centered" or "expressive"; that is, the motivation to develop new grammatical forms comes out of speakers' desire to express things that they feel cannot be easily expressed using the older forms.
• What could easily be explained as part of the syntactic system in LT can now best be explained as a more properly morphological element in ST, as in fact grammaticalization exactly specifies that material that was previously separate (lexically and syntactically) has become part of the morphology—that is, part of the internal grammar of the verbal *word*, not the verb *phrase*. This is also revealed by phonological processes. Certain rules must be considered word-internal, since they cannot occur across word boundaries; *v*-deletion is one of these. AMs that display these word-internal phonological reductions must therefore be part of the morphology.

Notes

1. There are inevitable kinds of interactions between grammaticalization and variability, variability that is sociolinguistic, a product of pragmatic and other kinds of discourse phenomena, but these are beyond the scope of this chapter.

2. There is no space here to demonstrate the dynamics of *v*-deletion (and also intervocalic *k*-deletion), since these processes are dependent on other phonological processes. It was through

Grammaticalization of Aspect in Tamil

my attempt to understand these variable processes, using a Lexical Phonology approach, that I came to the realization that aspect had been morphologized. For more details of this complex business, see Schiffman 1993.

3. English *have* and *be*, for example, exhibit some (but not all) of these meanings as lexical verbs and are thus easily explained as elements of the English aspectual system; the English verb *go* is also involved in expressing 'change of state', as in *go bananas, go bonkers, go crazy, go bad, go belly-up, go postal*, and so on.

4. Annamalai (1985) does include *kuDu* as an AM, which it seems to be in his dialect.

5. Ritually or ceremonially, the hands are certainly involved; drop-kicking a book into your neighbor's office or parachuting it from the roof of a building would not be considered "giving."

6. For a fuller discussion of modality, modal verbs, and the like, see Schiffman 1999, 77–80.

7. Note the phonological reduction of LT *koNDiru* to ST *kiTTiru* in "standard" (i.e., non-Brahman) dialect. In Brahman dialect, *koNDiru* is reduced to *-Ndiru*. In both dialects, in fact, intervocalic *-k-* is often deleted, and since this happens only word-internally, it is one of the signals that aspect is now a morphological process, and no longer a syntactic one.

8. The attitudinal AMs are not a closed set, and different dialects may use different verbs as markers of aspectual and attitudinal nuances. The more completely grammaticalized AMs are a closed set and show less variation from dialect to dialect, and indeed crosslinguistically within the Dravidian family.

9. Annamalai (1985) calls this the "verb of anticipated consequence."

10. Uninterrupted continuity is expressed by *koNDiru*.

11. This aspectual verb is often erroneously translated as English 'used to' (e.g., 'Many kings used to rule at that time'), whereas 'used to' probably ought to be reserved for translating habitual actions, which *vaa* does not express.

12. There is also a noun derived from this verb, *tolle*, which means 'trouble, care, vexation, perplexity'.

13. The intransitive *tole* is usually used with intransitive verbs, and probably originally the transitive was used only with transitive main verbs. But now transitive *tole* may occur with intransitive main verbs as well; there is variability according to dialect.

14. The short [o] in many forms of this morpheme is actually phonetically a schwa, a mid-central unrounded vowel.

15. The extreme variability of the phonology of this aspectual verb bespeaks a radical departure of some sort that is one of the symptoms of the process of grammaticalization.

16. Annamalai (1985) refers to this verb as "ego-benefactive." Many of the examples provided here are taken from Annamalai's book.

17. Many of the most interesting examples here and elsewhere are taken from Annamalai 1985, but converted from LT to ST.

18. One might find a parallel to this in the English "aspectual commentary" verbal expressions *manage to V* and *go and V*. For example, *Ramasamy **managed to** cut himself in the hand* and *Ramasamy **went and** cut himself in the hand* both imply that Ramasamy is not very competent or not very much in control of his life, whereas *Ramasamy **managed to** get his hair cut* implies that the incompetent Ramasamy finally got his act together and got his hair cut.

19. This characteristic is not unique to grammaticalization in Tamil or the Indian linguistic scene, of course; instead, it is typical of grammaticalization itself, as noted by various researchers, such as Hopper and Traugott (1993).

20. Again, as researchers like Hopper and Traugott (1993) note, metaphor is involved in the early stages of grammaticalization; but after "bleaching" and generalization of the meaning, the effect of metaphor is less clear than in early stages.

21. *tamiR enge katt-irukkiinga*, which literally means 'Where did you learn Tamil?', has sarcastic illocutionary force: 'Where [the hell] did you learn Tamil? (i.e., You don't know Tamil)'. By contrast, *tamiR enge kattu-kiTTiinga*, which also literally means 'Where did you learn Tamil?', with *koL* as its AM, has an obligatory implicature that the language was actually completely *acquired*, and therefore does not have an implicature of sarcasm.

22. That is, aspect marking is not obligatory, unlike inflection; but on the other hand, it does not create a new category. It is in some respects like causative marking in Tamil, in the sense that the formation of causative verbs is optional and somewhat limited in scope, but involves suffixation that augments the verb stem in various ways; and though causative verbs can be shown to be related to their noncausative analogues, they are usually listed separately in dictionaries, unlike inflected forms of the same verb. The fact that aspectually marked verbs often do become separate lexical items (e.g., *kattukko* 'learn'; the old LT root *kal-* 'learn' does not occur without some kind of aspectual "extender") shows another feature of grammaticalization: some items become *lexicalized* rather than grammaticalized; that is, they become new lexical items.

23. This problem is exacerbated by the fact that traditional Tamil grammarians did not identify aspectual distinctions as being operative in Tamil grammar, since it is not part of the Indian grammatical tradition to do so. The term *aspect* was not even used in descriptions of Tamil until my 1969 dissertation; the fact that LT spelling has not changed in seven or eight centuries also allows analysts of the literary language, at least, to ignore this phenomenon. But it must not be assumed that writing alone enables this ignorance, since Tamil was earlier written without word spaces (e.g., on specially treated palm leaves), and only with the introduction of movable-type printing by Europeans did the practice of separating words with spaces take hold.

24. I do not wish to imply here that researchers who use LT examples deny the existence of aspect marking; rather, I mean they are not forced to admit that it is *morphological*, because LT examples do not require this analysis.

25. Many studies of grammaticalization in English focus on the morphologization of items like *gotta*, *hafta*, and *gonna* and how they are becoming modal verbs; how *will* became a marker of future; and so on.

References

Annamalai, E. 1985. *Dynamics of verbal extension in Tamil*. Thiruvananthapuram: Dravidian Linguistics Association of India.

Arden, A. H. 1942. *A progressive grammar of Tamil*. Madras: Christian Literature Society.

Dale, Ian. 1975. Tamil auxiliary verbs. Doctoral dissertation, School of Oriental and African Studies, University of London.

Hopper, Paul, and Elizabeth Traugott. 1993. *Grammaticalization*. Cambridge: Cambridge University Press.

Lakoff, George, and Mark Johnson. 1980. *Metaphors we live by*. Chicago: University of Chicago Press.

Schiffman, Harold F. 1969. *A transformational grammar of the Tamil aspectual system*. Studies in Linguistics and Language Learning 8. Seattle: University of Washington, Department of Linguistics.

Schiffman, Harold F. 1993. Intervocalic V-deletion in Tamil: Its domains and its constraints. *Journal of the American Oriental Society* 113, 513–28.

Schiffman, Harold F. 1999. *A reference grammar of spoken Tamil*. Cambridge: Cambridge University Press.

Steever, Sanford B. 1983. A study in auxiliation: The grammar of the indicative auxiliary verb system of Tamil. Doctoral dissertation, University of Chicago.

Chapter 5

Causation and Tense in Subordinate Clauses: Conjunctive Participles and Conditionals in Bangla and Hindi

Tista Bagchi

5.1 Introduction

The purpose of this chapter is to examine and make explicit the semantics and pragmatics of causal and temporal dependence in two apparently unrelated syntactic construction types in the Indic languages Bangla (aka Bengali) and Hindi, namely, the conjunctive participial construction and the conditional construction. Both of these construction types crucially involve clausal subordination, in keeping with the jointly semantic, syntactic, and pragmatic approach to understanding linguistic expressions across languages advocated by Jim McCawley (notably in McCawley 1981/1993, 1988/1998). It is demonstrated that causation and temporal dependence play significant roles in the semantics and pragmatics of the two syntactic construction types both in Bangla and in Hindi. This is despite the fact that the syntax and semantics of Bangla verbs are strongly influenced by the phenomenon known as unaccusativity (in the sense of, e.g., Levin and Rappaport Hovav 1995), whereas the syntax and semantics of Hindi verbs are strongly governed by aspectually split ergativity.

An earlier version of this chapter was written when I was in residence as the Robert F. and Margaret S. Goheen Fellow at the National Humanities Center, Research Triangle Park, North Carolina, during the academic year 2001–2002. I am grateful to the participant Fellows of the Linguistics Discussion Group there for ideas that contributed to the themes developed in the chapter, and to Mitch Green, Kristin Hanson, Ursula Heise, and Brian Krostenko in particular. Discussion of many of the key ideas with William G. Lycan and Gert Webelhuth during my stay in North Carolina was also very helpful. To Connie Eble, Sally McConnell-Ginet, and Patrick O'Neill, I owe much by way of a supportive and encouraging environment that greatly facilitated the writing of this chapter. I am also very grateful to three anonymous reviewers for their detailed and insightful comments on an earlier version. Needless to say, none of these individuals are responsible for opinions and/or errors in the chapter, which are mine alone.

5.2 The Facts

5.2.1 The Conjunctive Participial Construction in Bangla and in Hindi

A significant subordinate-clause construction type under consideration in this chapter is the conjunctive participial construction, which occurs in both Bangla and Hindi, and indeed in most languages of the South Asian linguistic area. This construction is characterized by the conjunctive (sometimes also called the "perfective" or "absolutive") participle, a form of the verb that is (somewhat clumsily) translated into English as 'having V-ed'. The conjunctive participial suffix on the verb of the preceding of the two clauses in this construction possesses much of the logicosemantics and pragmatics of the connective AND (the conceptual counterpart of the two-place logical conjunction operator $\wedge/\&/\bullet$). The following examples illustrate this construction:

(1) *Bangla*
bulbul$_x$ baRi *phir-e* e_x bisram nebe
Bulbul home return-CONJ.PART   rest take-FUT.3
'Bulbul will return home and (then) rest.'

(2) *Hindi*
mistrii$_y$ ne e_y yahaaM *aa-kar*   sanduuq   banaayaa
carpenter ERG   here   come-CONJ.PART chest-M.SG make-PAST.M.SG
'The carpenter came here and made a chest.'
(Example based on Davison 1981)

The null subject of the conjunctive participle is coreferential with the subject of the main clause in both Bangla and Hindi. However, the two sister languages differ in whether or not they allow an overt subject to occur with the conjunctive participle, when the overt subject is *non*coreferential with the subject of the main clause: Bangla permits such an overt participial subject (Klaiman 1980; Bagchi 1993, 1997) in examples such as the following:

(3) *Bangla*
janla die   briSTi eSe   ghOr bhijeche
window by.means.of rain   come-CONJ.PART room be.wet-PRES.PERF.3
'The rain having come in through the window, the room has become wet.'

Klaiman (1980) proposes that two distinct volitional subjects for the conjunctive participial clause and the matrix (more generally, the next higher) clause are not allowed because of a "No-Double-Agent Condition" that holds for the conjunctive participial construction in Bangla. However, as I have pointed out in Bagchi 1997, this condition correlates with the requirement that the verb of the conjunctive participle be an unaccusative verb, so that its subject is necessarily nonagentive. The matrix clause

Causation and Tense in Subordinate Clauses

and the conjunctive participial clause cannot therefore each have an agentive subject of their own. The occurrence of unaccusative verbs in Bangla was noted by Dasgupta (1988), who demonstrated that two syntactic phenomena in Bangla—quantifier extraction and possibility passivization—are permitted only if the verb of the sentence subjected to these phenomena is unaccusative. As will be seen in section 5.3.1, two additional syntactic tests (adverb placement and placement of negation) support the claim that unaccusative verbs behave differently from other verbs in the conjunctive participial construction in Bangla.

5.2.2 Conditionals in Bangla and in Hindi

The syntax of conditional sentences exhibits interesting patterns of interaction with their semantics precisely because of the special significance of the logical connective IF (the conceptual counterpart of the material-implication operator → or ⊃ of standard propositional logic) in inference, which is attested crosslinguistically in pretty much all natural languages studied to date. This is observed for *if* in English, for instance, for the following chain of reasoning that illustrates the rule of ⊃-introduction presented by McCawley (1981/1993, 66):

(4) Whoever committed the murder left by the window.
Anyone who left by the window would have mud on his shoes.
Suppose that the butler committed the murder. Then he left by the window. In that case, he has mud on his shoes.
So if the butler committed the murder, he has mud on his shoes.

The logical properties of the material-implication operator in inference are likewise found to obtain in conditional sentences both in Bangla and in Hindi, even though both languages offer a choice among more than one conditional construction type.

In Bangla, the connective IF can be signaled by any one of the following:[1]

1. the lexical item *jodi* (optionally accompanied by *tObe* 'then' or *ta-hole* 'in that case', literally 'that-being-so'),
2. the conditional participial suffix *-le*,
3. (under special circumstances) the discourse particle *to*.[2]

The three devices are exemplified by sentences (5a–c).

(5) *Bangla*
    a. jodi ekhane keu   na aSe   (tObe) bEbSa TiMkbe   na
       if   here   anyone NEG comes (then) business survive-FUT NEG
       'If no one comes here, (the) business won't survive.'
    b. ekhane keu   na e-le   bEbSa TiMkbe   na
       here   anyone NEG come-COND business survive-FUT NEG
       'If no one comes here, (the) business won't survive.'

    c. ekhane eSecho   to morecho[3]
       here   come-PRES.PERF.2 PT die-PRES.PERF.2
       'If you come here, you're dead!'

In Hindi, the connective IF can be signaled by any one of the following:

1. the lexical item *agar* (usually in casual Hindi and in casual and formal Urdu),
2. the lexical item *yadi* (usually in formal, "learned" Hindi),
3. (additionally or, under special circumstances, by itself) the discourse particle *to*.[4]

The three devices are exemplified by sentences (6a–c).

(6) *Hindi*
    a. agar tum na   hote   to maiM mar jaataa
       if   you NEG be-PAST.IMPF PT I   die go-PAST.IMPF
       'If you weren't there, I would be dead.'/'Had you not been there, I would have died.'
    b. yadi hindii-paakii   samjhauta   na   ho   to dakSin eSiaa meM
       if   Indian-Pakistani understanding NEG be-SUBJUNCT PT south Asia in
       Saanti nahiiM rah paaYegaa
       peace not   stay get-to-FUT.3SG
       'If there is no mutual understanding between India and Pakistan, there will be no peace in South Asia.'
    c. yuuM na   hotaa   to kyaa hotaa?
       thus not be-PAST.IMPF PT what be-PAST.IMPF
       'What would have happened, had it not been this way?'
       (Quotation from Hindi-Urdu poem by Mirza Ghalib)[5]

As can be seen in both sets of sentences from the two sister languages, the following generalizations hold of the different conditional devices: a lexical connective for IF, such as *jodi* in Bangla or *yadi/agar* in Hindi, precedes, or occasionally follows, the first syntactic constituent of the antecedent clause or the *protasis* (the "IF-clause"), whereas the connective particle *to* (or, in Bangla, *tObe/ta-hole*) occurs between the protasis and the consequent clause or the *apodosis* (the "THEN-clause"). The order of the protasis and the apodosis can be inverted; that is, the apodosis can occur (without any connective particle or word for THEN) to the left and the protasis to the right, when the protasis occurs with a lexical connective such as *jodi* in Bangla or *agar* in Hindi (usually with some kind of "focusing" of the apodosis, such as an emphatic intonation), or when the verb of the protasis occurs with the Bangla conditional participial connective *-le*.

(7) a. *Bangla*
       [bEbSa *TiMkbe*   na] [jodi ekhane keu   na aSe]
        business last-FUT.3 NEG if   here   anyone NEG come-PRES.3
       'The business won't *survive* if no one comes here.'

b. *Hindi*
   [maiM *mar* jaataa]   [agar tum na   hote]
   I   die go-PAST.IMPF.M.SG if   you NEG be-PAST.IMPF.2
   'I would have *died* had you not been here.'
c. *Bangla*
   [phaguner   kuSum phoTa   hObe   phaMki], [amar ei   ekTi
    spring-GEN flowers bloom-VERBAL.NOUN be-FUT.3 in.vain my   this one
    kuMRi roi-le   baki]
    bud   stay-COND left.out
   'The blooming of spring flowers will be all in vain if this one bud of mine remains (unopened).'
   (Quotation from Bangla lyric poem by Rabindranath Tagore)

The relationship between the protasis and the apodosis in these conditional sentence types is moot. While the material-implication connective in logic is an asymmetric two-place connective—asymmetric, because a conditional formula such as $\supset pq$, where the protasis p and the apodosis q are (logical) propositions, is not logically equivalent to $\supset qp$, and two-place, because $\supset$ is an operator that requires two propositions p and q—there is no major need per se to determine the hierarchical relationship between p and q (or the lack of such a relationship) in the *logical* representation. However, what kind of *syntactic* representation the conditional construction has in these languages is still an open question.

It turns out that a good part of the evidence for a subordinate-clause analysis of the conditional construction—with the protasis as the subordinate clause—comes from the morphosyntax of the verb of the protasis in both Bangla and Hindi. In the conditional sentence types seen above with lexical connectives such as *jodi* or *agar/yadi*, the verb occurs in a special subjunctive form. The subjunctive form in Bangla is signaled largely by syntactic means: negation and the verb are ordered differently in the subjunctive than in the indicative pattern found in main clauses (Bagchi 1991; Bhattacharya, forthcoming). In Hindi, there is a morphological subjunctive, which notably shows up in the protasis of a conditional sentence when the apodosis is in either the present or the future tense. The following examples illustrate the difference between the indicative and the subjunctive (the latter in the protasis of conditional sentences) in Bangla and in Hindi:

(8) *Bangla*
   a. *Indicative*
      ram ekhane aSe   na
      Ram here   come-PRES.3 NEG
      'Ram does not come here.'

b. *Subjunctive*
ram jEno ekhane na aSe!
Ram as-if here   NEG come-PRES.3
'May Ram not come here!'

c. *Conditional*
jodi ram ekhane na aSe   tObe SObkichu Thik   thakbe
if   Ram here   NEG come-PRES.3 then everything all.right stay-FUT.3
'If Ram does not come here, everything will be all right.'

(9) *Hindi*
a. *Indicative*
raam yahaaM nahiiM/*na hai
Ram here   not   be-PRES.IND.3SG
'Ram is not here.'

b. *Subjunctive*
raam yahaaM *nahiiM/na ho!
Ram here   not be-PRES.SUBJUNCT.3SG
'That Ram not be here!'

c. *Conditional*
agar raam yahaaM na ho   to sab-kuch Thiik
if   Ram here   not be-PRES.SUBJUNCT.3SG PT everything all.right
rahegaa
remain-FUT.3SG
'If Ram is not here, everything will remain all right.'

Another piece of partial evidence comes from the Bangla conditional participial suffix: the verb of the protasis alone, but never that of the apodosis, occurs in the nonfinite conditional participial form with the suffix -*le*, and thus the conditional participial clause (i.e., the protasis) has the status of a subordinate clause in relation to the apodosis. The contrast between the perfectly well formed (10a) and the ungrammatical (10b) illustrates this, while (10c), with the conditional participial suffix occurring on the verb of the apodosis instead of the protasis, can only be interpreted as the converse conditional, with protasis and apodosis switched.

(10) *Bangla*
a. ram ekhane e-le   SObkichu Thik   thakbe
   Ram here   come-COND everything all.right stay-FUT.3
b. *ram ekhane e-le   SObkichu Thik   thak-le
   Ram here   come-COND everything all.right stay-COND
c. ram ekhane aSbe   SObkichu Thik   thak-le
   Ram here   come-FUT.3 everything all.right stay-COND
   (Only reading:) 'Ram will come here if everything remains all right.'

Causation and Tense in Subordinate Clauses

The third argument has to do with the tense of the protasis: this is less able to vary than the tense of the apodosis, and is dependent on the kind of tense taken by the apodosis. This argument will be examined in more detail in section 5.4.

Given all of these characteristics pointing to a subordinate-clause analysis of the conditional construction type in both Bangla and Hindi, one might proceed to examine what other characteristics differentiate conditionals in Bangla from those in Hindi. The most salient difference seems to lie in the relatively restricted occurrence of the simple past tense in the protasis of Bangla conditionals as contrasted with the flexibility of occurrence of the perfect participle in the protasis of Hindi conditionals. Thus, the Bangla sentence in (11) is at best odd, while the corresponding Hindi sentence in (12) does not appear to be so.

(11) *Bangla*
??jodi dOroja na   khullo   tObe ami kibhabe baRite   Dhukte
 if   door NEG open-PAST.3 then I   how   house-LOC enter-INF
pari?
be.able-PRES.1
'If the door doesn't open, how do I enter the house?'

(12) *Hindi*
agar darwaazaa na   khulaa   to maiM kaise makaan meM ghus
 if   door   NEG open-PERF.M.SG PT I   how   house   in   enter
sakuuM?
be.able-PRES.1SG
'If the door doesn't open, how can I enter the house?'

However, this restriction on the occurrence of the past tense in the Bangla finite conditional seems to hold less rigidly if the verb is agentive rather than unaccusative.

(13) *Bangla*
jodi *pro*₂ₛ𝓰 prem dile   na prane,   *pro*₂ₛ𝓰 kEno bhorer   akaS
 if   love give-PAST.2 NEG soul-LOC   why dawn-GEN sky
bhore +   dile⁶   Emon gane   gane?
fill-CONJ.PART + give-PAST.3 such song-INSTR song-INSTR
'If you did not give me love in the soul, why did you fill the dawn sky thus with song after song for me?'
(Quotation from Bangla poem by Rabindranath Tagore)

In the case of Hindi, no such constraint operates since Hindi is characterized not by unaccusativity but by split ergativity, with the verb displaying ergative morphosyntax in the perfective aspect. This is illustrated by the following contrast:[7]

(14) *Hindi*
   a. siitaa darwaazaa kholegii (nominative-accusative)
      Sita-F door-M open-FUT.3F.SG
      'Sita will open the door.'
   b. siitaa ne darwaazaa kholaa (ergative)
      Sita-F ERG *door-M* open-PERF.3M.SG
      'Sita opened the door.'

In sentence (14a), the verb (in the nonperfective future form) displays agreement in gender, number, and person with the feminine subject *siitaa*; the pattern of agreement in this sentence is thus nominative-accusative. In (14b), on the other hand, the verb, occurring in its perfective participial form to denote the simple past tense in Hindi, displays agreement in gender, number, and person with the masculine direct object *darwaazaa* 'door', while the agent *siitaa* occurs with the ergative postposition *ne*, the latter playing a "blocking" role as far as verb agreement is concerned. The pattern of agreement in this sentence is thus ergative, given its perfective aspect. In section 5.3.2, it will be shown that the split ergative pattern of agreement in Hindi can occur in the protasis of a conditional, but with some restrictions on the *nature* of the conditional rather than on the kind of verb (unaccusative or otherwise, as in Bangla) occurring in the conditional sentence.

5.3 The Correlations: Unaccusativity and the Conjunctive Participle in Bangla; Split Ergativity and the Conditional in Hindi

5.3.1 Unaccusativity and the Conjunctive Participle in Bangla

The subset of intransitive verbs that take a nonagentive subject (which typically has the thematic role theme) has come to be known as the class of *unaccusative* verbs.[8] The subject of an unaccusative verb is subcategorized for by the verb in the manner of an object or internal argument, but fails to get accusative Case from the verb as expected. While a number of European languages—including English, Italian, French, and German (Belletti 1988; Levin and Rappaport Hovav 1995)—have been examined in some detail for unaccusativity and found to possess it (though with varying syntactic effects crosslinguistically), the occurrence of unaccusativity as a syntactically significant phenomenon in the languages of South Asia has, on the whole, received relatively little attention. However, it has been postulated by Dasgupta (1988) for Bangla. In section 5.2.1, we saw that an unaccusative verb is tolerated less easily than a regular transitive verb in the protasis of a finite conditional in Bangla when the protasis occurs in the simple past tense. One might now proceed to examine the evidence supporting unaccusativity in Bangla in more detail, to ensure that this restriction on the protasis of Bangla conditionals does indeed have a substantive conceptual basis in unaccusativity in Bangla. The problem is, however, that the standard tests for unaccusativity in the literature apply only partially to Bangla. An overview of these tests, and whether or not they apply to Bangla, is presented in section 5.3.1.1.

5.3.1.1 Standard Tests for Unaccusativity The first standard test for unaccusativity involves *failure to assign accusative Case*. Belletti (1988) notes that, in Finnish, an indefinite direct object of a transitive unaccusative verb may fail to receive accusative Case from the verb. Instead, it is assigned partitive Case, a distinct Case in Finnish. The same partitive Case form is found on indefinite NP subjects of unaccusative verbs like those for 'be' and 'come' in Finnish, in that the indefinite NP subject of specifically an unaccusative verb in an inversion construction occurs in the partitive and not the accusative Case. Whether this Case form of an indefinite NP actually illustrates the definiteness effect in Finnish is open to question, since a definite NP can also receive partitive Case, provided it occurs as the sole argument of a telic predicate. The situation is different, however, in French and in English. Although these languages do not make a morphosyntactic distinction between the partitive and the accusative Cases, a distinction does show up in the *il*-inversion construction in French and the *there*-inversion construction in English, as Belletti also points out.

(15) *French*
    a.   Trois filles sont arrivées.
         three girls are arrived
         'Three girls (have) arrived.'
    b.   Il est arrivé trois filles.
         it is arrived three girls
         'There arrived three girls.'
    c.   *Il est arrivé la fille.
         it is arrived the girl
        *'There arrived the girl.'
        (Belletti 1988, 4)

The definiteness effect is observed only in *il*-inversion and *there*-inversion structures, which in turn are attested only with unaccusatives among (for French, nonreflexive) intransitive verbs. Since Bangla does not have anything like these structural types, this is not a diagnostic that can be used to test for unaccusativity in the language.

    The second standard test involves *auxiliary selection*. As Perlmutter (1978) and Davies and Rosen (1988) have observed, intransitive verbs in Italian can be identified as being unaccusative verbs if they occur with the auxiliary *essere* 'to be' in the perfective aspect (16a), as opposed to unergative verbs, which occur with the auxiliary verb *avere* 'to have' (16b).

(16) *Italian*
    a. Ugo è migliorato. (unaccusative)
       Ugo is improve-PERF.PART
       'Ugo (has) improved.'
    b. Ugo ha esagerato. (unergative)
       Ugo has exaggerated
       'Ugo (has) exaggerated.'
       (Davies and Rosen 1988, 62)

A similar, though not identical, distinction is attested in French, where a (nonvolitional) intransitive verb like *mourir* 'to die' selects the auxiliary *être* 'to be' in the perfect aspect, while a (volitional) intransitive verb like *sourire* 'to smile' selects the auxiliary *avoir* 'to have'. The phenomenon of auxiliary selection is, however, not attested in Bangla, and therefore this diagnostic is not applicable to the language.

The third standard test involves *resultative formation*. Levin and Rappaport Hovav (1995) demonstrate that the subject of an unaccusative verb can occur in a resultative construction. That is, it can be modified by a resultative predicate, as part of a resultative phrase (which is "an XP that denotes the state achieved by the referent of the NP it is predicated of as a result of the action denoted by the verb in the resultative construction"; Levin and Rappaport Hovav 1995, 34), in a manner similar to the possibility of occurrence of the direct object of a transitive verb in the resultative construction. Levin and Rappaport Hovav cite the examples in (17a–b), which have transitive verbs with the direct object in the resultative construction, and (18a–c), which have unaccusative verbs with the subject in the resultative construction.

(17) a. Woolite safely soaks all your fine washables clean.
    b. ... a 1,147 page novel that bores you bandy-legged ...
       (Levin and Rappaport Hovav 1995, 34)

(18) a. The river froze solid.
    b. The bottle broke open.
    c. The gate swung shut.
       (Levin and Rappaport Hovav 1995, 39)

In contrast, the resultative construction cannot be formed with the subjects of unergative verbs, as the ungrammatical examples (19a–c) illustrate, although of course if a "dummy" reflexive object is inserted after the verb, the examples become perfectly grammatical, as (19a'–c') illustrate.

(19) a. *We yelled hoarse.
    a'. We yelled ourselves hoarse.
    b. *My mistress grumbled calm.

b'. My mistress grumbled herself calm.
c. *The officers laugh helpless.
c'. The officers laugh themselves helpless.

This test is also inapplicable to Bangla in its present form, since Bangla does not have anything comparable to the resultative construction. Interestingly, such examples are most closely translatable by means of the conjunctive participial construction in Bangla. However, the kind of conjunctive participial construction that translates such examples is the regular null-controlled-subject conjunctive participial construction of Bangla, and therefore unaccusativity does not show up in this particular instance (though it does in the case of the other conjunctive participial construction type, the one with a lexical noncontrolled subject).

The fourth standard test involves the *causative alternation*. Unaccusative verbs participate in what Levin and Rappaport Hovav (1995) call the "causative alternation," illustrated by the transitive-intransitive pair (20a–b).

(20) a. The window broke.
     b. Pat broke the window.
        (Levin and Rappaport Hovav 1995, 79)

In contrast, prototypically unergative verbs such as *speak* do not participate in this alternation. Instead, a syntactic causative such as the *make V* construction has to be employed, as (21a–b) illustrate.

(21) a. The actor spoke.
     b. *The director spoke the actor.
        (cf. The director made the actor speak.)

This alternation is also found with certain intransitive verbs in Bangla. It turns out that these very verbs satisfy the tests for unaccusativity that work for Bangla, tests we will look at later in this section.

The fifth standard test involves *locative inversion*. This is a diagnostic that Levin and Rappaport Hovav call a "surface unaccusative diagnostic," as opposed to the last three diagnostics mentioned above. As they point out, "in the locative inversion construction the D-Structure object of an unaccusative verb does not become an S-Structure subject; instead, it maintains a postverbal position" (Levin and Rappaport Hovav 1995, 215). Examples of locative inversion sentences that they provide are (22a) and (23a); (22b) and (23b) are paraphrases without locative inversion.

(22) a. In the distance there appeared the towers and spires of a town which greatly resembled Oxford.
     b. The towers and spires of a town which greatly resembled Oxford appeared in the distance.
        (Levin and Rappaport Hovav 1995, 219)

(23) a. Here and there flourish groves of aged live oaks, planted to shadow the manor houses of the plantations that the road originally served.
  b. Here and there groves of aged live oaks flourish ...
     (Levin and Rappaport Hovav 1995, 221)

As Levin and Rappaport Hovav point out, intransitive verbs other than unaccusative (and passive) verbs do not undergo locative inversion.

(24) a. Many artists talk in the cafés of Paris.
  b. *In the cafés of Paris talk many artists.

(25) a. Half a dozen newborn babies smile in the nursery.
  b. *In the nursery smile half a dozen newborn babies.
     (Levin and Rappaport Hovav 1995, 222)

Bangla, like Hindi, displays a far greater flexibility of word order than does English. It turns out, therefore, that even if syntactic inversion of verb and direct object or subject *is* allowed in the language (and it is indeed allowed), such inversion is nothing like locative inversion, but is instead movement for certain discourse effects such as focusing or "afterthought" right-topicalization.

5.3.1.2 Tests for Unaccusativity in Bangla Dasgupta (1988) proposes two syntactic tests that Bangla unaccusative verbs do satisfy: quantifier extraction and "possibility passivization." Briefly, in Bangla a quantifier can be extracted out of the direct object NP of a sentence and right-fronted; a quantifier cannot be extracted out of an agentive (or unergative) subject NP and right-fronted; however, a quantifier can be extracted out of the (nonagentive) subject of an unaccusative verb. This is illustrated by the contrasts among the following examples:

(26) *Bangla*
  a. aj   ami [$_{NP}$ kOekTa ciThi]   likhechi
     today I   a.few   letter(s) write-PRES.PERF.1
     'I wrote a few letters today.'
  a'. aj   ami [$_{NP}$ t_i ciThi]   likhechi   kOekTa$_i$
     today I   letter(s) write-PRES.PERF.1 a.few
     'I wrote a few *letters* today.'
  b. bohudin e   maThe   [$_{NP}$ kono chele] dowRoYni
     many.day this field-LOC   any boy   run-PERF.NEG.3
     'No boy has run on this field for a long time.'
  b'. *bohudin e   maThe   [$_{NP}$ t_i chele] dowRoYni   kono$_i$
     many.day this field-LOC   boy   run-PERF.NEG.3 any
  c. Se din e   maThe   [$_{NP}$ Onek phul]   phuTechilo
     that day this field-LOC   many flower(s) blossom-PAST.PERF.3
     'Many flowers had bloomed in this field that day.'

c'. Se din e maThe [NP t_i phul] phuTechilo Onek_i
that day this field-LOC flower(s) blossom-PAST.PERF.3 many
'Many *flowers* had bloomed in this field that day.'

"Possibility passivization" is actually a negative test, in that an agentive transitive or unergative verb in Bangla undergoes this kind of passivization, but an unaccusative verb does not. This is illustrated by the following examples:

(27) *Bangla*
 a. aj kOekTa ciThi lekha gEche
 today a.few letter(s) write-PASS go-PRES.PERF.3
 'It has been possible to write a few letters today.'
 b. aj dowRono gEche
 today run-PASS go-PRES.PERF.3
 'It has been possible to run today.'
 c. *aj phoTa gEche
 today blossom-PASS go-PRES.PERF.3
 *'It has been possible to blossom today.'

To these, I add two somewhat weaker tests: when an unaccusative verb occurs in a conjunctive participial clause, it resists the placement of an adverb such as *hOThat* 'suddenly' within the clause, and (perhaps for pragmatic rather than syntactic reasons) it also resists placement of the negative marker *na* in the clause.[9] The test of *resistance to adverb placement* is illustrated in (28) and (29).

(28) *Intransitive/transitive verb (Bangla)*
 a. bulbul [VP ghOre Dhuke] [[Adv hOThat] [VP citkar korlo]]
 Bulbul room-LOC enter-CONJ suddenly scream make-PAST.3
 'Bulbul entered the room and all of a sudden (she/he) screamed.'
 b. bulbul [[Adv hOThat] [VP ghOre Dhuke]] [VP citkar korlo]
 Bulbul suddenly room-LOC enter-CONJ scream make-PAST.3
 'Bulbul entered the room all of a sudden and screamed.'

(29) *Unaccusative verb (Bangla)*
 a. ?(?)janla die briSTi [[Adv hOThat] [VP eSe]] [VP ghOr
 window via rain suddenly come-CONJ room
 bhijeche]
 become.wet-PRES.PERF.3
 'The rain having suddenly entered through the window, the room became/has become wet.'
 b. ??janla die briSTi [VP eSe] ghOr [[Adv hOThat]
 window via rain come-CONJ room suddenly
 [VP bhijeche]]
 become.wet-PRES.PERF.3

'The rain having entered through the window, the room suddenly became/has suddenly become wet.'

The test of *resistance to placement of negation* is illustrated in (30).[10] Ordinarily, negation can occur freely with a conjunctive participle, with or without the (additional) occurrence of negation with the matrix verb. When the conjunctive participle is the participle of an unaccusative verb, however, it seems to resist co-occurring with negation, and this is observed both when the matrix verb occurs with (additional) negation (30b) and when it does not (30a).

(30) *Bangla*
    a. ??janla   die briSTi [[Neg na] [VP eSe]]   ghOr
        window via rain   not   come-CONJ room
        [VP bhijeche]
           become.wet-PRES.PERF.3
        'The room became/has become wet without the rain having entered the room.'
    b. ?(?)janla   die briSTi [[Neg na] [VP eSe]]   ghOr
        window via rain   not   come-CONJ room
        [VP[V bheje-][Neg -ni]][11]
           become.wet-PERF.3+not
        'The room did not become wet without the rain having entered the room.'

These two tests thus constitute additional, if weaker, evidence for the special status of an unaccusative verb in a conjunctive participial clause: an unaccusative verb in the shape of a conjunctive participle resists both the placement of an adverb such as *hOThat* 'suddenly' and the placement of negation in Bangla.

5.3.2 Split Ergativity and the Conditional in Hindi

The nature of split ergativity in Hindi has already been touched upon briefly in section 5.2.2. What I would like to make clear, though, is that the term *ergativity* is to be understood as referring to a purely morphosyntactic phenomenon in Hindi. This clarification is necessary because the distinction between lexical and morphosyntactic ergativity has not always been drawn explicitly in the mainstream literature focusing on Case phenomena in syntax (as in Hale and Keyser 1993, Hendrick 1995, and Chomsky 1995, 2000, in which attempts are made to draw a structurally encoded distinction between transitive and unergative verbs on the one hand and unaccusatives on the other).[12] In this literature, unaccusative verbs have been dubbed "ergative" verbs, with the result that there has been an unfortunate conceptual conflation of genuinely ergative morphosyntax, the dually lexical and syntactic phenomenon of unaccusativity, and *lexical* ergativity (which Hindi in fact also displays in a small number of agentive intransitive verbs, in tandem with morphosyntactic ergativity in the perfective aspect).[13] To unpack these conflated notions of ergativity in the specific case of Hindi, one must begin by understanding the nature of morphosyntactic ergativity in Hindi. As indicated in section 5.2, Hindi displays morphosyntactic ergativity in the perfective aspect, in both its case and its agreement patterns.

(31) *Hindi*
    a. raam   roTii   khaa rahaa   hai[14]
       Ram-M bread-F eat   CONT.M.SG be-PRES.3SG
       'Ram is eating (the) bread.'
    b. raam   ne   roTii   khaaii
       Ram-M ERG bread-F eat-PERF.F.3SG
       'Ram ate (the) bread.'

(32) a. siitaa aam   khaa rahii   hai
      Sita-F mango-M eat   CONT.F.SG be-PRES.3SG
      'Sita is eating a/the mango.'
    b. siitaa ne   aam   khaayaa
      Sita-F ERG mango-M eat-PERF.M.SG
      'Sita ate a/the mango.'

Compare these sentences with the following sentences, with intransitive verbs:

(33) *Hindi*
    a. raam   dillii   meM rahtaa   hai
       Ram-M Delhi in   live-PRES.M.SG be-PRES.3SG
       'Ram lives in Delhi.'
    b. raam   dillii   meM rahaa   (thaa)
       Ram-M Delhi in   live-PERF.M.SG (be-PAST.3SG)
       'Ram lived in Delhi.'/'Ram had lived in Delhi (before).'

(34) *Hindi*
    a. siitaa dillii   meM rahtii   hai
       Sita-F Delhi in   live-PRES.F be-PRES.3SG
       'Sita lives in Delhi.'
    b. siitaa dillii   meM rahii   (thii)
       Sita-F Delhi in   live-PRES.F (be-PAST.3SG)
       'Sita lived in Delhi.'/'Sita had lived in Delhi (before).'

However, Hindi also has a small number of lexically ergative verbs (which, it must be emphasized, are *not* unaccusative verbs), for which the subject is marked by the ergative postposition *ne* in the perfective aspect and which take "default" (masculine third person singular) agreement, with no direct object either articulated or understood.

(35) *Hindi*
    a. kutiyaa bhauMk rahii   hai
       dog-F bark   PRES.CONT.F be-3SG
       'The (female) dog is barking.'
    b. kutiyaa ne bhauMkaa
       dog-F   ERG bark-PERF.M.3SG
       'The (female) dog barked.'

This distinction between morphosyntactic ergativity and lexical ergativity is an important one to make in light of the facts of Hindi. As it turns out, the distinction is of special explanatory significance for an otherwise unexplained contrast found in certain Hindi conditional sentence types. This is exemplified by the contrast in grammaticality between sentences (36a) and (37a): that is, between the inadmissibility of a zero pronoun in the apodosis that is coreferential with the subject of the morphosyntactically ergative protasis of (36a) and the considerably greater admissibility of such a zero pronoun in (37a), whose protasis has a lexically ergative subject. However, there is no such contrast in grammaticality between (36b) and (37b), both of which have an overt coreferential pronoun in the apodosis.

(36) *Hindi*
    a. *agar raam$_x$ ne kaam nahiiM   kiyaa   to e_x so rahaa hogaa
       if   Ram ERG work not.indeed do-PERF PT   sleeping be-FUT.M.3SG
    b. agar raam$_x$ ne kaam nahiiM   kiyaa   to vah$_x$ so rahaa hogaa
       if   Ram ERG work not.indeed do-PERF PT 3SG sleeping be-FUT.M.3SG
       'If Ram did not do the work, he must be asleep.'

(37) *Hindi*
    a. ?agar kutiyaa$_y$ ne nahiiM   bhauMkaa to e_y so rahii hogii
       if   dog-F   ERG not.indeed bark-PERF PT   sleeping be-FUT.F.3SG
    b. agar kutiyaa$_y$ ne nahiiM   bhauMkaa to vah$_y$ so rahii hogii
       if   dog-F   ERG not.indeed bark-PERF PT 3SG sleeping be-FUT.F.3SG
       'If the (female) dog did not bark, she must be asleep.'

The distinction between unaccusativity and both kinds of ergativity turns out to be an important one to make in light of the facts of Bangla, and in particular in the context of the Bangla conjunctive participial construction.[15]

5.4 Causation and Tense in the Conjunctive Participial and Conditional Constructions

5.4.1 Causation: A Conventional Implicature

The conjunctive participial and conditional constructions in both Bangla and Hindi turn out to have something in common, namely, that a conventional implicature of

Causation and Tense in Subordinate Clauses

(partial or total) causation is often generated by the subordinate clause. In the conjunctive participial construction, the conventional implicature of causation may or may not be there when the subject of the construction is a controlled null subject. This is by and large true of both Hindi and Bangla. The conventional implicature of causation is always generated in the case of the Bangla noncontrolled lexical-subject conjunctive participial construction, however: the occurrence of an overt subject with an unaccusative verb in this particular subtype of the conjunctive participial construction signals a special causal relationship between the event expressed by the conjunctive participial clause and that expressed by the main clause, the former event having a causal role in the occurrence of the latter. This is true, for instance, in the conjunctive participial sentence (38).

(38) *Bangla*
[khaT   bheNe]   Sita poRe+gElo
bedstead break-CONJ Sita fall-CONJ+go-PAST.3
'Sita fell down because the bedstead broke.'/'The bedstead having broken, Sita fell down.'

As for the conditional construction, given that the material-implication operator is one of the key elements in deductive inference as conducted through either symbolism or natural language, a conventional implicature of causation is necessarily conveyed by the conditional construction in natural language, with the protasis understood as playing a (partial or total) causal role in the occurrence of the apodosis. Bangla and Hindi conditionals are no exception in generating such a conventional implicature of causation.[16]

5.4.2 Tense Restrictions and Temporal Sequence

As indicated in section 5.2, the conditional and the conjunctive participial constructions display restrictions on the tense of the subordinate clause, in both Bangla and Hindi. The following patterns are observed in the case of Bangla:

(39) *Bangla*
    a. jodi ram ekhane aSe/*aSche/*aSbe   tObe
       if   Ram here   come-PRES.3/come-PRES.CONT.3/come-FUT.3 then
       SObkichu Thik   thake/thakbe
       everything all.right stay-PRES.3/stay-FUT.3
       'If Ram comes here, everything remains/will remain all right.'
    b. jodi ram ekhane aSto/*elo/*eSechilo/
       if   Ram here   come-PAST.HAB.3/come-PAST.3/come-PAST.PERF.3/
       ??aSchilo   tObe SObkichu Thik   thakto[17]
         come-PAST.CONT.3 then everything all.right stay-PAST.HAB.3

'If Ram came here, everything would remain all right.'/'If Ram had come here, everything would have been all right.'

Special cases involve the occurrence of the simple past and the future in the protasis of a conditional, but in those instances there is usually a special "emphasizer" particle occurring in the protasis, and the apodosis is a question, not a truth-evaluable declarative clause.

(40) *Bangla*
    a. ram jodi ekhane *elo+i*[18]   tObe ar   or   baRite
       Ram if   here   come-PAST.3+EMP then any.more 3SG.GEN house-LOC
       jaWa   kEno?
       go-VERBAL.NOUN why
       'If Ram *does* indeed come here, why go to his house?'
    b. ram jodi ekhane *aSbe+i*   tObe ar   oke
       Ram if   here   come-FUT.3+EMP then any.more 3SG.ACC
       ERano   kEno?
       avoid-VERBAL.NOUN why
       'If Ram *will* be coming here after all, why avoid him?'

There are similar tense restrictions in Hindi in truth-evaluable conditional sentences. The verb of the protasis occurs in the simple subjunctive form when the tense of the apodosis is present (with or without an aspectual category) or future; and it occurs in a special past conditional form, morphologically identical to the simple participial form in *-t-* (followed by a gender/number ending), with the verb of the apodosis also occurring in the special past conditional form, when the conditional sentence is to be interpreted as a past conditional or a counterfactual conditional sentence.

(41) *Hindi*
    a. agar raam yahaaM aaye/??aataa   hai   to
       if   Ram here   come-SUBJUNCT-3SG/come-PRES-M.SG be-PRES.3SG PT
       sab-kuch Thiik rahtaa   hai/rahegaa
       everything all.right stay-PRES.M.SG be-PRES.3SG/stay-FUT.M.3SG
       'If Ram comes here, everything remains/will remain all right.'
    b. agar raam yahaaM aataa/??aayaa   (thaa)   to
       if   Ram here   come-PAST.COND.3SG/come-PERF.M.SG be-PAST.M.SG PT
       sab-kuch Thiik rahtaa/??rahaa   (*thaa)
       everything all.right stay-PAST.COND/stay-PERF.M.SG   be-PAST.M.SG
       'If Ram came here, everything would remain all right.'/'If Ram had come here, everything would have remained all right.'

Causation and Tense in Subordinate Clauses

In Hindi, for conditionals that have the form of questions instead of truth-evaluable declaratives, with special emphasis marked by extra stress on a constituent of the protasis, typically a negative marker, the restrictions on the tense of the protasis are likewise relaxed somewhat.

(42) *Hindi*
    a. agar raam yahaaM *na* aayaa to corii kis-ne kii?
       if Ram here NEG come-PERF.M.SG PT theft-F who-ERG do-PERF.F.3SG
       'If Ram *didn't* come here, who committed the theft?'
    b. agar raam yahaaM *nahiiM* aayegaa to hame kyuuM bulaa
       if Ram here not.indeed come-FUT.M.3SG PT we-ACC why call
       rahe ho?
       CONT.2 be-PRES.2
       'If Ram *won't* be coming after all, why are you summoning us?'

Obviously, there is an asymmetric relationship of one-way dependence between the tense of the protasis and not just the tense but also the semantic/pragmatic status of the apodosis of the conditional in both Bangla and Hindi. It seems as though there is a "coindexing" of the tense of the protasis with that of the apodosis. This is much more obviously the case in the conjunctive participial construction in the two languages, the time of occurrence of the event expressed by the conjunctive participial clause always being construed as prior to the time of occurrence of the event expressed by the matrix clause. In both the conditional construction and the conjunctive participial construction, therefore, the tense of the subordinate clause is dependent on the tense of the matrix clause (the apodosis in the conditional construction). In McCawley's (1981/1993, 430–49) formalization of tense logic, he presents the tense operators T_p and T_f, which capture the simultaneity of some event or state of affairs with some other specified event or state of affairs at some past time and at some future time, respectively, as in the following examples:

(43) a. $T_p(B)$ = 'at the past time at which B', e.g.
      $T_p(j$ meet $d)$ (j be a student)
      = 'When John met Dora, he was a student.'
    b. $T_f(B)$ = 'at the future time at which B', e.g.
      $T_f(r$ arrive) (r will call you)
      = 'When Roger arrives, he will call you.'
    (McCawley 1981/1993, 440)

However, neither of these operators can satisfactorily capture the semantic interpretation of either the conditional construction or the conjunctive participial construction. Instead, McCawley's logical representation (12.2.19a) for his sentence (12.2.16a), repeated here as (44b) and (44a), respectively, with the addition of a missing logical conjunction, looks more promising.[19]

(44) a. When John married Amy, he had met Cynthia five years earlier.
   b. (ι: R_t (j marry a))$_t$ (ι: ∧ ($t' = t - 5$ years, $R_{t'}$))$_{t'}$ (j meet c)

Using the basic insight captured in this representation, the conditional construction and the conjunctive participial construction can both be represented logically as follows:

(45) (ι: $R_{t'}$ (rain come in through window)$^{t'}$)$_{t'}$ (ι: ∧ ($Pt't, R_t$))$_t$ (room get wet)^t
   where a superscript time variable t indicates that it is the time of occurrence of the event so superscripted, and a subscript time variable t indicates restricted quantification over t within the domain of reference times R_t.

There is, however, an additional need to give some sort of formal shape to the interaction between the temporal semantics and the causative-implicative pragmatics of conditional and conjunctive participial constructions in Bangla and Hindi, perhaps through a hybrid formalism. For this, one might draw upon McCawley's characterization of tense in terms of time-variable arguments (McCawley 1981/1993, 431) and the logicosemantic formalism employed by Sadock (1991) for the relationship between propositions and predicate-argument combinatorics. Schematically, one might capture the asymmetric dependence between the tenses of the two clauses of the conditional roughly as follows:

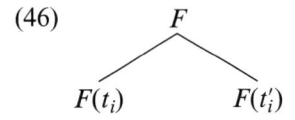

(46)
```
            F
           / \
       F(t_i)  F(t'_i)
```

where F stands for a propositional formula with or without a time argument specified for it, and $Pt_i t'_i$ (i.e., t_i temporally precedes t'_i).

Extending this idea further, the schematic representation of the temporal dependence relation between the two clauses in the conjunctive participial construction in Bangla and Hindi might, in the general case, be represented as in (47a), and the special-case unaccusative-verb conjunctive participial construction might be represented as in (47b).

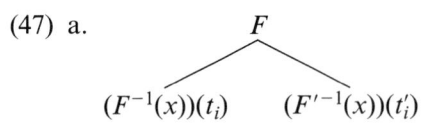

(47) a.
```
                F
               / \
     (F^{-1}(x))(t_i)  (F'^{-1}(x))(t'_i)
```

where F is a (composite) proposition; F^{-1} and F'^{-1} are one-place predicates, each missing an entity argument (the entity variable x is the missing argument); t_i is the time of occurrence of the conjunctive participial event; t'_i is the time of occurrence of the matrix event; and $Pt_i t'_i$ (i.e., t_i temporally precedes t'_i).

b.

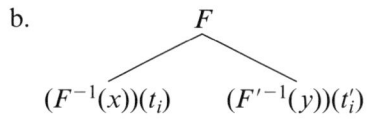

$$F$$
$$(F^{-1}(x))(t_i) \quad (F'^{-1}(y))(t'_i)$$

where x and y are entity variables, and $x \neq y$; F is a proposition; that $F^{-1}(x)$ causes $F'^{-1}(y)$ is conventionally implicated; t_i is the time of occurrence of the conjunctive participial event; t'_i is the time of occurrence of the matrix event; and $Pt_i t'_i$.

A caveat is in order here, however: the schemata (46) and (47a–b) are not meant to be representations that are licit within tense logic alone. Instead, they combine formulas licensed by tense logic—especially as formulated by McCawley (1981/1993, 430–49)—with structural and pragmatic information encoded in the conditional construction and the two different cases of the conjunctive participial construction.

A significant linguistic fact from the viewpoint of possible-world semantics as applied specifically to tense relations in conditionals seems to be that neither Bangla nor Hindi makes a formal distinction between past conditionals and counterfactual conditionals: the two kinds of conditionals thus constitute a single class of nonfuture "intensional" conditionals, that is, conditionals that are not evaluable extensionally in the present time against actual-world parameters. This, of course, raises the possibility of important implications for drawing conceptual distinctions among nonpast real conditionals (in the sense of Lycan 2001) and past and/or counterfactual conditionals in inferential discourse conducted in Bangla and Hindi, a matter that must await further detailed investigation.

5.5 Conclusion

This chapter has provided a necessarily sketchy overview of how the lexical and morphosyntactic phenomena of unaccusativity and ergativity interact with the largely semantic and pragmatic parameters of causation and tense in the grammar and interpretation of two salient subordinate-clause construction types in the Indic languages Bangla and Hindi, namely, the conditional construction and the conjunctive participial construction. While the effect of unaccusativity and ergativity on the grammar of conditionals in these two languages has been found to be relatively small, the effect of unaccusativity on the interpretation and pragmatics of the conjunctive participial construction in Bangla appears to be significant.

The aim of this chapter has also been to pay homage to the range of linguistic interests that Jim McCawley pursued, both in terms of the kinds of linguistic phenomena that he subjected to his astute scrutiny and in terms of the variety of language groups on which he focused his exceptional analytical abilities as a linguist and as a logician. The Indic languages of South Asia, and in particular the intricacies of the relationship between syntactic phenomena and interpretive phenomena in these languages, continued to attract his attention over the span of at least three decades. Evidence of this is to be found in his seminar lectures at the University of Chicago, in occasional conference papers, in his interactions with linguists (some of them former students of his) working on these languages, and in his detailed oral and written comments on their work. Jim set high standards indeed for linguists working on these and other languages to live up to.

Notes

1. For typographical convenience, the following special symbols are used to transcribe Bangla and Hindi phonemes:

a	central unrounded vowel (in Hindi)
VV	phonemically distinct long vowel (in Hindi)
E O	lower mid vowels (in Bangla)
Y W	mid semivowels
T D R	retroflex consonants (voiceless and voiced stops, voiced flap)
S	voiceless palatoalveolar fricative
N	velar nasal
M	nasalization of preceding vowel symbol

2. While the historical phonology and morphology of particles such as the conditional particles in Bangla have received detailed attention in Chatterji 1926/1970, to the extent that I have been able to verify there has been no systematic treatment of the conditional construction in Bangla in terms of either descriptive or generative syntax. Elsewhere (Bagchi 1991), I have examined certain aspects of the pragmatics of Bangla conditionals in interaction with the emphasizer clitics -*i* 'only, alone' and -*o* 'also, even'.

3. The expressive quality of this sentence is fairly close to that of "pseudocoordinate" conditional sentences in English as described by for instance McCawley (1988/1998, 708, 711), exemplified by his sentences (i) and (ii).

(i) Open the door and I'll give you a dollar.

(ii) Be careful or you'll have a lot of trouble.

McCawley (1988/1998, 738–39) presents a formal analysis of such sentences that develops further a suggestion by Dwight Bolinger that such sentences are formed through a "blend" of the protasis of a conditional and an imperative structure for the first conjunct of the pseudocoordinate conditional. Since neither a Bangla nor a Hindi conditional sentence marked solely by the particle *to* has an imperative clause as its "first conjunct" or protasis, McCawley's analysis as it stands is unlikely to be applicable to such a Bangla or Hindi conditional—with the important modification that the protasis not be underlyingly an imperative but instead a declarative (or, perhaps in the Hindi case, subjunctive) clause. However, in keeping with the spirit of McCawley's proposal, an analysis in terms of a corresponding "blend" of a conditional structure and a coordinate structure might not be altogether ruled out for this particular kind of conditional in Bangla or Hindi.

4. The conditional construction in Hindi has received surprisingly scant attention in standard reference grammars and handbooks of Hindi such as Guru 1920/1962, Fairbanks and Misra

Causation and Tense in Subordinate Clauses 131

1966, and McGregor 1972, 1997. The only standard reference on Hindi syntax that provides any kind of systematic description of the Hindi conditional construction is Kachru 1980, which nonetheless does not focus on tense patterns in this construction.

5. An anonymous reviewer cites McGregor 1997 as a source of general information about Hindi tenses. As mentioned in note 4, however, the constraints on tenses in the protasis and the apodosis of Hindi conditionals are not described in significant detail.

6. The conjunctive participle *bhore* 'having filled' is part of the compound verb *bhore dile* 'fill-PAST.2' (benefactive) and is thus not the head of an independent clause. The difference between the compound verb construction and the conjunctive participial construction in Bangla is accounted for in terms of Autolexical Syntax in Bagchi 1993.

7. The phenomenon of aspectually split ergativity in Hindi has received considerable attention in the literature on the generative syntax of Hindi; for a Principles-and-Parameters account of this phenomenon see, for example, Mahajan 1990.

8. According to Levin and Rappaport Hovav (1995), the notion of unaccusativity was proposed by Perlmutter (1978), although the subclass of intransitive verbs that cannot take an external argument and yet cannot assign accusative case to their only internal argument was anticipated by Barbara Hall (later Partee) in her 1965 doctoral dissertation.

9. I propose these two additional tests in Bagchi 1997 in more rudimentary form.

10. The relative unacceptability of these two examples probably arises from additional semantic/pragmatic considerations (Horn 1989) besides the occurrence of unaccusative verbs in both the finite clause and the conjunctive participial clause. While this makes the test of resistance to placement of negation correspondingly a weaker test for unaccusativity, I retain it nonetheless because its results for Bangla do partially support the presence of unaccusativity in this language, and certainly do not contradict it.

11. For some speakers, this sentence is marginally acceptable in a highly contrived discourse context, with the meaning 'The room did not become wet for some reason other than the rain entering through the window'—the implicature being that the room became wet precisely because of the rain entering through the window. As one can see, however, the context seems to force a certain kind of acceptability on the sentence; it is not a readily acceptable sentence for the average speaker of standard colloquial Bangla.

12. Chomsky (1995, 352), for instance, proposes that unaccusative verbs lack the *v*-shell that dominates VP in the case of transitive and unergative verbs; and he later (2000, 106–7) argues that an unaccusative verbal phrase cannot be a derivational phase. In no case, however, is morphosyntactic ergativity recognized as being a significant phenomenon. While Mahajan (1990) presents a Principles-and-Parameters account of the syntax of ergativity in Hindi, he does not draw the distinction between lexical and morphosyntactic ergativity sharply in this work.

13. A reviewer suggests Manning 1996 as a reference on syntactic ergativity. However, Manning focuses on languages such as Tagalog and Inuit whose ergative behavior is markedly different from that of Hindi, which manifests aspectually split ergativity as a morphosyntactic phenomenon and in which lexical ergativity is also subject to the same aspectual constraint.

14. The verb *rah-* means 'stay, live, remain' in its capacity as a main (lexical) verb. When it immediately follows a (bare) main-verb root such as *khaa* 'eat', however, *rah-* functions as the auxiliary denoting the continuous aspect. The form *rahaa* in sentence (31a) (and the

corresponding sentence (32a)) is therefore to be interpreted not as the perfect participle of the main verb *rah-* but as the continuous auxiliary.

15. A reviewer points out a restricted but nonetheless common use of the Hindi conjunctive participle in time statements in terms of hours and minutes, as in the following phrase:

(i) *Hindi*
    tiin *baj-kar*   biis   minaT
    three strike-CONJ.PART twenty minute
    'twenty minutes past three'

Here, of course, the usual constraint that holds of conjunctive participles in Hindi, namely, that the participle's subject be coreferential with the matrix subject, is violated. On the other hand, it is not even clear in phrases such as (i) that there *is* a matrix clause, much less a matrix subject. This phrasal pattern therefore seems to be something of an archaism in Hindi. However, the very fact that it is found in Hindi at all is significant: as the reviewer points out, it raises the possibility that Hindi is more similar to Bangla than it appears to be at first glance in regard to the conjunctive participle.

16. A reviewer asks for proof of defeasibility of this claimed implicature. However, defeasibility is a property of conversational rather than conventional implicature as originally defined by Grice. As McCawley (1981/1993, 318) points out, "[c]onversational implicatures can be **canceled** but conventional implicatures cannot" (boldface in original). It turns out that the implicature of causation in Bangla cannot be canceled; an attempt to do so results in something of a contradiction, which persists even if either of the two emphasizer clitics *-o* 'also, even' and *-i* 'only, alone' is added to the conjunctive participle *eSe* 'having-come'.

(i) *Bangla*
    !janla   die briSTi eSe   ghOr bhijeche,   kintu/eboN janla   die briSTi
    window via rain come-CONJ room be.wet-PRES.PERF.3 but/and   window via rain
    na eSe   (-o/-i)   ghOr bhijeche
    not come-CONJ (-also/-only) room be.wet-PRES.PERF.3
    'The room got wet because of the rain having come in through the window, but/and the room got wet even without the rain having come in through the window.'

That one cannot treat this conventional implicature of causation as being part of the regular meaning of the conjunctive participle is evident in the fact that, with a subject that is coreferential with the matrix subject, the conjunctive participle does not carry this obligatory sense of causation but merely one of temporal sequence.

17. The "habitual" past tense in Bangla, marked by the verbal suffix *-t-* followed by the person/honorificity verbal ending, is also used as the conditional past tense or the counterfactual "tense" in conditional sentences.

18. Two reviewers ask why the Bangla past tense verb-form (followed by emphasizer clitic) *elo(+i)* is not reflected in the English translation for sentence (40a). There seems to be a quasi-idiomatic use of the simple past tense in Bangla to affirm a present event, action, or state as being a fait accompli (as opposed to a purely hypothetical event/action/state, an event/action in progress, or a habitual event/action). Here, the occurrence of the emphasizer *-i* signals that Ram's coming here is such a fait accompli in the speech situation in addition to being the protasis of the conditional question.

19. McCawley (1981/1993, sec. 12.2) presents at least three different formal representational conventions for the logic of tense in English. Here, I attempt to follow just one of them, namely, the one he developed the most directly from the Reichenbachian representation of tense/aspect combinations and in particular Reichenbach's notion of reference time (R).

References

Bagchi, Tista. 1991. Conditionals and emphasizers in Bangla: Some pragmatic effects of their interaction. Paper presented at the Thirteenth South Asian Languages Analysis Roundtable Meeting (SALA XIII), University of Illinois at Urbana-Champaign, 29–31 May 1991. Summary in *Studies in the Linguistic Sciences* 20.3, 19–21.

Bagchi, Tista. 1993. Clausal subordination in Bangla: A cross-modular approach. Doctoral dissertation, University of Chicago.

Bagchi, Tista. 1997. On the (empty) subject of the conjunctive participle: Unaccusatives in the conjunctive participial construction in Bangla. Paper presented at the International Seminar on Null Elements, University of Delhi, 10–12 January 1997. To appear in a special number of the *South Asian Language Review*, ed. by Omkar N. Koul and K. V. Subbarao.

Belletti, Adriana. 1988. The Case of unaccusatives. *Linguistic Inquiry* 19, 1–34.

Bhattacharya, Tanmoy. Forthcoming. The Bangla subjunctive. In *The syntax and semantics of mood and tense*, ed. by Alexandra Giorgi, James Higginbotham, and Fabio Pianesi. Cambridge: Cambridge University Press.

Chatterji, Suniti Kumar. 1926/1970. *The origin and development of the Bengali language*. London: Allen & Unwin.

Chomsky, Noam. 1995. *The Minimalist Program*. Cambridge, MA: MIT Press.

Chomsky, Noam. 2000. Minimalist inquiries: The framework. In *Step by step: Essays in minimalist syntax in honor of Howard Lasnik*, ed. by Roger Martin, David Michaels, and Juan Uriagereka, 89–155. Cambridge, MA: MIT Press.

Dasgupta, Probal. 1988. Bangla quantifier extraction, unaccusative *in situ*, and the ECP. *Linguistic Inquiry* 19, 691–97.

Davies, William D., and Carol Rosen. 1988. Unions as multi-predicate clauses. *Language* 64, 52–88.

Davison, Alice. 1981. Syntactic and semantic indeterminacy resolved: A mostly pragmatic analysis of the Hindi conjunctive participle in *-kar*. In *Radical pragmatics*, ed. by Peter Cole, 101–28. New York: Academic Press.

Fairbanks, Gordon H., and Bal Govind Misra. 1966. *Spoken and written Hindi*. Ithaca, NY: Cornell University Press.

Guru, Kamta Prasad. 1920/1962. *Hindii vyaakaraṇ* [Hindi grammar]. Varaṇasi: Kashi Nagari Pracharini Sabha.

Hale, Kenneth, and Samuel Jay Keyser. 1993. On argument structure and the lexical expression of syntactic relations. In *The view from Building 20: Essays in linguistics in honor of Sylvain Bromberger*, ed. by Kenneth Hale and Samuel Jay Keyser, 53–109. Cambridge, MA: MIT Press.

Hall, Barbara. 1965. Subject and object in modern English. Doctoral dissertation, MIT.

Hendrick, Randall. 1995. Morphosyntax. In *Government and Binding Theory and the Minimalist Program*, ed. by Gert Webelhuth, 299–347. Oxford: Blackwell.

Horn, Laurence R. 1989. *A natural history of negation*. Chicago: University of Chicago Press.

Kachru, Yamuna. 1980. *Aspects of Hindi grammar*. New Delhi: Manohar.

Klaiman, Miriam H. 1980. Volitionality and subject in Bengali. Doctoral dissertation, University of Chicago. Distr., Bloomington: Indiana University Linguistics Club.

Levin, Beth, and Malka Rappaport Hovav. 1995. *Unaccusativity: At the syntax–lexical semantics interface*. Cambridge, MA: MIT Press.

Lycan, William G. 2001. *Real conditionals*. New York: Oxford University Press.

Mahajan, Anoop K. 1990. The A/A-bar distinction and movement theory. Doctoral dissertation, MIT.

Manning, Christopher D. 1996. *Ergativity: Argument structure and grammatical relations*. Stanford, CA: CSLI Publications. Doctoral dissertation, Stanford University, 1995.

McCawley, James D. 1981. *Everything that linguists have always wanted to know about logic—*but were ashamed to ask*. Chicago: University of Chicago Press. 2nd ed., 1993. References are to the 1993 edition.

McCawley, James D. 1988. *The syntactic phenomena of English*. Chicago: University of Chicago Press. 2nd. ed., 1998. References are to the 1988 edition.

McGregor, R. S. 1972. *Outline of Hindi grammar*. Delhi: Oxford University Press.

McGregor, R. S. 1997. *Outline of Hindi grammar*. 3rd ed. New York: Oxford University Press.

Perlmutter, David. 1978. Impersonal passives and the Unaccusative Hypothesis. In *Proceedings of the Fourth Annual Meeting of the Berkeley Linguistics Society*, ed. by Jeri J. Jaeger and Anthony C. Woodbury, 157–89. Berkeley: University of California, Berkeley Linguistics Society.

Sadock, Jerrold M. 1991. *Autolexical Syntax: A theory of parallel grammatical representations*. Chicago: University of Chicago Press.

Chapter 6

Independence in Subordinate Clauses: Analysis of Nonrestrictive Relative Clauses in English and Japanese

Etsuyo Yuasa

I give top billing to the phenomena and second billing to the theory, not because of any disdain for theory (much the contrary!) but because I think the greatest value of any theory is in the extent to which it makes phenomena accessible to an investigator: the extent to which it helps him to notice things that he would otherwise have overlooked, raises questions which otherwise would not have occurred to him, and suggests previously unfamiliar places in which to look for answers to those questions.

Jim McCawley, *The Syntactic Phenomena of English*

6.1 Introduction

Jim McCawley was a linguist who dealt with a tremendous amount of linguistic data bravely, honestly, and brilliantly. His theory was rationally constructed with the fewest assumptions, and he acknowledged that meanings of sentences play an important role in syntax. Among the syntactic phenomena that he investigated, he extensively examined nonrestrictive relative clauses (RCs) in English (McCawley 1988/1998). He concluded that although they appear to be subordinate to the head noun, nonrestrictive RCs and their antecedents actually form discontinuous constituent structures. That is to say, a nonrestrictive RC is in fact independent of the head noun or the main clause, and it is merely moved into a position next to a target without being combined with the target into a larger constituent.

In this chapter, I would like to address three issues. First, I show that the independence of English nonrestrictive RCs is further supported by five additional factors: scope, the interpretation of the gap in a nonrestrictive RC as an E-type pronoun, the distribution of certain adverbs, root transformations, and antecedent-contained deletion.

This chapter has benefited from comments and criticisms from anonymous reviewers; from Elaine Francis, Salikoko Mufwene, Barbara Luka, and Yoshio Ueno; and from audiences at the Third International Conference on Practical Linguistics of Japanese, San Francisco, 2002, and the annual meeting of the Linguistic Society of America, Washington, DC, 2001.

Second, I argue that Japanese nonrestrictive RCs should also be analyzed as independent of the main clause. The data include not only the above-mentioned phenomena but also tense interpretation and the occurrence of certain auxiliary verbs and polite forms unique to Japanese.

Finally, to explain why the properties of an independent clause occur in these seemingly subordinate constructions, I propose that a nonrestrictive RC should be considered an instance of mismatch in syntax and semantics. Elsewhere, Jerrold Sadock and I have examined unusual coordinate structures in various languages and proposed that the notions of subordination and coordination can be applied to syntax and semantics independently (Yuasa 1997, 1998; Yuasa and Sadock 2002). I extend this analysis and claim that the notion of independence can also be applied to syntax and semantics independently, and that the autonomy of different levels of grammar allows the association of incongruous syntactic and semantic representations (independence-subordination mismatch in syntax and semantics).

This chapter is organized as follows. In section 6.2, I review McCawley's analysis of English nonrestrictive RCs and provide additional evidence to support it. In section 6.3, I discuss Japanese nonrestrictive RCs and point out that McCawley's analysis is also applicable to Japanese. In section 6.4, I provide a multimodular analysis of these constructions; and in section 6.5, I offer closing arguments.

6.2 Nonrestrictive Relative Clauses in English

6.2.1 McCawley 1988/1998

From his extensive investigation of English nonrestrictive RCs, McCawley (1998, 446) concluded that a nonrestrictive RC is an independent S in the deep structure, associated with a certain speech act type and containing an item that is coreferential with some item in another S;[1] and that after the coreferential item is turned into a relative pronoun and moved to the S-initial position, the entire nonrestrictive relative clause is juxtaposed to the coreferential item in the main S without forming a constituent. Example structures and derivations are given in (1).

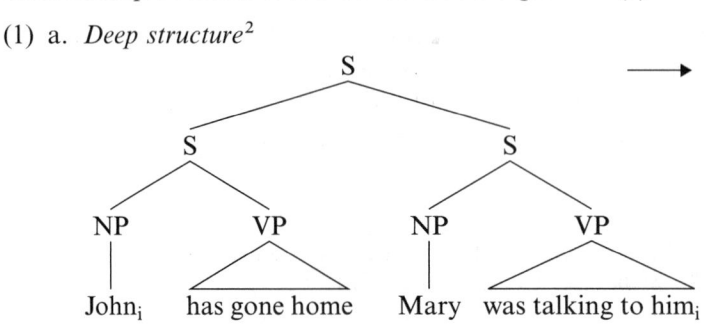

(1) a. *Deep structure*[2]

```
              S
           /     \
          S       S
         / \     / \
        NP  VP  NP  VP
        |   /\  |   /\
       John_i has gone home  Mary was talking to him_i
```

Independence in Subordinate Clauses

b. *Surface structure*

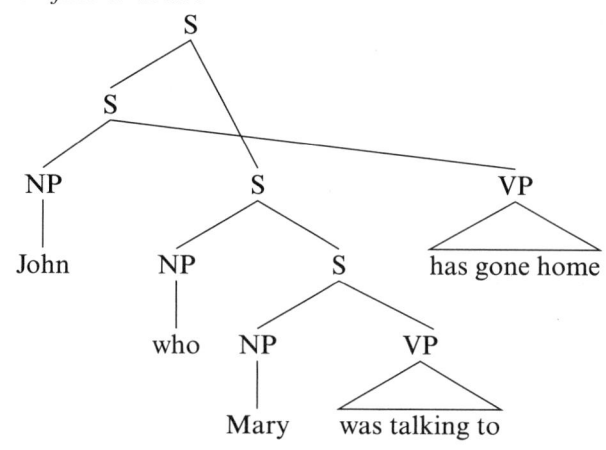

```
                    S
                   / \
                  S   \
                 /|    \
               NP S    VP
               |  |\    |
             John | \   has gone home
                  |  \
                 NP   S
                 |   /|
                who NP VP
                    |   \
                   Mary  was talking to
```

The basic claim of McCawley's analysis of nonrestrictive RCs is that although a nonrestrictive RC occurs next to its antecedent and seems to be subordinate to it just as a restrictive RC would be, the subordinate relation between the antecedent and the nonrestrictive RC is only apparent. His analysis is supported by the following arguments. First, an N′ and a restrictive RC form a unit and can be replaced by *one*, as shown in (2a); but an N′ and a nonrestrictive RC cannot be replaced by *one*, as shown in (2b), and therefore cannot be considered to form a constituent (McCawley 1998, 445).

(2) a. Tom has [a [violin that once belonged to Heifetz]], and Jane has *one* (= a violin that once belonged to Heifetz) too.
   b. Tom has [a [violin]], which once belonged to Heifetz, and Jane has *one* (= a violin) too.

Second, a nonrestrictive RC instantiates a separate speech act from the main clause (McCawley 1998, 448). In (3a), for example, while the main clause expresses a request for information, the nonrestrictive RC expresses a reminder that is independent of the request made in the main clause. The two separate speech acts in (3a) can be separated into two independent sentences, as shown in (3b).

(3) a. Has John, who was talking to Mary a minute ago, gone home?
   b. Has John gone home? He was talking to Mary a minute ago.

Third, even when the antecedent is a direct object, a nonrestrictive RC cannot be deleted in VP-deletion (McCawley 1998, 450). Since normally any item in the VP can be deleted by VP-deletion, (4a–b) show that a nonrestrictive RC is not part of the matrix VP, let alone the antecedent.[3]

(4) a. John sold Mary, who had offered him $600 an ounce, a pound of gold, and Arthur did (= sell Mary a pound of gold) too.
   b. John sold a violin, which had once belonged to Nathan Milstein, to Itzhak Perlman, and Mary did (= sell a violin to Itzhak Perlman) too.

McCawley claims that the gap in a nonrestrictive RC is underlyingly a pronoun. The pronoun in the nonrestrictive RC in (1a) coindexed with its antecedent in the host S is justified by the following arguments. First, an NP introduced by a quantifier such as *each*, *every*, or *no* cannot be the antecedent of a nonrestrictive RC, as shown in (5a) (McCawley 1998, 451). A variable must be bound by an antecedent that is a quantified NP; and a restrictive RC, as in (5b), or a pronoun in a sentential complement, as in (5c), can take a quantified NP as an antecedent. The ungrammaticality in (5a) parallels that in (5d), where the pronoun is located in a separate S.

(5) a. *The doctor gave a lollipop to each child, who she examined.
   b. The doctor gave a lollipop to each child that she examined.
   c. Every child$_i$ thinks he$_i$ should be given a lollipop.
   d. The doctor gave a lollipop to each child$_i$. *She examined him$_i$.

Second, unlike restrictive RCs, nonrestrictive RCs can take proper names, which form an entire NP, as their antecedent.[4] This parallels intersentential pronouns, which can also take a proper name as their antecedent, as shown in (6b) (McCawley 1998, 452).

(6) a. John$_i$ can't be trusted. You were talking to him$_i$ a minute ago.
   b. John, who you were talking to a minute ago, can't be trusted.

6.2.2 Additional Evidence for the Independent Status of Nonrestrictive Relative Clauses

In this section, I adduce five types of evidence to support McCawley's claim that nonrestrictive RCs are like independent clauses. First, nonrestrictive RCs cannot be under the scope of negation or a question in the main clause (Demirdache 1991). Therefore, while the nonrestrictive RC in (7a) cannot be negated like the independent clause in (7a′), the restrictive RC in (7b) can be negated, and the sentence presupposes that I beat a dog that my parents do not love.

(7) a. [I do not beat Fido], which my parents love.
   a′. I do not beat Fido$_i$. My parents love it$_i$.
   b. [I do not beat a dog that my parents love].

Second, there are cases where the antecedent of a nonrestrictive RC appears to be under the scope of a quantified NP, as shown in (8) (Sells 1986; Demirdache 1991).

(8) Each car has (exactly) two doors, which open only from the outside.
(Sells 1986, 435)

According to Sells (1986), the interpretation of the gap in (8) is different from that of restrictive RCs like the one in (9).

(9) Each car has (exactly) two doors that open only from the outside.

While the restrictive RC contributes to the meaning of the nominal *two doors*, the antecedent in the nonrestrictive RC in (8) is identified independently of the nonrestrictive RC. Sells claims that the gap in the nonrestrictive relative in (8) is what Evans (1980) calls an "E-type" pronoun, illustrated in (10).

(10) Each car has (exactly) two doors$_i$. They$_i$ open only from the outside.

The pronoun in (10) is neither referential nor coreferential; nor is it a bound variable. It can take a quantified expression or something under the scope of a quantified expression as its antecedent, but most importantly it does not need to be bound.

Characteristically, an E-type pronoun is said to show the maximality effect (Evans 1980; Sells 1986), in which all of the relevant objects are required to satisfy the predicate of the antecedent clause. Hence, examples (8) and (10) entail that all the doors that each car has open only from the outside, whereas (9) entails that there are other doors that open from the inside. Since an E-type pronoun does not need to be bound, the nonrestrictive RC in (8) shows another similarity to independent clauses like the one in (10) in terms of scope.

Third, Emonds (1979) observes that the speaker-oriented interpretation of adverbs is generally possible only in main clauses. Such an interpretation is also possible in nonrestrictive RCs, but not in restrictive RCs.

(11) a. The boys, who have *frankly* lost their case, should give up.
    b. *The boys who have *frankly* lost their case should give up.
(Emonds 1979, 239)

Fourth, although certain transformations are said to occur in independent clauses, Hooper and Thompson (1973, 489) report that they can also occur in nonrestrictive RCs. For instance, while locative inversion is possible with the nonrestrictive RC in (12a), it is not acceptable with the restrictive RC in (12b).

(12) *Locative inversion*[5]
    a. The rotunda, in which stands a statue of Washington, will be repainted.
    b. *The rotunda in which stands a statue of Washington will be repainted.

Finally, antecedent-contained deletion (Sag 1976) also supports the claim that nonrestrictive RCs are independent of the main clause. First, consider the antecedent-contained deletion with a restrictive RC in (13).

(13) Dulles suspected everyone who Angleton did.

If we assume that the antecedent of the VP-deletion is *suspected everyone who Angleton did*, then the antecedent contains the deleted VP; hence, an indefinitely regressive interpretation will result (i.e., 'Dulles suspected everyone who Angleton suspected everyone who Angleton suspected everyone...'). May (1985) claims that quantifiers like *everyone* in (13) are raised along with the restrictive RC at LF as shown in (14); hence, the interpretation of (13) is not indefinitely regressive.[6]

(14) [everyone who Angleton did [Dulles suspected e]] (LF representation of (13))

The example in (15a) is an instance of antecedent-contained deletion with a nonrestrictive RC. Unlike in the case of the restrictive RC with a quantifier in (13), however, May's Quantifier Raising is not available for (15a), since the antecedent noun of the nonrestrictive RC is not a quantifier (Hornstein 1994, 1995).

(15) a. Dulles suspected Angleton, who incidentally, Philby did as well.
    b. Dulles suspected Angleton, and Philby did as well.

However, if we assume that nonrestrictive RCs are independent of the host VP, as McCawley claims, the matrix VP no longer contains the deleted VP in the nonrestrictive RC in (15a). Hence, the example in (15a) will also avoid an indefinitely regressive interpretation, as the independent clause in (15b) does.[7]

In this section, I presented five more arguments that support the independent status of nonrestrictive RCs in English. In the next section, I turn to Japanese nonrestrictive RCs and show that many of the above arguments for English are also applicable to Japanese.[8] I also discuss tense interpretation and polite forms in Japanese RCs and claim that they also point to the independent status of nonrestrictive RCs.

6.3 Nonrestrictive Relative Clauses in Japanese

Examples of Japanese relative clauses are shown in (16).

(16) a. [ano daigaku-ga   yon-da]   gengogakusha (restrictive)
       that university-NOM invite-PAST linguist
       'the linguist that that university invited'
    b. [ano daigaku-ga   yon-da]   Suzuki-sensei (nonrestrictive)
       that university-NOM invite-PAST Prof. Suzuki
       'Prof. Suzuki, who that university invited'

In Japanese, RCs precede their heads, and they do not have relative pronouns. Furthermore, the distinction between restrictive and nonrestrictive RCs is ostensibly inconspicuous, and it is sometimes even said that Japanese does not have such a distinction (Kuno 1973; Collier-Sanuki 1999).[9] However, close examination reveals that Japanese nonrestrictive RCs are very different from restrictive RCs, and they

Independence in Subordinate Clauses 141

have various main-clause properties. Specifically, Japanese nonrestrictive RCs also behave like main clauses in terms of *no*-pronominalization, speech acts, VP-deletion, scope, E-type pronouns, and the distribution of adverbs. Furthermore, I argue that tense interpretation, modal adverbs, and polite forms also suggest the independent status of Japanese nonrestrictive RCs.

First, consider the following examples with the "nominal" *no*, which is translated as 'one' in English. In Japanese, the nominal *no* cannot be used unless an N′ modifier is present, as shown in (17c) (Kamio 1983).

(17) a. [Yasui sutereo]-ga are-ba ka-oo.
cheap stereo-NOM have-if buy-shall
'If they have a cheap stereo, let's buy it.'
b. [Yasui *no*]-ga are-ba ka-oo.
cheap one-NOM have-if buy-shall
'If they have a cheap one, let's buy it.'
c. *[*No*]-ga are-ba ka-oo.
one-NOM have-if buy-shall
(Kamio 1983, 81–82)

Example (18a) is ambiguous, and it can be interpreted either as a restrictive RC or as a nonrestrictive RC. However, if the nominal *no* is used, as in (18b), only the restrictive reading is possible. Recall that *no* cannot appear on its own without an N′ modifier. Kamio concludes that a nonrestrictive RC is not an N′ modifier; hence, it is not possible to interpret (18b) as a nonrestrictive RC.

(18) a. [asa-kara ban-made yoku hatara-ku] nihonjin
morning-from evening-to hard work-PRES Japanese
'Japanese who work hard from the morning to the evening' (restrictive)
'Japanese, who work hard from the morning to the evening' (nonrestrictive)
b. [asa-kara ban-made yoku hatara-ku] *no*
morning-from evening-to hard work-PRES one
'ones who work hard from the morning to the evening' (restrictive)
'*ones, who work hard from the morning to the evening' (nonrestrictive)
(Kamio 1983, 103–4)

Second, just like English nonrestrictive RCs, Japanese nonrestrictive RCs are independent of the speech act of the main clause. In (19), the nonrestrictive relative clause expresses a reminder, and the reminder is independent of the request for information expressed in the main clause.

(19) [Sakki-made koko-ni i-ta Sasaki-buchoo]-ni watashi-ta-no?
a.short.time.ago-until here-at be-PAST Sasaki-manager-to give-PAST-NOMZ
'Did (you) give (it) to Mr. Sasaki, who was here until a short time ago?'

Third, Japanese nonrestrictive RCs cannot be understood as part of VP-deletion either, even when the antecedent is the direct object of the main clause.[10] This suggests that Japanese nonrestrictive RCs are not part of VPs, let alone of NPs.

(20) a. *Restrictive RC*[11]
NBC-wa ototoi [mae-no hi-ni Nihon-kara
NBC-TOP the.day.before.yesterday previous-GEN day-on Japan-from
kaetteki-ta hito]-o shuzai shi-ta; NHK-mo kinoo *shi*-ta.
return-PAST person-ACC interview do-PAST NHK-also yesterday do-PAST
'NBC interviewed the day before yesterday the person who had come back from Japan on the previous day. NHK did (= interviewed the person who had come back from Japan on the previous day) yesterday too.'

b. *Nonrestrictive RC*
NBC-wa ototoi [mae-no hi-ni Nihon-kara
NBC-TOP the.day.before.yesterday previous-GEN day-on Japan-from
kaettekita paaruman]-o shuzai shi-ta; NHK-mo kinoo *shi*-ta.
returned Perlman-ACC interview do-PAST NHK-also yesterday do-PAST
'NBC interviewed Perlman, who came back from Japan on the previous day, the day before yesterday. NHK did (= interviewed Perlman) yesterday too.'

Fourth, the scope of the interrogative particle *ka* in the main clause does not extend to nonrestrictive RCs. In Japanese, as long as the interrogative *ka* has scope over it, a *wh*-expression can occur even in a restrictive RC (21a). However, the scope of *ka* does not extend to nonrestrictive RCs; hence, they cannot contain *wh*-expressions (21b) (Miyake 1995, 55–56).

(21) a. *Restrictive RC*
Anata-wa [[*dare*-ga yakushi-ta] Hamuretto]-o yomi-mashi-ta-*ka*?
you-TOP who-NOM translate-PAST Hamlet-ACC read-POL-PAST-Q
'lit., Who$_i$ did you read [the *Hamlet* that t$_i$ translated]?'

b. *Nonrestrictive RC*
*Anata-wa [[*dare*-ga kai-ta] Hamuretto]-o yomi-mashi-ta-*ka*?
you-TOP who-NOM write-PAST Hamlet-ACC read-POL-PAST-Q
'lit., Who$_i$ did you read *Hamlet*, which t$_i$ wrote?'[12]

Miyake also points out that the scope of negation in the main clause does not extend to nonrestrictive RCs. *Rokuna* in (22) is a negative polarity item (NPI henceforth), and it must occur within the scope of negation. The examples in (23) show that the matrix negative can license an NPI in a restrictive RC but not in a nonrestrictive RC.

Independence in Subordinate Clauses 143

(22) *Rokuna* senshu-ga tor-e-*na*-katta/*tor-e-ta.
 decent athlete-NOM recruit-can-NEG-PAST/recruit-can-PAST
 'We could not/*could recruit a decent athlete.'

(23) a. *Restrictive RC*
 Saikin-wa [*roku-na* shiai-o su-ru yatu]-ga i-*na*-i.
 these.days-TOP decent match-ACC do-PRES fellow-NOM be-NEG-PRES
 'There is nobody who can have a decent match.'
 b. *Nonrestrictive RC*
 *[*Rokuna* shiai-o su-ru Taison]-ga i-*na*-i.
 decent match-ACC do-PRES Tyson-NOM be-NEG-PRES
 'Tyson, who can have a decent match, is not here.'

Fifth, when the matrix subject is a quantified NP, the gap in a nonrestrictive relative clause can be interpreted as an E-type pronoun that occurs in independent clauses (Hoshi 1995).[13]

(24) Dono nooka-mo$_i$ [[kuni-ga maitoshi haru-ni *pro*$_i$ katteik-u] ni-too-no
 every farmer state-NOM annually spring-in buy-PRES two-CL-GEN
 ushi]-o kattei-ru.
 cow-ACC have-PRES
 'Every farmer owns two cows, which the state buys in spring every year.'

Because the gap in the nonrestrictive RC is an E-type pronoun, it also exhibits the maximality effect. Hence, sentence (24) unambiguously means that every farmer has two and a maximum of two cows. It cannot mean that every farmer has at least two cows.

Finally, there are many adverbs that can occur in nonrestrictive RCs (25a), but not in restrictive RCs (25b).

(25) a. *Nonrestrictive RC*
 [[Shigoto-de *tabun* Shikago-e it-ta] Tanaka-san]-ga denwa-shite
 on business probably Chicago-to go-PAST Mr. Tanaka-NOM phone-do
 ku-ru-deshoo.
 come-PRES-will
 'Mr. Tanaka, who probably went to Chicago on business, will call us.'
 b. *Restrictive RC*
 *[[Shigoto-de *tabun* Shikago-e it-ta] hito]-ga denwa-shite
 on business probably Chicago-to go-PAST person-NOM phone-do
 ku-ru-deshoo.
 come-PRES-will
 'Someone who probably went to Chicago on business will call us.'

Adverbs like *tabun* 'probably' commonly occur in independent structures such as main clauses (Minami 1974), and they normally do not occur in subordinate clauses such as adverbial clauses, as illustrated in (26).[14]

(26) [[**Tabun*/∅ Tanaka-san-ga kinoo Shikago-e it-ta-node] shinpai
  probably Mr. Tanaka-NOM yesterday Chicago-to go-PAST-because worry
  ir-ana-i-deshoo.
  need-NEG/PRES-might
  '*You do not have to worry, because probably Mr. Tanaka went to Chicago yesterday.'

Besides the nice parallelism between English and Japanese, tense interpretation and occurrence of various auxiliary verbs and polite forms also suggest the independent status of Japanese nonrestrictive RCs.

In Japanese, although there are some slight differences in meaning among different kinds of predicates, the tense of a main clause is generally determined in relation to the time of the utterance (Inoue 1976; Nakau 1976; Teramura 1984; Sunakawa 1986; Nakamura 1994). For example, the nonpast form of the stative predicate in (27a) shows that the state expressed in the clause exists at the time of the utterance, and the past form in (27b) shows that the state existed prior to the time of the utterance (Teramura 1984, 82).

(27) a. Uchi-no mise-wa yasumi des-*u*.
    my-GEN store-TOP closed COP-PRES
    'Our store is closed.'
  b. Uchi-no mise-wa yasumi deshi-*ta*.
    my-GEN store-TOP closed COP-PAST
    'Our store was closed.'

In subordinate clauses, however, the time of the main clause is taken as a reference (Inoue 1976; Nakau 1976; Sunakawa 1986; Ogihara 1989; Nakamura 1994). Hence, the nonpast form in adverbial clauses and complement clauses as in (28) indicates an action or a state that has not been completed at the time of the main clause. If the past form appears in a subordinate clause, it indicates that the event in the subordinate clause has been completed prior to the time when the event in the main clause takes place.

(28) a. *Adverbial clause*
    [Ryokoo-ni de-*ru* toki] juubun-ni suimin-o totte oi-ta.
     trip-to leave-PRES time enough sleep-ACC take have-PAST
    'When I was about to go on a journey, I had a good sleep.'
    (Nakau 1976, 437–38)

b. *Sentential complement*
John-wa [Mary-ga Austin-ni i-*ru*]-to it-ta.
John-TOP Mary-NOM Austin-at be-PRES-COMP say-PAST
'John said Mary was in Austin.'

Comparing the tense interpretation in restrictive and nonrestrictive RCs in Japanese, Miyake (1995, 58–59) points out that the tense in restrictive RCs, as in (29a), takes the time of the main clause as the reference time, while the tense in nonrestrictive RCs, as in (29b), takes the time of the utterance as the reference time.

(29) a. *Restrictive RC*
[Shuuron-o kaite i-*ru* gakusei]-ga sono gakkai-de
 master's.thesis-ACC write be-PRES student-NOM the conference-at
happyoo shi-*ta*.
presentation do-PAST
'The student who was writing a master's thesis (then) presented a paper at the conference.'
b. *Nonrestrictive RC*
[Shuuron-o kaite i-*ru* Iwasaki-san]-ga sono gakkai-de
 master's.thesis-ACC write be-PRES Mr. Iwasaki-NOM the conference-at
happyoo shi-*ta*.
presentation do-PAST
'Mr. Iwasaki, who is writing a master's thesis (now), presented a paper at the conference.'

In (29a), the nonpast form indicates that the event of the student's writing a master's thesis had not been completed when the event of presenting a paper at the conference expressed in the main clause took place. In (29b), on the other hand, the nonpast form in the nonrestrictive RC indicates that Mr. Iwasaki is writing his master's thesis not at the time of presenting a paper at the conference but at the time of the utterance.[15] Therefore, tense interpretation in nonrestrictive RCs also shows their similarity to independent clauses.

Japanese is an agglutinative language, and, as example (30) clearly shows, various auxiliary verbs or polite forms appear as morphemes attached to predicates.

(30) Sensei-wa Suzuki-san-o Shikago-daigaku-ni
Prof.-TOP Ms. Suzuki-ACC Chicago-university-to
ik-ase-ta-katta-yoo-desu-ne?
go-CAUS-want-PAST-seem-POL-SFP
'The professor seems to have wanted to make Ms. Suzuki go to the University of Chicago, doesn't he?'

As Minami (1974) points out, the various auxiliary verbs cannot just appear anywhere, and certain auxiliary verbs can occur only in independent structures. For example, the auxiliary verb *daroo* 'would' cannot appear in subordinate clauses, as shown in (31).[16]

(31) a. Mizu-o   nom-u-*daroo*.
       water-ACC drink-PRES-would
       '(She/He) would drink water.'

   b. [Mizu-o   nom-u/*nom-u-*daroo*   node] ookina koppu-o
       water-ACC drink-PRES/drink-PRES-would because big glass-ACC
       dashi-ta.
       take.out-PAST
       'Because (she/he) drinks/*would drink water, (I) took out a big glass.'

Masuoka (1997) reports that while restrictive RCs do not allow *daroo* (32a), nonrestrictive RCs can (32b).

(32) a. *Restrictive RC*
       ??[[Kondo-no   senkyo-de rakusen su-ru   *daroo*] kooho]-wa
           this.time-GEN election-in lose   do-PRES would candidate-TOP
           koonin-no   taishoo-kara hazus-are-ta.[17]
           endorsement-GEN subject-from remove-PASS-PAST
           'The candidates who would lose in the next election were removed from the endorsement list.'

   b. *Nonrestrictive RC*
       [[Kondo-no   senkyo-de rakusen su-ru   *daroo*] A kooho]-wa
           this.time-GEN election-in lose   do-PRES would A-candidate-TOP
           koonin-no   taishoo-kara hazus-are-ta.
           endorsement-GEN subject-from remove-PASS-PAST
           'The candidate A, who would lose in the next election, was removed from the endorsement list.'

When the predicate of the main clause appears with the polite form that shows deference to the addressee, the polite form can also occur in nonrestrictive RCs but not in restrictive RCs (Ueno 1994, 154–55).[18]

(33) a. *Nonrestrictive RC*
       [[CLS-e it-ta/iki-*mashi*-ta]   Suzuki-san]-ga   moosugu kaette
           CLS-to go-PAST/go-POL-PAST Ms. Suzuki-NOM soon   return
           ki-*mas*-u.
           come-POL-PRES
           'Ms. Suzuki, who went to CLS, will come back soon.'

Independence in Subordinate Clauses

147

b. *Restrictive RC*
[[CLS-e it-ta/??iki-*mashi*-ta] gakusei]-ga moosugu kaette ki-*mas*-u.
CLS-to go-PAST/go-POL-PAST student-NOM soon return come-POL-PRES
'The student who went to CLS will come back soon.'

In this section, I have shown that Japanese nonrestrictive RCs are like English nonrestrictive RCs, and they behave like independent clauses. In addition, I showed that tense interpretation and the occurrence of auxiliary verbs and polite forms whose behaviors are Japanese-specific also suggest that Japanese nonrestrictive RCs behave like main clauses. In the next section, I will analyze these constructions in a multimodular grammatical framework, inspired particularly by Sadock's (1991, 1993) Autolexical Syntax.

6.4 Analysis: Syntax-Semantics Mismatch

6.4.1 Mixed Properties of Nonrestrictive Relative Clauses

As clearly demonstrated above, English nonrestrictive RCs and Japanese nonrestrictive RCs have various main-clause properties. However, they also have some properties commonly found in subordinate clauses. Keenan (1985) points out that the form of nonrestrictive RCs is generally very similar to that of restrictive RCs. Especially, as noted by Haiman and Thompson (1984), RCs in English and Japanese occur in a prototypical subordinate-clause configuration, as shown in (34).

(34) [S_1 ... [S_2 ...] ...]

This is a configuration where S_2 is surrounded by the material of S_1, or S_2 can have grammatical morphology that marks it as a constituent of S_1. Disregarding differences in their branching peculiarities, both restrictive and nonrestrictive RCs in English and Japanese occur in the configuration of (34).

Furthermore, an adjectival noun at the end of a Japanese nonrestrictive RC takes the prenominal form as if the nonrestrictive RC directly modifies the antecedent (Yoshio Ueno, pers. comm., September 2000).[19]

(35) [yoku hatarak-u koto-de yuumei-*na*] Yamamoto-sensei
well work-PRES that-by famous Prof. Yamamoto
'Prof. Yamamoto, who is famous for working hard'

In order to accommodate the mixed properties of nonrestrictive RCs, I will show in the next section that properties and representations of prototypical independent clauses and prototypical subordinate clauses can be decomposed into syntactic and semantic levels. Furthermore, while the representations at different levels of grammar correspond straightforwardly in prototypical subordinate clause and prototypical independent clauses, they need not be congruent all the time, to the extent that different levels of grammar are autonomous and independent (Sadock 1991; Jackendoff 1997). I will conclude that nonrestrictive RCs are syntactically subordinate although they are semantically independent, and that they are instances of an independence-subordination mismatch in syntax and semantics.

6.4.2 Multimodular Analysis of Nonrestrictive Relative Clauses

The multimodular approach to grammar that I employ in this chapter assumes that different levels of grammar such as syntax and semantics are autonomous, and that they simultaneously exist without any derivation (Sadock 1991; Jackendoff 1997). The specific model that I adopt here is Autolexical Syntax (Sadock 1991). According to this approach, the syntax, employing primitives such as N, V, and P, is responsible for the composition of phrases, the order of heads and nonheads, case marking, certain aspects of agreement, and syntactic subcategorization, including the distinction between finite and nonfinite clauses. The semantic component employs semantic primitives such as proposition (PROP), predicate (PRED), argument (ARG), operator (OP), and quantifier (Q). It also specifies logical relations such as function-argument relations, variable-binder relations, and operator-nucleus relations. Although the theory assumes that different representations at different levels are often isomorphic (Sadock 1991; Sadock and Schiller 1993), it claims that the autonomy of these levels permits the association of incongruous representations. Hence, any systematic mismatch among different levels of grammar provides evidence regarding the autonomous levels of architecture in the grammar.[20]

Mismatch cases with mixed properties of different constructions are not unique to nonrestrictive RCs. In Yuasa and Sadock 2002, Jerrold Sadock and I examine idiosyncratic structures like the ones in (36) and argue that they are semantically coordinate, though syntactically subordinate.[21]

(36) a. *Japanese*
Ojiisan-ga yama-de *hatarai-te*, obaasan-ga mise-no ban-o
old.man-NOM mountain-at work-and old.woman-NOM store-GEN sitting-ACC
shi-ta.
do-PAST
'The old man worked at the mountain, and the old woman the store.'
(Teramura 1991, 221)
b. *Yiddish*
der tate mit der mamen
the-NOM father with the-DAT mother-DAT
'father and mother' (lit., 'the father with the mother')

Independence in Subordinate Clauses   149

Table 6.1
Prototypes and mismatches of coordinate and subordinate structures

	Syntax	Semantics
a. Simple coordination	coordinate	coordinate
b. Pseudocoordination	coordinate	subordinate
c. Simple subordination	subordinate	subordinate
d. Pseudosubordination	subordinate	coordinate

Table 6.2
Prototypes and mismatch of independent and subordinate structures

	Syntax	Semantics
a. Simple independent S	independent	independent
b. Simple subordinate S	subordinate	subordinate
c. Pseudosubordinate S	subordinate	independent

    c. *Greenlandic*
       Hansi-∅   ern-ni-lu   makip-put.
       Hans-ABS.SG son-ABS.REFL.SG-and arise-IND.3PL
       'Hans$_i$ and his$_i$ son got up.'

To explain the fact that these constructions have the mixed properties of subordination and coordination, we propose that while the syntactic and semantic representations of prototypical coordination and subordination are isomorphic, as in (a) and (c) of table 6.1, the syntactic and semantic representations can be incongruous, yielding coordination-subordination mismatches, as in (b) and (d) of the table. The examples in (36) are instances of pseudosubordination, corresponding to (d) of table 6.1, while the pseudocoordinate conditional in (37) is an instance of pseudocoordination, corresponding to (b) of the table.

(37) Big Louie sees you with the loot and he puts a contract out on you.
     (Culicover and Jackendoff 1997, 198)

    I propose that the notions of independence and subordination can be separately instantiated in syntax and semantics, just as in the case of coordination-subordination mismatch, and that nonrestrictive RCs are instances of independence-subordination mismatch, as shown in table 6.2.[22] More specifically, a simple independent clause is the highest S in syntax as well as the highest proposition at the semantic level. One type of simple subordinate clause, the simple (restrictive) RC, is syntactically adjacent to the head, which is an N′ in this case, and semantically a

Table 6.3
Syntactic and semantic representations of independence-subordination mismatch

	Syntax	Semantics
a. Simple independent S	highest S	highest proposition
b. Simple subordinate S		
(restrictive) RC$_E$	S, head [(Comp/Rel pro) ___]	M(CN)
(restrictive) RC$_J$	S, ___ head	M(CN)
c. Pseudosubordinate S		
nonrestrictive RC$_E$	S, head [Rel pro ___]	highest proposition
nonrestrictive RC$_J$	S, ___ head	highest proposition

common noun modifier (M(CN)).[23] In the case of simple independent clauses and simple subordinate clauses, the syntactic representations and semantic representations are isomorphic; hence, the association between their syntactic and semantic representations is predictable and straightforward. However, syntax and semantics are autonomous levels of grammar, and representations need not always be congruent. Consequently, the semantic representation of a simple independent clause, the highest proposition, can be paired with the syntactic structure of a simple (restrictive) RC, giving an instance of pseudosubordination, as shown in table 6.3.[24]

The multimodular representations for nonrestrictive RCs are given in (38) and (39).

(38) *English*
   a. John, who Mary was talking to, has gone home.
   b. *Syntax*

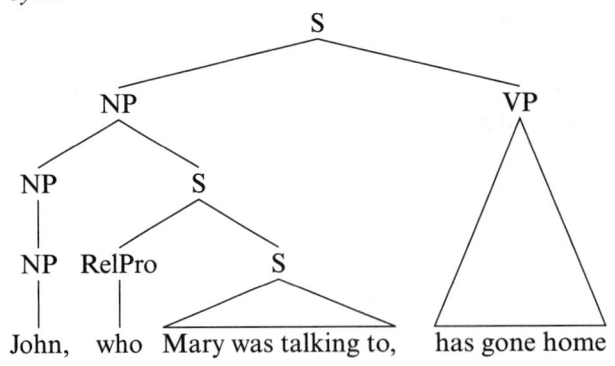

```
                        S
               _____/ _____
              NP                  VP
         ____/  \____              /\
        NP         S              /  \
        |       __/ \__          /    \
        NP   RelPro    S
        |      |      /\
      John,  who  Mary was talking to,  has gone home
```

   c. *Semantics*
     John$_i$ has gone home.   Mary was talking to him$_i$.
          Prop   Prop

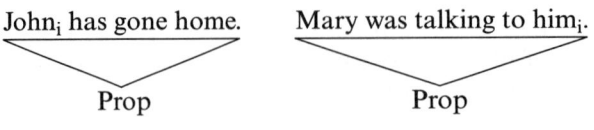

(39) *Japanese*
   a. Kinoo   Amerika-kara ki-ta   Tomu-san-ga ki-ta.
      yesterday America-from come-PAST Tom-NOM   come-PAST
      'Tom, who comes from America, came here yesterday.'
   b. *Syntax*

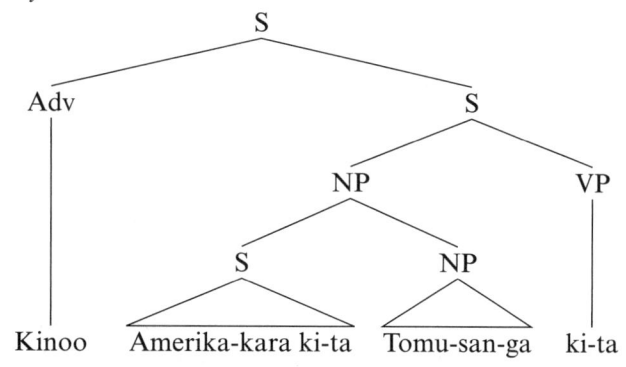

```
                    S
             ┌──────┴──────┐
            Adv            S
             │      ┌──────┴──────┐
             │      NP            VP
             │   ┌──┴──┐          │
             │   S    NP          │
             │   △    △           │
           Kinoo Amerika-kara ki-ta Tomu-san-ga  ki-ta
```

   c. *Semantics*

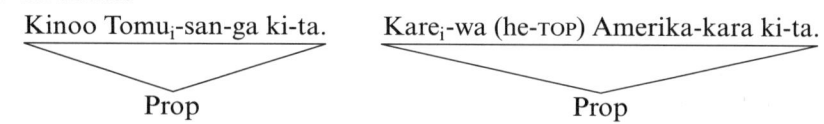

   Kinoo Tomu$_i$-san-ga ki-ta.   Kare$_i$-wa (he-TOP) Amerika-kara ki-ta.
   ⎵⎵⎵⎵⎵⎵⎵⎵⎵⎵⎵⎵⎵⎵⎵⎵⎵⎵⎵⎵   ⎵⎵⎵⎵⎵⎵⎵⎵⎵⎵⎵⎵⎵⎵⎵⎵⎵⎵⎵⎵⎵⎵⎵⎵⎵⎵
              Prop   Prop

In Autolexical Syntax, logical relations such as variable-binder relations and operator-nucleus relations are represented at the level of semantics. Therefore, semantic phenomena such as the scope of negation or quantified expressions discussed with respect to examples (7), (8), (21), (23), and (24) justify the semantic representations in (38) and (39).

Syntactically, nonrestrictive RCs appear next to the head, as shown by the syntactic representation of simple RCs in (b) of table 6.3. A restrictive RC appears adjacent to an N', and they form a constituent. However, the test of coordination that identifies syntactic constituents (McCawley 1988, 422) suggests that the head and a nonrestrictive RC do not form an N' constituent.

(40) a. Those [[linguists who wear sweatshirts] and [philosophers who wear suits and ties]] are having another big argument.
     b. *Those linguists, who wear sweatshirts, and philosophers, who wear suits and ties, are having another big argument.

In restrictive RCs, the head adjacent to an RC is an N', because the N' corresponds to a common noun that the RC modifies in semantics. In nonrestrictive RCs, a semantically independent proposition contains an anaphoric expression, and it refers to an item in another proposition. For example, in *Dr. Smith, who attended this conference, is from America*, the nonrestrictive RC, *he attended this conference*, contains an anaphoric expression, and it refers to *Dr. Smith* in *Dr. Smith is from America*. Therefore, I assume that the syntactic correspondent of the antecedent that an anaphoric expression in a nonrestrictive RC refers to in semantics is taken as the head in syntax, and the nonrestrictive RC appears next to it.

6.5 Discussion

In the multimodular approach to grammar, the syntactic and semantic representations of nonrestrictive RCs are not related by derivations; rather, they are generated concurrently and independently. The analysis proposed here claims that the mixed properties of a subordinate clause and of an independent clause manifested by nonrestrictive RCs are due to the fact that nonrestrictive RCs are just like restrictive RCs in syntax, while they are independent clauses in semantics. Such mixed representations of a subordinate structure and an independent structure can be nicely explained if we assume, as in the coordinate structures in (36) and (37), that the properties of prototypical constructions can be dissociated into syntax and semantics, and that representations can sometimes be associated even though they remain incongruous across different levels of grammar.

Before concluding this chapter, I would like to speculate on why grammar allows incongruity between representations such as independence-subordination mismatch, as in (38) and (39), or coordination-subordination mismatch, as in (36) and (37). In the view proposed here, the syntactic and semantic information about coordinate, subordinate, and independent clauses exists separately in different levels of grammar. Hence, while different representations are isomorphic in simple or prototypical cases, incongruous representations can be associated, and mismatches can arise. However, while one cannot predict which specific representations will associate isomorphically or incongruously across levels of grammar, the representations of these mismatch cases are not idiosyncratic within a given level. For example, while nonrestrictive RCs are like restrictive RCs in syntax, they are like independent clauses in semantics. That is to say, each representation of a nonrestrictive RC is based on the representations of restrictive RCs and independent clauses, and the repertoire of representations in grammar need not be expanded in order to accommodate nonrestrictive RCs.

The goal of reserving cognitive efficiency within each level of representation can explain why mismatches between levels are allowed. Lakoff's (1987) definition of *motivation* applies in these cases. Lakoff defines a structure as *motivated* when it inherits the information of another structure. Lakoff subsequently proposes that language tends to maximize motivation because it increases cognitive efficiency. Goldberg (1995) uses Lakoff's definition of motivation to explain that similarity of form aids language acquisition, pointing out the seemingly paradoxical finding that it is easier for children to learn complex forms that are similar to forms they already know than it is for them to learn simpler but novel forms. Goldberg (1995, 72) also claims that "speakers (unconsciously) seek out regularities and patterns, and tend to impose regularities and patterns when these are not readily available." To the extent that each representation in a mismatch case is based on the representations of other simple or prototypical structures, constructions of mismatch will be less taxing for cognitive processes compared to completely novel constructions. Although the reasons why mismatches arise or how they are constrained require further research, the analysis outlined here proposes that the properties of simple or prototypical constructions can be dissociated into levels, and that familiar representations are preferred within each level. Constraints of cognitive efficiency within each level can lead to incongruities between levels.[25]

Jim McCawley once said, "Languages are weird and wonderful things. As long as you are perceptive enough there is plenty to keep you happy and busy."[26] In the case of RCs, although nonrestrictive RCs appear very similar to restrictive RCs, their properties are actually quite different from those of restrictive RCs in a curious way. In this chapter, I have argued that one way of recognizing the differences and commonalities between these constructions is to assume autonomous levels of grammar and allow associations of incongruous representations across different levels. McCawley also said that the value of theories lies in the extent to which they make phenomena accessible to an investigator (1998, xvi). I hope I have shown that the use of a multimodular theory can help to make these phenomena indeed more accessible.

Notes

1. Deep structures in McCawley's theory "correlate fairly closely with at least one notion of meaning in that they involve constituents that play a semantic role in the sentence but do not necessarily correspond to any constituent of surface structure" (McCawley 1998, 38).

2. Although McCawley (1998, 450) tentatively gives a diagram where the host clause and the nonrestrictive RC in (1) make up a constituent, he actually speculates that the connection between the host and the nonrestrictive RC may not be syntactic. This matter could belong to "the realm of the structure of complex action."

3. An anonymous reviewer points out that the same argument can be constructed with pronouns. In (i), the pronoun *her* only refers to Mary, and it does not contain the nonrestrictive RC.

(i) John sold Mary, who had offered him $600 an ounce, a pound of gold, and Arthur sold her (= Mary) two pounds.

Also, observe the following examples:

(ii) a. John sold a pound of gold to Mary. She had offered John $600.
  b. John sold a pound of gold to Mary, who had offered John $600 an ounce.
  c. ?John sold a pound of gold to the woman who had offered John $600 an ounce.

In (iic), the second *John* is c-commanded by the first *John* and violates Binding Condition C. However, the independent clause in (iia) and the nonrestrictive relative clause in (iib) are perfectly grammatical. This shows that a nonrestrictive RC is not part of the matrix S, let alone the antecedent.

4. As McCawley (1998, 481) points out, a proper noun can be modified by a restrictive RC if it is used as a common noun.

5. An anonymous reviewer points out that locative inversion can also occur in some restrictive RCs.

(i) That spring she monopolized with her class the benches under the elm from which could be seen an endless avenue of dark pink May trees, and heard the trotting of horses in time to the turning wheels of light carts returning home empty by a hidden lane from their early morning rounds. (M. Spark, *The Prime of Miss Jean Brodie*, 104–5; cited in Levin and Rappaport Hovav 1995, 222)

The conditions for locative inversion in restrictive RCs like that in (i) are not clear.

6. Logical Form (LF) is a level of representation where linguistic form interfaces with interpretation, and quantificational structures are represented at this level (May 1985, 2–6).

7. May (1985) reports that antecedent-contained deletion with nonrestrictive RCs is ungrammatical.

(i) *Dulles suspected Philby, who Angleton did.

However, Hornstein (1994, 1995) points out that the ungrammaticality of (i) parallels that of the coordination of two independent clauses, as illustrated in (ii).

(ii) *Dulles suspected Philby, and Angleton did.

If we modify both (i) and (ii), Hornstein points out that their level of grammaticality improves equally.

(iii) a. Dulles suspected Angleton, who Philby did as well.
    b. Dulles suspected Angleton, and Philby did as well.

Therefore, instead of serving as a counterexample to my claim, (i) shows the similarity of nonrestrictive RCs to main clauses.

8. Root transformations are unique to English and cannot be directly applied to Japanese.

Using the example in (i), Takahashi (1993) claims that object antecedent-contained deletion is not permitted in Japanese (the example is from Hornstein 1995).

(i) John-ga/mo   [jibun-no hahaoya]-ni [[Mary-ga   [e] okut-ta]   dono hon]-mo okut-ta.
    John-NOM/also self-GEN mother-to   Mary-NOM   send-PAST every book   send-PAST
    'John sent his mother every book that Mary sent.'
    '≠ John sent John's mother every book that Mary sent to Mary's mother.'

As Ueno (1994) points out (see also note 10 below), the structure that Takahashi uses in (i) contains a null object, but it does not involve VP-deletion. The example in (ii) contains a restrictive RC with antecedent-contained VP-deletion (not with a null object), but it is also worse than the English counterpart.

(ii) *John-wa [Mary-ga   shi-ta]   dono-hanzaisha-mo kokuso shi-ta.
    John-TOP Mary-NOM do-PAST every-criminal   sue   do-PAST
    'John accused every criminal that Mary did.'

Example (iii) shows that a nonrestrictive RC is even worse.

(ii) *John-wa [Mary-ga shi-ta] Kubo-hikoku-o onajiyooni kokuso shi-ta.
   John-TOP Mary-NOM do-PAST Kubo-defendant-ACC as.well sue do-PAST
   'John accused Mr. Kubo, who Mary did as well.'

Currently, the status of antecedent-contained deletion in Japanese is not entirely clear.

9. These authors actually claim that the distinction does not exist in syntax, and that restrictive and nonrestrictive RCs should be distinguished in semantics. Although I concur with their position below, I also argue that the semantic differences between restrictive and nonrestrictive RCs play a more significant role than previously assumed in the grammar of RCs.

10. Different structures such as (i) and (ii) are proposed to be instances of VP-deletion.

(i) Taroo-wa CLS-de toogoron-no ronbun-o happyoo shi-ta. Ichi-nen-go-ni
   Taro-TOP CLS-at syntax-GEN paper-ACC present do-PAST one-year-after-at
   Hanako-mo (BLS-de) shi-ta.
   Hanako-also BLS-at do-PAST
   'Taro read a syntax paper at CLS. A year later, Hanako did (at BLS) too.'
   (Ueno 1994)

(ii) John-wa jibun-no tegami-o sute-ta. Mary-mo [e] sute-ta.
   John-TOP self-GEN letter-ACC discard-PAST Mary-also discard-PAST
   'John$_i$ threw out his$_i$ letters. Mary$_j$ also threw out his$_{i/j}$ letters.'
   (Otani and Whitman 1991)

In (i), a dummy verb is present both in the antecedent clause and in the clause that contains deletion. In (ii), the same verb that is used in the antecedent clause is also used in the second clause. Following Ueno (1994), I consider (i) as an instance of VP-deletion, and (ii) as containing a null object.

11. As an anonymous reviewer points out, (20a) is ambiguous. Hence, it can also have a strict identity reading and mean 'NBC interviewed the person the day before yesterday who came back from Japan on the previous day. NHK did (= interviewed him) yesterday too'. Even in the strict identity reading, however, the pronoun is coreferential with the NP including the restrictive RC in the first clause.

12. These examples were provided by an anonymous reviewer.

13. As Hoshi (1995, 237) claims, there are cases where a (zero) pronoun in a nonrestrictive RC can be coreferential with a quantified NP antecedent and have the bound variable interpretation.

(i) a. *Restrictive RC*
   Dono kurisuchan$_i$-mo [[pro$_j$ pro$_i$ keikokushitsuzuke-ru] hito$_j$]-o yurushitei-ru.
   every Christian keep.warning-PRES person-ACC forgive-PRES
   'Every Christian forgives a man who warns him.'
   b. *Nonrestrictive RC*
   Dono kurisuchan$_i$-mo [[pro$_j$ pro$_i$ keikokushitsuzuke-ru] John$_j$]-o yurushitei-ru.
   every Christian keep.warning-PRES John]-ACC forgive-PRES
   '*Every Christian forgives John, who warns him.'

In both (ia) and (ib), the zero pronouns, which are the direct objects of the RCs, have the bound variable interpretation. However, the following example shows that in Japanese, a zero pronoun in an independent clause can also receive a bound variable interpretation:

(ii) Dono kurisuchan$_i$-mo John-o   yurusitei-ru. Sore-wa John-ga   *pro*$_i$
    every Christian   John-ACC forgive-PRES it-TOP   John-NOM
    keikokushitsuzuke-ru nimokakawarazu da.
    keep.warning-PRES   despite   COP
    '*Every Christian forgives John. Despite the fact that John keeps warning him.'

14. Minami (1974) points out that there are some subordinate clauses such as the ones headed by *keredo* 'although', *ga* 'although', and *kara* 'because' that allow the adverb *tabun* and many other items that normally seem to occur only in independent clauses.

15. The tense interpretation of restrictive RCs is actually more complicated than Miyake (1995) assumes. See Mihara 1992 for detailed descriptions and analyses of restrictive RCs in Japanese. In any case, what is crucial to the discussion is that nonrestrictive RCs take the time of the utterance as the reference time, although it is generally assumed that not only restrictive RCs but also other subordinate clauses such as sentential complements and adverbial clauses take the time of the main clause as the reference time.

16. Although auxiliary verbs such as *daroo* typically occur in independent clauses, an anonymous reviewer points out that some subordinate clauses allow *daroo* (Minami 1974).

(i) [Rainen   Furansu-e i-ku-*daroo*-kara]   Furansugo-o benkyoo shi-yoo.
    next.year France-to go-PRES-will-because French-ACC study   do-will
    'I will study French, because I will go to France next year.'

As discussed in note 14, subordinate clauses headed by -*kara*, -*keredo*, and -*ga* allow items that normally occur in independent clauses. I assume that the occurrence of *daroo* in (i) is due to the peculiar independent nature of these subordinate clauses.

17. Masuoka provides only one question mark, but to me this example is worse than Masuoka judges it to be.

18. An anonymous reviewer points out that although nonrestrictive RCs allow numerous auxiliary verbs and polite forms that normally occur in independent clauses, they do not allow sentence-final particles such as *wa*, *yo*, and *ne* that also occur only in independent clauses.

(i) a. Sakki-made   koko-ni i-ta-wa/yo/ne.
       a.short.time.ago-until here-at be-PAST-SFP/SFP/SFP
       'She/He was here until a short time ago.'
    b. [Sakki-made   koko-ni i-ta-*wa/*yo/*ne] Sasaki-buchoo-ni watashi-ta-no?
       a.short.time.ago-until here-at be-PAST-SFP/SFP/SFP Sasaki-manager-to give-PAST-NOMZ
       'Did (you) give (it) to Mr. Sasaki, who was here until a short time ago?'

As I will show, I assume that the representations of nonrestrictive RCs are not entirely the same as those of independent clauses. This may explain the difference between (ia) and (ib), but I will leave this issue unresolved.

19. An anonymous reviewer also provides the following example, which is ambiguous and can be interpreted as both restrictive and nonrestrictive:

(i) [Nihonjin-yori hatarakimono-*no*] Amerikajin
    Japanese-than hard.worker-GEN   Americans
    'Americans who work harder than Japanese'
    'the Americans, who work harder than Japanese'

When an NP modifies a noun in Japanese, the genitive marker *no* must appear between the NP and the noun, as in *sensei-no pen* 'professor's pen'. Interestingly, the example in (i) interpreted as a nonrestrictive RC is also followed by the genitive *no* as if it directly modifies the following noun, *Amerikajin*.

20. As Newmeyer (1998) points out, mere differences or arbitrary association between syntactic and semantic representations do not justify the autonomy of syntax and semantics. See Yuasa and Francis 2003 for the criteria for systematic mismatch among different levels of grammar, and Yuasa 2003 for how the mismatch in nonrestrictive RCs satisfies these criteria.

21. We defined *subordination* as follows:

(i) A subordinate constituent is a node whose categorial information does not percolate to the mother node while that of at least one sister node does.

Diagrammatically, subordinate constituents can be represented as in (ii).

(ii) [$_X$[X Y ... Z]]

22. Three observations are in order here.

First, just as with the coordination-subordination mismatch, technically there should be pseudoindependent clauses that have subordinate properties in semantics and independent properties in syntax, but I will concentrate on pseudosubordinate clauses in this chapter.

Second, among the three types of subordinate clauses (RCs, adverbial clauses, and complements), I focus only on RCs here; but there are also cases of independence-subordination mismatch for adverbial clauses (Yuasa 2003).

Third, there is a question about the semantics of nonrestrictive RCs with respect to coordination. Nonrestrictive RCs are often assumed to be semantically coordinate (Ross 1967; Jackendoff 1977). It is clear that nonrestrictive RCs are like independent clauses in semantics. Given the evidence from truth conditions, however, it is not clear whether they should be considered conjuncts in a coordinate structure in semantics. For example:

(i) a. John is from Chicago, and he went to Japan to study Japanese.
    b. John is from Chicago. He went to Japan to study Japanese.
    c. John, who went to Japan to study Japanese, is from Chicago.

Any semantic coordination such as (ia) becomes false if one of the conjuncts is false. Therefore, if John is actually not from Chicago but from Boston, (ia) becomes false. However, (ib) is not an instance of semantic coordination; hence, both sentences do not automatically become false if John is actually from Boston. The same interpretation seems to apply to (ic). This point was brought to my attention by David Oshima (pers. comm., March 2002).

Furthermore, an anonymous reviewer points out that assuming that the Coordinate Structure Constraint is a semantic constraint (Culicover and Jackendoff 1997), sentences (ii) and (iii) show that nonrestrictive RCs are not conjuncts in semantics.

(ii) The knife that I've just bought ∅ from Mary, who carved the turkey with it, has a serrated blade.

(iii) *The knife that I've just bought ∅ from Mary, who carved the turkey with ∅, has a serrated blade.

In (ii), a gap coindexed with the head noun exists only in the matrix clause, but the entire sentence is grammatical. On the other hand, while across-the-board application of relativization is possible in coordinate structures, it makes the sentence in (iii) ungrammatical. Therefore, I conclude that nonrestrictive RCs are not part of a coordinate structure in semantics, and it is not possible to reduce the independence-subordination distinction to the coordination-subordination distinction.

23. In English, a relative pronoun can appear between the head N' and an RC. Also, there must be a gap that is coreferential with the N' in syntax and a variable that is coreferential with the common noun in semantics. The relation between the head and an RC is much looser in Japanese (Kuno 1973; Teramura 1993; Matsumoto 1989). Furthermore, the head of an RC precedes the RC in English but follows it in Japanese.

24. Elaine Francis (pers. comm., October 2002) points out that there are some minor structural differences between restrictive and nonrestrictive RCs. For example, McCawley (1998, 445) shows that restrictive RCs can have a relative pronoun, a complementizer, or zero, while nonrestrictive RCs can have only a relative pronoun.

(i) a. The person who/that/∅ John asked ∅ for help thinks John is an idiot.
 b. Mary, who/??that/*∅ asked ∅ for help, thinks John is an idiot.

In Yuasa 2003, I propose that when a mismatch case arises as a result of interaction between two different constructions, the mismatch case does not necessarily inherit all of the properties of the original constructions. This type of interrelation among constructions is also assumed in Construction Grammar (Goldberg 1995, 73).

25. As Salikoko Mufwene (pers. comm., August 2003) points out, the conception of structure sharing within a level of grammar assumed here is similar to McCawley's (1998, 315) surface gross combinatorics.

See Luka, this volume, for discussion of a close relation between familiarity and grammar.

26. Reported by Margalit Fox, *The New York Times*, 14 April 1999.

References

Collier-Sanuki, Yoko. 1999. Nihongo-rentaisetu ni okeru gentei/higentei [On the definitions of restrictive and nonrestrictive relative clauses in Japanese]. In *Gengogaku to nihongo-kyooiku* [Linguistics and Japanese language education], ed. by Yukiko Sasaki Alam, 275–90. Tokyo: Kuroshio.

Culicover, Peter, and Ray Jackendoff. 1997. Semantic subordination despite syntactic coordination. *Linguistic Inquiry* 28, 195–217.

Demirdache, Hamida K. 1991. Resumptive chains in restrictive relatives, appositives and dislocation structures. Doctoral dissertation, MIT.

Emonds, Joseph. 1979. Appositive relatives have no properties. *Linguistic Inquiry* 10, 211–43.

Evans, Gareth. 1980. Pronouns. *Linguistic Inquiry* 11, 337–62.

Goldberg, Adele E. 1995. *Constructions: A Construction Grammar approach to argument structure*. Chicago: University of Chicago Press.

Haiman, John, and Sandra Thompson. 1984. "Subordination" in Universal Grammar. In *Proceedings of the Tenth Annual Meeting of the Berkeley Linguistics Society*, ed. by Claudia Brugman and Monica Macaulay, 510–23. Berkeley: University of California, Berkeley Linguistics Society.

Hooper, Joan B., and Sandra Thompson. 1973. On the applicability of root transformations. *Linguistic Inquiry* 4, 465–97.

Hornstein, Norbert. 1994. An argument for minimalism: The case of antecedent-contained deletion. *Linguistic Inquiry* 25, 455–80.

Hornstein, Norbert. 1995. *Logical Form: From GB to minimalism*. Oxford: Blackwell.

Hoshi, Koji. 1995. Structural and interpretive aspects of head-internal and head-external relative clauses. Doctoral dissertation, University of Rochester.

Inoue, Kazuko. 1976. *Henkei-bunpoo to nihongo 2* [Transformational grammar and Japanese 2]. Tokyo: Taishuukan.

Jackendoff, Ray. 1977. *$\bar{X}$ syntax: A study of phrase structure*. Cambridge, MA: MIT Press.

Jackendoff, Ray. 1997. *The architecture of the language faculty*. Cambridge, MA: MIT Press.

Kamio, Akio. 1983. Meeshiku no koozoo [Structure of noun phrase]. In *Nihongo no kihon koozoo* [Basic structure of Japanese], ed. by Kazuko Inoue, 77–126. Tokyo: Sanseidoo.

Keenan, Edward L. 1985. Relative clauses. In *Language typology and syntactic description II*, ed. by Timothy Shopen, 141–70. Cambridge: Cambridge University Press.

Kuno, Susumu. 1973. *The structure of the Japanese language*. Cambridge, MA: MIT Press.

Lakoff, George. 1987. *Women, fire, and dangerous things*. Chicago: University of Chicago Press.

Levin, Beth, and Malka Rappaport Hovav. 1995. *Unaccusativity: At the syntax–lexical semantics interface*. Cambridge, MA: MIT Press.

Masuoka, Takashi. 1997. *Fukubun* [Complex clauses]. Tokyo: Kuroshio.

Matsumoto, Yoshiko. 1989. Grammar and semantics of adnominal clauses in Japanese. Doctoral dissertation, University of California, Berkeley.

May, Robert. 1985. *Logical Form: Its structure and derivation*. Cambridge, MA: MIT Press.

McCawley, James D. 1988. *The syntactic phenomena of English*. Chicago: University of Chicago Press. 2nd ed., 1998.

Mihara, Kenichi. 1992. *Jisei-kaishaku to toogo-genshoo* [Tense interpretation and syntactic phenomena]. Tokyo: Kuroshio.

Minami, Fujio. 1974. *Gendai-nihongo no koozoo* [Structure of modern Japanese]. Tokyo: Taishukan.

Miyake, Tomohiro. 1995. Nihongo no fukugoomeishiku no koozoo [Structure of Japanese complex NPs]. *Gendai Nihongo Kenkyuu 2* [Modern Japanese Studies] 2, 49–66.

Nakamura, Akira. 1994. On the tense system of Japanese. In *Japanese/Korean linguistics 4*, ed. by Noriko Akatsuka, 363–78. Stanford, CA: CSLI Publications.

Nakau, Minoru. 1976. Tense, aspect, and modality. In *Syntax and semantics 5: Japanese generative grammar*, ed. by Masayoshi Shibatani, 421–82. New York: Academic Press.

Newmeyer, Frederick. 1998. *Language form and language function*. Cambridge, MA: MIT Press.

Ogihara, Toshiyuki. 1989. Temporal reference in English and Japanese. Doctoral dissertation, University of Texas at Austin.

Otani, Kazuyo, and John Whitman. 1991. V-raising and VP-ellipsis. *Linguistic Inquiry* 22, 345–58.

Ross, John R. 1967. Constraints on variables in syntax. Doctoral dissertation, MIT. Published as *Infinite Syntax!* Hillsdale, NJ: Lawrence Erlbaum, 1986.

Sadock, Jerrold M. 1991. *Autolexical Syntax: A theory of parallel grammatical representations.* Chicago: University of Chicago Press.

Sadock, Jerrold M. 1993. An autolexical sketch of English. Manuscript, University of Chicago.

Sadock, Jerrold M., and Eric Schiller. 1993. The Generalized Interface Principle. In *CLS 29*. Vol. 1, *The Main Session*, ed. by Katharine Beals, Gina Cooke, David Kathman, Sotaro Kita, Karl-Erik McCullough, and David Testen, 391–401. Chicago: University of Chicago, Chicago Linguistic Society.

Sag, Ivan. 1976. Deletion and Logical Form. Doctoral dissertation, MIT.

Sells, Peter. 1986. Coreference and bound anaphora: A restatement of the facts. In *Proceedings of NELS 16*, ed. by Stpphen Berman, Jae-Woong Choe, and Joyce McDonough, 434–46. Amherst: University of Massachusetts, GLSA.

Sunakawa, Yuriko. 1986. Suru•shita•shiteiru [Do•did•is doing]. Tokyo: Kuroshio.

Takahashi, Daiko. 1993. On antecedent contained deletion. Manuscript, University of Connecticut.

Teramura, Hideo. 1984. *Nihongo no shintakusu to imi 2* [Syntax and meaning in Japanese 2]. Tokyo: Kuroshio.

Teramura, Hideo. 1991. *Nihongo no shintakusu to imi 3* [Syntax and meaning in Japanese 3]. Tokyo: Kuroshio.

Teramura, Hideo. 1993. *Teramura Hideo ronbunsyuu 1* [Collection of papers by Hideo Teramura 1]. Tokyo: Kuroshio.

Ueno, Yoshio. 1994. Grammatical functions and clause structure in Japanese. Doctoral dissertation, University of Chicago.

Yuasa, Etsuyo. 1997. An autolexical account of coordination-subordination mismatches. Paper presented at the annual meeting of the Linguistic Society of America, Chicago.

Yuasa, Etsuyo. 1998. Subordinate clauses in Japanese. Doctoral dissertation, University of Chicago.

Yuasa, Etsuyo. 2003. Modularity in language: Constructional and categorial mismatch in syntax and semantics. Manuscript, The Ohio State University.

Yuasa, Etsuyo, and Elaine J. Francis. 2003. Categorial mismatch in a multi-modular theory of grammar. In *Mismatch: Form-function incongruity and the architecture of grammar*, ed. by Elaine J. Francis and Laura A. Michaelis, 179–227. Stanford, CA: CSLI Publications.

Yuasa, Etsuyo, and Jerrold M. Sadock. 2002. Pseudo-subordination: A mismatch between syntax and semantics. *Journal of Linguistics* 38, 87–111.

Chapter 7

Syntactic Mimicry as Evidence for Prototypes in Grammar

Elaine J. Francis

7.1 Introduction

Jim McCawley was known for his empirically driven approach to syntactic theory. One of the many empirical problems that caught his attention was the fact that some members of a given syntactic category fail to display the full range of distributional properties typical of that category. For example, predicate noun phrases such as *an idiot* in (1a) are restricted in terms of the range of determiners they can accept, as shown in (1b), and in terms of the kinds of constructions in which they can occur, as illustrated in (1c).

(1) a. That salesman is an idiot.
    b. *That salesman is the idiot.
    c. *An idiot is easy for that salesman to be.

As McCawley (1982) and others have argued, this kind of defective grammatical behavior is closely related to the fact that predicate noun phrases (henceforth, *predicate NPs*) do not perform the typical semantic function of NPs. The NP *an idiot* in (1a) does not refer to any particular person but rather predicates a property of the salesman. Thus, predicate NPs serve a semantic function more commonly associated with adjectives or intransitive verbs.

Traditional notions of syntactic category in generative grammar do not distinguish predicate NPs from other kinds of NPs. Rather, all NPs are treated in the same way with respect to the application of grammatical rules that make reference to category information. Viewing this as a limitation of traditional approaches, McCawley (1982, 1987, 1988/1998) proposed a "prototype" theory of syntactic categories designed to more adequately accommodate these kinds of exceptional cases. According to McCawley, syntactic categories such as "noun" and NP are characterized by correspondences of independent syntactic and semantic factors. While certain typical or

---

I am grateful to Bob Knippen, Alex Francis, Adele Goldberg, and an anonymous reviewer for their helpful comments on an earlier version of this chapter.

canonical correspondences make up the "core" or "prototype" for a category, other correspondences are also possible. For example, the subject NP *that salesman* in (1a) instantiates the prototype for the category of NP in the sense that it has the usual syntactic form of NPs [Det N'], as well as the usual semantic function of NPs (i.e., it is an argument). In contrast, the predicate NP *an idiot* in (1) has the usual syntactic form of NPs, but not the usual semantic function. This unusual form-meaning correspondence results in the defective grammatical behavior of predicate NPs shown in (1b–c) (see McCawley 1982; Ross 1995).

Similar "prototype" approaches to syntactic categories have been developed within cognitive and functional schools of linguistics in response to similar observations (e.g., Hopper and Thompson 1984; Lakoff 1987b; Croft 1991, 2001; Taylor 1995). However, mainstream theories of formal syntax have either ignored or rejected the idea of prototypes, and Newmeyer (1998, 2000) has argued that a notion of prototype is unnecessary to account for the kinds of phenomena that have inspired prototype theories of syntactic categories. Instead, Newmeyer argues in favor of a modular approach according to which independently defined principles of syntax and semantics interact to produce the observed effects. Newmeyer's approach is insightful, and, in many ways, compatible with McCawley's. However, there is some evidence that a *purely* modular approach as advocated by Newmeyer cannot adequately account for the full range of data and that a notion of prototype is in fact needed.

In this chapter, I examine and defend McCawley's position that a notion of prototype is relevant to the representation of syntactic categories in grammatical competence. I first discuss some background on prototype theories of categorization, including McCawley's (1982, 1987, 1988/1998) theory of syntactic categories, in sections 7.2 and 7.3. Then, in section 7.4, I present linguistic evidence in support of a prototype theory of syntactic categories. The evidence is based on McCawley's (1987) analysis of English adjectival nouns and is further supported by data from Culicover and Jackendoff (1997) involving subordinating uses of the English conjunction *and*. Both cases involve unacceptable sentences that are neither syntactically nor semantically ill formed, but that deviate from the prototypical syntax-semantics correspondence. On the basis of this evidence, I argue that deviations from the prototypical syntax-semantics correspondence for a category can have consequences beyond those predictable from independent principles of syntax and semantics.[1] The notion of prototype is therefore significant for grammatical competence because it constitutes an *expectation* that, when violated in certain ways, has direct consequences for the grammar.

7.2 Classical versus Prototype Theories of Categorization

There is a long-standing debate in philosophy, cognitive psychology, and linguistics regarding the nature of categorization. Much of this debate has focused on concep-

Syntactic Mimicry and Prototypes in Grammar

tual (semantic) categories such as CAT, CHAIR, and BACHELOR. Proponents of "classical" theories of categorization hold that conceptual categories are discrete entities defined by a particular set of features that are necessary and sufficient for category membership. For example, an item is judged to belong to the category BACHELOR if it bears the features [human], [male], [adult], [never married], and [available for dating]. Furthermore, membership in a category is all or none. There is no sense in which one exemplar can be a "better" member of the category BACHELOR than any other. Something either is a bachelor or it isn't.

Other categories are not so clear-cut as the category BACHELOR, however. Even for a seemingly straightforward category such as CHAIR, it may be difficult to find a set of defining features common to all members of the category. For example, we might think of [having legs] as a defining feature of chairs, but on the other hand we would not want to deny that a recliner is still a chair. Proponents of "prototype" theories hold that conceptual categories are organized around typical combinations of features that make up a "prototype" rather than being defined by necessary and sufficient conditions. According to this approach, an item belonging to a particular category need not instantiate all of the features for that category. Thus, a recliner can be judged to belong to the category CHAIR even though it lacks the feature [having legs], provided that it still possesses enough of the other features of the category CHAIR to be sufficiently similar to the prototype. In addition, category membership is a matter of degree, such that some exemplars may be judged as "better" (or more representative) members of the category CHAIR than others. Chairs with legs, for example, might be considered "better" members of the category CHAIR than chairs without legs in the sense that chairs with legs instantiate more of the prototypical features than those without legs do. A consequence of this approach is that category boundaries may be unclear. Is an auditorium seat a kind of chair? Some people say yes, some say no, and others just aren't sure.

In support of a prototype approach to categories, researchers, most notably the psychologist Eleanor Rosch and her colleagues, have collected a large body of experimental evidence for so-called prototype effects (e.g., Labov 1973; Rosch and Mervis 1975; Rosch 1978; Smith and Medin 1981; Hampton 1995). In experiments in which people are asked to rate the "goodness" of an item as a member of a category, people reliably and consistently rate some items as better than others. For example, robins are consistently rated as good members of the category BIRD, while penguins are consistently rated as poor members. Other experiments have shown that such judgments can be predicted on the basis of the value of certain features (e.g., size, shape, ability to fly) and that goodness ratings are strongly correlated with performance in a number of psychological tasks. For example, participants are able to respond more quickly to the question "Is a robin a kind of bird?" than to the question "Is a penguin a kind of bird?"

Prototype effects have been interpreted in a number of different ways, and I will not attempt to survey the vast literature on this topic here. It is important to note, however, that these effects are not unambiguous evidence for prototypes—even classical categories show them. A famous study by Armstrong, Gleitman, and Gleitman (1983) found evidence of prototype effects in judgments about categories that are clearly definable in terms of necessary and sufficient conditions. For example, participants judged mothers to be better examples of the category FEMALE than comediennes even though both mothers and comediennes satisfy the necessary and sufficient conditions of the category. The authors of the study took these results as evidence against a prototype theory of categories, arguing that prototype effects must be distinct from actual category structure. After all, participants *know* that both mothers and comediennes are female to an equal degree, as demonstrated in an independent questionnaire.

What, then, do prototype effects indicate? Armstrong, Gleitman, and Gleitman argue that prototype effects result from the procedures people use in *identifying* categories, as distinct from the categories themselves. However, other authors, such as Taylor (1995, 71) and Pinker and Prince (1999, 255), interpret the results differently. These authors reject the idea that identification procedures can be separated from processes of categorization, and instead propose that in some cases, people may have alternative representations of the same category—one with a prototype structure and one with a classical structure. Thus, the same word *female* can be used to label two alternative conceptual representations, one of which is influenced by cultural stereotypes (e.g., female as caregiver) and has a prototype structure, and one of which is based on scientific knowledge and has a classical structure.

I assume following Taylor (1995) and Pinker and Prince (1999) that it is possible for a single concept to be represented in both classical and prototype forms. By the same token, I assume that it is possible for different categories to be represented in terms of different structures (see Pinker and Prince 1999 for additional arguments in favor of this position). Whether a particular category has a prototype structure, a classical structure, or some other structure, is therefore a matter of empirical investigation.[2] In the following sections, I investigate whether syntactic categories such as "noun" and NP have a prototype structure. What kinds of empirical evidence can shed light on this question? Unlike conceptual categories such as CHAIR, syntactic categories such as NP cannot be identified using ordinary words or pictures and are below the level of conscious awareness for most people. As a result, researchers have not (yet) made use of psychological experiments for testing the structure of syntactic categories, but have relied on purely linguistic evidence of the kind given in (1). Newmeyer (1998, 2000) argues that much of this linguistic evidence is actually ambiguous with respect to category structure and can be accommodated equally well or better in terms of a modular theory of grammar. I will elaborate on the nature of this evidence and its implications in section 7.3. Following McCawley (1987), I argue in section 7.4 that there is some linguistic evidence that not only suggests a prototype structure, but also appears to defy explanation in terms of a modular approach, thus supporting the plausibility of a prototype theory of syntactic categories.

7.3 Syntactic Categories as Prototype Categories

This section explores the notion of prototype as it has been applied to syntactic categories. I begin by looking at the motivation and development of various prototype theories of syntactic categories and then briefly discuss Jim McCawley's theory of syntactic categories. Finally, I discuss the modular approach to syntactic categories presented by Newmeyer (1998, 2000) as a possible alternative to prototypes.

7.3.1 The Development of Prototype Theories of Syntactic Categories

Building on his earlier proposal (Chomsky 1965), Chomsky (1970) proposed that syntactic categories are defined by sets of abstract syntactic features. For example, the category "noun" is defined by the features [+N] and [−V], and the category "verb" is defined by the features [+V] and [−N]. All members of the categories "noun" and "verb" are specified with the appropriate features in their lexical entries, thus ensuring their appropriate placement under N ("noun") and V ("verb") nodes in phrase structure. Implicit in this approach is a classical notion of category structure, according to which categories are defined by necessary and sufficient conditions for membership (i.e., a particular set of syntactic features). Some version of Chomsky's feature theory of syntactic categories is still in use today by most formal approaches to syntax.[3]

Ross (1972, 1973a,b) challenged Chomsky's approach to category structure on the basis of evidence for systematic variation among members of the same syntactic category. Ross (1973a) observed that some NPs fail to undergo certain transformations otherwise typical of NPs. For example, existential *there* acts like an ordinary NP in many ways, such as with respect to subject-auxiliary inversion in (2a) and subject raising in (2b). However, unlike ordinary NPs, it is defective with respect to topicalization (2c) and occurrence in *think of as*-constructions (2d), among other processes.

(2) a. Was there any news?
　　b. There seems not to have been any news.
　　c. *There, I don't consider ____ to be much point in this exercise.
　　d. *I thought of there as being alien invaders in the house.

Such variation among members of the same category is not readily accommodated within a Chomskyan feature theory, since all members of the same category share the same features. It is possible in a Chomskyan framework to list exceptional features in each lexical entry. For example, a lexical feature such as [−topicalization] could block the application of topicalization in examples like (2c). However, Ross preferred a more general solution. He proposed a graded continuum, or "category squish," to account for the kinds of variation he observed. The "nouniest" NPs are those that undergo the full range of transformations characteristic of NPs, while those (such as existential *there*) that fail to undergo certain transformations are relatively less nouny.

Although proposed independently of Rosch's psychological work on prototypes, Ross's approach resembles prototype theory in allowing graded category membership. The concept of "nouniness," for example, can easily be restated in terms of having more or fewer NP features. In addition, Ross (1973b) observed interesting correlations between syntax and semantics. Those NPs that undergo the fullest range of transformations (i.e., the nouniest NPs in terms of syntactic behavior) tend to refer to animate beings, while the least syntactically nouny NPs tend to refer to states of affairs, abstract entities, or (as in the case of existential *there*) nothing at all.

Ross's work was influential in the subsequent development of prototype theories of syntactic categories. Both gradedness of category membership and syntax-semantics correlations of the sort Ross observed play a role in several prototype theories of syntactic categories proposed in the 1980s and 1990s. McCawley (1982, 1987, 1988/1998), Hopper and Thompson (1984), Lakoff (1987a,b), Croft (1991), and Taylor (1995) explain apparent gradedness of category membership and regular correspondences between grammatical behavior and semantic (or discourse) function in terms of a prototype structure for syntactic categories. Of these theorists, all except McCawley adopted a cognitive-functionalist perspective on grammar, according to which syntax does not operate independently of semantics and discourse function.

According to Croft (1991), for example, each syntactic category is prototypically associated with a particular pragmatic function and a particular ontological class. Nouns and NPs are associated with the function of reference and with the class of concrete objects, while adjectives and APs are associated with the function of attribution and with the class of properties. Verbs and VPs are associated with the function of predication and with the class of actions. To the extent that a particular item instantiates these prototypical correlations, it is expected to display the full range of grammatical behavior typical of its category. To the extent that an item fails to instantiate these prototypical correlations, however, it may fail to display some of the typical grammatical properties of its category. For example, stative verbs in English such as *contain* and *belong* are nonprototypical of the category "verb" because they fail to denote actions. In accordance with this semantic nonprototypicality, these verbs usually fail to occur in the progressive (3a) or in the passive (3b).

(3) a. *Water is containing hydrogen and oxygen.
    b. *Hydrogen and oxygen are contained by water.

Exactly how this works is detailed by Croft (1991) in terms of a theory of typological markedness.[4] Similar, but less detailed prototype theories of syntactic categories are proposed by Hopper and Thompson (1984), Lakoff (1987a), and Taylor (1995), all of whom draw a connection between prototypicality of semantic or discourse function and relative degree of markedness in grammar.

7.3.2 McCawley's Prototype Theory of Syntactic Categories

Jim McCawley is one of the few linguists to have advocated a prototype theory of syntactic categories within a transformational-generative theory of grammar. In McCawley's view, syntactic categories are characterized in terms of prototypical correspondences of particular morphological, syntactic, and semantic attributes. As in other prototype theories, individual members of a category may or may not instantiate all of the features associated with that category. McCawley's (1982, 1987, 1988/1998) approach is inspired in part by that of Ross (1972, 1973a,b) and quite similar in spirit to that of Croft (1991). Like Ross and Croft, McCawley admits graded category membership. For example, McCawley characterizes a predicate NP such as *an idiot* in the sentence *That salesman was an idiot* as "only loosely speaking an NP" (1982, 198). His reasoning here is quite similar to that found in later work by Croft (1991): predicate NPs function as predicates rather than arguments, thus deviating from the prototypical pragmatic function (or "logical category" in McCawley's terms) of NPs.[5] As a result, predicate NPs are more restricted than argument NPs in terms of the range of determiners with which they can combine and in terms of the syntactic processes that can apply to them. Similarly, McCawley (1982, 198) observes that transitive stative verbs such as *contain* and *believe* are semantically nonprototypical of the category "verb," resulting in markedness effects such as limitations on passivization and occurrence with progressive aspect, as discussed with respect to (3a–b) above.

McCawley's approach differs from Croft's, however, with respect to the role of syntax in grammar. While McCawley assumes the existence of an autonomous formal syntax with its own units and combinatoric principles, Croft does not (see also Croft 1995, 2001). For McCawley, predicate NPs are *independently* constrained by distinct syntactic and semantic factors. In semantics, they obey the combinatoric principles of predicate logic, whereas in syntax, they conform to the "surface" combinatorics of English syntax. Although the semantics does not permit any (meaningful) quantifier or determiner to occur with an item functioning as a main predicate, the syntax of English requires a determiner to occur in the specifier position of an NP headed by a singular count noun. This (surface) syntactic requirement results in the occurrence of a determiner (usually the article *a*) that is semantically bleached and does not serve its usual referential function. As shown in (4a–d), singular predicate NPs require a determiner, while synonymous predicate APs do not allow any determiner.[6]

(4) a. That salesman is an idiot. (predicate NP)
    b. *That salesman is idiot.
    c. That salesman is idiotic. (predicate AP)
    d. *That salesman is an idiotic.

Thus, according to McCawley, what is unusual about predicate NPs is not the principles of grammar that apply to them, but the particular combination of syntactic and semantic properties that they display. In the terminology of Sadock (1990) and Bresnan (1995), predicate NPs instantiate a "categorial mismatch" between syntax and semantics—a specific kind of nonprototypical category structure in which syntactic properties prototypical of one syntactic category are combined with semantic properties prototypical of a different syntactic category (see Francis 1999 for detailed discussion).

The need for independent constraints on syntax and semantics is also supported in subsequent work on categorial mismatch within the tradition of parallel-architecture theories of grammar such as Autolexical Syntax (Sadock 1990; Yuasa 1998; Francis 1999; Yuasa and Francis 2003), Representational Modularity (Culicover and Jackendoff 1997; Jackendoff 1997), Lexical-Functional Grammar (Bresnan 1995), and Head-driven Phrase Structure Grammar (Malouf 2000). Much like McCawley's approach, these theories assume a modular grammatical architecture in which syntactic principles are independent from semantic and discourse principles, but interact with each other in complex ways. For example, drawing inspiration from McCawley's work, Yuasa (1996, 1998) discusses a class of grammaticalized nouns in Japanese that display the syntactic properties of nouns, but the semantic properties of subordinating conjunctions. As in McCawley's case of predicate NPs, the unusual behavior of these nouns can be predicted from the interaction of existing syntactic and semantic principles. Similarly, Bresnan (1995) discusses a class of lexical items in Chicheŵa that have syntactic and morphological properties of ordinary verbs but at the same time display semantic properties and grammatical functions more typical of complementizers. Bresnan argues that such items provide evidence for distinct structural and functional constraints on independent dimensions of grammar.

In sum, various prototype theories of syntactic categories have been developed to account for phenomena involving systematic variation among members of the same category. Because of the flexibility that a prototype structure allows, variation among category members is not only allowed but also expected. In contrast, a Chomskyan feature-based approach to syntactic categories is less flexible in that all category members share exactly the same features. Furthermore, exceptions must be listed individually in the lexicon, thus failing to predict the systematic clustering of features that we observe.[7]

McCawley's prototype theory of syntactic categories differs from functionalist prototype theories in that it posits independent constraints on syntax and semantics, as also advocated by proponents of various parallel-architecture theories of grammar. This allows McCawley to straightforwardly account for the existence of meaningless morphemes occurring with predicate NPs and similar cases of categorial mismatch. In the next section, I discuss Newmeyer's (1998, 2000) proposal that independent constraints on syntax and semantics might in fact be all that is needed to explain the observed patterns of data, and then in section 7.4, I test this proposal against linguistic evidence from two case studies.

7.3.3 Modularity as a Possible Alternative to Prototypes

Newmeyer (1998, 165–208) argues that a notion of prototype is not in fact needed to account for prototype effects. Although he acknowledges that there are certain semantic and pragmatic functions typically associated with the major syntactic categories, he denies that these associations have any privileged status within the grammar. All grammatical facts purported to be in favor of prototypes should, he argues, be explicable in terms of independent but interacting semantic, pragmatic, and syntactic principles of the sort described in work by McCawley (1982), Sadock (1990), Bresnan (1995), and others, and discussed above in section 7.3.2.

Newmeyer argues that all prototype effects can be given an alternative explanation in terms of factors independent of prototypicality. One example he discusses at some length is existential *there*. Existential *there* is highly limited in its distribution, leading prototype theorists to explain such facts in terms of its failure to conform to the NP prototype. Newmeyer explains these limitations instead in terms of the specific semantic and pragmatic properties of *there*-constructions. He argues, for example, that existential *there* cannot be topicalized, as shown in (4c), because it does not refer to a possible discourse topic. (In fact, it does not refer to anything.) He provides similar explanations for a number of other distributional limitations on existential *there*. Thus, Newmeyer shows that the distribution of certain defective items need not be explained in terms of prototypes (1998, 187–190).

Furthermore, Newmeyer argues that a prototype account of the sort proposed by Croft (1991) fails to account for certain patterns of data. For example, he observes that while typically, stative verbs disallow the progressive (as in (3a)), some stative verbs commonly occur in the progressive.

(5) a. The portrait is hanging on the wall of the bedroom.
    b. I'm enjoying my sabbatical year.
       (Newmeyer 1998, 183)

He conjectures that the difference between stative verbs like *contain*, which disallow the progressive (see (3a)), and stative verbs like *enjoy*, which commonly occur in the progressive, may be explained in terms of independent semantic or pragmatic principles. Although he does not give an account of this difference, he refers readers to some of the relevant literature on the topic. His main point, however, is that these patterns of data cannot be explained by appealing to the notion of prototypes or prototypicality: both *contain* and *enjoy* are nonprototypical (at least according to the criteria given in Croft 1991), and yet only one of them fails to occur in the progressive.[8]

Could it be that independent syntactic, semantic, and pragmatic factors are all that is needed to explain prototype effects? Newmeyer (1998) argues that a modular solution of this sort is in fact more economical than a solution that involves both modularity and prototypes. Since independent syntactic and semantic principles are needed anyway to account for cases of categorial mismatch (as discussed in section 7.3) and to account for cases such as (5a–b), it would appear superfluous to posit prototypes in addition. However, McCawley (1987) presents evidence that certain kinds of defective grammatical behavior are explicable in terms of a violation of the prototype, but not in terms of independent syntactic or semantic factors. I will discuss this and other evidence in the following section.

7.4 Syntactic Mimicry as Evidence for Prototypes in Grammar

In this section, I discuss two cases of what McCawley calls *syntactic mimicry*: adjectival nouns (ANs) and left-subordinating *and*. These cases involve a nonprototypical correspondence between a syntactic category and semantic type. For example, ANs such as *snap* in *That problem was a snap* belong to the syntactic category "noun," but function semantically like typical adjectives.

Cases of syntactic mimicry arise historically when a lexical item or structural pattern is extended to a new meaning, but retains many of its original syntactic properties. In the case of ANs, ordinary nouns have undergone a semantic extension to take on the meaning of a single property. For example, the word *snap* as in *That problem was a snap* has been extended to the meaning of 'easy' by means of the comparison *as easy as a snap of the fingers*. Although nearly synonymous with the adjective *easy*, the noun *snap* still retains nounlike syntactic properties (see discussion below). Similarly, the coordinate clause construction with *and* has undergone a semantic extension to take on an interpretation in which the first clause is a condition on which the second clause is predicated, as in *You make one more move and I call the police*. This semantic extension is consistent with the tendency noted by Hopper and Traugott (1993, 169–70) for subordinate clause constructions to be historically derived from constructions that show a lesser degree of dependency between clauses. As in the case of ANs, the subordinating *and*-construction retains many of the syntactic properties of the original coordinate construction, as discussed below.

While the synchronic grammar can readily accommodate these cases, it imposes limitations on their distributions. Some of these limitations are predictable from independently needed semantic and syntactic principles. However, others are not. I argue that certain distributional limitations in cases of syntactic mimicry result from

Syntactic Mimicry and Prototypes in Grammar

constraints on the manner in which the items in question can deviate from the prototypical syntax-semantics mapping.

7.4.1 Adjectival Nouns

McCawley (1987) investigates the class of nouns that includes words like *bitch*, *snap*, *breeze*, *pain*, and *murder* (pp. 459–61).[9]

(6) a. *Ulysses* is a bitch of a book to read.
   b. **Ulysses* is a bitch book to read.
   c. The last problem was a snap to solve.
   d. *The last problem was snap to solve.

Such nouns may be compared with the semantically similar adjectives *difficult* and *easy*.

(7) a. *Ulysses* is a difficult book to read.
   b. The last problem was easy to solve.

McCawley (1987) characterizes this class of words, which, following Ross (1972), he calls "adjectival nouns," as a kind of categorial mismatch akin to the case of predicate NPs discussed in McCawley 1982. ANs are prototypical of nouns with respect to morphology and syntax, but they are nonprototypical of nouns (but akin to prototypical adjectives) with respect to semantics. According to McCawley's analysis, ANs function as syntactic heads of NPs even though they are semantically modifiers.[10] Consistent with McCawley's idea that syntax and semantics operate according to independent principles, ANs co-occur with words that are syntactically relevant but semantically empty. In (6a), for example, the words *of a* contribute little or nothing to the meaning of the sentence, but their presence makes it syntactically felicitous for the noun *bitch* to modify and precede another noun.

Taking a purely modular approach along the lines of Newmeyer (1998), it might be possible to account for the distributions of ANs directly in terms of these independent syntactic and semantic principles. The grammatical differences between *snap* and *bitch* in (6) and *difficult* and *easy* in (7) would, according to this approach, be a simple consequence of the fact that they belong to different syntactic categories: *snap* and *bitch* are nouns, but *difficult* and *easy* are adjectives. Observe, for example, that (6b) is unacceptable because the noun *bitch* directly precedes the noun it modifies, in violation of the (surface) phrase structure rules of English. In contrast, (7a) is acceptable because as an adjective, the word *difficult* is allowed to directly precede the noun it modifies. This explanation is perfectly consistent with McCawley's theory and does not require reference to prototypes.

Similarly, we could describe many of the defective properties of ANs directly in terms of their lexical meanings.

(8) a. *The last problem was a loud snap to solve.
   b. **Ulysses* is an angry bitch of a book to read.

In (8a), *snap* cannot be modified by *loud* because its meaning 'easy' is not something that can be loud. Similarly, *bitch* cannot be modified by *angry* because its meaning 'difficult' is not something that can be angry.

ANs are a problem for a (purely) modular approach, however, because they display other defective patterns that do not seem explicable in terms of independent syntactic or semantic factors.

(9) a. **Finnegan's Wake* and *Ulysses* are a bitch of books to read.
   b. *Finnegan's Wake* and *Ulysses* are difficult books to read.
   c. *Finnegan's Wake* and *Ulysses* are a pair of (interesting) books to read.
   d. ?*Finnegan's Wake* and *Ulysses* are bitches of books to read.
      (McCawley 1987, 462)

(10) a. *John solved every bitch of a problem that they asked him to solve.
   b. John solved every difficult problem that they asked him to solve.
   c. John solved every part of the problem that they asked him to solve.

McCawley (1987, 464–65) observes that *bitch* is infelicitous in plural predicate NPs (9a) and quantified NPs (10a). However, the oddity of (9a) and (10a) does not seem explicable in lexical semantic terms. Examples (9b) and (10b) show that with minor adjustments for syntactic category, the synonymous adjective *difficult* is fully felicitous in such constructions, suggesting that there is no semantic incompatibility in (9a) and (10a) either. The oddity of (9a) and (10a) does not seem explicable in syntactic terms either. Examples (9c) and (10c) demonstrate that nouns that are not semantic modifiers can occur felicitously both in plural predicate NPs and in quantified NPs.

If the oddity of (9a) and (10a) is not caused by independent syntactic or lexical semantic factors, then what causes it? McCawley (1987) presents a compelling explanation. He argues that ANs participate in syntactic constructions in which constituent structures that allow nouns are used "to simulate syntactic constructions typical of adjectives"—hence the term *syntactic mimicry* (1987, 459). He then explains the defective properties of ANs in examples such as (9) and (10) as follows:

> ANs are most acceptable where they appear in a N position but do not call attention to the fact that semantically they are not nouns. The ideal contexts for that are those in which the semantic nounhood of a true noun would play the least role, i.e. as the head of a predicate NP with a semantically empty article.... Part of the camouflage involved in an AN construction is the use of the AN in a position where it looks like the head of a NP even though it is semantically a modifier. (McCawley 1987, 465)

McCawley reasons that in (9a), the syntactic configuration suggests that *bitch* is the semantic head, but the plural morphology on *book* (but not *bitch*) reveals that actually *book* is the semantic head, thus rendering the sentence unacceptable. Consistent with this analysis, (9d) is somewhat more acceptable because *bitch* also has a plural ending. Similarly, in (10a), the syntactic form suggests that *every* quantifies over *bitch*, thus clashing with the intended semantic interpretation in which *every* quantifies over *problem*. In singular predicate nominals such as those in (6a,c), however, the fact that the AN is a semantic modifier is not made so explicit: there is no plural inflection on *book*, and the determiner *a*, unlike the quantifier *every*, has little if any semantic content in this context. Therefore, these sentences are fully acceptable. In McCawley's terms, the ANs in (6a,c) do not blow their cover, whereas the ANs in (9a) and (10a) do.

If McCawley's explanation is correct, then the notion of prototype receives support. This is because it is the *expectation* for the syntactic head noun to also be the semantic head that renders (9a) and (10a) infelicitous. Because the word *bitch* 'difficult' violates this expectation, it can only occur in contexts in which the violation is not especially salient. In contrast, (9b) and (10b) are perfectly fine because the word *difficult* conforms to the expectation for adjectives to be semantic modifiers. Similarly, (9c) and (10c) are felicitous because the words *pair* and *part* conform to the expectation for syntactic head nouns also to be semantic heads. Thus, the case of ANs shows that the expectation for a particular syntactic category to be associated with a particular semantic function appears to limit the kinds of nonprototypical syntax-semantics mappings that can occur. If so, an account of these data requires the specification of prototypes (i.e., prototypical syntax-semantics mappings) in the grammar.

7.4.2 Left-subordinating *And*

Culicover and Jackendoff (1997) discuss a case of categorial mismatch similar to McCawley's case of ANs. They observe that in certain contexts, the English word *and* receives a subordinate rather than a coordinate interpretation. For example, on one reading, sentence (11a) receives approximately the same subordinate interpretation as sentence (11b). Culicover and Jackendoff refer to the interpretation of *and* in (11a) as "left-subordinating *and*," as distinct from the ordinary coordinating interpretation of *and* in (11c).

(11) a. Big Louie sees you with the loot and he puts a contract out on you. (left-subordinating *and*)
   b. If Big Louie sees you with the loot, he puts a contract out on you.
   c. Johnny stole the loot, and Big Louie went after him. (coordinating *and*)

Although left-subordinating *and* appears to resemble the subordinating conjunction *if* in meaning, Culicover and Jackendoff (1997, 199–200) argue that left-subordinating *and* is unlikely to be a subordinating conjunction in such contexts. First, it occurs clause-finally rather than clause-initially, as shown in (11a). Second, the purported subordinate clause cannot follow the main clause, as illustrated in (12a). In contrast, ordinary subordinating conjunctions such as *if* and *since* occur clause-initially and allow either order of clauses, as shown in (11b) and (12b).

(12) a. *Big Louie puts out a contract on you, he sees you with the loot and.
    b. Big Louie puts out a contract on you if he sees you with the loot.

Culicover and Jackendoff conclude that left-subordinating *and* is in fact a coordinating conjunction with respect to syntax, but receives a subordinating interpretation in certain contexts. Thus, left-subordinating *and* instantiates a case of categorial mismatch similar to that of McCawley's ANs.

Culicover and Jackendoff observe that left-subordinating *and* has distributional properties distinct from those of either subordinating conjunctions or coordinating *and*. Among the various properties they describe, many can be attributed to independent principles of syntax or semantics. For example, the ungrammaticality of (11a) can be attributed directly to syntactic factors. Because *and* is a coordinating conjunction, it lacks the syntactic properties characteristic of subordinating conjunctions. Similarly, Culicover and Jackendoff argue that many distributional properties of left-subordinating *and* can be attributed directly to its meaning. Similar to subordinate clauses with *if*, clauses with left-subordinating *and* can contain reflexive pronouns whose antecedents occur in the following clause, as shown in (13a–b) (1997, 201). This is not, however, true of syntactically similar coordinate clauses that receive a coordinate interpretation, as shown in (13c).

(13) a. Another picture of himself$_i$ appears in the newspaper, and Susan thinks John$_i$ will definitely go out and get a lawyer.
    b. If another picture of himself$_i$ appears in the newspaper, Susan thinks John$_i$ will definitely go out and get a lawyer.
    c. *Another picture of himself$_i$ has appeared in the newspaper, and Susan thinks John$_i$ is getting a bad reputation.

As Culicover and Jackendoff argue at length, these facts suggest that the possibility for binding a reflexive pronoun depends on semantic properties that are independent of syntactic structure.[11]

Culicover and Jackendoff's main goal is to argue for a modular analysis whereby syntactic and semantic principles operate independently. They do not mention any need for the idea of prototypes or prototypicality. However, they do in passing discuss some interesting data that are not readily explained in terms of independent syntactic or semantic principles. Consider the examples in (14a–b).

(14) a. Big Louie saw you with the loot and he put a contract out on you.
       (coordinate interpretation only)

b. If Big Louie saw you with the loot, he put a contract out on you. (subordinate interpretation)

Unlike in (11a), where a subordinate interpretation of the first clause is preferred, in (14a)—the past tense version of the same sentence—only a coordinate interpretation is possible. However, there is no obvious syntactic or semantic reason why this should be so. Simply changing the verb form to past tense should not change the constituent structure of the sentence. Likewise, there appears to be no semantic anomaly involved, as indicated by the fact that the past tense *if*-clause in (14b) is perfectly acceptable with a subordinate interpretation.

A similar problem is posed by the examples in (15a–d). The sentence in (15a) contains left-subordinating *and* and receives a subordinate interpretation similar to that of (15b). However, the subordinate interpretation disappears if we add a third clause, as in (15c). Since syntactically coordinate structures normally allow three conjuncts, there is no obvious syntactic reason why constructions with left-subordinating *and* should not also allow three conjuncts. Furthermore, there is no obvious semantic reason for this either. As shown in (15d), a three-clause sentence in which the first two clauses are subordinated to the third is perfectly acceptable when the first two clauses are *if*-clauses.

(15) a. You drink another can of beer and I'm leaving. (subordinate interpretation preferred)
b. If you drink another can of beer, I'm leaving. (subordinate interpretation)
c. You drink another can of beer, (and) Bill eats more pretzels, and I'm leaving. (coordinate interpretation only)
d. If you drink another can of beer, and if Bill eats more pretzels, I'm leaving. (subordinate interpretation)

As in the case of ANs, independent syntactic and semantic principles fail to predict the patterns of data described here. Although pragmatic factors and idiosyncratic conventions of the language may play some role in these cases, we can again argue that the lack of a subordinate interpretation for sentences such as (14a) and (15c) is at least partly the result of a deviation from the prototype. In sentences with left-subordinating *and*, a syntactically coordinate structure is used to express a subordinate relationship, thus violating the prototypical correspondence between coordinate structure and coordinate meaning. Although in many contexts, left-subordinating *and* is completely natural and fully grammatical, we have seen that some syntactically coordinate sentences with *and* cannot receive a subordinate interpretation. Why? Following McCawley's approach, I propose that such sentences call too much attention to the fact that left-subordinating *and* violates the prototypical syntax-semantics correspondence. As in the case of ANs, the *expectation* for certain prototypical form-meaning correspondences to apply contributes to the failure of left-subordinating *and* to occur in sentences such as (14a) and (15c).

In the case of (14a), past tense marking appears to preclude a subordinate interpretation. This fact is puzzling, since past tense marking is semantically compatible with a subordination relation, as shown in (14b). I propose that because a sequence of coordinated past tense clauses is normally used perfectively to express a sequence of events in a narrative, and because sequences of events are semantically coordinate, past tense marking strongly implicates a coordinate interpretation of (14a). Why, then, is present tense marking in (11a) fully compatible with left-subordinating *and*? Since present tense is rarely used to describe sequences of events but normally used to express subordination relations involving hypothetical situations, the violation of the prototype exhibited by left-subordinating *and* is less salient in present tense than in past. In other words, present tense is an expected form for expressing a subordinate meaning, whereas past tense is not.[12] Thus, present tense calls less attention to the mismatch involved with left-subordinating *and* than past tense does.

Interestingly, a subordinate interpretation is in fact compatible with past tense marking in certain discourse contexts in which a habitual or generic pattern of behavior is being described.[13]

(16) In those days, Big Louie saw you with his sister and he put a contract out on you. (subordinate interpretation preferred)

I conjecture that because the phrase *in those days* in (16) invokes a generic or habitual context and thus precludes a perfective interpretation involving a sequence of reported events, a conditional interpretation in which the first clause is subordinate to the second again becomes possible. Similar to what we find in the case of present tense, the mismatch involved with left-subordinating *and* is less salient in a generic past tense context as in (16) than in a nongeneric past tense context as in (14a), because the generic context does not implicate a coordinate meaning and so does not highlight the coordinate properties of the sentence.

We can understand the patterns in (15) in a similar manner. Sequences of three clauses normally express sequences of three events rather than subordination relations, whereas subordination relations are more typically expressed by two-clause sequences. Similar to what we find in (14), the violation of the prototype is less salient for two-clause sequences involving left-subordinating *and* than for three-clause sequences, contributing to the unacceptability of sentences like (15c) in a subordinate interpretation. This is because the two-clause structure in (15a) instantiates the expected form-meaning correspondence for expressing subordination (as much as is possible within the context of a syntactically coordinate sentence), thus downplaying the syntactically coordinate nature of left-subordinating *and*. In contrast, the three-clause structure in (15c) draws attention to the coordinate properties of the sentence, in effect excluding the possibility of a subordinating interpretation of *and*.

These two case studies of syntactic mimicry provide some evidence in favor of a modular approach to grammar in which independent principles apply to distinct levels of linguistic structure. Such an approach is helpful, for example, in explaining the binding facts for constructions with left-subordinating *and*, as well as the presence of semantically empty words in constructions with ANs. However, independently needed principles of syntax and semantics are apparently not enough to explain some of the distributional and interpretive properties of these items. I have proposed, following McCawley (1987), that these cases can best be handled with reference to prototypes. While relatively subtle violations of the prototype are allowed, more blatant violations are not.

7.5 Conclusions

In this chapter, I have reviewed some of the issues involved in evaluating prototype theories of syntactic categories and have argued in favor of a notion of prototype in grammar. Following McCawley (1982, 1987, 1988/1998), I contend that categories such as "coordinating conjunction," "noun," and NP are best understood not simply as syntactic feature sets, as in Chomskyan theories, but as prototypical correspondences of information from syntax, semantics, and possibly other independently defined domains of grammar. Like Newmeyer's (1998, 2000) approach, this approach can account for a wide range of distributional facts in terms of independent but interacting principles of syntax and semantics. I have shown that such principles are helpful for understanding otherwise puzzling phenomena, such as the occurrence of meaningless morphemes in some cases of categorial mismatch (e.g., McCawley 1982, 1987; Sadock 1990; Francis 1999). Like Croft's (1991) approach and similar cognitive and functionalist theories, however, this approach maintains the idea that there are privileged correspondences of categorial properties that people know and use in producing and understanding language.

The two cases of syntactic mimicry discussed in this chapter support the existence of prototypes in grammar. Armed with this notion of prototype, we can not only capture the generalization that some members of a category are "defective" or "marked" relative to other members, but also begin to understand why some manifestations of categorial mismatch are possible but not others. In short, prototypes constitute expectations that appear to constrain the manner and degree to which syntax and semantics can operate independently of each other, thus rendering more blatant deviations from the expected form-meaning correspondences ungrammatical. Ultimately, of course, syntactic categories are cognitive in nature, and additional psycholinguistic and neurolinguistic evidence will be needed to determine their structure. At the least, the linguistic evidence for prototypes discussed in this chapter provides a plausible hypothesis to test in future studies of syntactic categorization.

Notes

1. A reviewer points out that similar arguments regarding the inadequacy of a purely modular approach have been offered by proponents of Construction Grammar to support the existence of syntactic constructions (e.g., see Kay and Fillmore 1999). Although constructions do not necessarily have a prototype structure, they are similar to the prototypes discussed in this chapter in that they involve a conventional mapping between a form and a meaning.

2. Another possibility is that categorization decisions may be based on clusters of previously stored exemplars, as hypothesized in exemplar-based theories (e.g., see Dopkins and Gleason 1997). However, exemplar-based theories are beyond the scope of this chapter and will not be considered here.

3. But see Baker 2003 for an alternative proposal within generative grammar that seeks to define the lexical categories in a more substantial way.

4. Croft's theory predicts that crosslinguistically, nonprototypical correlations should result in either the same or more highly marked grammatical behavior than prototypical correlations, and that prototypical correlations should not be more marked than nonprototypical correlations (1991, 58–59).

5. Also similar to Croft's theory and unlike Ross's squishy category approach, categories in McCawley's view are structured around prototypes rather than along a linear continuum. This difference between prototypes and squishy categories will not concern us here.

6. As Bolinger (1980, 1–4) points out, the indefinite article *a* still specifies singular number in the context of predicate NPs, and it can have an individualizing function. However, it is semantically bleached in the sense that it does not serve its usual function of indicating indefinite reference. Salikoko Mufwene (pers. comm., September 2003) points out that the usage of *a* in predicate nominals may be related to its generic usage, as in *A lion kills its prey quickly*.

7. Other options are available for a classical theorist if additional assumptions are made regarding the interaction of syntax with other components of grammar. For example, Newmeyer (1998, 2000) advocates a classical approach to categories and assumes in addition a modular theory of grammar to accommodate prototype effects, as discussed in section 7.3.3 below.

8. See Mufwene 1984 for an explanation of the differences between those stative verbs that allow or require the progressive and those stative verbs that disallow the progressive. Mufwene argues that only a small, semantically defined subset of stative verbs is actually incompatible with the progressive. This is consistent with Newmeyer's position that a specific semantic explanation might account for these data. Mufwene's position is, however, also consistent with a prototype approach in which only a small subset of stative verbs is considered to be prototypical. Thus, if the verbal prototype were redefined in a manner consistent with Mufwene 1984, Newmeyer's argument would lose some of its force.

9. Many of the arguments and examples in this section also appear in section 7.3.2 of Francis 2002.

10. Aarts (1998) argues that ANs do not function as the syntactic head of the noun phrase but rather function as modifiers in both syntax and semantics. However, he agrees with McCawley

that these nouns display an unusual combination of syntactic and semantic properties, contributing to their defective distributions.

11. More generally, they propose in this and other work that conditions on binding are mostly stated at the level of conceptual structure (semantics) and that binding conditions only appear to be syntactic by virtue of the typical correlations between syntactic structure and conceptual structure (see Jackendoff 1992, 1997).

12. An anonymous reviewer points out that this generalization apparently does not hold when the coordinated clauses express states rather than events.

(i) She has two children and she's eligible for the tax credit. (coordinate reading only)

(ii) If she has two children, then she's eligible for the tax credit.

The reviewer suggests that perhaps (i) lacks a subordinate interpretation because there is a separate prototype for the coordination of simultaneously valid states, which specifies present tense. This seems to me to be a plausible interpretation of the facts.

13. I am grateful to Bob Knippen (pers. comm., 2002) for this interesting example.

References

Aarts, Bas. 1998. Binominal noun phrases in English. *Transactions of the Philological Society* 96, 117–58.

Armstrong, Sharon, Lila Gleitman, and Henry Gleitman. 1983. What some concepts might not be. *Cognition* 13, 263–308.

Baker, Mark C. 2003. *Lexical categories: Verbs, nouns and adjectives.* Cambridge: Cambridge University Press.

Bolinger, Dwight. 1980. *Syntactic diffusion and the definite article.* Bloomington: Indiana University Linguistics Club.

Bresnan, Joan. 1995. Category mismatches. In *Theoretical approaches to African linguistics*, ed. by Akinbiyi Akinlabi, 19–45. Trenton, NJ: Africa World Press.

Chomsky, Noam. 1965. *Aspects of the theory of syntax.* Cambridge, MA: MIT Press.

Chomsky, Noam. 1970. Remarks on nominalization. In *Readings in English transformational grammar*, ed. by Roderick Jacobs and Peter S. Rosenbaum, 184–221. Waltham, MA: Ginn.

Croft, William. 1991. *Syntactic categories and grammatical relations.* Chicago: University of Chicago Press.

Croft, William. 1995. Autonomy and functionalist linguistics. *Language* 71, 490–532.

Croft, William. 2001. *Radical Construction Grammar.* Oxford: Oxford University Press.

Culicover, Peter, and Ray Jackendoff. 1997. Syntactic coordination despite semantic subordination. *Linguistic Inquiry* 28, 195–217.

Dopkins, Stephen, and Theresa Gleason. 1997. Comparing exemplar and prototype models of categorization. *Canadian Journal of Experimental Psychology* 51, 212–30.

Francis, Elaine J. 1999. Variation within lexical categories. Doctoral dissertation, University of Chicago.

Francis, Elaine J. 2002. Form and function in syntactic theory: A reaction to Newmeyer. *Language Sciences* 24, 29–56.

Hampton, James A. 1995. Testing the prototype theory of concepts. *Journal of Memory and Language* 34, 686–708.

Hopper, Paul J., and Sandra A. Thompson. 1984. The discourse basis for lexical categories in Universal Grammar. *Language* 60, 715–17.

Hopper, Paul J., and Elizabeth Traugott. 1993. *Grammaticalization*. Cambridge: Cambridge University Press.

Jackendoff, Ray. 1992. Mme. Tussaud meets the binding theory. *Natural Language and Linguistic Theory* 10, 1–31.

Jackendoff, Ray. 1997. *The architecture of the language faculty*. Cambridge, MA: MIT Press.

Kay, Paul, and Charles J. Fillmore. 1999. Grammatical constructions and linguistic generalizations: The 'what's x doing y' construction. *Language* 75, 1–33.

Labov, William. 1973. The boundaries of words and their meanings. In *New ways of analyzing variation in English*, ed. by Charles-James N. Bailey and Roger Shuy, 340–73. Washington, DC: Georgetown University Press.

Lakoff, George. 1987a. Cognitive models and prototype theory. In *Concepts and conceptual development: Ecological and intellectual factors in categorization*, ed. by Ulric Neisser, 63–100. Cambridge: Cambridge University Press.

Lakoff, George. 1987b. *Women, fire, and dangerous things: What categories reveal about the mind*. Chicago: University of Chicago Press.

Malouf, Robert P. 2000. *Mixed categories in the hierarchical lexicon*. Stanford, CA: CSLI Publications.

McCawley, James D. 1982. The nonexistence of syntactic categories. In *Thirty million theories of grammar*, 176–203. Chicago: University of Chicago Press.

McCawley, James D. 1987. A case of syntactic mimicry. In *Functionalism in linguistics*, ed. by René Dirven and Vilém Frid, 459–70. Amsterdam: John Benjamins.

McCawley, James D. 1988. *The syntactic phenomena of English*. Chicago: University of Chicago Press. 2nd ed., 1998.

Mufwene, Salikoko S. 1984. *Stativity and the progressive*. Bloomington: Indiana University Linguistics Club.

Newmeyer, Frederick J. 1998. *Language form and language function*. Cambridge, MA: MIT Press.

Newmeyer, Frederick J. 2000. The discrete nature of syntactic categories: Against a prototype-based account. In *Syntax and semantics 32: The nature and function of syntactic categories*, ed. by Robert D. Borsley, 221–50. San Diego, CA: Academic Press.

Pinker, Steven, and Alan Prince. 1999. The nature of human concepts: Evidence from an unusual source. In *Language, logic, and concepts: Essays in memory of John Macnamara*, ed. by Ray Jackendoff and Paul Bloom, 221–61. Cambridge, MA: MIT Press.

Rosch, Eleanor. 1978. Principles of categorization. In *Cognition and categorization*, ed. by Eleanor Rosch and Barbara Lloyd, 27–48. Hillsdale, NJ: Lawrence Erlbaum.

Rosch, Eleanor, and Carolyn B. Mervis. 1975. Family resemblances: Studies in the internal representation of categories. *Cognitive Psychology* 7, 573–605.

Ross, John R. 1972. The category squish: Endstation Hauptwort. In *Proceedings of the Eighth Regional Meeting, Chicago Linguistic Society*, ed. by Paul M. Peranteau, Judith N. Levi, and Gloria C. Phares, 316–28. Chicago: University of Chicago, Chicago Linguistic Society.

Ross, John R. 1973a. A fake NP squish. In *New ways of analyzing variation in English*, ed. by Charles-James N. Bailey and Roger Shuy, 96–140. Washington, DC: Georgetown University Press.

Ross, John R. 1973b. Nouniness. In *Three dimensions of linguistic theory*, ed. by Osamu Fujimura, 137–258. Tokyo: TEC Company.

Ross, John R. 1995. Defective noun phrases. In *CLS 31*, ed. by Audra Dainora, Rachel Hemphill, Barbara Luka, Barbara Need, and Sheri Pargman, 398–440. Chicago: University of Chicago, Chicago Linguistic Society.

Sadock, Jerrold M. 1990. Parts of speech in Autolexical Syntax. In *Proceedings of the Sixteenth Annual Meeting of the Berkeley Linguistics Society*, ed. by Kira Hall, Jean-Pierre Koenig, Michael Meacham, Sondra Reinman, and Laurel A. Sutton, 269–81. Berkeley: University of California, Berkeley Linguistics Society.

Smith, Edward E., and Douglas L. Medin. 1981. *Categories and concepts.* Cambridge, MA: Harvard University Press.

Taylor, John R. 1995. *Linguistic categorization.* 2nd ed. Oxford: Clarendon Press.

Yuasa, Etsuyo. 1996. Categorial mismatches: An autolexical account of formal nouns in Japanese. In *CLS 32*, ed. by Lisa McNair, Kora Singer, Lise M. Dobrin, and Michelle M. Aucoin, 423–32. Chicago: University of Chicago, Chicago Linguistic Society.

Yuasa, Etsuyo. 1998. Subordinate clauses in Japanese. Doctoral dissertation, University of Chicago.

Yuasa, Etsuyo, and Elaine J. Francis. 2003. Categorial mismatch in a multi-modular theory of grammar. In *Mismatch: Form-function incongruity and the architecture of grammar*, ed. by Elaine J. Francis and Laura A. Michaelis, 179–227. Stanford, CA: CSLI Publications.

Chapter 8

Gerundive Modifiers in English and Korean Geoffrey J. Huck

8.1 Introduction

It has been standard in semantic analysis to recognize two classes of nominal modifiers (Kamp 1975; Siegel 1976; Dowty, Wall, and Peters 1981). *Absolute* modifiers (such as *nearby, carnivorous, naughty*) translate, in the terminology of formal semantics, as characteristic functions of sets of individual concepts, which means that a phrase like *nearby forest* receives an interpretation something like 'is an x such that x is a forest and x is nearby'. By contrast, *relative* modifiers (like *former, alleged, mere*) are generally translated as functions from properties of individual concepts to characteristic functions of sets of them. *Former girlfriend* is then, roughly, 'is an x such that x was a girlfriend at some prior point in time'.

Because of their intersective semantics, absolute modifiers are indistinguishable at the semantic level from relative or conjoined clauses. That is, *(be) a nearby forest*, *(be) a forest that's nearby*, *(be) a forest and nearby* would all have similar semantic translations. But relative modifiers do not have this property: to be *a former girlfriend* is not to be a girlfriend who is former, nor to be a girlfriend and to be former (whatever that might mean).

In this chapter, I will examine a class of gerundive modifiers in English and their analogues in Korean and show that they form a subtype of the general type of relative modifiers. There are peculiarities in the distributions of such modifiers, however, that suggest interesting differences in the way these modifiers are interpreted in the two languages.[1] In particular, these differences account for the fact that the acceptable English combination *reading glasses* has a generally unacceptable analogue in Korean (#*ilk-nun ankyeng*), while the generally unacceptable #*reading book* has an acceptable Korean counterpart (*ilk-nun chaek*).[2] Despite these differences, however,

---

An earlier version of this chapter was presented at the 1996 meeting of the Chicago Linguistic Society and appeared in the proceedings (Huck 1996). I would like to thank Younghee Na, Elaine Francis, and Salikoko Mufwene for helpful discussion of a number of issues raised in the present, revised version.

I will offer evidence that gerundives in the two languages should be assigned essentially the same semantic structure. Importantly, there is also good reason to assume that this structure is not isomorphic in either language with the syntactic structure with which it is paired.

8.2 Participial Modifiers

The English gerundive modifiers in which I am interested are formed by adding the suffix *-ing* to a bare verb stem. However, it is important to distinguish gerundive modifiers from participial modifiers, which are similarly formed. For example, the modifiers in the constructions in (1) are participial.

(1) singing detective   amusing incident   striking miners
     running water   going concern   rising temperature
     wilting flower   flowering plant   penetrating cold
     lingering illness   boring movie   falling rock
     insulting remark   daring move   dancing bear
     flaming sword   daunting problem   darkening skies

Participial modifiers have an intersective semantics (an *insulting* remark is a remark that is insulting) and behave morphosyntactically like deverbal adjectives; that is, they can be assigned a structure like [$_{NP}$[$_A$[$_V$ *insult*] *-ing*]] *remark*] (Jackendoff 1977; Abney 1987). Accordingly, participial modifiers can stack with ordinary adjectives (e.g., *a boring red hat*), and when a participial modifier is in construction with its head, phonological stress falls on that head: *amusing* INCIDENT, *lingering* ILLNESS, *boring* MOVIE. The facts concerning these modifiers appear for the most part to be straightforward, and I will not have much more to say about them.

8.3 Gerundive Modifiers as Purpose Clauses

Although gerundive modifiers look superficially like participial modifiers, they have different structural and semantic properties. We can in fact identify two subclasses of gerundive modifiers, which are distinguished by the type of relation the modifiers denote. Modifiers in the first subclass, as illustrated in (2), generally denote a three-place relation with respect to which the head noun serves an instrumental role: for example, a *drinking glass* is a glass intended to be used by someone for drinking something.

(2) drinking glass   potting soil   ironing board
     washing machine   cleaning fluid   marking pen
     polishing cloth   polishing wax   sketching pad
     frying pan   knitting needle   sealing wax
     rolling pin   measuring stick   lubricating jelly

Gerundive Modifiers in English and Korean 185

The second subclass, illustrated in (3), is like the first, but here the head noun fills a patient or locative role and the relation may be simply two-place: for example, a *waiting room* is a room that people can wait in.

(3)   drinking water   chewing tobacco   holding pen
    waiting room   swimming pool   breathing space
    sipping whiskey   spending money   saving plan
    warming hut   smoking area   chewing gum
    shooting gallery   eating apple   touring car

In either case, a fair paraphrase of these V-*ing* N combinations is 'N for V-*ing*', which suggests that the gerundive modifier is serving semantically as a kind of purpose clause (see Bach 1982; Jones 1991).[3] If so, then we might interpret such a modifier as a relative modifier that returns, for any common noun (CN), a subset of the set that the CN denotes, all of whose members are intended to be used for the purpose defined by the V-*ing*.

(4) drinking $\Rightarrow \lambda P \lambda x$ (((for' (drink' (..., x, ...))) ^P) (x))

(5) drinking glass $\Rightarrow \lambda x$ (((for' (drink' (..., x, ...))) ^glass') (x))

The notation in (5), following Bach (1982), is intended to suggest that a *drinking glass* is an entity x such that x is a glass that is intended to be used for the purpose indicated by a proposition involving x in the *drink*-relation to some other unspecified entities. (In the language of formal semantics, we would say that *for* denotes a function from sentence-type meanings to a function from CN-type meanings to CN-type meanings; in other words, it is a predicate that takes a proposition as an argument to restrict the meaning of a CN.) Moreover, although this is not indicated in (5), we will need to specify that x has to fill either an instrumental, a patient, or a locative role with respect to *drink*. This then should accord with the perception that *a drinking glass* is most naturally interpreted as a glass that someone can use for drinking something and *drinking water* as water that is intended to be drunk, although of course in each case other possibilities can be imagined.

In contrast with participial modifiers, gerundive modifiers behave morphosyntactically like deverbal nominals, so that we will want to assign them a structure something like [N[N[V *drink*] -*ing*] *glass*] (Jespersen 1937; Selkirk 1982; Abney 1987). Thus, they do not stack with adjectives (e.g., #*a drinking red glass*[4]), and when they are in construction with their head nouns, they take phonological stress: DRINKING glass, KNITTING needle, BATTING helmet.

In what follows, I will be concerned only with gerundive modifiers with this particular clustering of properties; note that there are other nonabsolute modifiers ending in -*ing* that do not appear to have these properties.[5]

(6) sinking feeling   turning point   teaching problems
    smacking sounds   cooking odors   walking tour
    asking price   growing pains   spending spree
    looking glass   purchasing power   foraging behavior
    acting dean   moving violation   dying words

8.4 Distributional Issues

A purpose clause analysis of prenominal gerundive modifiers in English receives support from the fact that such modifiers share semantic restrictions with their counterparts in purpose constructions. For example, prenominal gerundive modifiers, like the predicates of postnominal gerundive *for*-constructions, cannot comfortably denote achievements or accomplishments—witness *painting brush*, #*painting picture*, #*picture for painting*, *writing pen*, #*writing novel*, #*novel for writing*, *baking dish*, #*baking bread*, #*bread for baking*. And in general, where a *for*-construction paraphrase is acceptable, so is the corresponding prenominal gerundive modifier. However, there are cases where a moderately acceptable postnominal gerundive *for*-construction does not seem to have an acceptable prenominal gerundive counterpart. For example, the postnominal constructions in (7) seem fairly acceptable, although it also appears that when stripped of their adjectival and adverbial modifiers, as in (8), they become more difficult to contextualize.

(7) car for everyday driving
    good road for long-distance traveling
    clothes just for wearing around the house
    food for eating with friends
    bell for ringing during the ceremony
    chair for sitting and watching TV
    book for reading on the train
    (e.g., Do you have any clothes just for wearing around the house?)

(8) ?car for driving
    ?road for traveling
    ?clothes for wearing
    ?food for eating
    ?bell for ringing
    ?chair for sitting
    ?book for reading
      (e.g., ?Do you have any clothes for wearing?)

But there is an obvious difference between the postnominal gerundive constructions in (7) and their prenominal counterparts in (9), which are clearly odd in unmarked contexts.

(9) #driving car
#traveling road
#wearing clothes
#eating food
#ringing bell
#sitting chair
#reading book
   (e.g., #Do you have any wearing clothes?)

How is the oddity of the constructions in (9) to be explained? On the one hand, the source of the deviance cannot be purely structural, since there are contexts in which the constructions seem relatively acceptable.

(10) These are my MODELING clothes and those are my WEARING clothes.
This is my PAINTING fruit and that is my EATING fruit.

On the other hand, where the constructions in (9) are unacceptable, that unacceptability cannot be a consequence of universal pragmatic or semantic conditions either, since the analogous constructions in Korean are generally acceptable in similar contexts.

(11) wuncenha-nun cha 'lit., driving car'
ka-nun kil 'lit., traveling road'
ip-nun os 'lit., wearing clothes'
mok-nun umsik 'lit., eating food'
chi-nun cong 'lit., ringing bell'
an-nun uica 'lit., sitting chair'
ilk-nun chaek 'lit., reading book'
   (e.g., Ip-nun os-i iss-eyo? 'lit., Do you have any wearing clothes?')

Moreover, there are generally *unacceptable* constructions in Korean of this sort that have *acceptable* English analogues; compare (12) and (13).

(12) #ilk-nun ankyeng 'reading glasses'
#ilk-nun tungpwul 'reading lamp'
#yoliha-nun yangnyem 'cooking spice'
#talli-nun sin 'running shoes'
#sanyangha-nun heka 'hunting permit'
#ket-nun cipangi 'walking stick'

#koki-cap-nun moca 'fishing cap'
#wuncenha-nun cangkap 'driving gloves'
  (e.g., #Wuncenha-nun cangkap iss-eyo? 'Do you have any driving gloves?')

(13) reading glasses   reading lamp   cooking spice
     running shoes   hunting permit   walking stick
     fishing cap   driving gloves
     (e.g., Do you have any driving gloves?)

8.5 Gerundive Modifiers and Contrastive Focus

It was claimed above that English gerundive modifiers appear in noun-noun constructions. Selkirk (1984) argues that in noun-noun constructions in English like *apron string*, *death penalty*, and *house keeper*, the first noun is marked as a focus and therefore receives stress.

(14) [$_N$ N   N]
         [+Focus]

   (e.g., APRON string, DEATH penalty, WAGE freeze, SCHOOL teacher, HOUSE keeper, CHICKEN thief)

We will assume that gerundive modifiers in construction with their head nouns are similarly marked in English. Moreover, we will assume that the focus involved is specifically *contrastive* focus.

(15) *Contrastive focus*
   If X' is the semantic representation of a construction X and is identical to Y', the semantic representation of a distinct construction Y to which the speaker of X intends to draw attention for the purpose of comparison, except that, where X' contains C', Y' contains D' (C' not identical to D'), then C is a contrastive focus of X with respect to Y. (adapted from Huck and Na 1990, 1992)

According to (15), a syntactic element C is a contrastive focus if it is embedded in a construction whose interpretation is identical to that of another construction the speaker wants to draw attention to except at the point of the interpretation of C. What is important for our purposes is that contrastive focus is context-sensitive and that, with certain exceptions that are essentially irrelevant to our present concerns, a focused constituent receives an intonational accent (i.e., is stressed).

  Participial modifiers, such as those in (1), can of course be contrastively focused in appropriate contexts (*No, I said it was a DANCING bear, not a FANCY bear*). What distinguishes gerundive modifiers in English, like other nominal modifiers, is that they are inevitably loci of contrast: they distinguish a particular subset of the set of things denoted by the head in contrast with other subsets—thus, a *knitting* needle is set off against a *darning* needle or *sewing* needle, *chewing* tobacco is set off against *smoking* tobacco, and so on. With English gerundive modifiers, the force of contrast cannot be eliminated.[6]

If this is so, then this suggests why the phrases in (9) are generally unacceptable. For example, there is no obvious class of food that food for eating contrasts with. In the central cases, it is in fact part of the definition of food that it is for eating. Unusual contexts can nevertheless be imagined in which phrases like those in (10) are more or less acceptable.

The Korean gerundive modifiers in (11) and (12) are not inherently loci of contrast and in this respect resemble English infinitival relatives (see note 4). However, the interpretive principles that distinguish the constructions in (11) from those in (12) in Korean do not have robust counterparts in English.

8.6 The Syntax and Semantics of the Korean Gerundive Modifier

Unlike English noun phrases, Korean noun phrases are strictly right-headed; accordingly, modifiers in the Korean phrase, including clausal modifiers, appear uniformly to its left. Where the modifier of a nominal is headed by a predicative element (either a verb or an adjective), it is so marked by a special suffix, commonly *-nun*. This suffix does not distinguish between modifiers that are syntactically clausal, such as relative clauses, and other modifiers that are less obviously so, such as adjectives and gerundives.[7] Because verbal arguments can generally be deleted up to recoverability, gerundive modifiers in Korean, as in (16), are therefore sometimes difficult to distinguish from ordinary relatives, as in (17).

(16) [$_N$[$_M$[$_V$ masi]-nun] mwul]
    drink-MOD water
    'water for drinking, drinking water'

(17) [$_{NP}$[$_{S'}$ e$_i$ e$_j$ masi-koiss-nun] mwul$_j$]
    drink-PROG-MOD water
    'lit., water that *pro* is drinking'

However, gerundive modifiers, as in (18), unlike ordinary relatives, as in (20b), but like ordinary adjectives, as in (19), follow a genitive specifier.

(18) ku-uy masi-nun mwul
    his   drink-MOD water
    'his drinking water'

(19) ku-uy yeppu-n   yetongsaeng
     his   pretty-MOD sister
     'his pretty sister'

(20) a. *ku-uy masi-koiss-nun   mwul
        his   drink-PROG-MOD water
        'his water that he is drinking'
     b. masi-koiss-nun ku-uy mwul
        'his water that he is drinking'

One way to account for this would be to assume that gerundive modifiers in Korean, as in English, do not have a clausal structure at the level of surface syntax, where word order is significant. However, it is essential that at some level the argument structure of the verbal element of a gerundive modifier in Korean be explicitly recoverable. For example, to explain the contrast in acceptability between (21a) and (21b), we will want to make reference to the thematic roles that *cha* 'car' and *cangkap* 'gloves' respectively fill in the argument structure of the predicate *wuncenha-* 'drive'.

(21) a. wuncenha-nun cha
         'driving car'
     b. #wuncenha-nun cangkap
         'driving gloves'

That is, we will have to say that the semantic structure of Korean gerundive modifiers is in all relevant respects identical to that of English gerundive modifiers—that the semantic translations of *drinking water* and *masi-nun mwul* would be the same, both denoting the same entity x such that x is water that is intended to be used for the purpose indicated by a proposition involving x in the *drink*-relation to some other unspecified entities. Following the notation in (5), this translation would look like (22).

(22) $\lambda x\ (((for'\ (drink'\ (PRO,\ x)))\ ^\wedge water')\ (x))$

8.7 The Thematic Well-formedness Condition

Na (1991) distinguishes two types of relative clauses in Korean: those that contain a gap coindexed with the clause head and those that do not. She then argues in support of the following restriction on the semantic interpretation of gap-type relatives:

(23) *Thematic Well-formedness Condition (TWC)*
     A (gap-type) relative clause construction in Korean is semantically well formed only if the gap contained in the clause that is coindexed with the nominal head of the relative is assigned a thematic role within the thematic domain of the clause predicate.

Na assumes (following Jackendoff 1972, 1983, 1987; Culicover and Wilkins 1984, 1986; Wilkins 1988; Dowty 1988; Pinker 1989) that the *thematic domain* of a predicate consists of the obligatory and optional thematic roles associated with that predicate. Syntactically, elements of the thematic domain are realized as arguments of the predicate they are associated with, and obligatory roles are realized as subcategorized arguments. Other modifiers of the predicate appear as adjuncts to it.[8]

The TWC accounts for the difference between (24a) and (24b).

(24) a. Swuni-ka e_i wuncenha-koiss-nun cha_i
          Swuni-NOM drive-PROG-MOD   car
          'car that Swuni is driving'
     b. #Swuni-ka $e_{i/j}$ wuncenha-koiss-nun $cangkap_i$
          Swuni-NOM drive-PROG-MOD   gloves
          'lit., gloves such that Swuni is driving'

That is, (24a) satisfies the TWC because the conceptual structure of the predicate *wuncenha-* 'drive' contains at least two argument positions, one for an agent and one for a patient. In (24a), the agent role is most naturally interpreted as being filled by *Swuni* and the patient role by the empty element coindexed with *cha*; this makes sense because a person and a car are just the right kinds of entities to respectively drive and be driven. But only in the most bizarre of contexts can gloves be driven—thus the strangeness of (24b) if it is interpreted, like (24a), as containing a gap in the patient role coindexed with *cangkap*. Its English translation suggests that the relative clause of (24b) might perhaps be intended to refer to gloves in an instrumental role ('the gloves Swuni is driving with'); however, since the predicate *wuncenha-* does not have an instrumental argument associated with it,[9] the TWC correctly rules out this possibility in Korean.

We now see that if the TWC extends to Korean gerundive modifiers, it would explain the difference in acceptability between (21a) and (21b), indeed the differences in acceptability between all of the phrases in (11) and those in (12). Moreover, this approach is fully consistent with the intuition that the gerundive construction (21b), #*wuncenha-nun cangkap*, must be odd for the same reason that the relative clause construction (24b), #*wuncenha-koiss-nun cangkap*, is: in neither case is it plausible to assume a gap at the semantic level coindexed with the nominal head that fills one of the obligatory or optional argument roles associated with the predicate *wuncenha*.

It should be pointed out that there is an alternative in Korean to (21b) that falls outside the scope of the TWC. Example (25) is quite acceptable, although the *-yong* construction itself is restricted and not fully productive.

(25) $[_N[_N[_N$ wuncen$]$ $[_N$ -yong$]]$ cangkap$]$
              drive   usage   gloves
     'driving gloves'

Unlike the Korean gerundive constructions we have been considering, (25) has a noun-noun structure in surface syntax and behaves like the other noun-noun structures mentioned in section 8.5. In particular, the first element is contrastively focused and the construction as a whole has a contrastive interpretation. Thus, it might be concluded that the Korean *-yong* construction is actually more similar to the English gerundive modifier and that the Korean *-nun* construction shares more features with the English postnominal clause, as the distributions in (7), (9), and (11) suggest. But the parallels are not exact. Because the *-yong* construction is restricted, there are numerous English gerundive modifiers that have no *-yong* counterpart and can only be translated into Korean in the *-nun* form. Moreover, if English postnominal purpose clauses are subject to the TWC, its effects on them are surely much weaker than on Korean gerundives. This does not mean, however, that the TWC cannot have a universal basis, at least as regards relative clauses. For example, consider the contrasts in (26).[10]

(26) driving gloves / (#?)gloves I drive with / #gloves I drive
running shoes / (#?)shoes I run with / #shoes I run
reading glasses / (#?)glasses I read with / #glasses I read

The second alternative in each of these examples is certainly not wholly unacceptable, but still seems somewhat less preferable than the first in ordinary contexts where special gloves, shoes, and glasses are not perceived as necessarily *required* for driving, running, and reading, respectively. (Similarly, the meaning of a phrase like *gardening necklace* = 'necklace one wears while gardening' is more easily apprehended than that of *(#?)necklace she gardens with*.) The crucial difference between English and Korean in this respect is that Korean does not strand its postpositions or pied-pipe them with *wh*-expressions. So, the peculiarity of Korean #*ilk-nun ankyeng*, parsed as a relative clause construction, is much like that of English #*the glasses I read*, where the head noun wants to be interpreted as the patient of the clause predicate. In English, such an interpretation is forestalled when a preposition is left behind: *(#?)the glasses I read with* (or *(#?)the glasses with which I read*); but this strategy is not available in Korean.

There are several accounts in the literature that attempt to explain why preposition stranding is found as rarely as it is among the world's languages (see, e.g., Koster 1978; Hornstein and Weinberg 1981; Kayne 1981; Aoun et al. 1987). These accounts typically argue that there is a universal filter prohibiting extraction from prepositional phrases, but also that English and the handful of other languages that permit preposition stranding have available a rule that reanalyzes the structure of prepositional phrases in such a way that the filter can be circumvented in certain circumstances. Extended to Korean, which would be assumed not to permit reanalysis, such an approach might appear to account not only for the fact that postpositions do

Gerundive Modifiers in English and Korean   193

not strand in that language, but also for the fact that nonarguments cannot be relativized, as the TWC suggests.

However, it is not simply because nonarguments are found in construction with postpositions in Korean that they cannot be relativized: *any* argument can potentially be relativized, whether or not it is in construction with a postposition.[11] Put another way, in Korean it is the verb's marking properties that are important, while in English it is the preposition's. No account that depends exclusively on the particular marking properties of prepositions or postpositions would therefore appear sufficient to explain the distributions described by the TWC.

8.8 Discussion

We have seen with respect to Korean relative clause constructions like #*ilk-nun ankyeng* 'reading glasses' that there is strong motivation to associate a gap coindexed with the nominal head of the construction with some obligatory internal argument role, if this can be done in a way that is semantically plausible. Only when the relevant obligatory roles are discharged by being associated with some lexical nominal is a gap coindexed with the clause head free to be associated with an optional role. Exactly the same restriction applies in gerundive modifier constructions, as the examples in (27)–(29) illustrate.

(27) a. #kuli-nun   yenphil
        draw-MOD pencil
        'drawing pencil'
     b. kulim-kuli-nun   yenphil
        picture-draw-MOD pencil
        'picture-drawing pencil'

(28) a. #kkak-nun khal
        'paring knife'
     b. sakwa-kkak-nun khal
        'apple-paring knife'

(29) a. #kkuli-nun nampi
        'boiling pot'
     b. kwuk-kkuli-nun nampi
        'soup-boiling pot'

The situation is further complicated by the fact that Korean permits gapless relative clauses, where the head noun of the construction and the clause are in an "aboutness" relation.[12]

(30) nwun-i   kalsayki-n namca
     eyes-NOM brown-MOD man
     'man/men whose eyes are brown' (lit., 'man/men such that eyes are brown')

The phrase in (30) makes sense when it can be used to designate a particular individual or set of individuals. That is, an important aspect of the meaning of (30), interpreted as a restrictive relative clause construction, is that the relative clause distinguishes a subset of the set denoted by the clause head. A child who learns Korean must come to know that relative clauses, whether gapped like (24a), or gapless like (30), can have exactly this function. But the relative clause in (30) can distinguish a subset of the set denoted by the head only if the noun in the clause is assumed to stand semantically in a particular relationship to the head noun. And it can be shown that the noun in the relative clause that bears that relationship must serve to fill an argument position in the thematic domain of the clause predicate—which is to say that the correct formulation of the TWC will involve reference not just to gaps, but to nominals in gapless constructions as well (see Na and Huck 1993).

Why should the TWC apply in Korean but not in English? If the phrase *driving gloves* is not semantically restricted in English, why should #*wuncenhanun cagkap* be so in Korean? Consider the ways in which the two languages construct relations between nominals and propositions about them: because the syntax of Korean permits phonetically null arguments in most positions,[13] absent something like the TWC a phrase like (30) would be potentially many ways ambiguous—it could refer to the man whose father's (or sister's or mother's or brother's) eyes are brown, or to the man for whom all eyes appear or were made to appear brown, or to the man next to or above or below whom the eyes are brown, and so on. While one might simply assume that the restriction is given, it may also be productive to think of the TWC as a component of a strategy for reducing what would otherwise be pernicious ambiguity in the syntax-semantics mapping in Korean, the kind of strategy that we would expect to be highly valued in language design. It is furthermore not implausible a priori that secondary strategies of this sort, which allow for more rapid processing over the full domain of sentences, will become entrenched in language learning, so long as they are not in conflict with the more central, compositional rules of semantic interpretation.[14] By contrast, in English, the TWC would be rendered otiose by whatever separate, ambiguity-reducing mechanism allows for preposition stranding; in such circumstances, we would expect any English version of the TWC to be significantly weakened.

Na (1991) compares the TWC with Keenan and Comrie's (1977) proposal that there is a universal "accessibility hierarchy" of grammatical relations and that each language chooses a point on that hierarchy below which relativization is not possible. Na shows that any such hierarchy cannot account for the facts in Korean, since what is relevant in that language is the argument status of the nominal to be relativized and not the grammatical relation it bears.[15] Nevertheless, Keenan and Comrie's conclusion that what can be relativized in a language appears to be determined by recognition strategies designed to fit the grammar of that language is consistent with the position taken here.

I should emphasize that it is not my purpose to choose between a formal and a functional approach to the TWC; insofar as they are committed to explaining approximately the same range of facts, it seems reasonable to expect that both approaches will converge on a mutually useful set of results. However, it is perhaps worth pointing out that it is a consequence of the analysis undertaken above that gerundive modifiers cannot be assigned structurally analogous representations at the surface syntactic and semantic levels; the evidence we have seen suggests that these modifiers are nonclausal at the former level but propositional at the latter. More specifically, it has been demonstrated that a gerundive modifier is interpreted semantically as containing a variable that is coindexed with the nominal head that it modifies and that language-particular restrictions on this relationship apply. This, and the fact that a gerundive modifier in English, but not Korean, is interpreted as a contrastive focus, is crucial to an account of the behavior of these constructions in these languages.

Finally, although gerundive modifiers and relative clauses in Korean (as in English) must be assigned different surface syntactic structures, we have seen that they manifest essentially the same propositional structure at the level of semantic representation, where they are equally subject to the TWC. These facts raise some interesting questions about the nature of the syntax-semantics interface that I will not address beyond observing that any theory will have to come to grips with them. As Elaine Francis has pointed out to me, expressing the appropriate restrictions should be a fairly straightforward matter in multimodular theories like Sadock's (1991) Autolexical Syntax or Jackendoff's (1987, 1997) Representational Modularity, since in these and similar theories thematic roles are independently computed at the semantic level and constituents there need not match constituents at the syntactic level. However, I would not want to underestimate the ability of very different frameworks to accommodate the results in some conceptually parallel fashion.

Notes

1. There has been previous work (see especially Lapointe and Nielson 1994; Yoon 1996) that has pointed to distinct areas of contrast between English and Korean nominal gerund phrases. For example, Yoon (1996) observes that the deverbal element in a phrasal nominalization in English behaves morphologically as a verb, while the deverbal element in Korean behaves morphologically as a noun. Since the phrasal facts are not relevant to an analysis of the gerundive modifiers I'm interested in, I will ignore these differences in what follows.

2. In this chapter, "#" indicates anomaly relative to unmarked contexts or interpretations.

3. Bach (1982) and Jones (1991) are both primarily concerned with problems of control in English infinitival adjuncts, as in *Mary brought John along to talk to (her)*. However, Jones does attempt to subsume at least some constructions involving what are usually called "infinitival relatives," as in *That's an easy pan to fry eggs in*, under his account of purpose clauses. There are obvious similarities between postnominal gerundive constructions, as in *water for drinking*, and infinitival relative constructions, as in *water to drink*—as well as obvious differences: for example, all of the phrases in (8) in the text distinctly improve if the preposition + gerundive forms are replaced by infinitival relatives (*food to eat*, *chair to sit in*, etc.). The difference between gerundive constructions like *?bell for ringing* and infinitival constructions like *bell to ring* appears to be that an infinitival clause is taken to indicate the specific use to which the referent of the head noun is to be put by the implicit subject of the predicate, whereas the gerundive phrase restricts the set of objects denoted by the head noun to the subset whose members are designed or intended to be used for the purpose designated by that phrase. Compare *Do you have a clean shirt to wear/??for wearing to the party tonight?* with *Do you have any solvent for removing/??to remove marine enamel from wood surfaces?* While one might want to try to capture this distinction as a concomitant of control in a framework like Jones's, I will not pursue this issue here. I should point out, however, that in the case of the Korean gerundive modifiers I will consider below, this semantic distinction is not made via separate syntactic structures; that is, in Korean there is a single syntactic structure that can potentially serve either interpretation.

4. It is of course possible to interpret *drinking* as a participial modifier in this construction, which would then have the strange interpretation of a red glass that is drinking. Note that the examples in (9) in the text would be similarly odd under a participial interpretation. As Salikoko Mufwene has pointed out to me, the phrase *a red drinking glass* is perfectly acceptable, but that is an ordinary case of an adjective modifying a noun-noun nominal.

5. It might be assumed that the existence of phrases like those in (6) alongside the gerundive phrases we are interested in indicates that there is no regularity to be captured (see Gleitman and Gleitman 1970 and Clark 1992, among others, for arguments that there is no denumerable set of rules for interpreting noun-noun compounds). However, whether or not the phrases in (6) are idioms or there exist distinct rules for producing them, it is clear that gerundive phrases are produced by productive rule and that one can coin new instances ad libitum.

6. As Elaine Francis has pointed out to me, compounds like *ironing board* are susceptible to conventionalization, so that explicit contrast with other kinds of boards may not have to be intended, just as such contrast would not be assumed if the word denoting an ironing board were, say, *blick*. This phenomenon is not restricted to gerundives, but also is seen in Selkirk's noun-noun compounds like *death penalty* and *house keeper*, as well as in adjective-noun compounds like *blackboard* and *greenhouse*. It is important to note, however, that in all these cases, the first element of the compound is still stressed as if it were marked as a contrastive focus at the morphophonological level, even if in the semantics a conventionalized meaning overrides what would otherwise be arrived at compositionally. This is typical of conventionalization: an idiom like *kick the bucket*, for example, receives a standard analysis at the lower levels but in the semantics an overriding conventionalized interpretation applies.

7. I have been following standard practice in calling modifiers like *masinun* in the phrase *masinun mwul* (with the meaning 'water for drinking'; see (16)) gerundives. What is crucial here is that Korean gerundives, like English gerundives, are syntactically nonfinite, nonclausal dever-

bals. The nominalizations that Korean linguists generally call "gerunds" (see, e.g., Yoon 1996) are undoubtedly nominals, but whether Korean gerundive modifiers are syntactically nominals like English gerundive modifiers, I will leave open. As Salikoko Mufwene has pointed out to me, there is something less than fully satisfactory about calling *masinun* in (16) a gerundive modifier on a parallel with English gerundive modifiers like *drinking* in the phrase *drinking glass*, since the two constructions do not behave in all relevant respects the same (as we clearly see in this chapter), nor is there any reason to expect, prima facie, that they should. However, I will continue to refer to the constructions in both languages as "gerundives" for three reasons: first, the term is relatively well established in both traditions; second, the constructions are usually employed to translate one from the other in the two languages; and third, they share crucial properties that allow for a uniform analysis of the problem under discussion.

8. Na (1991, 30) suggests the following methodological principle to distinguish obligatory arguments from optional arguments: "the subcategorization frame of a predicate will be established on the basis of what arguments are necessary for a sentence with that predicate to be well-formed in discourse-initial position." As regards optional arguments, these are to be determined by inferential possibility; for example, although by the "discourse-initial" test *kyelho-nha* 'marry' subcategorizes only for a theme argument, the fact that (ii) can be inferred from (i) suggests that the predicate also takes an argument associated with the role of the person the theme argument's referent marries.

(i) Jane-i onul kyelhonhayssta.
    Jane today got.married
    'Jane got married today.'

(ii) Kulemulo, Jane-un namphyen-ul etessta.
     therefore Jane-TOP husband acquired
     'Therefore, Jane acquired a husband.'

The TWC thus correctly predicts the acceptability of (iii).

(iii) [Sally-ka kyelhonhan] namca
      Sally-NOM married man
      'the man Sally married'

Korean allows empty elements in both obligatory and optional positions, but, logically, obligatory arguments must be discharged (i.e., assigned a reference in accordance with the appropriate semantic rules) before optional arguments. Where there is an explicit lexical element like a nominal head of a relative clause or a gerundive modifier and more than one gap, it will be coindexed with one that is assigned an obligatory role if one is free. For example, in (iv), *cha* 'car' can be coindexed only with the gap filling the patient role of *wuncenha-koiss-nun* 'is driving', since that is the only open obligatory role that can be filled by an inanimate object like a car.

(iv) e_i e_j wuncenha-koiss-nun cha$_j$
     drive-PROG-MOD car
     'lit., car that *pro* is driving'

Although the predicate *wuncenha-* may take an optional argument filling the role of location, *cha* cannot be coindexed with a gap associated with that role.

(v) #e_i e_j e_k wuncenha-koiss-nun cha$_k$
    drive-PROG-MOD car
    'lit., car where *pro* is driving *pro*'

However, if the obligatory roles have been discharged by explicit lexical items, the head is free to be coindexed with a gap associated with an optional argument.

(vi) Swuni-ka   cha-lul   e$_i$ wuncenha-koiss-nun   tosi$_i$
      Swuni-NOM car-ACC   drive-PROG-MOD   city
      'city that Swuni is driving her car in'

9. That is, from the fact that Swuni is driving, it cannot be inferred that Swuni is driving *with something* (like gloves). In contrast, there are other action verbs, such as *draw*, *peel*, and *boil* (see below in the text), that seem to take optional instrumental arguments.

10. The construction *X that Y Zs in* appears unrelated; for example, there is no #*appearing wig* with the meaning of *wig that he appears in*. The same is true of comitative *with*: there is no #*arriving woman* with the meaning of *woman that he arrives with*.

11. When an argument that would normally be associated with a nominal in construction with a postposition is relativized, the postposition is deleted along with the nominal (see, e.g., examples (iiia) and (iiib) of note 15).

12. This relation can be made precise: see Na and Huck 1993.

13. In particular, the distribution of these elements in Korean does not appear to be uniformly constrained by independent structural restrictions like the Generalized Control Rule (Huang 1982, 1984), the Empty Category Principle (Chomsky 1981), or Subjacency (Chomsky 1986). For example, phrases like (i) and (ii) are generally acceptable, given the appropriate context.

(i) [[e$_i$ e$_j$ ip-koiss-nun]   os-i$_j$ metci-n]   namca$_i$
         wear-PROG-MOD clothes-NOM be.stylish-MOD man
     'man such that the clothes that he is wearing are stylish'

(ii) [[e$_i$ e$_j$ a-nun]   saramtul-i$_j$ motwu hwakatuli-n]   namca$_i$
         know-MOD people-NOM all   be.painters-MOD man
     'man such that everyone he knows is a painter' or 'man such that everyone who knows him is a painter'

For extensive discussion, see Na 1986 and Na and Huck 1993.

14. There have been suggestions that positive evidence can be sufficient to establish such strategies. For example, if a paraphrase is generally employed by adult speakers where a core construction would otherwise be expected, the language learner may be able to infer the relevant constraint from that fact alone. See Pinker 1984 and Goldberg 1995 for discussion. Independently of the success of such arguments in particular cases, we would still like to know what inherent properties of the system as a whole might give rise to or guarantee these effects.

15. Keenan and Comrie (1977) propose a set of three "hierarchy constraints." As applied to relativization, they are (1) a language must be able to relativize subjects; (2) any relative-clause-forming strategy must apply to a continuous segment of the accessibility hierarchy; and (3) strategies that apply at one point of the accessibility hierarchy may in principle cease to apply at any lower point. But while subjects and direct objects do consistently relativize in Korean (ignoring constructions with so-called free heads), Na (1991) shows that whether other grammatical relations relativize cannot be predicted simply by reference to the position in the hierarchy of the target nominal. For example, not all indirect objects relativize equally successfully.

(i) a. Sinay-ka   ku salam-eykey phyenci-lul ssessta.
       Sinay-NOM DET person-DAT letter-ACC wrote
       'Sinay wrote a letter to the person.'
    b. #Sinay-ka   phyenci-lul ssu-n   salam
       Sinay-NOM letter-ACC wrote-MOD person
       'the person Sinay wrote a letter to'
(ii) a. Sinay-ka   ku salam-eykey ton-ul   cwuessta.
        Sinay-NOM DET person-DAT money-ACC gave
        'Sinay gave money to the person.'
     b. Sinay-ka   ton-ul   cu-n   salam
        Sinay-NOM money-ACC gave-MOD person
        'the person Sinay gave money to'

Similarly, no uniformity is observed with respect to the relativizability of what Keenan and Comrie (1977) call "major oblique NPs."

(iii) a. Sinay-ka   ku tosi-ey tochakhassta.
         Sinay-NOM DET city-LOC arrived
         'Sinay arrived in that city.'
      b. Sinay-ka   tochakha-n tosi
         Sinay-NOM arrived-MOD city
         'the city Sinay arrived in'
(iv) a. Sinay-ka   ce kenmwul-ccok-ulo   kelessta.
        Sinay-NOM DET building-direction-LOC walked
        'Sinay walked in the direction of that building.'
     b. #Sinay-ka   kel-un   kenmwul
        Sinay-NOM walked-MOD building
        'the building Sinay walked toward'

All these facts, however, are consistent with the TWC.

References

Abney, Stephen. 1987. The English noun phrase in its sentential aspect. Doctoral dissertation, MIT.

Aoun, Joseph, Norbert Hornstein, David Lightfoot, and Amy Weinberg. 1987. Two types of locality. *Linguistic Inquiry* 18, 537–77.

Bach, Emmon. 1982. Purpose clauses and control. In *The nature of syntactic representation*, ed. by Pauline Jacobson and Geoffrey K. Pullum, 35–57. Dordrecht: Reidel.

Chomsky, Noam. 1981. *Lectures on government and binding*. Dordrecht: Foris.

Chomsky, Noam. 1986. *Barriers*. Cambridge, MA: MIT Press.

Clark, Herbert H. 1992. *Arenas of language use*. Chicago: University of Chicago Press; Stanford, CA: CSLI Publications.

Culicover, Peter, and Wendy Wilkins. 1984. *Locality in linguistic theory*. New York: Academic Press.

Culicover, Peter, and Wendy Wilkins. 1986. Control, PRO, and the Projection Principle. *Language* 62, 120–53.

Dowty, David R. 1988. On the semantic content of the notion of "thematic role." In *Properties, types, and meaning*, ed. by Gennaro Chierchia, Barbara H. Partee, and Ralph Turner, 2:69–129. Dordrecht: Kluwer.

Dowty, David R., Robert E. Wall, and Stanley Peters. 1981. *Introduction to Montague semantics*. Dordrecht: Reidel.

Gleitman, Lila, and Henry Gleitman. 1970. *Phrase and paraphrase*. New York: Norton.

Goldberg, Adele E. 1995. *Constructions: A Construction Grammar approach to argument structure*. Chicago: University of Chicago Press.

Hornstein, Norbert, and Amy Weinberg. 1981. Case theory and preposition stranding. *Linguistic Inquiry* 12, 55–91.

Huang, C.-T. James. 1982. Logical relations in Chinese and the theory of grammar. Doctoral dissertation, MIT.

Huang, C.-T. James. 1984. On the distribution and reference of empty pronouns. *Linguistic Inquiry* 15, 531–74.

Huck, Geoffrey J. 1996. Gerundive modifiers in English and Korean. In *CLS 32*. Vol. 1, *Papers from the main session*, ed. by Lise M. Dobrin, Kora Singer, and Lisa McNair, 125–39. Chicago: University of Chicago, Chicago Linguistic Society.

Huck, Geoffrey J., and Younghee Na. 1990. Extraposition and focus. *Language* 66, 51–77.

Huck, Geoffrey J., and Younghee Na. 1992. Information and contrast. *Studies in Language* 16, 325–34.

Jackendoff, Ray S. 1972. *Semantic interpretation in generative grammar*. Cambridge, MA: MIT Press.

Jackendoff, Ray S. 1977. *$\bar{X}$ syntax*. Cambridge, MA: MIT Press.

Jackendoff, Ray S. 1983. *Semantics and cognition*. Cambridge, MA: MIT Press.

Jackendoff, Ray S. 1987. The status of thematic relations in linguistic theory. *Linguistic Inquiry* 18, 89–150.

Jackendoff, Ray S. 1997. *The architecture of the language faculty*. Cambridge, MA: MIT Press.

Jespersen, Otto. 1937. *Analytic syntax*. Chicago: University of Chicago Press.

Jones, Charles. 1991. *Purpose clauses: Syntax, thematics, and semantics of English purpose constructions*. Dordrecht: Kluwer.

Kamp, Hans. 1975. Two theories about adjectives. In *Formal semantics of natural language*, ed. by Edward L. Keenan, 123–55. Cambridge: Cambridge University Press.

Kayne, Richard S. 1981. ECP extensions. *Linguistic Inquiry* 12, 93–133.

Keenan, Edward L., and Bernard Comrie. 1977. Noun phrase accessibility and Universal Grammar. *Linguistic Inquiry* 8, 63–99.

Koster, Jan. 1978. *Locality principles in syntax*. Dordrecht: Foris.

Lapointe, Stephen G., and Sarah Nielson. 1994. A reconsideration of type III gerunds in Korean. In *Japanese/Korean Linguistics 5*, ed. by Noriko Akatsuka, Shoichi Iwasaki, and Susan Strauss, 305–20. Stanford, CA: CSLI Publications.

Na, Younghee. 1986. Syntactic and semantic interaction in Korean: Topic, focus, and relative clause. Doctoral dissertation, University of Chicago.

Na, Younghee. 1991. Relativizability in Korean. Manuscript, University of Toronto.

Na, Younghee, and Geoffrey J. Huck. 1993. On the status of certain island violations in Korean. *Linguistics and Philosophy* 16, 181–229.

Pinker, Steven. 1984. *Language learnability and language development.* Cambridge, MA: Harvard University Press.

Pinker, Steven. 1989. *Learnability and cognition: The acquisition of argument structure.* Cambridge, MA: MIT Press.

Sadock, Jerrold M. 1991. *Autolexical Syntax: A theory of parallel grammatical representations.* Chicago: University of Chicago Press.

Selkirk, Elisabeth. 1982. T*he syntax of words.* Cambridge, MA: MIT Press.

Selkirk, Elisabeth. 1984. *Phonology and syntax: The relation between sound and structure.* Cambridge, MA: MIT Press.

Siegel, Muffy. 1976. Capturing the adjective. Doctoral dissertation, University of Massachusetts, Amherst.

Wilkins, Wendy. 1988. Thematic structure and reflexivization. In *Syntax and semantics 21: Thematic relations*, ed. by Wendy Wilkins, 191–213. New York: Academic Press.

Yoon, James H. S. 1996. A syntactic account of category-changing phrasal morphology: Nominalizations in English and Korean. In *Morphosyntax in generative grammar*, ed. by Heedon Ahn, Myung-Yoon Kang, Yong-Suck Kim, and Sookhee Lee, 63–86. Seoul: Hankuk.

Chapter 9
Multiple Mechanisms Underlying Morphological Productivity

Yoko Sugioka

9.1 Introduction: Productivity of Word Formation

In a number of his papers, Jim McCawley discussed how lexically derived forms contrast in usage with syntactically derived expressions. For instance, in McCawley 1978a he accounts for the division of labor between a lexically simple word and its periphrastic counterpart by Gricean conversational implicature, and in McCawley 1978b he carefully applies this idea to analyzing lexical and syntactic causatives of Japanese clothing verbs. In this chapter, I will address a similar division of labor within the domain of word formation, and I will examine and attempt to account for different types of productivity in word formation in a manner compatible with the notion that linguistics is part of cognitive psychology, a notion that Jim McCawley held to be extremely important but found difficult to do justice to in actual linguistic research (e.g., McCawley 1979, 1986).

I will focus on the following question: are the differences in productivity found with word formation only a matter of degree, or are some word formation rules different in kind from others? Many recent works in psycho- and neurolinguistics have

---

I started looking into the Japanese nominal affixes discussed in section 9.4 at the beginning of my dissertation research supervised by Jim McCawley, and his great enthusiasm for my casual observations at the time gave me the much-needed confidence to continue. I am forever thankful to Jim for his encouragement and guidance.

Part of this chapter is based on work conducted with Hiroko Hagiwara (Tokyo Metropolitan University) and Takane Ito (University of Tokyo), to whom I would like to express my gratitude for insightful discussion and support. I am also grateful to Taro Kageyama, Yoko Yumoto, and the members of the Lexicon Study Circle of Tokyo for valuable comments on earlier versions of the materials incorporated here. I would also like to thank anonymous reviewers for helpful comments on an earlier version of this chapter, and Rebecca S. Wheeler and Salikoko S. Mufwene for invaluable editorial help.

This research was supported in part by grants from Keio University and by the Japanese Ministry of Education (Grants-in-Aid for Scientific Research #14310225, #14510620, #08CE1001).

spoken to this point. In the sections to follow, I will first review proposals made concerning the mental mechanisms behind the regular and irregular inflections in English. I will then discuss the possibility of extending such proposals to derivational morphology in Japanese, both affixation and compounding. I hope to show that the two different modes of creating new words—by rule and by analogy—must be distinguished in the consideration of morphological productivity.

9.2 Regular versus Irregular Inflection in English

9.2.1 Different Approaches to English Inflection

In languages such as English that show a dichotomy between regular and irregular inflection, it has been assumed that the forms with regular inflection (*boys* PL, *walked* PAST) are generated by rules (here, rules that attach -*s* and -*ed* to the stem), while those with irregular inflection (*teeth* PL, *ran* PAST) are memorized. In other words, the irregularly inflected forms are listed in the lexicon item by item, whereas the outputs of regular inflection (e.g., *boys, walked*) are not necessarily memorized.

This idea of a regular/irregular dichotomy in inflections has been disputed from two different angles. The connectionist group in psychology claims that since regular and irregular inflection are basically the same process, no clear dichotomy exists between the two. From their vantage point, no suffixation rule attaches plural or past endings to the stem; rather, the base word (*run, walk*) is connected to the inflected word (*ran, walked*) in a network, and it is this network that sustains such inflectional relations (Rumelhart and McClelland 1986). This idea is partially motivated by the fact that the so-called irregular inflection paradigm is not totally random but actually consists of some prominent patterns, such as $XinY \to XanY$ for *sing/sang, ring/rang, drink/drank, sink/sank* (Bybee and Slobin 1982). Such patterns in the inflectional paradigm have been shown to have some psychological reality by experiments involving novel words (Bybee and Moder 1983). For example, when asked to produce a past form for a novel word belonging to the pattern $XinY$, subjects answered $XanY$ (e.g., *spling → splang*). Connectionists argue that if each irregular inflection belongs to a certain pattern, then the so-called regular inflection can be considered another such pattern, $X \to X\text{-}ed$, the one in which the majority of verbs participate. Under this account, there is no dichotomy between regular and irregular inflection. A single mechanism of network connection can handle all inflections; the distinction between regular and irregular inflections consists only in the number of verbs belonging to each pattern.

Pinker and his colleagues also claim that inflection in English does not consist of a regular/irregular dichotomy. However, they see it as consisting of three different mechanisms, as listed in (1) (Pinker and Prince 1991; Pinker 1991, 1999).

(1) a. *Computation rule (listed)*
       V+ed: walk/walked, laugh/laughed
   b. *Associative memory*
       sing/sang, ring/rang, drink/drank, sink/sank,... sleep/slept, keep/kept, feel/felt, mean/meant, etc.
   c. *Rote memory listed (listed)*
       go/went, be/was

Rule-governed processes such as English past participle formation with *-ed* illustrated in (1a) are derived by pure concatenation of the stem and the affix. They are productive and compositional in meaning, and they apply to nonce words. On the other hand, the so-called irregular inflection forms consist of two groups, (1b) and (1c). Associative memory links patterns or types and handles the irregular forms that show "subregularities" or family resemblance, as exemplified in (1b). This process is semiproductive, as it allows analogical extension such as *spling → splang*. Rote memory links item to item without any association of patterns, so the suppletive pairs in (1c) are simply listed in the lexicon. This process is completely unproductive.

Since there is little controversy over the claim that the suppletive pairs of (1c) are listed in rote memory, the controversial question is whether (1a) and (1b) are different mechanisms or not. While connectionist theorists claim that they are, Pinker and his colleagues claim they are not; hence, the latter is called the *dual-mechanism* approach. Let us look at the reasoning behind it in more detail.

9.2.2 Rule and Associative Memory in Inflection

According to the dual-mechanism view, rule and associative memory represent two distinct mechanisms behind production and comprehension of inflected forms; rules (suffixation of *-ed* and *-s*) are responsible for regular inflections, and associative memory for irregular inflections (the $XinY \sim XanY$ pattern for *sing/sang, sink/sank*, etc., and $XooY \sim XeeY$ for *tooth/teeth, foot/feet*, etc.). The major differences between them, as noted by Prasada and Pinker (1983), Pinker and Prince (1991), and Pinker (1999), can be summarized as follows.

First, associative memory maintains the links between the existing forms in the lexicon, while a rule applies "online" to a given item. From this follows the fact that when a new form enters the lexicon, it almost always takes the regular inflection. For instance, as pointed out by a reviewer, the plural form of the French loanword *chief* is *chiefs*, not *chieves, in contrast with Germanic words such as *handkerchief~handkerchieves* and *thief~thieves, leaf~leaves*. Second, associative memory, but not rules, shows the frequency effect. That is, irregular inflection is found only with words of high frequency, since the association link is strengthened by frequency. It is well known that irregular forms (*give~gave, hide~hid*) are the ones frequently used, while less frequent words such as *cleave~clave, chide~chid* tend to be overgeneralized to *-ed* forms. Furthermore, some irregular verbs used less frequently in the past tense sound awkward in that tense: for example, *I can't **bear** it/ ??I **bore** it*. This contrast is not found with regular-inflection verbs: *afford* is not frequently used in past tense, but *afforded* is just as fine. Third, associative memory is based on similarity (or recognized pattern) of the linked items; thus, we find some patterns of resemblance within the family of irregularly inflected forms, as shown in (1b). This point was demonstrated by the experiments using nonce words: *splung* was accepted as the past form of *spling* because of its similarity to the pattern observed with *spring~sprung, string~strung*, and so on. In contrast, *nust* was not accepted as the inflected form of *nist* because there is no extant verb with the same inflection pattern.

This last point is significant in that associative memory can be the basis for formation by analogy. In nonexperimental situations, we find some speech errors that are based on analogy (e.g., when the rote memory that links *bring* and *brought* fails, *brang may be uttered by analogy to the registered pattern of *sing~sang, ring~rang*). Thus, as will be discussed below, analogy based on associative memory provides a way of deriving new words, which is distinct from deriving new words by rule.

The regular/irregular dichotomy also manifests itself with regard to level-ordering in word formation (Kiparsky 1982). In level-ordered morphology, word formation processes are classified into more idiosyncratic level 1 processes and more regular level 2 processes. Level 1 processes such as *go~went, sing~sang*, and *keep~kept* precede level 2 processes such as *-ed* suffixation, so the former can block the application of the latter, preempting *goed, *singed, and *keeped. In other words, regular inflection such as *-ed* suffixation functions as the default rule. For instance, the verb *fly*, in the sense 'to hit a fly ball', is a denominal verb and its [+irregular] verbal feature has been lost, so it undergoes regular inflection: *flied*. Similar reasoning explains why irregular plural inflections do not appear with exocentric words and proper names: *low-lifes, Mickey Mouses*, and *Batmans*. Furthermore, since compounding belongs to level 2, only irregular inflection can occur inside a compound: *mice-infected* (vs. *rats-infected), *teeth-marks* (vs. *claws-marks), and *men-bashing* (vs. *guys-bashing). This contrast has been attested in the grammars of 3- to 5-year-old children (Gordon 1985).

In short, the dual-mechanism theory claims two distinct processes—rule and associative memory—are involved in inflection, while the single-mechanism theory claims only the latter is involved.

9.3 Rule and Associative Memory in Derivational Morphology

Recently, the debate between the single- and dual-mechanism theories has been very intense in the domain of inflectional morphology. This naturally raises the question whether derivational morphology involves both rule and associative memory. If that turns out to be true, the dual-mechanism theory can encompass all types of complex word formation strategies, not just inflection.

There have been very few attempts to extend the debate to processes of derivational morphology. One exception is the study in progress by Alegre and Gordon (1999). They have tested whether "neutral" affixes (e.g., *-er*, *-ness*, *-able*), which do not affect the internal phonology of the stem to which they attach, behave like regular inflections, as opposed to "nonneutral" affixes (e.g., *-ion*, *-al*, *-ity*). Testing the acceptability ratings for nonce derived forms with different degrees of similarity to existing forms that take the affixes in question, they found that the acceptability ratings for the nonneutral affixes were affected by similarity to some extent and those for the neutral affixes were not. The correlation, however, was not perfect. Thus, the question of whether the dual-mechanism theory can also apply to derivational morphology has not sufficiently been explored.

In the following section, I will discuss the different degrees of productivity found in affixation and compounding in Japanese and provide evidence suggesting that the rule/associative memory dichotomy is indeed present in derivational morphology.

9.4 Japanese Nominal Affixation

9.4.1 *-sa* versus *-mi*

The Japanese affixes *-sa* and *-mi* attach to adjective stems and derive nouns. While *-sa* can attach to virtually all adjectives and adjectival nouns, *-mi* is found with only a small subset of frequently used adjectives (about 30 of them), so there are numerous lexical gaps. For example, it is not uncommon for only one member of an antonym pair to allow *-mi* affixation.

(2) a. akaru-mi 'bright-ness' / #kura-mi 'dark-ness' (cf. kura-gari 'darkness')
　　b. atataka-mi 'warmth' / #tumeta-mi 'coldness'
　　c. atu-mi 'thickness' / #usu-mi 'thinness'

It is thus plausible to differentiate these two suffixes on the basis of level ordering, taking *-mi* as a level 1 affix and *-sa* as a level 2 affix. In fact, there is some concrete evidence showing that they belong to different levels of derivation (Sugioka 1984, 1992; Kageyama 1993). Namely, *-sa*, but not *-mi*, can attach to adjectives derived by various affixes, as in (3), as well as compound adjectives, as in (4).

(3) a. urayam-asi-sa 'envy-causing-ness, enviousness' / *urayam-asi-mi
   b. kodomo-rasi-sa 'child-like-ness' / *kodomo-rasi-mi
   c. sirooto-ppo-sa 'amateur-ish-ness' / *sirooto-ppo-mi
   d. kaki-yasu-sa 'write-easy-ness, ease of writing' / *kaki-yasu-mi
   e. asobi-ta-sa 'play-want-ness, desire to play' / *asobi-ta-mi

(4) a. oku-huka-sa 'end-deep-ness, profoundness' / *oku-huka-mi (cf. huka-mi 'depth')
   b. tyuui-buka-sa[1] 'attention-deep-ness, carefulness' / *tyuui-buka-mi
   c. nebari-zuyo-sa 'stick-strong-ness, tenacity' / *nebari-zuyo-mi (cf. tuyo-mi 'strength')
   d. sakana-kusa-sa 'fish-smelly-ness, fishy smell' / *sakana-kusa-mi (cf. kusa-mi 'smelly-ness')

The contrast in (3) and (4) follows naturally from the assumption that -*mi* belongs to level 1 and thus cannot follow other affixation or compounding, while -*sa* follows those processes at level 2. Here, we see a parallel between these affixes, on the one hand, and regular and irregular inflections in English, on the other hand, as briefly discussed in section 9.2.

It also follows that -*sa* affixation, like English regular inflections, functions as the default rule and applies to foreign borrowings, as in (5a–b),[2] or newly coined words, as in (5c–d).

(5) a. nau-na, nau-i '(lit. now) hip' → nau-sa / *nau-mi
   b. hotto-na 'hot, trendy' → hotto-sa / *hotto-mi
   c. keba-i 'flashy' → keba-sa / *keba-mi
   d. dasa-i 'tacky' → dasa-sa / *dasa-mi

Differences between -*sa* affixation and -*mi* affixation also involve syntactic and semantic factors, as we will now see.

9.4.2 Thematic Constraints on Nominals

When inherited arguments appear with derived nominals, the preposition accompanying the argument NP expresses the thematic relation it bears to the base verb (Rappaport 1983).

(6) a. The soldiers invaded *the city* (theme).
   b. the soldiers' invasion of the city

(7) a. The soldiers entered *the city* (goal).
   b. the soldiers' entry to the city
   c. *the soldiers' entry of the city

Comparing (7b) and (7c), note that *the city*, which is the direct argument NP in the corresponding sentence (7a), cannot appear with *of*. Since it bears the goal thematic role, it must appear with *to*. It is the thematic relation rather than the syntactic position of the argument NP that determines the choice of preposition.

Turning to the Japanese nominalized adjectives in question, we find that *-mi* nominals appear only with theme arguments, while *-sa* nominals can appear with arguments bearing various roles.

(8) a. karada no atataka-mi 'the body's warmth' (theme)
   b. *heya no atataka-mi 'the room's warmth' (locative)

(9) a. karada no atataka-sa 'the body's warmth' (theme)
   b. heya no atataka-sa 'the room's warmth' (locative)
   c. watasi no tura-sa 'my painfulness' (experiencer)
   d. wakare no tura-sa 'painfulness of parting' (theme)

Note that *-sa* can attach to theme or locative NPs (9a–b) and theme or experiencer (9c–d) of the corresponding adjective. This indicates that an NP corresponding to the argument NP (subject NP) of the base adjective can appear as argument to the *-sa* nominal, regardless of its thematic relation.

Furthermore, if the argument NP is in a nonthematic position, the derived nominal cannot inherit the argument (Baker 1985). See the following cases of exceptional case marking and raising.

(10) a. John believes Mary to be insane.
    b. *John's belief of Mary to be insane

(11) a. John is easy to please.
    b. *John's easiness to please
       (cf. John's eagerness to please)

Again, *-sa* nominalization allows raised NPs to appear, as in (12c) and (13c).

(12) a. [Baka o damasi]-yasui.
       fool ACC deceive-easy
       'It is easy to deceive a fool.'
    b. Baka$_i$ ga [t$_i$ damasi]-yasui.
       fool NOM deceive-easy
       'A fool is easy to deceive.'
    c. baka no damasi-yasu-sa
       fool GEN deceive-easy-ness
       'lit., a fool's easiness to deceive'

(13) a. [Kono beddo de nemuri]-yasui.
      this bed LOC sleep-easy
      'It is easy to sleep in this bed.'
   b. Kono beddo$_i$ ga [t$_i$ nemuri]-yasui.
      this bed NOM sleep-easy
      'This bed is easy to sleep in.'
   c. kono beddo no nemuri-yasu-sa
      this bed GEN sleep-easy-ness
      'this bed's easiness to sleep in'

This indicates that -*sa* nominalization is not subject to thematic constraints on the realization of the argument NPs, in contrast to derived nominals, including -*ness* nominals in English.

9.4.3 Semantic Transparency of Nominals

Inflection does not change the meaning of the base except for marking it for a certain grammatical feature such as tense or number. In derivational morphology, however, the derived word often acquires a meaning different from that of the base. If the process in derivational morphology is completely productive, the semantics of the output is compositional; by contrast, less productive processes tend to involve more lexical idiosyncrasy. This holds true for -*sa* affixation as opposed to -*mi* affixation (Sugioka 1984). Deadjectival nominals with -*sa* denote an abstract state or property and mean 'the degree of [ADJ]-ness / the fact of being [ADJ]'. Nominals with -*mi*, on the other hand, can refer to various tangible objects bearing the property denoted by the base adjective: for example, *maru-mi* 'round shape', *huka-mi* 'deep point (in water)', *ama-mi* 'sweet taste', *ita-mi* 'pain', *tuyo-mi* 'strong point'. Thus, while the meaning of -*sa* nominals is transparent, that of -*mi* nominals is not predictable and so they must be listed in the lexicon with their meanings.

Because of this meaning difference, nominals with the two affixes appear in slightly different discourse contexts.

(14) a. Kawa no huka-mi/*huka-sa ni hamat-ta.
       river GEN dep-th deep-ness LOC fell-PAST
       'I fell in the deep section of the river.'
    b. Kawa no *huka-mi/huka-sa o hakat-ta.
       river GEN dep-th deep-ness ACC measure-PAST
       'I measured the depth of the river.'

Note that -*mi* nominals do not block -*sa* nominals, unlike in the case of inflection, where irregular forms always block regular forms because they denote exactly the same thing.

9.4.4 Limited Productivity of *-mi* Affixation: Analogy

As we saw in (5), *-sa* can attach to virtually all adjectives and adjectival nouns including new loanwords and coinages. The fact that it can attach mechanically to any morphologically appropriate base can also be seen in the way it attaches to verbs. The negation affix in Japanese (*-(a)nai*) is morphologically an adjective, and so if the negated verb denotes a property rather than an action, it can be nominalized by *-sa*, as shown in (15).

(15) a. suugaku ga wakar-anai → suugaku no wakar-ana-sa
math NOM understand-NEG math GEN understand-NEG-SA
'don't understand math' 'not understanding math'
b. okane ga tari-nai → okane no tari-na-sa
money NOM suffice-NEG money GEN suffice-NEG-SA
'there is not enough money' 'there being not enough money'
c. keikaku ga susum-anai → keikaku no susum-ana-sa
plan NOM advance-NEG plan GEN advance-NEG-SA
'the plan does not advance' 'the plan's not making progress'

Similarly, *-sa* can attach to adjectives that have lost their literal meanings in idiom chunks.

(16) a. atama ga yawarakai → atama no yawaraka-sa
head NOM soft head GEN soft-ness
'flexible' 'flexibility (in thoughts)'
b. kao ga hiroi → kao no hiro-sa
face NOM wide face GEN wide-ness
'has many acquaintances' 'having many acquaintances'
c. ten ga karai → ten no kara-sa
grade NOM salty grade GEN salty-ness
'gives low grades' 'giving low grades'

In contrast, *-mi* cannot appear in any of the above contexts.

Nevertheless, limited cases of *-mi* forming new words under specific conditions do exist. Studying those conditions reveals that the limited productivity involves analogical formation, in contrast to the default-type productivity of *-sa* affixation. As briefly discussed in section 9.2.2, the dual-mechanism model maintains that irregular inflection in English is supported by associative memory, which is sensitive to frequency and similarity. The limited productivity exhibited by *-mi* affixation seems to display the same features.

First, a number of *-mi* nominals denote some flavor.

(17) a. ama-mi 'sweetness'
b. kara-mi 'saltiness, spiciness'

c. niga-mi 'bitterness'
d. sibu-mi 'astringency'
e. uma-mi 'tastiness'
f. egu-mi 'bitterness'

In addition, the following nominals are somewhat acceptable, although derived adjectives reject -*mi* as was shown in (3) and (4).

(18) a. su-ppai   → suppa-mi
       vinegar-ish   'sourness'
     b. syo(< sio)-ppai → syoppa-mi
        salt-ish   'saltiness'

Furthermore, although -*mi* does not attach to native Japanese adjectival nouns as mentioned earlier, the following example of an adjectival noun followed by -*mi* has been attested in a TV commercial.

(19) karee ni   koku to   *maroyaka-mi* o   ataeru tyoomiryoo
     curry DAT flavor and mildness   ACC give   seasoning
     'the seasoning that gives flavor and mellow taste to curry'

The stem *maroyaka* is not an adjectival noun and takes a copula ending: *maroyaka-na* (cf. **maroyaka-i*). We can conjecture that these limited cases of -*mi* affixation are made possible by analogy to the existing and frequently used -*mi* nominals denoting some flavor (e.g., *ama-mi* 'sweetness', *kara-mi* 'salty taste'). Since *maroyaka* also refers to a flavor, it belongs to the same semantic field as other adjectives that can take -*mi*.

In addition to being influenced by semantic affinity, the acceptability of *maroyaka-mi* in (19) may be affected by its phonological similarity to existing forms, which again suggests that it is formed by analogy rather than rule. Although -*mi* does not generally attach to adjectival nouns, the -*mi* nominals in (20) are derived from adjectives that also have adjectival noun forms with the copula; such dual-category membership is found with only a small number of adjectives.

(20) a. atataka-mi 'warmth' < atataka-i (cf. atataka-na) 'warm'
     b. yawaraka-mi 'softness' < yawaraka-i (cf. yawaraka-na) 'soft'

Thus, although the -*mi* nominals in (20a–b) are based on adjectives, it is possible to reanalyze them as -*mi* affixation to the homomorphic adjectival-noun base shown in parentheses. It is then conceivable that *maroyaka-mi* in (19) is formed on the basis of the phonological similarity schematized as follows:

(21) atataka-mi / yawaraka-mi : ____ (C)aka-mi → maroyaka-mi

In fact, attaching -*mi* to adjectival nouns ending with -*(C)aka* yields acceptable forms (22a–b), unlike attaching it to other adjectival nouns (22c).[3]

(22) a. ___ yaka
Seikaku ga *odayaka-mi* o masita.
personality NOM calm-MI ACC increased
'[The person] became more calm in personality.'
?sawayaka-mi 'freshness'
?hanayaka-mi 'flamboyance'
b. ___ raka
?nameraka-mi 'smoothness'
?nadaraka-mi 'flatness'
c. *Others*
#shizuka-mi 'quietness'
#nodoka-mi 'peacefulness'
#tasika-mi 'sureness'
#oroka-mi 'foolishness'

Note that some of the forms in (22a–b) are less than fully acceptable. In fact, this is expected because analogy is applied to fill lexical gaps (i.e., possible but nonexistent words) in the outputs of semiproductive word formation. As Thompson (1975, 347) points out, "The main features of these coinages [by analogy] is their awkwardness."[4]

Finally, we find a small number of *-mi* nominals where affixation of *-sa* to the same base is not possible.

(23) yasei 'wild [N]' -mi 'wildness' (cf. *yasei-sa)
genzitu 'reality' -mi 'reality' (cf. *genzitu-sa)
ningen 'man' -mi 'humanity' (cf. *ningen-sa)
sizen 'nature' -mi 'sense of nature' (cf. sizen-sa 'naturalness')

In these examples, the base is a noun, though each denotes some property rather than a concrete entity.[5] In such cases, *-mi* can be attached to form a nominal with the meaning 'a sense of (property)'. Other such cases include a nominal derived from a verb stem, as in (24a), and an onomatopoeic morpheme denoting some sort of feeling or sensation, as in (24b–c).

(24) a. enzyuku 'to mature' -mi 'maturity' / *enzyuku-sa (cf. enjuku-suru 'to mature')
b. toro 'thick and sticky' -mi 'thickness (of liquid)' / *toro-sa
(cf. onomatopoeia: toro-toro 'thick' (used for liquid))
c. zara 'rough, gravelly' -mi 'roughness (of touch)' / *zara-sa
(cf. onomatopoeia: zara-zara 'coarse to touch')

Thus, in the extended use of the affix *-mi*, the semantic notion of '(tangible) property' is relevant rather than the morphosyntactic category of the base. In contrast, the otherwise productive affix -*sa* can never go beyond the morphosyntactic category boundary even if the semantics of the base denotes a property. Hence, -*mi* appears to be more productive for the very limited cases just observed.

These observations on -*mi* affixation follow naturally, if we assume that it is supported by associative memory, which is sensitive to frequency and phonological similarity, and that it is governed by semantic factors rather than strict categorial selection.

9.4.5 Nominal Affixation to Novel Adjectives

The claim that the innovative application of -*mi* affixation involves analogy to existing words has been confirmed by an experiment using novel adjectives, as reported in Hagiwara et al. 1999.[6] In these experiments, three different discourse contexts were used: one in which the -*mi* form is preferred to the -*sa* form ((25a): -*mi* discourse), one in which both forms are equally possible ((25b): neutral discourse), and one in which the -*sa* form is preferred to the -*mi* form ((25c): -*sa* discourse).

(25) a. Rebaa wa *kusa-i* node   tabe-nikui. Gyuunyuu ni tukete oku to sono
liver   TOP smelly because eat-difficult milk   LOC soak   if that
?kusa-sa/kusa-mi ga   nukeru.
  smelly-ness   NOM be-gone
'Liver is difficult to eat because it is smelly (has a distinct smell).
If you soak it in milk, you can remove the smell.'
   b. Kono yasai   wa sukosi *niga-i*. Sono *niga-sa/niga-mi* ga   wahuu no
this   vegetable TOP a.little bitter that bitter-ness   NOM Japanese
azituke   ni   yoku au.
seasoning DAT well match
'This vegetable tastes a little bitter.
Its bitterness goes well with Japanese seasoning.'
   c. Burokku-bei   wa zisin   ni *yowai*. Sono *yowa-sa/?yowa-mi* ga
concrete.block-wall TOP earthquake to weak that weak-ness   NOM
konkai no   sinsai   de syoomei-sare-ta.
recent GEN earthquake in prove-PASS-PAST
'Concrete block walls are weak against earthquakes.
Their weakness was proved by the recent earthquake.'

Two discourse sets were used, one with existing adjectives and another with novel (nonce) adjectives. In the latter set, in order to examine the similarity effect, two types of novel adjective forms were used: "familiar" ones that phonologically resemble existing adjectives, and "unfamiliar" ones that sound odd as Japanese adjectives (i.e., stems ending with /i/, /e/, /n/, etc.). Familiar novel adjectives included *toka-i*, *simaka-i*, *maku-i*, *sano-i*, *meka-i*, *taso-i*, and *kunaro-i*; unfamiliar ones included *gome-i, yati-i, rahi-i, dotiki-i, pameri-i, mebene-i,* and *katon-i*. Participants were asked to judge the naturalness of the noun in the second sentence as the nominalized form of the adjective in the first sentence.

In the experiment, *-sa* nominals based on novel adjectives were judged highly acceptable, equaling the results with existing adjectives. In contrast, *-mi* nominals derived from novel adjectives were judged much less acceptable compared with those derived from existing adjectives even in the *-mi* discourse (see Hagiwara et al. 1999 for details). This result indicates that the outputs of *-mi* affixation are listed in the lexicon; so *-mi* cannot attach freely to novel adjectives. On the other hand, *-sa* affixation, being a default rule, applies freely to novel forms. In addition, *-sa* nominals were judged highly acceptable regardless of the familiarity of the base adjective, while the acceptability for *-mi* nominals depended on the familiarity of the novel stem: familiar novel adjectives yielded more acceptable nominals, but *-mi* nominals based on unfamiliar novel adjectives were judged significantly less acceptable. This result indicates that *-sa* affixation is not affected by phonological similarity, while *-mi* affixation is. These findings are consistent with the observations in section 9.4.4 and the assumption that innovative *-mi* affixation involves analogical extension supported by associative memory.

9.4.6 Rule and Analogy in Affixation

As we have seen, two nominal affixes in Japanese show contrastive features suggesting that different mechanisms, rule and associative memory, are involved in affixation. Nominalization by *-sa* is mechanically applied as a default rule, which explains its extremely high productivity and ability to attach to new coinages. Furthermore, *-sa* nominals are semantically transparent, so they need not be listed in the lexicon. In contrast, the suffix *-mi* displays relatively low productivity and more semantic idiosyncrasy, and is very limited in its extension to new coinages. An experiment using novel adjective bases has also shown that *-mi* affixation is sensitive to phonological similarity. These observations indicate that *-mi* affixation is supported by associative memory that links the base forms and the derived nominals in the lexicon.

The different types of productivity found in these Japanese affixation processes can therefore be relegated to rule and analogy. As a result, the dual-mechanism model proposed for English inflection can also account for derivational word formation.[7]

9.5 Rule versus Analogy in Compound Formation

In this section, I will show that the rule/analogy dichotomy is also valid for analyzing the productivity of deverbal compound formation in Japanese.

Compound formation is generally perceived as a rule for simple concatenation of two items (e.g., [*computer*]$_N$ + [*desk*]$_N$), just like regular inflection or derivational affixation (base + suffix: *walk* + *-ed*, *taka* + *-sa*). Alternatively, it is possible to say that in some cases a new compound is formed, as schematized in (26).

(26) XZ → YZ (X → Y on the basis of XZ)

Here, a new compound YZ is formed by analogy to the existing XZ by supplying a different nonhead Y. The following examples are clearly formed this way:

(27) a. firewoman < fireman
 b. chairperson < chairman
 c. airsick < seasick
   (Becker 1993)
 d. seascape, cloudscape, waterscape < landscape
   (Bauer 1983)

Now look at the following cases of Japanese novel compounds derived by analogy to existing forms:

(28) a. kyabetu no *hyaku-giri* (< *sen-giri* 'lit., thousand-cut, finely cut')
      cabbage GEN hundred-cut
      'coarse cutting of cabbage'
      (Sawaki 1989)
 b. Zassi   no tati-yomi to *suwari-yomi* o
    magazine GEN stand-read and sit-read   ACC
    kinziru. (< *tati-yomi* 'browse')
    forbid
    'We forbid standing or sitting around reading magazines (in the bookshop).'
    (Satake 1989)

Clearly, for the new compounds in (28) to be understood, the existing compounds in parentheses must be evoked either by memory or by juxtaposition.

On the other hand, there are new compounds that do not seem to be based on existing compounds. For example:

(29) a. Syanai ga   atui node *mado-ake*   ni gokyooryoku kudasai.
      in-train NOM hot so   window-open DAT cooperate   please
      'It is hot in the train, so please cooperate in opening the windows.
      (announcement on the train)'
 b. tyoonooryoku   niyoru *supuun-mage*
    supernatural power by   spoon-bend
    'spoon-bending by a supernatural power'
 c. Muri na *kisyu-age* ga   hikooki-ziko   no gen'in da.
    reckless nose-lift NOM plane-accident GEN cause COP
    'Reckless nose lifting caused the plane crash.'

d. puroguramu no *bagu-hiroi*
program   GEN bug-hunt
'debugging of a computer program'

These compounds are created when a name for a certain action ('open the window', 'bend a spoon', 'lift the nose of an airplane') is necessary.

The compounds in (28) and (29) consist of a verbal head preceded by the verb's argument or adjunct. As pointed out in Sugioka 1996, deverbal compounds formed with direct object arguments are very productive.

(30) a. *Act*
tegami-kaki 'letter writing', takara-sagasi 'treasure hunting', gohan-taki 'rice cooking', sakana turi 'fish fishing', tuna-hiki 'rope tugging', pan-yaki 'bread baking', mizu-kumi 'water fetching', kihukin-atume 'donation collecting', yasai-zukuri 'vegetable growing'
b. *Agent*
hana-uri 'flower vender', gekkyuu-tori 'salary earner', sinario-kaki 'scenario writer', hituzi-kai 'sheep herder'
c. *Instrument*
tume-kiri 'nail cutter', kawa-muki 'skin peeler', hae-tataki 'fly swatter', nezi-mawasi 'screw driver'

Note that it is also very easy and common to coin a new word in this category; the novel examples of (29) all belong to this type. In contrast, compounds with adjuncts are possible but not fully productive.

(31) a. *Goal + V*
Pari-iki 'Paris-going (bound)' / *Pari-tuki 'Paris-arriving'
b. *Instrument + V*
te-gaki 'hand-writing (handwritten)' / *te-nuki 'hand-pulled'
c. *Locative + V*
Amerika-umare 'American-born' / *Amerika-zini 'America-died'
d. *Cause + V*
sigoto-zukare 'work-tired' / *sigoto-nayami 'work-troubled'
e. *Manner Adv + V*
haya-gui 'fast-eating' / *haya-nomi 'fast-drinking'
f. *Result state + V*
usu-giri 'thin-cutting' / *usu-nobashi 'thin-pounding'

These observations suggest that deverbal compound formation involving direct object arguments enjoys rulelike productivity, while that involving adjuncts has lexical gaps. In fact, the somewhat odd-sounding new coinages *hyaku-giri* and *suwari-yomi* in (28) involve adjuncts. Such oddness is not present in the novel examples in

(29) although they are also new coinages. As noted earlier for a subclass of deadjectival nominals, Thompson (1975, 347) states that

> the main feature of these coinages [by analogy] is their awkwardness [for an example, see note 4].... I think this contrasts sharply with coinages created according to productive rules, which I claim are not generally noticed by the participants in a discourse.

The same type of contrast can be observed between the compounds in (28) and (29), a finding consistent with the contention that they are formed by analogy and rule, respectively.

We have seen that both irregular inflection and semiproductive affixation exhibit some characteristics of "lower-level" derivation, as opposed to regular inflection and productive affixation. There is in fact a salient phonological alternation that distinguishes the two types of compounding. Rendaku, the voicing of the first consonant of the head (see note 1 and Vance, this volume), takes place in all possible cases of deverbal compounds with adjuncts, but not in most cases of deverbal compounds with arguments. For example, in the following pairs with the same verb base, the initial consonant of the verb in adjunct compounds is voiced while that of argument compounds is not:

(32) *Rendaku (voicing)*
 a. kak-u 'write': (adjunct) pen-gaki 'writing with a pen', hasiri-gaki 'hastily written'; (argument) tegami-kaki 'letter writing', syoosetu-kaki 'novel writer'
 b. kir-u 'cut': (adjunct) usu-giri 'thin-sliced', te-giri 'hand-cut', yotu-giri 'cut into four'; (argument) pan-kiri 'bread cutting', kan-kiri 'can opener'
 c. tur-u 'fish': (adjunct) umi-zuri 'ocean fishing', ippon-zuri 'single-hook fishing'; (argument) sakana-turi 'fishing', ika-turi 'squid fishing'
 d. kar-u 'cut, mow': (adjunct) maru-gari 'completely mowed'; (argument) kusa-kari 'weed mowing'
 e. huk-u 'wipe': (adjunct) te-buki 'hand-wipe', zookin-buki 'mop-wipe', kara-buki 'dry-wipe'; (argument) ase-huki 'sweat wiper, towel', mado-huki 'window wiping'

Although the exact nature of rendaku is unclear (see Sugioka 2002 for some discussion and an analysis), considering the fact that the lower-level affixation induces phonological change (cf. *-ity* vs. *-ness* in English), the contrast between the two types of compounds is consistent with the claim here that adjunct compounding is the lower-level process.

Another piece of evidence comes from "blocking," whereby more lexical (or lower-level) word formation processes preempt more productive ones if the outputs compete for the same slot: for example, *glory/glorious/#gloriousity* (Aronoff 1976). It is crucial here that the blocking element (*glory*) is listed in the lexicon. Now look at the following examples of adjunct compounds:

(33) a. inaka-zumai/#inaka-zumi
country live   country live
'living in the country'
b. apaato-zumai/#appato-zumi
apartment live apartment live
'living in an apartment'

Sumau is an archaic verb seldom used now except for an honorific nominal form *o-sumai*. The modern verb is *sumu* 'live in', but compounds containing it are not well formed. Instead, the compound pattern "(place)-*zumai*" is very productive, so any location or type of residential building can be the nonhead.

(34) a. mansyon-zumai 'living in a condo'
b. syataku-zumai 'living in company housing'
c. amerika-zumai 'living in the United States'
d. nyuuyooku-zumai 'living in New York'

Since this kind of productivity is typical of analogical formation, it is plausible to say that the compound pattern "(place)-*zumi*" in (33a–b) is not well formed because it is blocked by the pattern "(place)-*zumai*" already in the lexicon. If adjunct compounding is based on associative memory, it is natural that such blocking should occur.

On the other hand, we can find virtually synonymous pairs of verbs forming argument compounds without blocking each other.

(35) a. tug-u/sas-u 'pour'
b. abura-sasi/abura-tugi 'oil pitcher'
c. mizu-sasi/mizu-tugi 'water pitcher'
d. syooyu-sasi/syooyu-tugi 'soy sauce pitcher'

This is expected under the contention that these argument compounds are rule-based.[8]

Thus, we have seen evidence pointing to the rule-based nature of deverbal compounds involving direct object arguments and the memory-based nature of those involving adjuncts. If the argument compounds can be created "online" by rule, it is not surprising that they can sometimes involve phrases as nonheads. In fact, the following types of examples are not uncommon:

(36) a. [senzo   no haka] -mairi (cf. haka-mairi)
ancestor GEN grave visit
'visiting the ancestor's grave'
(Kageyama 1993)
b. [heiwa na kuni]   -zukuri (cf. kuni-zukuri)
peaceful country build
'building a peaceful country'

c. [yuunoo na sin-zin]   -sagasi (cf. sinzin-sagasi)
      able   new-person search
      'searching for an able new employee'
   d. [konpyuuta no yoosi] -ire (cf. yoosi-ire)
      computer GEN paper put
      'container for computer paper'

These examples can be seen as an expansion on the simple form (shown in parentheses), expressing a more complex idea in combination with the modified nonhead. In contrast, the adjuncts that can appear in deverbal compounds are usually limited to words, often just to monomorphemic ones.

(37) a. *[osanai te]   -zukuri (cf. te-zukuri)
         young hand make
         'made by a child's hand'
     b. *[akai pen] -gaki (cf. pen-gaki)
         red pen   write
         'written with a red pen'
     c. *[hidari te]   -gaki (cf. te-gaki)
         left   hand write
         'written with the left hand'

It seems, then, that the type of semiproductivity found with adjunct compounds is restricted to replacing the nonhead with another word of the same semantic category; "expanding" it by modification is not possible.

We have seen in this section that compounds are formed in two different ways: via rule-based and extremely productive argument compounding on the one hand, and via memory-based and only semiproductive adjunct compounding on the other. The relatively limited productivity of the latter involves analogy with existing forms.

9.6 Concluding Remarks

Compound formation is often said to be closer to syntax than other types of word formation in that it combines words to form a more complex expression. Nevertheless, the different types of productivity observed in Japanese deverbal compounds suggest that even within compound formation there is a clear division between processes that exhibit rulelike behavior and those that do not. It is quite possible, then, that the rule/memory dichotomy outlined in sections 2 and 4 also exists in compound formation, so that the dichotomy cuts across all word formation processes.

Likewise, productivity itself can be divided into two types, one based on rule and the other based on analogy, for both derivational and inflectional morphology. Analogy plays a less significant role in inflection because inflectional paradigms provide virtually no "new slot." In derivational morphology, however, the complex words derived by affixation and compounding can take on different meanings and be lexicalized, so there are ample "new slots" to be filled. Here analogy plays a larger role in creating new words. That factor may have made it difficult to confirm the existence of rule-based processes in derivational morphology. The observations made here, however, indicate the significance of rule and analogy as separate factors affecting productivity in derivational morphology. We can thus conclude that multiple mechanisms underlie productivity in word formation.

Notes

1. Voicing of the initial consonant in the second element (*huka* → *buka*) is called "rendaku" and is very common in Japanese compounds. It is especially common when the second element is a noun: for example, *kutu bako* (< *hako*) 'shoe box'. For details of rendaku, see chapter 10 of Vance 1987 and Vance, this volume.

2. Here, *foreign borrowing* refers to vocabulary borrowed from English or other European languages, which is much more recent than the vocabulary borrowed from Chinese (*Sino-Japanese borrowings*), which forms very large part of the Japanese lexicon. Foreign borrowings and Sino-Japanese borrowings with adjectival meaning are mostly used as adjectival nouns, which do not inflect like regular adjectives and take a copula: *na* in adnominal form and *da* in predicate form. Thus, *nau-i* in (5a) is a rare case.

3. The number of moras in the base also seems relevant here, as suggested by a reviewer. Specifically, the unacceptable examples in (22c) have bases with three moras, while those claimed to be based on analogy in (19) and (22a–b) have a four-mora base, just like the existing forms in (20). It is conceivable that the phonological similarity includes mora structure as well.

4. Thompson (1975, 347) gives the following example of coinage by analogy in deadjectival nominalization in English:

... so, if we're talking about the ideal communicator, it would be concern, credibility, sincerity, and being seemingly involved for your involvement. Now, Nixon doesn't match warmth, does he? What do we get? *Coolth.* (*Esquire,* August 1974, 68)

5. Jim McCawley keenly observed and discussed this type of mismatch in category class on various occasions. For instance, at one point (McCawley 1988/1998, 764) he discusses what he calls "syntactic mimicry" in the construction *X is a bitch (of a problem)*. Here, *a bitch* is a noun (syntactically) but functions semantically as an adjective because it denotes a property. The analogical extension of *-mi* affixation in (23) and (24) involves a similar disparity between the syntactic and semantic categories of the base word.

6. This section is based on collaborative work conducted over several years with Hiroko Hagiwara and Takane Ito. For more details and discussion of the experiment mentioned here, see section 3 of Hagiwara et al. 1999. The main part of the paper discusses results from another experiment on brain-damaged patients and what they imply about the neurological bases of the different mental mechanisms of rule and associative memory.

7. Evidence for the dual-mechanism model from German inflection can be found in Clahsen et al. 1992.

8. This does not mean that argument compounds are not listed in the lexicon at all. It is conceivable that many deverbal compounds involving direct object arguments are listed in the lexicon, especially when their meaning and use are fixed. It is also natural that which specific compounds enter the lexicon differs greatly from speaker to speaker.

References

Alegre, Maria, and Peter Gordon. 1999. Rule-based vs. associative processes in derivational morphology. *Brain and Language* 68, 347–54.

Aronoff, Mark. 1976. *Word formation in generative grammar*. Cambridge, MA: MIT Press.

Baker, Mark. 1985. Syntactic affixation and English gerunds. In *Proceedings of the Fourth West Coast Conference on Formal Linguistics*, ed. by Jeffrey Goldberg, Susannah MacKaye, and Michael T. Wescoat, 1–11. Stanford, CA: CSLI Publications.

Bauer, Laurie. 1983. *English word-formation*. Cambridge: Cambridge University Press.

Becker, Thomas. 1993. Back formation, cross-formation, and "bracketing paradoxes" in paradigmatic morphology. *Morphology Yearbook 1993*, ed. by Geert Booij and Jaap van Marle, 1–25. Dordrecht: Kluwer.

Bybee, Joan, and Carol Lynn Moder. 1983. Morphological classes as natural categories. *Language* 59, 251–70.

Bybee, Joan, and Dan Slobin. 1982. Rules and schemes in the development and use of the English past tense. *Language* 58, 265–89.

Clahsen, Harald, Monica Rothweiler, Andreas Woest, and Gary F. Marcus. 1992. Regular and irregular inflection in the acquisition of German noun plurals. *Cognition* 45, 225–55.

Gordon, Peter. 1985. Level-ordering in lexical development. *Cognition* 21, 73–93.

Hagiwara, Hiroko, Yoko Sugioka, Takane Ito, Mitsuru Kawamura, and Junichi Shiota. 1999. Neurolinguistic evidence for rule-based nominal suffixation. *Language* 75, 739–63.

Kageyama, Taro. 1993. *Bumpoo to gokeisei* [Grammar and word formation]. Tokyo: Hituzi Syobo.

Kiparsky, Paul. 1982. Lexical morphology and phonology. In *Linguistics in the morning calm: Selected papers from SICOL-1981*, ed. by Linguistic Society of Korea, 3–91. Seoul: Hanshin.

McCawley, James D. 1978a. Conversational implicature and the lexicon. In *Syntax and semantics 9: Pragmatics*, ed. by Peter Cole, 245–59. New York: Academic Press.

McCawley James D. 1978b. Notes on Japanese clothing verbs. In *Problems in Japanese syntax and semantics*, ed. by John Hinds and Irwin Howard, 68–78. Tokyo: Kaitakusha.

McCawley, James D. 1979. Some ideas not to live by. In *Adverbs, vowels, and other objects of wonder*, 234–46. Chicago: University of Chicago Press.

McCawley, James D. 1986. Today the world, tomorrow phonology. *Phonology Yearbook* 3, 27–43.

McCawley, James D. 1988. *The syntactic phenomena of English*. Chicago: University of Chicago Press. 2nd ed., 1998. References are to the 1998 edition.

Pinker, Steven. 1991. Rules of language. *Science* 253, 530–35.

Pinker, Steven. 1999. *Words and rules: The ingredients of language*. New York: Basic Books.

Pinker, Steven, and Alan Prince. 1991. Regular and irregular morphology and the psychological status of rules of grammar. In *Proceedings of the Seventeenth Annual Meeting of the Berkeley Linguistics Society*, ed. by Laurel A. Sutton and Christopher Johnson, 230–51. Berkeley: University of California, Berkeley Linguistics Society.

Prasada, Sandeep, and Steven Pinker. 1983. Generalization of regular and irregular morphological patterns. *Language and Cognitive Processes* 8, 1–56.

Rappaport, Malka. 1983. On the nature of derived nominals. In *Papers in Lexical-Functional Grammar*, ed. by Beth Levin, Malka Rappaport, and Annie Zaenen, 113–42. Bloomington: Indiana University Linguistics Club.

Rumelhart, David E., and James L. McClelland. 1986. On learning the past tenses of English verbs. In *Parallel distributed processing: Explorations in the microstructure of cognition*, ed. by James L. McClelland, David E. Rumelhart, and the PDP Research Group, 2:216–71. Cambridge, MA: MIT Press.

Satake, Hideo, ed. 1989. *Gengo-seikatu no me* [Eyes of everyday language]. Tokyo: Chikuma Shoboo.

Sawaki, Mikie, ed. 1989. *Gengo-seikatu no mimi—Hanasi-kotoba memo-choo* [Ears of everyday language—Notebook of spoken language]. Tokyo: Chikuma Shoboo.

Sugioka, Yoko. 1984. Interaction of derivational morphology and syntax in English and Japanese. Doctoral dissertation, University of Chicago. Publ., New York: Garland, 1986.

Sugioka, Yoko. 1992. On the role of argument structure in nominalization. *Language, Communication and Culture* 10, 53–80. Tokyo: Keio University.

Sugioka, Yoko. 1996. Regularity in inflection and derivation: Rule and analogy in Japanese deverbal compound formation. *Acta Linguistica Hungarica* 43, 1–2, 231–53. Budapest: Akadémiai Kiadó.

Sugioka, Yoko. 2002. Incorporation vs. modification in Japanese deverbal compounds. In *Japanese/Korean linguistics 10*, ed. by Noriko M. Akatsuka and Susan Strauss, 496–509. Stanford, CA: CSLI Publications.

Thompson, Sandra A. 1975. On the issue of productivity in the lexikon. *Kritikon Litterarum* 4, 332–49.

Vance, Timothy J. 1987. *An introduction to Japanese phonology*. Albany, NY: SUNY Press.

Chapter 10

How Many *Be*s Are There in English?

Salikoko S. Mufwene

10.1 Introduction

In this chapter, I reexamine McCawley's (1988/1998) analysis of the English copula *be* as a semantically empty auxiliary analogous to auxiliary *do*. Like *do*, copular *be* is not represented in his syntactic deep structure but is inserted transformationally, in order to create a verb phrase where the actual predicate phrase is headed by a nonverb. Following Dik (1983), I argue that the same kind of analysis can be extended to all instances of *be* identified as progressive, passive, modal, and existential; they are all copular and the copula itself is an auxiliary verb. I submit that *be* is in complementary distribution with auxiliary *do*: the latter combines with verb phrases or is used elliptically for them, whereas the former combines with nonverbal predicates or is used elliptically for them. Nonverbal predicate phrases are those headed by nouns, adjectives, prepositions, or, in some cases, locative adverbs (e.g., *outside* and *outdoors*). They also include "weird things like *up to no good*" (Jerry Sadock, pers. comm., August 2003).

An ancestor of this chapter was presented at the 40th meeting of the Southeastern Conference on Linguistics (SECOL), at Old Dominion University, VA, in 1989. Although I discussed the ideas a couple of times with Jim McCawley, I never got around to writing them up for publication. Jim saw the point of this alternative but perhaps did not find it compelling enough to revise his discussion of the subject matter in the 1998 corrected version of *The Syntactic Phenomena of English*. Since I joined the faculty at the University of Chicago in January 1992, I have presented my position on the copula in English a few times in my Syntax-1 classes as an alternative worth considering. It is in the same spirit that I am publishing it here to celebrate the legacy of a teacher, mentor, and friend who encouraged me to read critically, pay attention to as much relevant data as possible, and speak my mind after careful consideration of the issues. I am grateful to Elaine J. Francis, Jerry Sadock, Rebecca Wheeler, and an anonymous reviewer for constructive comments on an earlier version of this chapter. Remaining shortcomings are my sole responsibility.

The analysis proposed below is a bit more abstract than Jim McCawley may have wanted it, especially in the case of "modal" and "existential" *be*, which would require positing underlying predicates that do not surface as verbs, hence the insertion of *be* in the s-structure. In his later work, Jim seems to have shied away from his earlier, more abstract representations of the Generative Semantics days. However, the analysis is quite consistent with his acknowledgment of mismatches, or lack of isomorphism, between deep structure and surface structure configurations, similar to the analysis in Sadock 1991 and later, improved versions of Autolexical Syntax. I defend my theses within McCawley's own syntax framework, perhaps to show indirectly, as was McCawley's own practice, that it is not so much the particular framework of one's analysis that matters but the particular insights it articulates—which can be translated into any other framework—that deserve attention, especially now when approaches to syntax have proliferated.

It is perhaps not by accident that I have already invoked three frameworks that could enable me to defend the same theses equally successfully. Sometimes the choice of a particular framework is more a matter of which one a researcher has greater facility with for expressing his or her ideas than a matter of which one will yield the most significant insights. This is also in keeping with McCawley 1977, which highlights some insights captured in Montague Grammar, shows how they are equally captured, or can be, in Generative Semantics, and explains why McCawley felt he did not have to abandon his own framework. He wrote *The Syntactic Phenomena of English* (1988/1998) in the same spirit. The book is marked in part by an impressive theoretical eclecticism regarding the origins of ideas that inspired his discussions of various aspects of English syntax. I try to do the same here, and I conclude the chapter with some theoretical considerations.

10.2 Background

Syntacticians have traditionally distinguished between the following kinds of *be* in English: the progressive, the passive, the copular,[1] the modal (as in *He was to come*), and the existential *be*s. Although they are all distinguished from each other by their morphosyntactic peculiarities (viz., by how their complements are inflected or introduced), the progressive, the passive, and the modal *be*s have all been considered as auxiliary verbs, whereas the copular and existential *be*s have been assumed to be main verbs. Even studies as recent as Rothstein 1999 assume this position. One of the facts that require explanation is that these main verbs behave like auxiliary verbs in the following constructions:

(1) a. Is Paul tall?
    a'. *Does Paul be tall?[2]

b. Is there a book on the coffee table?
b'. *Does there be a book on the coffee table?

Since the 1970s, the literature on the topic has generally favored a position suggesting, or claiming, that the copular and existential *be*s behave like auxiliary verbs simply because they are homophonous with the auxiliary *be*s.[3] This is basically the position advocated particularly by Akmajian and Wasow (1975), Emonds (1976), and Iwakura (1977). Akmajian and Wasow are aware of the inconsistency of the proposed analysis in relation to modal and main verb *have*s, which undergo Subject-Auxiliary Inversion and Auxiliary Ellipsis in some dialects of English but not in all, as illustrated in (2).

(2) a. I have not to go.
   a'. I don't have to go.
   b. I have not many books.
   c. I don't have many books.

In this respect, they are similar to the modal verb *need*, which in some dialects, notably of American English, selects auxiliary *do* and behaves like a regular main verb.

(3) a. I need not go.
   b. I don't need to go.

Nowadays, one may explain such inconsistent grammatical behavior by claiming that the modals *have* and *need* are not fully grammaticalized yet and continue to behave like main verbs by selecting auxiliary *do*. Copular and existential *be*s can be said to have evolved at a faster pace than modal *have* and *need* toward the status of "auxiliary verbs" (items that behave syntactically like main verbs—and carry tense markers in finite clauses—but function semantically as modifiers of their syntactic complement verbs, those typically identified as "main verbs"; see Mufwene 1994). However, "Standard Theory" syntacticians, who subscribed to extrinsic ordering of ad hoc transformational rules designed to account for the well-formedness of surface structures, stuck to the *Be*-Shift transformation (a precursor of V-to-I movement in Government-Binding syntax; Elaine J. Francis, pers. comm., 2003), which moves copular and existential *be*s from their main-verb position in the deep structure into AUX (the ancestor of INFL) when this node dominates no modal or other auxiliary verb.

Like Bach (1967), Rosenbaum (1967), and Dik (1983), McCawley (1988/1998) sought his solution to this issue in the fact that, unlike main-verb *have*, copular *be* is a semantically empty constituent required by the surface combinatoric principles of English syntax to head a predicate phrase otherwise headed by a nonverbal constituent (viz., an adjective, a noun, a preposition, or an adverb). Typologically, English is different from languages such as Russian, Chinese, and several creoles, in which even main clauses can also have predicate phrases that are not headed by verbs and have copulaless constructions in which English would require a copula.[4] In English, this surface combinatoric requirement is not restricted to main verbs, because there are nonfinite clauses other than small clauses that also require a copula.

(4) a. Mary always wanted to be an astronaut.
  b. Being an astronaut is something that Peter never dreamt of.

Therefore, the presence of the copula is not required just for holding tense and agreement marking in finite clauses, as has typically been argued, but is needed to meet the surface phrase-structure requirements of English in both finite and nonfinite clauses. Small clauses such as those in (5) can thus be considered exceptional in that they do without the copula. However, they play a central role in determining whether copulaless deep structures should (or should not) be preferred to the conventional alternative of representing the copula underlyingly, even though they apparently contribute nothing to the semantics of the relevant sentences.[5]

(5) a. John found *Susan smart*.
  b. The police wanted *the criminal in jail/there*.
  c. The students wished for *Alice as their teacher*.

In his syntax framework, McCawley (1988/1998) posits a deep structure that, under the influence of his earlier practice of Generative Semantics, represents all the semantically relevant information for understanding an utterance and nothing that is semantically empty.[6] Thus, items such as *of* in *the development of a hypothesis* and copular *be* have no place in his deep structure. He posits transformations that have the power to generate new structures and therefore to account for discrepancies between the surface and the deep structures. He also sees no point in using exactly the same kind of lexical categories in the deep structure as in the surface structure. A consequence of having structure-building transformations is to assign particular lexical categories to constituents that are unspecified for lexical category in the deep structure but function as predicates. Accordingly, McCawley devises an unspecified syntactic category O′ that is headed by an unspecified lexical category O with which some nonverbal predicates such as tense markers are associated. He posits rules that convert English tenses to suffixes in finite clauses but the marker of PAST to the lexical verb *have* in nonfinite clauses. For some reason, in the case of predicate phrases headed by adjectives, prepositions, nouns, or adverbs, he departs from the Generative Semantics abstract representations and resorts to the compromise of having underlying phrase structures such as (6) (for *The child is afraid of dogs*), in which the lexical categories are clearly identified.

How Many *Be*s Are There in English? 229

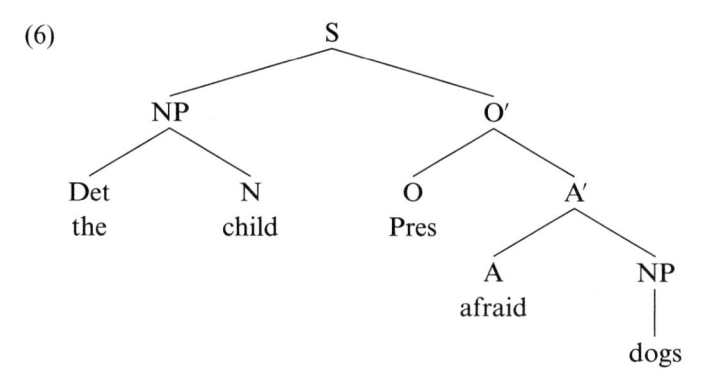

(6)
```
                S
         ┌──────┴──────┐
        NP             O'
      ┌──┴──┐       ┌───┴───┐
     Det    N       O       A'
     the  child    Pres  ┌───┴───┐
                         A       NP
                       afraid    │
                                dogs
```

The application of McCawley's *Be*-Insertion rule, similar to Dik's (1983) Copula Support (see below), has the effect not only of generating a verb phrase headed by the copula in the surface structure but also of providing a carrier for tense.[7] An advantage of the Dik-McCawley approach is the seemingly elegant way in which it handles VP-Deletion or VP-Ellipsis in the following example:

(7) Jim was tall but George is/was not ∅.

As noted above, the application of the rule in this particular case seems exceptional if one considers the fact that main verbs leave an auxiliary *do* behind if they do not follow an auxiliary verb in the antecedent clause.

(8) a. Bill plays the harmonica, and Larry does ∅ too.
    b. Phil has bought a new car, and Jane has ∅ too.

The way McCawley (1998) handles the whole proposal regarding *Be*-Insertion and V'-Deletion in chapters 5, 6, and 8 is unfortunately not fully consistent. He identifies nonverbal predicates as acceptable governors of transformations, including *Tough*-Movement and Extraposition, which must apply before *Be*-Insertion (1998, 141). Whether or not the latter transformation applies postcylically, in a way similar to *Do*-Insertion (= *Do*-Support), he states that it must apply after V'-Deletion (1998, 171)—my Predication Phrase Deletion—which he refuses to treat as a precyclic rule (1998, 172). He lists *Do*-Support but not *Be*-Insertion among postcyclic rules. Despite the following observation, he proceeds in the rest of the book with deep structures that include verb phrases headed by *be*, a practice that leads him away from the insight that he did not want to miss:

> A second way requires a significant alteration of our underlying structures but provides insights that would otherwise be missed. Suppose that copula *be* were not included in deep structures (and thus that there was a transformation inserting copula *be*). Predicate adjectives would be in the same deep structure position as any other governors, that is, the governor would in every case be the head of the X' of a [s NP X'] structure. (1998, 141)

If one follows this appealing insight (as I do below) and what McCawley also proposes about the interaction of *Be*-Insertion with cyclic rules, there is every reason to infer that he assumes *Be*-Insertion to apply after Predicate Phrase Deletion simply because he espouses Akmajian and Wasow's position that "V's whose head is extracted retain the status of V'" (McCawley 1998, 208). This entails that deleted nonverbal predicate phrases leave behind a copy that triggers *Be*-Insertion, on the model of *Do*-Support, at some level of the derivation. Without this assumption, McCawley's proposal would require that Predicate Phrase Deletion apply after *Be*-Insertion; otherwise, there would be nothing to trigger the insertion. Thus, as an inserted auxiliary, *be* would have to undergo Attraction to Tense, unlike support *do*.

However, in the rest of the book McCawley actually reopens the door to the problem that Akmajian and Wasow's analysis created: because he posits, or simply represents, a main-verb *be* (or at least he does not identify it as an auxiliary verb) in the deep structure, he lets it undergo Attraction to Tense before the application of Predicate Phrase Deletion. As I show below, the insight being lost is that there is no evidence that the grammar of English has such isomorphism between its deep and surface structures or that the copula as a semantically empty verb is a main verb in the same capacity as verbs such as *become* and *go*. Nor is there evidence that the copula is distinct from all those other forms of *be* identified as "auxiliary" or "existential."

It is also interesting that McCawley does not stick to an alternative analysis that he considers very briefly:

It is thus necessary to revise the above characterization of "governor" to allow for predicate adjectives as governors. One way of doing this is simply to give a disjunctive definition: the governor in a structure [s NP [v' V X]] is the V unless the V is *be* and the X is A', in which case it is the A of the A'. (1998, 141)

This approach to the problem is consistent with my own position (Mufwene 1992b) that grammars are not monolithic, that syntactic rules need not all be triggered by syntactic factors, that "V'-Deletion" is a misnomer for Predicate Phrase Deletion, and that its application conditions are semantic rather than syntactic, at least not exclusively so. However, because copular *be* is not clearly identified as an auxiliary verb, the inconsistency problem that arises from Akmajian and Wasow's analysis survives this solution too. If copular *be* were assumed to be an auxiliary, then McCawley would have to adopt a different kind of deep structure showing that the auxiliary combines not with a V' but with a nonverbal predicate phrase. (It is immaterial now how different this conceivable deep structure would be from the *be*-less alternative that I favor.)

To be sure, it makes sense to assume that like main-verb, or possessive, *have* in British English, the copula behaves like an auxiliary verb in interrogative, emphatic, negative, and elliptical constructions because it is phonetically similar to auxiliary *be* or *be*s in progressive, passive, and modal constructions. However, it would really be informative to determine whether there is no other, more plausible explanation. The same is true of existential *be*. And indeed, every piece of evidence presented below in section 10.3 militates for Dik's (1983) position that copular *be* is nothing more than an auxiliary verb. Copular and existential *be*s are one and the same auxiliary verb and their syntactic behavior is consistent with this identification.

Claiming that *be* is not present in the deep structure but is inserted transformationally has the advantage of providing a unified solution for copular, existential, and other auxiliary *be*s, suggesting that they are all the same, namely, auxiliary constituents (Dik 1983). Here too, one would wish that McCawley had stuck to Dik's conclusion, from which he departs by maintaining a conservative distinction between progressive *be* (which is represented in the deep structure), passive *be* (which is transformationally inserted during the formation of the passive construction), and copular *be* (also transformationally inserted for the reasons discussed above). In chapter 8, McCawley (1998) chooses to distinguish progressive *be* from passive *be* in two ways: first, by representing the former in the deep structure (p. 218) but inserting the latter transformationally (p. 228), and second, by considering the form *be* sufficient in all of the underlying structures and inserting the appropriate suffix on the modified verb in the s-structure. Transformations intended to satisfy English surface morphosyntactic requirements attach the suffix *-ing* to verbs modified by progressive *be* and the suffix *-en* (to be reinterpreted phonetically into the relevant past participial form) to verbs modified by passive *be*.

McCawley's solution is consistent with the identification of modal *be* as an auxiliary verb distinct from the copula, because it combines with an infinitival clause (a matter that I discuss below) but not with a nonverbal predicate.

(9) a. John was to meet Mary here but didn't make it.
    b. John was to *(be) with Mary here but is nowhere to be found.

The meaning of (9b) obviously changes if *to* is also omitted, which can certainly lead to the conclusion—questionable, as I argue below—that modal *be* is different from copular *be*. One winds up with the impression that it is only the copula that McCawley (1998) considers to be semantically empty and that there are as many auxiliary *be*s in English as there are syntactic functions. There is as yet no particular reason why a language would not use the same morpheme, *be* in the case of English or *être* in the case of French, for all the different functions associated with the copula. Nor is there any a priori reason why a morphological distinction must be made between the different syntactic functions that *be* is associated with, or even only between auxiliary *be*s and copular or main-verb *be*. After all, one of McCawley's own assumptions about syntactic representations is that surface structure distinctions need not be isomorphic with deep structure distinctions. In the case of English, he shows that there are many more possibilities in the deep structure than in the surface structure, and norms of well-formedness are not identical for both levels of representation. Thus, *afraid dogs* (or some more abstract representation) may be well formed in the deep structure but not in the surface structure.

In the next section, I argue that McCawley could have chosen a more reductionist approach, in which one and the same copular auxiliary *be* could be inserted transformationally in progressive, passive, modal, and copular constructions, and perhaps also in existential ones.

10.3 Evidence for a Reductionist Analysis of *Be* in English

English does not seem short of evidence for reducing auxiliary and main-verb *be*s to one single, copular case of a semantically empty verb inserted to form a verb phrase out of a predicate phrase headed by a nonverb. If, after examining facts of English discourse, one were to choose intuitively which of the surface discontinuous markers of a progressive construction is for all practical purposes more basic or critical, one's candidate would be the participial suffix *-ing* rather than *be*. That is, some abstract representation such as -ING or PROGRESSIVE would be the ideal candidate in McCawley's kind of deep structure, with *be* inserted in the surface structure only to satisfy the surface combinatoric requirement that he invokes to explain the insertion of copula *be*. Following Ross (1972), the rationale for this is that the participial suffix makes the verb less "verby," or (somewhat) adjective-like; therefore, another item that is more "verby" (and could carry tense in a finite clause) should head the predicate phrase without changing the meaning of the construction. A copula is the designated morphosyntactic item for this function. There are, however, plenty of constructions that indicate that the copula can be omitted under specific pragmatic or sociolinguistic conditions.

In casual speech and in nonstandard varieties such as African American Vernacular English (AAVE), the suffix is retained (albeit with an alveolar, rather than velar, nasal: *-in*) whereas *be* is typically reduced or omitted, as evidenced in Labov 1969 and several studies on copula absence since then. Constructions such as (10a) are common, whereas (10b) is unattested.

(10) a. The boys ('re) goin' there.
     b. *The boys are go there.

Headlines and photo captions are more likely to contain a copulaless construction with a present participial form, such as in (11a), than the alternative in (11b).

(11) a. Bush Heading for the Middle East
     b. *Bush Be Head for the Middle East

The same is true of passive *be*, as illustrated in (12) and (13).

(12) a. Larry('s) *Buried Here/(Being) Driven out of Power*
     b. *Larry's Bury Here/Drive out of Power[8]

(13) a. Prince Driven out of Power
     b. *Prince Be Drive out of Power

In the case of the modal *be* construction, the choice is between, on the one hand, a *be*-less alternative with *to* alone marking the modal function (consistent in some ways with Radford's (1997, 49–54) analysis of this *to* as a nonfinite modal auxiliary) and, on the other, a *to*-less alternative, with *be* alone marking the function.

(14) a. John ∅ to Be with Mary Here[9]
     b. *John ∅ Be with Mary Here
     c. *John ∅∅ with Mary Here

Construction (14b) cannot be interpreted modally, though one may choose to interpret *be* here as a consuetudinal auxiliary in relation to, for instance, Hiberno/Irish English, or as "invariant *be*," as in the literature on AAVE. Unlike all the other instances of *be* discussed so far, this one would not be interpreted as semantically empty. As observed in note 2, the verb would be identified here as a specific aspectual marker, which, consistent with Green's (1998) analysis, does not have the same syntactic behavior as tense and modal auxiliaries. It is used in interrogative, emphatic, and negative constructions with the semantically empty auxiliary *do*.

Construction (14c) cannot be assigned a modal interpretation either. The only conceivable interpretation in this case is 'John is/was with Mary here'. Likewise, (15a) is a conceivable headline or caption whereas (15b) is not, at least not with the intended modal meaning and with *meet* intended as an infinitive. Interestingly, (15c) reports an event that has already taken place, the tense of *meets* having the value of historical present.

(15) a. President Bush to Meet Prime Minister Blair
     b. ?President Bush Meet Prime Minister Blair
     c. President Bush Meets Prime Minister Blair

All these examples illustrate the fact that in headlines and captions, writers select the surface structure parts of predication that preserve the essential meaning and dispense with those that are not essential to interpreting the meaning, including all cases of *be* in would-be finite clauses. The constraints that bear on the above cases also seem to bear on cases of predication traditionally associated with the copula, to the extent that the omission of the copula does not affect the interpretation of the construction, as can be extensively observed in the literature on the absence of the copula in AAVE.

(16) a. Larry is out.
  b. Larry's out.
  c. Larry out.
  d. *Larry is.
  e. *Larry's.

(16d–e) cannot be used nonelliptically with the meaning associated with (16a–c). However, the constructions in (17) would be well-formed photo captions.

(17) a. Crown Prince Out of Power
  b. Bill Tall, Smart, and Highly Appreciated
  c. "The Rock" Fit and Brimming with Enthusiasm

All these examples show that the absence of *be* does not affect the overall meaning of the construction and that it is a kind of "cosmetic constituent" needed to meet a specific target construction in the surface syntax of English, namely, to form a verb phrase where one is needed in finite and nonfinite clauses other than small clauses. *Be* in all these cases seems to be the same morpheme connecting a non- or less-"verby" predicate to the subject noun phrase. It is indeed plausible to assume that the present participial form of the progressive is less "verby." This participial form can carry neither tense nor agreement markers, though it is not fully adjectival either. For instance, in comparative constructions, it behaves like a verb in being followed by its modifier phrase, but not like an attributive adjective, whose modifier precedes it.

(18) a. We heard kids singing louder/more than adults.
  a'. We heard kids sing louder/more than adults.
  b. We heard louder/more kids.
  b'. *We heard kids louder/more singing.
  c. A new gang of kids, noisier than the earlier cohort, passed by.
  c'. *A new gang of kids, more noisily singing than the earlier cohort, passed by.

Adjectives sometimes display a pattern similar to verbs and present participial forms in following, without a copula and in the style of secondary predication, the noun phrase they modify, as shown in (18c–c'). However, they remain different in that their own modifiers must precede them. We can thus safely conclude that the verb *be* used in the progressive is the same copular *be* used before adjectival, prepositional, nominal, adverbial, and less "verby" predicates. The same conclusion can be drawn about the past participial form of the passive construction, which actually displays more similarities with adjectives.

(19) a. Lynn's arguments (were) more easily accepted (by the audience).
  b. Lynn's arguments (were) more easily acceptable (to his audience).

The question about the modal construction is whether *to* is a complementizer or a modal in its own right that requires a bare infinitive. Is it different from the *to* that combines with *able* and *have* in the alternative modal constructions illustrated in (20)?

(20) a. Surprisingly, I could reproduce the narrative intact from my dream.
   a'. Surprisingly, I was *able to* reproduce the narrative intact from my dream.
   b. Andrew must resign.[10]
   b'. Andrew *has to* resign.

Incidentally, (20b) can function as a headline, though it is less clear whether (20b') can. If it can, the omission of *to* would produce an ill-formed headline. Recall, however, that McCawley's conception of syntax allows deep structure material to surface as zero markers. This is true of, for instance, preposition phrases without preposition heads, as in *John wrote a poem (*on/*at) last Tuesday*. Could we therefore assume that modal constructions with *be to* are derivations from some deep structure nonverbal modal material that must combine with an infinitival clause when the complementizer *to* and *be* are inserted to form a verb phrase? Or is it more plausible to assume, like Radford (1997, 49–54), that *to* is a nonfinite modal? As Elaine J. Francis reminds me (pers. comm., September 2003), the modal analysis of *to* (which seems to apply to all cases where it has been identified as a complementizer) is justified, partially at least, by the fact that *to* always combines with a verb phrase, not with a sentence. Much to the credit of the proposed alternative, the relevant, modal *be* precedes *to* (unlike the *be* that sometimes follows the same modal to form a verb phrase out of its complement). Radford's analysis also entails acknowledging the lexical status of modal *to* as nonverbal.

Both analyses have their own merits and undoubtedly some shortcomings that need not be discussed here. What is particularly significant is that neither analysis speaks against treating modal *be* as a copula qua semantically empty auxiliary. There is thus ample support for the reductionist approach that I argue McCawley (1998) could have considered. Although McCawley (1976) also cautions linguists against speciously claiming "significant generalizations" that seem to lack psychological realism, my hypothesis is justified by uses of the same phonetic form, *be* (and its conjugated variants), for what appears to be the same syntactic function.

Dixon (2002, 7) seems to propose a similar reductionist analysis for existential *be*. He states:

[I]n other languages, there is an alternative copula construction in which the C[opula]-C[omplement] is omitted. This applies to Ancient Greek (where one can say 'god is' with the meaning 'god exists, there is a god'), and also to Jarawara.

The analysis seems quite applicable to English, except that the inversion rule associated with *There*-Insertion must apply. However, McCawley (1998, 94–97) reminds us that *There*-Insertion is not restricted to existential *be*. It also applies to several other verbs when the subject has an "existential interpretation" and the verb "ascribes existence or 'visibility' to the subject" (1998, 95), as in (21b–d).

(21) a. There is a Santa Claus.
    a′. *A Santa Claus is.
    b. There arose a commotion.
    b′. A commotion arose.
    c. Yesterday there occurred a tragic event.
    c′. Yesterday a tragic event occurred.
    d. There barked a dog.
    d′. A dog barked.

What makes the existential construction with *be* different is the fact that *There*-Insertion applies obligatorily, a behavior that McCawley seems to associate with its "pure existential" interpretation (1998, 96). There are, in any case, two good reasons for not treating existential *be* as a regular, intransitive main verb: (1) in elliptical constructions, it may not be replaced by the supportive *do* (unlike the verb *exist*); (2) if it is a one-argument predicate, it does not behave like one in most cases where it is used—it cannot be used alone, nonelliptically, after an indefinite subject, as shown in (21a′).

The evidence seems to suggest that existential *be* is a copula, in other words, a semantically empty support/auxiliary verb that should not occur clause-finally unless the construction is elliptical, as in (22).

(22) Was there a car in the driveway? —Yes, there was.

The syntactic behavior is similar to what can also be observed in the following example in which a different verb is used:

(23) Did there arise a commotion after the speech? —Yes, there did/*arose.

The evidence shows that existential *be* behaves like an auxiliary verb and may in fact be one—that is, the copula.

It is difficult to argue strongly for or against the above proposal, even if we can assume a lexically null variant of *exist*. As in the case of modal *be*, the evidence is rather weak, lying essentially in the fact that there is no strong argument against the proposed analysis, which is very reductionist. Support for this reductionism also comes from the fact that the same phonetic form is used for a syntactic function that is the same in all cases, namely, to form a verb phrase where the surface syntax of English requires one. And one particular consideration that seems to favor the conclusion that one and the same copular *be* is used in all the cases considered so far is this: it is curious that in a language that has lexicalized fine distinctions in the semantics of auxiliary verbs (e.g., different ways of expressing obligation), so many different functions would be associated with what appears to be one and the same verb *be*. The case would seem peculiar even under the nonmonolithic conception of grammar outlined in Mufwene 1992b, which cautions that grammatical principles of a language need not be consistent with each other. I conclude that all the *be*s traditionally identified as copular, progressive, passive, modal, and existential are all the same copular *be*; moreover, as pointed out by Elaine J. Francis (pers. comm., September 2003), the meanings associated with these different functions can be attributed to other elements present in each construction.

The remaining question is whether copular *be* is a main verb or an auxiliary verb. I have suggested so far that it is an auxiliary, because, like other auxiliary verbs in English, it is used elliptically and as a support element in inverted, negated, emphatic, and tag question constructions. I have also pointed out analogies with the auxiliary *do*, with which it seems to be in complementary distribution,[11] and I have highlighted the fact that it is a semantically empty surface-structure constituent, at least in the functions traditionally identified as a copula and as progressive and passive auxiliaries, and conceivably also as a modal auxiliary and as an existential verb. It can be omitted without loss of meaning in the predicate phrase in small clauses and in headlines. In the present modification of McCawley's (1988/1998) conception of syntactic derivations, it is after the formation of the verb phrase that *be* in any of the above functions can also be used elliptically to stand for the nonverbal predicates that it would otherwise appear with.

One can see why Akmajian and Wasow (1975) had to devise a *Be*-Shift rule to move copular *be* from its main-verb position to an auxiliary position. However, this was an approach that must have also had to invoke a more ad hoc deletion rule to account for the absence of *be* in headlines and photo captions, as well as in small clauses, especially in those contexts where there is no conceivable alternative in which the secondary predicate phrase would be headed by *be*.

(24) a. Mary caught *Larry$_i$ $\emptyset_i$ naked in her room.*
 a'. *Mary caught *Larry$_i$ $\emptyset_i$ be/was naked in her room.*
 b. *Bill$_i$ could be seen $\emptyset_i$ standing on the table.*
 b'. *Bill$_i$ could be seen $\emptyset_i$ be/was standing on the table.*
 c. John$_i$ stood on the platform $\emptyset_i$ *singing the national anthem.*
 c'. *John$_i$ stood on the platform $\emptyset_i$ *be/was singing the national anthem.*
 d. *The body$_i$ lay on the ground $\emptyset_i$ covered with blood.*
 d'. *The body$_i$ lay on the ground $\emptyset_i$ be/was covered with blood.*
 e. He wiped *the dust$_i$ $\emptyset_i$ off the table.*
 e'. *He wiped *the dust$_i$ $\emptyset_i$ be/was off the table.*

The proposed analysis is admittedly quite abstract, of the kind that syntacticians have been moving away from since the late 1970s, and I can see why McCawley

(1988/1998) would have avoided it. Truly, the complication in the analysis arises only with regard to modal and existential *be* that some linguists may prefer to treat as exceptional. On the other hand, the argument that there must be some good reason why the same phonetic form *be* (and all its allomorphs) is used for all these seemingly different functions is not without its merits. In the next section, I will articulate more benefits to be gained from this analysis.

10.4 Conclusions

One of the peculiarities of McCawley's (1988/1998) syntax is its dual interest in, on the one hand, language-particular facts and, on the other, typological and language-universal considerations. One can recognize this strength also in Dixon's (2002) discussion of the copula in Australian languages, which starts with typological considerations, some of which were discussed above. I conclude this chapter with such observations. The most significant difference between English and languages that allow nonverbal predicate phrases is that English requires a verb phrase in all but small clauses. It differs from some languages that likewise show a strong preference for VP-orientation (like Swahili) in using what appears to be one and the same verb, *be*, identified in the proposed analysis as a copula. It behaves in all respects like a semantically empty auxiliary verb and is thus similar to *do*, with which it seems to be in complementary distribution. The latter combines with, or replaces, verb phrases, whereas *be* combines with, or replaces, nonverbal predicate phrases.

The proposed analysis also helps us understand why in English creoles and others that have developed from Western European languages (whose predication pattern is VP-oriented), the copula has been lost especially before adjectival and prepositional predicates. Concurrent with their tendency to dispense with redundant and/or semantically empty surface-structure fillers, they have also dispensed with the copula. Like languages such as Mandarin Chinese, these new vernaculars prefer that adjectives and prepositions not combine with a copula when they head a predicate phrase. One can say that they are PredP-oriented in the sense that whatever heads the predicate phrase in the deep structure remains its head in the surface structure. The exception is noun phrases, which in most of these languages must then be headed by a copula. In the case of creoles such as Jamaican, there is also a specialized locative copula, as in (25c), which can be argued not to be semantically empty and can be treated as a regular verb.[12]

(25) a. Kieti taal.
 Katie tall
 'Katie [is] tall.'

b. Ingrid (de) ina di hows.
     Ingrid be in the house
     'Ingrid [is] in the house.'
  c. Maria de huom.
     Maria is home
     'Maria is home.'

Sentence (25b) illustrates the same point, although *de* is optional before a locative preposition, simply because it becomes redundant before a more specific locative marker. This optionality is a consequence of the fact that a predicate phrase can also be headed by a preposition in the surface structure.

Regardless of whether substrate influence is taken into account, an important factor in this particular evolution from the English system is the loss of the finite/nonfinite distinction (Mufwene and Dijkhoff 1989) and the expression of tenses with periphrastic markers rather than with verbal affixes, which would certainly make the copula useless. It has been retained most in equative/identificational clauses, where it is typically followed by a noun phrase, and, as noted above, in locative contexts. In both cases, it carries no tense inflections. In some creoles, the forms are also different. For instance, in Jamaican Creole, the identificational copula is *a* (pronounced [a]), whereas the locative one is *de* (pronounced [dɛ]).

These creole data confirm a reason why the English verb *be* has been identified by so many different names. It has been associated with different syntactic functions, which in some languages are served by different lexical items. From an evolutionary point of view, the data also show that even these grammatical distinctions bore on language-restructuring processes that produced creoles, regardless of whether substrate influence is invoked. Syntacticians may have seen all such typological evidence as justification for positing so many different *be*s in English. Yet the language-specific evidence adduced in section 10.3 is compelling enough to posit one and the same *be*, a copula or a semantically empty auxiliary, in all the contexts. It is actually sound typology to show that not exactly the same surface-syntactic distinctions are made from one language to another.

My analysis also enables us to take a closer look at previous analyses of the variable absence of the copula in AAVE. First, it was not necessary for Labov (1969) to discuss copula absence in terms of "low-level," phonological deletion. As argued in Mufwene 1992b, a Copula-Insertion rule, subject to the same phonological constraints as the Copula-Deletion rule, can also account adequately for the same facts. One must remember that the distributional patterns of copula absence are not parallel to those of copula contraction; and, contrary to Labov's claims, the copula is not "deleted" just in a subset of those contexts where it can be contracted. A redisplay of Labov's own statistics shows copula absence to be in inverse proportion to both the full copula and contractions (Mufwene 1992a; for a more elaborate discussion, see Kautzsch 2002, chap. 4).

To be sure, Labov was influenced by syntactic analyses of the 1960s that all represented *be* underlyingly. However, it is now obvious that copula insertion analyses of *be* could perhaps account more insightfully, or just less ad hoc–ly, for the behavior of the copula in standard English itself, especially in regard to Predicate-Phrase Deletion (traditionally identified as Verb-Phrase Deletion) and Subject-Auxiliary Inversion. What Labov needed then is what he accomplishes in Labov 1998 with the notion of "coexistent systems"—that is, a conception of grammar that, like the non-monolithic grammar proposed in Mufwene 1992b, allows two or more (partial) grammars, with different typological orientations, to coexist and therefore compete with each other in the same language variety. In the present case, this view holds that speakers alternate between dominant VP orientation, typical of standard English, and PredP orientation, also attested in some English creoles (among others), thus accounting for the variation that has been the subject of so many investigations in variationist sociolinguistics (see Rickford 1998).

Second, Labov (1969) need not have apologized for lumping all instances of *be* (progressive, passive, and copular) together. It appears that they all belong together in English (a dialect of which is AAVE, after all): they are all copular, according to the definition given by Dixon (2002, 8):

[F]or a verb to be identified as a copula, it must occur with two core arguments, C[opula]-S[subject] and C[opula]C[omplement], with CC including at least the identity/equation relation, (a), or the attributive relation, (b).

Assuming that present and past participial forms function as CCs, as they are not fully "verby," we can reexamine why the rate of copula absence is the highest before progressive verbs. The discussion in section 10.3 suggests that the present participle is more "verby" than the past participle, which is more adjectival. The copula would thus seem maximally redundant before it, the *-ing* suffix being sufficient to express the progressive meaning. Since the different grammatical principles of a language need not be monolithically integrated, some may be semantically motivated and others may be motivated by purely syntactic factors (Mufwene 1992b). In AAVE, progressive constructions may be the cutoff line in patterns of predication between VP orientation and PredP orientation, the fact that there is strong variation between absence and presence of the copula notwithstanding.[13]

We must bear in mind that predication is also an area of considerable nonmonolithicity in the sense that VP orientation, marked by copula presence, and PredP orientation, allowing copula absence, coexist significantly in AAVE, although the variationist literature clearly shows that in the case of predicative adjectives, prepositions, and noun phases, instances of copula absence are in the minority relative to instances of full and contracted copula combined. The fact that the rate of copula absence is the lowest before predicative noun phrases is something that AAVE shares not only with English creoles but also with Mandarin Chinese, in which the predicative noun phrase is almost obligatorily linked to the subject by a copula. All these cross-systemic considerations appear to support the analysis proposed in this chapter.

Notes

1. According to the same tradition, the copula applies to functions that are identificational (e.g., *Monica is the lady he wanted to meet*) and equative (e.g., *Vesper is the Evening Star*), and it also links adjectival and locative predicates to the subject. (See also Dixon 2002.) I assume the *be* of cleft-focused constructions to be identificational too, although there are languages in which a specialized focus marker is used for this function, in a construction that is not a literal translation of the English. One such language is Kikongo-Kituba (spoken in the Democratic Republic of Congo), in which the focus marker *si* is clearly different from the copula *ké(l)e*, as illustrated in (i) and (ii).

(i) *Si* Mobútu (ya) bantu zól-áká vé.
    FOC Mobutu (CON) people like-PAST not
    'It's Mobutu (that) people didn't like.'

(ii) Péteto *ké(l)e* muntu ya mubúlú.
    Peter COP person CON trouble
    'Peter is turbulent/Peter causes trouble.'

2. There are nonstandard English dialects, such as African American Vernacular English (AAVE), in which it is possible to ask questions similar to those identified as ill formed in (1a′) and (1b′).

(i) Do Paul be loud?

(ii) Do Paul be talkin' a lot?

This *be* is known as "consuetudinal," denoting repeated processes. As Green (1998) explains it, in the case of AAVE consuetudinal *be* is an aspectual marker, which is not subject to the Subject-Auxiliary Inversion rule. In such varieties, the copula still undergoes Subject-Auxiliary Inversion, as in (iii) and (iv).

(iii) Is Paul tall?

(iv) *Do/Does Paul be tall?

Consistent with the position to be defended in the text, *be* in (i)–(ii) is considered as the (primary) marker of the relevant aspect, not as a copula. The construction changes its meaning, and is therefore no longer the same, once consuetudinal *be* is omitted. Sentences (v) and (vi) are not synonymous.

(v) Paul be loud. (i.e., 'Every time I visit or see Paul, I find him speaking loud, though he may not be a loud person.')

(vi) Paul (is) loud. (i.e., 'Paul speaks loud—that's his characteristic.')

3. Some studies (e.g., Dowty 1979; Partee 1977, 1986) have suggested even more distinctions, recognizing for instance an equative or identificational *be*, which raises the same syntactic problem as the copular and existential *be*s. See Dixon 2002 for a fuller catalogue of the

distinctions. They are relevant typologically, to the extent that there are languages such as Swahili that indeed use different verbs for some of the meanings conveyed by these putatively different *be*s. However, the reductionist conclusion of this chapter makes it unnecessary to consider the full range of these distinctions here, at least in McCawley's (1988/1998) transformational framework, in which the surface structure sometimes contains forms that correspond to no particular constituents in the deep structure, as in the case of *of* in *the development of a hypothesis*.

4. For a history of the role of the copula in the debate on predication since Aristotle, see Lenci 1998. I wish to underscore the fact that copular *be* in particular is not used in English constructions to carry tense, contrary to what has often been suggested in the syntax literature. Rather, its function is to form a verb phrase where one is required, in both finite and nonfinite clauses. (For a similar observation, see also Dixon 2002, 9.) The only exception seems to be small clauses, in which a copula is not used and which appear to give us an idea of what the required elements of predication are in English. What makes my observation significant here is the fact that nonfinite clauses, such as those in (i) and (ii), do not seem to carry any particular tense, at least not morphologically, even if one invoked McCawley's (1988/1998) own Tense Replacement rule, which would allow for a "zero morpheme."

(i) Everybody wants to be happy.

(ii) Jane wouldn't mind being alone during the next few months.

Considering (ii), one might want to argue that the role of the copula is actually to carry verbal inflections, without which predication would be incomplete (Lenci 1998). Such a position makes sense only if one also assumes that *be* in (i) is inflected as well (say, with a null form). Otherwise, the position I advocate makes more sense, assuming that secondary predication is as informative as primary predication, with some temporal information having to be inferred from semantic properties of the main verb. My position is further supported by the common assumption since Emonds 1976 that modal verbs and other auxiliary verbs take verb phrases as their objects. Copular *be* can be interpreted to play precisely the role explained above, to avoid ill-formed constructions such as (iv).

(iii) Billy can be noisy.

(iv) *Billy can noisy.

This is the kind of explanation that McCawley (1988/1998) provides in chapter 8—namely, nonfinite *be* occurs where the preceding verb requires a VP complement, regardless of whether the infinitive is introduced by the complementizer *to* or not.

5. Rothstein (1999) argues against the position that the copula is a semantically empty constituent that is motivated only by the surface syntax of typologically English-like languages. According to her, sentences like (i) and (ii) are not completely synonymous, because "it has often been commented that small clauses like in [(i)] 'feel' more 'individual level', inherent, or general than their inflected verbal [i.e., infinitival] counterparts" in (ii), which "[are] used [simply?] to make an individual level predication" (p. 349).

(i) Mary believes/considers Jane very clever.

(ii) Mary believes/considers Jane to be very clever.

Yet the following alternatives suggest that this putative semantic difference may have more to do with specific semantic or pragmatic properties of the predicate *clever* or its particular co-occurrence with the matrix verbs *believe* and *consider* than with the alternation of small and infinitival clauses per se:

(iii) I expect Jane *(to be) very nice.

(iv) I believe/consider the duty nurse *(to be) Rina.

In any case, although these contrasts are relevant to understanding when copulaless constructions are permitted in English, Rothstein's basic position is peripheral to the main arguments of this chapter. Since I do not find her arguments compelling, I will leave the matter alone and focus here on insights that can be gained from studying what I will identify as the Dik-McCawley syntactic approach to the copula.

6. Until he gets to chapter 8, which plays a kind of "magical role" in the articulation of his framework, he is apologetic about including *be* in some deep structures:

> ... however, copula *be* will be included in the deep structures presented below even though it strictly speaking need not—in fact, should not—be there. (McCawley 1998, 142)

7. Had McCawley opted to remain closer to the more abstract representations of Generative Semantics, the meaning of FEAR in *afraid* would be represented in a rather abstract way that captures the partial synonymy between the adjective *afraid* and the verb *fear* and only the syntactic derivation, under specific pragmatic specifications, would determine the choice of *afraid* and its identification in the surface structure as Adjective. This would motivate the insertion of the semantically empty preposition *of* between this surface adjectival predicate head and its object. Thus, *of*-Insertion prevents violating a surface combinatoric constraint of English that does not allow an object complement to combine directly with an adjective, contrary to what happens in the case of verbs. Likewise, the deep structure of *development* in *development of a hypothesis* would be something that captures its partial synonymy with the verb *develop*. A nominalization transformation, under specific pragmatic conditions, would yield the surface form *development*. As surface combinatoric principles of English disallow combining a noun directly with its direct object, except in compounds (in which case the object precedes the noun), the preposition *of* is inserted between the noun and its object.

8. In the case of *bury*, it is possible that the final consonant could be omitted here in AAVE, but this is also one of those environments where the omission rule is the least likely to apply, because the word-final consonant is not part of a consonant cluster. Also, because semantically empty elements are more likely to be deleted than morphemes that carry meanings, it would be surprising to see the past participle marker omitted while the copula is retained even in the contracted form.

9. The *be* that is retained in these examples is not modal *be*. Although it is a copula, it is not the item under discussion in these examples. It must occur here because the complementizer *to* (for this seems to be the identity of *to* that follows modal *be*) must combine with an infinitival clause. It is thus a second *be* that is inserted in the complement clause. The full clause contains two *bes*: *John was|is to **be** with Mary*.

10. It is worth noting that modal auxiliaries behave differently from the nonmodal auxiliary *have*, which McCawley characterizes as a lexicalization of PAST tense in nonfinite contexts (including the present perfect, where PAST is underlyingly in the scope of PRESENT). Modal auxiliaries are typically retained in headlines, whereas the tense auxiliary is omitted. For instance, one could not form headlines (i) and (iii), rather than (ii) and (iv), corresponding to sentences (v) and (vi).

(i) House (Finally) Passed Gun Control Bill

(ii) House (Finally) Passes Gun Control Bill

(iii) Harper Elected Mayor (with the intended meaning corresponding to ((iv) and (vi))

(iv) Harper to Be Elected Mayor

(v) The House has finally passed the gun control bill

(vi) Harper will be elected mayor

The fact that (ii) rather than (i) is the correct headline for (v) indicates that the present perfect definitely bridges the past and present tenses, bearing in mind that (ii) can also be interpreted to mean 'The House finally passed the gun control bill'. Headline (ii) cannot refer to a future (irrealis) tense. Note also that the correct headline for (vi) is (iv) but not (iii) and that *will* is replaced in such cases by something reminiscent of modal *be*, which is omitted in (iv). Passive *be* is retained here only because *to* must combine with a verb phrase, as observed in note 9.

11. The anonymous reviewer asks why, unlike auxiliary *do*, the copula is obligatory in affirmative constructions (except of course in small clauses). That it is obligatory in standard English (but not in some nonstandard dialects, at least not in all environments) is a consequence of VP orientation, as opposed to PredP orientation, in the surface structure combinatoric rules of English. That *Do*-Support is required in interrogative sentences, for instance, is a consequence of the fact that English, unlike French, does not allow the inversion of main verbs. There are simply so many different principles that interact in a grammar.

12. I am aware of positions such as Lenci's (1998, 234) that claim a "copulative function" applicable to a wide range of verbs (e.g., *become*) and identify *be* as the copula par excellence (in Lenci's own words, "*primus inter pares*"), because it is semantically empty. It is not clear to me that my statement that the "locative copula" can be treated as a regular, noncopular verb is at odds with this view.

13. Things are certainly more complex in AAVE, where phonological considerations cannot be completely ignored. Labov (1969) was correct in highlighting the phonological constraints that seem to apply the most when the copula has the form *is* and are so similar to those that apply also to genitive *'s* and to third person singular verbal forms in the present tense. This all shows how nonmonolithic the structure of a language can be.

References

Akmajian, Adrian, and Thomas Wasow. 1975. The constituent structure of VP and AUX and the position of the verb *be*. *Linguistic Analysis* 1, 205–45.

Bach, Emmon. 1967. The algebra of events. *Linguistics and Philosophy* 9, 5–16.

Dik, Simon C. 1983. Auxiliary and copula *be* in a functional grammar of English. In *Linguistic categories: Auxiliaries and related puzzles*. Vol. 2, *The scope, order, and distribution of auxiliary verbs*, ed. by Frank Heny and Barry Richards, 121–43. Dordrecht: Reidel.

Dixon, R. M. W. 2002. Copula clauses in Australian languages: A typological perspective. *Anthropological Linguistics* 1, 1–36.

Dowty, David. 1979. *Word meaning and Montague Grammar*. Dordrecht: Reidel.

Emonds, Joseph E. 1976. *A transformational approach to English syntax: Root, structure-preserving, and local transformations*. New York: Academic Press.

Green, Lisa. 1998. Aspect and predicate phrases in African-American Vernacular English. In *African-American English: Structure, history and use*, ed. by Salikoko S. Mufwene, John R. Rickford, Guy Bailey, and John Baugh, 37–68. London: Routledge.

Iwakura, Kinihiro. 1977. The auxiliary system in English. *Linguistic Analysis* 3, 101–36.

Kautzsch, Alexander. 2002. *The historical evolution of earlier African American English: An empirical comparison of early sources*. Berlin: Mouton de Gruyter.

Labov, William. 1969. Contraction, deletion and inherent variability of the English copula. *Language* 45, 714–62.

Labov, William. 1998. Co-existent systems in African-American Vernacular English. In *African-American English: Structure, history and use*, ed. by Salikoko S. Mufwene, John R. Rickford, Guy Bailey, and John Baugh, 110–53. London: Routledge.

Lenci, Alessandro. 1998. The structure of predication. *Synthese* 114, 233–76.

McCawley, James D. 1976. Some ideas not to live by. *Die neueren Sprachen* 75, 151–65. Reprinted in *Adverbs, vowels, and other objects of wonder*, 234–46. Chicago: University of Chicago Press, 1979.

McCawley, James D. 1977. Evolutionary parallels between Montague Grammar and transformational grammar. In *Proceedings of the Seventh Annual Meeting of the Northeastern Linguistic Society*, ed. by Judy Anne Kegl, David Nash, and Annie Zaenen, 219–32. Amherst: University of Massachusetts, GLSA. Reprinted in *Adverbs, vowels, and other objects of wonder*, 122–32. Chicago: University of Chicago Press, 1979.

McCawley, James D. 1988. *The syntactic phenomena of English*. Chicago: University of Chicago Press. 2nd ed., 1998.

Mufwene, Salikoko S. 1992a. Ideology and facts on African American English. *Pragmatics* 2, 141–66.

Mufwene, Salikoko S. 1992b. Why grammars are not monolithic. In *The joy of grammar: A festschrift for James D. McCawley*, ed. by Diane Brentari, Gary N. Larson, and Lynn A. MacLeod, 225–50. Amsterdam: John Benjamins.

Mufwene, Salikoko S. 1994. Double modals in American Southern English: How peculiar are they? In *Contemporary linguistics*, ed. by John A. Goldsmith, Salikoko S. Mufwene, Barbara Need, and David Testen, 1:89–109. University of Chicago Working Papers in Linguistics. Chicago: University of Chicago, Department of Linguistics.

Mufwene, Salikoko S., and Marta B. Dijkhoff. 1989. On the so-called "infinitive" in Atlantic creoles. *Lingua* 77, 319–52.

Partee, Barbara. 1977. John is easy to please. In *Linguistic structures processing*, ed. by Antonio Zampolli, 281–312. Amsterdam: North-Holland.

Partee, Barbara. 1986. Ambiguous pseudoclefts with unambiguous "be." In *Proceedings NELS 16*, ed. by 354–66. Amherst: University of Massachusetts, Amherst.

Radford, Andrew. 1997. *Syntactic theory and the structure of English: A minimalist approach*. Cambridge: Cambridge University Press.

Rickford, John R. 1998. The creole origins of African-American Vernacular English: Evidence from copula absence. In *African-American English: Structure, history and use*, ed. by Salikoko S. Mufwene, John R. Rickford, Guy Bailey, and John Baugh, 154–200. London: Routledge.

Rosenbaum, Peter S. 1967. *The grammar of English predicate complement constructions.* Cambridge, MA: MIT Press.

Ross, John R. 1972. The category squish: Endstation Hauptwort. In *Proceedings of the Eighth Regional Meeting, Chicago Linguistic Society*, ed. by Paul M. Peranteau, Judith N. Levi, and Gloria C. Phares, 316–28. Chicago: University of Chicago, Chicago Linguistic Society.

Rothstein, Susan D. 1999. Fine-grained structure in the eventuality domain: The semantics of predicate adjective phrases and *be*. *Natural Language Semantics* 7, 347–420.

Sadock, Jerrold M. 1991. *Autolexical Syntax: A theory of parallel grammatical representations.* Chicago: University of Chicago Press.

PART III
Tense, Aspect, and Mood

Chapter 11
On McCawley on Tense — Robert I. Binnick

11.1 Introduction

Given that much of Jim McCawley's Generative Semantics work of the late 1960s and early 1970s is relevant to the study of Aktionsart (i.e., "lexical" or "situation" aspect), it is striking how little he actually published concerning the allied topics of tense and verbal ("grammatical" or "viewpoint") aspect. His work in this area is remembered today chiefly for his account of the English present perfect in "Tense and Time Reference in English" (henceforth TTRE), a 1969 conference paper (published in 1971), but also for his anticipation in that paper of Barbara Hall Partee's (1973) famous observation (in "Some Structural Analogies between Tenses and Pronouns") that tenses act like pronouns. Indeed, it is upon this one paper, TTRE, and its sequel, "Notes on the English Present Perfect" (1981b), that McCawley's not inconsiderable reputation as a scholar of tense and aspect chiefly rests.

It is unfortunate that McCawley never produced a book on semantics parallel to his major works on logic (1981a/1993) and English syntax (1988/1998). Though there is, naturally enough, a great deal of material of a semantic nature in both books, his treatment of tense and verbal aspect shows little influence of the mainstream of the semantic literature. While his approach to these phenomena is sometimes that of the logician, concerned with the translation of natural language

---

The personal voice of Jim McCawley can often be heard in his academic prose, but his writings provide merely a hint of the living presence of the man, which survives now only in the memories of those who were fortunate enough to have known him. He always seemed to be getting fifty percent more out of life than anyone else, and perhaps he was. The genius of the man is amply exhibited in his works, but the rest—the sartorial eccentricities, the strident walk, the gestures (the rolled-back eyes and thrown-back head; the quavering, deictic finger), the stutter (in English, but surprisingly absent from the several other languages he spoke), the Scottish/American accent, the sheer good humor—is gone, along with the stack of woks on the kitchen floor, the music scores in the coat pocket, the briefcase full of offprints. We are left to console ourselves for the incomprehensible loss of the man with the brilliance of the works he left us. They're not enough, but they'll have to do.

expressions into formulae of an unambiguous formal language, and sometimes that of the syntactician, concerned with the mappings between levels of linguistic representations, it is only infrequently that of the semantician, whose principal concern is with the interpretation of linguistic expressions.

It is possibly for this reason that Partee's 1973 paper has had much more impact on the field than McCawley's 1969 one. Although TTRE scooped Partee's paper, the latter can justifiably be said to have introduced into the study of tense and aspect the contrast between temporal deixis and temporal anaphoresis, since it influenced or engendered quite a large number of other works by some of the most prominent scholars of tense and aspect, including, but by no means restricted to, Bennett (1977), Hinrich (1986), Hornstein (1990), Janssen (1996), Kleiber (1993), Lo Cascio (1986), and Vetters (1993), though Houweling (1986), for example, credits the distinction to McCawley, and Moens and Steedman (1988) refer to both authors.

In fact, the first three sentences of the quotation in (1) must be among the most frequently cited passages in the tense literature, being quoted by, among others, Baüerle (1979, 228), Dowty (1979, 330–31), Nerbonne (1984, 11), and Saurer (1984, 41).

(1) The deictic use of the Past tense morpheme appears in a sentence like [*I didn't turn off the stove*]. When uttered, for instance, halfway down the turnpike, such a sentence clearly does not mean either that there exists some time in the past at which I did not turn off the stove or that there exists no time in the past at which I turned off the stove. The sentence clearly refers to a particular time— not a particular instant, most likely, but a definite interval whose identity is generally clear from the extra-linguistic context, just as the identity of the *he* in [*He shouldn't be in here*, accompanied by a gesture to point out the referent] is clear from the context. In the case of deictic Past tense there is no analog to the pointing gesture that is often used with deictic pronouns. But deictic pronouns need not be accompanied by gestures; the referent may be understood from the context without being physically present, as in [*She left me*]. (Partee 1973, 602–3)

To this deictic use of tenses, Partee contrasts (1973, 605) their anaphoric use, found in sentences like (2). In this example, the past tense of *got* has as antecedent the past tense of the preceding clause; but a tense can also, she observes, take as antecedent an entire clause, as in sentence (3), in which the *when*-clause serves as antecedent to the past tense verb *left*.[1] That is, Sam in (2) got drunk *when* Sheila had a party, and Peter left in (3) *when* Susan walked in.

(2) Sheila had a party last Friday and Sam got drunk.

(3) When Susan walked in, Peter left.

On McCawley on Tense

Although, as noted above, McCawley's primary perspective was generally syntactic or logical rather than semantic, the treatment of tenses as bound variables (see section 11.3) in TTRE and in the above-mentioned books is in some respects more attuned to natural language and less grounded in purely abstract logic than is Partee's approach in either her 1973 paper or (to a lesser extent) its 1984 successor, "Nominal and Temporal Anaphora."

The present chapter examines McCawley's theory of tense in TTRE and contrasts it with that in Partee's 1973 paper, thereby implicitly evaluating McCawley's place in the development of the theory of tense. What I propose is that McCawley's (1969) approach is superior in certain regards to Partee's, and avoids criticisms that have been leveled at the latter work.

11.2 Partee on Temporal Deixis and Anaphora

The starting point for both Partee and McCawley is Priorian tense logic (Prior 1967), which is less than optimal for the analysis of natural language, in part because it defines the past and future tenses indefinitely. A past-tensed sentence is translated into a formula of the logical translation language having the form $P\alpha$, constructed from the past tense operator P and some formula α. Such a formula $P\alpha$ is interpreted as true just in case α obtains at *some* point in time t prior to the present moment; likewise, one formed with the future tense operator F (i.e., $F\alpha$) is true if and only if α is true at some point later in time than the present. This has the undesirable result, for example, of rendering the simple past synonymous with the present perfect tense, since both *John has been happy* and *John was happy* are true if and only if *John is happy* has ever been true.

It is interesting to note that in the theory of tense developed by Partee in collaboration with Michael Bennett in their 1972 report (published in a revised version in 1978), tenses are analyzed in an essentially Priorian way, so that *John ate the fish yesterday* is held to be true if and only if *John eats the fish* is true of *some* interval of time I within yesterday. In a sense, the inability of Bennett and Partee at that time to supply a compositional account of such expressions—failing, that is, to separate out the interpretation of the temporal adverbial from that of the tense itself—covers over to a great extent the deficient Priorian analysis of the past as an indefinite tense, for the adverbial supplies a *definite* interval within which the event in question transpires.

In the 1973 paper, however, Partee treats the past tense in a non-Priorian way. She observes that the past tense in sentence (4) points to a definite, given period of time, so that (4) does *not* mean 'I have never turned off the stove'.

(4) I didn't turn off the stove.

In the quotation presented in (1), Partee offers up sentence (4) as an example of a use of the past tense parallel to the deictic use of a pronoun such as that of *he* in sentence (5).

(5) He shouldn't be in here.

In doing so, she effectively identifies temporal deixis with definiteness, for the deicticness of (4) consists in the temporal reference of the tense in (4) being supplied not by an antecedent but by context, as is the referent of *he* in (5). But in the case of indefinite tenses such as the present perfect, where there is no definite temporal referent, there can be no question of deixis, since there is no referent to be supplied by context or otherwise.

That Partee was considering the *uses* of tenses and not their *meanings*, unlike many of the scholars who followed her, is made clear by her observation that the tenses in sentences like (6) have both anaphoric and deictic readings.

(6) If you were king, you could cut off the hands of everyone who offended you.

In (6), *offended*, on a deictic reading, refers to actual past acts of offense: in the hypothetical world in which the interlocutor is king, he could punish those who offended him in the past in the real world. On an anaphoric reading, however, it refers to present and/or future offenses in the hypothetical world in which the addressee is king: the king could punish anyone who might in future offend him.

As Kleiber (1993) observes, there are many ways in which the distinction of the temporal deictic and anaphoric has been interpreted, some mutually contradictory, and many not at all in line with Partee's intention. In syntactic theory, an anaphoric pronoun is classically one that refers to an antecedent *within* the sentence, and a deictic pronoun one that does not. From this point of view, the past tenses of *got* and *left* in (2) and (3), taking as their points of reference the preceding verb and clause respectively, are anaphoric, while the past tense of (4), which has no such referent within the sentence, is not. Thus, in the 1973 paper, a tense is considered deictic to the extent that there is no antecedent for it within the sentence and definite insofar as there is a given time at which the eventuality takes place.

As Kleiber points out, however, deixis has had various definitions, including the introduction of a new referent into a discourse or text, and from that point of view an example such as (4) cannot be both deictic and definite at the same time, since definiteness requires an already given time, which deixis precludes. To identify deicticness with definiteness thus requires a rather different conception of deixis than many scholars of pronominal reference have adopted.

As it happens, Partee is in error when she relates example (4) to pronominal examples in which the referent is somehow understood from the context. For example, (4) is precisely parallel to examples in which a pronoun lacks an antecedent in the sentence, but has one in *another* sentence of the discourse or text. Thus, the relevant comparison to (4) is not example (7), in which the pronoun *she* could receive its referent by ostension (pointing out), but an example such as (8), in which the pronoun *she* refers back to *Emma Woodhouse*, found in the preceding sentence.[2]

(7) She left me.

(8) Emma Woodhouse, handsome, clever, and rich, had lived nearly twenty-one years with very little to distress or vex her. She was the youngest of the two daughters of a most affectionate, indulgent father.

This is one reason why in her 1984 paper Partee adopts a discourse-based approach that resolves the apparent contradiction between the newness and the givenness of the referent. If we identify temporal deixis with the introduction into a discourse of a new reference point, and anaphoresis with the maintenance of the current reference point, then a tense may legitimately have an antecedent *outside* the sentence. Accordingly, it is quite possible to view tenses as bound variables without their in fact being anaphoric in the way pronouns are taken to be in syntactic theory.

As it happens, McCawley in TTRE (p. 110) anticipates this same position by explicitly adopting a version of temporal anaphoresis in which the referents of tenses may occur outside the sentence. Thus, in the very passage quoted in (9), in which he anticipates Partee's treatment of tenses as pronouns, he refers to the "antecedent" of the past tense in the sentence *The farmer killed the duckling*.

(9) [T]he tense morpheme does not just express the time relationship between the clause that it is in, and the next higher clause—it also refers to the time of the clause that it is in, and indeed, refers to it in a way that is rather like the way in which personal pronouns refer to what they stand for. For example, a past tense normally requires an antecedent: [*The farmer killed the duckling*] is odd unless the prior context provides a time for the past tense to refer to; the oddity of [this sentence] without an antecedent for the past tense is exactly the oddity that is left in [*He resembles Mike*] when uttered in a context which has not provided any prior mention of a person for the *he* to refer to.

Over time, many scholars have reinterpreted Partee's purely pragmatic distinction as a semantic one and classified tenses as deictic or anaphoric.

This reinterpretation, along with the differing conceptions of deixis and anaphoresis in the 1973 and 1984 papers, has led to a number of controversies, precisely because tenses belonging to one of the categories may have *uses* characteristic of the other type. One such controversy involves the narrative (hence "deictic" or "definite") use of the *imparfait*, the imperfect tense of French, as in Ducrot's (1979) example (10), where *achetais* 'purchased' advances reference time in narrative and hence, on one definition of temporal deixis, constitutes an example of a deictic tense—or at least the deictic use of an otherwise anaphoric tense. Hence, Lo Cascio (1986) groups the "imparfait" both with definite tenses such as the past and with indefinite tenses such as the pluperfect, while Houweling (1986), in the same volume, groups it only with the "nonautonomous" tenses.

(10) Idiot que je suis! L'année dernière j'achetais un appareil de photo dont je n'avais besoin et cette année, je n'ai même pas de quoi de me payer le cinéma. 'What an idiot I am! Last year I bought (*j'achetais*) a camera which I didn't need and this year, I don't even have enough to pay for a movie.'

Partee's argument against analyzing tenses in terms of Priorian operators and in favor of treating tenses as bound variables itself proved a source of controversy. For if tenses are just like pronouns, then when they are interpreted anaphorically, they must be bound by their antecedents just as pronouns are. Hence, Partee translates (11) into (12), which can be read as in (13), capturing thereby the fact that the time of John's leaving is not just *any* time in the future, but a time t' in the immediate future of the time t at which Susan comes in.

(11) If Susan comes in, John will leave immediately.

(12) $(\exists t)\varphi(t) \supset \Psi((\text{Imm}(\text{Fut}))((\iota t)\varphi(t)))$

(13) There is a time t at which Susan's coming in at t implies John's leaving at a time that is in the immediate future of the time t of Susan's coming in.

At the time of the 1973 paper, some philosophers interpreted Partee's replacement of Prior's tense operators by bound variables as merely an issue of representation. Partee's paper is followed by an interesting critique by Terence Parsons in which he argues (1973, 609) that it is not obvious that tenses represented by the use of quantifiers and variables that range over times "cannot be represented by operators ... for tense operators are in fact capable of manifesting at least some pronoun-like behavior." Furthermore, if operators do not provide as powerful a notation as does quantification over times, this is actually in their favor, in Parsons's view, to the extent that "the expressive resources of English tenses do not exploit this extra expressive power." Parsons concludes (p. 610) that "all the examples in Partee's paper can be adequately symbolized using only tense operators." Another critique, by Robert C. Stalnaker (1973), similarly expresses doubt whether there is any difference between the two systems of representation, especially given that "sentence operators are themselves explained [*sic*] in terms of quantifiers and variables" (p. 611).

The formula in (12) illustrates that there *is* a difference between quantifiers-and-variables and operators. It is precisely intended to capture the relatedness of tenses to *other tenses* and hence reveals the inadequacy of operators, which cannot capture this, for representing tenses in a logical translation language. But while the representation in (12) does capture the dependence of the time of John's leaving on the time of Susan's entrance, it fails at the same time to capture the futurity of Susan's coming in, that is, the dependence of the time of Susan's entrance on the time of the speech act. What Partee's (1973) treatment shares with Priorian tense logic, that is, is the failure ultimately to capture the inherent relationality of temporal deixis, and it is this failure that renders the treatment vulnerable to the argument that a representation in terms of operators is just as good as one in terms of bound variables.

As we will see in section 11.3, McCawley's account of tense in TTRE, as exemplified by his treatment of the present perfect tense, integrates the use of quantifiers precisely into a theory of tenses in which temporal deixis *is* fully relational in the intended sense.

11.3 McCawley's Theory of Tense

McCawley's theory of tense, and especially his account of the English present perfect tense, is intended to do three things. First, as he notes in the logic book (1981a/1993, 349), it is strange that Reichenbach (1947) should not have provided, in a book about logic and full of logical representations, a formal account of his theory of tense. McCawley wishes to make up for this lack. TTRE is one of the very earliest attempts, if not *the* earliest attempt, in the linguistic literature to apply formal semantics to the problems of tense and verbal aspect.

Second, McCawley wishes to reconcile the apparent compositionality of verbal expressions, in which auxiliary verbs apparently take verbal complements, with the unitary interpretation of verbal complexes implied by Reichenbach's theory: syntactically, *will leave* in (11) is not a constituent in almost anyone's theory, but semantically it is, insofar as *will leave* is the "future tense" of the verb *leave*. In McCawley's syntactic theory, a verbal complex such as the future or the present perfect tense is a derived constituent resulting from syntactic transformation, and the semantics of that derived complex falls out from the interaction of the semantics of its individual components forming part of the underlying syntactic—in McCawley's theory, also semantic—representation.

Finally, he wishes to account for the multitudinous interpretations of the present perfect verbal complex. McCawley sees the two major senses of the present perfect as resulting from a difference in quantification. He says (TTRE, 105):

(14) The universal and existential perfects appear both to involve a quantifier which ranges over an interval stretching from the past into the present and differ as regards whether that quantifier is universal or existential.

What he has in mind is an analysis in which the "universal" present perfect (*I have been here for an hour*) is analyzed as involving all of the times within a period of time stretching from some point in the past up to the present moment, what McCoard (1978) calls the "extended now," and therefore is representable using the universal quantifier, as in (18), while the "existential" present perfect (*He has been to Rome at least once*) involves *some* time within the extended now and hence the existential quantifier, as in (20). But how, precisely, do these uses of the tense "involve" this quantifier?

McCawley argues that natural language semantics involves restricted rather than unrestricted quantification of the kind familiar from symbolic logic, so that (15), for example, is best translated into a logical language as (16), rather than with the standard, unrestricted quantification seen in (17).

(15) All men are mortal.

(16) $\forall_{x:\text{man}(x)}$ mortal(x)
'for everything that is a man, it is mortal'

(17) $\forall_x$ man$(x) \supset$ mortal(x)
'for everything, if it is a man, then it is mortal'

That is, "a quantifier joins two propositional functions, one giving the 'range' of the variable[3] and one giving the property that is being asserted of things in that range"[4] (TTRE, 105). So if tenses "involve" a (restricted) quantifier, they do so by dint of "involving" both a propositional function supplying the range of a variable and one giving a property of things in that range.

McCawley analyzes the present perfect as involving two tenses. The reference time, as in Reichenbach's (1947) account, is the present. The second tense is the past, the time of the eventuality, capturing the intuition that the present perfect represents the aftermath of a past event. The requisite two propositional functions are the sources respectively of these two tenses: "the range provides the present tense, since it must be an interval containing the present, and the function being asserted provides the past tense, since it is being asserted of events or times that are in the past" (TTRE, 105). Further, he assumes "that the tense morpheme corresponding to the range would be put in the clause corresponding to the quantifier" (idem).

While this is fairly explicit, McCawley does not show any actual representations of this type in TTRE. He does, however, in the logic book (McCawley 1981a/1993, 353), in which *Mary has always lived in Milwaukee* is analyzed as in (18).[5]

(18) $(\forall t: t \leq \text{now}) R_t$(Mary live in Milwaukee)

This can be read as 'for all times t such that t is either past or present, "Mary lives in Milwaukee" is true at t'. On the other hand, (19) is translated as in (20).[6]

(19) John has read *War and Peace*.

(20) $(\exists t: t \leq \text{now}) R_t$(John read War and Peace)

This means 'there is some time *t* that is either past or present such that "John reads *War and Peace*" is true at *t*'.

McCawley's account implicitly addresses Parsons's critique insofar as he shows that natural languages like English do make use of the expressive power of the representational system and that an analysis of natural language tenses in terms of operators would not in and of itself be adequate. For not only is there a distinction between the universal and existential present perfects, which therefore require (on his view) different logical representations involving universal and existential quantifiers, but that distinction is explicitly manifested in the propositional function restricting the scope of the temporal variable.

There is a real difference, then, between McCawley's analyses and analyses in terms of operators such as "has been" that yield representations such as (21) and (22), since the role of the reference time and the relativity of the time of the eventuality to the reference time are not captured in such representations, and, furthermore, the relationship of the two meanings and their coincidence in one and the same verbal form cannot be accounted for by operators, each of which is a primitive of the representational system.

(21) Always(HasBeen(Mary live in Milwaukee))
    'Mary has always lived in Milwaukee.'

(22) HasBeen(John read *War and Peace*)
    'John has read *War and Peace*.'

There are important differences between what McCawley means by saying that the tense morpheme "refers to the time of the clause that it is in" and "refers to it in a way that is rather like the way in which personal pronouns refer to what they stand for" and what Partee means by saying that "if pronouns have to be treated as variables and not as sentence operators ... the same must be true of tenses" (1973, 609).

Specifically, Partee does not address in the 1973 paper the question of *what* time the time at which the past or future event occurs is. To be sure, this time may be given deictically or anaphorically, just as a pronoun may have its reference fixed by ostension or by context as well as by an antecedent within the sentence. But to build a theory of tense requires an account not only of the relation of the two tenses to one another (antecedent and anaphor) but also of their relation to their context, and Partee's (1973) account provides no approach to this, while McCawley in TTRE specifically identifies the antecedent as a reference time.

Perhaps the greatest weaknesses of Partee's 1973 paper are its failure to relate the theory of temporal reference to the Reichenbachian notion of reference point, and to provide a formal theory of tense that incorporates its insights. In the 1984 paper, Partee set out to make up for both of these lacks via an analysis in terms of Discourse Representation Theory. But McCawley's treatment had already served to bring what had been vague notational categories into the precise world of formal logic.

What in the end is the legacy of Jim McCawley in the realm of tense and verbal aspect? His approach to the logical representation of tense has not been widely followed, though his theory of the present perfect has proven extremely influential and has generated a number of both refinements and critiques (such as Bauer 1970 and Matthews 1987). But it is not at all clear that the present perfect is ambiguous in the sense of requiring different semantic representations, as opposed to simply receiving different contextual interpretations. Nor is it clear that tense complexes such as the present perfect are compositional in the sense McCawley intends.

In the third of a century since the publication of TTRE, issues, methods, and theories in the study of the temporal phenomena of natural language have all changed quite a bit. It is increasingly likely that the persisting relevance of his work in this area, and indeed of all of his work, will be the way in which it marries an extraordinarily keen sensitivity to the myriad details of natural language phenomena with a profound and precise concern with formal linguistics.

Notes

1. More generally, a tense may take as antecedent an adverbial expression, as McCawley observes (TTRE, 110) in regard to the example (i), in which the tense of *couldn't sleep* refers back to *last night.*

(i) Although Max was tired last night, he couldn't sleep.

2. (8) is an abridgment of the first two sentences of Jane Austen's novel *Emma.*

3. For example, 'for everything that is a man', $\forall_{x:man(x)}$.

4. For example, 'it is mortal', mortal(x).

5. In this book, in fact, the restricted quantifier is given as "($\forall t$:past t)," but this fails to capture the present-tenseness (the "extended now"-ness) of the expression. The formulation with "$\leq$ now" is used for the analysis of (20) in the 1981b paper (p. 82).

6. In TTRE, McCawley uses I (for *interval*) in the analysis of (19) rather than t, but he uses t in the 1981b paper (p. 82). He assumes there that an accomplishment such as reading *War and Peace* takes place over an interval of time I and not at a moment of time t. There are two problems with this, however. First, (i)

(i) read *War and Peace*

is ambiguously either an activity or an accomplishment, or at least has an activity reading: 'John read *War and Peace* for an hour' as opposed to 'John read *War and Peace* in an hour'. Second, the existential reading of (ii)

(ii) John has read *War and Peace.*

clearly does not allow for the continuance of John's reading of *War and Peace* into the present; but if we translate, as McCawley does, ($\exists I$: past I), then parallelism is lost between the universal quantifier in (18) and the existential one in (20).

References

Bauer, Gero. 1970. The English "perfect" reconsidered. *Journal of Linguistics* 6, 189–98.

Baüerle, Rainer. 1979. Tense logics and natural language. *Synthese* 40, 225–30.

Bennett, Michael. 1977. A guide to the logic of tense and aspect in English. *Logique et analyse* 80, 491–517.

Bennett, Michael, and Barbara Hall Partee. 1978. *Toward the logic of tense and aspect in English*. Bloomington: Indiana University Linguistics Club. Revised and extended version of 1972 System Development Corporation (Santa Monica, CA) report.

Dowty, David. 1979. *Word meaning and Montague Grammar*. Dordrecht: Reidel.

Ducrot, Oswald. 1979. L'imparfait en français. *Linguistische Berichte* 60, 1–23.

Hinrich, Erhard. 1986. Temporal anaphora in discourses in English. *Linguistics and Philosophy* 9, 63–82.

Hornstein, Norbert. 1990. *As time goes by*. Cambridge, MA: MIT Press.

Houweling, Frans. 1986. Deictic and anaphoric tense morphemes. In *Temporal structure in sentence and discourse*, ed. by Vincenzo Lo Cascio and Co Vet, 161–90. Dordrecht: Foris. Originally in *Journal of Italian Linguistics* 7, 1–30, 1982.

Janssen, Theo. 1996. Deictic and anaphoric referencing of tenses. In *Anaphores temporelles et (in)coherence*, ed. by Walter De Mulder, Liliane Tasmowski-De Ryck, and Carl Vetters, 70–107. Amsterdam: Rodopi.

Kleiber, Georges. 1993. Lorsque l'anaphore se lie aux temps grammaticaux. In *Le temps, de la phrase au texte: Sens et structure*, ed. by Carl Vetters, 117–66. Lille: Presses Universitaires de Lille.

Lo Cascio, Vincenzo. 1986. Temporal deixis and anaphor in sentence and text: Finding a reference time. In *Temporal structure in sentence and discourse*, ed. by Vincenzo Lo Cascio and Co Vet, 191–228. Dordrecht: Foris. Originally in *Journal of Italian Linguistics* 7, 31–70, 1982.

Matthews, Richard. 1987. Present perfect tenses: Towards an integrated functional account. In *Essays on tensing in English*. Vol. 1, *Reference time, tense and adverbs*, ed. by Alfred Schopf, 111–76. Tübingen: Niemeyer.

McCawley, James D. 1971. Tense and time reference in English. In *Studies in linguistic semantics*, ed. by Charles Fillmore and D. Terence Langendoen, 96–113. New York: Holt, Rinehart and Winston.

McCawley, James D. 1981a. *Everything that linguists have always wanted to know about logic—but were ashamed to ask*. Chicago: University of Chicago Press. 2nd ed., 1993. References are to the 1981 edition.

McCawley, James D. 1981b. Notes on the English present perfect. *Australian Journal of Linguistics* 1, 81–90.

McCawley, James D. 1988. *The syntactic phenomena of English*. Chicago: University of Chicago Press. 2nd ed., 1998.

McCoard, Robert W. 1978. *The English perfect: Tense-choice and pragmatic inferences*. Amsterdam: North-Holland. Based on a Doctoral dissertation, UCLA, 1976.

Moens, Marc, and Mark Steedman. 1988. Temporal ontology and temporal reference. *Journal of Computational Linguistics* 14, 15–28.

Nerbonne, John. 1984. German temporal semantics: Three-dimensional tense logic and a GPSG fragment. Doctoral dissertation, Ohio State University. Publ., New York: Garland, 1985.

Parsons, Terence. 1973. Tense operators versus quantifiers. *Journal of Philosophy* 70, 609–10.

Partee, Barbara Hall. 1973. Some structural analogies between tenses and pronouns. *Journal of Philosophy* 70, 601–9.

Partee, Barbara Hall. 1984. Nominal and temporal anaphora. *Linguistics and Philosophy* 7, 243–86.

Prior, Arthur. 1967. *Past, present and future.* Oxford: Oxford University Press.

Reichenbach, Hans. 1947. *Elements of symbolic logic.* London: Macmillan.

Saurer, Werner. 1984. *A formal semantics of tense, aspect and aktionsarten.* Bloomington: Indiana University Linguistics Club. Doctoral dissertation, University of Pittsburgh, 1981.

Stalnaker, Robert C. 1973. Tenses and pronouns. *Journal of Philosophy* 70, 610–12.

Vetters, Carl. 1993. Temps et deixis. In *Le temps, de la phrase au texte: Sens et structure*, ed. by Carl Vetters, 85–115. Lille: Presses Universitaires de Lille.

Chapter 12

On the Fuzzy Boundary between Tense and Aspect in Japanese

Wesley M. Jacobsen

12.1 Introduction

In a footnote to his discussion of tense logic, McCawley (1981/1993, 595) notes that much of what he finds of interest on this topic, "though crucially involving temporal notions, has little to do with tense per se." He further notes that many languages lack tense systems, strictly defined, and yet manage quite well to express the full range of temporal relationships available in languages having such tense systems. McCawley's comments point to the difficulty of defining clearly the range of temporal meanings encompassed by the category of tense, and in particular of demarcating the boundary between tense and the other domain of temporal meaning commonly referred to by the name of aspect. Tense is widely understood to refer to the means languages employ for ordering the time of occurrence of one situation with respect to another, typically the act of speech. Aspect is understood to refer to the qualitative structure, or lack of it, that a situation is seen to have in time. Yet exactly where the distinction lies between these two is not always apparent, making it sometimes difficult to identify a particular token of temporal meaning as belonging to one of these categories or the other.

In this chapter, I will examine several temporal phenomena in Japanese that appear to involve both tense and aspect in an attempt to better understand how these two realms of meaning are interconnected and whether they should in fact be treated

---

Jim McCawley's love of the Japanese language was no secret among his students, although it was but one manifestation of the infectious enthusiasm for life and learning that he invested in his teaching and that first drew me into the field of linguistics as a graduate student. More specifically, it was Jim's eclecticism and iconoclasm that taught me to look with a skeptical eye at traditional ways of drawing boundaries between phenomena of language, either within linguistics proper or between linguistics and other disciplines, and that gave me the intellectual freedom to explore interconnections among otherwise disparate interests I brought to my graduate work in mathematics, philosophy, and the Japanese language. That spirit has been an inspiration and guiding principle to much of my work since, as is hopefully evident in this chapter. It is with fondness that I dedicate this chapter to Jim's memory.

as ultimately distinct from one another. While I will reject the view espoused in certain native traditions of Japanese grammar that the language contains no markers of tense, I will argue that the numerous areas of interaction observed between tense and aspect in the language follow as a natural consequence from the latent presence of tense relationships in the very notion of aspectual structure, and vice versa. Furthermore, I will argue that this interaction is mediated at the cognitive level by the phenomenon of change, a central organizing concept in human experience wherein notions of tense and aspect are inextricably bound to one another.

12.2 The Traditional Debate: Does Japanese Have Tense Markers?

Given the lack of a clear boundary between the domains of tense and aspect, it is perhaps no surprise that there exists a long-standing debate in traditional Japanese grammar regarding the very existence of tense in Japanese.[1] The debate has focused in particular on what the exact distinction is in meaning that underlies the morphological opposition between the affixes RU and TA lying at the heart of the Japanese temporal system.[2] In main clauses, these affixes appear to encode a straightforward distinction between nonpast and past tense, as can be seen in the present and future interpretations received by the RU forms in (1) and (2), respectively, versus the past interpretation received by the TA form in (3).

(1) Teeburu no ue ni hon ga sansatu *aru*. (RU form: present meaning)
    table GEN top LOC book NOM three exist-RU
    'There *are* three books on the table.'

(2) (Kyoo wa) gakkoo e *iku*. (RU form: future meaning)
    today TOP school LOC go-RU
    '(Today) I'*m going* to school.'

(3) (Kyoo) gakkoo e *itta*. (TA form: past meaning)
    today school LOC go-TA
    '(Today) I *went* to school.'

In subordinate contexts such as (4) and (5), however, these forms appear to behave quite differently. Contrary to its apparent nonpast interpretation in (1) and (2), the RU form in (4) marks a situation that at the time of speech has already occurred in the past; and the TA form in (5), contrary to its past interpretation in (3), marks a situation that has yet to occur in the future.

(4) Saisyo ni mensetu o *ukeru* gakusei ga kintyoosoo ni rooka o
    first TEMP interview ACC receive-RU student NOM nervous ADV hall ACC
    ittari kitari site-ita.
    go come do-PROG-TA

Tense and Aspect in Japanese

'The student who *interviewed* (lit., was to interview) first was walking nervously back and forth in the hall.'

(5) *Karita* mono wa kanarazu kaesite-kudasai.
borrow-TA things TOP without-fail return-please
'Please make sure you return things that you *borrow* (lit., have borrowed).'

In the subordinate temporal clauses in (6) and (7),[3] both the RU and TA forms are possible, with no corresponding change in the tense orientation of the event in question to the time of speech—future in the case of (6) and past in the case of (7).

(6) Uti e *kaeru/kaetta* toki ni denwa site-kudasai.
home LOC return-RU/return-TA time TEMP phone do-please
'Please give me a call when (at the time) you *return* home.'

(7) Yuube uti e *kaeru/kaetta* toki ni kaisya no zyoosi kara
last-night home LOC return-RU/return-TA time TEMP company GEN boss from
denwa ga atta.
phone-call NOM be-TA
'When (at the time) I *returned* home last night, I got a call from my company boss.'

This is not to say that the two forms are synonymous in these contexts. In (6), the use of RU in the subordinate clause indicates that the phone call is to occur before the addressee returns home (e.g., while the addressee is still at work), while the use of TA indicates that it is to occur at a time after the addressee has returned home. In (7), the use of RU in the subordinate clause conveys that the phone call came from the speaker's boss at a time prior to the speaker's returning home (while the speaker was not yet home), while the use of TA conveys that the call came at a time following the speaker's return home (when the speaker was at home). Note that this distinction is not obligatorily reflected in English. In (6), the English subordinate verb takes the nonpast form *return* regardless of the relative ordering of the main and subordinate events, and in (7), it takes the past tense form *returned*, again regardless of the ordering of the events in question.

When the predicate occurring in such subordinate contexts is stative, the interpretation received by the RU form is one where the subordinate situation occurs simultaneously with the time of the main event. This is so, once again, even when the main clause imposes a past tense context, as in (8).

(8) Tonari ni *iru* hito wa Tanaka-san datta.
alongside LOC exist-RU person TOP Tanaka COP-TA
'The person who *was* next to me was Tanaka.'

The temporal interpretation of RU and TA in such subordinate contexts furnishes the principal argument for advocates of the aspectual interpretation of these affixes. Since TA is capable of marking a future situation in contexts such as (5) and (6), and RU a past situation in contexts such as (4), (7), and (8), the reasoning goes, the temporal function of these affixes cannot be that of expressing tense. Under the assumption that all temporal meaning that is not tense must be aspect, the conclusion is drawn that these affixes are fundamentally aspectual in function, and that the apparent tense meanings they exhibit in main clauses like those in (1)–(3) are derivative of an underlying aspectual function. Specifically, TA is seen in this view to mark a situation that is "complete" (*kanryoo*) and RU a situation that is "noncomplete" (*mikanryoo*). Other types of evidence adduced to support this view include main-clause uses of TA like those in (9)–(10), where the apparent focus of the utterance is on a present situation rather than a past event.

(9) Aa, *tukareta*!   Sibaraku   yasumoo.
    INTJ become-tired-TA for-a-while rest-VOL
    'Oh, I'*m tired* (lit., became tired/have become tired). Let's rest a while.'

(10) Tadaima sanzi ni   *narimasita*.
     now   3:00 DAT become-TA
     'It *is* (lit., became/has become) now 3:00.'

A further piece of evidence for this view is provided by various anomalous "modal" uses of TA, such as those in (11), where it conveys an urgent imperative, and in (12), where it serves to highlight the immediacy of an event of discovering a lost or hidden item.[4] In neither case does TA apparently mark a situation that is past relative to the time of speech.

(11) Moo   hatizi da   yo. Saa, *okita*,   *okita*!
     already 8:00   COP SFP INTJ get-up-TA get-up-TA
     'It's already 8:00. *Get up, get up!*'

(12) (Looking for a lost item in a drawer)
     A! Koko ni   *atta*!
     INTJ here LOC exist-TA
     'Oh, here it *is*!'

The behavior of RU and TA in the subordinate and other contexts illustrated in (4)–(12) clearly departs from that of nonpast (present and future) and past tense forms in English. This in itself, however, is insufficient grounds for abandoning the view that they are fundamentally tense markers. What these data do call into question is defining tense in terms of relative ordering with respect to the time of speech. Viewing tense in more basic terms as a linguistic device for ordering the time of occurrence of one situation with respect to another, while leaving open the question of what particular point in time is taken as a reference for the ordering, allows a notion of *relative* tense that is fully adequate to account for the behavior of RU and TA seen in these examples.[5] Specifically, the reference point adopted in Japanese for tense forms in subordinate contexts such as (4)–(8) may be seen to be the time of occurrence of the situation or event of the *main* clause.[6] Thus, the use of RU in (4) indicates that the time of the interview is nonpast (more specifically, future) with respect to the past time of the event of walking up and down the hall, and the use of TA in (5) indicates that the time of the act of borrowing is past relative to the future time of the returning of the item. Subordinate TA in (6) and subordinate RU in (7) and (8) can be treated similarly.

Therefore, while exhibiting apparently different behavior in main-clause and subordinate-clause contexts, RU and TA in fact impose ordering relationships in a consistent fashion in all contexts. The apparent differences are due not to the nature of the ordering but to the reference point to which the ordering is anchored. The parallel functions of absolute and relative tense encoded by RU and TA can be summarized as in (13), where < indicates 'occurs at a time earlier than' and ≤ indicates 'occurs at a time earlier than or simultaneous with'.

(13) Absolute tense: relates time of main-clause event (t_{em}) to time of speech (t_s).
   Nonpast (RU): $t_s \leq t_{em}$ (see examples (1), (2))
   Past (TA): $t_{em} < t_s$ (see example (3))
   Relative tense: relates time of subordinate event (t_{es}) to time of main-clause event (t_{em})
   Subordinate nonpast (RU): $t_{em} \leq t_{es}$ (see examples (4), (6), (7), (8))
   Subordinate past (TA): $t_{es} < t_{em}$ (see examples (5), (6), (7))

In the case of so-called nontense functions of RU and TA in main-clause contexts such as (9) and (10), care is required to distinguish between a present state and a prior event leading up to that state. While the English predicates appearing in these examples are statives, the corresponding Japanese predicates *tukareru* 'become tired' and *naru* 'become' are in fact eventive, indicating a change in state. In order for the state in question to be seen as obtaining at the moment of speech, the event that results in that state will necessarily have occurred prior to the moment of speech, an ordering relationship that falls precisely under the domain of tense marking.

Nor are the main-clause uses of TA in (11) and (12), while perhaps anomalous, necessarily lacking in tense function. The sense of urgency expressed by the imperative-like use of TA in (11) can be seen to arise from a modal shift in the perspective of the speaker to an idealized possible world wherein the event in question has already occurred,[7] and the sense of discovery in (12) may be seen as arising from the simple past function of TA to mark a stative situation obtaining prior to the moment of speech. Specifically, the item discovered is seen in such cases to have been in a state of existing at a particular location prior to the time it is discovered to be in that location just prior to the moment of speech.

None of the uses of RU and TA considered above thus requires a nontense analysis. But even if not required, might such an analysis not at least be possible? Could these uses of RU and TA, for example, not be seen to express a distinction between a situation that is respectively noncomplete versus complete, as in certain traditional viewpoints? One critical flaw with the latter analysis has been pointed out by Suzuki (1976), who notes that TA occurs without any difficulty on stative as well as eventive main-clause predicates, but to speak of a stative situation as being "complete" borders on incoherence. In what sense, for example, is the state of the empty lot existing said to be "complete" in an example such as (14)?

(14) Tiisai toki sundeita   ie   no tonari ni akiti   ga *atta*.
     small time live-PROG-TA house GEN alongside LOC empty-lot NOM exist-TA
     'Next to the house I lived in when I was small *was* an empty lot.'

The aspectual analysis is also not able to account for uses of the TA form to mark stative situations that occur over an interval of time extending from a point of time in the past up to and (crucially) including the time of speech. Example (15) is fully natural even in a context where the chair still exists at the location in question at the time of speech, and where the stative situation has therefore not been terminated or "completed" in any coherent sense.[8]

(15) Sono isu wa kinoo   kara zutto   soko ni *atta*   yo.
     that chair TOP yesterday from all-the-time there LOC exist-TA SFP
     'That chair *has been* there since yesterday.'

Even granted that, ignoring cases like (14) and (15), it is possible in many cases for a past situation to be treated as a "completed" situation, is the notion of completeness itself truly devoid of any tense meaning, given the basic notion of ordering we have seen to be central to tense? The notion of completeness in fact seems to involve an implicit ordering between the prior termination of a state of affairs and some point in time following that termination. An apparently aspectual category may therefore involve inherent reference to a tense category, which once again raises the question of whether it is indeed possible to draw a clear distinction between tense and aspect in such cases. The answer to this question, and a possible explanation, will be offered in what follows.

12.3 Phenomena of Interaction between Tense and Aspect in Japanese

As we have seen, tense is, understood in its broadest sense, a linguistic means for ordering one situation in time with respect to another. Tense is therefore an inher-

Tense and Aspect in Japanese 267

ently relational notion that necessarily involves reference to a plurality of situations. It goes without saying that for such a relationship to obtain, it must be possible for the situations in question to be treated as distinct from one another. Aspect, by contrast, is defined as the particular qualitative structure, or lack of it, that a singular situation is seen to have in time.[9] Conceived of in this way, aspect may be seen to encompass situations that lack any internal structure (punctual situations) or lack any complexity in internal structure (stative situations), as well as those having a more complex internal structure.

To the extent, however, that temporal structure of any kind is realized on a unidimensional time line, there will necessarily arise ordering relationships, either internally among constituent elements making up the structure, or, in the case of a situation conceived without internal structure (such as punctual situations), between the situation itself and regions of the time line external to the situation. Relationships of tense are, in that sense, latent within the very notion of aspect. The particular ordering relationships possible either among elements internal to a situation or between the situation itself and elements external to the situation will naturally vary depending on the particular aspectual structure involved. Differences in aspectual structure can therefore be expected to impose constraints on the particular tense interpretation associated with a particular situation. Conversely, if the situations or elements ordered in a tense relationship lose their distinct character and come to be seen as constituents of a more encompassing structure, they may come to aggregately define temporal structures that are aspectual in character. Tense and aspect may in this way each be seen to encroach on the meaning territory of the other. Some concrete illustrations of this from Japanese will be taken up below.

12.3.1 Tense Interpretations of Nonpast RU

Consider first the conditions under which the nonpast marker RU receives either a future or a literal present interpretation, noted in connection with examples (1)–(2), repeated here for convenience.

(1) Teeburu no ue ni hon ga sansatu *aru*. (RU form: present meaning)
    table GEN top LOC book NOM three exist-RU
    'There *are* three books on the table.'

(2) (Kyoo wa) gakkoo e *iku*. (RU form: future meaning)
    today TOP school LOC go-RU
    '(Today) I'*m going* to school.'

As seen in these examples, the unmarked tense interpretation for RU is literal present with stative predicates and future with nonstative, event predicates. The crucial property distinguishing these two groups of predicates is the homogeneous character of states, often described in terms of the subinterval property. States are seen to obtain over intervals of time in such a way that the state in question can be predicated of any arbitrary subinterval of the larger interval, no matter how small, down to a single moment within the interval. States therefore have the property of being able to be predicated either of intervals or of points in time, as seen in (16).

(16) a. The book was on the table between 2:00 and 4:00.
b. The book was on the table at 2:15.[10]

As the time of speech is merely a special case of a momentary time frame, no difficulty arises in predicating a state of the moment of speech, resulting in the literal present interpretation with nonpast stative predicates, as in (1).

The situation is quite different in the case of nonhomogeneous situations expressed by event predicates. Such predicates involve aspectual structures of varying complexity, but are characterized minimally by the presence of a change of state as part of that aspectual structure. In the case of the predicate *iku* 'go' in (2), the relevant change is from a state of not being at a specified location to a state of being at that location.[11] In general, the aspectual structure of such change-of-state predicates can be rendered as follows, where ^Q and Q represent the nonexistence and existence, respectively, of a state Q on a time line, mediated by a unique interval (X) representing the occurrence of the change event itself.

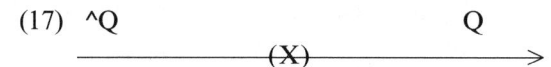

(17) ^Q   Q
   ─────────────(X)─────────────▶

In the idealized situation, the interval (X) can be seen to shrink to the size of an instantaneous moment without extension in time. Such a momentary treatment may indeed be adequate for change events such as *sinu* 'die', *tuku* 'arrive', and *(denki ga) kieru* '(the lights) go out'. The change expressed in predicates such as *hutoru* 'get fat', *sameru* 'cool down', and *tukareru* 'get tired', by contrast, is better treated as occurring over intervals of time. I leave aside here the question of where to locate the upper and lower bounds of such intervals, some of the complexities of which are discussed for English by Dowty (1979).

The necessity of a future tense interpretation for change-of-state predicates becomes clear when we consider the difficulty of associating (X) with the moment of speech.[12] In the case that (X) consists of an interval, it cannot by definition be seen to obtain at a moment. Even when (X) is seen to consist in a moment, it is existentially impossible to guarantee a perfect overlap between that moment and the moment of speech, at least to the extent that the utterance is intended to be descriptive of an event in the outside world and not, for example, a performative speech act where the event is "created" by the utterance itself. It is impossible, that is, to time the speech act in such a way that it coincides perfectly with a moment up to which Q does not obtain and immediately following which Q obtains in the real world, for any given state Q. Whether (X) is an interval or a moment, then, it must be seen as disjoint from the moment of speech: one must precede the other, thus excluding a literal present interpretation. Given that the meaning of the nonpast form excludes the possibility of (X) preceding the time of speech, which is expressed by the past form, a nonpast change-of-state predicate must by default receive a future interpretation.

12.3.2   Nascent Tense in the Aspectual Structure of TE-I(ru)
The example just considered illustrates how aspectual structure places constraints on ordering relationships between a situation expressed in a linguistic form and elements external to the situation, in this case the moment of speech. Aspectual structure may also be seen to impose ordering relationships on elements wholly internal to a situation expressed by a given linguistic form. An example of this can be seen in the various interpretations associated with the verb affix TE-I(ru) in Japanese.[13] Beginning with the pioneering work of Kindaichi (1950), a considerable body of descriptive and theoretical literature has been devoted to the treatment of this affix,[14] particularly with regard to the question of how to account for what appear to be two quite different meanings it expresses, those of progressive and resulting state. These are illustrated in (18) and (19).

(18) Kodomotati wa   rooka o   *hasitTE-Iru.*
      children   TOP hall   ACC run-PROG-RU
      'The children *are running* along the hall.'

(19) Kodomotati wa   gakkoo ni   *itTE-Iru.*
      children   TOP school LOC go-RES-RU
      'The children *have gone* to school (are at school).' (NB: not '... are going to school')

The approach presented in Jacobsen 1992, a modified form of which I will adopt here, treats these apparently different meanings as resulting from an interaction between the aspectual structure inherent to a predicate and a basic invariant meaning in TE-I(ru), which is to impose a homogeneous interval from within which a situation is viewed. This homogeneous meaning is defined in terms of the subinterval property considered earlier, so that when a predicate is attached to TE-I(ru), the resulting form may be considered to be a variety of stative predicate. The particular way in which the homogeneous interval is realized will be dictated in each case by the particular aspectual structure borne by a predicate type, as schematized in (20) for the classic Vendler (1957) categories of situation aspect.[15] Recall from (17) that Q and ^Q represent the presence and nonpresence, respectively of a state Q, and (X) represents either a point or an interval of change mediating between the nonpresence and presence of a state.

(20) States: ----------------------------
    Activities: ~~~~~~~~~~~~~~~
    Change-of-state predicates (achievements):   ^Q (X) Q
    Accomplishments: ~~~~~~(X) Q

States, first of all, are inherently homogeneous in character to begin with and therefore do not allow the attachment of TE-I(ru), as the ability to impose a homogeneous interval on a situation presupposes that the situation is not homogeneous. This is illustrated in (21).

(21) *Teeburu no ue ni hon ga   sansatu *atTE-Iru*. (cf. (1))
     table   GEN top LOC book NOM three   exist-PROG-RU
     '*Three books *are being* on the table.'

Activities, represented by predicates such as *hasiru* 'run', *asobu* 'play', and *hataraku* 'work', are defined in terms of the repetition of a subroutine of bodily movements (each subroutine represented as a single ∼ in the schema in (20)), which, taken alone, is internally nonhomogeneous. In the activity of running, for example, the subroutine consists of a cycle beginning with one foot on the ground and extending through the interval of time during which that foot is in the air until it is on the ground again. Activities are therefore not purely homogeneous, but the multiple repetition of an unchanging subroutine over an extended interval nevertheless imparts to that interval a "quasi-homogeneous" character represented as ~~~ in (20). The subinterval property may be seen to hold of this interval in that any arbitrary subdivision will yield an interval with a uniformly similar quality to that resulting from any other subdivision, at least insofar as the divisions are not made too small—smaller, that is, than the size of a single constituent subroutine. Activities are therefore not homogeneous in the pure sense applicable to states, for which the subinterval property holds down to arbitrarily small intervals and even instants of time. Nevertheless, this quasi-homogeneous character of activities licenses an interpretation by which the homogeneous interval introduced by TE-I(ru) may be seen to coincide with the interval over which an activity occurs, resulting in the progressive interpretation seen in (18), repeated here for convenience.

(18) Kodomotati wa rooka o   *hasitTE-Iru*.
     children   TOP hall ACC run-PROG-RU
     'The children *are running* along the hall.'

With achievements, by contrast, the unique point/interval of (X) constituting the change of state conflicts with the character of a homogeneous interval required by TE-I(ru), and the interval in question must therefore be interpreted as disjoint from (X) itself. The interval is consequently seen to coincide with the state that follows from the occurrence of (X), indicated by Q in (20), so that a resulting-state (perfect) interpretation obtains.[16] This is illustrated in (22) for the instantaneous achievement predicate *kieru* 'go out, become extinguished'.

(22) Denki ga   *kieTE-Iru*.
     lights NOM go-out-RES-RU
     'The lights *are out* (lit., are in the state of having gone out).'

Example (19), repeated here, also involves an achievement predicate indicating a unique change of state. Recall that the predicate *iku* 'go' is unlike its English counterpart in focusing on the point of arrival at a destination, not the process leading up to the arrival.

(19) Kodomotati wa gakkoo ni   *itTE-Iru*.
     children   TOP school LOC go-RES-RU
     'The children *have gone* to school (are at school).' (NB: not '... are going to school')

The fourth category in (20) is that of accomplishments, represented by examples such as *syoosetu o kaku* 'write a novel'. These may be construed as having a composite meaning structure, consisting both of an activity and of an achievement corresponding to the culmination of the activity. Not surprisingly, then, accomplishments are capable of either a progressive or a resulting-state interpretation, depending on which component—the activity leading up to the achievement or the achievement itself—is highlighted. (23a) is a case where the interval defined by TE-I(ru) is seen as coterminous with the activity leading up to an achievement, resulting in a progressive interpretation, in contrast to (23b), where the interval in question is the state resulting from the achievement (represented by Q in the schema of (20)).

(23) a. Murakami Haruki wa atarasii syoosetu o   *kaiTE-Iru*.
       Murakami Haruki TOP new   novel   ACC write-PROG-RU
       'Murakami Haruki *is writing* a new novel.'
    b. Murakami Haruki wa syoosetu o   takusan *kaiTE-Iru*.
       Murakami Haruki TOP novel   ACC many   write-RES-RU
       'Murakami Haruki *has written* many novels.'

The incompatibility of the aspectual character of the interval introduced by TE-I(ru) with the aspectual structure of achievements is thus resolved by means of ordering (X) (the moment or interval of the change event constituting the achievement) prior to that interval, which is effectively to introduce a nascent tense relationship. Although this ordering does not in itself involve the moment of speech, the nonpast RU affix on TE-I(ru) will link the interval in question to the moment of speech in a literal present interpretation, as it is associated with a statelike homogeneous situation. The result is a past-of-a-present relationship as in (23b). When the RU affix is replaced by TA in TE-I(ta) constructions such as (24), the homogeneous interval is shifted to a reference time prior to the moment of speech, resulting in a past-of-a-past tense relationship.

(24) Gakkoo ni tuita toki, Tanaka-sensei wa (moo) *kaetTE-Ita*.
 school LOC arrive-TA time Prof.-Tanaka TOP (already) leave-RES-TA
 'When I arrived at the school, Prof. Tanaka *had* (already) *left*.'

This variety of TE-I(ru) construction (the resultative/perfect variety) thus exhibits characteristics of the English present perfect and its past counterpart, the pluperfect. The range of tense interpretations of this construction is, however, broader than that of the English perfect. It allows, on the one hand, an exclusive focus on the resulting state, to the extent that the achievement event giving rise to the state is ignored, giving rise to a tense interpretation parallel to the English simple present. As seen in (25), this construction is even licensed in cases where no prior achievement event (here, an event of the road "coming to be curved") can conceivably have taken place in the real world.

(25) Kono hen de miti ga *magatTE-Iru*.[17]
 this area LOC road NOM become-curved-RES-RU
 'The road *curves* (lit., is in a state of having become curved) in this area.'

On the other hand, this construction licenses the use of temporal adverbs directly referring to the prior achievement event, in a fashion that can be rendered in English only as a simple past.

(26) Kisinzyaa-si wa 1950nen ni Haabaado-daigaku o *sotugyoo siTE-Iru*.[18]
 Kissinger TOP 1950-TEMP Harvard-University ACC graduate do-RES-RU
 'Kissinger *graduated* from Harvard in 1950.'

TE-I(ru) constructions of the resultative type thus exhibit a variety of tenselike functions deriving from a basic past-of-a-present meaning structure similar to the English perfect, although broader in the range of tense interpretations allowed than in the latter. The perfect in English and other European languages has of course itself long been the focus of debate for its quasi-tense, quasi-aspectual character.[19] Whether a primarily tense analysis or a primarily aspectual analysis of this form is adopted seems to depend on whether the component temporal elements of the perfect are seen to constitute distinct situations in themselves, and are therefore conceived of as mutually ordered in a tense relationship, or as together constituting a singular situation with a complex inner structure. The classic treatment of the former variety is that of Reichenbach (1947), who treats the perfect on a parallel level with basic tenses such as the present and past, by varying the order of three temporal primitives—time of speech (t_s), time of event (t_e), and time of reference (t_r), as in (27).

Tense and Aspect in Japanese   273

(27) a. Ken is at home. $t_s = t_r = t_e$
      b. Ken left home. $t_e = t_r < t_s$
      c. Ken has left home. $t_e < t_r = t_s$
      d. Ken had left home when I called. $t_e < t_r < t_s$

Of the four patterns above, the resultative use of TE-I(ru) can be seen to correspond most closely to $t_e < t_r = t_s$, where the reference point t_r is provided by the interval established by TE-I(ru) (which in turn is seen to overlap with the time of speech, given the semantics of RU), and t_e is identified with the time of occurrence of the change-of-state event (the achievement event). The fact that this construction also overlaps to some extent with a simple past interpretation representable as $t_e = t_r < t_s$, as in (26), nevertheless underlines the ease with which a shift in time of reference obtains and is reminiscent of the famous historical shift that the perfect construction has undergone in certain Romance and Germanic languages from a past-with-present-relevance interpretation to a simple past interpretation (e.g., French *Il a lu le livre*, German *Er hat das Buch gelesen*, both 'He read the book (lit., he has read the book/he has the book read, respectively)'). What would be analyzed in Reichenbach's framework as a shift in reference point away from the moment of speech might in this case equally be seen as a shift toward viewing the prior event as an event less unified with, and more distinct from, the time of speech. The result is a shift toward a stronger tenselike and correspondingly less aspectlike character in this construction, even while maintaining the same fundamental ordering relationships between the time of event and the time of speech.

12.3.3 Nascent Aspect in the Tense Structure of TA

A mirror image of this shift, one where a tenselike function shifts to an aspectlike function, can be seen in the TA affix. I noted earlier that, while all uses of TA may be seen to share a common tense function of ordering an event prior to some point of reference (most commonly the time of speech in main-clause contexts), certain uses of TA appear to highlight a state resulting from a past event more prominently than the past event itself. Examples of this were given in (9) and (10), repeated here:

(9) Aa, *tukareta*!   Sibaraku   yasumoo.
     INTJ become-tired-TA for-a-while rest-VOL
     'Oh, I'*m tired* (lit., became tired/have become tired). Let's rest a while.'

(10) Tadaima sanzi ni   *narimasita*.
     now   3:00 DAT become-TA
     'It *is* (lit., became/has become) now 3:00.'

These can, in Reichenbach's terms, be seen to represent the ordering $t_e < t_r = t_s$, a departure from the more basic $t_e = t_r < t_s$ pattern seen in standard main-clause uses of TA as in (3), repeated here:

(3) (Kyoo) gakkoo e   itta. (TA form: past meaning)
    today school LOC go-TA
    '(Today) I *went* to school.'

The examples in (9) and (10) therefore overlap in their basic temporal character with the resultative use of TE-I(ru), and, although not synonymous, constructions similar in meaning to those in (9) and (10) can in fact be constructed with TE-I(ru) as well.

(28) Kodomo ga   *tukareTE-Iru*.   Sorosoro   nekaseyoo.
     children NOM become-tired-RES-RU about-now put-to-bed-VOL
     'The children *are tired* (lit., are in a state of having become tired). It's about time we put them to bed.'

(29) Sanzi ni   *natTE-Iru*.
     3:00 DAT become-RES-RU
     'It *is* (lit., is in a state of having become) 3:00.'

In order to license the usage of TA illustrated in (9) and (10), two conditions must be met. The first is that the predicate constitute a change event associated with a subsequent resulting state (indicated by Q in (20)). This is of course the same requirement that licenses the resultative use of TE-I(ru) as in (28) and (29). The second requirement, not shared by the corresponding TE-I(ru) construction, is that the change event must be seen to have occurred with some immediacy relative to the time of speech. This feature of immediacy is reflected, among other ways, in the fact that predicates expressing the onset of a mental or emotional state can be used in this way with TA only with first person subjects, as in (9). The attribution of the same mental or emotional state to a third person requires a more distant, objective form of expression such as is made possible by the corresponding TE-I(ru) construction, as in (28). The more aspectlike, less tenselike quality that is ascribed in much of the literature to this use of TA may be seen to arise from this sense of immediacy, as it binds the change event closely to a present state in a way that facilitates viewing the two components as together making up a singular situation, unlike the clearer distinction made between the two in the more standard tenselike functions of TA.

This distinction between two types of TA, corresponding respectively in temporal shape to $t_e < t_r = t_s$ and $t_e = t_r < t_s$, manifests itself in a variety of grammatical phenomena in Japanese, two of which will be considered here. The first is in differing possible negative responses to questions involving the two types of TA, illustrated here:

(30) a. Yuube   no   "Ryoori no Tetuzin"   mita? Iie, minakatta.
        last-night GEN cooking GEN iron-man see-TA no see-NEG-TA
        'Did you watch last night's "Iron Chef" [a TV program]? No, I didn't.'

b. Nimotu todoita?　Iie, mada todoiTE-Inai.
   baggage arrive-TA no yet　arrive-RES.NEG-RU
   'Did the luggage arrive? No, it didn't (hasn't) yet.'

In (30a), the temporal frame within which the event in question (watching a program that aired on TV) is seen to have either occurred or not is restricted to an interval of time in the past that is disjoint from the present moment, an interpretation forced by the presence of *yuube* 'last night'. This is the "standard" tenselike use of TA of the $t_e = t_r < t_s$ variety, and the corresponding negative answer takes the form of a simple past negation *-nakatta*. The TA form in (30b), by contrast, is of the more aspectlike $t_e < t_r = t_s$ variety and marks a question whose focus is on a present circumstance rather than on a past event, albeit a present circumstance that is brought about by a past event. This is directly reflected in the shape of the corresponding negative response, which is a negation formed on a TE-I(ru) construction. The negative response is a denial, in other words, of the existence of a currently existing state. Although both types of TA involve the same ordering relationship between a prior event and a situation obtaining at the time of speech, whether this is construed more as a relationship of tense or more as an aspectual structure is correlated, here again, with the degree to which the two are viewed as either disjoint or bound together in a singular situation.

A second manifestation of the distinction between these two types of TA is seen in contexts of adnominal (relative clause) modification. I noted earlier that TA appearing in subordinate contexts is normally given a relative past interpretation, whereby the subordinate event is seen to occur prior to a temporal point of reference established by the main-clause event. A markedly different interpretation arises in subordinate contexts, however, between the TA form of change-of-state predicates licensing the aspectlike $t_e < t_r = t_s$ interpretation in main clauses and the TA form associated with the standard tenselike $t_e = t_r < t_s$ interpretation in main clauses, such as that of state and activity predicates. Keeping in mind that the role of the time of speech (t_s) in main-clause contexts is replaced in subordinate contexts by the time of occurrence of the main-clause event (t_{em}), prior to which the time of occurrence of the subordinate event (t_{es}) is ordered,[20] the $t_e < t_r = t_s$ and $t_e = t_r < t_s$ main-clause patterns may be reformulated in subordinate contexts as $t_{es} < t_r = t_{em}$ and $t_{es} = t_r < t_{em}$, respectively. Some examples of the former are given in (31) and of the latter in (32).

(31) *Change-of-state (achievement) predicates:* $t_e < t_r = t_s$ *(in subordinate contexts,* $t_{es} < t_r = t_{em}$*)*
   a. tukareta　　　　kao[21]
      become-tired-TA face
      'a tired face'

  b. nureta   kooto
    become-wet-TA court
    'a wet court'
  c. aita   mado
    become-open-TA window
    'an open window'
  d. ana ga aita   bubun
    hole NOM become-open-TA part
    'the part with a hole open(ed) in it'
  e. sugureta   nooryoku
    become-outstanding-TA ability
    'outstanding ability'
  f. arihureta   gensyoo
    become-commonplace-TA phenomenon
    'a commonplace phenomenon'

(32) *Activity or state predicates*: $t_e = t_r < t_s$ *(in subordinate contexts $t_{em} = t_r < t_{es}$)*
  a. hataraita hito
    work-TA people
    'people who worked'
  b. oyoida gakusei
    swim-TA students
    'students who swam'
  c. (sakki   made) atta okane
    little-while-ago until exist-TA money
    'money that was there (until just a little while ago)'
  d. (kodomo no toki) dekita   gengo[22]
    child GEN time be-able-TA languages
    'languages that I knew as a child'

Although the constructions in both (31) and (32) are tokens of a sentential clause (consisting in most of these examples of a predicate alone) modifying a head noun and are thus structurally identical, there is a marked difference in the "eventive" character of the subordinate event in the two cases. The TA-marked predicates in (31) do not characterize their head noun in terms of a prior event that has taken place, but merely in terms of a property corresponding to the state that, in main-clause contexts, would be understood to result from the event in question. This is directly reflected in the adjectival character of the corresponding English glosses. While the property attributed in some of these cases is likely to have in fact arisen from a prior occurrence of a change event, such as 'becoming tired' or 'becoming wet' in the case of (31a) and (31b), the occurrence of this event is defocused, making it possible for this type of construction to be used even when no such event in fact occurred or could possibly have occurred.[23] (31d), for example, could be used to characterize a piece of sheet metal that was manufactured from the start with a hole in it. (31e) and (31f) are tokens of this construction where an originating event for the property in question cannot even be conceptualized—the TA form has in effect become frozen in an adjective-like function.[24]

The situations denoted by the TA-marked predicates in (32), by contrast, fully retain their status as events. The difference between (31) and (32) is overtly reflected in two forms of grammatical behavior. First, the TA form of the predicates in (31) can typically be replaced by TE-I(ru) with little or no change in meaning: *nureta kooto* and *nureTE-Iru kooto* are both possible for 'a wet court'. Such is not the case with the predicates in (32), where replacing the TA form with TE-I(ru) would result in an aspectually different meaning: *hataraiTE-Iru hito*, for example, would mean 'people who are working', not 'people who worked'. Second, the TA predicates in (32) allow the co-occurrence of a temporal adverb making reference to the time of the event in question, but those in (31) do not. Thus, *kinoo hataraita hito* 'people who worked yesterday' is beyond reproach, whereas **kinoo tukareta kao* 'a face that became tired yesterday' cannot be construed in any natural way. The TA forms in (32) thus exemplify once again the characteristic feature of TA in its tenselike function, that of viewing the two situations ordered in time as distinct situations, in contrast to the forms in (31), where the distinction has been weakened or lost.

12.4 Conclusion

The varying temporal interpretations associated with the Japanese affixes RU, TA, and TE-I(ru) do not, as we have seen, admit of a neat dichotomy between tense and aspectual meaning, but reveal upon examination a fundamental interconnection between the two. This is, I have argued, a natural consequence of the inherent presence of temporal ordering—the defining characteristic of tense—within temporal structure—the defining characteristic of aspect. Conversely, it is a consequence of the inherent possibility of temporally ordered elements being viewed, given the right conditions, as collectively bound together in a singular encompassing structure. Whether temporal elements are viewed as individually distinct or as constituting parts of a larger whole is not itself a determination that admits of a strict dichotomy. As a result, tense meaning often appears to shade into aspectual meaning and vice versa, as in the case of simple past versus present perfect meaning in English or of corresponding differences in interpretation seen in the affix TA in Japanese. Reichenbach's "time of reference," and the shifts it is seen to undergo between t_e and t_s, may in fact be seen as an index of the degree to which situations associated with these temporal primitives are viewed as either distinct or bound together.

While the boundary between tense and aspect is thus a fuzzy one, it is nevertheless possible to categorize specific linguistic forms in terms of which of the two functions—temporally ordering distinct elements or binding erstwhile distinct elements into a singular structure—is relatively primary. Viewed from that perspective, RU and TA clearly tend to the former, tenselike function, much as they may also exhibit aspectlike properties in some uses, while TE-I(ru) tends to the latter, aspectlike function, much as it may also impose a temporal order among the elements internal to the aspectual structure it conveys. Japanese cannot therefore be seen as formally lacking either tense or aspect markers, but this discussion has suggested ways in which it may be possible for both tense and aspect meaning to be fully expressible even in languages that lack formal expression of one or the other, such as Chinese, which lacks formal marking of tense.

Central to many of the interactions observed here between tense and aspect has been the mediating role of the change-of-state event, the event I take to define the Vendlerian category of achievement predicates. On a cognitive level, the occurrence of change may be seen to be bound up with the very concept of time, as an awareness of the flow of time is predicated on the ability to perceive change in the phenomenal world. The existence of a unique interval or moment of time bridging two distinct states, as schematized in (17), highlights in a particularly salient way a sequential relationship between these states, inherently tying together considerations of temporal order and temporal structure. In the context of actual utterance, furthermore, a basic incompatibility arises in identifying the moment or interval of change with the moment of speech, forcing a disjoint, and therefore sequential, relationship between the two. Change thus provides us with a key to account for interactions of tense and aspect on many levels, pointing to a deeply rooted link between these two realms of meaning in human cognition and experience and reinforcing the inherent connection between the two that we have seen to exist on a purely notional level.

Notes

1. Teramura (1984) lists Matsushita 1930, Sagawa 1972, Kunihiro 1982, and Ando 1982 as works representative of this viewpoint.

2. Among verbs, the affix RU is in complementary distribution with its allomorphic variant U, the former occurring after vowel-final verb stems (e.g., *tabe-ru* 'eat', *oki-ru* 'get up') and the latter after consonant-final verb stems (e.g., *ik-u* 'go', *yom-u* 'read'). The verbal opposition of RU versus TA is manifested in the case of adjectives by the endings I versus KATTA, and, in the case of the copula, by DA versus DATTA. For the sake of convenience, the term *RU form* will be used in this chapter to include not only RU/U in verbs, but also I in adjectives and DA in the copula. Likewise, *TA form* will be used as a cover term for TA in verbs, KATTA in adjectives, and DATTA in the copula.

3. Temporal clauses in Japanese are structurally a variety of relative clause with a head noun indicating temporal orientation, such as *toki* 'the time (at which)', *mae* '(the time) before', *ato* '(the time) after', and so on.

4. The fact that the English counterpart corresponding to each of the predicates in (9)–(12) is a nonpast form is likely also a factor motivating this analysis. Since the Japanese TA form is used to convey what is manifestly a present situation (manifestly, that is, from the standpoint of the tense form used in English), the Japanese form must express something other than tense.

5. A relative tense analysis of subordinate RU and TA has been adopted in various guises in works such as Soga 1983 and Ogihara 1999.

6. Even in subordinate contexts, cases can be found where RU and TA are interpreted as markers of absolute tense, taking as their reference the time of speech. A full discussion of the conditions that license an absolute, rather than relative, tense reading in such contexts is not within the scope of this chapter, but one factor that may be pointed out as playing a role is the degree of subordination involved. Clauses marked by the conjunction *kara* 'because', for example, exhibit a lower degree of subordination, tending more toward a coordinating function than the clearly subordinating function of *toki* 'when' as seen in (6)–(7). Tense forms in *kara* clauses therefore have the potential of being interpreted in the same way as main-clause tense forms, that is, as marking absolute tense. Note how in example (i), the RU predicate in the *kara* clause allows either an absolute tense reading (where my mother's coming is still future at the time of speech) or a relative tense reading (where her coming is future with respect to the main-clause event, but past with respect to the time of speech).

(i) Haha ga *kuru* kara heya o katazukete-oita.
    mother NOM come-RU because room ACC clean-leave-TA
    'Because my mother *is/was* coming, I cleaned up my room.'

7. This is in essence what is proposed in Soga 1983 for such imperative-like uses of TA.

8. This example is a modified version of an example provided in Nakatani 2002, to which I owe this observation.

9. Smith (1997) draws the helpful distinction between situation aspect and viewpoint aspect. The former refers to temporal qualities that are inherent to a situation (such as the Vendlerian qualities of activity, state, and achievement). The latter refers to different options for viewing one and the same situation, such as the options of viewing it as a complete whole with endpoints (perfective viewpoint) or viewing only part of it without reference to endpoints (imperfective viewpoint). Whether a matter of inherent meaning or of viewpoint imposed from the outside, however, both types of aspect crucially involve reference to the qualitative structure of a situation.

10. Note that even in the case where a state is predicated of a moment, the state is not understood to obtain uniquely at that moment; rather, it is understood to obtain also at other moments forming an interval surrounding the moment in question.

11. Note that Japanese *iku*, unlike English *go*, must be treated as a change-of-state predicate belonging in the category of achievement, rather than activity, verbs (in Vendler's sense). It does not, for example, allow progressive formation.

12. For the sake of simplicity, I limit my focus here to cases of singular occurrence, ignoring habitual or generic readings.

13. The designation TE-I(ru) represents the union of the so-called TE form of a verb (the form into which a verb is converted in order to allow the attachment of certain auxiliary verbs) followed by the auxiliary verb I(ru) derived from an independent verb meaning 'to exist'. TE-I cannot occur morpheme-finally, but must be followed by either of the RU or TA affixes discussed earlier: for example, *taberu* 'eat' → *tabeTE-Iru* 'is eating'.

14. Some representative works in English on the analysis of TE-I(ru) include Soga 1983, Jacobsen 1992, Ogihara 1999, and Shirai 2000. For those unfamiliar with Japanese, an accessible introduction to the linguistic issues surrounding the treatment of this affix may be found in Tsujimura 1996, sec. 6.4.

15. The schematization I adopt here is a slightly modified form of that used in Shirai 2000.

16. Technically speaking, the requirement of homogeneity could equally be met by construing the interval in question to coincide with the interval *prior* to the occurrence of (X), in a way analogous to the futurelike interpretation of English *-ing* with achievement predicates (e.g., *The runner is (just) reaching the goal line*). Such an interpretation does not, however, obtain in Japanese, where the interval in question can only be associated with the state following, not preceding, (X). The reason for this has to do with an independent feature of the meaning of TE-I(ru), pointed out in Soga 1983, namely, that the interval it represents is always associated with a state of affairs that is "realized." The predicate to which TE-I(ru) is attached must, in other words, be seen as representing a state of affairs that actually obtains in the real world, thus obviating a futurelike modal interpretation such as is possible with English *-ing*.

17. This example corresponds to the category of "type 4" verbs in the classic treatment of Kindaichi (1950): verbs expressing a simple state with TE-I(ru) where no event leading up to the state can be conceptualized in the real world.

18. (26) is a token of a use of TE-I(ru) commonly seen in a journalistic style where biographical reference is made to the past career of an individual.

19. McCawley's (1981/1993) treatment of tense, for example, devotes considerable space to this construction.

20. Although the time of occurrence of the main-clause event (t_{em}) acts in this way as a reference point governing the tense of the subordinate predicate, this should, strictly speaking, be distinguished from the time of reference (t_r) in Reichenbach's framework. Reichenbach's t_r was designed to distinguish between simple and complex tenses, but not to function as a reference point for relative tenses. Two types of reference point must therefore be distinguished in the subordinate contexts here: t_{em}, which serves as the anchor for the tense of the subordinate predicate, and t_r, which is seen to alternate between t_{em} and t_{es} in the two interpretations of TA considered here, parallel to the way it alternates between t_e and t_s in the main-clause contexts considered in Reichenbach's analysis.

21. For the sake of simplicity, only tokens of the adnominal predicate and head noun are given here. In a full sentence, these will of course be incorporated into a main-clause structure where the final predicate provides the reference point to which the relative past reading of the subordinate TA is anchored. For example, (31a) might appear in a sentence such as the following:

(i) Kanozyo wa tukareta kao o siTE-Ita.
    she TOP become-tired-TA face ACC do-PROG-TA
    'She had a tired face (lit., she had a face which had become tired) (=She looked tired).'

22. The verb *dekiru* in Japanese is homophonous for two senses: a stative sense of 'be able to' and an achievement sense of 'become completed'. Compare (32d) with *yoku dekita sigoto* 'a job well done', where the verb is used in its achievement sense and the resulting adnominal construction therefore fits into the class of constructions in (31).

23. In his treatment of TA expressions in noun-modifying contexts such as (31) and (32), Kinsui (1994) posits a derivation whereby predicates with a composite semantic structure consist-

ing of an event component and a resulting-state component—predicates that correspond in aspectual terms to achievement or accomplishment predicates—may have their event component excised from the meaning structure under certain conditions, leaving behind a purely state component with an adjective-like character such as in (32). In Kinsui's view, contexts of noun modification lend themselves particularly well to this derivation, as they tend to highlight the head noun as an entity bearing a property of some sort, and properties are typically stative in character. In terms of the argument put forth here, this derivation may be seen as having the effect of removing one of two distinct elements necessary for a tenselike interpretation of temporal ordering, thereby yielding a singular temporal structure of the sort associated with a more aspectlike interpretation.

24. The predicates *sugureru* 'be(come) outstanding' and *arihureru* 'be(come) commonplace' are tokens of Kindaichi's (1950) "type 4" category of verbs referred to in note 17. These verbs cannot be used in main-clause position without TE-I(ru) attached to them.

References

Ando, Sadao. 1982. Nihongo doosi no asupekuto—nitieigo taisyoo kenkyuu [Aspect in Japanese verbs—a comparative study of Japanese and English]. *Gengo* 11:9, 84–108.

Dowty, David. 1979. *Word meaning and Montague Grammar.* Dordrecht: Reidel.

Jacobsen, Wesley M. 1992. *The transitive structure of events in Japanese.* Tokyo: Kurosio.

Kindaichi, Haruhiko. 1950. Kokugo doosi no itibunrui [A classification of Japanese verbs]. Reprinted in Haruhiko Kindaichi, ed. *Nihongo doosi no asupekuto* [Aspect in Japanese verbs], 5–26. Tokyo: Mugi Shobokan, 1976.

Kinsui, Satoshi. 1994. Rentaisyuusyoku no '~ta' ni tuite [On '~ta' modifying nouns]. In *Nihongo no meisi syuusyoku hyoogen* [Noun-modifying expressions in Japanese], ed. by Yukinori Takubo, 29–65. Tokyo: Kurosio.

Kunihiro, Tetsuya. 1982. Tensu-asupekuto—nihongo-eigo [Tense and aspect—Japanese and English]. In *Koza nihongogaku* [Lectures in Japanese linguistics], vol. 11, ed. by Kenji Morioka, Hiroshi Miyaji, Hideo Teramura, and Yoshiaki Kawabata, 2–18. Tokyo: Meiji Shoin.

Matsushita, Daizaburo. 1930. *Hyoozyun nihon koogohoo* [Standard Japanese colloquial grammar]. Tokyo: Chubunkan Shoten.

McCawley, James D. 1981. *Everything that linguists have always wanted to know about logic—but were ashamed to ask.* Chicago: University of Chicago Press. 2nd ed., 1993. References are to the 1993 edition.

Nakatani, Kentaro. 2002. Lexical rules in syntax: A case study of V-concatenation in Japanese. Doctoral dissertation, Harvard University.

Ogihara, Toshiyuki. 1999. Tense and aspect. In *Handbook of Japanese linguistics*, ed. by Natsuko Tsujimura, 326–48. Oxford: Blackwell.

Reichenbach, Hans. 1947. *Elements of symbolic logic.* New York: Macmillan.

Sagawa, Masayoshi. 1972. Nihongo no tensu ni tuite [On Japanese tense]. *Gengo kenkyu* 61, 40–56.

Shirai, Yasuhiro. 2000. The semantics of the Japanese imperfective -*teiru*: An integrative approach. *Journal of Pragmatics* 32, 327–61.

Smith, Carlota. 1997. *The parameter of aspect.* Dordrecht: Kluwer.

Soga, Matsuo. 1983. *Tense and aspect in modern colloquial Japanese*. Vancouver: University of British Columbia Press.

Suzuki, Shigeyuki. 1976. Nihongo doosi no toki ni tuite [On tense in Japanese verbs]. *Gengo* 5:12, 50–58.

Teramura, Hideo. 1984. *Nihongo no sintakusu to imi* 2 [Syntax and meaning in Japanese 2]. Tokyo: Kurosio.

Tsujimura, Natsuko. 1996. *An introduction to Japanese linguistics*. Cambridge, MA: Blackwell.

Vendler, Zeno. 1957. Verbs and times. Reprinted in Zeno Vendler, ed. *Linguistics in philosophy*, 97–121. Ithaca, NY: Cornell University Press, 1967.

Chapter 13

Counterfactuality in Burmese   Lynn Nichols

13.1 Introduction

The truth evaluation of a proposition with counterfactual interpretation has been argued to have at least two components. First, a proposition such as *John took the medicine* in the antecedent clause of the conditional in (1) is false in the actual world but true in some other possible world(s). The consequent clause then makes a prediction based on the state of affairs in those worlds the antecedent proposition picks out.

(1) If John had taken the medicine, he would have gotten better.

Second, the worlds in which *P* is true are assumed to be otherwise very much like the actual world, differing only in the value of *P* (and any other propositions whose truth is necessary for *P* to hold (Lewis 1973)). This relationship between these worlds of evaluation and the actual world is captured according to Kratzer (1981) by the actual world *w* functioning as an *ordering source*: all worlds in which *P* holds are ordered with respect to how similar they are to the actual world, that is, how many true propositions they share. In counterfactual cases, we are understood to be talking about those worlds that are closest to the actual world *w* and so share the largest number of propositions with it, except for the value of *P*. (The set of worlds in which the truth of *P* is evaluated is referred to as the *evaluation context* for *P*. Each possible world corresponds to a set of propositions that hold in that world.)

In this explanation of counterfactuality, the character of the evaluation context for *P* derives from the conversational context. There appears to be no role for any

---

I am grateful to be able to dedicate this research to Jim's memory and hope that he would find the confluence of Burmese and counterfactuality pleasing. I have particularly regretted not being able to discuss this ongoing research on counterfactuality with Jim and keenly feel the loss of his enthusiasm and ideas to the field of linguistics.

An earlier version of this chapter was presented at the 2002 annual meeting of the Linguistic Society of America in San Francisco.

additional semantic contribution of the counterfactual conditional verb morphology. This stance may stem from the assumption that the morphology simply reflects semantic properties already present, originating in the conversational context and the set of evaluation worlds it specifies.

There are semantic properties of counterfactual interpretation whose source is unaccounted for, however. It is problematic to assume, for example, that the ordering interpretation that turns the actual world *w* into an ordering source is contributed by the conversational context or the nature of the particular context set itself. With certain context sets of worlds corresponding to normative or legal ideals, this may be unproblematic; but for context sets such as those based on expectations, knowledge, beliefs, and so on, or even the actual world/common ground, all of which may function simply as straightforward evaluation contexts, as in (2a–b), no ordering is inherently specified.

(2) a. It is expected that John will take first prize.
    Evaluation context for subordinate clause supplied by attitude predicate: set of speaker's expectations
  b. Mary broke her leg.
    Evaluation context supplied by context: conversational common ground

We should therefore consider the ordering relation an independent aspect of counterfactual interpretation. There are then three components to counterfactual meaning: (1) the base context of evaluation, the actual world; (2) the worlds in which the truth of *P* is evaluated; and (3) the relationship between the evaluation world(s) for *P* and the actual world. In this chapter, I focus on the semantic contribution of counterfactual morphology and show that the morphology supplies the missing piece; that is, it is the morphology that ultimately contributes the ordering component to counterfactual interpretation. I make the case on the basis of a detailed study of the semantics of Burmese counterfactual morphology, showing that the semantic contribution of this counterfactual morphology is the indication of the nature of the relationship between the two contexts of evaluation. Specifically, Burmese morphology conveys counterfactuality by means of an attitude evaluation of distance, indicating that some proposition *P* is true in some world or set of worlds that is far from the actual world.

Burmese counterfactual morphology, expressing the relation between two contexts of evaluation, therefore does *not* function to directly indicate the truth value of the proposition it marks (cf. the claim of Giorgi and Pianesi (1997, 260) that the subjunctive in Italian counterfactuals marks a proposition as false in the worlds closest to the ordering source).[1]

13.2 Contexts

Since part of the meaning of Burmese counterfactual morphology includes reference to contexts, in this section I discuss some of the foundational assumptions I will be making regarding the nature of contexts and context sets of evaluation before treating the Burmese data in detail in section 13.3.

I assume that truth value is determined in the manner proposed in Stalnaker 1978, where the truth value of any proposition is evaluated with respect to some context C, where C is defined as a set of propositions (each proposition Q corresponding to a set of worlds in which Q holds). Two kinds of evaluation contexts are distinguished that play a role in propositional evaluation in the course of a conversation, normal contexts and modal contexts. A *normal context* is the default context in play in the course of a conversation (i.e., when a context of a specific character has not explicitly been specified) and is sometimes referred to as a normal conversational context. All participants in a conversation bring to the conversation a set of assumptions (presuppositions) about the world; the background assumptions that participants share are referred to as the *common ground* of the conversation.[2] Assertions evaluated as true are added to this common ground context set in the course of the conversation; therefore, it is a dynamic set. Modal contexts differ from normal conversational contexts in that they do not simply define a context set in terms of the sum of presupposed propositions thus far.

Two additional factors may determine how a modal context is set up. A selection function may characterize a particular set of worlds for the evaluation of a proposition, a characterization that can depart from the common ground. This selection function, picking out kinds of sets of worlds, is referred to as a *modal base* (Kratzer 1981, 1991) and can be determined contextually, introduced by adverbial phrases like *based on what has been learned about John*, *based on what we suspect*, *based on what John believes*, or by propositional attitude verbs such as *believe* and *suspect* (Giorgi and Pianesi 1997).

In addition to picking out a particular kind of context set of worlds for the evaluation of a proposition, it has been argued that the worlds in this context set can be ordered with respect to how closely they reflect the state of affairs in some world/set of worlds selected as the ideal case or basis of comparison (Kratzer 1981). The *ordering source* is the function that orders worlds in this manner;[3] the worlds sharing more propositions with the base world(s) are located closest to the base, those sharing fewer propositions are located further away. Examples of ordering sources include *what the law allows* and *what is normally the case*; like modal bases, they may be introduced by overt phrases, adverbs, or attitude predicates such as *wish*, or they may be understood from context. The notion of an ordering appears to be valid for modalized sentences like *John usually arrives on time* or *Mary should leave now*; since a proposition is equivalent to a set of worlds in which that proposition is true, a proposition may be evaluated according to whether the state of affairs it describes is close to or far from the ideal state of affairs. This study will challenge the idea, however, that ordering sources (as they are discussed in Kratzer 1981 and work drawing on this research) play a role in counterfactual interpretation.

With this background, consider how the interpretation of conditionals and counterfactuals is determined. In simple conditionals, such as (3), a direct relationship is established between the truth of the two clauses, since the truth of the consequent is dependent on the truth of the antecedent. Example (3) starts out with the common ground as the modal base context set. The role played by the antecedent consists in restricting the modal base evaluation context for the consequent, by adding one more proposition to it.

(3) If John takes the medicine, he'll get better.

In the case of counterfactual conditionals such as the past counterfactual in (4), the common ground context set of propositions serves as the ordering source for the proposition *John took the medicine* in the antecedent. This proposition is evaluated as false in a set of worlds that are otherwise similar to the actual world w (the world described by the propositions in the common ground) and therefore are those worlds closest to w.

(4) If John had taken the medicine, he would have gotten better.

With the notion that contexts (as sets of propositions or sets of sets of worlds) play a role in conditional and counterfactual interpretation, I turn to the properties of Burmese counterfactual morphology.

13.3 Attitude Evaluation in Burmese Counterfactuals

The morphology used to convey counterfactuality in Burmese indicates the relationship between the base context (the actual world) and the context of evaluation for P by means of an attitude evaluation that the worlds of the latter context set are located far from the actual world. I will show that this same morphology used in both modal and nonmodal domains makes similar reference to context in both domains, indicating the basic meaning underlying the interpretation of the morphology in its various grammatical contexts. I first describe the form of Burmese counterfactuals, focusing on the form and interpretation of the antecedent alone (there are additional complexities in the consequent not relevant to the current discussion). I then turn to nonmodal uses of the same morphology, where the crucial aspects of the semantic interpretation of this morphology can be most clearly brought out.

Counterfactuality in Burmese   287

13.3.1 The Form of Burmese Counterfactuals

The basic form of a conditional in Burmese is illustrated in (5).[4] The subordinate antecedent bears *yin* 'if', and the verb in the antecedent is plain; the main-clause consequent is marked with irrealis morphology, here *me*. (Burmese marks predicates for the realis/irrealis distinction rather than tense.)

(5) *Simple conditional*
    shèi   θauʔ *yin*, nei   kàun la   me
    medicine drink *if*   stay good come IRREALIS
    'If he takes the medicine, he'll get better.'

Two counterfactual conditional types are illustrated below, a present counterfactual in (6) and a past counterfactual in (7). Note that the presence of the morpheme *khé* following the predicate stem in (6) is responsible for the difference between simple conditional interpretation in (5) and counterfactual interpretation in (6).[5] (I will treat examples (5) and (6) as parallel for current purposes, abstracting away from the telic/nontelic difference, which leads to a complication in interpretation that is not relevant for the current discussion.) The base context of evaluation in the antecedents of both present and past counterfactuals is the common ground context set.

(6) *Present counterfactual*
    to   *khé* yin chànθa hma   phè
    clever *KHE* if rich   IRREALIS EMPHATIC
    'If he were smart, he would be rich.'

(7) *Past counterfactual*
    shèi   θauʔ *khé* yin, nei kàun la   *khé* me
    medicine drink *KHE* if   stay good come *KHE* IRREALIS
    'If he had taken the medicine, he would have gotten better.'

Burmese present and past counterfactuals differ in the presence of a second *khé* in the consequent in the past counterfactual; this *khé* conveys the past tense interpretation and has scope over both clauses.

13.3.2 The Source of the Ordering Interpretation

The key to interpreting the distribution (and meaning) of *khé* in the counterfactual paradigm is the semantic interpretation of *khé* in nonmodal main clauses. In simple main clauses, *khé* has an aspectually completive interpretation. Comparing sentences with and without *khé*, speakers report that (8a) without *khé* is simply past—that is, noncommittal about whether this event is a subevent in a series of ongoing conversations. (8b) with *khé* indicates that the event is over and done with; the event is not relevant to other current events.

(8) a. ingyìn né zəkà pyò <u>te</u>
    Ingyin with word speak REALIS
    'He spoke with Ingyin.'
  b. ingyìn né zəkà pyò <u>khé</u> te
    Ingyin with word speak *KHE* REALIS
    'He spoke to Ingyin [a while back; he hasn't spoken to her since then].'

Khé has a second interpretation in simple main clauses, however, which is particularly noteworthy: a geographically distal interpretation. Speakers use *khé* in (9) to mean that the past event is remarkable for the fact that it took place at some distance from the current speech context.

(9) mʷei chauʔ *khé* <u>te</u>
    snake scare *KHE* REALIS
    '[I] scared a snake [in another place before I arrived here].'

Khé cannot be used geographically where a past event or a state resulting from a past event holds over to the current speech context, as in 'I brought some grammars from Burma' or 'Maphyu came back from Burma last fall'. In contrast, 'I left my bicycle in Burma' is a context for using *khé*.

(10) *Contexts for* khé
    a. 'I brought some grammars from Burma.'   *
    b. 'Maphyu came back from Burma last fall.'   *
    c. 'I left my bicycle in Burma.'   *khé*

Similarly, *khé* can be used with imperatives as in (11a), but only with 'come' imperatives where the movement starts in a location different from the speaker's (Okell and Allott 2001), and not with 'go' imperatives where movement starts at the speaker's location.

(11) a. la   <u>khé</u>
        come *KHE*
        'Come!'
   b. *θwa <u>khé</u>
        go   *KHE*
        'Go!'

Because of this locational aspect of its interpretation, *khé* has been described in the grammatical literature on Burmese as a directional auxiliary (Wheatley 1982) and as a distal/perfective aspect (Soe 1999). These descriptions do not explain the use of *khé* in counterfactual antecedents, however, nor do they capture all aspects of the interpretation of *khé*.

Counterfactuality in Burmese 289

First, both completion and distance interpretations do not occur obligatorily with every instance of *khé*. Example (12) is in fact three-ways ambiguous between (a) just completed past, (b) just simple past distal, or (c) both completed past and distal.

(12) zəkà pyò p̲h̲yiʔ *khé* t̲e
word speak happen *KHE* REALIS
'(I) managed to speak to (her).'
 a. 'I managed to speak to her [here last year].'
 b. 'I managed to speak to her [in New York just before I came].'
 c. 'I managed to speak to her [last year in New York].'

Second, *khé* is optional even in the appropriate semantic context. As (13) indicates, *khé* is not obligatory when a geographically distant event is involved, and, despite the absence of *khé*, this example can also refer to a completed past event.

(13) ingyìn né zəkà pyò t̲e
Ingyin with word speak REALIS
'He spoke with Ingyin [a while back when they were both in New York].'

The chart in (14) illustrates in more detail what this optionality looks like for the past completed interpretation. A number of Burmese temporal adverbial specifications are listed (which may appear overtly or be understood from context) along with an indication of the appropriateness of *khé* for each temporal context.[6] On the one hand, the use of *khé* is more likely in certain temporal contexts, namely, the more distant past (14f–k). In addition, the use of *khé* is nonetheless optional in these distant past contexts. This behavior contrasts with that of canonical past tense inflection, where there is no choice with respect to marking an event that occurs prior to the speech time.

(14)			Likelihood of temporal *khé*
a.	lun gé dé tə nayi	'an hour ago'	*
b.	di néi mənèʔ	'this morning'	*
c.	mə néi nyá	'last night'	?OK
d.	mə néi	'yesterday'	?OK
e.	lun gé dé hnə yeʔ	'two days ago'	?OK
f.	ʔəyin də baʔ	'last week'	±
g.	ʔəyin lá	'last month'	±
h.	mò dʷin hma	'in the (last) rainy season'	±
i.	nʷei hma	'in the (last) summer'	±
j.	mə hniʔ	'last year'	±
k.	lun gé dé she hniʔ	'10 years ago'	±

Finally, the semantic profile is completed by important information from speakers on interpretations involving *khé*. Speakers report that when *khé* is used, completedness or geographical distance is somehow noteworthy to the speaker. In the words of one speaker (Ingyin Zaw, pers. comm., 2001), "You [the speaker] feel something about the fact that it's not going to happen again."

The apparent optionality of *khé* as well as these interpretive comments can be explained if *khé* not only expresses semantic distance (temporal or geographical) with respect to a proposition but also does this by expressing the speaker's attitude concerning the distance, in other words, a propositional attitude evaluation. An event may be distant in time and place, but if this is not considered significant by the speaker, simple indicative realis inflection can be used.

The meaning of Burmese *khé* then is something like 'be distant, be far', akin to the class of attitude evaluations expressed as predicates such as 'be interesting', 'be odd', 'be surprising'.[7] A single meaning can now straightforwardly be identified for *khé* that captures both its temporal and its geographical nonmodal uses as well as its interpretation in counterfactual cases: for some proposition P, for some context set of worlds C_i = the base context, and for some context set of worlds C_P = the context in which the truth of P is evaluated, the interpretation of *khé* (P) is such that C_P is far from C_i.

(15) *Meaning of Burmese* khé
    a. For some proposition P,
    b. For some context C_i and some context C_P,
    c. *khé* (P): far (C_i, C_P)
       that is, P is assertable with respect to C_i if there is a context C_P in which P is true and C_P is far from C_i.

The indicative and counterfactual interpretations for *khé* follow from the two types of contexts possible for the situation of an utterance.

In the case of the nonmodal interpretation, C_i is the current utterance context and *khé* expresses the speaker's evaluation that P is true in some context C_P distant from the current utterance context. Since an utterance context may be located by the values of two different kinds of variables, ⟨time⟩ of the utterance and ⟨speaker⟩;[8] it is in fact expected that there might be two distinct senses of distance for *khé* in the indicative, temporal and geographical. Burmese *khé* indicates that some proposition P is true in a context that is evaluated by the speaker as temporally and/or spatially distant from the current speech context.

In the counterfactual conditional, the base context of reference C_i is the common ground, the set of propositions the participants assume characterize the actual world. In counterfactuals, *khé* indicates that proposition P must be true in some context (set of worlds) that the speaker evaluates to be distant from the actual world.

Counterfactual interpretation in Burmese is therefore not a direct contrary-to-fact assertion for *P*, nor does *khé* mark *P* as false in the worlds closest to the base context of reference (the ordering source of Kratzer 1981), contrary to the standard model of counterfactuality based on the work of Lewis (1973). Rather, counterfactual interpretation arises from the speaker's assertion that *P* is true only in a world distant from the actual world. Worlds close to the actual world *w* are those that are most like *w* and share the truth value of *P* with it. The further away a world is from *w*, the fewer propositions it shares with *w*. Therefore, if *P* is true in a world evaluated as distant from *w*, *P* must be false (counterfactual) in *w*.

In counterfactuals, *khé* characterizes the nature of the relationship between C_P (evaluation context for *P*) and C_i (base context of reference), or in other words, conveys the nature of the ordering between these two contexts of evaluation. The ordering component of meaning in Burmese counterfactuals is therefore not derived from context as in Kratzer's treatment of counterfactuality but rather is overtly contributed by counterfactual morphology. The distance evaluation of *khé* is responsible for the base evaluation context functioning as an ordering source.

Finally, while challenging one component of the earlier approach to counterfactuality, the interpretation of Burmese *khé* confirms another. Burmese counterfactual *khé* evaluates distance with respect to some *context* even in the indicative domain (to convey PAST). We appear to have independent empirical support for the idea that contexts are a key semantic component of counterfactual interpretation.

13.3.3 Similarity of Worlds

Worlds that are most similar to the actual world *w* are those that share the greatest number of propositions with *w*. These similar worlds are assumed to be located closest to *w*. The greater the distance of some world *w'* from *w*, the greater the number of propositions whose truth value will differ in *w'* and *w*. As for counterfactual worlds, they are assumed to be maximally similar to the actual world except for the value of *P*. In characterizing counterfactuality as a truth evaluation in the world(s) furthest from the base context of reference as we have done here, however, we appear to lose the notion that the worlds in which a counterfactual proposition *P* holds differ from the actual world *w* (the base context) in just that proposition *P* (along with any other propositions whose truth is necessary for *P* to hold). Presumably worlds further away from *w* would differ in the value of other propositions as well.

The analysis of the interpretation of Burmese *khé* offered here is independently grounded in the empirical facts; therefore, it seems premature to reject the analysis on the above conceptual grounds. Instead, the results from Burmese provocatively suggest that the representation of counterfactual worlds in natural language may differ from the proposals made in the similarity model. In addressing the Burmese evidence for the evaluation of counterfactual truth in far worlds by considering alternative ways in which the similarity of the actual world w and counterfactual worlds might be captured, we may ultimately be led to an alternative view of counterfactuality. Further discussion of this interesting problem is unfortunately beyond the scope of the current chapter but is developed in detail in Nichols 2003.

13.4 More on Attitudes in Burmese Conditionals

Interestingly, the morpheme *khé* is part of a more general morphologically expressed propositional attitude category in conditionals. For instance, as an alternative to *khé* in the present counterfactual (16), *shou* 'say' may be used, as in (17), giving a more hypothetical flavor to the interpretation. *Shou* characterizes the antecedent as a supposition context rather than as contrary to fact.

(16) máphyu ká shèi né mə té *khé* yin
Maphyu FOC medicine with NEG agree KHE if
'if Maphyu were allergic to the medicine'

(17) máphyu ká shèi né mə té phù *shou* yin
Maphyu FOC medicine with NEG agree NEG say if
'if Maphyu were allergic (lit., if we say she is allergic) to the medicine'

A more complex paradigm of conditional antecedents is laid out in (18) involving the use of *shou* 'say', *khé* 'far', or both. All the antecedents in this paradigm have hypothetical interpretation.[9] This paradigm confirms the interpretation of *khé* discussed in the preceding section, since *khé* is always used to form the furthest degree of hypothetical. Compare (18a–c) and again (18d–f).

(18) *Antecedents of Burmese hypothetical conditionals*
Least hypothetical
    a. ... mə té yin   'if she is allergic'
    b. ... mə té phù ***shou*** yin   'if we say she is allergic'
    c. ... mə té *khé* yin   'if she were allergic'
    d. ... mə té *khé* bù ***shou*** yin   'if we said that she was allergic'
    e. ... mə té bù lóu ***shou*** *khé* yin   'if we were to say that she is allergic'
    f. ... mə té *khé* bù lóu ***shou*** *khé* yin   'if we were to say that she was allergic'
Most hypothetical

Though I have limited the discussion to the morpheme *khé*, and to only certain usages of *khé*, the paradigm in (18) suggests that attitude evaluation plays a more extensive role in Burmese conditional interpretation beyond that indicated by the brief discussion here.

13.5 Concluding Remarks

It should be noted that the specific conclusion for Burmese, that an attitude evaluation of distance indicates the nature of the relationship between the evaluation world(s) for *P* and the actual world, thus far holds only for that language. It is hypothesized that while counterfactual morphology crosslinguistically functions to indicate the nature of the relationship between the two evaluation contexts, there is expected crosslinguistic variation in the particular semantics of the morphology used to express this relationship, depending on the particular morphological resources (e.g., tense/aspect/mood/attitude) a language brings to the problem of counterfactuality. An attitude evaluation of distance is simply one strategy.

This chapter suggests then that although the basic semantic components of counterfactual interpretation—C_i, C_P, expression of the relation between the two—may be universal, there is nonetheless much interesting individual variation in the expression of counterfactuality, and that we are now able to be more precise about the locus and nature of this variation.

Notes

1. This may also be incorrect for Italian, since if *P* is false in the actual world, then *P* should be *true* in these close counterfactual worlds.

2. The participants need not share exactly the same presuppositions in order for a conversation to proceed normally. Rather, participants recognize that they share the subset of presuppositions salient to the actual conversational context and topic (including the presupposition that they may differ with respect to particular propositions); nonsalient presuppositions (including differing nonsalient presuppositions) remain vague (Lewis 1973; Stalnaker 1978). Information may come up in the course of the conversation that makes any presuppositional differences apparent.

3. The term *ordering source* is used here to refer both to the function ordering a set of worlds in a context set and to the output of the function, that is, the set serving as the basis of comparison.

4. I am grateful to Ingyin Zaw for extensive ongoing discussion of the Burmese data. Unattributed Burmese data come from my own field notes.

5. The underline notation on *kh* and other segments in the Burmese examples is the traditional grammar method of indicating the base form of a voiceless consonant that undergoes voicing in certain contexts.

6. "*" indicates the use of *khé* is prohibited; "?OK" indicates speakers' judgment that the use of *khé* is doubtful in this context; "±" indicates that *khé* may be used optionally, with both options having fully grammatical status.

7. However, *khé* is not a predicate but inflectional and therefore perhaps similar to "evidential" marking in languages like Quechua (Cole 1982). See especially Faller 2003 for an insightful discussion of Quechua evidential marking that makes apparent certain similarities between that morphology and the Burmese morphology discussed here.

8. The utterance is also situated with respect to ⟨world⟩; since the value of this variable is always *w* (actual world) for indicatives, and the assertion context for *P* is in *w*, the application of *khé* to this variable would be vacuous. Additionally, in Burmese conditionals, it is modal *yin* 'if' that determines that *khé* ranges over worlds. For both of these reasons, *khé* in a simple main clause like (i) does not apply to the ⟨world⟩ variable of the utterance context and so here does not result in any of the * interpretations indicated below (i).

(i) sà *khé* te
   eat *KHE* REALIS
   'He ate.'
   a. *'It's unlikely that he ate.'
   b. *'It's far from the case that he ate.'
   c. *'He didn't eat.'

9. As with the case of English "past" marking in conditional antecedents, the Burmese conditional antecedent marked with *khé* is ambiguous between a contrary-to-fact interpretation as in (16) and a hypothetical interpretation as in (18c), depending on the conversational context. This is similar to English [We don't know anything about John's health but] *if John were sick he would take the medicine* (= hypothetical) versus [We know John is not sick but] *if John were sick he would take the medicine* (= counterfactual).

References

Cole, Peter. 1982. *Imbabura Quechua*. Amsterdam: North-Holland.

Faller, Martina. 2003. Spatio-temporal deixis and evidentiality in Cuzco Quechua. In *Proceedings of SULA 2 (Semantics of Underrepresented Languages in the Americas)*, ed. by Jon Anderssen, Paula Menéndez-Benito, and Adam Werle, 87–98. Amherst: University of Massachusetts, GLSA.

Giorgi, Alessandra, and Fabio Pianesi. 1997. *Tense and aspect, from semantics to morphosyntax*. Oxford: Oxford University Press.

Kratzer, Angelika. 1981. The notional category of modality. In *Words, worlds and contexts: New approaches to word semantics*, ed. by Hans-Jürgen Eikmeyer and Hannes Rieser, 38–74. Berlin: de Gruyter.

Kratzer, Angelika. 1991. Modality. In *Semantik/Semantics: Ein internationales Handbuch der zeitgenössischen Forschung/An international handbook of contemporary research*, ed. by Arnim von Stechow and Dieter Wunderlich, 639–50. Berlin: de Gruyter.

Lewis, David. 1973. *Counterfactuals*. Cambridge, MA: Harvard University Press.

Nichols, Lynn. 2003. Locating counterfactual worlds: The morphosemantics of counterfactuality. Manuscript, University of California, Berkeley.

Okell, John, and Anna Allott. 2001. *Burmese/Myanmar dictionary of grammatical forms*. London: Curzon Press.

Soe, Myint. 1999. A grammar of Burmese. Doctoral dissertation, University of Oregon.

Stalnaker, Robert. 1978. Assertion. In *Syntax and semantics 9: Pragmatics*, ed. by Peter Cole, 315–32. New York: Academic Press.

Wheatley, Julian K. 1982. Burmese: A grammatical sketch. Doctoral dissertation, University of California, Berkeley.

Chapter 14

Retrospective Mood in Korean: Suk-Jin Chang
A Constraint-based Approach

14.1 Introduction

The Korean sentence type dubbed *retrospective* is one formally marked with the suffix *-te* (or its variants *-tey* and *-ti*), in the verbal predicate of a sentence.[1] It denotes a recollection of the speaker's past cognition of a state of affairs expressed in the sentence. When viewed from the perspective of form and meaning, it is unparalleled in many languages including typologically and structurally similar languages like Japanese, let alone English, French, or German. The proper descriptive domain of the retrospective extends from lexicon to discourse. This chapter aims at elucidating some of its salient speech act constraints in the framework of Constraint-based Unified Grammar of Korean (CUG/K; Chang 1999, 2002) by way of interfacing them with morphosyntactic and semantic constraints. As an outgrowth of HPSG (Head-driven Phrase Structure Grammar), CUG is lexicon-oriented, type-hierarchical, and above all sign-based. Unlike HPSG, however, it consolidates contextual and pragmatic information into its core. Abundant work has been done on Korean retrospectives from the viewpoint of traditional and functional grammars,[2] but none from that of constraint-based grammar.

This chapter is divided into two parts. The first provides a general exposition of the retrospective mood in descriptive and functional terms, beginning with the retrospective morpheme *te* in the sequence of verbal suffixes and its distributional constraints (section 14.2) and looking into the functioning of the retrospective in terms of temporal, aspectual, and modal constraints involving the discourse participants and the semantic content (section 14.3).

The second part, based on the general and informal account of the retrospective in the first part, presents the speech act properties in the framework of CUG/K. It begins with the sign-based type hierarchy and feature inheritance (section 14.4); explicates them in the form of attribute-value matrices, pinpointing the interactions of syntax, semantics, and pragmatics; and makes explicit the constraints on emotive predicates and the thematic roles of observers and experiencers (section 14.5).

This chapter has been nurtured by the legacy of Jim McCawley. It is immensely indebted to his conception of semantics, logic, and pragmatics as inseparable from each other—a guiding principle underlying CUG. Specifically, it owes much to Jim's pioneering work on decomposing a word into semantic primes, his treatment of each event time as a time index, and his account of speech acts.

14.2 Retrospectives

We will look first at the retrospective morpheme in the sequence of inflectional suffixes and then at illustrative examples of retrospective and nonretrospective sentences.

14.2.1 The Retrospective Morpheme

A Korean verbal—verb, adjective, or copula—consists of a stem and a word-final suffix, with optional intermediate suffixes as ordered in (1).[3]

(1) *Sequence of positions of verbal inflections*

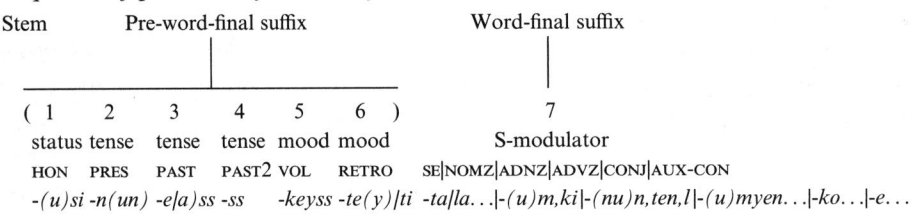

```
Stem     Pre-word-final suffix              Word-final suffix

         ( 1      2      3       4     5     6  )       7
         status  tense  tense  tense  mood  mood         S-modulator
         HON    PRES   PAST   PAST2   VOL   RETRO       SE|NOMZ|ADNZ|ADVZ|CONJ|AUX-CON
         -(u)si -n(un) -e/a)ss -ss    -keyss -te(y)/ti  -ta/la...|-(u)m,ki|-(nu)n,ten,l|-(u)myen...|-ko...|-e...
```

For example, the stem *ka-* 'go', with the RETRO (retrospective) suffix attached, yields word forms like those in (2).

(2) *Retrospective word forms*

     ka   ⟨stem⟩ 'go'
a. ka-te   ⟨stem-RETRO⟩
b. ka-si-te   ⟨stem-HON-RETRO⟩
c. ka-ss-te   ⟨stem-PAST-RETRO⟩
d. ka-ss-keyss-te   ⟨stem-PAST-VOL-RETRO⟩
e. ka-te-la   ⟨stem-RETRO-SE⟩
f. ka-te-nya   ⟨stem-RETRO-SE⟩

Notice that in (2e–f) the SE (sentence ending) morpheme, which is required in order to constitute a finite form of a sentence, has the forms *la* (plain-declarative) and *nya* (plain-interrogative).[4]

    RETRO sentence-final forms are restricted to declarative and interrogative sentences; future-oriented imperative and propositive sentences are nonexistent.

Retrospective Mood in Korean 297

(3) *Major retrospective SE word forms*
    a. te-la (= (2e)) ⟨retrospective plain-declarative⟩
    b. te-nya/ni (= (2f)) ⟨retrospective plain-interrogative⟩
    c. tey ⟨retrospective intimate-declarative⟩
    d. tey? ⟨retrospective intimate-interrogative⟩
    e. tey-yo ⟨retrospective polite-declarative⟩
    f. (su)p-ti-ta ⟨retrospective deferential-declarative⟩
    g. (su)p-ti-kka ⟨retrospective deferential-interrogative⟩

In addition to those in (3), retrospective word forms include declarative *ten-tey(yo)*; interrogative *ten?*, *ten-ka(yo)?* In exclamative sentences, the sentence-final marker *kwun!* (or the polite form *kwun-yo!*) is added to the retrospective word forms: *te-kwun!* (plain) and *te-kwun-yo!* (polite). Note that the retrospective intimate-interrogative *tey?* (3d) is distinguished from (3c) by a rising intonation, while the retrospective polite-declarative (3e) has no corresponding interrogative (*tey-yo?*).[5] The retrospective morpheme *te*, when combined with the adnominal suffix *(u)n*, gives rise to *ten* (retrospective adnominal modifier) and *ess-ten* (past retrospective adnominal modifier), which denote durative and complete events in the past, respectively. The use of the retrospective modifiers, however, is not taken into account in this chapter: the speech act properties of recollection and cognition, which are typically manifest in retrospective declarative and interrogative sentences (see section 14.3), are obscure, if not absent, in adnominal clauses with *ten* (or *ess-ten*).[6]

14.2.2 Retrospective Sentences

To facilitate the presentation in the following sections, simple retrospective sentences—declarative (4a) and interrogative (4b)—are presented and illustrated in parallel with the corresponding nonretrospective sentences.

(4)   *Retrospective*   *Nonretrospective*
    a. Mia-ka ka-te-la.   Mia-ka ka-ss-ta.
        Mia-SM go-RETRO-PL.DEC   Mia-SM go-PAST-PL.DEC
        'Mia went, I recall.'   'Mia went.'
    b. Mia-ka ka-te-nya?   Mia-ka ka-ss-nya?
        Mia-SM go-RETRO-PL.INT   Mia-SM go-PAST-PL.INT
        'Did Mia go, do you recall?'   'Did Mia go?'

The presence of the suffix *te* conveys the additional meaning 'I recall' in the declarative (4a), and 'do you recall' in the interrogative (4b), though the English parenthetical phrases 'I recall' and 'do you recall?' are not fine-grained enough to convey that the recollection is focused on the speaker's (or the hearer's) *observation* of Mia's going in the past. The Korean retrospectives denote such a cognitive meaning in addition to the meaning of recalling. By contrast, the nonretrospective sentences of Korean impart no such cognitive sense on the part of the discourse participants. The nonretrospective declarative simply conveys a speech act of assertion or one of its subtypes,[7] such as telling, reporting, or informing; likewise, the nonretrospective interrogative conveys a speech act of questioning. Notice that when the interrogative is answered negatively, what is negated is the content of the sentence, not the parenthetical part of recalling, as the two answers in (5) illustrate.

(5) a. Mia-ka ka-te-nya? (= (4b))
'Did Mia go, do you recall?'
 b. Ani-yo.
not-POL.DEC
'No.'
 c. Ani-yo   an ka-tey-yo.
not-POL.DEC not go-RETRO-POL.DEC
'No, she didn't go, I recall.'

If the retrospective question (5a) were given the translation (6a), it would get a wrong answer, as indicated in (6b).

(6) a. Do you recall that Mia went?
 b. No. I don't (recall it).

As illustrated above, the English renditions of the Korean retrospectives are supplemented with parenthetical phrases like 'I recall' and 'do you recall?'. But these tags do not precisely impart the speech act meaning inherent in the Korean retrospectives. What is mentally recalled is not the semantic content of the utterance itself but the cognitive act of observing it. In the examples in (7), the additional cognitive meaning is provided parenthetically—'I observed'—in addition to 'I recall'.

(7) a. Mia-ka ka-ss-te-la.
Mia-SM go-PAST-RETRO-PL.DEC
'Mia was gone, I observed, I recall.'
 b. Pi-ka o-keyss-te-la.
rain-SM come-will-RETRO-PL.DEC
'It looked like rain, I observed, I recall.'
 c. Mia-ka ca-ko-iss-te-la.
Mia-SM sleep-ing-be-RETRO-PL.DEC
'Mia was sleeping, I observed, I recall.'
 d. Mia-ka keki-ey wa-iss-te-la.
Mia-SM there-at come-be-RETRO-PL.DEC
'Mia was there, I observed, I recall.'

e. Mia-ka nayil ka-n-ta-te-la.
Mia-SM tomorrow go-PRES-DEC-RETRO-PL.DEC
   i. 'They said Mia will go tomorrow, I observed, I recall.'
   ii. 'Mia said she will go tomorrow, I observed, I recall.'

The modal auxiliary *keyss* in (7b) denotes predictive, not volitive, meaning; it is categorized as future tense by many grammarians. (7c) and (7d) show two aspects, progressive ⟨V-*ko-iss-ta*⟩ (*be* V-*ing*) and resultative (or perfective) ⟨V-*e-iss-ta*⟩ (*hav*e (or *be*)-V-*en*). As the parenthetical 'I recall' is a cover term—representative of a set of mental parentheses including 'I remember' and 'I recollect',[8] likewise, the cognitive expression 'I observed' is a cover term for expressions including 'I noticed' and 'I saw'. In English, the cognitive verb *see* may be used directly as a main verb, rather than parenthetically: the English sentence corresponding to (7c) would be *I saw Mia sleeping*. What type of cognitive act is involved in (7c)? Is it observing, seeing, noticing, or hearing? The answer depends on the context of use: the speaker directly saw Mia sleeping when he visited her at the hospital, he was told by her mother that she was in bed when he visited her house, and the like. (7e) is ambiguous with respect to who said it—either Mia or some other person.

Let us consider the examples in (8). (8c), which indicates that the speaker saw himself sleeping, is odd in normal situations, but it is quite acceptable in the context where the speaker *objectivizes* himself as an observer: for instance, watching a videotape of himself, he observed he was sleeping—he watched his "counterpart" in the video world.[9]

(8) a. Mia-ka ca-ko iss-te-la.
       Mia-SM sleep-ing be-RETRO-PL.DEC
       'Mia was sleeping, I observed, I recall.'
    b. Ney-ka ca-ko iss-te-la.
       you-SM
       'You were sleeping, I observed, I recall.'
    c. #Nay-ka ca-ko iss-te-la.
       I-SM
       'I was sleeping, I observed, I recall.'

By contrast, nothing seems to be wrong with the English translation 'I was sleeping, I recall'.[10] In English, what was recalled is the fact of the speaker's sleeping in the past, not his own observation of his sleeping in the past. Think of the following retrospective construction, which consists of a declarative sentence ending with a *wh*-question word. The speech act denoted is a sort of self-addressed question, which may be expressed in English with a parenthetical like 'I wonder'.

(9) a. Ce salam-i nwukwu-te-la?[11]
    that man-SM who-RETRO-PL.INT
    'Who was he? I wonder.'
  b. Ku ttay-ka meych-si-te-la?
    the time-SM what-time-RETRO-PL.INT
    'What time was it then? I wonder.'

In (9a), the observation time is placed implicitly as a reference point in the past and the speaker's recollection goes back to that time, at which he saw someone whose identity he now cannot recall. In (9b), the reference point is explicit (*ku ttay* 'the time'), and the speaker cannot recall what time it was then. This type of dubitative speech act is in contrast with the genuine *wh*-retrospectives in (10).

(10) a. Ce salam-i nwukwu-te-nya?
        'Who was he, do you recall?'
   b. Ku ttay-ka meych-si-te-nya?
        'What time was it, do you recall?'

14.3 Retrospectives and Speech Act

We will now look at some major constraints on temporal and modal relations pertaining to retrospectives. As observed and illustrated in section 14.2, the discourse participants—the speaker and the hearer—and temporal, aspectual, and modal relations are essential for the proper understanding of Korean retrospective expressions. The constraints on tense, aspect, and mood will be examined in that order.

14.3.1 Temporal Constraints

Five temporal reference points are relevant to the discussion: three basic ones (utterance time t_u, event time t_e, and reference time t_r; see Reichenbach 1947) and two new ones (retrospection time t_{retro} and observation time t_{obs}). These two additional time references are cover terms for the times of perceiving/experiencing and recalling/remembering, respectively. McCawley (1981/1993, 341) suggests three ways of expressing time considerations in logical structure: (1) treating time as an extra argument in a propositional function, representing, for example, Bald(*x*) as a two-place predicate Bald(*x, t*); (2) using a temporal operator R_t, as for example in R_t(Bald(*x*)), expressing that the proposition it is combined with is true at the indicated time *t*; (3) treating time as indices $(t_1, t_2, \ldots, t_n)$ relative to which a proposition is evaluated. Each event is assigned a specific time index in a feature structure in section 14.4. McCawley's two time references (PRIOR and NOW) are represented as a temporal relation (PRECEDE-REL) and a contextual index attribute UT (utterance time) with its value t_u.

The retrospection and cognition times are unique to the retrospective. There are two fundamental temporal constraints on the retrospective: (1) retrospection time overlaps with utterance time ($t_{retro} = t_u$); (2) observation time precedes retrospection time ($t_{obs} \succ t_{retro}$). In addition, the retrospective mood *te* manifests temporal constraints of the kind presented in (11), when combined with morphemes expressing tense and/or volitive or predictive mood.

(11) *Verbal form* *Temporal constraints*
    a. -te (RETRO)
        i. $t_e \succ t_{retro}$
        ii. $t_e \succ t_{obs}$
        (iii. $t_{retro} \succ t_e$)
    b. -ss-te (PAST-RETRO) $t_e \succ t_{obs}$
    c. -ss-ss-te (PAST-PAST2-RETRO) $t_e \succ t_r \succ t_{obs}$
    d. -keyss-te (VOL-RETRO)
        i. $t_{obs} \succ t_e \succ t_{retro}$
        ii. $t_{obs} \succ t_{retro} \succ t_e$
    e. -ess-keyss-te (PAST-VOL-RETRO) $t_r \succ t_e \succ t_{obs}$
    f. -ess-ess-keyss-te (PAST-PAST-VOL-RETRO) = (11e)

14.3.2 Aspectual Constraints

Syntactically, two distinct aspectual classes are set up: ⟨V-*ko-iss-ta*⟩[12] and ⟨V-*e-iss-ta*⟩.[13] Unlike tense and mood, aspect is not a suffix-based category, and it is restricted to verbs, excluding adjectives and the copula. The two classes bear compositional similarities with the corresponding aspectual classes of English: ⟨*be* V-*ing*⟩ (progressive) and ⟨*have* V-*en*⟩ (perfect).

The progressive aspect form ⟨V-*ko-iss-ta*⟩ primarily denotes an activity in progress or a durative state. It is productive: the auxiliary part ⟨-*ko-iss-ta*⟩ can be attached to any verb stem; moreover, the auxiliary *iss-* 'be' can fully inflect, yielding multiple progressive tense/mood word forms or sentence types including imperatives and propositives.

(12) a. Mia-ka ca-ko-ss-ta.
      Mia-SM sleep-ing-be-PL.DEC
      'Mia is sleeping.'
   b. Mia-ka ca-ko-iss-te-la.
      Mia-SM sleep-ing-be-RETRO-PL.DEC
      'Mia was sleeping, I recall.'

The perfect aspect form ⟨V-*e-iss-ta*⟩, which denotes continuation of a state resulting from the completion of an activity, is nonproductive, limited to some intransitive verbs.[14] Historically, most of the verbs in the form ⟨V-*e-iss-ta*⟩ were contracted to the past tense form ⟨V-*ess-ta*⟩ (i.e., *e-iss-ta* → *ess-ta*). Some verbs have both V-*ess-ta* (past tense) and V-*e-iss-ta* (perfect aspect) forms: for example, *o-ta* 'come':

wa-ss-ta (← *o-ass-ta*) (past) versus *wa-iss-ta* (← *o-a-iss-ta*) (perfective); *anc-ta* 'sit': *anc-ass-ta* (past) versus *anc-a-iss-ta* (perfective); *ca-ta* 'sleep': **ca-iss-ta* (perfective) versus *ca-ss-ta* (past). Now consider sentences in the perfect and compare them with the corresponding progressive retrospective and past sentences.

(13) a. Mia-ka yeki-ey w-a-iss-ta. (perfect)
    Mia-SM here-at come-en-be-PL.DEC
    'Mia is/has come here. → Mia is here.'

  b. Mia-ka yeki-ey wa-ss-ta. (past)
    Mia-SM here-at come-PAST-PL.DEC
    'Mia came here.'

  c. Mia-ka yeki-ey o-ko-iss-ta. (progressive)
    Mia-SM here-at come-ing-be-PL.DEC
    'Mia is coming here.'

(14) a. Mia-ka yeki-ey w-a-iss-te-la. (perfect retrospective)
    Mia-SM here-at come-en-be-RETRO-PL.DEC
    'Mia was here, I recall.'

  b. Mia-ka yeki-ey wa-ss-te-la. (past retrospective)
    Mia-SM here-at come-PAST-RETRO-PL.DEC
    'Mia came here, I recall.'

  c. Mia-ka yeki-ey o-ko-iss-te-la. (progressive retrospective)
    Mia-SM here-at come-ing-be-RETRO-PL.DEC
    'Mia was coming here, I recall.'

Some verbs with both ⟨*-e-iss-ta*⟩ and ⟨*-ko-iss-ta*⟩ forms convey different meanings. For example, *sal-ta* has two senses: 'live' and 'reside'.[15] The progressive form ⟨*sal-ko-iss-ta*⟩ means 'be living', in the sense of 'be residing', whereas the perfect form ⟨*sal-a-iss-ta*⟩ means 'be living', in the sense of 'be alive'. Form determines meaning in this case; that is, the meanings of the retrospective sentences in (15) are predictable.

(15) a. Mia-ka acik sal-ko-iss-te-la. (progressive retrospective)
    Mia-SM still live-ing-RETRO-PL.DEC
    'Mia was still residing, I recall.'

  b. Mia-ka acik sal-a-iss-te-la. (perfective retrospective)
    Mia-SM still live-en-be-RETRO-PL.DEC
    'Mia was still alive, I recall.'

14.3.3 Modal Constraints

The salient feature of the retrospective is the speaker's mode of retrospection based on his cognitive activity in the past.[16] The speaker's cognition may be defined as 'the psychological result of perception and learning and reasoning' (WordNet).

Retrospective Mood in Korean

Ontologically, the cognitive type COGNITION may be assumed to have two subtypes, OBSERVATION and EXPERIENCE.[17] Furthermore, the type PERCEPTION may be viewed as intermediate between COGNITION and OBSERVATION. A partial type hierarchy of COGNITION is represented in (16), where the cognitive verbs in small capital letters are meant to be metalinguistic or interlingual verbs—in the guise of English words, so to speak.

(16) *A partial hierarchy of cognition*

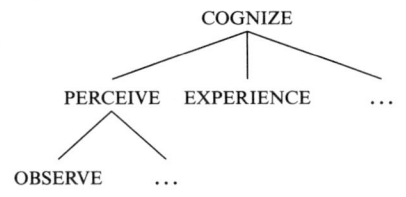

```
              COGNIZE
            /    |    \
      PERCEIVE EXPERIENCE  ...
       /   \
   OBSERVE  ...
```

In the vein of lexical decomposition pioneered by McCawley (1968),[18] the retrospective morpheme *te* is recast as in (17), where RECALL, OBSERVE, EXPERIENCE, and PRIOR are, as noted above, metalinguistic predicates.[19] The logical structure (17a) expresses that the proposition '*x* COGNIZED a state of affairs (SOA)' is realized in the form of *te* and it subsumes (17b) and (17c) according to the type hierarchy in (16).[20]

(17) a. $\text{RECALL}(x(\text{COGNIZE}(x, \text{SOA}, t_1), t_2)) \wedge \text{PRIOR}(t_1, t_2) \Rightarrow te$
   b. $\text{RECALL}(x(\text{OBSERVE}(x, \text{SOA}, t_1), t_2)) \wedge \text{PRIOR}(t_1, t_2) \Rightarrow te$
   c. $\text{RECALL}(x(\text{EXPERIENCE}(x, \text{SOA}, t_1), t_2)) \wedge \text{PRIOR}(t_1, t_2) \Rightarrow te$

The use of the same variable *x* indicates that the "recaller" and the "observer/experiencer" are identical (equi-subject constraint); furthermore, *x* is identical to the speaker in the discourse (equi-speaker constraint).[21] These constraints are represented by means of coindexation in CUG. The two cognitive types OBSERVE and EXPERIENCE underlie the realization of the retrospective morpheme *te* and are kept distinct in terms of emotive predicates it is suffixed to, as will be shown in section 14.3.5.

Retrospectives are also constrained by sentence types (declarative and interrogative) and by the thematic roles of the discourse participants (speaker and hearer): (1) in declaratives, what is recalled is the speaker's cognition; (2) in interrogatives, it is the hearer's; (3) the speaker/hearer is coreferential with the cognizer; (4) the subject referent in the sentence is noncoreferential with the cognizer (non-equi-subject constraint), unless the cognizer is assumed to play an observer's (not participant's) role.

14.3.4 Discourse Participants and Semantic Content

The entity that recalls and observes a state of affairs in the past is the speaker in declaratives and the hearer in interrogatives; the speech acts may be represented as the topmost illocutionary act of asserting (for declaratives) and questioning (for interrogatives), with modal acts of recalling and cognizing embedded in the order indicated in (18).

(18) a. *Retrospective declarative S*
    I ASSERT that
        I RECALL that
            I COGNIZED that
                S

b. *Retrospective interrogative S*
    I QUESTION (you to TELL me if)
        you RECALL that
            you COGNIZED that
                S

14.3.5 Korean Emotive Predicates and Retrospectives

Korean emotive predicates deserve special treatment in the retrospective. In terms of parts of speech, there are two: emotive adjectives and emotive verbs. Morphologically, some emotive verbs are derived from emotive adjectives with the auxiliary *hata* 'do', as shown in (19).

(19)   *Emotive adjective*   *Emotive verb (stem-hata)*
    a. mip-ta 'hateful'   miwe-hata 'hate'
    b. mwusep-ta 'fearful'   mwusewe-hata 'fear'
    c. coh-ta 'lik(e)able'   coha-hata 'like'
    d. kippu-ta 'glad'   kippe-hata 'pleased'

A default constraint on these emotive adjectives, which are normally one-place predicates, is that the speaker and the subject referent in declaratives must be identical, as must the hearer and the subject referent in interrogatives. The speaker-subject plays an experiencer's role. The corresponding emotive verbs with *hata* are not subject to an equi-speaker/subject constraint; they are normally two-place predicates.[22] The subject plays an actor's role (Davis 2001).

(20) a.   Kippe-yo.
       glad-POL.DEC
       'I am glad.'
    b.   Na-nun kippe-yo.
       I-TOP
       'I am glad.'
    c.   #Ney-ka kippe.
       you-SM
       'You are glad.'

Retrospective Mood in Korean 305

d. #Mia-ka kippe(-yo).
   Mia-SM
   'Mia is glad.'

The emotive adjectival sentences with non–first person subjects (20c–d) are quite odd, when used in the present and assertive mode. The first person subject is normally unexpressed, as in (20a). An explanation for this sort of constraint on emotive predicates may lie in the interaction between a psychological state of affairs and the speech act of assertion; that is, only the speaker is rightfully in a position to assert his current emotional state. Korean is one language prohibiting a speaker from asserting emotions other than his own. Another is Japanese.[23] To Koreans, for the speaker to assert someone else's current psychological state would appear grossly presumptuous unless the speaker is omniscient or has foolproof empathy with the other person.[24] The same kind of constraint applies to the interrogative with an emotive adjective predicate. This time it is the hearer (the second person subject referent) whose psychological state is questioned.

(21) a. Kippe-yo?
       glad-POL.DEC
       'Are you glad?'
    b. #Ce-nun kippe-yo?
       I-TOP
       'Am I glad?'
    c. Ne kippu-ni?
       you glad-PL.INT
       'Are you glad?'
    d. #Mia-ka kippe(-yo)?
       Mia-SM
       'Is Mia glad?'

By contrast, emotive verbs formed from ⟨emotive adj.-*hata*⟩ impose no constraint on the discourse participants. They are nonstative and have no constraint on subject selection. The subject referent plays an actor's role, not an experiencer's.

(22) a. Na-nun kippe-ha-ko-iss-ta.
       I   glad-do-ing-be-PL.DEC
       'I am showing gladness.'
    b. Ney-ka kippe-ha-ko-iss-ta.
       you
       'You are showing gladness.'
    c. Mia-ka kippe-ha-ko-iss-ta.
       Mia-SM
       'Mia is showing gladness.'

What is the difference in meaning between stative and nonstative emotives? Consider (23a–c), with their English translations.

(23) a. (Na-nun) kippe-yo. (= (20b))   'I am glad.'
    b. Na-nun kippe-hay-yo.   'I show gladness.'
    c. Na-nun kippe-hako-isse-yo.   'I am showing gladness.'

The English translations in (23b–c), which appear unnatural, are intended to show that the speaker is in the state of "showing" his gladness—showing or evincing his internal feeling externally. This process of "externalizing an internal feeling" (see Yeon 1994; Chang 1996) is manifested by turning emotive adjectives to emotive verbs with the auxiliary *hata* 'do'.[25] The speaker plays an actor's role, not an experiencer's.

Let us now examine retrospective constructions with emotive predicates.

(24) a. Kippu-te-la.
      glad-RETRO-PL.DEC
      'I was glad, I felt—I recall.'
   b. Paym-i   mwusep-te-la.
      snake-SM fearful-RETRO-PL.DEC
      'The snake was fearful, I felt—I recall.'
   c. Kippu-te-nya?
      glad-RETRO-PL.INT
      'Were you glad, did you feel?—do you recall?'
   d. Paymi-i mwusep-te-nya?
      'Was the snake fearful, did you feel?—do you recall?'

With nonstative emotive verbs, the subject referent plays the role of an actor and the speaker plays the cognitive role of an observer, not an experiencer.

(25) a. Mia-ka kippe-ha-te-la.
      Mia-SM glad-do-RETRO-PL.DEC
      'Mia showed gladness, I observed—I recall.'
   b. Mia-ka paym-ul   mwusewe-ha-te-la.
      Mia-SM snake-OM fearful-do-RETRO-PL.DEC
      'Mia feared the snake, I observed—I recall.'

(26) a. Mia-ka kippe-ha-te-nya?
      Mia-SM glad-do-RETRO-PL.INT
      'Did Mia show gladness—did you observe and do you recall?'
   b. Mia-ka paym-ul   mwusewe-ha-te-nya?
      Mia-SM snake-OM fearful-do-RETRO-PL.INT
      'Did Mia fear the snake—did you observe and do you recall?'

Compare the following pair and notice the difference in the state of cognition. (27a) is a stative emotive in the retrospective mood and (27b) is a nonstative emotive; in both, the speaker is the subject referent.

(27) a. Na-nun paym-i   mwusep-te-la.
         I-TOP   snake-SM fearful-RETRO-PL.DEC
         'The snake was fearful, I felt—I recall.'
     b. Na-nun paym-ul   mwusewe-ha-te-la.
         I-TOP   snake-OM fearful-do-RETRO-PL.DEC
         'I showed fear to the snake, I observed—I recall.'

Here (27b) behaves the same as the corresponding sentence with an ordinary nonemotive predicate; it is acceptable when the speaker acts like a bystander, not a direct experiencer or feeler in the given state of affairs.

We have extensively examined Korean retrospective sentences, beginning with the retrospective morpheme and its interactions with other verbal suffixes in the predicate and its use in sentences, cross-cutting the domains of syntax and speech act, focusing on the discourse participants' mental and cognitive activities. The primary speech act function of the retrospective is paraphrased in plain English as 'I recall that I observed that S' (where the subject referent expressed in S is non-I (i.e., not the speaker); otherwise, the speaker-subject is the experiencer in the emotive adjectival S). We might be tempted to suppress one of the mental and cognitive phrases from our informal speech act account, as in (28a) or (28b).

(28) a. I recall that S
     b. I observed that S
     c. I recall that I observed that S

Recalling may be replaced by another mental act (remembering, recollecting, or reminding); likewise, observing may be replaced by another cognitive act of perceiving (seeing or feeling)—all depending on the context of use. However, the cognitive act is properly embedded in the mental act as shown in (28c).

14.4 Retrospectives in Constraint-based Unified Grammar

Having looked at retrospective mood in descriptive and functional terms in the first part of this chapter, in the second part we will consider how to represent salient speech act properties of retrospective sentences in the general framework of Constraint-based Unified Grammar of Korean (CUG/K).[26] In this framework, such properties are explicitly expressed in the form of attribute-value matrices, notably in the pragmatic component PRA. From the outset, CUG was conceived of as incorporating contextual information—traditionally relegated to the "wastebasket of pragmatics" (Bar-Hillel 1954)—into the matrix of feature structures as an integral part. Speech act information relevant to the retrospective construction is properly located in the tense-aspect-mood component TAM interacting with the morphosyntactic component. It is a sign-based (Sag and Wasow 1999), type-theoretic (Carpenter 1992), lexicon-oriented (Koenig 1999) approach to grammar—a grammar extending from morpheme to discourse and further characterized by structure sharing, a multiple inheritance hierarchy, default constraint inheritance, and underspecification (Lascarides and Copestake 1999).

Section 14.4.1 gives an overview of CUG/K, outlining the notions of type hierarchy and lexical type inheritance and illustrating with the feature structure of a retrospective word form. Section 14.4.2 then presents the feature structure of the retrospective interfaced with SA (speech act), SEM (semantics), and SYN (syntax), elaborating emotive predicates with their two subtypes and building up a retrospective construction from a word to a phrase and eventually to a sentence.

14.4.1 Type Hierarchy and Feature Inheritance

Adhering to the sign-based conception of grammar, according to which grammar is a set of constraints on *signs*, CUG places *signs* at the top of the type hierarchy. In the type hierarchy of *sign*, its immediate subtypes are *lexical sign* and *phrase*. The *lexical sign* is partitioned into *lexeme* and *word*, as shown in (29a) and in a tree structure in (29b).[27]

(29) *Subtypes of* sign *(top level)*
    a. Partitions:
        Partition of *sign*: *lex sign, phrase*
        Partition of *lex sign*: *lexeme, word*
        Partition of *lexeme*: ...
        Partition of *word*: ...
    b.
```
              sign
             /    \
        lex sign   phrase
        /    \
    lexeme   word
      ⋮       ⋮
```

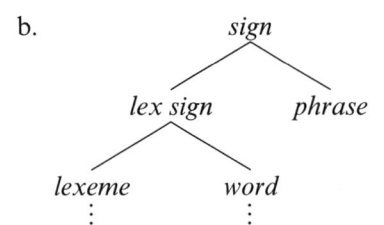

The *lexeme* type is assumed to have two subtypes: *part-of-speech* (*pos*) and *argument-selection* (*arg-select*). Arg-select specifies the number of arguments in the argument-structure (*arg-st*): *1-place-lexeme, 2-place-lexeme,* and *3-place-lexeme. Pos* is partitioned into *verbal-lexeme, nominal-lexeme, adverbial-lexeme,* and *particle-lexeme. Verbal-lexeme* is partitioned into *verb-lexeme, adjective-lexeme,* and *copula-*

Retrospective Mood in Korean 309

lexeme. Adjective-lexeme has the subtypes *emotive adjective-lexeme* and *nonemotive adjective-lexeme* (provisionally, for the explication of retrospectives).

Following the convention of the multiple inheritance hierarchy, lexical types of Korean verbals are subtyped along multiple dimensions, as illustrated in (30).[28]

(30) *Lexeme hierarchy (partial)*

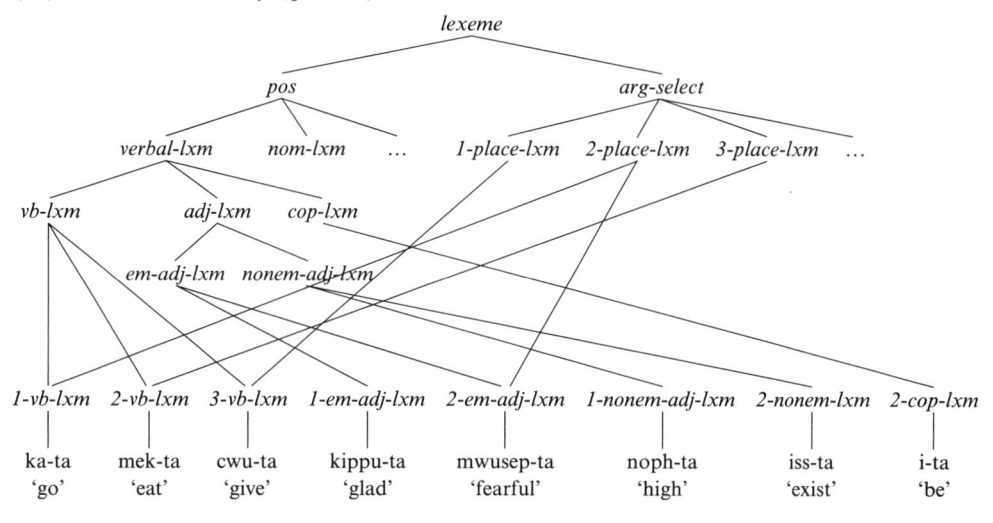

```
                          lexeme
                   /                \
                 pos               arg-select
              /   |              /    |      \
      verbal-lxm  nom-lxm ...  1-place-lxm  2-place-lxm  3-place-lxm ...
     /    |    \
  vb-lxm adj-lxm cop-lxm
          /    \
    em-adj-lxm  nonem-adj-lxm

  1-vb-lxm  2-vb-lxm  3-vb-lxm  1-em-adj-lxm  2-em-adj-lxm  1-nonem-adj-lxm  2-nonem-lxm  2-cop-lxm
     |         |         |          |             |              |               |           |
   ka-ta    mek-ta    cwu-ta     kippu-ta     mwusep-ta        noph-ta        iss-ta       i-ta
   'go'     'eat'     'give'      'glad'       'fearful'        'high'        'exist'       'be'
```

14.4.2 Feature Structures

In CUG, a *sign* is specified for two attributes: PPM (prosody-phonology-morphology) and SSP (syntax-semantics-pragmatics),[29] which are inherited by the subtypes *lexeme-sign* and *word*. The values of PPM and SSP are specified as types: *ppm* and *ssp*, respectively. The feature structures of *sign*, *ppm*, and *ssp* are each specified as in (31).

(31) a. *FS of* sign

$$sign: \begin{bmatrix} \text{PPM } ppm \\ \text{SSP } ssp \end{bmatrix}$$

b. *FS of* ppm

$$ppm: \begin{bmatrix} \text{PROS } pros \\ \text{PHON list}(phone\text{-}string) \\ \text{MORPH } morph \end{bmatrix}^{30}$$

c. *FS of* ssp

$$ssp: \begin{bmatrix} \text{SYN } syn \\ \text{SEM } sem \\ \text{PRA } pra \end{bmatrix}$$

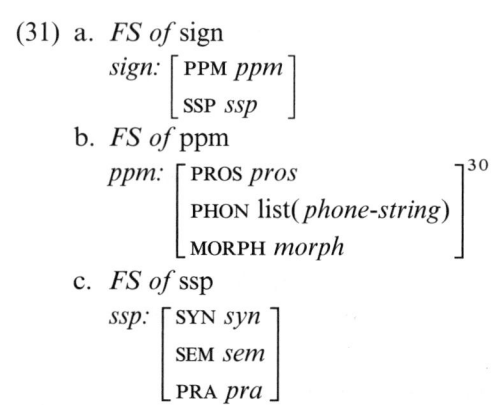

The FSs of *syn*, *sem*, and *verbal-lexeme* are as shown in (32).

(32) a. *FS of* syn
$$syn: \begin{bmatrix} \text{HEAD } pos \\ \text{COMPS list}(ssp) \\ \text{SPR list}(ssp) \\ \text{MARKING } marking \\ \text{GAP list}(ssp) \end{bmatrix}$$
b. *FS of* sem
$$sem: \begin{bmatrix} \text{INDEX } i \\ \text{RESTR list}(soa) \end{bmatrix}$$
c. *FS of* verbal-lexeme
$$vbl\text{-}lxm: \begin{bmatrix} \text{SYN} \begin{bmatrix} \text{HEAD } verb \text{ [FORM } vform] \\ \text{SPR } \langle [\ ] \rangle \end{bmatrix} \\ \text{ARG-ST } \langle \text{NP}, \ldots \rangle \\ \text{SEM } [\ldots] \\ \text{PRA } [\ldots] \end{bmatrix}$$

The *morph* type consists of two attributes, STEM and AFFIX, as shown in (33).

(33) a. *FS of* morph
$$morph: \begin{bmatrix} \text{STEM } stem \\ \text{AFFIX } affix \end{bmatrix}$$
b. *FS of* affix
$$affix: \begin{bmatrix} \text{SUFFIX } suffix \\ \text{PREFIX } prefix \end{bmatrix}^{31}$$

(34) *FS of* suffix
$$suffix: \begin{bmatrix} \text{HON } binary \\ \text{TNS } tns \\ \text{MD } md \\ \text{SM } sm \end{bmatrix}$$

The *vform* type has the following subtypes: *stem, hon, tns, md,* and *se*. With the subtypes of *tns, md,* and *se* fully specified, *vform* yields multiply inherited forms like *stem-hon-se, stem-retro-se,* and *stem-vol-retro-se*. For ease of reference, they will be called respectively *hon, retro,* and *vol-retro*.

Consider now the FS of the *word* type. It inherits the FSs of PPM and SSP. As represented in (35), the value of STEM is specified as the FS of the *lexeme* type and the values of its PHON and SSP are inherited by those of *word*'s PHON and SSP, respectively. This is a way of building the word-lexeme relation into a single FS and doing away with lexical rules (Koenig 1999; Sag and Wasow 1999, chap. 16).

(35) *FS of* word
word: $\begin{bmatrix} \text{PPM} & \begin{bmatrix} \text{PHON} / \boxed{1} \\ \text{MORPH} & \begin{bmatrix} \text{STEM} & \begin{bmatrix} \textit{lexeme} \\ \text{PPM [PHON} / \boxed{1}] \\ \text{SSP} / \boxed{2} \end{bmatrix} \\ \text{AFFIX } \textit{affix} \end{bmatrix} \end{bmatrix} \\ \text{SSP} / \boxed{2} \end{bmatrix}$

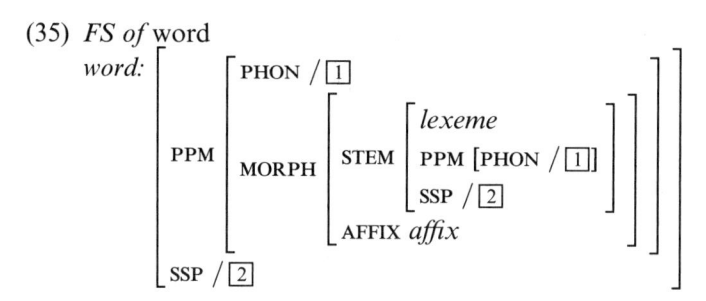

The FS of *word* in (35) is input to multiple word forms including retrospective word forms. By multiple feature inheritance, the *vform* type gives rise to as many verbal forms of a verbal as its inflection allows in the verbal morpheme sequence in (1).

14.5 Retrospectives in Attribute-Value Matrices

14.5.1 The Feature Structure of *pra*

What makes CUG/K unique in HPSG-style constraint-based grammars is the inclusion of speech acts, discourse functions, and background information.[32] The *pra* type is declared to have the FS shown in (36).

(36) *FS of* pra
pra: $\begin{bmatrix} \text{SA } \textit{speech-act} \\ \text{DF } \textit{discourse-function} \\ \text{BKG } \textit{background} \end{bmatrix}$

The *speech-act* (*sa*) type is specified for four attributes: C-INDS, TAM, IA, and DL, as in (37). A partial classification of the *tam* attribute, conceived of as a relation type, and its subtypes is shown in (38).

(37) *FS of* speech-act
sa: $\begin{bmatrix} \text{C-INDS} & \begin{bmatrix} \text{SP } \textit{ref} \\ \text{HR } \textit{ref} \\ \text{UT } \textit{t-ref} \end{bmatrix} \\ \text{TAM} & \begin{bmatrix} \text{TEMP list}(\textit{t-rel}) \\ \text{ASP list}(\textit{a-rel}) \\ \text{MDL list}(\textit{m-rel}) \end{bmatrix} \\ \text{IA list}(\textit{i-act}) \\ \text{DL list}(\textit{d-level}) \end{bmatrix}$

(38) *Partitions of* tam-relations *(incomplete)*
 a. Partition of *t-rel*: *precede-rel, overlap-rel*
 b. Partition of *a-rel*: *ongoing-rel, complete-rel, resultant-rel*

c. Partition of *m-rel*: *intend-rel, predict-rel, recall-rel, cognize-rel*
   d. Partition of *cognize-rel*: *perceive-rel, experience-rel*
   e. Partition of *perceive-rel*: *observe-rel, notice-rel, see-rel*

Notice that the subtypes of *modal-relation* (*m-rel*) are named differently from those in verbal morphology (e.g., *intend-rel* vs. *volitive suffix*; *predict-rel* vs. *predictive suffix*; *recall-rel* vs. *retrospective suffix*), so as to keep the two sets of terminology apart—one referring to the semantic type, the other to the morphosyntactic type. The *cognize-relation* is assumed to have subtypes including *perceive-relation* and *experience-relation*, as illustrated in (17). Likewise, the *perceive-relation* is assumed to have subtypes including *observe-relation*, *notice-relation*, and *see-relation*. The partial type hierarchy of cognition may help account for the cognitive and emotive properties of the retrospectives under discussion.[33]

Now the retrospective form and its interaction with speech act meaning are represented as constraints linking SYN and PRA, as shown in (39).

(39) *Linking: form and speech act*

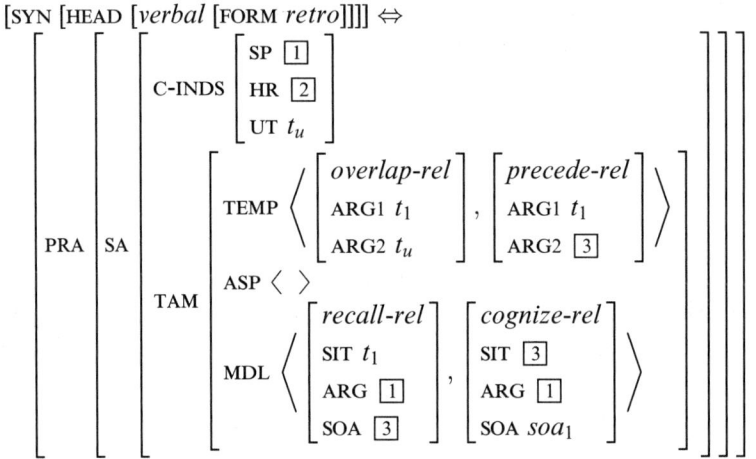

$$[\text{SYN } [\text{HEAD } [\textit{verbal } [\text{FORM } \textit{retro}]]]] \Leftrightarrow$$

$$\begin{bmatrix} \text{PRA} & \begin{bmatrix} \text{SA} & \begin{bmatrix} \text{C-INDS} & \begin{bmatrix} \text{SP} & \boxed{1} \\ \text{HR} & \boxed{2} \\ \text{UT} & t_u \end{bmatrix} \\ \text{TAM} & \begin{bmatrix} \text{TEMP} & \left\langle \begin{bmatrix} \textit{overlap-rel} \\ \text{ARG1 } t_1 \\ \text{ARG2 } t_u \end{bmatrix}, \begin{bmatrix} \textit{precede-rel} \\ \text{ARG1 } t_1 \\ \text{ARG2 } \boxed{3} \end{bmatrix} \right\rangle \\ \text{ASP } \langle \; \rangle \\ \text{MDL} & \left\langle \begin{bmatrix} \textit{recall-rel} \\ \text{SIT } t_1 \\ \text{ARG } \boxed{1} \\ \text{SOA } \boxed{3} \end{bmatrix}, \begin{bmatrix} \textit{cognize-rel} \\ \text{SIT } \boxed{3} \\ \text{ARG } \boxed{1} \\ \text{SOA } soa_1 \end{bmatrix} \right\rangle \end{bmatrix} \end{bmatrix} \end{bmatrix}$$

The *illocutionary-act* (*ia*) and *discourse-level* (*dl*) types, partitioned in (40),[34] are also interfaced with verbal forms as shown in (41).

(40) *Partitions of* ia *and* dl *(incomplete)*
   a. Partition of *illocutionary-act*: *assert-rel, question-rel, request-rel, propose-rel, suppose-rel, wonder-rel*
   b. Partition of *discourse-level*: *plain-rel, polite-rel, deferential-rel, intimate-rel, familiar-rel, blunt-rel, honorific-rel*

(41) *Linking:* SE *to* IA *and* DL *(partial)*
[SYN [HEAD *verb* [FORM *pl.dec*]]] ⇔

$$\begin{bmatrix} \text{SA} & \begin{bmatrix} \text{C-INDS} & \begin{bmatrix} \text{SP} & \boxed{1} \\ \text{HR} & \boxed{2} \\ \text{UT} & t_1 \end{bmatrix} \\ \text{IA} & \left\langle \begin{bmatrix} assert\text{-}rel \\ \text{ARG1} & \boxed{1} \\ \text{ARG2} & \boxed{2} \\ \text{SOA} & soa \end{bmatrix} \right\rangle \\ \text{DL} & \left\langle \begin{bmatrix} plain\text{-}rel \\ \text{ARG1} & \boxed{1} \\ \text{ARG2} & \boxed{2} \end{bmatrix} \right\rangle \end{bmatrix} \end{bmatrix}$$

14.5.2 Emotive Predicates and Thematic Roles

We will now closely look into the properties of Korean emotive predicates in retrospective sentences along with the thematic roles of the discourse participants. The speaker and the recaller/observer/experiencer are identical, which is shown by coindexation. Emotive predicates are divided into INTERNAL and EXTERNAL types: the internal consisting of one-place (by default) or two-place emotive adjectives and the EXTERNAL consisting of emotive verbs. In sentences with internal emotive adjectives, the speaker plays an experiencer's role by default, whereas in sentences with external emotive verbs, the speaker plays an observer's role. Internal emotion can be "externalized"—that is, manifested externally when the speaker assumes an observer's role, as discussed earlier in connection with (27b).

(42) a. *Internal emotives*
(one- or two-place emotive adjectives)
   i. kippu-ta 'glad'
   ii. mwusep-ta 'dreadful'
   iii. coh-ta 'lik(e)able'

b. *External emotives*
(two-place emotive verbs)
   i. kippe-hata 'show gladness'
   ii. mwusewe-hata 'fear'
   iii. coha-hata 'like'

The FS of an *internal emotive retrospective adjective* has an experiencer's role specified in the modal (MDL) relation interfaced with an *internal-emotive relation* in the semantic content (SEM|RESTR); by contrast, the FS of an *external emotive retrospective verb* has an observer's role in the modal relation interfaced with an *external-emotive relation*, as well as *nonemotive relation* in the semantic content. (43) shows the FS of *internal emotive adjectives* (e.g., *kippu-ta* 'glad'). *External emotive verbs* are treated like those belonging to the general verbal type, with an observer role assigned to the subject referent, which is not constrained by the identity condition with the speaker.

(43) *FS of* internal emotive retro-adjective *type (e.g., kippu-ta)*

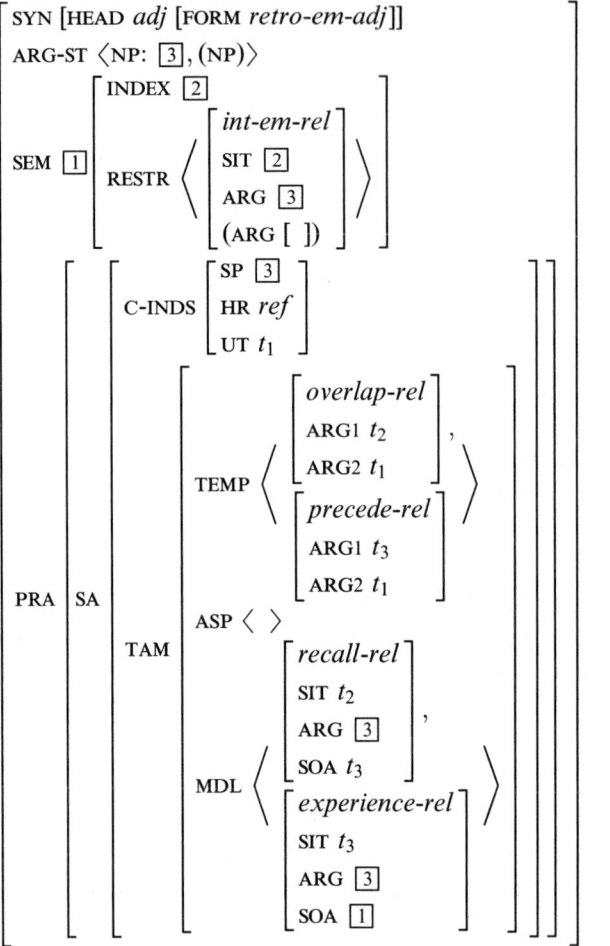

$$\begin{bmatrix} \text{SYN [HEAD } adj \text{ [FORM } retro\text{-}em\text{-}adj\text{]]} \\ \text{ARG-ST } \langle \text{NP: }\boxed{3}, (\text{NP}) \rangle \\ \text{SEM }\boxed{1} \begin{bmatrix} \text{INDEX }\boxed{2} \\ \text{RESTR } \left\langle \begin{bmatrix} int\text{-}em\text{-}rel \\ \text{SIT }\boxed{2} \\ \text{ARG }\boxed{3} \\ (\text{ARG [ ]}) \end{bmatrix} \right\rangle \end{bmatrix} \\ \text{PRA } \begin{bmatrix} \text{SA} \begin{bmatrix} \text{C-INDS} \begin{bmatrix} \text{SP }\boxed{3} \\ \text{HR } ref \\ \text{UT } t_1 \end{bmatrix} \\ \text{TAM} \begin{bmatrix} \text{TEMP } \left\langle \begin{bmatrix} overlap\text{-}rel \\ \text{ARG1 } t_2 \\ \text{ARG2 } t_1 \end{bmatrix}, \begin{bmatrix} precede\text{-}rel \\ \text{ARG1 } t_3 \\ \text{ARG2 } t_1 \end{bmatrix} \right\rangle \\ \text{ASP } \langle \rangle \\ \text{MDL } \left\langle \begin{bmatrix} recall\text{-}rel \\ \text{SIT } t_2 \\ \text{ARG }\boxed{3} \\ \text{SOA } t_3 \end{bmatrix}, \begin{bmatrix} experience\text{-}rel \\ \text{SIT } t_3 \\ \text{ARG }\boxed{3} \\ \text{SOA }\boxed{1} \end{bmatrix} \right\rangle \end{bmatrix} \end{bmatrix} \end{bmatrix} \end{bmatrix}$$

When the adjectival retrospective sentence is of the *internal emotive* type, its modal relation is that of *experience* and identity between the speaker and the subject referent is required, which is marked by coindexing—the tag [3] in (43). When the retrospective sentence is of the *external emotive* type (e.g., *kippe-ha-ta* 'glad' and *ka-ta* 'go'), the modal relation is that of *perception* (or its subtype *observation*) from the outset and no equi-speaker/subject constraint is imposed, as shown by the nonidentical tags [4] (speaker) and [1] (subject) in (44).

(44) *FS of (general)* retrospective-verb *type (e.g.,* kippe-ha-ta, ka-ta*)*

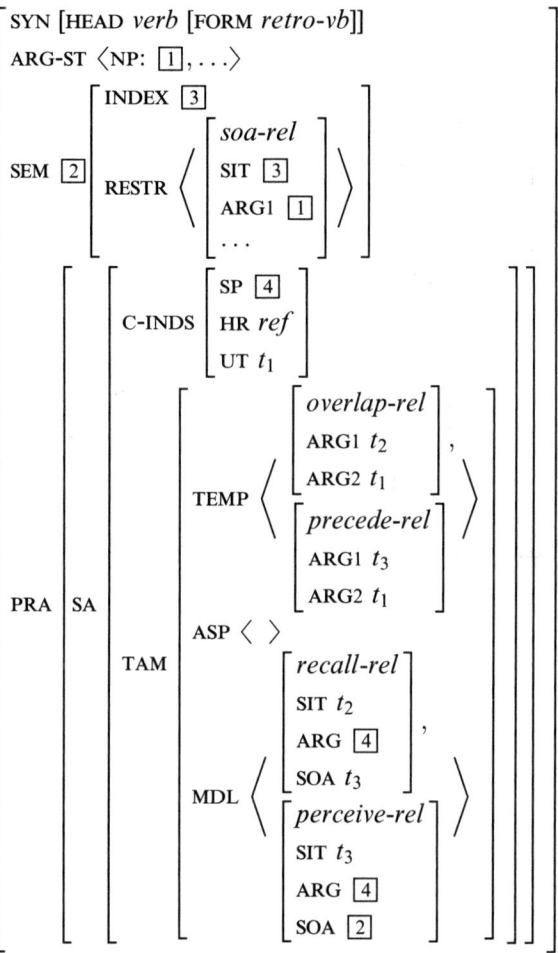

$$\begin{bmatrix} \text{SYN } [\text{HEAD } \textit{verb } [\text{FORM } \textit{retro-vb}]] \\ \text{ARG-ST } \langle \text{NP: } \boxed{1}, \ldots \rangle \\ \text{SEM } \boxed{2} \begin{bmatrix} \text{INDEX } \boxed{3} \\ \text{RESTR } \left\langle \begin{bmatrix} \textit{soa-rel} \\ \text{SIT } \boxed{3} \\ \text{ARG1 } \boxed{1} \\ \ldots \end{bmatrix} \right\rangle \end{bmatrix} \\ \text{PRA } \begin{bmatrix} \text{SA} \begin{bmatrix} \text{C-INDS} \begin{bmatrix} \text{SP } \boxed{4} \\ \text{HR } \textit{ref} \\ \text{UT } t_1 \end{bmatrix} \\ \text{TAM} \begin{bmatrix} \text{TEMP } \left\langle \begin{bmatrix} \textit{overlap-rel} \\ \text{ARG1 } t_2 \\ \text{ARG2 } t_1 \end{bmatrix}, \begin{bmatrix} \textit{precede-rel} \\ \text{ARG1 } t_3 \\ \text{ARG2 } t_1 \end{bmatrix} \right\rangle \\ \text{ASP } \langle \ \rangle \\ \text{MDL } \left\langle \begin{bmatrix} \textit{recall-rel} \\ \text{SIT } t_2 \\ \text{ARG } \boxed{4} \\ \text{SOA } t_3 \end{bmatrix}, \begin{bmatrix} \textit{perceive-rel} \\ \text{SIT } t_3 \\ \text{ARG } \boxed{4} \\ \text{SOA } \boxed{2} \end{bmatrix} \right\rangle \end{bmatrix} \end{bmatrix} \end{bmatrix} \end{bmatrix}$$

14.5.3 Illustrations: From Morpheme to Sentence

Given the interface constraints (39) and (41), we will now build up the FS of a retrospective sentence step by step: ⟨*ka-te*⟩ (V-STEM-RETRO; 'went, (I) recall') (45), ⟨*ka-te-la*⟩ (V-STEM-RETRO-PL.DEC; 'went, I recall') (46), ⟨*Mia-ka ka-te-la*⟩ ('Mia went, I recall') (48).

(45) *FS of word form* ka-te

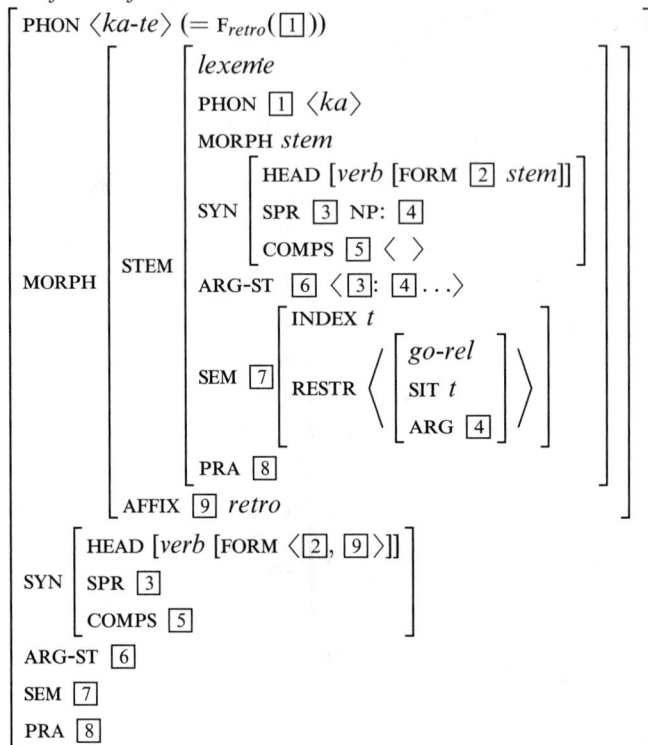

$$\begin{bmatrix} \text{PHON} \ \langle \textit{ka-te} \rangle \ (= F_{retro}(\boxed{1})) \\ \text{MORPH} \begin{bmatrix} \text{STEM} \begin{bmatrix} \textit{lexeme} \\ \text{PHON} \ \boxed{1} \ \langle \textit{ka} \rangle \\ \text{MORPH} \ \textit{stem} \\ \text{SYN} \begin{bmatrix} \text{HEAD} \ [\textit{verb} \ [\text{FORM} \ \boxed{2} \ \textit{stem}]] \\ \text{SPR} \ \boxed{3} \ \text{NP:} \ \boxed{4} \\ \text{COMPS} \ \boxed{5} \ \langle \ \rangle \end{bmatrix} \\ \text{ARG-ST} \ \boxed{6} \ \langle \boxed{3}: \boxed{4} \ldots \rangle \\ \text{SEM} \ \boxed{7} \begin{bmatrix} \text{INDEX} \ t \\ \text{RESTR} \ \langle \begin{bmatrix} \textit{go-rel} \\ \text{SIT} \ t \\ \text{ARG} \ \boxed{4} \end{bmatrix} \rangle \end{bmatrix} \\ \text{PRA} \ \boxed{8} \end{bmatrix} \\ \text{AFFIX} \ \boxed{9} \ \textit{retro} \end{bmatrix} \\ \text{SYN} \begin{bmatrix} \text{HEAD} \ [\textit{verb} \ [\text{FORM} \ \langle \boxed{2}, \boxed{9} \rangle]] \\ \text{SPR} \ \boxed{3} \\ \text{COMPS} \ \boxed{5} \end{bmatrix} \\ \text{ARG-ST} \ \boxed{6} \\ \text{SEM} \ \boxed{7} \\ \text{PRA} \ \boxed{8} \end{bmatrix}$$

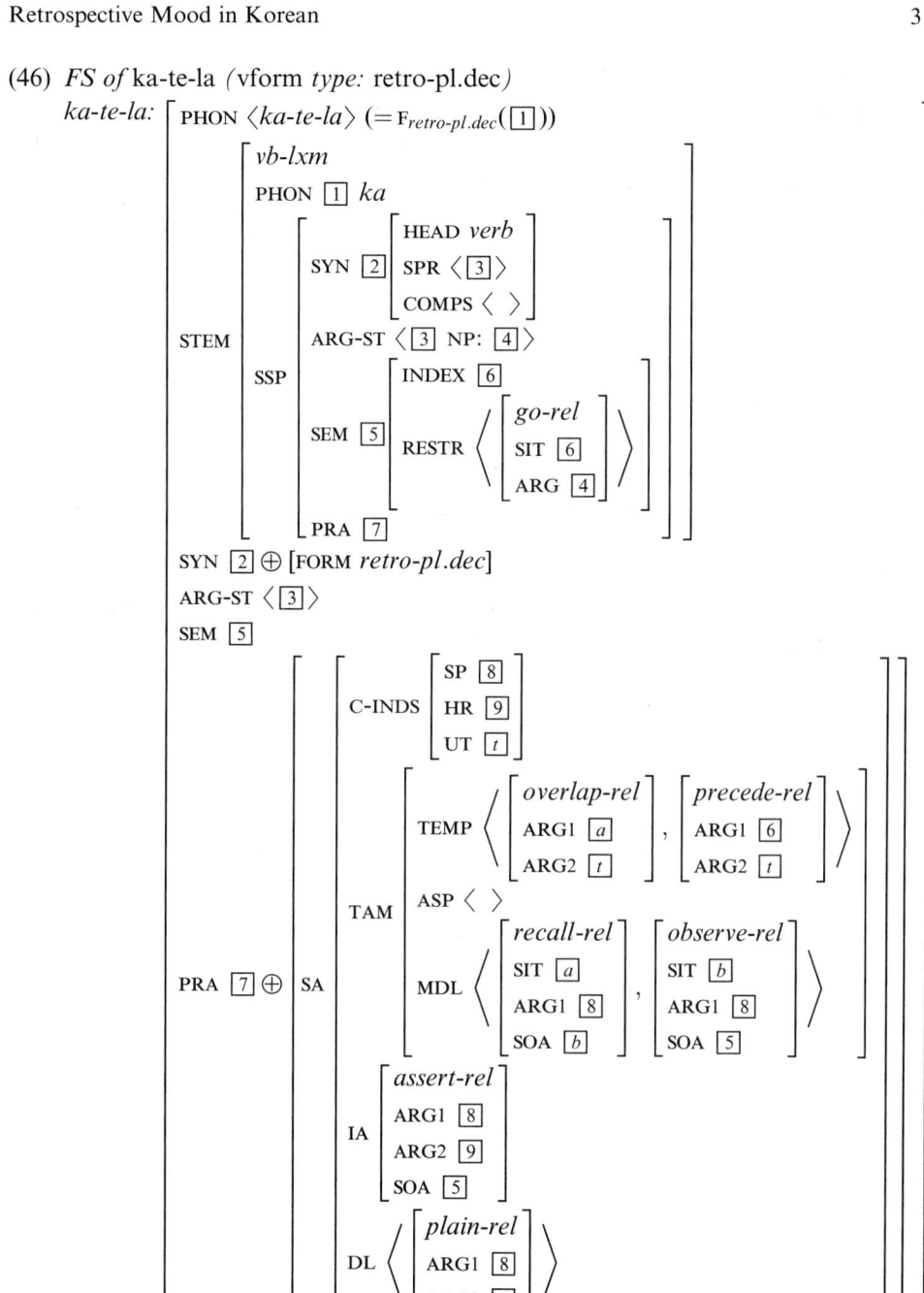

Retrospective Mood in Korean

(46) *FS of* ka-te-la *(*vform *type:* retro-pl.dec*)*

$$\text{ka-te-la:} \begin{bmatrix} \text{PHON} \langle \textit{ka-te-la} \rangle \; (= F_{retro\text{-}pl.dec}(\boxed{1})) \\ \text{STEM} \begin{bmatrix} \textit{vb-lxm} \\ \text{PHON} \; \boxed{1} \; \textit{ka} \\ \text{SSP} \begin{bmatrix} \text{SYN} \; \boxed{2} \begin{bmatrix} \text{HEAD } \textit{verb} \\ \text{SPR} \langle \boxed{3} \rangle \\ \text{COMPS} \langle \; \rangle \end{bmatrix} \\ \text{ARG-ST} \langle \boxed{3} \; \text{NP:} \boxed{4} \rangle \\ \text{SEM} \; \boxed{5} \begin{bmatrix} \text{INDEX} \; \boxed{6} \\ \text{RESTR} \left\langle \begin{bmatrix} \textit{go-rel} \\ \text{SIT} \; \boxed{6} \\ \text{ARG} \; \boxed{4} \end{bmatrix} \right\rangle \end{bmatrix} \\ \text{PRA} \; \boxed{7} \end{bmatrix} \end{bmatrix} \\ \text{SYN} \; \boxed{2} \oplus [\text{FORM } \textit{retro-pl.dec}] \\ \text{ARG-ST} \langle \boxed{3} \rangle \\ \text{SEM} \; \boxed{5} \\ \text{PRA} \; \boxed{7} \oplus \text{SA} \begin{bmatrix} \text{C-INDS} \begin{bmatrix} \text{SP} \; \boxed{8} \\ \text{HR} \; \boxed{9} \\ \text{UT} \; \boxed{t} \end{bmatrix} \\ \text{TAM} \begin{bmatrix} \text{TEMP} \left\langle \begin{bmatrix} \textit{overlap-rel} \\ \text{ARG1} \; \boxed{a} \\ \text{ARG2} \; \boxed{t} \end{bmatrix}, \begin{bmatrix} \textit{precede-rel} \\ \text{ARG1} \; \boxed{6} \\ \text{ARG2} \; \boxed{t} \end{bmatrix} \right\rangle \\ \text{ASP} \langle \; \rangle \\ \text{MDL} \left\langle \begin{bmatrix} \textit{recall-rel} \\ \text{SIT} \; \boxed{a} \\ \text{ARG1} \; \boxed{8} \\ \text{SOA} \; \boxed{b} \end{bmatrix}, \begin{bmatrix} \textit{observe-rel} \\ \text{SIT} \; \boxed{b} \\ \text{ARG1} \; \boxed{8} \\ \text{SOA} \; \boxed{5} \end{bmatrix} \right\rangle \end{bmatrix} \\ \text{IA} \begin{bmatrix} \textit{assert-rel} \\ \text{ARG1} \; \boxed{8} \\ \text{ARG2} \; \boxed{9} \\ \text{SOA} \; \boxed{5} \end{bmatrix} \\ \text{DL} \left\langle \begin{bmatrix} \textit{plain-rel} \\ \text{ARG1} \; \boxed{8} \\ \text{ARG2} \; \boxed{9} \end{bmatrix} \right\rangle \end{bmatrix} \end{bmatrix}$$

Notice that the values of STEM's SYN and PRA (i.e., those tagged [2] and [7], respectively) are passed to the top-level SYN and PRA and additional FS values pertaining to the morpheme sequence ⟨*retro-plain.declarative*⟩ are appended, as indicated by the *append* operator ⊕. The retrospective predicate *ka-te-la* in (47) now needs a subject to qualify as a sentence.[35] The construction type moves from *word* to *phrase*. The *phrase* type has two subtypes: *headed-phrase* and *nonheaded-phrase*. They are specified as in (47) (Sag and Wasow 1999, 372).

(47) a. *phrase*: [NHD-DTRS list(*sign*)]
 b. *headed-phrase*: [HD-DTR *sign*]

The subject ⟨*Mia-ka*⟩ is added to FS (46) and the information that the subject referent is named *Mia* is entered as a piece of background information (Pollard and Sag 1994).[36] The expanded FS is phrasal and sentential at the same time.

The HD-DTR ⟨*ka-te-la*⟩ takes the subject ⟨*Mia-ka*⟩ as NHD-DTR. This is represented as a HD-SPR (HEAD-SPECIFIER) PHRASE in (48). Note also that the PHON value is a list ⟨*Mia-ka, ka-te-la*⟩, which is the outcome of the PHON value of HD-DTR ⟨*ka-te-la*⟩ appended to that of NHD-DTR ⟨*Mia-ka*⟩. It is a simplified FS; the tags [5] and [7] refer to those in (46). (Circled numbers are the new tags in (48).)[37]

(48) *FS of* Mia-ka ka-te-la

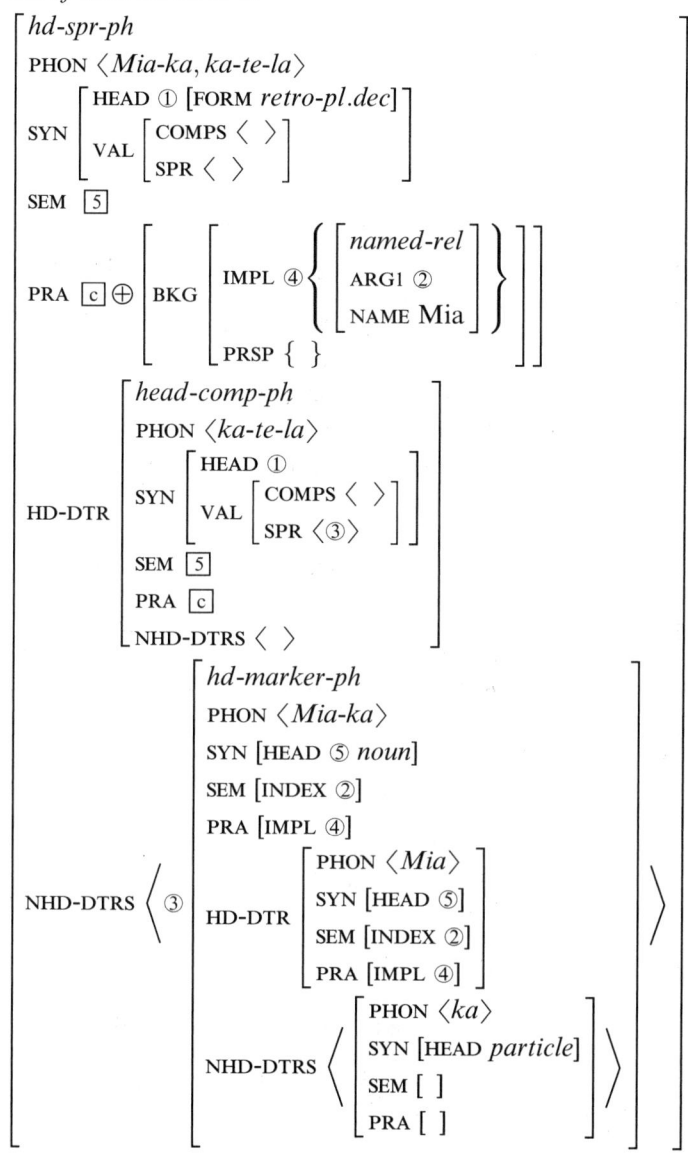

$$\begin{bmatrix} \textit{hd-spr-ph} \\ \text{PHON } \langle \textit{Mia-ka, ka-te-la} \rangle \\ \text{SYN} \begin{bmatrix} \text{HEAD } ① \text{ [FORM } \textit{retro-pl.dec}] \\ \text{VAL} \begin{bmatrix} \text{COMPS } \langle \; \rangle \\ \text{SPR } \langle \; \rangle \end{bmatrix} \end{bmatrix} \\ \text{SEM } \boxed{5} \\ \text{PRA } \boxed{c} \oplus \begin{bmatrix} \text{BKG} \begin{bmatrix} \text{IMPL } ④ \left\{ \begin{bmatrix} \textit{named-rel} \\ \text{ARG1 } ② \\ \text{NAME Mia} \end{bmatrix} \right\} \\ \text{PRSP } \{ \; \} \end{bmatrix} \end{bmatrix} \\ \text{HD-DTR} \begin{bmatrix} \textit{head-comp-ph} \\ \text{PHON } \langle \textit{ka-te-la} \rangle \\ \text{SYN} \begin{bmatrix} \text{HEAD } ① \\ \text{VAL} \begin{bmatrix} \text{COMPS } \langle \; \rangle \\ \text{SPR } \langle ③ \rangle \end{bmatrix} \end{bmatrix} \\ \text{SEM } \boxed{5} \\ \text{PRA } \boxed{c} \\ \text{NHD-DTRS } \langle \; \rangle \end{bmatrix} \\ \text{NHD-DTRS } \left\langle ③ \begin{bmatrix} \textit{hd-marker-ph} \\ \text{PHON } \langle \textit{Mia-ka} \rangle \\ \text{SYN [HEAD } ⑤ \textit{ noun}] \\ \text{SEM [INDEX } ②] \\ \text{PRA [IMPL } ④] \\ \text{HD-DTR} \begin{bmatrix} \text{PHON } \langle \textit{Mia} \rangle \\ \text{SYN [HEAD } ⑤] \\ \text{SEM [INDEX } ②] \\ \text{PRA [IMPL } ④] \end{bmatrix} \\ \text{NHD-DTRS } \left\langle \begin{bmatrix} \text{PHON } \langle \textit{ka} \rangle \\ \text{SYN [HEAD } \textit{particle}] \\ \text{SEM [ ]} \\ \text{PRA [ ]} \end{bmatrix} \right\rangle \end{bmatrix} \right\rangle \end{bmatrix}$$

14.6 Concluding Remarks

In the general framework of CUG/K, the speech act properties of Korean retrospectives are represented explicitly in the form of attitude-value matrices as constraints cutting across the FSs of MORPH, SYN, SEM, and PRA. TAM, where the temporal and modal properties of the retrospectives are properly treated, is placed under SA in PRA.[38]

CUG can be readily adapted to the grammar of English (CUG/E) or Japanese (CUG/J) by adjusting type hierarchies and their constraints with language-specific value assignments. CUG is eclectic and ever growing—with prospects in (1) morpho-lexical theory (e.g., Koenig 1999), for developing feature-structured morphology; (2) constraint-based syntax (e.g., Sag and Wasow 1999), for deepening sign-theoretic phrase structure grammar; (3) Minimal Recursion Semantics (e.g., Copestake et al. 1999), for constructing flat semantics for discourse analysis; and (4) Optimality Theory (e.g., Barbosa et al. 1998), for ranking and overriding default constraints.

Notes

1. It has been termed variously: Choi (1961) calls it "retrospective tense" and Suh (1996) "reportive mood." The English term *retrospective* was introduced by Martin (1954) as an aspect category along with indicative, subjunctive, and processive—those suffixes in the penultimate position of a verbal. Grammatical notions of tense, aspect, and mood, as reflected in the use of these terms, have always been murky in the description of Korean grammar.

2. For various grammatical treatments of Korean retrospectives, see Suh 1996. For an elaborate exposition on the functioning of the retrospective, see Sohn 1975, where the conceptual structure of TE is posited as convergence of REPORTER (speaker/hearer), PAST, and PERCEIVE with due constraints.

3. There are co-occurrence restrictions among the prefinal suffixes: (1) PAST2 is bound to PAST1; (2) PRES cannot co-occur with another tense or mood suffix. When the final S-modulator position is taken into account, the co-occurrence restrictions in the whole sequence increase. We are not concerned with S-modulators other than SE (sentence ending) in this chapter.

For the Korean verbal inflections presented in (1), see Chang 1996, sec. 4.1.1. The word-final position labeled "S-modulator" is what is called "mood" in Martin 1954. Suh (1996) distinguishes two types of mood: sentence-final mood (= Martin's mood) and prefinal mood (= positions 5 and 6 in (1)); in Martin 1954, the volitive and retrospective moods are called "future tense" and "retrospective aspect," respectively. Suh's sentence-final mood is termed "sentence-ending (SE)" in Chang 1996 and CUG/K.

Throughout the chapter, ⟨V-ta⟩ (not the stem V-) is given as the citation form of a verbal.

4. The SE morpheme, which is called "mood" in Martin 1954 and Suh 1996, is the conflation of SL (sentence level) and ST (sentence type), as shown in the following table (Chang 1996, 42). The SL terms *deferential*, *polite*, and so on, are semantically based; alternatively, SLs are termed, as indicated in the table, *p-SL*, *yo-SL*, and so on, on the basis of their phonological shapes.

Retrospective Mood in Korean

(i) Sentence ending: SL ⊗ ST (conflate(SL,ST))

ST\SL	Deferential **p**	Polite **yo**	Blunt **o**	Familiar **ey**	Intimate **e**	Plain **a**
Declarative (DEC)	(su)pnita	(e)yo	(si)o	ney	e	ta
Interrogative (INT)	(su)pnikka	(e)yo?	(si)o?	na	e?	nya/ni
Imperative (IMP)	psio	(e)yo	(si)o	key	e	(u)la
Propositive (PRP)	(u)psita	(e)yo	(si)o	sey	e	ca

5. The word form -*tey-yo?* is acceptable as an echo question, though. Why the interrogative retrospective *V-*tey-yo?* is not allowed is puzzling. Its absence may be related to the unacceptability of *V-*ca-yo* 'Let's V' and *V-*la-yo* 'V!' or *V-*ni-yo?* / *V-*nya-yo?* (vs. V-*na-yo?*) '... V?'

6. Contrast a retrospective sentence (i) with a retrospective adnominal clause (ii) and a nonretrospective adnominal clause (iii). The parenthetical 'I recall', denoting a retrospective speech act, is present in (i), obscure in (ii), and absent in (iii).

(i) *Retrospective declarative*
Ay-ka cip-ey iss-te-la.
child-SM house-at be-RETRO-PL.DEC
'(The) child was at home, I recall.'

(ii) *Retrospective adnominal clause*
cip-ey iss-te.n ay
house-at be-RETRO.ADNZ child
'(the) child who (I recall) was at home'

(iii) *Nonretrospective adnominal clause*
cip-ey iss-nun ay
house-at be-ADNZ child
'(the) child who is at home'

7. The default speech act of a declarative sentence is "assertive" (Fraser 1975; Searle 1976; Bach and Harnish 1979) or "expositive" (Austin 1962; McCawley 1979). An interrogative is often paraphrased performatively: '(I) request (you) to tell (me)' (Searle 1976).

8. For the ontological typology involving cognitive acts, Princeton University's WordNet (version 2.0; see Fellbaum 1998) is referenced in this chapter. For example, in WordNet *recall*-1 (sense-1) is in the synset (synonym set) {*remember, retrieve, recall, call back, call up, recollect, think*} and defined as 'recall knowledge from memory; have a recollection'.

9. (7c) is thus reminiscent of George Lakoff's well-known example: *I dreamt that I was B.B. and I kissed me/?myself.*

10. It may be odd even in English to say #*I saw myself/me sleeping, I recall.*

11. This example is provided by Sohn (1975, 144); his English rendering is 'I wonder whom I observed him to be'.

12. ⟨V-*ko iss-ta*⟩ consists of ⟨V-stem-*ing be*-SE⟩. *Ko* is called "complementizer" by generative grammarians and the "gerundive *ko*" by Martin (1954), corresponding to the term gerundive *te* that he uses for Japanese (Martin 1987). Here, *ing* is given as a gloss for *ko*.

(i) V-*ko*-*iss*-SE
| |
ing be

13. Korean has a number of aspectual verbs or auxiliaries: for example, *sicak-hata* 'begin', *toyta* 'change', *cita* 'become'. The aspect system adopted here is motivated syntactically—not morphologically or lexically (Chang 1996, sec. 5.8.2).

14. The *e* in ⟨*-e-iss-ta*⟩ is another complementizer, called "infinitive" by Martin (1954).

15. English *live* also has the sense of 'reside', which is more basic than the sense of 'exist' (WordNet lists the sense of 'reside' on top, as *live*-1; the sense of 'exist' is *live*-4).

16. Similarly, in volitive or predictive sentences, the suffix *keyss* expresses the speaker's volition or prediction. *Keyss*, akin to English *will*, denotes two distinct moods: volition and prediction.

17. In WordNet, *cognize* is synonymous with *know* (*know*-1): 'be cognizant or be aware of a fact or a specific piece of information; possess knowledge or information about'.

18. Following McCawley's famed lexical decomposition CAUSE(x, BECOME(NOT(ALIVE y))) → *kill*(x, y), Dowty (1979, 51) analyzed the English inchoative morpheme *-en* as a realization of BECOME: BECOME → *-en*.

19. EXPERIENCE in the sense of 'undergo an emotional sensation' (*experience*-4 in WordNet). Similarly, OBSERVE in the sense of *observe*-1, forming a synset {*detect, observe, discover, find, notice*}. *P(rior)* is used in McCawley 1981/1993, together with time indices: for example, $P_{t_1 t_2}$ 't_1 is prior to t_2'.

20. I will use RECALL rather than RETRO when the retrospective mood is paraphrased. See note 8 for the synset of *recall*-1 in WordNet.

21. The two constraints together may be termed the equi-speaker/subject constraint.

22. Some emotive verbs with *hata* retain the same valence value as the corresponding emotive adjectives: for example, both *kippe-hata* 'pleased' and *kippu-ta* 'glad' are one-place predicates. While English has two-place verbs corresponding to one-place adjectives (though some of the adjectives do allow a second argument introduced by *of*, as in *John is afraid of snakes*), its emotive predicates are morphologically irregular (**fearable-fearful-afraid* vs. *fear*; *sad* vs. *sadden*; *lik(e)able-*likeful* vs. *like*; *lov(e)able-*loveful* vs. *love*; **loath(e)able-loathful-loathsome* vs. *loathe*; *pleasing-pleasant-pleased-*pleaseful* vs. *please*).

23. The Japanese counterparts of (20a–d) are provided here for comparison.

(i) a. Uresii.
 glad
 'I am glad.'
 b. Watasi-wa uresii.
 I-TOP
 'I am glad.'
 c. #Anata-wa uresii.
 you-TOP
 'You are glad.'
 d. #Hanako-ga uresii.
 Hanako-SM
 'Hanako is glad.'

24. English seems to lack such a psychological constraint. One can say *Mia is happy* in English, whereas in Korean it is normal to say 'Mia looks/appears happy'.

25. In Japanese, a similar kind of metamorphosis takes place by suffixing *-garu* 'want' (desiderative verbalizer; Martin 1987, sec. 7.2) to emotive adjectives.

(i) Watasi-ga uresi-ga-tte iru.
I-SM glad-want-ing be
'I am showing gladness.'

(ii) Anata-ga uresi-ga-tte iru.
you-SM
'You are showing gladness.'

(iii) Hanako-ga uresi-ga-tte iru.
Hanako-SM
'Hanako is showing gladness.'

26. CUG/K, also called KDG (Korean Discourse Grammar; Chang 1999), has been in development since the mid-1990s (Chang 1993, 1994, 1999, 2001, 2002; Chang and Choe 1993). The three parts of HPSG (Pollard and Sag 1994)—category, content, and context—are dubbed SYN, SEM, and PRA, respectively.

27. For a different partitioning of Korean verbal types and inflectional suffixes, see Kim 1998, where a *sign* is declared to have three subtypes: *morph-sign*, *word*, and *phrase*.

28. The type *verb-lexeme* might be partitioned into *emotive* and *nonemotive* subtypes; however, as *verb-lexemes* are immune to the speech act constraint of retrospectives noted in the case of *emotive adjectives*, they are not partitioned into such subtypes here.

29. The attribute is written in small capitals; its value, as well as the type name, in lowercase italics. Here the term *attribute* is used interchangeably with *feature*.

30. The FS of PROS (prosody) is omitted from the attribute-value matrix for ease of exposition. For TC (terminal contour) and STR (stress) in PROS, see Chang 2002.

31. *Suffix* and *prefix* are further subtyped into *v-suffix* (*verbal suffix*) and *n-suffix* (*nominal suffix*), *v-prefix* (*verbal prefix*) and *n-prefix* (*nominal prefix*).

32. In Sag and Wasow 1999, contextual information such as "naming" (e.g., *x is named Mia*) is treated as part of SEM in contradistinction to its treatment as part of CONTEXT (as background information) in Pollard and Sag 1994.

33. Ontologically, *recalling-relation* may well be placed under *cognize-relation* as its subtype.

34. IA and DL features are now assumed to have list values. Classification of illocutionary acts, which is left incomplete here, is based on Austin's (1962) classification, amended and expanded by Searle (1976), McCawley (1979), Bach and Harnish (1979). The major *ia* types should be further partitioned; for example, the *assert-rel* type, which is called "expositive" (by Austin and McCawley) and "constative" (by Bach and Harnish) is subdivided into 15 types by Bach and Harnish (1979, 41–46): *assertive*, *predictive*, *retrodictive*, *descriptive*, and so on. The "deferential" DL is also called "formal" (Martin 1954, 1992; Chang 1973). Notice that the *honor-rel* type is added to the list of *dl* subtypes and it interacts with the form *hon* in SYN. The *honor-rel* will be the second element in the list of *dl*.

35. Note that in (46) the semantic content [5] is what was observed. What is *recalled* is the situation of the speaker's observing a state of affairs in the past, not the semantic content [5]. In the temporal relation, the event time of "going" precedes the utterance time by default. As (i) indicates, however, the event may take place in the future.

(i) Mia-ka nayil   sicip   ka-te-la.
   Mia-SM tomorrow marrying go-RETRO-PL.DEC
   'Mia is getting married tomorrow, I noticed/I recall.'

On the basis of the speaker's cognition or knowledge such as reading a newspaper or receiving an invitation, he has come to understand that Mia is getting married tomorrow. Without a future-indicating adverb like 'tomorrow', the event is normally interpreted as a past one.

(ii) Mia-ka sicip ka-te-la.
   'Mia got married, I saw/I heard/I recall.'

(iii) Mia-ka ku ttay sicip ka-te-la.
             the time
   'Mia got married then, I saw/I heard/I recall.'

(iv) Mia-ka ku taum nal sicip ka-te-la.
            the next day
   'Mia got married the next day, I saw/I heard/I recall.'

36. *Mia-ka*, which is composed of ⟨noun + case particle⟩, is treated as a noun phrase of the type *head-marker phrase*. Phrases with noncase particles such as ⟨N-*ey*⟩ 'at N', ⟨N-*eykey*⟩ 'to N', and ⟨N-*pwuthe*⟩ 'from N' are particle phrases functioning as adverbials.

37. The value of PRA [c] is identical to the value of PRA in (46), not to that of its STEM's PRA [7].

38. One might argue that TAM should be placed under SEM rather than under SA in PRA. CUG, taking a rather conservative stance, views the field of semantics as limited by the truth-conditional aspects of meaning and entrusts temporal and modal, as well as contextual, aspects of meaning to pragmatics (Levinson 1983).

References

Austin, J. L. 1962. *How to do things with words.* Oxford: Oxford University Press.

Bach, Kent, and Robert M. Harnish. 1979. *Linguistic communication and speech acts.* Cambridge, MA: MIT Press.

Barbosa, Pilar, Danny Fox, Paul Hagstrom, Martha McGinnis, and David Pesetsky, eds. 1998. *Is the best good enough?* Cambridge, MA: MIT Press.

Bar-Hillel, Yehoshua. 1954. Indexical expressions. *Mind* 63, 359–79.

Carpenter, Robert L. 1992. *The logic of typed feature structures.* Cambridge: Cambridge University Press.

Chang, Suk-Jin. 1973. A generative study of discourse: Pragmatic aspects of Korean with reference to English. Supplement to *Language Research* 9 (Seoul National University).

Chang, Suk-Jin. 1993. *Information-based Korean grammar* [in Korean]. Seoul: Hanshin.

Chang, Suk-Jin. 1994. *Unified grammar: Discourse and pragmatics* [in Korean]. Seoul: Seoul National University Press.

Chang, Suk-Jin. 1996. *Korean.* Amsterdam: John Benjamins.

Chang, Suk-Jin. 1999. Where grammar meets pragmatics: A constraint-based approach to Korean discourse. Paper presented at the 1999 LSA Conference on Korean Linguistics, University of Illinois at Urbana-Champaign.

Chang, Suk-Jin. 2001. Interlingual representation for natural language understanding [in Korean]. *The Journal of the National Academy of Sciences: Humanities and Social Science Edition* 40, 43–85. Seoul: National Academy of Sciences, Republic of Korea.

Chang, Suk-Jin. 2002. Information unpackaging: A constraint-based grammar approach to topic-focus articulation. In *Japanese/Korean linguistics 10*, ed. by Noriko M. Akatsuka and Susan Strauss, 451–64. Stanford, CA: CSLI Publications.

Chang, Suk-Jin, and Jae-Woong Choe. 1993. Toward understanding discourse structure: Flow of contextual information in spoken Korean. In *Language, information and computation*, ed. by Chungmin Lee and Bummo Kang, 1–13. Seoul: Taehaksa.

Choi, Hyon-Bai. 1961. *Our grammar* [in Korean]. Seoul: Yenhi College Press / Ceongum SA.

Copestake, Ann, Dan Flickinger, Rob Malouf, Susanne Riehemann, and Ivan A. Sag. 1995. Translation using Minimal Recursion Semantics (ACQUILEX II WP NO. 61). In *Proceedings of the 6th International Conference on Theoretical and Methodological Issues in Machine Translation* (TM195). Leuven, Belgium.

Copestake, Ann, Dan Flickinger, Carl Pollard, and Ivan A. Sag. 1999. Minimal Recursion Semantics: An introduction. Manuscript.

Davis, Anthony R. 2001. *Linking by types in the hierarchical lexicon*. Stanford, CA: CSLI Publications.

Dowty, David. 1979. *Word meaning and Montague Grammar*. Dordrecht: Reidel.

Fellbaum, Christiane, ed. 1998. *WordNet*. Cambridge, MA: MIT Press.

Fraser, Bruce. 1975. Hedged performatives. In *Syntax and semantics 3: Speech acts*, ed. by Peter Cole and Jerry Morgan, 187–210. New York: Academic Press.

Kim, Jong-Bok. 1998. Interface between morphology and syntax: A constraint-based and lexicalist approach. *Language and Information* 2, 177–213.

Koenig, Jean-Pierre. 1999. *Lexical relations*. Stanford, CA: CSLI Publications.

Lascarides, Alex, and Ann Copestake. 1999. Default representation in constraint-based frameworks. *Computational Linguistics* 25, 55–105.

Levinson, Stephen C. 1983. *Pragmatics*. Cambridge: Cambridge University Press.

Martin, Samuel E. 1954. *Korean morphophonemics*. Baltimore: Linguistic Society of America.

Martin, Samuel E. 1987. *A reference grammar of Japanese*. Tokyo: Tuttle.

Martin, Samuel E. 1992. *A reference grammar of Korean*. Rutland: Tuttle.

McCawley, James D. 1968. Lexical insertion in a transformational grammar without deep structure. In *Proceedings of the Fourth Regional Meeting, Chicago Linguistic Society*, ed. by Bill J. Darden, Charles-James N. Bailey, and Alice Davison, 71–80. Chicago: University of Chicago, Chicago Linguistic Society.

McCawley, James D. 1979. *Adverbs, vowels, and other objects of wonder*. Chicago: University of Chicago Press.

McCawley, James D. 1981. *Everything that linguists have always wanted to know about logic—but were ashamed to ask*. Chicago: University of Chicago Press. 2nd ed., 1993. References are to the 1981 edition.

Pollard, Carl, and Ivan A. Sag. 1994. *Head-driven Phrase Structure Grammar*. Stanford, CA: CSLI Publications.

Reichenbach, Hans. 1947. *Elements of symbolic logic*. New York: Free Press.

Sag, Ivan A., and Thomas A. Wasow. 1999. *Syntactic theory: A formal introduction*. Stanford, CA: CSLI Publications.

Searle, John R. 1976. The classification of illocutionary acts. *Language in Society* 5, 1–24.

Sohn, Ho-min. 1975. Retrospection in Korean. *Language Research* 11, 87–103.

Suh, Cheong-Soo. 1996. *Korean grammar* [in Korean]. Seoul: Hanyang University Press.

Yeon, Jae-Hoon. 1994. Grammatical relation changing constructions in Korean: A functional-typological study. Doctoral dissertation, University of London.

PART IV
Semantics and Pragmatics

Chapter 15

An *Un-* Paper for the Unsyntactician

Laurence R. Horn

15.1 Introduction

Moravcsik and Wirth 1980 comprises the proceedings of the Great Milwaukee Syntax Bake-Off of 1979, an event pitting various grammatical theories against one another in a kind of intersyntactic precursor of the CBS *Survivor* show. The table of contents to that volume includes—among standard entries like Robin Cooper's "Montague's Syntax," Susumu Kuno's "Functional Syntax," and David Perlmutter's "Relational Grammar"—an entry for "An Un-syntax" submitted by (who else?) Jim McCawley.[1] As it happens, I was the designated discussant for this presentation; my contribution was later published as "Giving *Un* to Others" (Horn 1980). In this memorial volume, I propose to honor the immortal unsyntactician with a somewhat more comprehensive *un-* paper.

More specifically, I shall seek to account for the increasingly productive word formation process resulting in a brood of *un-*nouns, the semilegitimate offspring of Humpty Dumpty's *unbirthday present* (1872) and 7-Up's commercial incarnation as *the Uncola* (1968). Drawing on a large corpus of novel *un-*nouns I have been assembling jointly with Beth Levin (see the appendices in Horn 2002a), I will seek to motivate a set of constraints on the formation of these lexical items by invoking Rosch's prototype semantics and Aristotle's theory of opposition, in which *privation* is defined in terms of a marked exception to a general class property, to explain why 7-Up is a better candidate for an uncola than tea or chocolate milk, and more generally why a given *un-*noun refers either to an element just outside a given category

I am grateful to Yasuhiko Kato for the invitation that led to my first oral presentation on *un-*nouns (Tokyo, May 1999) and to SOLIFIC, the publishers of *Sophia Linguistica*, in which an earlier published version of some of this material previously appeared as Horn 2002a. Thanks also to those attending later oral presentations at the University of Massachusetts at Amherst, the University of Chicago, and Stanford University, to Barbara Abbott for her comments on an earlier written version of this chapter, and to the anonymous reviewers. None of these individuals are any more responsible than Aristotle for the outcome.

with whose members it shares a salient function (e.g., *uncola*) or to a peripheral member of a given category (an *unhotel* is a hotel but not a good exemplar of the category—not a "HOTEL hotel"). I conclude with some remarks in defense of the conceptual necessity for a lexical pragmatics, a field whose ancestry traces back to McCawley 1978.

15.2 Varieties of Opposition

The genus of opposition, as developed in Aristotle's *Categories* (11b17), is divided into four apparently disjoint species:

(1) a. *Contrariety* (between two *contraries*): for example, *good* versus *bad*
 b. *Contradiction* (*affirmative* to *negative*): for example, *He sits* versus *He does not sit*
 c. *Correlation* (between two *relatives*): for example, *double* versus *half*
 d. *Privation* (*privative* to *positive*): for example, *blind* versus *sighted*

Aristotle proceeds to offer detailed diagnostics for distinguishing "the various senses in which the term 'opposite' is used" (11b16–14a25).

Contradictory opposites are mutually exhaustive as well as mutually exclusive, while contrary opposites do not mutually exhaust their domain (for details, see Horn 1989, chap. 1). This distinction is originally drawn for statement types, as depicted in the system later schematized by Apuleius and Boethius in the square of opposition in figure 15.1.

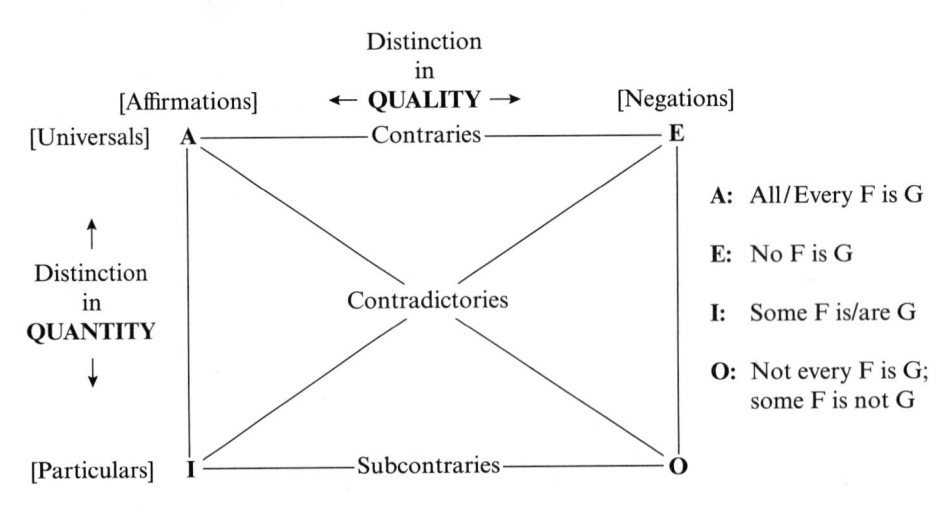

A: All/Every F is G
E: No F is G
I: Some F is/are G
O: Not every F is G; some F is not G

Figure 15.1
Traditional square of opposition

Corresponding A and E statements are contraries in that they cannot be simultaneously true (though they may be simultaneously false). Corresponding A and O (and I and E) statements are contradictories; members of each pair cannot be true *or* false simultaneously. In Aristotle's terms, contradictories "divide the true and the false between them." Contradictory terms (*black/nonblack*, *odd/even*, *male/female*) exclude any middle term, an entity satisfying the range of the two opposed terms but falling under neither of them: a shirt that is neither black nor not-black, an integer that is neither odd nor even. Contraries, by definition, admit a middle: my shirt may be neither black nor white, my friend neither happy nor sad.

Correlation is essentially converseness: A is the double of B if and only if B is the half of A. Other pairs include *parent* versus *child*, *above* versus *below*, *own* versus *belong to*, and *eat* versus *be eaten by*; I shall have nothing further to say here about correlates. But privation, the fourth mode of opposition, will be our capstone.

For Aristotle, privatives and positives always apply to the same subject and are defined in terms of the presence or absence of a default property for that subject:

We say that that which is capable of some particular faculty or possession has suffered privation when the faculty or possession in question is in no way present in that in which, and at the time in which, it should be naturally present. We do not call that toothless which has not teeth, or that blind which has not sight, but rather that which has not teeth or sight at the time when by nature it should. (*Categories*, 12a28–33)

On this understanding, a newborn kitten is no more blind than is a chair, and a baby is not toothless.

Privation as the absence of what would be expected by nature to be present is revisited in the *Metaphysics* (1022b23–1023a8), where Aristotle—noting that privation can range over predictable absence, accidental removal, or deliberate "taking away by force" of the relevant property—distinguishes privation "with respect to genus," as in the blindness of moles, from privation "with respect to self," as in the blindness or toothlessness of an old man. In the end, Aristotle concedes, there may be as many senses of privation as there are *a*-prefixed terms in Greek (1022b33).[2] Indeed, privation may be reanalyzed as a marked contrary bearing an *a*-prefix: "the primary contrariety is that of possession and privation" (1055a34).

15.3 Contrariety, E-negativity, and the *Un*-adjective

The prefix *un*- attaches to English adjectives, verbs, and nouns, in each case yielding a lexical item of the same category as the original base. The standard characterization of the semantics associated with this prefix (or family of prefixes) is in terms of either *negation* or *antonymy*, but it is not clear what sense of negation is involved or whether there *is* a single sense (however generally defined), even within a single category. What is clear is that few *un*-words of any category correspond to the contradictory opposition of the sentential negative.

It has long been recognized (see, e.g., Sigwart 1895, 138, for citation of *unhappy*, *unwise*, *unfeeling*, and *speechless*, and more recently Kruisinga 1931, sec. 1620; Zimmer 1964; Funk 1971; Horn 1989, sec. 5.1) that negative affixation, especially when it involves the English prefixes *un-* and *iN-* and their crosslinguistic analogues, tends to develop a contrary rather than merely contradictory interpretation when such a strengthened reading is possible. Here is Jespersen's take on the semantics of *un*-prefixed adjectives:

The modification in sense brought about by the addition of the prefix is generally that of a simple negation: *unworthy* = 'not worthy', etc.... The two terms [*X*, *unX*] are thus contradictory terms. But very often the prefix produces a "contrary" term or at any rate what approaches one: *unjust* generally implies the opposite of *just*; *unwise* means more than *not wise* and approaches *foolish*, *unhappy* is not far from *miserable*, etc. (Jespersen 1917, 144; cf. 1942, 466–67)

As Jespersen observes, this strengthened, contrary reading correlates with the often observed fact that the same prefixes tend to yield derived forms that are associated with a pejorative or evaluatively negative content: "The same general rule obtains in English as in other languages, that most adjectives with *un-* or *in-* have a depreciatory sense: we have *unworthy*, *undue*, *imperfect*, etc., but it is not possible to form similar adjectives from *wicked*, *foolish*, or *terrible*" (1917, 144).

Jespersen (1917) and Zimmer (1964, 10ff.) review a number of early discussions of negative affixation that demonstrate what Wundt (1886) labels the *Unlustaffekte* of negatively affixed forms in particular and negation in general. In German, Swedish, French, and English, as these lexical studies demonstrate, disproportionately many negatively affixed adjectives are depreciatory, derogatory, or evaluatively negative in denotation or connotation. Following Cruse (1980), I adopt *e-pos* and *e-neg* as shorthand for evaluatively/emotively positive and negative, respectively. The formula expressing the relevant generalization can be given as in (2).

(2) negative affix + e-pos base → e-neg derived output
    [*un*]   [*happy*]   [*unhappy*]

Thus, in English we have *unhappy* but not *unsad*, *unwise* but not *unfoolish*, and the parallel examples in (3).

(3) uncivilized   *unboorish, *unbarbarian
     unclean   *undirty
     unclear   *unfuzzy, ?unconfused
     unfriendly   *unhostile, *unantagonistic
     unhealthy, unwell *unsick, *unill

unintelligent	*unstupid
uninteresting	*unboring, *undull
unjust, unfair	*unwrongful
unkind, uncivil	*unrude
unsympathetic	*unantipathetic
untrue	*unfalse
infertile	*unbarren

In these examples, only an e-pos or neutral stem can serve as a natural base for a negatively affixed adjective, and only e-neg derived adjectives are therefore possible.

Elsewhere, as in (4), we find an (e-neg) *un-* or *iN-*prefixed adjective based on an e-pos stem where there is no corresponding e-neg stem to serve as a source for an e-pos derived form.

(4) impossible   inconsequential   unfit
    improper   inconsistent   unfortunate/unlucky
    inappropriate irrelevant   unfree
    incoherent   unapt/inept   unsuitable

There are also a number of "orphaned" *un-*adjectives with no extant positive counterpart whatsoever: *unabashed, unassuming, unbending, uncouth, unflagging, unheard-of, unkempt, unparalleled, unprecedented, unruly, unscathed, untouched, untoward,* and so on.[3] Significantly, most such orphans (many of which are evaluatively positive) represent the productive *un*+V+participle pattern; those that fail to reflect this pattern do seem to share the e-neg quality of the adjectives in (3) and (4).

As Cruse (1980) notes, e-pos adjectives are semantically heterogeneous. A given pair of e-pos/e-neg adjectives will constitute *antonyms* (gradable contraries) if there is a midinterval between the unmarked and marked qualities. In such cases, the unmarked term (*happy, wise, interesting*) denotes a positive attribute or property that can be present in varying degrees, and there are no literal endpoints of the relevant scales (#*absolutely {happy/sad/wise/foolish/interesting/dull}*). With *gradable complementaries* (contradictories), there is by definition no midinterval, and the unmarked term denotes the absence of some negative or undesirable property (*clean* vs. *dirty, safe* vs. *dangerous*) and allows a scalar endpoint (*absolutely {clean/#dirty, safe/#dangerous}*). With antonyms, the e-pos term is also *q-pos* (quantitatively positive, denoting a salient property such as wisdom or interest), and it is this term that forms the basis for *un-*adjectives (*unhappy, unwise, uninteresting*); with gradable complementaries, it is the e-neg term that is q-pos: "All gradable complementaries denote degrees of some undesirable property, like dirtiness, or danger; antonyms always indicate degrees of either a neutral property, like length, or weight, or a desirable one, like beauty, merit, or intelligence" (Cruse 1980, 21). But, as shown by pairs like *unclean/*undirty, unsafe/*undangerous*, and by the existence of unpaired neg-prefixed adjectives from q-neg but e-pos bases (e.g., *unfaithful, dishonest, imperfect, impure*), it is e-polarity rather than q-polarity that determines the availability of an adjective for negative prefixation. (For further discussion of antonymy, markedness, and gradable adjectives, see Sapir 1944; Givón 1970; Lehrer 1974, 1985; Ljung 1974; Lyons 1977; Lehrer and Lehrer 1982; Horn 1989.)

The asymmetry illustrated in (3)—and indirectly in (4)—does not extend to all negatively prefixed adjectives. The key correlation is formulated by Zimmer (1964): the less productive the affixation process, the more likely its output is to be interpreted as a contrary (rather than contradictory) of its base, and the stronger the restriction to e-pos bases (and, correspondingly, to e-neg resultant meanings for the derived negative adjective). This correlation emerges especially clearly when we turn to more productive subrules for *un-*. At least since the *Oxford English Dictionary* (*OED*), it has been noticed that *un-* attaches freely to stems with three deverbal suffixes, *-able* and participial *-ed* and *-ing*. Indeed, *un-* prefixation is virtually unrestricted in these cases, constrained only by the existence of lexicalized *iN-* forms occupying the same slot.[4] But in just these contexts, the affixation rule produces derived forms that are strictly contradictory and emotively either neutral, as in (5a), or positive, as in (5b).

(5) a. imperceptible   b. unbeaten   untarnished
       irreducible   unbigoted   unblamable
       undecidable   unblemished   unconquerable
       uneaten   undaunted   incorruptible
       unexpired   undefeated   indomitable
       unprefix{able/ed}   undeterred   unimpeachable
       unxerox{able/ed}   unharmed   unobjectionable
       un-cross-examined   unscathed   irreproachable
       un-mouse-eaten   unsullied   invulnerable

Thus, "the negative content of simplex words differs from the negative content of forms derived according to some synchronically productive and frequently encountered pattern" (Zimmer 1964, 38). It is for this reason that Jespersen, in discussing the tendency for *un-* negatives to be read as contraries, explicitly exempts "words in *-able* and participles"; his examples (1917, 144) include *unabsorbable, unadaptable, unabbreviated, unadapted, unavailing,* and *unbefitting*.

Additional confirmation of the semantic asymmetry of *un-* formations is provided by the history of English. A number of potentially occurring *unX* adjectives are ruled out, presumably blocked or preempted by a previously existing and more lexicalized simple contrary with the same meaning; but this was not always the case. Here again is the *OED* (**un-**[1], 7):

There is ... considerable restriction in the use of *un-* with short simple adjectives of native origin, the negative of these being naturally supplied by another simple word of an opposite signification. There is thus little or no tendency now to employ such forms as *unbroad, undeep, unwide, unbold, unglad, ungood, unstrong, unwhole,* [etc.] which freely occur in the older language.

These cited examples, like those of (3) and (4), are e-neg forms with e-pos bases; no *unshallow, unnarrow, unsad, unbad,* or *unweak* seems to have occurred even "in the older language" (cf. Zimmer 1964, 41).

The Avoid Synonymy principle ("The output of a lexical rule may not be synonymous with an existing lexical item": Kiparsky 1983) or its generalization as the Division of Pragmatic Labor (see Horn 1984) predicts that the meaning of derived adjectives such as *unhappy* and *unintelligent* must be different from (characteristically, weaker than) those of the corresponding underived *sad* and *stupid* (see Zimmer 1964; Lehrer 1985). But despite this difference in strength between derived and simple e-neg adjectives, *unhappy* and *unintelligent* still constitute contrary rather than contradictory opposites of their bases *happy* and *intelligent*: someone who is neither happy nor sad may be, but need not be, unhappy.

As noted by Jespersen and Marchand, *un-* and *iN-* derivatives tend to negate the emotive senses of the stems to which they attach, while *non-* negates objective or descriptive content. Among the minimal pairs that have been cited to illustrate this contrast are those in (6).

(6) immoral : nonmoral   unprofessional : nonprofessional
    irrational : nonrational   unprofitable : nonprofit
    un-American : non-American   unremunerative : nonremunerative
    un-Christian : non-Christian   unrhythmical : nonrhythmical
    unnatural : nonnatural   unscientific : nonscientific

In each case, the *iN-* or *un-* form is understood pejoratively and is in contrary opposition with the corresponding positive stem, while the *non-* derivative is a simple, evaluatively neutral contradictory.[5] As Algeo (1971, 90–91) describes the contrast:

A Moslem is a *non-Christian,* but only a Christian can be *un-Christian* in behavior. A *nonrealistic* novel is one whose goal is other than a realistic view of the world, but an *unrealistic* novel is likely to be one that aims at, and fails to achieve, realism.

In each case, the emergence of the contrary reading also implies that the adjectival stem can be regarded as a *gradable* or *scalar* value (see Sapir 1944; Horn 1989, chap. 4). Applying the standard tests for gradability, we get the correct prediction that *iN-* and (usually) *un-*adjectives but not the *non-* forms can be inserted into the appropriate scalar frames.

(7) downright {un/#non}-American   very {un/#non}-Christian
    extremely {un/#non}natural   awfully {immoral/#nonmoral}
    somewhat {irrational/#nonrational}   rather {un/#non}scientific

Hence also the impossibility of *un-* prefixation for binary ungradables (*unmale, *unfemale, *unodd) and the semantic restriction of other derived forms to scalar senses or contexts: the surface of my table can be *uneven*, but the number 7 cannot be; your decision may be *unfair*, but not your complexion. *Uneven* (for integers) is, of course, blocked by *odd*, and the same blocking effect explains why *uncool* could mean 'not hip' but not 'warm', while *unyoung* (attested but not yet lexicalized) will imply '... but not yet old', as when the *New York Times* uses it in an article entitled "Where Age 40 Doesn't Mean the End of Everything" to describe a film about the comeback of an aging ballerina.

The evaluative versus descriptive parameter yields some striking lexical gaps. Alongside *unmaternal*, *nonmaternal*, and *unmotherly*, we have no adjective *nonmotherly: while the stem *maternal* may be construed as either a descriptive or an evaluative adjective, *motherly* can only be evaluative (Zimmer 1964, 33). Similarly, we have *nonmale* but *unmanly*, while their counterparts *unmale and *nonmanly do not occur. The same consideration rules out *nondecent and *nonrespectable.

The other side of the coin, as pointed out by Funk (1971), is that adjectives formed with *iN-* and *un-*, even when they originate as evaluatively neutral and semantically contradictory senses, tend to develop a contrary, affective, and typically depreciatory meaning or connotation. Funk's examples of this process include *inadequate*, *inappropriate*, *inconvenient*, *incorrigible*, *infertile*, *irrelevant*, *uninteresting*, and *unsatisfactory*. Thus, color terms do not ordinarily sponsor *un-* contraries (*unred, *unyellow), but we do get *ungreen* with the specific meaning 'environmentally incorrect', as in *ungreen politicians* or *ungreen power sources*. And, as with Algeo's observations on "unrealistic" novels, only a failed comedy may be *unfunny*, not a successful tragedy. The *New Haven Advocate* "Film Clips" section in 1993 that excoriated *Sister Act 2* as "Wretched, unfunny, soporific; quite likely the year's worst movie" while hailing *Schindler's List* just above it in the alphabetic listings as "Stunning, superb, far and away the year's best movie, and a deeply emotional experience," could not have used the descriptor *unfunny* for the latter film, although whatever might be said about *Schindler's List*, funny it surely wasn't.

Apparently nonscalar categories can be coerced into scalarity via *un-* attachment. The scientific adjective *nuclear* ('of, relating to, or forming a nucleus') is binary— either a particle or reaction is nuclear or it's not; there are no two ways (more strictly, no third way) about it. But its metaphorically extended sense, in which we speak of nuclear families, is more admitting of scalar gradations, and thus while we have no unnuclear bomb, physics, power, and the like, and while this adjective is not

An *Un-* Paper for the Unsyntactician

listed in conventional dictionaries, we are not too surprised to find a grouping that consists of the protagonist of a novel (*Mapping the Edge*, by Sarah Dunant) along with her 6-year-old daughter, her confidante, and her best friend and his boyfriend, described as "a strange unnuclear family" (*New York Times Book Review*, 18 February 2001, 34).

Similarly, one of the conventional examples of contradictory adjectives is *alive/dead*; nothing can be both and nothing capable of being either can be "in between." But is this really true? In fact, *undead* has been around since Bram Stoker's *Dracula* (1897) as both an adjective and a zero-derived occupational noun to describe zombies, vampires, and other creatures that are, as the *OED* puts it, 'not quite dead but not fully alive, dead-and-alive'. Note that the someone or something that is undead, such as a vampire, fails to conform to one's expectation that it *should* be dead. But if something appears to be alive but does not quite fulfill that expectation, it must be not *undead* but *unalive*: "I wait for them [artificial flowers] to droop as in a natural cycle. But they are stubbornly unalive and therefore unwilting" (Baxter 2000, 106). Both the undead (but not quite alive) vampire and the unalive (but not dead) artificial flowers conform to Aristotle's notion of a privative opposite, in lacking a property associated by default rules with the respective subject.[6]

The poet E. E. Cummings (1972), notorious for his willingness to cajole and twist the English language to create new morphological, syntactic, and orthographic fault lines, found the *un*-adjective, not to mention the *un*-verb and *un*-noun, an unending source of inspiration. Cureton (1996) points out that Cummings's innovative *un*-verbs include reversatives like *unteach* and *ungrow* that undo what are not normally taken to be undoable actions along with statives like *unbe*, *unexist*, and *unsit*. Cummings's novel *un*-adjectives—*unalive*, *unbig*, *unslender*—strive, by overriding the normal blocking constraints, to induce a finer partition of the physical world.

More generally, the poet envisions an entire *unworld* inhabited by *unthings*, a domain of *unmen* going through the motions, not quite living but "unexisting" in an *unlife* filled with *unlove* ("unlove's the heavenless hell and homeless home/of knowledgeable shadows"). Noting that "Cummings uses *un*- with nominal bases as a major thematic device," Cureton observes that "the advertising industry has resorted to this use of *un*- as well," notably in 7-Up's self-promotion as the Uncola. "Has industry resorted to poetry?" wonders Cureton.

15.4 Privation, Prototype, and the *Un*-noun

Before either poets or advertising copywriters resorted to them, *un*-nouns were amply attested in English word formation. Most of the earlier examples, however, can be rationalized as deadjectival formations: *untruth* as a nominalization of *untrue* (rather than a negation of *truth*), *unhappiness* from *unhappy*, and so on. A number of cases appear to involve a blend of an irregular nominalization and an *un*-adjective (as in the *OED* citations *Unintelligentsia* (G. B. Shaw 1930) or *unmotherhood* (Bushnell 1947)) or the more recent *unprivacy*. Nouns like *unrest, undismay,* and *unconcern* can be seen as back-formed from the corresponding adjective or participle (see Horn 1989, sec. 5.1, for complications). In still other cases, the nominalization works off an implicit reversative *un*-verb, even when that verb (*uncircumcise, uncopy, unverify*) is not otherwise attested.[7]

(8) a. **uncircumcision**
Many men who have been circumcised as infants feel mutilated and robbed of their birthright, hence the growing "uncircumcision" movement.
("Ask Isadora" sex advice column, *New Haven Advocate*, 5 June 1997, 55)

b. **uncopier**
Headline: Un-copier Technology Draws a Blank on Used Paper
Heard of the Un-Cola? Now there's the Un-Copier, a kind of reverse photocopier that produces blank pieces of paper from documents published on a photocopier or a laser printer.
(Article by David Akin, *Ottawa Citizen*, 27 June 1998, Business, H3; the machine, manufactured by ImageX Technologies, is officially the "Decopier," although the write-up refers to it as an Un-copier for expository purposes.)

c. **unverification**
I was recently involved in an appeals case in which the question arose as to whether voice recognition had ever been used to show (prove?) that two different recorded voices were made by two different individuals. One might call this voice unverification.
(R. Rodman, posting to Language & Law e-mail list, 11 April 2001)

Suffixless cases of *un*-noun formation are not so easy to explain away, including these cited by the *OED*:

(9) a. **unbook**
Another un-book.
(1965 Probl. Communism July/Aug. 56 (heading))

b. **uncountry**
In this un-country there was blue sky and light, consent and so sin.
(1964 W. Golding Spire ix. 178)

c. **uncrime**
All that the State can aim at is un-crime, whereas the work of the Church is to inculcate virtue.
(1882 Ch. Times XX. 938)

d. **undeath**

The sum of the first and second sign Shall be undeath of the moon.
(1933 L. Riding Poet v. 125)
There is, every now and then, a film that escapes this sort of un-death.
(1974 *Globe & Mail* (Toronto) 24 July 13/4)

e. **unlight**

A cloak of darkness she wove about them ... an Unlight, in which things seemed to be no more, and which eyes could not pierce, for it was void.
(1973 J. R. R. Tolkien Silmarillion (1977) viii. 74)

f. **unphilosophy**

Every single fall or rise of nature's work ... led her into various veins of inductive unphilosophy.
(1877 Blackmore Cripps II. ii. 23)

—and the most historically significant member of the class:

g. **unperson** [introduced by George Orwell]

A person who, usu. for political misdemeanour, is deemed not to have existed and whose name is removed from all public records. In extended use, a person whose existence or achievement is officially denied or disregarded; a person of no political or social importance.
Syme was not only dead, he was abolished, an unperson.
(1949 G. Orwell *Nineteen Eighty-Four*, 159)
Beria is already an "unperson," the record of his career "unfacts."
(1954 *Economist* 18 Sept. 883/2)

In each case, we are dealing with a simplex base where there is no plausible source for the nominal in an *un*-adjective or *un*-verb and the meaning involves antonymy or, more specifically, *privation* in Aristotle's sense: the absence of something that might have been expected to inhere in the referent.

Some attested *un*-nouns seem to have been facilitated by a priming effect.

(10) a. **unpublicity**

The publicity or unpublicity of the process.
(1802–12 Bentham Ration. Judic. Evid. (1827) II. 140)

b. **unshapes**

The English noses in their shapes and unshapes.
(C. 1843 Carlyle Hist. Sk. Jas. I & Chas; I (1898) 269)

Other cited forms allude to a tacit version of the priming effect, where the reader is invited to recall "the land of promise" or "promised land" in the former case and the hackneyed rhetorical query "What kind of society ...?" in the latter.

(11) a. **unpromise**
Gaze down into the future upon the hateful Land of Unpromise.
(1866 Pall Mall G. 12 May 12)
b. **unsociety**
What kind of unsociety we suffer when we have about us only persons very unequal.
(1872 H. Bushnell Serm. Living Subj. 335)

It will be noticed that the *OED un*-nouns sampled here and especially the members of the Cummings collection have a palpable e-neg flavor to them. Given this, it may seem surprising that the 7-Up team should have sponsored an ad campaign identifying its product as the *un*- anything. Unlight, unpromise ... and Uncola? Crucially, though, it is the privative function of the *un*-noun that the advertisement exploited: if the "expected" beverage has undesirable qualities—caffeine, heaviness, or just plain old-hattitude—then the privation of this e-neg "positive" term can only be (e-)positive.

Kicking off in 1968, the Uncola campaign appealed to the nonconformist urges (or pretenses) of the intended audience in those heady days of the counterculture, and even decades later was still spreading to other businesses. In 1991, the *New York Daily News* introduced what its editor called a new supplement, of which its editor claimed, "It's not quite like anything else we do. It's an un-magazine, like an un-Cola" (quoted in Crain's *New York Business*, 2 September 1991). John Hull, developing his SanFax Systems in Angels Camp, California, also alluded to 7-Up's ad campaign and proclaimed, "We're the 'Un-dot-com'" (*Modesto Bee*, 10 October 2000). The cola companies can even dispense uncolas of their own: "Coke is diversifying, with plans to introduce a line of fashion and sports clothing and a rollout this summer of the ultimate un-cola—a bottled water called Dasani" (*Boston Globe*, 28 March 1999).

15.5 Class A and Class B *Un*-nouns

To gain a perspective on the sudden increase in productivity of these forms, which have exploded into the lexicon since the inauguration of the Uncola campaign, consider these forms:[8]

(12) *Class A* un-*nouns*
a. **unhit**
Un-hit of the week: Cardinals pitcher Garrett Stephenson came into last Saturday's game with Atlanta 1 for 36 at the plate. Then he lined what looked like a single to right. But Brian Jordan charged, fielded it and threw him out at first.

(Baseball "Week in Review" column by Jayson Stark at espn.com, 11 August 2000)

b. **unkids**

Getting a Life, Episode One: The Un-Kids

(Title of NYC column by Clyde Haberman, *NYT*, 14 May 1999, comparing young girls screaming for Latin teen idol Ricky Martin with the 20- and 30-somethings who ought to know better lining up for days at the Ziegfeld, dueling with plastic light sabers while waiting to buy tickets for *The Phantom Menace*. One woman, explaining "We're kids," admits to being 28.)

c. **unmartini**

Photo caption: UNMARTINI—A Ginger Citrus Snap, with pomegranate seeds, at Tabla.

(*NYT*, 20 January 1999, F1, "The Aperitif Moment: Sip or Flinch")

d. **unpotato**

Photo caption: THE UNPOTATO: Jerusalem artichokes are roasted with thyme at Craft.

(*NYT*, 14 March 2001, F3)

e. **unpublications**

The main unpublications of H. P. Grice

(Heading for column in bibliographic addendum to *PGRICE* (Grandy and Warner 1986, 495), facing page listing "The Publications of H. P. Grice")

f. **unturkey** (and **unbird**)

The Great UnTurkey. Let One of Now & Zen's featherless friends be the centerpiece of Your Holiday table! This impressive creation is completely vegan and offers 5 solid pounds of boneless eating (enough for 8 hungry adults)! Made of delicately flavored tender seitan, dressed in a delectable 'skin' made from yuba (beancurd skin),... this innovative creation will delight vegetarians and non-vegetarians alike. This frozen "unbird" comes fully cooked, and needs only reheating to be enjoyed.

(Ad for Now & Zen, San Francisco, November 1999)

The *un*-noun coinages of (12) represent one of two closely related contexts distinguished in figure 15.2. As exemplified by the *Uncola* of the 7-Up ad and the *unmartini* consisting of a citrus ginger snap, sans gin or vermouth, served in a martini glass, the class A *unX* is not structurally a member of the category *X*, but it shares a significant functional status with *X*s. The innovation of *unX* invites the hearer to construct a category that contains the sets denoted by both *X* and *unX* as subsets. Such class A *un*-nouns include *unhit* (a batted ball that bounces into the outfield but is thrown to first before the batter arrives is not a hit, although it starts out resembling one),

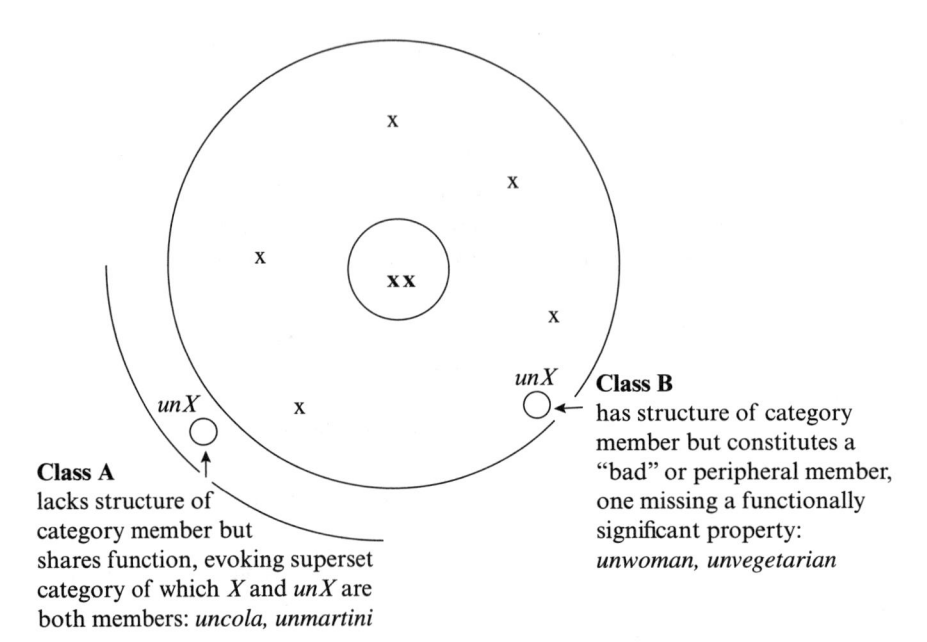

Class A
lacks structure of category member but shares function, evoking superset category of which *X* and *unX* are both members: *uncola, unmartini*

Class B
has structure of category member but constitutes a "bad" or peripheral member, one missing a functionally significant property: *unwoman, unvegetarian*

Figure 15.2
Classes of *un*-nouns

unkids (a 20- or 30-year-old doesn't become a kid by acting like one), and *unpotato* (however roasted and served, a Jerusalem artichoke doesn't turn into a potato). An *unturkey* (one of Now & Zen's featherless vegan "creations") isn't a turkey even if it looks like one and gets eaten at Thanksgiving.[9] Nor, as one's tenure committee is quick to remind one, do *unpublications*, however impressive and copious, truly count.

Note the crucial role of Aristotelian privation in establishing the common ground against which the class A *un*-noun is coined.[10] Just as it is its shared properties with Coke or Pepsi that make 7-Up a better candidate for an uncola than tea or chocolate milk would be, so too it's only when it's docked near Coney Island or another amusement park that a blighted garbage barge would qualify as an *unamusement*.

(13) **unamusement**
 Sometimes she talked about the garbage barge, which was now docked off Coney Island, an unamusement.
 (Lorrie Moore, "Places to Look for Your Mind," in *Like Life*, 1990, 115)

The ancestral role of the Uncola here is recognized by those who have developed the device for their own commercial purposes. Here is Washington consultant Jay Jaffe explaining his strategy for repositioning an Atlanta law firm:

The point, says Jaffe, was that Atlanta had two main players: King & Spalding and Alston & Bird. The next four or five firms down the line blended together, and Kilpatrick was looking for a way to distinguish itself.... The marketing costs of making Kilpatrick another King & Spalding—if that was what the firm wanted—would have been too high, he says. "We can't make you the Coca-Cola of Atlanta, but we can make you the **Un-Cola** of Atlanta," he says. (*American Lawyer Media*, Fulton County Daily Report, 12 July 1999)

The key is to exploit the target's tacit knowledge:

A television commercial for the United Jersey Banks shows a loan officer from "Lethargic National Bank" on the telephone assuring a customer in an unhurried manner than approval for his loan should be in "any day now—any day." After a narrator explains how large organizations often are "slow moving" when it comes to processing transactions such as loans, the commercial shows how United Jersey, "the fast moving bank," processes loans for its customers swiftly.

The ad clearly illustrates how one bank holding company has used positioning to gain market share, said Al Ries, who is the coauthor of *Positioning: The Battle for Your Mind* and the chairman of Trout & Ries Advertising Inc., a New York ad agency.... "The battle doesn't take place in the banking retail establishment," he said. "The battle takes place in the minds of consumers." ...

In planning marketing strategies, Mr. Ries suggested, bankers should "cherchez le creneau" (look for the opening) in consumers' heads. The best way, he added, is by "relating what you say to what's already in their mind. The mind accepts whatever information it already agrees with," he said. "Even 7-Up ["the Uncola"] got into people's minds by relating to colas," he said. (*The American Banker*, 29 April 1986, 14)

But while relating to colas, the Uncola is not one. Most instances of novel *un*-nouns fall into class B of figure 15.2, in which an *unY* is a bona fide—but (in the sense of Rosch 1978) not prototypic or stereotypic—member of category *Y*; the *unY* is a "bad example" of the category, lacking a functionally significant property. For instance:

(14) *Class B* un-*nouns*
   a. **unbank**
      Banking on the Unbanks: Tellerless Wonders Are Reinventing Small-Business Lending
      (Headline, *NYT*, 4 February 1999)
   b. **uncollege**
      Even though many Mids [= Midshipmen, students at the U.S. Naval Academy] refer to their school with bemused affection as "the uncollege," it remains one of the great bastions of "old college spirit" in its pristine form. (*Washington Post*, 22 November 1977, D1, "Navy Revives College Spirit for the Game; Mids Rally 'Round for the Game")

c. **unelection**

Numerous Google hits after the irregular Gore-Bush election of November 2000. For example: Twelve days after the unelection, no one knows how to keep a rendezvous with destiny—not the politicians, not the lobbyists, not the chatterers in the press, not the hangers-on, not the sycophants, not even the White House interns.
(*NYT*, 19 November 2000, Week in Review, 1)
Our unelection is superior to our election in every way. The campaign was never about anything. Lockbox, prescription drugs, blah, blah. Now we are fighting over bedrock principles of freedom. The sanctity of the vote, the idea that every vote counts.
(Maureen Dowd column, *NYT*, 10 December 2000, 15)

d. **unplace**

[Referring to E. B. White's essay "Here Is New York"]
And what he made just as clear was that any place else was just, well, any place else. Or perhaps an un-place. The closest of these is New Jersey.
(Charles Strum, "Garden State? The Image Is Closer to Crab Grass," *NYT*, 27 October 1996, Arts, 33)

e. **unplan**

Of course, a plan is a plan, even if it calls itself an "unplan."
(Herbert Muschamp, "42nd Street Plan: Be Bold or Begone!" *NYT*, 19 September 1993, Arts, 33)

f. **unpolitician**

Reference to Victor Morales, schoolteacher and surprise Democratic nominee for U.S. Senate seat opposite Phil Gramm
(*NYT*, 30 April 1996; many other examples since)

g. **unsheets**

Now that the big names in bedding—Cannon, Fieldcrest and J. P. Stevens—are bringing out their own versions of unsheets, suggestible types can go see natural [unbleached, untreated cotton sheets] displayed ... in department stores around town.
(Liz Logan, "New Bed Linen," *NYT*, 10 October 1991, Home, 1)

h. **unsuperstar**

Meet Tom Cruise, the unsuperstar of superstardom.
(TV ad for *Access Hollywood*, 8 January 2000)

i. **unvegetarian**

The Unvegetarian
(Headline of article in the *Los Angeles Times*, 5 July 1990, by Charles Perry profiling Deborah Madison, whose restaurant and gourmet cookbooks "have made meatless cooking chic" but who "hates being called a vegetarian")

An *Un-* Paper for the Unsyntactician   345

The chic unvegetarians targeted by Deborah Madison are still vegetarians, although "bad" members of the tribe. Similarly, the Naval Academy is a college (as well as an uncollege), Bush prevailed over Gore in an election (even if it was also an unelection), the archetypal unplace New Jersey is nevertheless a place, Tom Cruise is undeniably a superstar (if also an unsuperstar), and, as their description implies, unbleached natural cotton sheets are not only unsheets but also sheets.

The "badness" of the category member may be made explicit, as in the Ungame® marketed at http://www.educationalmedia.com/bookfiles/ungame.html:

> The world's most popular self-expression game is a cooperative adventure in communication. Two to six players, ages 5 through adult, progress along the playing board as they answer questions such as "What do you think life will be like in 100 years?" This noncompetitive game can be a great icebreaker or a serious exchange of thoughts, feelings, and ideas.

Customer reviews posted on amazon.com highlight the noncompetitive, and thus exceptional, nature of the Ungame:

- "There is no winner and no loser—so everybody feels good!"
- "It's therapeutic"
- "There's a gameboard, but it's non-competitive"

Of course, it is the problem of defining *game* that provided Wittgenstein (1958, secs. 66–67) with the motivation for rejecting the traditional necessary-and-jointly-sufficient criterion for category membership and for introducing the notion of family resemblance, as well as his theory of language games.

In some cases, the assignment of an *un*-noun to class A or class B depends on the definition of the relevant (non-natural-kind) categories.

(15) *Class A or B?*
  a. **unbreakfast**
     Among the "un-breakfasts" that the experts suggest, besides a bean burrito, are a ham or turkey sandwich (try it on a toasted English muffin) and a bowl of soup.
     (Sheryl Julian, "Which of the Above Is a Nutritious Breakfast? A. All of Them. When It Comes to Kids, the Rules on Eating Right Are Changing," *Boston Globe*, 11 October 2000, E1)
  b. The **Un-Chocolate**
     (Title of piece on white chocolate, *Better Homes and Gardens*, December 1995, 182)
  c. **unhotel**
     I don't always wear a suit. And I don't always stay in a hotel. Business is not my whole life. But it can seem that way when I'm on an extended out of town assignment. That's why I choose Oakwood Corporate Apartments. The Un-Hotel.
     (Magazine advertisement)

The Ventana at Big Sur, California, is variously called the Ventana Hotel, the Ventana Inn and the Ventana Retreat. Lacking the quasi-mystic aura of the nearby Tassajara Zen guest facility, lacking the countercultural improvementalism of nearby Esalen, the Ventana seems to be merely a tasteful, luxurious, expensive, hot-tubbed, advanced-Sybaritic, getaway, redwood and cedar lodge on its magnificent site up a slope of the Santa Lucia mountains just above the bravely foaming Pacific Ocean.... At one point, in the way of such matters, bankruptcy loomed. Professionals took over—but professionals who seemed to understand the nature of an unhotel—and now the place, like its cedar grayed by salt winds, has worn comfortably, perhaps even profitably, into the special world of Big Sur. (Herbert Gold, *NYT*, 29 January 1984, Travel, 16)

d. **unprizes**
Presenting the IgNobels, UnPrizes Satirizing Weak Science
(Headline of story on awards ceremony of the *Annals of Improbable Research, NYT*, 5 October 2000, 8)

e. **unseason**
It was a typical California *un*season, but it *felt* like fall.
(Sue Grafton, *D Is for Deadbeat*, 1987, 1)

f. **unwomen**
(Label for women in Margaret Atwood's *The Handmaid's Tale* (1985) who, because they are not fertile, are shipped to the colonies as slave labor)

Is a ham sandwich eaten in the morning a breakfast (as well as an unbreakfast)? Is an unhotel—whether corporate apartments for un-suit-wearing business types or the redwood-and-cedar lodge at Big Sur for well-off eco-boomers—a hotel? The unwomen of Margaret Atwood's dystopian future are technically women, albeit peripheral members of the category (i.e., class B unwomen)—but that is by our definition: within the world of *The Handmaid's Tale*, to be infertile is arguably to be not quite a woman at all. And what of Jim McCawley's unsyntax—a syntax or not a syntax? It depends on your syntactic theory. And indeed, the outcome of the 2000 (un)election hinged on whether those dimpled, chad-hung unvotes were technically votes or (as it turns out) not.[11]

Having distinguished class A and class B *un*-nouns, I should note that these labels are not mere alphabet-initial placeholders. An *un*-noun *unX* of class **A** is ALMOST an *X*, while an *un*-noun *unY* of class **B** is BARELY a *Y*. As argued in Horn 2002b, *almost* and *barely* both *entail* their polar and proximal components; yet in each case only the proximal component is *asserted*.

(16) a. Gore almost won.
       Proximal component: Gore approximated winning.
       Polar component: Gore did not win.
    b. Bush barely won.
       Proximal component: Bush approximated not-winning.
       Polar component: Bush won.

This explains why *barely* but not *almost* is a trigger for negative polarity items.

(17) a. #She almost {budged/slept a wink/touched a drop/spoke to anyone}.
    b. She barely {budged/slept a wink/touched a drop/spoke to anyone}.

Assertorically inert material (like the positive component of *barely VP* or *only NP*) is irrelevant to NPI (negative polarity item) licensing. While *almost* doing something is akin to *not quite* doing it, so that *almost* and *not quite* are equivalent at the level of what is entailed, they differ at the level of what is asserted: it is the negative polar (and not the positive proximal) component of meaning that the *not quite* version asserts, whence the rhetorical opposition in (18a–b) and the contrast in NPI licensing in (18c).

(18) a. It's too bad you almost died in there. [now you'll need therapy]
    b. It's too bad you didn't quite die in there. [now I'll have to finish you off, heh heh]
    c. I {didn't quite make it/*almost made it} to any of your papers.

In a number of approximative constructions crosslinguistically, the proximal component is retained but the polar component effectively flip-flops, depending on the context of utterance and interpretation. Thus, consider the Mandarin particle variously transliterated as *cha-yidiar/chadianr* and literally glossed as 'miss-a-little' (Li 1976; Biq 1989). While its ordinary interpretation is 'almost', when it has scope over a negative predicate it can be rendered either as 'almost not' (= 'barely') or as 'almost', with the negation essentially pleonastic.

(19) Wo chadianr mei chi.
     I   almost   not eat
    a. 'I almost didn't eat.' 'I barely ate.'
    b. 'I almost ate.' [= Wo chadianr chi le.]

When the verb shifts from 'eat' to 'bump into' or 'die', the 'almost' reading predominates. Similarly, as Li (1976) notes (citing Bolinger), for Spanish *por poco no*.

(20) a. Por poco   me ahogo.
       by a little I-drown
       'I almost drowned.'

b. Por poco no me ahogo.
   by a little not I-drown
   'I almost/?barely drowned.'

Even more dramatic is the evidence Schwenter (2002) presents on "inverted" *casi* in Spanish. Normally *casi* has the same analysis as English *almost*, as illustrated in (21).

(21) María casi terminó la cena.
   Maria almost finished the dinner
   'Maria almost finished dinner.'
   Proximal component [entailed and asserted]: She approximated finishing it.
   Polar component [entailed, not asserted]: She did not finish it.

In this respect, the relation between *casi* and *apenas* is essentially akin to that between *almost* and *barely*. But consider the emergence of an "inverted" use of *casi* in the Valencian dialect. A man impatiently awaiting his friend at the auditorium door sees her arrive a minute before the session starts and exclaims ¡*Casi llegas!* 'You just barely made it!' (lit., 'You almost arrive!'). In such a context, restricted to simple present tense and utterance-initial occurrence, *casi p* clearly does not entail ~*p*, since the truth of *p* is obvious in the context. Instead, *casi p* = canonical *casi + no (p)* or *apenas (p)*.

Other crosslinguistic analogues can be found in Swiss German *fasch* (normally similar to standard German *fast* 'almost' but allowing an inverted 'barely' sense), or English *near miss*, which for airplanes implies a bare miss but elsewhere suggests an almost miss.

(22) **near miss**
   Martin's Near Miss
   A stomach problem nearly ruled Martin out.... Great Britain curling skip Rhona Martin almost missed the Winter Olympics because of a stomach problem. The gold medallist, who delivered the stone of destiny, spent time in hospital a week before the Salt Lake City Games began.
   (http://news.bbc.co.uk/winterolympics2002/hi/english/curling/newsid_1836000/1836528.stm)

It is thus not too surprising that affixal morphology also allows the crossing of the same boundary, in which proximality is held constant but the polar component (being almost an *X* vs. barely an *X*) can be relaxed, leading to the permeability of the circumferential membrane in figure 15.2.

One feature that does distinguish the class A *un*-noun is the fact that against all expectation, an *unX* of this stripe is for better or worse simply not an *X*. This exclusion may often be used as a means of irony, subtle or not. In this respect, consider the role of *propositional denial* (*A genius he's not*) and *epitomization* (*Einstein he's not*), which are, in the words of Birner and Ward (1998, 65ff.) "used to deny a salient proposition in the discourse for ironic effect," an effect associated with the preposing. Thus, try adding the proposition-denial coda *an X it's not* to each of the citations for the relevant class A *un*-noun in (23).

(23) a. **unmartini**
UNMARTINI: A Ginger Citrus Snap, with pomegranate seeds, at Tabla.
—*A martini it's not*
b. **unpotato**
THE UNPOTATO: Jerusalem artichokes are roasted with thyme at Craft.
—*A potato it's not*
c. **unturkey** (and **unbird**)
The Great UnTurkey. Let One of Now & Zen's featherless friends be the centerpiece of Your Holiday table!... Made of delicately flavored tender seitan, dressed in a delectable "skin" made from yuba (beancurd skin),... this innovative creation will delight vegetarians and non-vegetarians alike.
—*A turkey/bird it's not*

As listeners and readers have pointed out to me, these italicized codas do not necessarily, as ordinary scalar nouns generally do, convey that it is unfortunate that the *unX* in question is outside the realm of the *X*s; in this respect, the evaluative dimension of propositional denial with *un*-nouns is contextually flexible: ... *an X it's not, {much as it pains me to admit it/and a good thing too}!*

But what of epitomization for proper names? The *un*-nouns we have considered to this point, whether class A or class B, are common nouns, so let us expand our database to the proper names in (24), labeling categories denoting individuals rather than kinds.

(24) *The* un-*proper name*
a. **un-Agassi**
Normally, Agassi's reflexes are quick, his instincts have an edge and the crafty angles of his shots appear choreographed by a pool shark.... Normally, he wouldn't go down like this. But this was the un-Agassi yesterday. In the end, Clement, who is ranked 37th in the world, seized upon Agassi's distracted performance on his way to a straight-set upset of the Open's top-seeded player.
(Selena Roberts, "U.S. Open: Agassi Is Unable to Defend against Clement," *NYT*, 1 September 2000, D1)

b. **un-Clinton**
Mr. Dole provides such a contrast to the talkatively gifted President that Republicans insist their man will finally prevail as "the un-Clinton," the reassuring politician of oak-solid yeps and nopes. They are hoping for a voters' verdict first prescribed by Cicero: "I prefer tongue-tied knowledge to ignorant loquacity."
(Francis X. Clines, "It's a War of Words (Say What?)," *NYT*, 30 June 1996, Week in Review, 16; later candidates for the un-Clinton role include John McCain, Bill Bradley, Al Gore, and George W. Bush)

c. **un-Hamptons**
We had bought a second home on this picturesque island two hours from the city because it was a "real place"—the avowed "UnHamptons"—where the Catholic Church hosts a Blessing of the Pets parade and year-rounders keep livestock pens with children's-book farm critters.
(Diane McWhorter, "Raising a Stink," *NYT Magazine*, 19 August 2001, 68)

d. **un-Hong Kong**
The Un-Hong Kong: This Colony Can't Wait for the Chinese
(Headline of article on how Macao, with its triads and turf battles, looked forward to takeover by China, *NYT*, 7 August 1998, Week in Review, 14)

e. **un-Oscars**
Once, the Golden Globes were the *un*-Oscars. Now they're becoming respectable.
(*NYT*, 16 January 1994, Arts, 11)

f. **un-Provence**
Friends are envious when they hear that my wife, Rynn, and I have built a family retreat in the Ecuadorian Andes, with two mature orange trees in the yard and flocks of parrots flying by. The house is located in an "un-Provence" called Zona de Intag, a rural county that tends more toward fried yucca than white truffle omelets.
(Stephen P. Williams, "Family Retreat in the Andes," *NYT*, 10 August 2000, Home, 1)

g. **un-Titanic**
Hideous Kinky is the un-*Titanic*.
(Gael Greene in *New York*, 26 April 1999, 74, reviewing Kate Winslet's post-*Titanic* release, in which she portrays an English mother who flees London with her two young daughters to wander through the zonked-out "all-spice exotica" of 1972 Marrakech)

h. **un-Zermatt**
The Un-Zermatt: Saas-Fee Lacks the Flash of Grander Resorts, and Its Village Air Is Real
(Headline and subhead from *NYT*, 20 January 2002, Travel)

Since there can be only one (relevant) person or place named Bill Clinton or Hong Kong, *un-Clinton* or *un-Hong Kong* will naturally enough be taken as a class A *un-* noun, referring to an *unX* that shares features with *X* but not its identity, and in each case inducing a supercategory that encompasses both of them. Both Hong Kong and Macao (the *un-Hong Kong*) are former European colonies that were or are to be absorbed into China, Clinton and the various *un-Clintons* are (un)candidates, the Oscars and *un-Oscars* (the Golden Globes) are annual film awards. The lone class B coinage in this group is *un-Agassi*, representing not a rival player but an incarnation of Andre himself that lacked the prototypical features of the normally resolute and focused tennis star—the man simply wasn't himself that day. The *un-* names exemplified in this group appear to be gradually encroaching on the territory of the previously well established *anti-* in this frame:

(25) **un-Clinton** and **un-Yeltsin**
George W. Bush and Vladimir Putin have this in common: They got where they are by promising to be unlike their larger-than-life predecessors. Both say Russian-American relations will also be different, based on hard-boiled scrutiny of national interests, not on personal ties dressed up as grand strategy. So when the un-Clinton meets the un-Yeltsin tomorrow, post-cold-war diplomacy officially enters its post-heroic phase.
(Op-ed column by Stephen Sestanovich, *NYT*, 15 June 2001, A39)

Similarly, we have the *un-Arafat* (for Salam Fayyad, the Palestinian finance minister, a "starched-shirt economist" with a Ph.D. from the University of Texas, *Newsweek*, 12 August 2002, 38) and the *un-Samaranch* (for Dr. Jacques Rogge, the successor to the ethically suspect Samaranch as the head of the International Olympic Committee, *NYT*, 1 August 2002, D1). We anxiously await the first coming of the *un-Christ*.

As with proposition denial for the common nouns, epitomization reigns for the proper noun examples.

(26) a. Macao: the colony that can't wait for the Chinese—*Hong Kong it's not*
b. those funky Golden Globes—*the Oscars they're not*
c. the down-to-earth Zona de Intag—*Provence it's not*

As with proposition denial per se, the target of epitomization may constitute either a positive or a negative exemplar, depending on the context.[12] And again, the expectation established by the common ground is crucial. Given our shared knowledge about Provence or Zermatt, it is possible to situate the Zona de Intag or Saas-Fee as their respective Aristotelian privative, but not vice versa.

(27) a. #Provence: the un-Zona de Intag!
　　 b. #Zermatt: Saas-Fee it's not!

If proposition denial and epitomization mark class A *un*-nouns, is there a comparable diagnostic for the class B *un*-noun? At the center of the circle in figure 15.2 is a small circle containing an iterated *x*. This represents not only the core membership of category *X* (perhaps Bill Clinton for political candidates, a clear-punched machine-readable ballot for votes, Coke for colas) but also what appears literally as *XX*—that is, the construction variously labeled the double (Dray 1987; Horn 1993), contrastive focus reduplication (Ghomeshi et al. 2004), or (as I shall refer to it here) the *lexical clone*. In a neutral context, clones pick out the prototype members of a category: a *SALAD salad* is (in our culture) a green salad with lettuce and perhaps tomatoes, not a chicken or potato salad; a *DOG dog* may be a golden retriever or German shepherd but hardly a chihuahua or Peke (much less a hot dog); a *DOCTOR doctor* has an M.D., not a Ph.D. in linguistics; and so on.[13] With this in view, we can predict that the peripheral members of a category picked out by a class B *un*-noun will be at the opposite extreme from the core members picked out by the lexical clone: the *uncollege* as opposed to the *COLLEGE college* of leafy lawns, fraternities, a high-powered football team, and binge drinking, the *unpolitician* versus the *POLITICIAN politician* (Bill Clinton?). Notice in particular that in (28), the trend toward *undesign* is explicitly contrasted with the aggressive "signature" style of rooms that are, according to (un)designer Nancy Agrest's lexical clone, "DESIGN designed."

(28) Undesign: Moving Away from Aggressive Décor
　　　(Headline, *NYT*, 2 June 1988, C6)
　　　"Nothing is 'design designed.' Nothing has a signature."
　　　(New York architect Diana Agrest)

Similarly, compare the *MOVIE movie* in (29) (a classic Hollywood production) with the *unmovie* in (30).

(29) a. It's almost certainly the best movie-movie Hollywood has produced since *Saving Private Ryan* and maybe since *Titanic*.
　　　　(Stephen Holden's review of *Cast Away*, *NYT*, 5 January 2001, E1)
　　 b. This is what they used to call a real MOVIE-MOVIE.
　　　　(Rex Reed's review of *Charlotte Gray*, *The New York Observer*, blurb quoted in January 2002 ads)

(30) **unmovie**
　　　UNEARTHLING, THE (1984). Really bad E.T. imitation, of the it-came-from-outer-space school. A meteor crashlands on Earth in a forest that just

happens to be full of (1) dumb teenagers, (2) some nightingale egg poachers and (3) a young boy who has seen the crash. Out of the crash hulks a plastic-suited creature with the nose of an anteater. This is the father alien, who goes around killing everyone. Meanwhile, the insufferable kid finds an alien egg and hatches it. Out pops a cute version of the father, who goes "Coo" to tug at your heartstrings. The script by J. Piquer Simon (who also directed) and Jack Gray goes nowhere. THE UNEARTHLING is the unmovie of the decade. (http://tilt.largo.fl.us/critic/mst3k/ss3303f.html)

The ambivalent cases of (15) are similar in this respect: whatever an *unhotel* is, it's in a different league from the four-star Sheraton or Hilton *HOTEL hotel*, and an *unbreakfast* is explicitly designed to provide a change of pace from the cornflakes or scrambled eggs of the all-American *BREAKFAST breakfast*.

15.6 Humpty Dumpty and the *Un*-attributive

Another class of apparent *un*-names, sampled in (31), turns out on closer inspection not to involve *un*-nouns at all, but zero-derived adjectives that have undergone conventional affixal negativization.

(31) *The pseudo* un-*noun: adjectives in nominal clothing*
  a. **undesert**
     The estate had a lush green lawn in front, flowers blooming in neatly tended beds, huge weeping willows trailing ferny branches onto the grass, a pebbled circular drive with an offshoot that led to a three-car garage in front of which a Mercedes was parked. The house featured white stucco and ornate grillwork balconies. It was so beautiful. And so undesert.
     (Nancy Herndon, *Time Bombs*, 1997, 202)
  b. **un-Disney**
     For a show that is attracting family audiences, this one [*The Producers*] is about as un-Disney as you can get. It's multicultural only in the sense that it makes fun of blacks and the Irish as well as Jews.
     ("Springtime for Adolf and Tony," op-ed by Frank Rich, *NYT*, 12 May 2001, A15)
  c. **un-Florida**
     So what does one wear to a place that looks like home? Your best. No T-shirts (which may seem un-Florida to some), sneakers, jerseys, shorts or baseball hats allowed.
     (Babita Persaud, "Get Comfortable in the Living Room," *St. Petersburg Times*, 12 October 2000, 38W)

d. **un-Garcia**
Why a Star Is Spinning in the Grave.
Very Un-Garcia: Bitter Estate Fight
(Headline, *NYT*, 3 January 1997)

e. **un-Porsche**
Porsche blew everyone out of the water with its 558-horsepower Carrera GT—with a shape as dramatically un-Porsche as could possibly be—leaving Ferrari to ponder about the timing of the launch of its beautiful 550 Barchetta.
(Adrian Low, "BMW's New Mini Cooper Steals the Paris Show," *Business Times (Singapore)*, 5 October 2000, 30)

f. **un-rock'n'roll**
One problem is that so many bona fide rock stars are beyond parody. How, for example, could you hope to better the magisterial buffoonery of Primal Scream, who failed to show up for a booking on Top of the Pops because it would have meant passing through Luton Airport, a prospect which the band's leader Bobby Gillespie declared was simply too un-rock'n'roll to contemplate?
(David Sinclair, "You Couldn't Make It Up," *The Times (London)*, 13 October 2000, Features)

g. **un-VH1**
Two of the former Shaggs [sisters who were forced into becoming a rock band in the late 1960s by their father after the girls' grandmother read his palm and predicted that the girls would play in a band] meet Orlean at a Dunkin' Donuts in New Hampshire for a look behind the music that is very un-VH1. One sister cleans houses for a living, the other works in a kitchen goods warehouse. The former Shagg who didn't show up suffers from depression.
(Blaine Harden, review of Susan Orlean's *The Bullfighter Checks Her Makeup*, *NYT Book Review*, 28 January 2001, 11)
Apparently they even give props to MC5 and Sonic Youth . . . how very un-VH1.
(Web site)

This is shown by the standard adjectival diagnostics: *so (undesert)*, *very (un-Garcia, un-VH1)*, *dramatically (un-Porsche)*, *too (un-rock'n'roll)*, *seem (un-Florida)*. In each case, the same construction is equally possible with the positive base of the *un*-adjective (*so desert*, *very VH1*). While lacking an overt suffix, these *un*-adjectives are otherwise quite close to the plebian instances of word formation resulting in *un-Dickensian*, *un-Chomskyan*, *un-chocolaty*, or, for some un-adjective-worthy eponyms, [$_{Adj}$ *un* [$_{Adj}$[$_N$ *X*] *like*]], as in

(32) **un-Queen Amidala-like**

Novalee (Natalie Portman, looking radiant but very un-Queen Amidala-like)
...
(*NYT*, 23 April 2000, Arts, 11, on actress Portman's role in *Where the Heart Is*, after playing female lead in the Star Wars epic *The Phantom Menace*)

A more significant category of apparent *un*-nouns traces back to the famous Looking Glass exchange (Carroll 1872, chap. 6).

(33) **unbirthday present**

Humpty Dumpty [on his cravat/belt, a gift from the White King and Queen]: "They gave it me—for an un-birthday present"...
Alice: "What is an un-birthday present?"
Humpty Dumpty: "A present given when it isn't your birthday, of course."

If the seed of today's *un*-noun was donated (for a fee) by the copywriter of *Uncola* fame, the egg was undoubtedly contributed a century earlier by Humpty Dumpty. But Messrs. Carroll and Dumpty did not hatch the unbirthday present *ab ovo*. The *OED* files several other examples of this usage under **un-**[1] 12b, remarking that "the prefixing of *un-* to nouns used attributively is rare and usually not intended seriously." The cited examples are largely nonce forms.

(34) a. **unquality Ladys**

The reason of the discontent of the unquality Ladys is that they were laugh'd at by the great Ladys.
(1771 Lady Mary Coke Jrnl. 13 Aug.)

b. **uncountry gentlemen**

Alas, the country! how shall tongue or pen Bewail her now uncountry gentlemen?
(1823 Byron Age of Bronze xiv)

c. **uncompany costume**

It was a whim of the artist to sketch his subject in that occasional, uncompany costume.
(1852 S. R. Maitland Eight Ess. 236)

d. **unbusiness men**

Single women, widows, and unbusiness men, are those on whom the blow chiefly fell.
(1880 Spectator 3 Jan. 9/2)

In these cases and others (*uncurrency-style* (1852), *undining-room* (1845), *unhousehold-name* (1894), *unsociety-people* (1898)), the negation affixes to the first noun of a nominal compound. What is *structurally* an *un*-nominal is *functionally* a prefixed quasi-adjectival modifier; these are *un*-nouns in name only.

The Age of Uncola is also the age of the *un*-attributive nominal, as seen in the progeny of Mr. Dumpty on display in (35).

(35) *The* un-*attributives*

    a. **un-Brooklyn crime**
        An Un-Brooklyn Crime; Army Officer Charged in Killings in Land Fraud ... In Brooklyn, where many killings stem from drug dealing and domestic disputes, investigators said that murders that arise from white-collar crime are uncommon. A suspect who is a decorated Army officer accused of committing the crime during a short furlough from foreign soil is unheard of.
        (Headline of article about unusual murder case for Brooklyn, NY; Kevin Flynn, *NYT*, 17 May 2000, B1)

    b. **un-Christmas turkey**
        "Thank you. An un-Christmas turkey is a great treat," he said.
        (Elizabeth Taylor, *In a Summer Season*, 1961, 98)

    c. **undate movie**
        Of things already in town do not miss the blackly comic, spiritually desolate undate movie *In the Company of Men.*
        (Article on current films in *The (Montreal) Gazette*, 19 September 1997)

    d. **un-dressing room**
        It was an un-dressing room, Thérèse thought.
        (Michèle Roberts, *Daughters of the House*, 1992, 60)

    e. **unengagement hand**
        "And I don't think I'm old enough to be engaged to anyone really, so I am going to wear his ring on my unengagement hand."
        (Angela Thirkell, *Miss Bunting*, 1996, 322)

    f. **unguy sentiment**
        Layne sympathized with Black and the Super Smokers about the whole hog contest. (This sympathy is a very un-guy sentiment. After the disastrous news, Black said he would be razzed unmercifully by some friends. Sure enough, as he took his ribs to the judging area, someone called out: "Hey, Terry, leave those ribs with us. The judges don't want them—just like they didn't want that skanky pig of yours.")
        (Joe Holleman, "Where There's Smoke ... There's a Man Firing Up the Grill," *St. Louis Post-Dispatch*, 8 October 2000, E1)

    g. **unhealth food**
        "I'm into un-health food," Miss Stockbridge said. "I love Ben & Jerry's vanilla-and-Oreo chunk ice cream. I have it with Diet Coke so I can feel good about myself."
        (*NYT*, 3 August 1988, C3)

h. **un-Miss Manners stack**
"Done with your dinnah?" asks the waitress. A rhetorical question since she is slapping dishes together in a very un-Miss Manners stack.
(Mameve Medwed, *Host Family*, 2000, 44–45)

i. **un-Mister Rogers tone of voice**
The more he was called Mister Rogers, the more his face grew red. One day last month, in a very un-Mister Rogers tone of voice, Fassel turned and said, "You know, I hate that."
(Bill Pennington on character makeover of New York Giants' mild-mannered football coach Jim Fassel, *NYT*, 10 January 2001, D1)

j. **unmother mother**
"After I've gotten him as prepared as I can for his un-mother mother, I'll try to hammer a few pounds of sense into his head about taking on Henri Forquet."
(J. M. Redmann, *Lost Daughters*, 1999, 258; narrator is a detective who is about to reunite someone with the birth mother who gave him up for adoption and is not a prototypical mother figure)

k. **unpetroleum lip jelly**
Un-Petroleum™ Lip Jelly™
Un-Chap® your lips
(Label on product manufactured by Autumn Harp, Bristol, VT)

l. **"unpotato" latkes**
(Heading for recipe at http://www.oz.net/~csrh/new_page_1.htm in which the usual potato latkes are made with pureed cauliflower instead)

m. **unreal estate**
Unreal Estate: Internet Stocks May No Longer Be Soaring, but the Market for Web Addresses Is Getting Tighter All the Time
(Headline and subhead of "The New Economy," column in *NYT Magazine*, 22 August 1999)

n. **unrealpolitik**
On Russia's Far East Fringe, Unrealpolitik
(Headline of article on Vladivostok, *NYT*, 14 February 1999, 1; several other instances of *Unrealpolitik* attested)

o. **unvalley idea**
A [Silicon] Valley Enterprise with an Un-valley Idea: There Is Life outside the Office
(Headline, *NYT*, 28 May 2000, Business, 9)

p. **unwelcome mat**
New York's Public Areas Roll Out Unwelcome Mat for Homeless
(Headline, *NYT*, 18 November 1989, 32)

Closer examination, however, indicates that the *un*-compounds in this list are structurally heterogeneous, depending on whether the prefixed nominal is a true *un*-noun or an *un*-adjective in nominal garb. While an unbirthday present is indeed a gift for one's unbirthday, an *undate movie* is not a movie that one sees on an *undate* but a movie that is not a date movie. Similarly, an *un-dressing room* is not a room where one does not dress (much less a room where one undresses, that being a hyphenless *undressing room*) but a room other than a dressing room. In these cases, the innovation of the *unA B* presupposes the prior establishment of the *A B* in the common ground. Such *un*-attributives may well introduce antonymy, but do not simply yield the antonym of the attributive noun itself. Rather, the entire nominal compound is effectively *un*-ned, in the manner of the class A *un*-noun. To posit an *unguy sentiment* is to evoke a superset encompassing two kinds of sentiments: the guy kind and the unguy kind. (The *very* modification here suggests that *unguy* is in fact functioning adjectivally here, and that thus we're dealing in this case with a pseudonoun.) Notice also the anticlone: we have the *unmother mother* above and elsewhere the *undiet diet*, which promises untold gustatory delights that don't weigh against one's waistline.

Similarly for the examples in which the attributive noun is a proper name: while *an un-Christmas turkey* is, Humpty-Dumpty-style, a turkey to be enjoyed on a day other than Christmas, an *un-Brooklyn crime* is not a crime that takes place out of Brooklyn but an atypical Brooklyn crime, an *un-Miss Manners stack* of dishes is one of which the eponymous etiquette guide would not approve, and an *un-Mister Rogers tone of voice* one that the children's television show host would not have been caught dead using. In each of these three cases, a *very* intensifier would again be eminently plausible.

Like their simplex *un*-noun cousins, these compounds are novel lexical items, constructed online, which are not destined for the permanent lexicon. In fact, it is this very feature that bears out the robust productivity of the process of *un*-noun formation in contemporary English (see Clark and Clark 1979 for a similar observation about denominal verbs).

15.7 Lexical Pragmatics and the *Un*-noun: Toward an Unconclusion

Uniting the *un*-attributive heirs of Humpty Dumpty's unbirthday present with the class A and class B *un*-nouns (and *un*-proper names) and the pseudo-*un*-nouns reviewed earlier is the Aristotelian semantics of privation and markedness, the same asymmetric conceptual structure invoked in section 15.3 to describe the distribution of semiproductive adjectival *un*- formation.[14] It is only when the speaker can assume (or pretend to assume) an expected or "natural" property associated with a given referent or with the set to which that referent aspires to belong that she can felicitously invoke the corresponding *un*- form. Antonymy is generally defined as a symmetric lexical relation; if *hot* is the antonym of *cold, cold* is equally the antonym of *hot*. But the antonymy reflected in the *un*-word—whether adjective, noun, or even verb (see Horn 2002a)—is a conceptually asymmetric relation, just as is Aristotle's opposition between the positive and the privative.

While pragmatics was defined by its founders Charles Morris, Rudolf Carnap, and C. S. Peirce as "the science of the relation of signs to their interpreters" in opposition to the pure domains of syntactics and semantics (Morris 1938), the relatively simple trichotomy envisioned in the *Encyclopedia of Unified Science* has gradually given way to a more complex picture in which syntax, semantics, and pragmatics are applicable to both sentential and lexical domains, as schematized roughly in figure 15.3. The field of lexical pragmatics originated with McCawley 1978, a memorable study of the penetration of Gricean implicature into word formation and word use; it was largely an attempt to extend this work (along with related morphological studies by Aronoff (1976) and Kiparsky (1983) that bypass pragmatic modes of explanation)

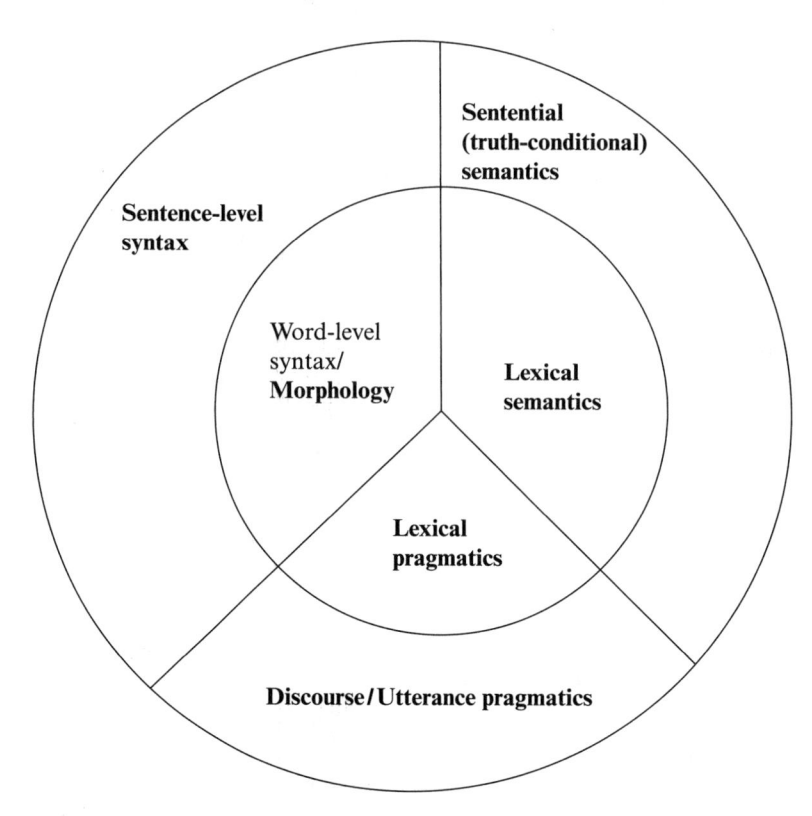

Figure 15.3
Lexical pragmatics in the expanded trichotomy

that inspired my own dialectic model of language (Horn 1984) in which an R-based principle of least effort squares off against a Q-based principle of sufficiency of information. The application of this model to the analysis of redundant *un*-verbs is explored in Horn 1988, 1993. (For a lucid introduction to current trends in lexical pragmatics, see Blutner 1998, 2004; and for some applications to lexical change, see Traugott 2004.)

In this study in lexical pragmatics focusing on the behavior of the partially productive prefix *un-*, I have drawn from a wide variety of sources, beginning with the notions of opposition developed by Aristotle and schematized in the logical square of Apuleius and Boethius. I reviewed the widespread tendency for contradictory negation to develop (pragmatically and/or conventionally) strengthened contrary interpretations as recognized by Sapir and others (see Horn 1989, chap. 5), and more specifically for affixal negation—as represented canonically in English *un-* adjectives on simplex bases—to lexicalize a contrary and evaluatively negative meaning, as detailed by Jespersen and Zimmer. This, in turn, can be linked to the more general phenomenon of R-based strengthening as realized in euphemism and related politeness strategies surveyed in Brown and Levinson 1987 (see also Shuman and Hutchings 1960 for related historical background and Horn 2000 for additional applications). Finally, the lexical pragmatics of *un*-adjectives and especially of *un*-nouns can only be understood against a general background of the markedness of negation (see Horn 1989, sec. 1.2 and chap. 3, for various formulations by philosophers, psychologists, and linguists from Parmenides and Kant to Wason and Givón) and, in particular, of the recognition of the role played by the Aristotelian concept of privation.

Descending from these shoulders on which I stand, a methodological hand should be waved in the direction of the technological resources that make it feasible to undertake a study of this kind. Without the services provided by Lexis/Nexis, Google, and the online *OED*, the observations offered here could not have been carried out with any systematicity, and without the human resources provided by Beth Levin, my co-principal *un*-vestigator, this study would be an unalive shadow of its current self.

Notes

1. McCawley explains (1980, 168) that this admittedly "disposable title" was intended to suggest that "much of what has been thought of as syntax is largely a reflection of other things, such as morphology, logic, production strategies, and principles of cooperation."
2. In the free translation of Apostle (1966, 167), "Privation has as many senses as there are negations of terms which are prefixed by '*un*' or '*in*' ... or suffixed by '*less*.'"
3. See Winter 1994 for an impressive collection of invented (back-formed) positives of just this sort, in his tale of a *maculate* and *flappable* but relatively *sipid* gentleman with a *wieldy* um-

brella but *peccable* manners, who strenuously avoids any *toward* and *heard-of* behavior to win the heart of a *descript* and *gainly* young woman with *kempt* hair and a *sheveled* appearance.

4. The more lexicalized and less productive *iN-* forms always have the potential to "restrict the domain of *un-*": hence, we have no **unpossible*, **unactive*, and so on (Zimmer 1964, 30). (See *OED*, **un-**[1], 7; Jespersen 1942, sec. 26.1; Marchand 1969; and—on the general phenomenon of blocking or preemption by synonymy—Bréal 1900, 27; Aronoff 1976, 43ff.; McCawley 1978; Clark and Clark 1979, sec. 4.4; Horn 1984, 25ff.)

5. The situation is actually somewhat more complex; see Horn 1989, sec. 5.1, for more on the structural and semantic distinctions among *iN-*, *un-*, and *non-* prefixation.

6. For reasons of space, I restrict discussion here to the adjectival- and nominal-deriving *un-* prefix. The reversative and denominal *un-* of *unzip*, *unskin*, *unthaw* may be assimilable to the general account of Aristotelian privation as well, although its etymological source is different. For discussion, see Horn 1988, 2002a.

7. As a reviewer points out, *uncircumcision* and *unverification* may also be back-formed from the corresponding participle.

8. See Horn 2002a, 46–64, for a comprehensive inventory of attested *un-*nouns culled from newspapers, magazines, and observation of life over the last several years, constructed jointly with Beth Levin (now of Stanford University). In these and subsequent citations, *NYT* = *The New York Times*.

9. Class A uncomestibles in the *unturkey* mold are legion. Thus, we have *unbologna* (for the suspected filling of a child's sandwich in *The Nanny Diaries*), *unbutter* (for margarine), *uncheese* (for the nondairy substitute: 1,930 Google hits, including Uncheese Cookbooks), *unBLTs* (with faux bacon), and the *unsushi* (for a Japanese restaurant's serving of katsu don, pork on a stick with egg and onion over rice), all washed down with either *uncoffee* (either tea or Postum) or some nonalcoholic *unbeer*. In each case, the context of presentation of the *unX* is one in which *X* would be normal or anticipated.

10. As Aristotle would no doubt have predicted, what counts as the default will vary with context. Thus, in an article "The Un-Beats: Lawrence Ferlinghetti and His Pals Aren't the Only Bay Area Poets, Just the Noisiest" (*San Francisco Magazine*, July 2002, 91), the Stanford School of Poets is described as follows: "Their work is restrained, elegant, classical, and insistently metrical, everything that Beat poetry is not." In the context of San Francisco and poetry, *beat* represents the unmarked or "expected" category.

11. When other polysemies are factored in, the explosion of possible meanings for a given *un-*prefixed noun can be daunting indeed. As demonstrated by a roundup of Google sites, the lexical item *unmarriage*—if we do consider it a single lexical item—has been variously evoked as a class A *un-*noun (= a committed same- or mixed-sex relationship that does not attain legal wedlock), as a class B *un-*noun (= a marriage in name only, whether one deteriorated into that status or one designed to obtain one partner a green card), as a deverbal reversative (= a divorce or annulment), or for the (un)ceremony resulting in any of the above (as in the dream recounted at http://whither.blogspot.com/2002_08_01_whither_archive.html).

12. In his discussion of ironic preposing, Ward (1985, 289–90) notes that the height of a value on the relevant scale—and hence its eligibility as a target of epitomization—is determined by the context, thus yielding the difference in acceptability between (i) and (ii), where Hitler counts as a low and high scalar value, respectively.

(i) A: Do you think Bill is a nice guy?
   B: #Hitler he's not.

(ii) He's a powerful demagogue, but Hitler he's not.

Similarly, consider the role of Patrick Ewing as an epitome of failure in the following text:

(iii) Coach Fassel tried to tell us this, but we were weak and disbelieving and forgot that when it came to playoff guarantees, Patrick Ewing he isn't. We should have known better. The next time the deacon of December says that his seemingly mediocre 6-6 team is capable of running the table and making the playoffs, we will fold our hands and say, "Amen!"
(Harvey Araton column, *NYT*, 24 December 2002, D1)

The key here is the assumption of a common ground for the New York sports fan, who will immediately recognize that unlike Joe Namath, Mark Messier, or Coach Jim Fassel, who were each locally celebrated for fulfilling their guarantees of victory for the 1969 Jets, 1994 Rangers, and 1999 Giants, respectively, Ewing is remembered for his many unfulfilled guarantees as the team leader of the Knicks in the 1990s. "Patrick Ewing he isn't" thus plays off Ewing's status as the standard bearer for the disappointed and unrequited.

13. The clones here are of the *prototype* variety; see the cited references for the role of context in distinguishing among the other possible variants. These additional examples of prototype clones were provided by Yale University undergraduates:

(i) A: Did you *hook UP hook up*? (value-added clone)
   B: No, we just *hooked up hooked up*. (prototype clone)

(ii) *SEX sex:* "refers to regular intercourse, not variations or imitations such as oral or vaginal [*sic*] sex"

14. This extends to novel *un*-phrase generation, as in (i).

(i) a. **unfooled around with**
      Simply Orange—unfooled around with
      (In TV commercials)
   b. **un-what-I-expected**
      She was very un-what-I-expected.
      (A reference to women's studies scholar Mary Cathryn Cain)
   c. **un-up your alley**
      This is not un-up your alley.
      (Don DeLillo, *Underworld*, 1997, 202)

In a sense, *every* novel *un*-word is very un-what-one-expected.

References

Algeo, John. 1971. The voguish uses of *non-*. *American Speech* 46, 87–105.

Apostle, Hippocrates, ed. 1966. *Aristotle's* Metaphysics, *translated with commentaries.* Bloomington: Indiana University Press.

Aristotle. *Categories. The works of Aristotle*, vol. 1, ed. by W. D. Ross. Trans. by E. M. Edghill. London: Oxford University Press, 1928.

Aronoff, Mark. 1976. *Word formation in generative grammar.* Cambridge, MA: MIT Press.

Baxter, Charles. 2000. *The feast of love*. New York: Pantheon Books.

Biq, Yung-O. 1989. Metalinguistic negation in Mandarin. *Journal of Chinese Linguistics* 17, 75–94.

Birner, Betty, and Gregory Ward. 1998. *Information status and non-canonical word order in English*. Amsterdam: John Benjamins.

Blutner, Reinhard. 1998. Lexical pragmatics. *Journal of Semantics* 15, 115–62.

Blutner, Reinhard. 2004. Pragmatics and the lexicon. In *Handbook of pragmatics*, ed. by Laurence R. Horn and Gregory Ward, 488–514. Oxford: Blackwell.

Bréal, Michel. 1900. *Semantics*. Trans. by Mrs. H. Cust. New York: Henry Holt.

Brown, Penelope, and Stephen C. Levinson. 1987. *Politeness*. Cambridge: Cambridge University Press.

Carroll, Lewis. 1872. *Through the looking glass, and what Alice found there*. London: Macmillan and Co.

Clark, Eve, and Herbert Clark. 1979. When nouns surface as verbs. *Language* 55, 767–811.

Cruse, D. A. 1980. Antonyms and gradable complementaries. In *Perspektiven der lexikalischen Semantik*, ed. by Dieter Kastovsky, 14–25. Bonn: Herbert Grundmann.

Cummings, E. E. 1972. *Complete poems 1913–1962*. New York: Harcourt, Brace & Jovanovich.

Cureton, Richard. 1996. E. E. Cummings: A study of the poetic use of deviant morphology. Posted on the web 29 February 1996 at http://Spinoza.tau.ac.il/hci/pub/poetics/art/eec12.html.

Dray, Nancy. 1987. Doubles and modifiers in English. Master's thesis, University of Chicago.

Funk, Wolf-Peter. 1971. Adjectives with negative prefixes in Modern English and the problem of synonymy. *Zeitschrift für Anglistik und Amerikanistik* 19, 364–86.

Ghomeshi, Jila, Ray Jackendoff, Nicole Rosen, and Kevin Russell. 2004. Contrastive focus reduplication in English. *Natural Language and Linguistic Theory* 22, 307–57.

Givón, Talmy. 1970. Notes on the semantic structure of English adjectives. *Language* 46, 816–37.

Grandy, Richard, and Richard Warner, eds. 1986. *Philosophical grounds of rationality: Intentions, categories, ends ["PGRICE"]*. Oxford: Clarendon Press.

Horn, Laurence R. 1980. Giving *un* to others: A reply to J. D. McCawley's "Epiphenomenal (un-)syntax. In *Current syntactic theories: Discussion papers from the 1979 Milwaukee Syntax Conference*, ed. by Michael Kac, 41–50. Bloomington: Indiana University Linguistics Club.

Horn, Laurence R. 1984. Toward a new taxonomy for pragmatic inference: Q-based and R-based implicature. In *Meaning, form, and use in context: Linguistic applications*, ed. by Deborah Schiffrin, 11–42. Washington, DC: Georgetown University Press.

Horn, Laurence R. 1988. Morphology, pragmatics, and the un-verb. In *Proceedings of the Fifth Eastern States Conference on Linguistics (ESCOL '88)*, ed. by Joyce Powers and Kenneth de Jong, 210–33. Columbus: The Ohio State University, Department of Linguistics.

Horn, Laurence R. 1989. *A natural history of negation*. Chicago: University of Chicago Press.

Horn, Laurence R. 1993. Economy and redundancy in a dualistic model of natural language. *SKY 1993: 1993 Yearbook of the Linguistic Association of Finland*, ed. by Susanna Shore and Maria Vilkuna, 33–72. Helsinki: Linguistic Association of Finland.

Horn, Laurence R. 2000. From *if* to *iff*: Conditional perfection as pragmatic strengthening. *Journal of Pragmatics* 32, 289–326.

Horn, Laurence R. 2002a. Uncovering the un-word: A study in lexical pragmatics. *Sophia Linguistica* 49, 1–64.

Horn, Laurence R. 2002b. Assertoric inertia and NPI licensing. In *CLS 38*. Part 2, *The Panels*, 55–82. Chicago: University of Chicago, Chicago Linguistic Society.

Jespersen, Otto. 1917. *Negation in English and other languages*. Copenhagen: A. F. Høst.

Jespersen, Otto. 1942. *A modern English grammar on historical principles*. Part 6, *Morphology*. Copenhagen: Einar Munksgaard.

Kiparsky, Paul. 1983. Word-formation and the lexicon. In *Proceedings of the 1982 Mid-America Linguistics Conference*, ed. by Francis Ingemann, 47–78. Lawrence: Kansas University, Department of Linguistics.

Kruisinga, E. 1931. *A handbook of present-day English*. 5th ed. Groningen: P. Noordhoff.

Lehrer, Adrienne. 1974. *Semantic fields and lexical structure*. Amsterdam: North-Holland.

Lehrer, Adrienne. 1985. Markedness and antonymy. *Journal of Linguistics* 21, 397–429.

Lehrer, Adrienne, and Keith Lehrer. 1982. Antonymy. *Linguistics and Philosophy* 4, 483–501.

Li, Charles. 1976. A functional explanation for an unexpected case of ambiguity (S or −S). In *Linguistic studies offered to Joseph Greenberg on the occasion of his sixtieth birthday*, ed. by Alphonse Juilland, 527–35. Saratoga, CA: Anma Libri.

Ljung, Magnus. 1974. Some remarks on antonymy. *Language* 50, 74–88.

Lyons, John. 1977. *Semantics*. Cambridge: Cambridge University Press.

Marchand, Hans. 1969. *The categories and types of present-day English word formation*. 2d ed. Munich: Beck.

McCawley, James D. 1978. Conversational implicature and the lexicon. In *Syntax and semantics 9: Pragmatics*, ed. by Peter Cole, 245–59. New York: Academic Press.

McCawley, James D. 1980. An un-syntax. In *Syntax and semantics 13: Current approaches to syntax*, ed. by Edith Moravcsik and Jessica Wirth, 167–93. New York: Academic Press.

Moravcsik, Edith, and Jessica Wirth, eds. 1980. *Syntax and semantics 13: Current approaches to syntax*. New York: Academic Press.

Morris, Charles W. 1938. *Foundations of the theory of signs*. Chicago: University of Chicago Press.

Rosch, Eleanor. 1978. Principles of categorization. In *Cognition and categorization*, ed. by Eleanor Rosch and Barbara B. Lloyd, 27–48. Hillsdale, NJ: Lawrence Erlbaum.

Sapir, Edward. 1944. Grading: A study in semantics. Reprinted in *Selected writings*, ed. by David Mandelbaum, 122–49. Berkeley: University of California Press, 1951.

Schwenter, Scott. 2002. Discourse context and polysemy: Spanish *casi*. In *Romance phonology and variation: Selected papers from the 30th Linguistic Symposium on Romance Languages*, ed.

by Caroline Wiltshire and Joaquim Camps, 161–75. Current Issues in Linguistic Theory 217. Amsterdam: John Benjamins.

Shuman, R. B., and H. C. Hutchings II. 1960. The *un-* prefix: A means of Germanic irony in *Beowulf*. *Modern Philology* 57, 217–22.

Sigwart, Christoph. 1895. *Logic*, vol. 1. 2nd ed. Trans. by H. Dendy. New York: Macmillan.

Traugott, Elizabeth. 2004. Pragmatics and historical linguistics. In *Handbook of pragmatics*, ed. by Laurence R. Horn and Gregory Ward, 538–61. Oxford: Blackwell.

Ward, Gregory. 1985. The semantics and pragmatics of preposing. Doctoral dissertation, University of Pennsylvania.

Winter, Jack. 1994. How I met my wife. *New Yorker*, 25 July 1994.

Wittgenstein, Ludwig. 1958. *Philosophical investigations*. Trans. by G. E. M. Anscombe. New York: Macmillan.

Wundt, Wilhelm. 1886. Das Sittliche in der Sprache. *Deutsche Rundschau* 47, 70–92.

Zimmer, Karl. 1964. Affixal negation in English and other languages. Supplement to *Word* 20.

Chapter 16

Semantic Noun Phrase Typology   Donka F. Farkas

16.1 Introduction

This chapter deals with the general question of what semantic types of noun phrase (NP) could and should be distinguished.[1] This endeavor falls into "category" typology rather than "language" typology in the sense that the domain of classification is constituted by a syntactic category rather than by a set of languages. "Language" typology aims at predicting crosslinguistic borders; it concerns itself with the question of how morphosyntactic distinctions cluster within particular languages. Within the confines of NP semantics, Chierchia (1997), for instance, deals with the issue of how semantically relevant morphosyntactic NP types are distributed across natural languages. The approach taken here is different. Put in most general terms, we will be concerned with the following two questions: (1) what semantic types of NPs are there crosslinguistically? and (2) how are these types grammatically encoded?

When pursuing category typology, one is caught in the tension between having to account for the semantic traits that unite all items in the category and having to account for the various distinctions between the subtypes. What categories and subcategories one can establish depends in large part on the general framework assumed. The state one aims toward is to have one's theory lead to exactly those distinctions that are necessary in accounting for actual natural language phenomena.

Work grounded in Montague-based type theory has tended to focus on accounting for what is common across NPs. Gross distinctions within this framework concern

---

The roots of the present chapter, and of my longstanding interest in noun phrase semantics, are in Jim's "Where Do Noun Phrases Come From?"—which happens to be the first work of his that I ever read, in 1974, in Bucharest, Romania. At the time, thinking of studying with James D. McCawley would have been a futile exercise in absurd daydreaming. From that memorable afternoon on, Jim's vision, and, later, his teaching and inspiration (as well as my fear of disappointing him), have always been with me.

I am grateful to two anonymous reviewers for helpful suggestions on a previous draft of this chapter.

the semantic type assigned to an NP and the mode of combination used when the NP is combined with expressions in its immediate linguistic environment. Finer distinctions can be drawn within members of the same semantic type by considering logical properties of the expression in question (see Barwise and Cooper 1981) or other type-neutral properties such as those having to do with lattice-theoretic properties of the denotation of an NP involved in the semantics of number.

The starting point of this chapter is different. We will explore here the semantic nominal typology we are led to in a representational framework, namely Discourse Representation Theory (DRT). The relevant features of the version of DRT I adopt are given in section 16.2, where I point out the affinity between NP semantics in DRT and proposals made in McCawley 1970, an early and lasting answer to the question of what the semantic contribution of noun phrases is. In sections 16.3 and 16.4, I pursue the issue of the semantic nominal typology this framework leads to. In sections 16.5 and 16.6, I provide evidence that this typology is needed to account for natural language phenomena by examining the way the semantic distinctions it draws are encoded grammatically.

16.2 Essentials of Discourse Representation Theory

DRT is a representational semantic theory in the sense that semantic representations are constructed on the basis of syntactically interpreted expressions, and it is these representations, called discourse representation structures (DRSs), that are assigned truth (or satisfaction) conditions relative to a model. In the version of DRT presented in Kamp and Reyle 1993, with which I am assuming basic familiarity, a minimal DRS K is made up of a set U_K of discourse referents and a set Con_K of conditions on them. Generally, these conditions are predicative; that is, they are made up of an n-ary predicate followed by n discourse referents, all of whom are elements of U_K. Complex DRSs are structures whose elements are simple DRSs and expressions that combine them.

The semantic representation of (1) in Kamp and Reyle's system is given in (2), where issues concerning tense and aspect are ignored, as they will be throughout this chapter, given that they are irrelevant to our purposes.

(1) A student arrived.

(2)
$$\begin{array}{|l|}\hline d_1 \\ \text{student}(d_1) \\ \text{arrive}(d_1) \\ \hline \end{array}$$

The contribution of the NP *a student* is the discourse referent d_1 and the predicative condition *student(d_1)*; the contribution of the verb phrase is the predicative condition *arrive(d_1)*. Note that this representation is essentially identical to the deep structure representations proposed in McCawley 1970. The structure of (1) in McCawley's notation is given in (3).

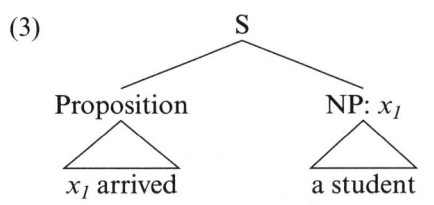

(3)
```
                    S
           ┌────────┴────────┐
      Proposition         NP: x₁
        ╱    ╲             ╱  ╲
    x₁ arrived          a student
```

The DRS in (2) differs from what one finds in Kamp and Reyle 1993 in that the contribution of the NP is separated from that of the main predicate, thereby being closer in both spirit and form to McCawley's original proposal. I am following here suggestions made in Farkas 1997b and Corblin 2000, in separating main predicative conditions, contributed by the main predicate of a clause (here *arrive(d_1)*), from restrictive predicative conditions (here *student(d_1)*), contributed by the predicative part of the NP. This distinction is relevant to the way truth conditions of DRSs are established.

Truth (or satisfaction) conditions of DRSs are defined relative to a model M consisting, minimally, of a set of entities, E, a set of worlds W, and an interpretation function I assigning to each n-ary predicate at each world w a set of n-tuples each member of which is in E. A DRS K is true in M if one can assign values to U_K in such a way as to satisfy the conditions in Con_K. More precisely, there must be an assignment function f from discourse referents and worlds to elements in E such that the values of the discourse referents in U_K satisfy the conditions in Con_K. In what follows, modal issues will not be relevant and therefore the world parameter will be ignored.

I adopt here a view in which discourse referents are analogous to restricted variables, as advocated in McCawley 1981/1993. The role of restrictive conditions, which are provided by information within the nominal, is to provide the subdomain of E from which the discourse referent can be given values. In (2), d_1 is restricted to taking values from the elements of the denotation of *student*. This DRS is true in a model M if there is an assignment function f that assigns to d_1 a value in $I(student)$, such that $f(d_1) \in I(arrive)$. The role of restrictive conditions is to delimit the assignment functions relevant to the interpretation of a DRS to those that assign to the relevant discourse referents values that meet these conditions. Note that the DRS in (2) is equivalent to the expression in (4), using the notation in McCawley 1981/1993, where restrictive expressions are separated from the variable they restrict by a colon.

(4) d_1: student(d_1) arrive(d_1)

Here d_1 is a free variable that is given existential force via the truth condition requiring there to be an assignment function that satisfies the DRS.

A further departure from classical DRT that is relevant to what follows concerns the distinction between discourse referents and thematic arguments advocated in Farkas and de Swart 2003. Following earlier suggestions (Kamp and Rossdeutcher 1994; Koenig and Mauner 2000), Farkas and de Swart propose that lexical predicates enter semantic representation as *n*-ary predicates followed by *n* thematic arguments, denoted by x, y, z. Discourse referents, on the other hand, are introduced by NPs, as before. A discourse referent introduced by the syntactic argument of a predicate replaces a particular thematic argument of the latter by a process called *Argument-Instantiation* (A-Instantiation), formulated in (5).

(5) *A-Instantiation*

Replace the *n*th thematic argument of a predicative condition with the discourse referent contributed by the argument of the predicate.

A-Instantiation occurs at that point of the meaning construction when the syntactic node dominating the predicate and its argument is interpreted.[2] Under these assumptions, the VP of (1) contributes the condition in (6).

(6) arrive(x)

The contribution of the NP *a student* is given in (7).

(7) d_1: student(d_1)

At the point at which the whole sentence is interpreted, A-Instantiation applies, replacing x by d_1 and resulting in the final representation in (2).

In the case of descriptive NPs like *a student*, which contribute a predicative restrictive expression, the determiner introduces the discourse referent, d_1, while the description introduces a predicative condition, *student(y)*. At the point when the NP node is reduced, another instance of instantiation applies, called *D-Instantiation*, whereby the thematic argument of the description (here, y) is replaced by the discourse referent introduced by the determiner (here, d_1).

A further innovation is that thematic arguments may remain uninstantiated in final DRSs, accounting for instance for the interpretation of the agent in agentless passives exemplified in (8), whose final DRS is given in (9) (see Koenig and Mauner 2000).

(8) The painting was stolen.

Semantic Noun Phrase Typology

(9)
d_2
painting(d_2)
steal(x, d_2)

Unlike discourse referents, uninstantiated thematic arguments, such as x here, are not part of the universe of DRSs and are not given values by assignment functions. Their interpretation is part of the interpretation of the predicative condition in which they occur. To put informally the proposal made by Farkas and de Swart (2003, chap. 3), the DRS in (9) is true in a model M if there is a function f restricted on d_2 to paintings, such that $f(d_2)$ is the second element of a pair in $I(steal)$. If this condition is met, there must be some entity that is the first element in this pair, thus deriving the existential entailment on the implicit agent.

The fact that the uninstantiated thematic argument here is interpreted as part of the predicative condition in which it occurs rather than given values by assignment functions is responsible for its being interpreted as scoping with the predicate, for its being less prominent than discourse referents and therefore a weaker supporter of discourse anaphora, as well as for details of its number interpretation. This last issue will be discussed in detail below.[3]

To conclude this section, let us consider the typological dimensions this framework leads to. One such dimension concerns the nature of the contribution an expression makes to semantic representation and the way it relates to the rest of that representation. I will call such distinctions *structural*. With respect to nominals, these issues concern whether the nominal introduces a discourse referent or not, how it combines with the rest of the semantic structure, and, in case a discourse referent is introduced, what the nature of the restriction placed on it is. Another dimension concerns *fine* distinctions, differentiations that have to do with the details of the evaluation of the discourse referent introduced (in case there is one). The next two sections examine these in more detail.

There is an important aspect of interpretation that remains outside the (arbitrary) limits of this discussion, namely, "information structure," which concerns the way propositional content is organized in terms of topic and comment as well as issues having to do with various types of focus.

16.3 Structural Distinctions

In this section, I will consider distinctions that involve the basic contribution of nominals to semantic representation and the way this contribution combines with other elements of the representation.

16.3.1 Argumental versus Predicative Noun Phrases

The most fundamental distinction between expressions in a DRS concerns the distinction between main predicative conditions, made up of a predicate and n thematic arguments, and information that affects the thematic arguments of this condition. The main predicative part of a clause contributes the former, and its syntactic arguments contribute the latter. The canonical role of verbs is to contribute main predicative conditions, while that of NPs is to contribute argumental expressions. The canonical relation between the two is A-Instantiation.

The most fundamental structural distinction between nominal types concerns the distinction between predicative and argumental nominals, characterized in (10).[4]

(10) *Argumental NPs* contribute information that affects the thematic argument of a main predicative condition.
Predicative NPs contribute a main predicative condition.

The NP *a student* is argumental in (1), while in (11) it is predicative.

(11) This guy is a student.

The role of *a student* in the construction of the meaning of (11) is parallel to the role of *arrived* in (1), while the role of *this guy* in (11) is parallel to that of *a student* in (1). The contribution of *a student* to the semantic representation of (11) is the main predicative condition $student(x)$, where x is instantiated by the discourse referent contributed by the subject. The final representation of (11) is given in (12).

(12)
$$\begin{array}{|l|} \hline d_2 \\ guy(d_2) \\ student(d_2) \\ \hline \end{array}$$

Predicate nominals are predicative NPs. In the rest of this chapter, I deal exclusively with argumental nominals.

16.3.2 Full-fledged Noun Phrases versus Incorporated Nominals

Within the category of argumental nominals, a major structural division is that between full-fledged arguments and incorporated ones. (Whether incorporated nominals are fully projected NPs or not is a language-particular issue; the term *nominal* is used to cover both fully projected NPs and nominals with reduced structure. I am concerned here only with cases where the nominal is visible at the level of clausal semantics and syntax.)

Full-fledged NPs introduce a discourse referent and some restrictive condition(s) on it. They combine with their predicate by A-Instantiation, as a result of which the discourse referent introduced by the NP replaces a particular thematic argument of the main predicative condition. Within this category of NPs further classifications can be made concerning the nature of the restrictive condition(s) contributed, but I will not pursue this issue further here. In languages that use determiners, their main role is to introduce a discourse referent.

Under the analysis proposed by Farkas and de Swart (2003), *incorporated* argumental nominals contribute a predicative condition and no discourse referent.[5] Unlike in the case of predicate nominals, however, this is not a main predicative condition. Rather, such nominals fall under the argumental category because their contribution affects a particular thematic argument of a main predicative condition. The way this happens is not by A-Instantiation but rather by *Unification*, characterized as in (13).

(13) *Unification*
Replace the nth thematic argument of a predicative condition by the thematic argument contributed by the nominal.

As a result of Unification, two predicative conditions end up sharing a thematic argument. Note that Unification, like Instantiation, involves the substitution of a thematic argument of a predicate by a discourse entity contributed by the argument of that predicate. The difference lies only in what that entity is.[6]

I exemplify with articleless singulars in Hungarian.

(14) A   lány bélyeget   gyüjt.
     the girl stamp.ACC collect.3
     'The girl collects stamps.'

What is special here is that the direct object, *bélyeget* 'stamp.ACC', occurs without an article. Farkas and de Swart analyze such bare singulars as contributing a predicative condition based on their lexical head, in this case *stamp(x)*. At the point of combination with the main predicative condition (here *collect(y, z)*), Unification applies, replacing z by x. The subject, as before, is a full-fledged NP that combines with the predicate by A-Instantiation. The final DRS for (14) is given in (15).

(15)
$$\begin{array}{|l|} \hline d_2 \\ \text{girl}(d_2) \\ \text{stamp}(x) \\ \text{collect}(d_2, x) \\ \hline \end{array}$$

The thematic argument affected by Unification, x, remains uninstantiated but restricted by the contribution of the predicate modifier.

In the typology being developed here, the category of full-fledged NPs includes all the NPs whose contribution to semantic representation involves the introduction of a discourse referent, and which combine with their predicate by A-Instantiation. Pronouns, proper names, all kinds of descriptions, and quantificational NPs belong to this category.

The crucial distinction between full-fledged NPs and incorporated ones is that the latter contribute a predicative condition only. The fact that they combine via Unification rather than Instantiation is a result of this property.

16.3.3 Quantificational versus Nonquantificational NPs

Within the category of full-fledged NPs, the fundamental structural distinction is that between quantificational and nonquantificational NPs. Recall that in DRT, quantificational NPs are NPs that lead to tripartite complex DRSs where the quantifier and the information in the NP is part of the restrictor, while the main predication is in the nuclear scope.[7] NPs in this class are those with essentially quantificational determiners, such as *every*, as well as certain NPs with numeral determiners when interpreted distributively. Quantificational determiners introduce a discourse referent, just like nonquantificational determiners, but in addition they contribute a quantifier. Thus, the contribution of *every student* in (16),

(16) Every student arrived.

after D-Instantiation, is the expression in (17).

(17) every d_1: student(d_1)

The contribution of the VP is the main predicative condition *arrive(x)*. When the VP and the subject combine, A-Instantiation replaces x by d_1. Given that this verb has a quantificational argument, the main predicative condition goes into the nuclear scope. The final DRS is given in (18) in the notation used in DRT and in (19) in the formalism introduced in McCawley 1981/1993, which has the advantage of keeping the quantifier and the restrictive condition as one semantic constituent.

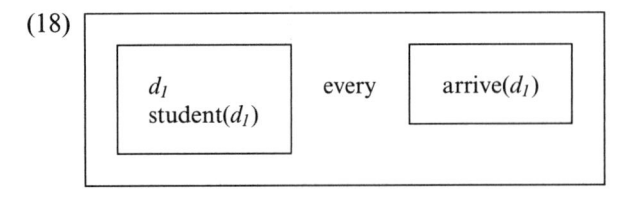

(18)

| d_1 student(d_1) | every | arrive(d_1) |

(19) [d_1: student(d_1)] arrive(d_1)

The truth conditions of complex representations such as these are also complex. The source of the complexity is the fact that a function f satisfies the DRS in (18) if each d_1-version f' of f that satisfies the restrictor is such that it satisfies the nuclear scope as well. A function f' is a d_1-version of f that satisfies the restrictor if f' is just like f except for the value it assigns to d_1, the discourse referent contributed by the quantificational determiner. Quantificational NPs introduce this complex structure associated with complex satisfaction conditions. Nonquantificational NPs do not. The NPs in (20) are all argumental and nonquantificational under this view.

(20) a. John/He arrived.
 b. A (certain)/Some/The/This/ student(s) arrived.

To sum up, the structural classification we have arrived at is the one given in (21).

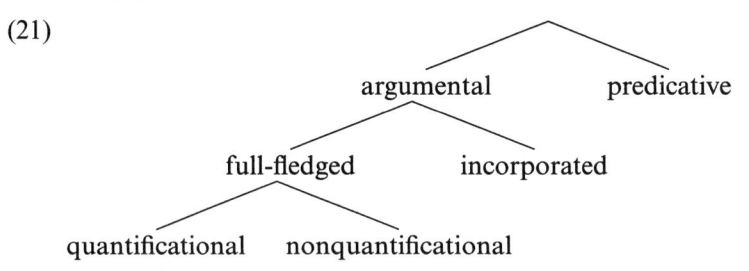

(21)
```
                    argumental              predicative
              full-fledged    incorporated
      quantificational   nonquantificational
```

I turn back to this classification in section 16.5, where I examine ways in which it relates to syntactic structure, thereby justifying the need for recognizing these semantic categories.

16.4 Fine Distinctions

I turn now briefly to fine semantic differentiations that affect full-fledged NPs and concern the mapping of a discourse referent to the model. There are at least three categories of fine distinctions. First, *ontological distinctions* involve the categorization of entities in the model. NPs may bring with them restrictions concerning the ontological category of the entity that may serve as their value, and these restrictions may serve as nominal categorization parameters. Second, NPs may encode restrictions on the mapping process itself. In the framework sketched above, such *mapping distinctions* concern the properties of the functions that end up giving values to the relevant discourse referent. Third, there are *contextual distinctions* that involve the properties of the discourse referent introduced by the NP with respect to the immediately preceding context or with respect to projected future contexts. Below, I restrict attention to one type of ontological distinction only, which is relevant to number interpretation. (For discussion pertinent to other fine distinctions, see Farkas 1997a, 2002.)

Ontological distinctions in their turn may be structural or not. Nonstructural ontological distinctions concern categorization of entities in terms of properties such as animacy or properties involving contexts such as the relation of the entity in question to the speaker.

Structural ontological distinctions concern the internal structure of the entities in the model. One such distinction concerns the kind/individual divide, having to do with whether the entity has individuals as realizations or not, brought onto the linguistic scene by the seminal work of Carlson (1977). Kinds are entities of the former type, individuals are entities of the latter. Another distinction concerns whether the potential values are elements of a lattice structure or not. This difference is at the root of the count/mass distinction. In the case of entities of the former type, the question arises whether they are atoms in the lattice structure or groups, a question directly relevant to the semantics of number. It is this issue that concerns us below, and therefore I give here the basic insights, due to Link (1983).

I assume that the set associated by the function I to "count nouns" (i.e., predicates such as *chair* or *student*) has a join semilattice structure. To exemplify, in a model in which there are three students, a, b, and c, the set $I(student)$ will have the structure in (22).

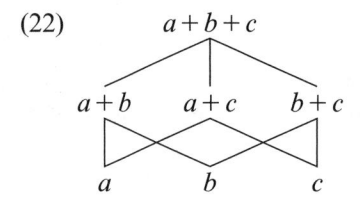

(22)
$$\begin{array}{c} a+b+c \\ a+b \quad a+c \quad b+c \\ a \quad b \quad c \end{array}$$

Here a, b, and c are the atoms in the set of students, while $a+b$, $a+c$, $b+c$, and $a+b+c$ are the groups of students. Positing such a structure is useful in dealing with the semantics of number: the discourse referents introduced by singular NPs whose head noun is *student* take values from the set of atoms in (22), while discourse referents introduced by plural NPs may (or must) take values from the set of groups. I will come back to the details of number interpretation in section 16.5.2. For now, I have only established an ontological distinction between nominals that are associated with atoms in a lattice structure and those that are associated with groups.

16.5 Grammatical Encoding

In this section, I turn to the question of how the various meaning distinctions discussed above are encoded in the grammar. If the typology set up so far is on the right track, the classes it distinguishes should be among the ones that various formal markings are sensitive to. I provide evidence for the relevance of the classifications distinguished above by first looking at clausal and NP-internal syntax and then turning to morphology and more specifically to number interpretation.

16.5.1 Connection with Syntax

A plausible hypothesis is that structural distinctions may be encoded in syntactic structure only. More particularly, I will attempt to show in this section that what McCawley (1988/1998, 314) calls "surface gross combinatorics" of a language may be sensitive to the semantic structural distinctions drawn in section 16.3.

There are three ways in which a syntactic position may be sensitive to a semantic category. (1) The strongest connection between a syntactic position p and a semantic category α exists when a constituent occurs in p if and only if it is of semantic category α. In this case, p will be said to be *dedicated* to the semantic category α: being of semantic category α is a sufficient and necessary condition for occurrence in p. (2) The connection may be weakened to stating that property α is a necessary but not sufficient condition for occurrence in p: if a constituent occurs in p, it must be of semantic category α, but constituents of category α may occur elsewhere as well. In this case, p will be said to be RESERVED for α. (3) A third type of connection may require all constituents with semantic property α to occur in p without α being necessary for occurrence in p. In this case, α will be said to be TIED to p. The rest of this section will recall Szabolcsi's (1997) argument according to which there is a position in Hungarian clausal syntax that is reserved for quantificational NPs, and Farkas and de Swart's (2003) arguments showing that there is a syntactic position in Hungarian that is tied to incorporated nominals. These two points lend support to the need for these two semantic categories, showing that clausal syntax may be sensitive to these structural semantic distinctions.

Szabolcsi (1997), distilling much previous work, proposes that the basic clausal positions in Hungarian are as shown in (23).

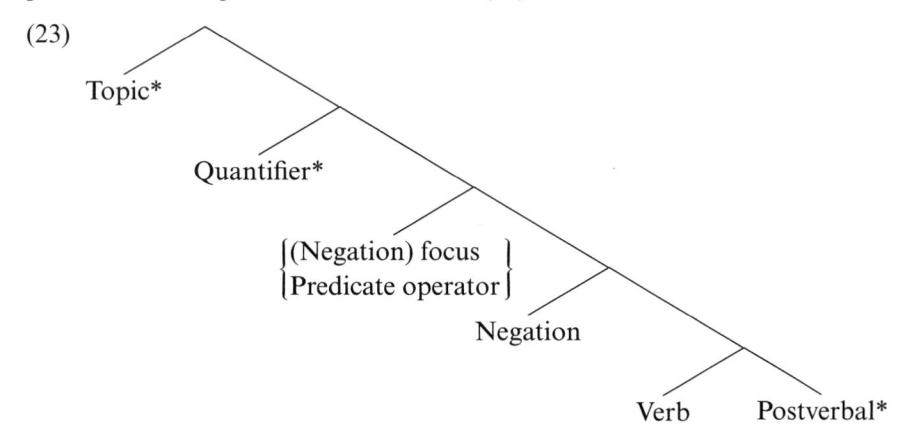

(23)
```
       Topic*
           Quantifier*
                {(Negation) focus }
                {Predicate operator}
                        Negation
                            Verb   Postverbal*
```

The positions of interest here are the Quantifier and the Focus/PredOp nodes. With respect to the former, Szabolcsi's arguments amount to the claim that this syntactic position is reserved for quantificational NPs—in other words, NPs that in DRT terms involve a tripartite structure.[8] Thus, NPs that are necessarily quantificational in this sense, namely, those whose determiner is *minden* 'every' and *valamennyi* 'each', may occur only in two positions: either in Quantifier or postverbally.

(24) a. Mari tegnap   minden gyereket meg-látogatott.
        Mari yesterday every   child.ACC PT-visit.PAST
     b. Mari tegnap   meg-látogatott minden gyereket.
        Mari yesterday PT-visit.PAST   every   child.ACC
        'Yesterday, Mari visited every child.'

Here *Mari* is in Topic position and the universal occurs in Quantifier in (24a) and in a postverbal position in (24b). Adverbs like *tegnap* 'yesterday' may separate the Topic and Quantifier but no other nodes in the preverbal field. The morpheme *meg* is a particle that occurs preverbally when the Focus/PredOp position is empty, but after the verb when that position is filled. The fact that the particle occurs before the verb here shows that *minden gyereket* 'every child.ACC' does not occur in Focus/PredOp. From the position of the adverb, we conclude that it does not occur in Topic either. Note that because these NPs may occur postverbally, Quantifier cannot be said to be dedicated to quantificational NPs.

Szabolcsi (1997) also shows that NPs such as *több, mint hat fiú* 'more than six boys', which can be interpreted either as predicate operators or as quantifiers, may occur in either of the two positions one would expect them to. Interpretation is subtly different depending on where they occur: when in Quantifier, they are necessarily distributive; when in PredOp, they are necessarily collective. (This last fact follows from the assumption that the relation between the restrictor and the nuclear scope is necessarily distributive.)

Turning now to the (Neg/)Focus/PredOp position, the claim defended by Farkas and de Swart (2003) is that this position is tied to incorporated nominals in Hungarian in the sense that if a nominal is incorporated, it must occur in PredOp, but constituents other than incorporated nominals, such as focused constituents, may occur there as well. Obviously, if negation and focused constituents can be shown to occur in a different preverbal position after all, PredOp would be dedicated to incorporated nominals, rather than just tied to them. I will not consider focused nominals further here.

Nominals that occur in PredOp position in Hungarian are bare in the sense that they are not preceded by an article.

(25) A   lány verset   olvas fel.
     the girl poem.ACC   read-PT
     'The girl is reading aloud a poem/poems.'

The postverbal occurrence of the particle shows that the nominal is in PredOp.

Adopting Farkas and de Swart's proposal, the only contribution of a bare singular is a predicative condition. Unlike predicate nominals, however, these nominals are argumental and combine with their predicate by Unification.

Now claiming that the preverbal position where the bare nominal occurs in (25) is tied to incorporated nominals amounts to claiming that bare singulars may not occur anywhere else in Hungarian. This is so because, given that they may only contribute a predicative condition, they may only combine with their predicate by Unification, and that semantic operation is tied to the PredOp position in Hungarian. (26) illustrates that indeed a bare singular may not occur in other positions in the sentence.

(26) a. *Verset   tegnap   Mari olvasott fel.
       poem.ACC yesterday Mari read.PAST-PT
    b. *Mari verset   fel-olvasott.
       Mari poem.ACC PT-read.PAST
    c. *Mari fel-olvasott   verset.
       Mari PT-read.PAST poem.ACC

I conclude, then, that at least some of the semantic structural classes identified in section 16.3 may have a direct tie to clausal syntax. This provides support for semantic theories such as DRT, in which these distinctions can easily be drawn.

With respect to nominal-internal matters, since our claim is that an essential semantic job of determiners is to introduce a discourse referent, we would expect nominals that do not introduce discourse referents—namely, incorporated and predicate nominals—not to necessarily require a determiner. Since the two types of predicate nominals belong to different semantic categories, we do not expect their syntax to be parallel, however. The facts in Hungarian conform to these expectations. In Hungarian, as in many other languages, incorporated nominals must be determinerless. Predicate nominals may occur without a determiner, as exemplified in (27a), as well as with a determiner, as in (27b).

(27) a. Mari orvos.
       Mari doctor
       'Mari is a doctor.'
    b. Mari egy jó   orvos.
       Mari a   good doctor
       'Mari is a good doctor.'

Going into further details of the morphosyntax of predicate nominals would take us too far afield. I have brought them up only to make the point that the approach argued for above predicts that there may be languages that require articles with full-fledged arguments but not necessarily with incorporated nominals or predicate nominals. Given that in the present approach, predicate nominals and incorporated nominals are differentiated both semantically and syntactically, they may well differ in when and how they require or allow articles. The obligatory presence of an article with singular predicate nominals in English has to be explained, under present assumptions, as a syntactic requirement rather than as a semantic one, since the article makes no semantic contribution here.

16.5.2 Connection with Morphology and the Interpretation of Number

A further hypothesis to be explored briefly here is that fine distinctions are encoded in the morphology. The rest of this section deals with the details of number interpretation the framework developed so far allows us. A major concern is to account for McCawley's (1968) observation, later discussed by Ojeda (1992), that plurals are simultaneously the formally marked and the semantically unmarked members of the singular/plural opposition. My proposal involves a further distinction, that between semantically number-neutral nominals and nominals with number entailments. The account is based on Farkas and de Swart 2003.

I assume here that common nouns that may head count NPs denote sets with the internal structure of a join semilattice as in (22), while mass nouns do not. The lack of articles with mass nouns would follow if we assumed that articles and determiners in general presuppose a structured value domain. In what follows, mass nouns will not be dealt with any further.

To capture the fact that in languages that involve a singular/plural distinction the plural is the formally marked member of the pair, let us assume that there is no singular morpheme. NPs that are unmarked for number receive an atomic interpretation owing to the default atomicity entailment in (28).

(28) In the absence of requirements to the contrary, a discourse referent is assigned an atomic value.

Thus, in the default case, the value domain of a discourse referent is the set of atoms of the join semilattice associated with the restrictive predicate contributed by the NP. The contribution of the NP *a chair* when argumental is as given in (29).

(29) d_1: chair(d_1)

The singular interpretation of such an NP is due to (28).

The default atomicity requirement is lifted in the presence of any condition that contradicts it. A determiner such as *two*, for instance, comes with an extra requirement on the discourse referent it introduces, namely, that of being a group consisting of two members. This requirement contradicts and therefore overrides (28). This approach predicts the possibility of interpreting formally singular NPs as plural in case the determiner entails nonatomicity. This, in fact, is the situation in Hungarian. For example, the Hungarian noun phrase *két szék* combines the determiner *két* 'two' and the singular form of *szék* 'chair'. The contribution of this NP (when argumental) is as in (30),

(30) d_1: two(d_1) chair(d_1)

where the value of d_1 is restricted to being chosen from groups of chairs of cardinality two.

The fact that morphologically singular NPs carry a singularity entailment in the absence of special conditions is responsible for the fact that they support singular anaphoric reference only as well as for the fact that they cannot be used in cases where the context or the predicate requires group reference. These two properties are exemplified in (31) and (32).

(31) Mary brought *a chair$_i$*. *It/The chair$_i$* she brought was green./*The chairs she brought$_i$/*They$_i$ were green.

(32) *The student gathered in the square.

As expected, in Hungarian, NPs whose determiners entail nonatomicity may only support plural anaphoric expressions.

(33) Mari hozott   két széket$_i$.   Az asztal mellé tette   őket$_i$.
     Mari bring.PAST two chair.ACC the table near put.PAST 3PL.ACC
     'Mari brought two chairs. She put them near the table.'

The italicized pronoun is third person plural. Using the singular pronoun *azt* would not be appropriate under the relevant interpretation. This is as expected under the assumption that anaphorically linked discourse referents must be given the same value.

Turning now to plural NPs, Farkas and de Swart (2003) propose that the plural marker in a nominal contributes a presupposed discourse referent d_n and a predicative condition of the form *Plural(d_n)*, where d_n is to be bound by the discourse referent introduced by the determiner. Such a condition lifts the default atomicity restriction on this discourse referent and thereby allows groups into its denotation domain.

The question that arises now is how to reconcile this analysis with the claim that the plural is the semantically unmarked member of the singular/plural opposition. This observation is based on the fact that at least in some contexts, the denotation domain of a plural NP may include not only the groups but also the atoms of the relevant structure. Thus, the question in (34)

(34) Have you seen giraffes at the zoo?

may be truthfully answered in the affirmative even if one has only seen a single giraffe at the zoo. The use of the plural exemplified in (34) will be called *inclusive*. It contrasts with the *exclusive* plural, exemplified in (35).

(35) I brought you some presents.

Here, we would be justified to protest the use of the plural, were the speaker to give us a single present. The denotation domain of the plural in (35) is the set of groups in the structure denoted by *present* with the exclusion of its atoms. The question that arises now is whether to assume that plural nominals are ambiguous between an inclusive and an exclusive interpretation, or to leave the choice between these two interpretations to pragmatics. In the former case, we would have to posit two plural conditions: a more general one requiring the value domain to include groups, and a more specific one requiring it to include groups and exclude atoms. Under the pragmatic approach, the plural condition would have the effect of lifting the default atomic interpretation requirement and would thereby necessarily include groups in the denotation domain of the relevant discourse referent, but it would leave the question of whether atoms are excluded or not to pragmatic considerations. In the absence of evidence to the contrary, a nonambiguous treatment of the plural morphology is to be preferred and so I will assume this view here. What is crucial is that the use of a morphologically plural nominal has a number entailment, namely, that the domain from which values are chosen for the discourse referent includes groups. Thus, plural marking is incompatible with situations where a group interpretation is excluded. This explains why plural NPs support only plural anaphoric reference, as illustrated in (36).

(36) Mary saw *some students$_i$. They$_i$/The students she saw$_i$/*She$_i$/*The student she saw$_i$* had graduated from UCSC.

Note also that a plural NP is unacceptable in the presence of contextual atomicity entailments.

(37) a. Mary has a brother and *no other siblings$_i$. Mary's brother$_i$/*Mary's brothers$_i$* must have a hard time.
   b. #Do you have spouses in the U.S.?

The atomic interpretation of discourse referents is the default one, I assume, because, as suggested in McCawley 1968, singular (atomic) reference is the more frequent case, while the plural is the formally marked member because it represents the less frequent one. The analysis given so far, however, correctly predicts that the plural is not semantically unmarked for number since it requires groups to be possible values for the relevant discourse referent.

Two related questions arise at this point: (1) are there instances where number entailments are absent? and (2) what happens in the case of uninstantiated thematic arguments? The combined answer to these questions is that uninstantiated thematic arguments are *number-neutral* in the sense of not contributing any semantic number

Semantic Noun Phrase Typology 383

entailments whatever. Uninstantiated thematic arguments, recall, are not discourse referents and therefore they do not fall under the default atomicity evaluation the latter are subject to. They are interpreted together with the predicate they are an argument of. As such, they may be subject to various predicate entailments, some of which may involve atomicity. In the absence of such external entailments, however, they do not involve any number entailment whatsoever; that is, they are number-neutral.

Under this analysis, uninstantiated thematic arguments are predicted to support either singular or plural anaphoric reference. That this is correct is shown by (38), which contrasts with (39).

(38) The painting was stolen. The person(s) who did it will soon be caught.

(39) a. The painting was stolen by *someone$_i$*. The person(*s)$_i$ who did it will soon be caught.
  b. The painting was stolen by *clever thieves$_i$*. *He$_i$/*The person who did it$_i$/ They$_i$/The people who did it$_i$ will soon be caught.

Incorporated nominals that are not specifically marked as plurals are also predicted to be number-neutral; that is, they are predicted to be fine both in case there is a contextual or lexical atomicity entailment and in case of a group entailment. This is an important characteristic of such nominals that has not figured prominently in previous treatments of semantic incorporation (but see Dayal 1999 for a programmatic proposal along different lines).

The Hungarian examples in (40) and (41) show that this prediction is correct.

(40) A lány bélyeget gyüjt.
 the girl stamp.ACC collect
 'The girl collects stamps.'

(41) János feleséget keres.
 Janos wife.ACC seek
 'Janos is looking for a wife.'

The predicate in (40) has a group entailment on the direct object, yet this direct object can be realized by a morphologically singular incorporated nominal. In (41) a morphologically singular incorporated nominal is used in a situation where there is a contextual atomicity entailment, assuming (41) is uttered in a monogamous society. These nominals then contrast with plurals in being semantically number-neutral.

In conclusion, we have established a three-way distinction with respect to number: singular, plural, and number-neutral. Full-fledged NPs always involve a semantic number entailment (in languages that mark number). They are either morphologically marked (plural), in which case they entail at least the possibility of a group referent, or morphologically singular (unmarked), in which case they either are subject to the default atomicity entailment or entail nonatomic reference. The plural is the unmarked element of the pair in the sense that it has inclusive uses, where group reference is allowed but not required. Morphologically singular incorporated nominals on the other hand, as well as the implicit agent in agentless passives, are number-neutral in the sense that they do not involve any number entailments. At the representational level, we have an opposition between discourse referents and uninstantiated thematic arguments.

In sum, discourse referents and uninstantiated thematic arguments differ under this analysis in that the former but not the latter have atoms as default values, which accounts for the default atomic interpretation of nonincorporated singular NPs as well as for the special cases of morphologically singular but semantically plural NPs, where the D is responsible for the nonatomicity requirement.

The plural morpheme of morphologically plural NPs lifts this default by contributing a condition whose effect is to allow the value domain to include groups. Consequently, plural NPs cannot be used in case group reference is excluded.[9] Uninstantiated thematic arguments, on the other hand, are number-neutral. They may be subject to number entailments from their predicate or the context, but in the absence of such entailments their interpretation is neutral with respect to number. Morphologically singular incorporated nominals are appropriate both when predicate or contextual entailments exclude atoms and when they exclude groups.

16.6 Possible and Impossible Encodings

In the previous sections, we have established a structural typology of nominal expressions as well as one based on fine distinctions and we have seen that the surface gross syntactic combinatorics of a language may be sensitive to the former, while the latter distinctions are encoded within the morphology. At this point, we can speculate that this correlation is not accidental. A hypothesis that captures it is formulated in (42).

(42) Surface gross clausal combinatorics are insensitive to fine nominal distinctions.

Taking "sensitivity" here to include the various types of connections between a syntactic position and a semantic category, (42) means that there will be no gross clausal syntactic position dedicated to, reserved for, or tied to a nominal category defined in terms of a fine semantic distinction. What (42) then excludes is a language where clausal structure is just like in Hungarian except that a syntactic position has a mark such as *atomic*, *animate*, or *kind* indicating that only nominals with these semantic properties may occupy them or that if a nominal has these properties, it must occur in those positions.

Semantic Noun Phrase Typology

Under this hypothesis, fine distinctions would be encoded in nominal syntax, morphology, and the lexicon. These distinctions are involved in selectional restrictions and therefore may end up playing a role at the clausal level. Certain semantic properties that involve such fine distinctions, such as animacy, definiteness, and certain brands of specificity, are crucial in the characterization of grammatical relations and thus are central to matters involving case marking, as work on differential case marking has shown (Bossong 1985; Aissen 2003 and references cited therein). Fine distinctions involving contextual properties of nominals (such as familiarity of reference) are relevant to issues concerning the articulation of information into topic and focus and other matters of information structure.

An interesting hypothesis would involve strengthening (42) to the claim that features encoding fine distinctions are not visible to clausal syntax at all. Fine distinctions then could affect syntax only indirectly, through selectional restrictions, or through their connection to grammatical relations, or through their connection to structural distinctions (including information structure), which in turn affect clausal structure directly. Pursuing this hypothesis is left for the future.

Notes

1. The term *NP* is used here as a cover term for both NPs and DPs.

2. Which argument is replaced by which discourse referent is a matter decided by linking theory, of which nothing will be said in what follows.

3. The implicit agent of agentless passives is one of the many types of implicit arguments found in English. Other types of implicit arguments place particular interpretive constraints on features of the discourse to which they are added, functioning more like anaphoric elements. Consequently, their interpretive properties will be significantly different from those of the agent in agentless passives, whose lack of associated constraints makes it similar to an ordinary indefinite.

4. The distinction between arguments and adjuncts, though relevant, is outside the scope of the present discussion.

5. See Van Geenhoven 1998 for the first detailed account of semantic incorporation. Here, I restrict attention to morphologically singular incorporated nominals. For details of the complex issues raised by incorporated plurals, see Farkas and de Swart 2003, chap. 5.

6. The operation of Unification is similar to Restrict in Chung and Ladusaw 2003.

7. The issue of how the contribution of the other elements of the clause is distributed between the restrictor and the nuclear scope will not concern us here.

8. Szabolcsi also argues, persuasively, that such NPs also introduce a set-level discourse referent. I will ignore this issue here, however.

9. There are various special lexical exceptions that I leave out of the discussion. One is the use of the morphologically plural *they* in cases where groups are excluded, as in (i).

(i) If you marry *someone$_i$*, *they$_i$* will expect to move in here.

Another case is "plural only" NPs such as *scissors* and *trousers*.

References

Aissen, Judith. 2003. Differential object marking: Iconicity vs. economy. *Natural Language and Linguistic Theory* 21, 435–83.

Barwise, Jon, and Robin Cooper. 1981. Generalized quantifiers in natural language. *Linguistics and Philosophy* 4, 159–219.

Bossong, Georg. 1985. *Differentielle Objektmarkierung in den neuiranischen Sprachen.* Tübingen: Gunter Narr Verlag.

Carlson, Greg. 1977. Reference to kinds in English. Doctoral dissertation, University of Massachusetts, Amherst.

Chierchia, Gennaro. 1997. Reference to kinds across languages. *Natural Language Semantics* 6, 339–405.

Chung, Sandra, and William Ladusaw. 2003. *Restriction and saturation.* Cambridge, MA: MIT Press.

Corblin, Francis. 2000. *Représentation du discours et sémantique formelle.* Paris: Presses Universitaires de France.

Dayal, Veneeta. 1999. Bare NPs, reference to kinds and incorporation. In *Proceedings of SALT 9*, ed. by Tanya Matthews and Devon Strolovitch, 58–76. Ithaca, NY: Cornell University, CLC Publications.

Farkas, Donka. 1997a. Dependent indefinites. In *Empirical issues in formal syntax and semantics*, ed. by Francis Corblin, Danièle Godard, and Jean-Marie Marandin, 243–68. Bern: Peter Lang.

Farkas, Donka. 1997b. Evaluation indices and scope. In *Ways of scope taking*, ed. by Anna Szabolcsi, 183–215. Dordrecht: Kluwer.

Farkas, Donka. 2002. Varieties of indefinites. In *Proceedings of SALT 12*, ed. by Brendan Jackson, 59–83. Ithaca, NY: Cornell University, CLC Publications.

Farkas, Donka, and Henriëtte de Swart. 2003. *Semantic incorporation: From argument structure to discourse transparency.* Stanford, CA: CSLI Publications.

Kamp, Hans, and Uwe Reyle. 1993. *From discourse to logic.* Dordrecht: Kluwer.

Kamp, Hans, and Antje Rossdeutcher. 1994. Remarks on lexical structure and DRS construction. *Theoretical Linguistics* 20, 97–167.

Koenig, Jean-Pierre, and Gail Mauner. 2000. A-definites and the discourse status of implicit arguments. *Journal of Semantics* 16, 207–36.

Link, Godehard. 1983. The logical analysis of plurals and mass terms: A lattice-theoretical approach. In *Meaning, use and interpretation of language*, ed. by Rainer Bäuerle, Christoph Schwarze, and Arnim von Stechow, 302–23. Berlin: Walter de Gruyter.

McCawley, James D. 1968. Review of *Current trends in linguistics 3. Language* 44, 556–93.

McCawley, James D. 1970. Where do noun phrases come from? In *Readings in English transformational grammar*, ed. by Roderick A. Jacobs and Peter S. Rosenbaum, 166–83. Waltham, MA: Ginn.

McCawley, James D. 1981. *Everything that linguists have always wanted to know about logic—but were ashamed to ask.* Chicago: University of Chicago Press. 2nd ed., 1993.

McCawley, James D. 1988. *The syntactic phenomena of English.* Chicago: University of Chicago Press. 2nd ed., 1998. References are to the 1998 edition.

Ojeda, Almerindo. 1992. The markedness of plurality. In *The joy of grammar*, ed. by Diane Brentari, Gary N. Larson, and Lynn A. MacLeod, 275–89. Amsterdam: John Benjamins.

Szabolcsi, Anna. 1997. Strategies for scope taking. In *Ways of scope taking*, ed. by Anna Szabolcsi, 109–55. Dordrecht: Kluwer.

Van Geenhoven, Veerle. 1998. *Semantic incorporation and indefinite descriptions.* Stanford, CA: CSLI Publications.

Chapter 17

The Paradox of Mass Plurals   Almerindo E. Ojeda

So we have plural mass nouns, a fact that we'll have to live with.
Jim McCawley, "Lexicography and the Count-Mass Distinction"

17.1 Introduction

The noun *clothes* is somewhat of an embarrassment for semantic theory. On the one hand, it is considered a mass noun. As such, it would gloss as Spanish *ropa* and refer to discrete entities (one or more articles of clothing) taken in bulk rather than collectively. On the other hand, *clothes* is said to be a plural noun. As such, it would refer, like its French equivalent *vêtements*, to discrete entities (two or more articles of clothing) taken collectively rather than in bulk. In short, *clothes* should refer to discrete entities taken in bulk rather than collectively and, at the same time, to discrete entities taken collectively rather than in bulk. This embarrassing predicament is the *paradox of mass plurals*.

The paradox of mass plurals cannot be ignored, as it leads to incorrect empirical predictions. Since mass plurals place incompatible demands on their reference, they would refer either incoherently or vacuously and would therefore be ill-formed on semantic grounds. But there is nothing ill-formed about these nouns. In fact, the reference of the mass plural *clothes* of English is the same as that of the unproblematic Spanish *ropa* mentioned above.

Notice that nothing really changes if we adopt any of the more nuanced interpretations of mass nouns found in the literature. Thus, it has been said that mass nouns refer not to entities that *must* be taken in bulk, but only to entities that *may* be taken in bulk (McCawley 1979; Link 1983). It has also been said that mass nouns may even refer collectively rather than in bulk, but that the entities thus referred to are just

---

I am indebted to Salikoko Mufwene and to Rebecca Wheeler, as well as to an anonymous reviewer, for suggestions that improved significantly the draft of this chapter. Needless to say, this does not make them responsible for any of the remaining shortcomings.

"too small to count" (Quine 1964). The problem is that these analyses still contrast mass nouns and plurals. Thus, plurals refer to entities that *may not* be taken in bulk (or to entities that *are not* too small to count). So mass plurals would refer to entities that both may and may not be taken in bulk (or to entities that both are and are not too small to count). The paradox of mass plurals thus reappears in the more nuanced interpretations of mass reference.

To resolve this paradox, mass plurals are sometimes deemed to be plural only in form, not in content. Here the idea is that there are two kinds of plurality: formal plurality and semantic plurality. Semantic plurality applies to regular plural nouns like *garments* but not to regular mass nouns like *clothing*. Moreover, semantic plurality means what it says and ensures that semantically plural nouns refer to sets of two or more discrete entities taken collectively. Formal plurality, on the other hand, applies only to certain mass nouns, for example *clothes*, and does *not* mean what it says, as it does not ensure that formally plural nouns refer to sets of two or more discrete entities taken collectively. In fact, formal plurality means nothing at all, so its presence on nouns is puzzling, if not outright paradoxical. It follows that regarding mass nouns like *clothes* as pro forma plurals does not quite eliminate our paradox; it just replaces the paradox of mass plurals by the paradox of vacuous plurals.

The purpose of this chapter is to resolve the paradox of mass plurals. To do so, I will build on certain ideas advanced by Salikoko Mufwene in a series of papers (Mufwene 1980a,b, 1981, 1984) and split the received opposition between the singular and the plural in two: an opposition between the singular and the cosingular, and an opposition between the plural and the coplural. Plural mass nouns like *clothes* can then be regarded as cosingular rather than plural. As we will see, cosingular nouns can refer to entities taken in bulk—but without having to refer, at the same time, to entities taken collectively.

Mass plurals like *clothes* should not be confused with nouns like *beers*, *wines*, or *whiskeys*. As explained by Pelletier and Schubert (1989) and others, these nouns refer to discrete entities, here kinds or units of alcoholic beverages, taken collectively two or more at a time. They do not refer to beer, wine, or whiskey taken in bulk. Consequently, they are count plurals that derive from mass nouns; they are not examples of the paradoxical mass plurals that will be investigated here. Yet my proposals for mass plurals will have a bearing on these count plurals. I will therefore address them below, in section 17.5.

Interestingly, variants of the paradox of mass plurals arise with mass nouns in general. Consider *clothing*, a slightly more general mass noun than *clothes*.[1] This noun is generally considered singular. But the notion of a singular mass noun is just as paradoxical as that of a plural mass noun. Being singular, *clothing* would be expected to refer to discrete entities taken individually rather than in bulk. And, being a mass noun, it would be expected to refer to discrete entities taken in bulk rather than indi-

Paradox of Mass Plurals

vidually. It follows that *clothing* should refer to entities that are taken individually rather than in bulk and, at the same time, in bulk rather than individually. These requirements are, of course, impossible to meet concurrently.

To avoid this second paradox—call it the *paradox of mass singulars*—one might claim that singularity is really unmarkedness with respect to number. But this will not do. Although singularity may be unmarked in form, it is not unmarked in meaning. Consider simple pairs like *the man* and *the men* (or *your man* and *your men*, or *some man* and *some men*, or *what man* and *what men*). All of these pairs exhibit equipollent contrasts between one man and more than one man; they do not show markedness contrasts between more than one man (the marked option) and an unspecified number of men (the unmarked one). But if the singular were semantically unmarked with respect to number, where would the equipollent contrasts come from? Spurious ambiguities in the determiners? Transderivational constraints making underspecified nouns singular if they have plural counterparts? Instead of claiming that a mass noun like *clothing* is singular or unmarked, I will describe it as being *coplural*. As we will see, coplural nouns will be able to refer to entities taken in bulk, but without having to refer, at the same time, to entities taken individually.

Consequently, I will propose that linguistic theory should not limit itself to the traditional opposition between singularity and plurality, but should avail itself of the full square of numerical opposition shown in (1) (in addition to the opposition between count and mass reference).

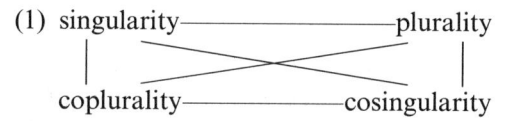

(1) singularity─────────plurality
     │   ╲   ╱   │
     │   ╳   │
     │   ╱   ╲   │
     coplurality──────cosingularity

Only then will it do justice to the interaction between mass reference and grammatical number and resolve the paradox of mass plurals.

It should be clear that, in order to be meaningful, the proposals made here depend on theories of number and countability that will actually back the distinctions between the *plural* and the *cosingular* and between the *singular* and the *coplural* with real differences. The development of such theories will therefore be a central part of this chapter. But before we turn to them, it will be helpful to get a sense of the robustness of the paradox we are trying to resolve. Let us therefore look at the pervasiveness of mass plurals in three unrelated languages (English, Lingala, and Zuni).

17.2 The Importance of the Paradox of Mass Plurals

Clothes is just one of the many mass plurals of English. Other common examples are *cattle*, *brains* (in the sense of *smarts*), and *guts* (in the sense of *balls*). Jespersen (1954, sec. 5.28) presents the following list of mass plurals—and he points out that this list is only partial:

(2) chattel(s), effects, stocks, victuals, cates (Scottish), vivers, sweetmeats, molasses, oats, hops, weeds, brains, bowels, cinders, curds, embers, grounds, dregs, hards, lees, proceeds, remains, vails, contents, belongings, (paper) hangings, leavings, sharings, sweepings, winnings, ashes, chemicals, vegetables, greens, eatables, drinkables, sweets, sours, bitters, cordials, movables, valuables, necessaries, dues, assets, goods, wages, measles, mumps, hysterics, shingles, shivers, rickets, chills, throes, vives, earlier uses of pox and smallpox (cf. pock marks, pock pitted, cowpock), blues, creeps, dumps, jumps, sulks, sullens

The plurality (or the nonsingularity) of these nouns is clear from their agreement and their anaphora.

(3) a. *The clothes is dirty.
    b. The clothes are dirty.

(4) a. *Pick up this clothes.
    b. Pick up these clothes.

(5) a. *I need a clothes.
    b. I need some clothes.

(6) a. *I need clothes that will take care of itself.
    b. I need clothes that will take care of themselves.

As to their mass nature, notice that these nouns reject all forms of modification in terms of number, be they definite (7a) or indefinite (7b–c) (see McCawley 1979, 172).

(7) a. *I've just bought five clothes.
    b. *I've just bought several clothes.
    c. *Many clothes are too expensive for me to buy.

Only if the nouns in (7) are taken as taxonomical count nouns (i.e., nouns referring to kinds of clothes) can the sentences that contain them make any sense. So the sentences in (7) make sense only if the relevant nouns do not have mass interpretations. Moreover, consider the following scenario:

If Fred's wardrobe consists of 2 pairs of shoes, 2 pairs of socks, 1 pair of swimming trunks, and 4 T-shirts, and mine consists of 1 pair of shoes, 1 pair of socks, 1 pair of levis [*sic*], 2 shirts, and 1 jacket, it would be strange to say that Fred has more clothes than I do, even though Fred has 9 or 13 articles of clothing (depending on whether a pair of shoes or of socks counts as 1 or 2 articles of clothing) but I have only 6 or 8. I conjecture that the reason for this is that Fred's 9 or 13 articles of clothing don't clothe him as fully as my 6 or 8 articles clothe me. (McCawley 1979, 171)

Paradox of Mass Plurals 393

What this shows is that the amount of clothes, like the amounts expressed by all extended mass nouns, is measured in terms of volume rather than number. Given all these facts, it looks like we must conclude that *"clothes* is evidently a plural mass noun, as are such words as *brains*, *guts*, and *intestines*.... So we have plural mass nouns, a fact that we'll have to live with" (McCawley 1979, 172). But mass plurals are not limited to English. As we will see in (10), they can also be found in Lingala, a Bantu language of Central Africa.

Being Bantu, Lingala assigns nouns to noun classes and forces them to bear prefixes and trigger agreements based on this assignment. Following Bwantsa-Kafungu (1970, 44), the nominal classes of Lingala and their prefixes are as laid out in (8).[2]

(8) Class   Prefix
    1   mo (or zero)
    2   ba
    3   mo
    4   mi
    5   li
    6   ma
    7   e
    8   bi
    9   N (or zero)
    10   N (or zero)
    11   lo
    (12   attested in Bantu languages other than Lingala)
    (13   attested in Bantu languages other than Lingala)
    14   bo
    15   ko

Glossed and parsed examples of these noun classes are given in (9).

(9)   1   mo-bóti   'parent'   (or ∅-tatá 'father')
    2   ba-bóti   'parents'   (or ba-tatá 'fathers')
    3   mo-sapi   'finger'
    4   mi-sapi   'fingers'
    5   li-táma   'cheek'
    6   ma-táma   'cheeks'
    7   e-lòkò   'thing'
    8   bi-lòkò   'things'
    9   n-dáko   'house'   (or ∅-zando 'market')
    10   n-dáko   'houses'   (or ∅-zando 'markets')
    11   lo-kolo   'leg'

6	ma-kolo	'legs'
12	*	*
13	*	*
14	bo-ndóki	'rifle'	(or bo-bóto 'tenderness')
6	ma-ndóki	'rifles'	(but *ma-bóto 'tendernesses')
15	ko-linga	'to love'

In light of the contrasts in (9) and many others like them, it is tempting to regard the odd-numbered classes in (8) as *singular* and the even-numbered ones as *plural*. This, in fact, is the standard view. But subscribing to it leads us directly into the paradox of mass plurals. Consider the nouns in (10). As can be seen from the *ma* prefix they all bear, these nouns must be assigned to class 6 of the table in (8). Under the standard view, they would all be plural.

(10) ma-í   'water'
     ma-sanga   'drink, beverage'
     ma-kilá   'blood'
     ma-súba   'urine'
     ma-fúta   'oil, fat'
     ma-lási   'perfume'
     ma-belé   'earth, dirt, soil'
     ma-kála   'charcoal'
     ma-keléle   'noise'
     ma-táta   'trouble'
     ma-wa   'sadness'
     ma-yéle   'wisdom'
     (Mufwene 1980b, 1033)[3]

Yet, as one might gather from their glosses, all of the forms in (10) are mass nouns; they name "stuff" or "entities taken in bulk." One way to make this point is to observe that these nouns are, like true mass nouns, outside the opposition of number; for, although these nouns are generally considered plural, they are also known to lack singular counterparts. Indeed, what *could* be the singular counterpart of *water*, *drink*, *blood*, *clothes*, *cattle*, and so on? Nouns like *maí*, *masanga*, and *makilá* lack singulars for the same reason that *clothes*, *cattle*, and *brains* do: they are all mass nouns.

Although the nouns in (10) lack singular counterparts, they still have what we may call corresponding *singulatives*, essentially measure nouns naming appropriate units of the stuff in question, but taken individually.[4] These counterparts are nouns that take the *li* prefix, thereby signaling their membership in class 5 of the table in (8).

(11) a. ma-nkundú   'tripe'
        li-nkundú   'unit or cut of tripe'
     b. ma-kémba   'plantain'
        li-kémba   'single plantain or bunch of plantains'
     c. ma-sángó   'corn'
        li-sángó   'ear or grain of corn'

Interestingly, these singulatives may then pluralize as class 6 nouns bearing a *ma* prefix. These plurals would therefore be *homophones* of the mass nouns we started with, so that *maí* should be glossed either 'water' or 'units of water'. This is perhaps clearest when the usual units of the stuff in question are spatially disjoint.

(12) a. ma-lálá   'mass of orange'/'two or more oranges'
     b. ma-ngoló   'mass of mango'/'two or more mangoes'
     c. ma-tungúlu   'mass of onion'/'two or more onions'

The ambiguity persists in certain environments, as shown in (13).

(13) a. to-sómb-í   ma-lála
        we-buy-PERF CL6-orange
        'We bought orange.'/'We bought oranges.'
     b. to-sómb-í   ma-lálá   míngi
        we-buy-PERF CL6-orange a-lot
        'We bought a lot of orange.'/'We bought a lot of oranges.'

But it is resolved in others, notably in conjunction with numerals. Consider for example (14), where *malálá* and *makála* can only have the plural senses 'oranges' and 'pieces of charcoal', not the mass senses 'orange' and 'charcoal'.

(14) a. to-sómb-í   ma-lálá   mineí
        we-buy-PERF CL6-orange four
        'We bought four oranges.'
     b. to-sómb-í   ma-kála   mibalé
        we-buy-PERF CL6-charcoal two
        'We bought two pieces of charcoal.'

But avoidance of direct construction with numerals is, of course, a property of mass nouns, if not the criterial one. This is therefore a second way of making the case that the forms in (10) are true mass nouns (see Mufwene 1980b, sec. 2.6). A third would invoke the well-known inability of mass nouns to undergo modification in terms of size.

(15) *ka (mwá) malálá
      small/tiny orange

So, if the nouns in (10) are plural, then we would have plural mass nouns in Lingala—a paradox that we would again have to live with.[5]

It should be pointed out that the features of Lingala described above are not exceptional in Bantu. According to Welmers (1973, 159), there is a semantic correlation in the large Bantu family between being a noun that denotes masses or liquids and being a noun that belongs to the plural class 6. There is even some awareness of the peculiarities these plural mass nouns exhibit, as Welmers (1973, 163, 166, 206) proposes the creation of a special subclass "6a" for those nouns in class 6 that lack singular counterparts (and are excluded, for example, from numerical environments like the ones in (14)).

Beyond English and Lingala, the paradox of plural mass nouns appears also in Zuni.[6] To see this, notice first that Zuni uses the suffix (or suffixes) *we* and *:we* to mark plurality. This is borne out by the contrasts in (16) and the *pluralia tantum* in (17).

(16) a. sa-'le   'dish'
        sa-we   'dishes'
     b. he-'le   'coin'
        he-we   'coins'
     c. 'achiya-nne   'knife'
        achiya-:we   'knives'
     d. simi-nne   'needle'
        simi-:we   'needles'

(17) a. lhashshina-:we   'parents'
     b. moha-:we   'testicles'
     c. 'atuna-:we   'eyeglasses'

Notice next that, although Zuni leaves some mass nouns uninflected for number (18), it seems to have a definite preference for marking them plural, as indicated in (19) by the presence of the plural suffix (or suffixes) mentioned above.

(18) 'ate   'blood'
     uwaku   'coal'
     he'sho   'pine resin, rubber, chewing gum'
     ma:k'ose   'salt'
     ma:chikwa   'sugar'

(19) 'o-we   'flour, powder'
     'ohe-:we   'brains, marrow'
     'u-we   'wool'
     'uhe-:we   'cotton'
     ha-we   'alfalfa, hay'

Paradox of Mass Plurals

397

haytoshna-:we	'procedure'
k'oli-:we	'metallic taste or smell'
kyasilili-:we	'oats'
k'ya-:we	'water'
k'yali-:we	'honey'
k'ya'opi-:we	'beer, vinegar'
k'yachikwa-:we	'soda'
k'yapali-:we	'whiskey'
lhashshi-:we	'old age'
lheya-:we	'clothes'
ma-we	'salt'
mahe-:we	'feces'
maso-:we	'muscle'
nochapi-:we	'coffee'
poche-:we	'garbage'
kwik'a-:we	'milk'
so-we	'dust, sand, soil'
sho-we	'sperm'
yak'o-:we	'vomit'

17.3 Models for the Interpretation of Mass Nouns

We will resolve the paradox of mass plurals by interpreting them model-theoretically. To do so, we will need to characterize the models (or ontologies) against which these nouns will be interpreted. The interpretation of the mass nouns in question, and the resolution of the paradox of mass plurals, will be proposed in section 17.4 and extended in section 17.5. Potential objections to this resolution will be addressed in section 17.6.

Let us say that the *universe of discourse* of a particular occasion of linguistic use is the set of entities one can talk about on such an occasion. One can talk about an entity in a variety of ways: say, by mentioning it with a proper name (*Cerberus*), by referring to it with a definite description (*the three-headed dog held in classical mythology to guard the entrance of Hades*), by referring back to it anaphorically (*the aforementioned dog*), or by pointing to it deictically (*that dog*), possibly in conjunction with pointing to it gesturally. As these examples imply, one can talk about things that do not exist in the real world. And there may also be things in the real world that one cannot talk about.

Next, let us say that the *partitive relation* of a particular occasion of linguistic use is the *be-part-of* or *be-some-of* relation (compare the Spanish *formar-parte-de* relation and the French *faire-partie-de* relation). Technically, it is a binary relation on the universe of discourse for that occasion, namely, the one that applies to an ordered pair if and only if one can say, on that occasion, that the first member of the pair is part of the second. To illustrate: Consider an occasion of linguistic use in which one may talk, both individually and collectively, about the keys of my piano. One may say, on that occasion, that the keys of my piano taken individually are part of the keys of my piano taken collectively. Or, consider an occasion of use in which one may talk both about the coffee each of us had this morning and about the coffee all of us had this morning. One may say, on such an occasion, that the coffee each of us had this morning is part of the coffee all of us had this morning.

It should again be pointed out that the partitive relation holds if and only if one can *say* that some entity is part of another (on a particular occasion of linguistic use). It does not require that the former in fact *be* part of the latter, or indeed that any entity truly be part of the latter. All that is needed is that the partitive relation can be asserted in ordinary use. As Link (1983) insisted, in matters of ontology, semantics must follow use.

Armed with these two notions, we now say that the model for the interpretation of mass nouns on a particular occasion of linguistic use is simply the ordered pair formed by the universe of discourse of such an occasion followed by the partitive relation of that occasion. Since this term is rather cumbersome, we will refer to these models simply as *models for the interpretation of mass nouns*. If we bear in mind that these models are always relative to occasions of use, no confusion should arise from this abbreviatory convention.

Models for the interpretation of mass nouns have a number of important properties.[7] Chief among them is atomlessness. Intuitively, models for the interpretation of nouns are *atomless* if and only if any time one can talk about any given entity, one can also talk about part of it; so models do not have any minimal parts or *atoms*. To illustrate: Take the keys of my piano. Any time one may talk about them, one may talk about part of them (20a), about part of part of them (20b), about part of part of part of them (20c), and so on.

(20) a. The white keys of my piano are part of the keys of my piano.
 b. The first white key of my piano is part of the white keys of my piano.
 c. The front of the first white key of my piano is part of the first white key of my piano.

And what we can say about the keys of my piano holds in general. Notice, for example, that we can even talk about part of a speaker, an entity commonly regarded as prototypically individual (e.g., *part of me agrees with part of you; part of the part of me that agrees with you likes part of the part of you that agrees with me . . .*). A case can therefore be made that models for the interpretation of nouns are in general atomless.

Since the atomlessness of models for the interpretation of mass nouns will play a large role in resolving the paradox of mass plurals, it might be worthwhile to address potential objections to it right away. It might be objected, for example, that there are entities—call them *elementary particles*—that cannot be split. Perhaps. But the point is not that they can be *split*, but that parts of them can be *talked about*, and this can always be done (e.g., *the core of an elementary particle*, *the core of the core of an elementary particle*,...). Or it might be objected that some entities cannot be split without ceasing to be what they are (part of a key is not a key anymore; part of me is not me anymore). True but irrelevant. All we need to establish atomlessness is that everything may have parts (that one can talk about) ad infinitum, not that parts will preserve essences.

Although these objections can be disposed of cleanly at this point, they will have to be faced again when we interpret mass nouns as atomless. In the meantime, let us recapitulate this section by saying that we have defined "model for the interpretation of mass nouns on a particular occasion of linguistic use" as a relational structure $(E, <)$ in which E is the universe of discourse for that occasion and $<$ is the partitive relation on E. We have also made a case that this relational structure is *atomless* in the sense that for every $x \in E$ there will be some $y \in E$ such that $y < x$.

17.4 The Paradox of Mass Plurals Resolved

Let M be a model for the interpretation of mass nouns. This means that there exist a set E and a binary relation $<$ on E such that $M = (E, <)$. Pick any $F \subseteq E$ such that F either is the empty set or else consists of nothing more and nothing less than some $x \in E$ together with every $y \in E$ such that $y < x$. F is commonly said to be an "ideal of M."

Ideals are prima facie candidates for the interpretation of mass nouns. Take for example the mass noun *clothing*. It should refer vacuously (i.e., to the empty set) on any occasion of linguistic use in which one cannot talk about clothing; on all other occasions, it should refer to all the clothing one can talk about together with anything that can be said to be part thereof. In short, *clothing* should refer to an ideal. Included in this ideal will be every individual item of clothing, every combination of individual items of clothing, every part of any individual item of clothing, and any combination of parts of individual items of clothing. In other words (and if models for the interpretation of mass nouns are indeed atomless), this ideal will contain, as desired, nothing more and nothing less than discrete items of clothing taken in bulk.

To ensure that mass nouns are interpreted as ideals, we will first constrain the interpretation of their stems as indicated in (21).

(21) *Mass stems*
   The reference of any *mass stem* relative to a model for the interpretation of mass nouns is an ideal of the model.

This will already ensure that all the bare mass stems of Zuni given in (18) will be interpreted as ideals. It will also ensure that the stems inside the inflected mass nouns of Zuni given in (19) will be interpreted as ideals. And the same can be said for the stems inside the prefixed nouns of Lingala given in (10). But what about the inflected mass nouns of these languages? For these, we will introduce a notion of *relative minimality*.

Let E be the universe of discourse of some model M for the interpretation of mass nouns. Let x be an element of E, and let F be a subset of E. We will say that x is a *minimal element* of F if and only if (1) x is an element of F, and (2) no element of F can be said to be part of x. We will also say that F has *minimal elements* if and only if there is at least one element of E that is a minimal element of F.

To illustrate: Notice that F will not have minimal elements if it is empty. Otherwise, it will have minimal elements if it is finite. If F is infinite, then it may or may not have minimal elements depending on the choice of F. Thus, F may have minimal elements if it forms, for example, an infinitely ascending chain with the partitive relation of M, and it will not have minimal elements if it forms an infinitely descending chain with it.

The notion of minimality as just defined is relative in the following sense. Since models for the interpretation of nouns are all atomless, no element of the universe of discourse of any model can be a minimal element of that universe ("absolute minimality"). Yet it may be a minimal element of any number of subsets of the universe; it will be minimal relative to them ("relative minimality").

Our interest in whether subsets have minimal elements or not stems from the fact that no ideal of a model for the interpretation of mass nouns has minimal elements. This fact follows directly from the definition of *ideal* and from the fact that models for the interpretation of nouns are atomless.

Equipped with this notion of relative minimality, we may be tempted to interpret singular nouns as relative minima taken individually and plural nouns as relative minima taken collectively. One way to do so is to interpret number inflections as follows:

(22) *Number inflections (part 1)*
   a. The reference of a *singular inflection* relative to a model for the interpretation of mass nouns is a function that assigns, to each subset of the universe of discourse of the model, its set of minimal elements taken individually one at a time.

Paradox of Mass Plurals 401

b. The reference of a *plural inflection* relative to a model for the interpretation of mass nouns is a function that assigns, to each subset of the universe of discourse of the model, its set of minimal elements taken collectively two or more at a time.[8]

Unfortunately, this will not do for mass nouns. We have seen that ideals do not contain minimal elements. This means that the semantic effect of applying the singular inflection as interpreted in (22a) to a mass stem as interpreted in (21) will necessarily be vacuous.

(23) $[\![\text{MASS STEM} + \text{SG}]\!] = [\![\text{SG}]\!]([\![\text{MASS STEM}]\!]) = \varnothing$

It would follow that so-called singular mass nouns should be ill formed on semantic grounds. But, as we have seen, there is nothing ill formed about these nouns. The perfectly well formed *clothing* is one of them. We thus arrive at the paradox of mass singulars.

Moreover, if ideals do not have minimal elements, then they can hardly have two or more of them. This means that the semantic effect of imposing the plural inflection as interpreted in (22b) on a mass stem as interpreted in (21) should be vacuous as well.

(24) $[\![\text{MASS STEM} + \text{PL}]\!] = [\![\text{PL}]\!]([\![\text{MASS STEM}]\!]) = \varnothing$

It would again follow that so-called plural mass nouns should be ill formed on semantic grounds. But, as we have seen, there is nothing ill formed about these nouns. The perfectly well formed *clothes* is one of them. This, of course, is the paradox of mass plurals.

But suppose we had, in addition to the number inflections in (22), the inflections in (25).

(25) *Number inflections (part 2)*
  a. The reference of a *cosingular inflection* relative to a model for the interpretation of mass nouns is a function that assigns, to each subset of the universe of discourse of the model, the set-theoretic difference between the subset and its minimal elements taken individually one at a time.
  b. The reference of a *coplural inflection* relative to a model for the interpretation of mass nouns is a function that assigns, to each subset of the universe of discourse of the model, the set-theoretic difference between the subset and its set of minimal elements taken collectively two or more at a time.

Now take any of the so-called plural mass nouns we have been talking about. Suppose that it is formed by a mass stem plus a number inflection. Suppose further that this inflection is the cosingular (COSG) inflection interpreted in (25a) rather than the plural inflection interpreted in (22b). Given (21) and (25a), the reference of such a noun would be the set of nonminimal elements of an ideal. But, as we have seen, all the elements of an ideal are nonminimal relative to it. So the reference of any "plural mass noun" would just be the original ideal the mass stem referred to.

(26) $[\![\text{MASS STEM} + \text{COSG}]\!] = [\![\text{COSG}]\!]([\![\text{MASS STEM}]\!])$
$= [\![\text{MASS STEM}]\!] - [\![\text{SG}]\!]([\![\text{MASS STEM}]\!])$
$= [\![\text{MASS STEM}]\!] - \varnothing$
$= [\![\text{MASS STEM}]\!]$

It follows that so-called plural mass nouns may have a coherent meaning after all; they can refer to a *set of entities taken in bulk* (but without having to refer, at the same time, to entities taken collectively). The paradox of mass plurals is thus resolved. All that was needed was to reanalyze their plurality as cosingularity (in the context of atomless models and ideal-denoting mass stems).

Notice that the interpretations in (25) can also resolve the paradox of singular mass nouns. Take any of the so-called singular mass nouns we have talked about. Suppose that it is formed by a mass stem plus a number inflection. Suppose further that this inflection is the coplural (COPL) inflection interpreted in (25b) rather than the singular inflection interpreted in (22a). Given (21) and (25b), the reference of such a noun would be the set of elements of an ideal that are not minimal elements of the ideal taken collectively two or more at a time. But, since none of the elements of an ideal are minimal, none can be taken collectively two or more at a time. So the reference of any singular mass noun would just be the original ideal the mass stem referred to.

(27) $[\![\text{MASS STEM} + \text{COPL}]\!] = [\![\text{COPL}]\!]([\![\text{MASS STEM}]\!])$
$= [\![\text{MASS STEM}]\!] - [\![\text{PL}]\!]([\![\text{MASS STEM}]\!])$
$= [\![\text{MASS STEM}]\!] - \varnothing$
$= [\![\text{MASS STEM}]\!]$

Incidentally, notice that both of the inflections in (25) can combine meaningfully with any mass stem and yield the same result when they do. This is a mixed blessing. On the one hand, it allows us to account for the fact that the English cosingular *clothes* is synonymous with the Spanish coplural *ropa*. It is problematic, however, in that no mass nouns can ever be both cosingular and coplural. Thus, while English *clothes* calls for cosingular agreement (28a), Spanish *ropa* requires coplural agreement (28b).

(28) a. My clothes *is/are here.
    b. Mi ropa   está/*están aquí.
       my clothes is/are   here
       'My clothes are here.'

Paradox of Mass Plurals 403

Unless the grammatical number of mass nouns can be predicted on general grounds (see Wierzbicka 1988), we would have to explicitly indicate this information for them, say, as lexical stipulations. This would allow us to handle contrasts like that in (28) and at the same time account for synonymies like that of *clothes* and *ropa*.

It should be pointed out that the interpretations of number inflections given in (22) and (25) do not work only with mass nouns. They work with count nouns as well. To see this, we will first need two definitions. Let M be a model for the interpretation of mass nouns. Let E be the universe of discourse of M. Let F be a subset of E. We will say that the elements of F are *discrete* if no element of E can be said to be part of any two of them.

Now, let F be a subset of E whose elements are discrete. Let G be the set consisting of (1) the elements of F taken individually one at a time, and (2) the elements of F taken collectively two or more at a time. We will call G an *individuation* of M. To illustrate: Let a, b, c be three discrete garments taken individually, say, the three pieces of a three-piece suit. Gather these garments into a set. Add to this the set $\{ab, ac, bc, abc\}$, consisting of the said garments taken collectively two or more at a time. The resulting set is an individuation that we may represent as in (29).

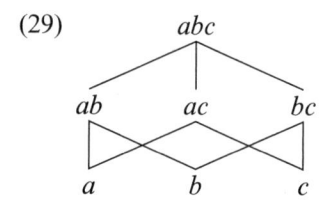

(29)
```
         abc
        / | \
      ab  ac  bc
       ><    ><
      a   b   c
```

Intuitively, an individuation is a set of discrete entities taken either individually (a, b, c) or collectively (ab, ac, bc, abc). Individuations are so called because they represent the ways in which a collective entity like abc can be split into the three discrete entities a, b, c. Since the discrete entities of an individuation will be indivisible relative to the individuation, individuations correspond to ways of *individuating* collective entities, that is, to ways of splitting them into the individuals that make them up.

Individuations play a central role in the interpretation of count nouns. Suppose we were to constrain the interpretation of count stems as indicated in (30).

(30) *Count stems*

The reference of any *count stem* relative to a model for the interpretation of mass nouns is an individuation of the model.

Thus, if we apply the singular inflection (22a) to a count stem like *garment*, we will get the set of individual garments taken individually one at a time, which is what we would want the singular noun *garment* to denote.

(31) $[\![\text{garment} + \text{SG}]\!] = [\![\text{SG}]\!]([\![\text{garment}]\!])$
$= [\![\text{SG}]\!](\{a, b, c, ab, ac, bc, abc\})$
$= \{a, b, c\}$

And if we apply the plural inflection (22b) to this count stem, we will get the set of individual garments taken collectively two or more at a time, which is also what we would want the plural noun *garments* to denote.

(32) $[\![\text{garment} + \text{PL}]\!] = [\![\text{PL}]\!]([\![\text{garment}]\!])$
$= [\![\text{PL}]\!](\{a, b, c, ab, ac, bc, abc\})$
$= \{ab, ac, bc, abc\}$

Interestingly, if we inflect a count stem for cosingularity, we will get the same result as if we had inflected it for plurality. And if we inflect a count stem for coplurality, we will get the same result as if we had inflected it for singularity. These results would also seem to be as desired.

Note that the account we have just developed predicts, correctly, that, while count nouns will participate meaningfully in the opposition of number (compare [31] and [32]), mass nouns will not. If a mass noun is cosingular, then its singular counterpart will be vacuous, and if it is coplural, then its plural counterpart will likewise be vacuous. Mass nouns will therefore stand, as desired, outside the opposition of number.

The account just developed will also support an account of all the other, well-known differences between count nouns and mass nouns (tolerance of enumeration, ordering, *one*-pronominalization, modification in terms of size and shape, etc.), as all of these differences can be predicated on the fact that count nouns refer to individuations whereas mass nouns refer to ideals.

17.5 The Metamorphosis of Mass Nouns

It is well known that mass nouns may morph into count nouns. Thus, even though *beer*, *wine*, and *whiskey* are normally mass nouns, they can turn into count nouns, be they singular or plural, in contexts like the following:

(33) a. I'll have another beer/wine/whiskey.
   b. I had too many beers/wines/whiskeys already.

These count nouns are, in fact, what we called *singulatives* in (11)–(12).

To account for these metamorphoses, it is natural to propose a family of operations that map ideals into individuations whose minimal elements partition the maximal element of the ideal. To be more precise, let E be the universe of discourse of some model M. Let x be an element of E. Let I be the ideal of M consisting of some entity x and anything that can be said to be part of x. Split x into two or more discrete parts. Take these parts and construct the individuation that has these entities as its minimal elements. This is an operation that maps an ideal into an individuation.[9] We will call it *singulative formation*. There will be as many operations of singulative formation as there are ways of splitting x into a set of discrete entities.

To illustrate: Let us say that all the clothes we can talk about are contained in a particular three-piece suit. On this occasion of linguistic use, *clothes* will refer to the ideal consisting of this three-piece suit and anything that can be said to be part of it. This ideal is, of course, atomless. Included in this ideal are, for example, half of these clothes, half of half of these clothes, and so on without end. Now, it is natural to split this three-piece suit into the three pieces that make it up—the pants, the vest, and the jacket. These three garments are discrete, as no two of them have any part in common. We may therefore construct an individuation that has the pants, the vest, and the jacket as its minimal elements. The operation that maps the ideal into the individuation is an operation of singulative formation. Other singulative formations would map the ideals of beer, wine, or whiskey into the individuations based on the glasses or servings thereof. These individuations would be involved in the count nouns of (33). To be more specific, the individuations involved in the count nouns of (33) would be the referents of the count *stems* contained therein, and the number inflections in (22) or (25) would pick the minimal or nonminimal portions of these individuations as called for in (33a) and (33b).

Thus, given the proposals made so far, the count senses in (33) will arise as follows. Recall that the mass stems in *beer/wine/whiskey* are specified (coplural) for number. This will happen either predictably via general principles or idiosyncratically via lexical specification. In either case, these mass stems will not be able to bear any number specification other than cosingular. But they may also undergo singulative formation as indicated above. If they do, they will morph into count stems. As things stand, these count stems would be unmarked for number. They may therefore inflect for singular (or coplural) or plural (or cosingular). As it turns out, they would be *coerced* to inflect in one of these ways in (33), as *another* requires a singular nominal and *too many* calls for a plural head. And similar solutions are available for the Bantu count nouns in (11) and (12).

It should be added that nothing said so far prevents *cosingular* mass nouns from morphing into count nouns under contextual pressure. And this is as desired. Metamorphoses of cosingular mass nouns can be documented with the following examples, all of which are taken from simple Google searches:

(34) a. He had a hard time finding a clothes to fit.
 b. There are too many clothes in that suitcase.

(35) a. The U.S. Department of Agriculture has estimated that it takes as many as 34 acres to raise a cattle in arid Arizona, as opposed to 2.6 acres in Wisconsin.

b. In 1998, despite a growing wolf population, only three cattle and four sheep were lost to wolf predation.

(36) a. I've got a brains to go with what you see!
b. I'm the perfect kind of person they need in the auto industry these days because I am a practical kind of guy with a few brains. Technology is really changing cars these days—so they need guys and girls with a few brains to be able to roll with all the techno stuff.

Finally, although *beer/wine/whiskey* occur as count nouns in (33), this is not their typical behavior, as they usually occur as mass nouns. Conversely, although *apple/house/chicken* tend to occur as count nouns, they may occur as mass nouns as well.

(37) a. Put more apple in the salad.
b. You can buy a lot of house with that money.
c. There is still a lot of chicken on your plate, young man.

Note that we could easily account for this alternation the same way we did for *beer/wine/whiskey*, that is, by invoking an operation that maps an ideal into an individuation. But, given the preference for count status displayed by these nouns, perhaps another alternative would be more natural: namely, to treat the count senses of *apple/house/chicken* as basic and to derive their mass senses from them by means of an operation that turns individuations into ideals. This would be an operation that takes the set of all apples/houses/chickens *taken collectively* and returns the same set of entities, but *taken in bulk*.[10] This operation would not be a function from elements of the individuation to elements of the ideal (there are too few of the former to map into the latter). Yet it would be a function from individuations to ideals, as there could be one and only one of these ideals per individuation.

17.6 Anticipating Potential Objections

It is sometimes argued that, contrary to what has been said throughout this chapter, mass nouns must name entities that have minimal parts. This argument is typically based on the noun *furniture*, which is supposed to refer to entities that have the various pieces of furniture as minimal parts. Thus, "furniture comes in 'pieces,' and a part of a piece of furniture is not furniture: an arm of a chair or a nail in a bookcase is not furniture" (McCawley 1981/1993, 233). Similar points could be made about *water* and molecules of water, about *gold* and atoms of gold, or about *matter* and elementary particles of matter.

But if *furniture* named entities whose minimal parts were pieces of furniture, then the mass term *furniture* would be referentially indistinguishable from the count term *piece or pieces of furniture*. But this is plainly wrong. While the mass noun *furniture* may refer to discrete pieces of furniture taken in bulk, the count term *piece or pieces of furniture* may only refer to discrete pieces of furniture taken discretely. In fact, if the mass term *furniture* had the same reference as the count term *piece or pieces of furniture*, then we would be unable to account for all the well-known differences between them regarding tolerance of enumeration, ordering, *one*-pronominalization, modification in terms of size and shape, and so on. The reason we speak of furniture rather than of piece(s) of furniture is that we want to disregard the fact that furniture forms functional units and refer to it in bulk.

We may even follow McCawley's discussion of *clothes* cited above and devise a thought experiment that yields positive evidence that *furniture* names entities without minimal parts. Suppose we were selling furniture in bulk. Notice that it is entirely possible to say what every part of every piece of furniture would cost—indeed, down to the arm of a chair or a nail of a bookcase. This would not be possible, of course, if we were selling furniture by the piece. This is because *furniture* taken in bulk, which is *furniture* pure and simple, refers to furniture down to the arms of chairs and the nails of bookcases, while *piece or pieces of furniture* does not.

In addition to making a case for the atomlessness of furniture, this thought experiment reveals that there is a purpose to speaking about furniture rather than about piece(s) of furniture. It is that sometimes we want to speak without regard to individuation, in this case of furniture without regard to the fact that furniture consists of functional units. As pointed out by one of the reviewers for this chapter, the point could perhaps be made more clearly with contrasts like *kitchen utensils* versus *kitchenware* or *leaves* versus *foliage*.

The same could be said of *water* and molecules of water, about *gold* and atoms of gold, and about *matter* and elementary particles of matter. In particular, *water* does not mean the same thing as *molecules of water*, *gold* does not mean the same thing as *atoms of gold*, and *matter* does not mean the same thing as *elementary particles of matter*. One good way to bring these points out is to notice that water, gold, and matter have many properties that their scientific construals do not, and cannot, have (see McCawley 1981/1993, 232–33). Thus, although water is liquid, molecules of water are not. In fact, molecules of water cannot be liquid, as being liquid is a property that a collection of molecules may acquire by virtue of its density, the tightness with which the molecules in the collection are packed together. Similarly, while gold may be dirty or impure, atoms of gold may be neither; atoms of gold are pure gold. Or, while some amount of matter may be acidic, the elementary particles constituting it cannot be.

It might be objected at this point that, if we subscribed to scientific theories of the structure of matter, then mass terms would fail to refer (there is no water outside molecules of water, no gold outside atoms of gold, and no matter outside elementary particles). But all this means is that mass nouns would fail to refer if we interpreted them against models that are consistent with scientific theories of the structure of matter; they would remain fully referential if we interpreted them relative to the models for the interpretation of mass nouns characterized in this chapter. Notice that there is no need for these two models to be compatible in every respect. It is true that we use these two models when we (purport to) talk about the real world. But, to do this, all we need is that these models be consistent at the macroscopic level of human experience, which they are. There is no need for them to be consistent all the way down to the microscopic level at which the structure of matter is decided.

In conclusion, then, the paradox of mass plurals can be resolved if we interpret the grammatical number of mass nouns in terms of cosingularity and coplurality rather than singularity and plurality—or, more generally, if we interpret it in terms of *subcontrariety* rather than *contrariety* in the square of oppositions in (38).

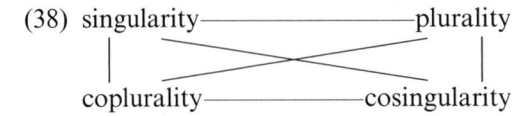

(38) singularity————————plurality

coplurality————————cosingularity

The resolution proposed here applies both to the notorious paradox of plural mass nouns and to the little-noticed paradox of singular mass nouns, at least if we interpret the stems of these nouns as ideals in atomless models.

So, is having plural mass nouns a fact that we'll have to live with? Only if by *plural* we mean *cosingular*, which is not the same thing!

Notes

1. While *clothing* refers to anything that can clothe, *clothes* refers to anything that can clothe a human. Thus, speaking of the *clothes on a cable* (as opposed to *the clothing on a cable*) or of *a wolf in sheep's clothes* (as opposed to *a wolf in sheep's clothing*) evokes a slightly humorous situation in which a cable or a wolf is wearing human apparel.

2. *N* stands for nasals. To facilitate comparisons, Bantuists give corresponding noun classes the same numbers in all Bantu languages, even if some of these classes are empty in some of these languages. In Lingala, for example, classes 12 and 13, as well as any classes over 15, are unattested.

3. Unless stated otherwise, all the Lingala facts in the following discussion are drawn from Mufwene 1980b.

4. The term *singulative* comes from the Celtic and Arabic grammatical traditions (see Greenberg 1977, 287).

5. The grammatical number of mass nouns in classes other than class 6 is a bit more complex. According to Mufwene (1980b, sec. 7), Lingala mass nouns may be found also in classes 4, 7, 8, 10, and 14. The mass nouns in classes 4, 8, 10 will behave like the class 6 nouns discussed in the text (the nouns of all these classes have been considered plural in the literature). Class 7, on the other hand, is supposed to have at least one mass noun: *e-sengo* 'pleasure'. Yet the nouns of this class have been traditionally considered singular. Is it possible that *e-sengo* is actually a

singular count noun that should be glossed as 'type of pleasure', 'degree of pleasure', or 'pleasurable event' instead? As for the mass nouns of class 14, they are considered not just singular but in fact *singularia tantum* in the literature (see Bwantsa-Kafungu 1970, 48). But could they have been misanalyzed as well? According to Mufwene (1980b, 1045), these nouns do not behave entirely like singulars, as they may be specified by *míngi* 'a lot' but not by *mókó* 'one'.

6. I am indebted to Lynn Nichols (pers. comm., 20 March 2001, 22 and 26 July 2002), who provided me with all the Zuni data in this chapter.

7. They are (the irreflexive portions of) mereologies. See for example Ojeda 1993, as well as much other work deriving from Link 1983.

8. Technically, this is the set of least upper bounds for the sets of two or more minimal elements of the subset.

9. Alternatively, sort x into discrete kinds. Take these kinds and construct the individuation that has them as minimal elements. This is an operation that maps ideals into individuations. This operation is, like the one described in the text, a *homomorphism* from an ideal into an individuation. It maps every element of an ideal into an element of an individuation, that is, the least inclusive of the elements that include it.

10. To be more precise, it would be an operation that takes an individuation and returns the smallest ideal that includes it. This ideal is the set-theoretic intersection of all the ideals that include the individuation (or the ideal *generated* by the maximal element of the individuation).

References

Bwantsa-Kafungu, S. Pierre. 1970. *Esquisse grammaticale de Lingala*. Kinshasa: Publications de L'Université Lovanium.

Greenberg, Joseph. 1977. Numeral classifiers and substantival number: Problems in the genesis of a linguistic type. In *Linguistics at the crossroads*, ed. by Adam Makkai, Valerie Becker Makkai, and Luigi Heilmann. Padua: Liviana Editrice; Lake Bluff, IL: Jupiter Press.

Jespersen, Otto. 1954. *A modern English grammar on historical principles*. Part 2, *Syntax. First volume*. London: George Allen and Unwin.

Link, Godehard. 1983. The logical analysis of plurals and mass terms. In *Meaning, use, and interpretation of language*, ed. by Rainer Bäuerle, Christoph Schwarze, and Arnim von Stechow, 302–23. Berlin: Walter de Gruyter.

McCawley, James D. 1979. Lexicography and the count-mass distinction. In *Adverbs, vowels, and other objects of wonder*, 165–73. Chicago: University of Chicago Press.

McCawley, James D. 1981. *Everything that linguists have always wanted to know about logic— but were ashamed to ask*. Chicago: University of Chicago Press. 2nd ed., 1993. References are to the 1993 edition.

Mufwene, Salikoko S. 1980a. Bantu class prefixes: Inflectional or derivational? In *Papers from the Sixteenth Regional Meeting, Chicago Linguistic Society*, ed. by Jody Kreiman and Almerindo Ojeda, 246–58. Chicago: University of Chicago. Chicago Linguistic Society.

Mufwene, Salikoko S. 1980b. Number, countability and markedness in Lingala LI-/MA- noun class. *Linguistics* 18, 1019–52.

Mufwene, Salikoko S. 1981. Non-individuation and the count/mass distinction. In *Papers from the Seventeenth Regional Meeting, Chicago Linguistic Society*, ed. by Roberta A. Hendrick,

Carrie S. Masek, and Mary Frances Miller, 221–38. Chicago: University of Chicago, Chicago Linguistic Society.

Mufwene, Salikoko S. 1984. The count/mass distinction in the English lexicon. In *Papers from the Parasession on Lexical Semantics*, ed. by David Testen, Veena Mishra, and Joseph Drogo, 200–21. Chicago: University of Chicago, Chicago Linguistic Society.

Ojeda, Almerindo E. 1993. *Linguistic individuals.* CSLI Lecture notes 31. Stanford, CA: CSLI Publications.

Pelletier, Francis Jeffry, and Lenhart Schubert. 1989. Mass expressions. In *Handbook of philosophical logic.* Vol. 4, *Topics in the philosophy of language*, ed. by Dov Gabbay and Franz Guenthner, 327–407. Dordrecht: Reidel.

Quine, Willard van Orman. 1964. *Word and object.* Cambridge, MA: MIT Press.

Welmers, William. 1973. *African language structures.* Berkeley: University of California Press.

Wierzbicka, Anna. 1988. Oats and wheat: Mass nouns, iconicity, and human categorization. In *Semantics and grammar*, ed. by Anna Wierzbicka, 499–557. Amsterdam: John Benjamins.

Chapter 18

Everything That Linguists Have Always Wanted to Know about Ironic Presuppositions and Implicatures but Were Ashamed to Ask

Katharine Beals

18.1 Introduction

John is a genius, said of an idiot, or *It seems to be raining*, uttered in a downpour, are typical examples of verbal irony, stemming as they do from some sort of ludicrous incompatibility between background assumptions and what a speaker says or implies. Many sorts of implied propositions, it turns out, lend themselves to irony. Ironic implications can arise whenever what is implied is ludicrously at odds with background assumptions. But how is it possible to imply indirectly a proposition that everyone presupposes to be false? This chapter explores how.

18.2 The Relationship between Irony and Implicature

The oft-cited discussion of irony in Grice 1975 treats ironic utterances as involving deliberate floutings of the Conversational Maxim of Quality, or truthfulness. Grice's example, *X is a fine friend*, if mutually known by speaker and hearer to be false, must convey some related proposition—otherwise, Grice says, it would be pointless. The "most obviously related proposition," Grice concludes, "is the contradictory." As McCawley (1981/1993) obliquely points out in one of his exercises, however, this analysis will accept as ironic such cases as (1).

My interest in irony and implicatures and, by extension, in irony and presuppositions originated in an exercise in Jim McCawley's *Everything That Linguists Have Always Wanted to Know About Logic—but Were Ashamed to Ask* (1981/1993), discussed at length in section 18.2. This exercise, which is the springboard for what follows, contains, to my knowledge, the only observations Jim published on irony—observations I have found far more astute and inspiring than anything else I have encountered on this much underresearched topic in linguistics.

(1) George and Martha are eating in a Chinese restaurant, talking about baseball. George says *I don't want any soy sauce*, intending thereby to get Martha to pass him the soy sauce, which is on Martha's side of the table. (McCawley 1981/ 1993, 234)

Assuming that the proposition most obviously related to *I don't want any soy sauce* is its contradictory, then Martha, if familiar with George's taste, should deduce his actual intention to be to convey that he *does* want soy sauce. Why, then, does George's utterance sound not ironic, but awkward?

According to the analysis in Beals 1995, ironic utterances are so because they convey a ludicrous falsity. Many falsities are simply not ludicrous enough, in most contexts, for irony. This observation applies to utterances such as *Larry Summers is president of the United States*, *You own twenty cats*, and *World War III has started*. Unless George's urge for soy sauce on Chinese food is so strong that the proposition that he doesn't want any is ludicrously false even when the topic at hand is baseball, the irony in (1) falls flat.

But McCawley's exercise hints at a second, more subtle problem with Grice's analysis. As Grice seems to recognize, an ironic utterance succeeds only if the ludicrous falsity it conveys is, a priori, mutually recognized by speaker and addressee. If Martha doesn't view George's enormous predilection for soy sauce on Chinese food as given, she will have no idea that he's been ironic, let alone how he wants her to react. In other words, the proposition that Grice would say George is implicating in (1), that he *does* want soy sauce, must already be a background assumption. In all of Grice's other, much-cited examples of conversational implicature, by contrast, the addressee uses what is said, together with background assumptions, to calculate new information—whether about the garage around the corner, the possibility of Smith having a girlfriend in New York, or the opinion of the writer of the recommendation letter that the student in question is no good at philosophy (Grice 1975, 155–56). These observations lead to the conclusion in Beals 1995 that ironic utterances do not convey their contradictories as propositions that the addressee must calculate as she would an implicature; rather, they index or *highlight* as ludicrously false a proposition that the discourse context already presupposes as such.[1]

Implicature, however, does interact with irony, for without it we would have no explanation for the ironies in utterances like (2) and (3).

(2) [Uttered outside as a torrential downpour begins.] It seems to be raining.

(3) [A and B are stuck in winter in a hot, stuffy room with no climate control, within a condemned building known by both of them to be in danger of collapsing if any windows are opened. A is standing by the window.]
A: Can I do anything else for you?
B: Well, it's really hot and stuffy in here.

Ironic Presuppositions and Implicatures 413

Unlike the examples most often cited by linguists, including Grice's *X is a fine friend*, these ironies are relatively subtle; correspondingly less obvious is their source, though under close scrutiny it becomes apparent.

As is discussed at length in Beals 1995, irony has, over many centuries of definition and analysis, traditionally been conceived of as arising when the speaker says the opposite of what she intends to convey. This reflects our strong intuition that some sort of opposition or clash between the speaker's utterance and her actual beliefs is crucial. But the notion of irony as an opposition, specifically, between what is said and what is intended fails to explain that of (2) and (3). The former arises not because it doesn't seem to be raining, but because the rain is egregiously obvious. The latter arises not because it's not really hot and stuffy (indeed it *is*), but because it would be a really bad idea to open a window.

As pointed out in Beals 1995, there is only one treatment of irony that at once is unitary, reflects our specific intuitions about its source in examples like (2) and (3), and captures our general sense that at its core lies an opposition between an utterance and what its speaker actually intends. This is to allow that the falsity that an ironic utterance highlights may sometimes be found not in its propositional content, as it is in *X is a fine friend*, but in a proposition that the utterance presupposes or conversationally implicates.

And this is precisely how irony works in (2) and (3). The speaker of (2) conveys, through a scalar Quantity implicature (i.e., through the assumption that she is being as informative as is required), that it's not obviously raining. In (3), B suggests, through Relation (i.e., through the assumption that B's response is relevant to A's question), that he wants A to open the window. Thus, irony is not a specific kind of conversational implicature that connects an untruthful statement to its contradictory; rather, different kinds of implicature that apply independently of irony can convey the ludicrous falsity that makes an utterance ironic. More generally, irony arises whenever a speaker highlights something as ludicrously false by pretending to embrace it as true—most often, through her words and what they directly or indirectly commit her to believing.

18.3 The Mystery: How Do Ironic Implicatures and Presuppositions Survive?

That irony can stem from a conversational implicature is actually rather remarkable, raising new questions that are the focus of this chapter. Recall that it is, after all, only from the assumption that the speaker is being conversationally cooperative, and specifically not misleading, that implicatures are calculated. And yet, in the above examples, it is only if the implicated propositions are already assumed by speaker and hearer to be ludicrously false that irony is possible in the first place. Indeed, not only is irony possible in utterances like (2) and (3); it is in fact difficult to interpret either one in its given context as anything other than ironic. How is it that ironic implicatures can arise, even inevitably, rather than being blocked a priori by their ludicrous falsity?

Equally mysterious are ironic presuppositions, as in (4), which presupposes, via *back*, that to call someone a bitch is a compliment.

(4) George called Martha a bitch and she complimented him back.

Somehow this presupposition goes through, despite being contradicted by background assumptions about compliments, and even though Gazdar (1979), Levinson (1983, 2000), and others have suggested that such assumptions can undo presuppositions. In Levinson's words, "... when it is mutually known that certain facts do not obtain, we can use sentences that might otherwise presuppose those facts, with no consequent presuppositions arising" (1983, 187). However, so freely and inevitably does the presupposition in (4) apply that its irony seems inescapable.

18.4 Reevaluating Presuppositions with Contradictory Background Assumptions

The persistence of the presupposition in (4), despite assumptions about compliments, raises suspicions that something is wrong with Levinson's and others' claims that contradictory background assumptions trump presuppositions. We begin our investigation of the mystery of ironic presuppositions and implicatures, thus, with a closer look at Levinson's analysis and supporting examples.

Noting that propositions expressed by *before*-clauses are normally presupposed, Levinson (1983, 187) contrasts the following utterances:

(5) Sue cried before she finished her thesis.

(6) Sue died before she finished her thesis.

The presupposition that Sue finished her thesis obtains in (5) but not in (6), because (6) asserts that she died beforehand, and because "we generally hold that people ... do not do things after they die." Similarly, he (1983, 187–88) contrasts utterances (7) and (8) from Karttunen 1973.

(7) If the vice-chancellor invites the U.S. president to dinner, he'll regret having invited a feminist to his table.

(8) If the vice-chancellor invites Simone de Beauvoir to dinner, he'll regret having invited a feminist to his table.

The sentence in (7) presupposes, via the factive verb *regret*, that the vice-chancellor has invited a feminist to his table. In contrast, assuming as background knowledge that Simone de Beauvoir is a well-known feminist, we tend to interpret *a feminist* in (8) as referring specifically to her. Since, as Levinson notes (1983, 188), "the use of the conditional ... specifically indicates that the speaker does not know for certain that the Vice-Chancellor has invited Simone de Beauvoir, the presupposition ... is canceled."

Finally, Levinson (1983) considers (9).

(9) Either Sue has never been a Mormon or she has stopped wearing holy underwear.
(Karttunen 1974)

Here, he says, the presuppositions "depend on one's beliefs about whether Mormons wear holy underwear" (Levinson 1983, 188). The second clause presupposes, via *stop*, that Sue used to wear holy underwear, but this presupposition "evaporates" if we assume that only Mormons wear holy underwear, because the utterance as a whole, via its first clause, suggests that Sue might not be a Mormon.

As Levinson's specific analysis of each example in fact makes clear, however, it is not background assumptions alone, but background knowledge *in conjunction with* something that each of the above utterances independently entails or implies, that undoes its presupposition. Thus, (6) asserts that Sue died prior to her dissertation's completion; the *if*-clause in (8) indicates the speaker's uncertainty about whether a particular feminist was invited; the *either*-clause in (9) suggests that perhaps Sue has never been a Mormon.

Consider, now, what happens if we replace these linguistic contributions with corresponding background assumptions. Can this extralinguistic knowledge alone cancel presuppositions? Suppose, for example, that we know that Sue died before finishing her dissertation, and that her death had no connection with her restaurant venture, and consider the following counterpart to (6):

(10) ??Sue opened a Chinese restaurant before she finished her thesis.

However true this statement might be, it is an odd thing to utter in the given context, precisely because it presupposes that Sue finished her thesis.

The presuppositions of *regret* and *stop* likewise survive contradictory background assumptions in cases like (11) and (12), where there's no linguistic contribution to the contradiction.

(11) [Said of a well-known atheist.] ??Sue has stopped wearing holy underwear.

(12) [The vice-chancellor infamously avoids all feminists, never inviting them anywhere.] ??The vice-chancellor will regret having invited a feminist to his table.

It should be noted, though, that (11) and (12) are awkward not just because their presuppositions—that Sue used to wear holy underwear, and that the vice-chancellor has invited a feminist to his table—stubbornly survive the antagonistic background.

They are also awkward because it is bizarre to say that someone stopped, or will regret, doing something he never did. There is, however, a less awkward interpretation of these utterances, namely, that they are meant ironically—but in that case, as in (4), their presuppositions must survive, for they are the source of the irony.

Levinson cites two examples in which he argues that background assumptions alone can block presupposition.

(13) At least John won't have to regret that he did a PhD.

(14) Kissinger ceased to be secretary of state before World War III started.

While (13) normally presupposes, via *regret*, that John got a PhD, Levinson argues that this presupposition does not apply "if participants mutually know that John failed to get into a doctoral course" (1983, 187). Background knowledge also cancels, Levinson says, the presupposition in (14) that World War III has started.

According my own informal survey, though, (13) is not a completely normal thing to say in Levinson's hypothetical scenario, precisely because it still faintly presupposes, in spite of the background assumptions, that John got, or will get, a PhD. It is, furthermore, a misleading example, because there's something about embedding the clause headed by *regret* in the complement of the modal *have to* predicate that softens its presupposition. Remove the *have to*, as in (15), and the proposition that John got/will get a PhD defies even more strongly Levinson's hypothetical discourse context. Now replace *regret* with a predicate like *realize*, which more strongly presupposes its complement, and the presupposition becomes more defiant still.

(15) ?(?)At least John won't regret that he did a PhD.

(16) ??At least John won't realize that he got a useless degree.

In the case of (14), certain background assumptions remain crucial; indeed, we need them to make sense of the utterance. If we assume that the speaker takes Kissinger to be so much of a hawkish foreign affairs adventurist that his departure from office could have been seen as preventing a war that was otherwise inevitable, then what she says makes sense in the same way that (17) does.

(17) Both sides backed off before World War III started.

Here the presupposition that World War III began may be canceled, more obviously than in (14), by the assumption that the backing off has blocked the war's otherwise apparent inevitability—in the same way that, in (6), knowledge of Sue's death blocks the presupposition that she finished her dissertation.

Without such an assumption about the speaker's potential view of Kissinger, (14) is as odd as (18), where we replace Kissinger with a successor who has no such reputation for brinkmanship.

(18) ??Warren Christopher ceased to be secretary of state before World War III started.

Even in the absence of mutual assumptions about Kissinger's foreign policy, the proposition that World War III has started is so clearly presupposed in (14) that it, together with the matrix clause and background knowledge about how reckless Kissinger's policies are deemed to have been by some people, can actually occasion a conversational implicature to the effect that the speaker himself must share these views. In this case, the presupposition assists in its own demise, but, once again, only with the additional help not just of background knowledge, but of what else the speaker has actually said.

Thus, so strongly are presuppositions attached to the linguistic expressions that bear them, that speakers are committed to them even in the face of contradictory background assumptions. Committed, that is, unless they supplement their utterances with other expressions, such as qualifying or clarifying assertions, *if-then* clauses and *either-or* clauses, that commit them to overriding, alternative beliefs. In other words, presupposition-bearing expressions are a kind of linguistic convention that only a fellow linguistic convention can undo. And it is, in turn, because the linguistic conventions of presupposition-bearing expressions are independent of non-linguistic context that they can be exploited for irony, allowing one to highlight a mutually recognized ludicrous falsity by committing oneself, in pretense, to the idea that it is true.

While background assumptions alone cannot prevent the communication of a contradictory presupposition, they remain unaffected by it. People do not respond to the presupposition in (4), for example, by adjusting their understanding of what a compliment is. But in cases where the contradictory proposition is intended ironically, it is also the irony, highlighting as ludicrously false something already presupposed as such, that blocks such changes to the common ground.

18.5 Reevaluating Conversational Implicatures with Contradictory Background Assumptions

Now what of the possibilities for irony in conversational implicatures in examples like (2) and (3)? Conversational implicature, as a function not of particular linguistic expressions but of Grice's Conversational Maxims, should not be as conventionalized, let alone as context-free, as presupposition. That irony can reside in these examples raises the possibility that conversational implicatures are nevertheless somewhat conventionalized, and somewhat independent from discourse context.

Let us return to the scalar Q-implicature that is the basis for irony in (2), repeated as (19).

(19) [Uttered outside as a torrential downpour begins.] It seems to be raining.

The implicature that it's not obviously raining follows from the assumption that the speaker is conversing cooperatively—observing, inter alia, Grice's Maxim of Quantity, and thus not going out of the way to be underinformative. If it is obviously raining, it would be more informative to forego the *seems*.

18.5.1 Generalized Implicatures

Now Levinson (1983, 2000) argues that certain conversational implicatures, what he calls "generalized conversational implicatures," are, in fact, partially conventionalized, obtaining in general unless certain unusual circumstances apply. Included in this category are scalar implicatures, like that of *some*, which implies *not all*; *similar*, which implies *not identical*; *three*, which implies *not more than three*; and, as in (19), *seems to be*, which implies *isn't obviously*. Perhaps it is because of this partial conventionalization that the irony in (19) is possible. On the other hand, shouldn't the torrential rain, which contradicts the implicature outright, qualify as the sort of unusual circumstance that can cancel it?

The failure of this salient circumstance to cancel the implicature it so egregiously contradicts raises the possibility that, as with presuppositions, nonlinguistic background assumptions alone cannot cancel generalized conversational implicatures. And indeed, as with presupposition, most of Levinson's examples of unrealized generalized conversational implicatures involve a cancellation that is, at least in part, linguistically based. In (20)–(22), *some* → *not all* is canceled, respectively, by a parenthetical that asserts *all*, by a matrix clause that does not entail its complement, and by a subsequent *either-or* construction that expresses uncertainty; in (23), *three* → *not more than three* is canceled by a similar uncertainty expressed by the subsequent *if*-clause.

(20) Some Saudi princes, and in fact all of them, are pretty wealthy.
(Levinson 2000, 50)

(21) John says that some of the boys went.
(Levinson 2000, 134)

(22) Some of the Elgin Marbles are fakes, and either the rest of them are too, or they're inferior originals.
(Levinson 2000, 144)

(23) John has three children, if not four.
(Levinson 2000, 88)

The same behavior with respect to cancellability is seen with another sort of generalized conversational implicature: that occasioned by the linguistic conjunction. This implies that the events expressed are temporally successive and occur in the order in

Ironic Presuppositions and Implicatures 419

which they are listed. Thus, B's utterance in (24) implicates that George and Martha got married first, and then had a baby.

(24) A: Which of our classmates have followed a more conventional life since college?
B: Well, there's George and Martha, who got married and had a baby.

Even if this implicature is ludicrously false—suppose George and Martha were well known to have had an out-of-wedlock child who was later their flower girl—it still goes through, now being grounds for an ironic understanding of B's utterance.

And, indeed, Levinson's examples of the failure of implicatures of temporal succession all involve linguistically based, rather than knowledge-based, cancellations, as in (25).

(25) Hans wrote a novel and sold the rights to Macmillan, but not necessarily in that order.
(Levinson 2000, 123)

Furthermore, Levinson himself notes that even when background assumptions dictate otherwise, we still tend to prefer the implicated order of events, as in (26), where we tend to assume that he opened the door before receiving the key.

(26) He opened the door and she handed him a key.
(Levinson 2000, 123)

Finally, as Levinson points out, even when background assumptions do help cancel the implicature, special prosody is also crucial. For example, without the emphasis and rising intonation on *she*, (27) sounds odd, precisely because it would suggest that her birth and childhood followed her Olympic victory.

(27) But *she* won an Olympic medal and she was born in a slum and undernourished as a child.
(Levinson 2000, 123)

A final sort of generalized conversational implicature whose defeasibility Levinson discusses is that of the clausal implicatures of *if-then* structures. These implicate, among other things, that the speaker does not know whether the embedded propositions are true or false. For example, (28) implicates that the speaker thinks that the world might have been created in seven days.

(28) Oh, dear. If the world was created in seven days, then I'd better toss out all my science books.

As with the other generalized conversational implicatures discussed above, this one, too, can survive contradictory background assumptions to serve as a source of irony, as it does when the speaker is known to scorn creationism.

In Levinson's one example (1983, 142) of the cancellation of such an implicature, it is the discourse context rather than a background assumption that is responsible.

(29) A: I've just heard that Chuck has got a scholarship.
  B: Oh dear. If Chuck has got a scholarship, he'll give up medicine.

Here, A's preceding assertion, inasmuch as it informs B that Chuck got a scholarship, cancels the potential implicature in the latter's utterance that he doesn't know whether this happened.

A more subtle discourse-based cancellation, where there is no explicit linguistic contribution, occurs through a mutual understanding of conversational goals, as in (30) and (31), where we return to scalar implicatures.

(30) A: It's going to cost us 10 dollars to get in and I didn't bring a cent.
  B: Don't worry, I've got 10 dollars.
    (Levinson 2000, 52)

(31) C: On many occasions?
  W: Not many.
  C: Some?
  W: Yes, a few.
    (Levinson 1983, 121)

The discourse context in (30) shows A to be interested only in whether B has 10 dollars, not in how much more she might have. In the legal cross-examination in (31), W, as a hostile witness, is not expected to be cooperating with legal counsel C beyond giving answers that are literally true. In particular, one cannot assume that his *not many* implies *some*, and thus C has to explicitly extract that clarification from him.

As these examples show, an implicature may be canceled not just by what is actually said, but by the broader context of communicative intentions. In none of these examples, however, do we see a case where background assumptions alone cancel implicatures.

Levinson, however, cites one (just one) purported example.

(32) A: A Saudi prince has just bought Harrods.
  B: Some Saudi princes must be pretty wealthy.
    (Levinson 2000, 50)

Levinson claims that background knowledge about the assets of Saudi royalty cancels an implicature that would otherwise obtain, that not all Saudi princes are wealthy. But Levinson has overlooked the subtle irony in B's utterance that is, nonetheless, inescapable so long as the wealth of all Saudi princes really is background knowledge. This irony, which depends on the contradictory implicature, requires

Ironic Presuppositions and Implicatures 421

only the simple addition of a *wow*, *gee*, or *gosh* to the beginning of the utterance to become more transparent. Still less subtle, thanks to the fact that its implicature contradicts more basic, salient common knowledge, is the irony of the corresponding utterance in (33).

(33) A: A dog just barked.
     B: Some dogs must know how to bark.

In sum, then, generalized conversational implicatures appear to be just as immune to contradictory background assumptions as are presuppositions. Once again, it takes a linguistic convention to undo a linguistic convention.

18.5.2 Particularized Implicatures

More mysterious are the possibilities for irony in less conventionalized—what Levinson would call "particularized"—conversational implicatures. These implicatures are sensitive to particular nonlinguistic contexts, for it is only under specific circumstances that they obtain.

18.5.2.1 Relation Implicatures
Consider, first, the implicature in (3), repeated here as (34).

(34) [A and B are stuck in winter in a hot, stuffy room with no climate control. A is standing by the window.]
     A: Can I do anything else for you?
     B: Well, it's really hot and stuffy in here.

The implicature in question, that B wants A to open the window, is particularized in that in a different context—for example, one where the room has no windows, or where B is locked inside a trunk—it does not go through. The question, then, is why, while not arising in most contexts, the implicature nonetheless arises in one in which it is manifestly false: one where the room is in a condemned building known by A and B to be in danger of collapsing if any windows are opened, and B is speaking ironically.

As the sincere and ironic versions of (34) in fact suggest, perhaps when a particularized conversational implicature applies in a given context (e.g., with A by the window in a hot, stuffy room), it also applies, as the source of irony, in a context that differs from the original only in being obviously at odds with the implicature (e.g., with A by the window in a hot, stuffy room in a condemned building).

Further support for this theory comes from a classic example from Grice 1975.

(35) A: I am out of petrol.
     B: There is a garage round the corner.

As a response to A's statement, B's utterance implicates that she thinks it possible that the garage is open and selling gas. If all else is equal, but A and B both know that the garage around the corner was recently fire-bombed, B's utterance still carries the implicature, now the basis for irony.

And, indeed, a survey of Levinson's examples of particularized conversational implicatures bears out the hypothesis that whenever a sincere implicature applies, an ironic one, with just enough alteration of context as to render it an obvious ludicrous falsity, is also possible.

Consider, for example, two more Relation implicatures carried by answers to questions.

(36) A: What time is it?
    B: Well, some of the guests have already left.
       (Levinson 2000, 16)

(37) A: Where's Bill?
    B: Well, there's a shiny white Lexus outside Sue's house.
       (adapted from Levinson 1983, 102)

Uttered at a party in response to A's question, B's utterance in (36) implicates that it may be getting late. Adjust the circumstances such that it's in fact still quite early, and that the few guests that have already left have done so well ahead of schedule because of unusual circumstances (perhaps one of them suddenly went into labor). Then B's utterance still implicates, now ironically, that it may be getting late. Similarly, in (37), B's implication that the Lexus outside Sue's house indicates where Bill is still holds, ironically, if Bill is famous for always driving an ancient, beat-up Oldsmobile.

Other particularized Relation implicatures bridge successive statements that would otherwise appear disjoint, and these too can be the basis for irony, as in (38)–(40).

(38) She needed the beer for a health reason. Whisky made her sick.
    (Mike Royko, cited in Beals 1995)

(39) [Upon entering Maxim's restaurant in Paris and addressing the maître d'.] I decided to be as suave as possible. "Hiya," I said.
    (Mike Royko, cited in Beals 1995)

(40) [Quoting a family restaurant menu.] "For over 50 years the Ferri family has enjoyed serving the finest food to nice people like you." They like me.
    (Andy Rooney, cited in Beals 1995)

Connecting the two statements in (38) is the implicature that a health reason for drinking beer is when whisky makes you sick; similarly, the two statements in (39) imply that *Hiya* is a suave greeting, and those in (40), that the complimentary words in the menu are addressed to Andy Rooney personally.

Ironic Presuppositions and Implicatures   423

A third sort of particularized Relation implicature involves a connection not between specific utterances, but between an utterance and a salient, nonlinguistic element of the discourse context; and this, too, can be a ludicrously false proposition that is the basis for irony, as in (41)–(43).

(41) [A quotation from Robert Browning, "Home Thoughts from Abroad," uttered during a cold, wet, April morning in London.] Oh, to be in England, Now that April's there.
(Sperber and Wilson 1992, 55)

(42) [Uttered by a driver who has just been held up by a nonsignaling, left-turning driver.] It's great when people signal.

(43) [Peter has just left the classroom in shame after walking into the wall, spilling his books, and then splitting his pants while stooping down to collect them.] Peter's my star student.

What is especially interesting about the last two is that they could, even in their given contexts, conceivably be taken as sincere rather than as ironic. For instance, the speaker in (42) might be reacting to the nonsignaling driver not by ironically praising his signaling habits, but by sincerely appreciating those who do signal. Similarly, rather than ironically suggesting that what Peter just did was evidence of his stellar scholarship, the speaker in (43) might be conveying that, in spite of what just happened, or in spite of a general lack of coordination, Peter is a star student. In other words, these two utterances each carry two different potential Relation implicatures, one that does not contradict background assumptions and one that does. And yet it is the contradictory implicatures that more obviously obtain here, for both (42) and (43) are more apparently ironic than sincere.

While this heightens the mystery of particularized conversational implicatures, it also suggests the beginnings of an explanation. Note that it is the ironic implicatures of (42) and (43) that relate most directly to the circumstance to which each speaker is most obviously responding. Only in the ironic interpretation does the speaker allude directly to the nonsignaling driver in (42) or to Peter's mishap in (43). Perhaps our expectation of Relation in discourse is so strong that we look for whichever implicatures yield the most obvious, direct connections, even when these contradict background assumptions.

If so, then we also have an explanation for the ironic Relation implicatures borne by responses to questions or assertions, as in (34)–(37), and by otherwise disjointed assertions, as in (38)–(40). Hand in hand with the hearer's quest for the greatest fulfillment of Relation, however, is also the speaker's observance of certain linguistic conventions that apply even in the case of particularized conversational implicatures. Note, first of all, that most of the above responses to questions begin with *well*—a conventional signal that what follows is an answer. Without the *well* all of these sound slightly awkward, because literally they are not direct answers and thus, minus an overt signal to the contrary, initially come across as non sequiturs. Compare, for example, B's utterance in (44), which, though Levinson cites it as a perfectly natural exchange, is less so than its counterpart in (36).

(44) A: What time is it?
     B: ?Some of the guests have already left.

Note that, as an instance of irony (e.g., in the context of two guests leaving early because one of them suddenly went into labor), B's utterance here is more awkward still—in fact, it's not at all clear that he is being ironic. If they are likewise stripped of their *well*s, the same is true of the ironies in (34) and (37).

One could argue that, when it introduces an utterance that follows a question, *well* carries a mostly context-independent (i.e., generalized) conversational implicature that the utterance is a response to the question. If so, then the irony in (34) and (36)–(37), dependent as it is on this *well*, stems from generalized, rather than from particularized, conversational implicatures.

Another Relation-based speaking convention is that we generally do not juxtapose unrelated assertions: habitually violating this rule, indeed, is one of the classic symptoms of schizophrenia. Without the implicated connections, (38)–(40) would indeed be even more awkward than examples like (44); (45), for example, is a counterpart to (38) without any apparent connection between assertions.

(45) ??She needed the beer for a health reason. Whisky is the same color as her dress.

In these cases, then, the ironic implicature arises because it is the most obvious way to satisfy the assumption that the speaker is speaking in connected prose.

Levinson himself treats at least one type of implied connection between juxtaposed utterances as a generalized conversational implicature, namely, the "bridging inferences" that locate an antecedent for a definite noun phrase in a preceding clause, as in (46) and (47) (from Levinson 2000).

(46) Harold bought an old car. The steering wheel was loose.

(47) Patience walked into the dining room. The French windows were open.

As he puts it (2000, 126–27), these inferences

seem to be forced by the attempt to find coherence across the two conjoined or adjoined clauses. Note that although they may utilize background knowledge as in [(46)] (where we all know that every car has a steering wheel), or activate frames as in [(47)] (all dining rooms have windows and some dining rooms have French windows), they are completely independent of such information.

Ironic Presuppositions and Implicatures 425

Thus, Levinson himself allows for the possibility that some Relation implicatures are context-free yet underspecified enough to require, in their specific instantiations, fleshing out by the contents of the specific clauses together with background knowledge.

One can debate about just how comparably generalized are other sorts of Relation implicatures that stem from the presumption of connected prose, as in (38)–(40), or from the use of *well* in responses to questions, or from attempts, as in (41)–(43), to connect an utterance as directly as possible to its surrounding circumstances. Clearly, in the latter case in particular, the immediate nonlinguistic context plays an intimate role in the fleshing out of implicatures. As in our discussion of generalized conversational implicatures, however, it is useful to keep the immediate discourse context, or what has just been said and what the ostensible communicative intentions are, distinct from other aspects of context, particularly from background assumptions. As with presuppositions and generalized conversational implicatures, discourse plays a far greater role in allowing and generating these particularized conversational implicatures than does the general background.

18.5.2.2 Nonscalar Quantity Implicatures Another major class of particularized conversational implicature are nonscalar Quantity implicatures, generated by the assumption that the speaker is being as informative as required, but not involving contrasting, scalar terms like *some* versus *all*. Like their particularized Relation counterparts, these, too, can serve as the source for irony whenever the context is minimally adjusted so as to render the implicature ludicrously false. Consider (48)–(50).

(48) A: How did Harry fare in court the other day?
 B: Oh, he got a fine.
 (Levinson 1983, 106)

(49) A: Did you get any autographs?
 B: I got Joanne Woodward's.
 (Levinson 2000, 105)

(50) A: How did McBain get in here?
 B: He opened the door.
 (Levinson 2000, 113)

Given general background assumptions about the relative severity of different legal sentences, or the relative fame of movie stars, B's utterance in (48) implicates that Harry did not also receive a life sentence, and in (49) that he did not also get Paul Newman's autograph. In (50), as pointed out by Levinson, B implicates that McBain opened the door in the normal way, and not, say, by ramming himself into it until it burst open.

Now imagine that these utterances are addressed not just to A, but also to C, a third party who knows what actually happened; and suppose, in fact, that Harry did also get a life sentence, that B also got Paul Newman's autograph, and that McBain rammed the door open. Then these utterances are all examples of ironic omissions directed at C (A being as oblivious to the omission as the uncertainty in her questions indicates).

What is special about ironic omissions, and why they are possible in the first place, is that they are a sort of metalinguistic irony. That is, the basis for these ironies is not what the speaker pretends to believe about an actual event, but what he pretends to believe about what he says. In (48), for example, what's most ludicrously false isn't that Harry didn't get a life sentence or that a life sentence isn't as serious as a fine,[2] but that the speaker thinks that this mention of Harry's fine is an adequate answer to the question. In general, then, what's ludicrous in these examples isn't that the speaker thinks that what he has omitted didn't actually happen or is unimportant, but that he believes that what he said is an adequate response to the question at hand.

This sort of metalinguistic irony can arise, perhaps more transparently, with certain expressions bearing generalized conversational implicatures.

(51) George: Did anything interesting happen at work today?
Martha: Well, a man came and brought me flowers.

If George and Martha are married, and George happens himself to have brought Martha flowers today, Martha's utterance may ironically implicate, through her choice of *a man*, over *my husband* or *you*, that the flower-bearer was someone other than George. But the source of her irony isn't in this not particularly ludicrous proposition, but in the notion that *a man* is an appropriate way to refer to George.

Manner implicatures lend themselves to a similar sort of metalinguistic irony, for example, to describing ordinary, well-understood occurrences in ironically fancy, prolix, or precise ways, as does B in (52).

(52) A: How did he open the door?
B: By walking up to the door, reaching for the handle, turning it clockwise until he heard the latch click, and then pulling the handle towards him while moving out of the way.

The question in our earlier examples was why an implicature goes through when contradicted by background assumptions—that is, why this interpretation isn't overridden by an alternative understanding that lacks the contradictory implication. Metalinguistic irony is less mysterious: here there is no way to construe the utterance as nonironic because the basis for its irony is a brazenly inappropriate use of linguistic conventions. If it could be construed in some other way, then it simply would not qualify as brazenly inappropriate.

Ironic Presuppositions and Implicatures 427

18.6 Conclusion: The Dependence of Irony on Linguistic Conventions

Some sort of linguistic convention, however, has turned out to be common to all the vehicles for irony we have visited. Even non-metalinguistic Relation-based particularized implicatures arguably involve some sort of convention relating to connections between utterances or between an utterance and salient circumstances. The proposed account, in particular of Relation-based ironies, predicts one area where irony should not be possible, namely, cases where an utterance has only weak ties to the circumstance or discourse context that triggers its implicature. And, in fact, we have already witnessed just this in the failure of irony in indirect responses to questions that lack, as in (44), the explicit connecting signal of *well*. Consider, in addition, the following counterparts to some of the other Relation-based ironies we reviewed above:

(53) There's a shiny white Lexus outside Sue's house.

(54) There's a garage round the corner.

(55) It's really hot and stuffy in here.

Imagine (53) as a counterpart to (37) that does not respond to an immediately preceding question about Bill's whereabouts, but whose audience is still wondering where he is, and knows him to drive an ancient, beat-up Oldsmobile. Or, suppose that (54) is a similarly out-of-the-blue counterpart to (35), in which the garage is still dysfunctional after a recent fire-bombing. Finally, consider (55) as a counterpart to (34) in which the person by the hazardous window hasn't just asked if there's anything she can do. In none of these cases does irony succeed, because the implicatures on which it depends are not sufficiently obvious. In contrast, in sincere contexts, where Bill does drive a Lexus, the garage is functioning, or the window can safely be opened by an addressee who stands next to it, these implicatures are still somewhat apparent even if time has passed since the utterances that trigger them. Contradictory background assumptions, therefore, can help block implicatures that are only weakly connected to the circumstances that might trigger them, by further distancing them from those circumstances.

The generalized, partially generalized, and metalinguistic implicatures that do allow irony do so because their propositions, in contrast, are so strongly, immediately, and inevitably conveyed as to be as immune to contradictory background assumptions as those expressed through outright assertion. Underlying this, in turn, is our awareness that speakers, even those we think we can trust, may sometimes purport to believe things that contradict what we assume is true. Thus, even before we learn what irony is, we are still as aware of implausible presuppositions and implicatures as is the child speaking in (56).

(56) Child: A dog just barked.
　　　Parent: Some dogs must know how to bark.
　　　Child: But *all* dogs know how to bark!

Then, as we learn to appreciate irony, we may also come to esteem the deliberate highlighting of ludicrous falsities through pretended beliefs as a reasonable behavior that the maxims of conversation must somehow accommodate. At that point, asked what Jim McCawley was known for, we can confidently proclaim to an audience that includes linguists:

(57) He was a great amateur chef, and his Chinese food was so damn tasty that it never required additional soy sauce.

Linguists who knew him will recognize our ironic omission of the rest of Jim's myriad feats, culinary and other.

　Ironic omissions of Jim's tremendous linguistic legacy aside, even irony, about which he published so little, inspired him with significant insights. At the drop of a hat, he could craft clever ironic turns of phrase, broadening vastly my appreciation for the extent to which this phenomenon pervades language—whether in "Twinkle Toes," said of a klutz; "haute cuisine" for meals from Harold's Chicken Shack; or, uttered on one in a series of cold, rainy days, the truthful yet ironic statement "It's just as warm and sunny today as it was yesterday." The insight that irony and implicature are distinct but overlapping phenomena, suggested by Jim in the soy sauce example with which we began, lays a crucial foundation for all that has followed.

Notes

1. Other linguistic devices that may highlight what is given rather than introducing new material are referring expressions and negative polarity items. For such an analysis of the latter, see Linebarger 1987, 1992.

2. Such propositions would, in their respective contexts, make for ironies as awkward and ineffectual as George's *I don't want any soy sauce* in (1).

References

Beals, Katharine. 1995. A linguistic analysis of verbal irony. Doctoral dissertation, University of Chicago.

Gazdar, Gerald. 1979. *Pragmatics: Implicature, presupposition, and logical form*. New York: Academic Press.

Grice, H. P. 1975. Logic and conversation. In *Syntax and semantics 3: Speech acts*, ed. by Peter Cole and Jerry L. Morgan, 41–58. New York: Academic Press. Reprinted in Steven Davis, ed. *Pragmatics: A reader*, 305–15. New York: Oxford University Press, 1991.

Karttunen, Lauri. 1973. Presuppositions of compound sentences. *Linguistic Inquiry* 4, 169–93.

Karttunen, Lauri. 1974. Presuppositions and linguistic context. *Theoretical Linguistics* 1, 3–44.

Levinson, Stephen C. 1983. *Pragmatics.* Cambridge: Cambridge University Press.

Levinson, Stephen C. 2000. *Presumptive meanings: The theory of generalized conversational implicature.* Cambridge, MA: MIT Press.

Linebarger, Marcia C. 1987. Negative polarity and grammatical representation. *Linguistics and Philosophy* 10, 325–87.

Linebarger, Marcia C. 1992. Negative polarity as linguistic evidence. In *CLS 27: Papers from the 27th Regional Meeting of the Chicago Linguistic Society*, ed. by Lise M. Dobrin, Lynn Nichols, and Rosa M. Rodriguez, 165–88. Chicago: University of Chicago, Chicago Linguistic Society.

McCawley, James D. 1981. *Everything that linguists have always wanted to know about logic— but were ashamed to ask.* Chicago: University of Chicago Press. 2nd ed., 1993. References are to the 1981 edition.

Sperber, Dan, and Deidre Wilson. 1992. On verbal irony. *Lingua* 87, 53–76.

PART V
Knowledge of Language

Chapter 19

**Deficits in Pronoun Interpretation: William O'Grady
Clues to a Theory of Competence
and Acquisition**

Consideration of language acquisition can provide solid arguments for or against particular linguistic analyses only when facts about the behavior of real children are marshalled in support of the assumptions that are made about how children acquire their language.

Jim McCawley, "A Note on Auxiliary Verbs and Language Acquisition"

19.1 Introduction

It is widely acknowledged that much can be learned about the nature of the human language faculty by studying its operation under a variety of conditions. Even though the first concern of contemporary linguistics is to account for how fully fluent adults ("ideal speaker-hearers") are able to form and interpret the sentences of their native language, substantial attention has also been paid to the study of first language acquisition, second language learning, and aphasia. Moreover, it is widely agreed not only that an eventual theory of the language faculty in fluent adults should shed light

The last e-mail message that I received from Jim McCawley, about a year before his death, was an inquiry about whether I thought that language learners could make "real mistakes" on core linguistic principles, such as the binding principles, constraints on extraction, and so forth. This question occurred to me often as I pursued the particular line of investigation that constitutes the focus of this chapter. I am not sure what Jim would have made of the facts reported here or of the interpretation that I put on them. He made relatively little use of "psychological evidence" in his own work, although he did consider it "essential if one is to know how to interpret putative linguistic facts and whether to take them seriously" (McCawley 1980, 27). I regret never having had the opportunity to seek out Jim's views on these matters. This chapter is dedicated to his memory.

I am grateful to Kevin Gregg and two anonymous reviewers for their comments on an earlier version of this chapter and to Miseon Lee for first drawing my attention to the existence of possible parallels between agrammatism and second language acquisition. I would like to express my thanks to audiences at the annual conference of the Japan Society for Language Sciences and at the Pacific Second Language Research Forum, at which much longer versions of this chapter were presented. (The version of the chapter presented to the Japan Society for Language Sciences appears in the society's journal, *Second Language Studies*.)

on the nature of language acquisition and language deficits, but also that an understanding of language learning and language loss could contribute in tangible ways to a theory of the language faculty.

The purpose of this chapter is to begin the investigation of a set of parallel deficits that are manifested in first language acquisition, in second language learning, and in the agrammatism associated with Broca's aphasia. My goal will be to offer an account of these parallels while at the same time providing support for a particular view of the language faculty that I have been trying to develop in recent years.

I will begin in section 19.2 by briefly outlining that view and comparing it with the more traditional perspective. In section 19.3, I consider a representative set of deficits involving pronoun interpretation that are observed in first language acquisition, second language learning, and agrammatism, offering an account of their properties and considering their relevance to our understanding of how language works. In section 19.4, I attempt to take these ideas one step further by tying them in a preliminary way to recent advances in the study of the structure and development of the human brain.

19.2 Contrasting Views of the Language Faculty

At least two cognitive systems are central to language acquisition and use. On the one hand, there is a conceptual-symbolic system that is concerned with the properties of words and morphemes, including their role in expressing linguistically relevant notions such as definiteness, tense, aspect, agency, causality, affectedness, and so forth. On the other hand, there is a computational system that operates on these words and morphemes, combining them in particular ways to construct phrases and sentences, including some that are extraordinarily complex. The computational system corresponds more or less to what is traditionally thought of as "syntax."

As a first approximation at least, I think it is possible to distinguish between two types of theories of what the computational system for language looks like. (McCawley (1974, 179–80) makes a similar distinction, following Derwing (1973).) First, there are theories that take the computational system to consist of a dedicated, faculty-specific *grammatical* system that includes categories and principles common in one form or another to all human languages: Universal Grammar (UG), in other words. The best-known versions of the UG theory have been formulated within the so-called Principles-and-Parameters framework associated with the work of Noam Chomsky and his colleagues—first Government-Binding Theory and more recently the Minimalist Program. However, versions of UG are at least implicit in a variety of other frameworks, including most obviously Lexical-Functional Grammar and Head-driven Phrase Structure Grammar.

A defining feature of all UG approaches is that they essentially equate the language faculty with an autonomous grammatical system that is primarily concerned with issues of well-formedness, not parsing or processing (e.g., Newmeyer 1998). The latter issues are relegated to a theory of performance that deals with actual sentence production and comprehension by positing a separate set of processing strategies and production algorithms.

The second view, which I hold, is quite different. It maintains that the mechanisms that are required to account for the traditional concerns of syntactic theory (word order, pronoun interpretation, control, agreement, contraction, constraints on extraction, etc.) are identical to the mechanisms that are independently required to account for how sentences are processed from "left to right" in real time. According to this view, then, the theory of processing simply subsumes syntactic theory. Let us refer to this as the *processing theory* of the computational system for language. As noted by McCawley (1974, 180), agreeing with Derwing (1973, 55), this sort of approach offers the greatest hope of explaining language acquisition in terms of a more general theory of learning.

The processing theory is not without precedents of various sorts, beginning with work by MacWhinney (e.g., 1987). More recently, Steedman (1996, 2000) and Phillips (1996) have both proposed that the grammatical operations of particular syntactic theories (Categorial Grammar and the Minimalist Program, respectively) can be used for the left-to-right processing of sentence structure. And, of course, there is a long tradition of work that proposes processing mechanisms for production and/or comprehension that complement particular syntactic theories (e.g., Levelt 1989 and Frazier and Clifton 1996, among many others) and that play a role in explaining both language acquisition and language loss (see below). In addition, it is frequently suggested that particular grammatical phenomena may be motivated by processing considerations of various sorts (e.g., Kluender and Kutas 1993; Hawkins 1999).

My proposal goes one step further in suggesting, essentially, that there is no grammar per se at all. Space does not permit a full exposition of this idea here or of how it can account for the traditional problems of syntactic theory, but a few brief illustrations are in order. A more in-depth treatment can be found in O'Grady 2002, forthcoming.

19.2.1 Argument Dependencies

The core of the computational system that I propose consists of a simple combinatorial operation that brings together functors (i.e., argument-taking categories such as verbs) and their arguments. The system operates in a linear manner (i.e., from "left to right"), combining functors and their arguments at the first opportunity in accordance with the *Efficiency Requirement* outlined in (1).

(1) *The Efficiency Requirement*
"Dependencies" (lexical requirements) must be resolved at the first opportunity.

As I see it, the Efficiency Requirement is motivated by the need to minimize the burden on working memory since unresolved dependencies must be held in working memory, obviously an undesirable outcome if it can be avoided.

But what exactly counts as "the first opportunity"? In the case of a functor's argument requirements, information in the argument grid is crucial. As depicted in (2), for instance, the argument grid for a transitive verb such as *speak* indicates that it has two nominal arguments (an agent and a patient) and that the functor is to look to the left for its first argument and to the right for its second argument.

(2) speak: V, ⟨N, N⟩
$\qquad\quad\;\;\leftarrow \;\rightarrow$
$\qquad\quad\;\;$ag pat

Take the sentence *Mary speaks French* as an example. Proceeding from left to right,[1] the noun-verb sequence *Mary speaks* presents the computational system with an immediate opportunity to resolve the verb's first argument dependency by combining it with *Mary*. The Efficiency Requirement demands that advantage be taken of this opportunity, giving the representation depicted in (3).

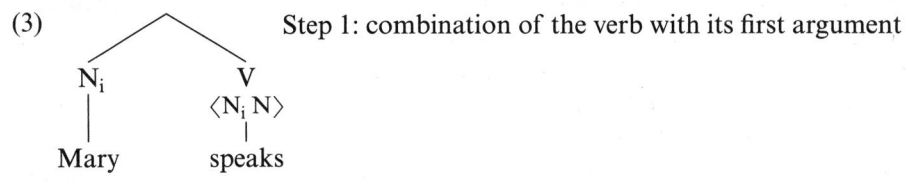

(3)　　　　　　　　　Step 1: combination of the verb with its first argument

$\quad\;\;$ N_i　　V
$\quad\;\;$ |　　⟨N_i N⟩
$\quad\;$ Mary　speaks

The resolution of an argument dependency is indicated by copying the index associated with the nominal into the verb's argument grid, as in Stowell 1981 and Starosta 1988, for instance. Thus, the index of *Mary* is copied into the first position of the grid of *speak* at the point where the two are combined.

The computational system then proceeds to resolve the verb's second argument dependency by combining it directly with the nominal to its right, giving the result depicted in (4).

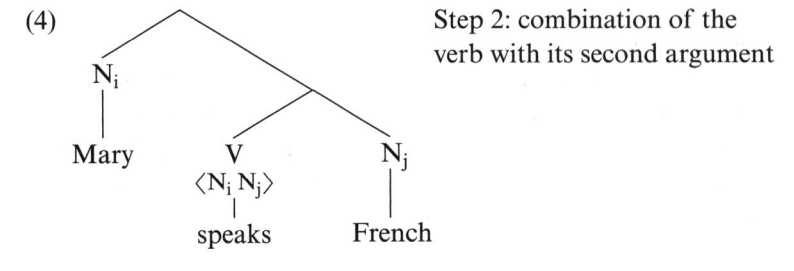

(4)　　　　　　　　　Step 2: combination of the
　　　　　　　　　　 verb with its second argument

$\;\;N_i$
$\;\;$|
$\;$Mary　　V　　　N_j
$\qquad\;$⟨N_i N_j⟩　|
$\qquad\;$speaks　French

Deficits in Pronoun Interpretation 437

It might help to think of this second combinatorial operation as unfolding in two substeps, as in (5).

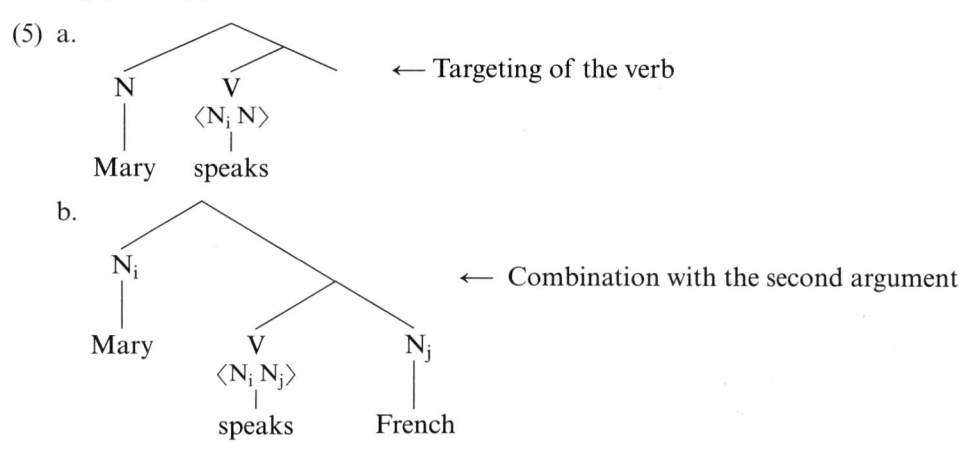

(5) a.
```
      N      V         ← Targeting of the verb
      |    ⟨Nᵢ N⟩
      |      |
     Mary  speaks
```
b.
```
      Nᵢ
      |                ← Combination with the second argument
     Mary   V      Nⱼ
          ⟨Nᵢ Nⱼ⟩    |
            |       French
          speaks
```

The syntactic representations produced in this manner manifest the familiar SVO order and binary-branching design, with the subject higher than the direct object—but not as the result of an a priori grammatical blueprint such as the X-bar schema. Rather, the configurational properties of syntactic representations are "emergent," to use a term currently in vogue (e.g., MacWhinney 1999): they follow from something more basic.

As I see them, "trees" like the ones above are not representations of sentences per se. Rather, they are simply a fleeting residual record of how the computational system goes about combining words, one at a time and from left to right, in accordance with their lexical properties and the demands of the Efficiency Requirement. The structure in (3) exists only as a reflex of the fact that the verb has combined with the nominal to its left. And the structure in (4) exists only because the verb then goes on to combine with the nominal to its right. A more transparent way to represent these facts might be as in (6).

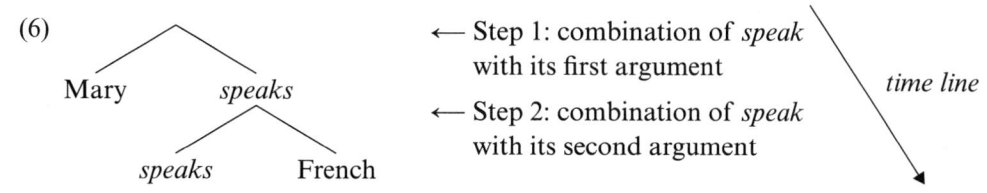

(6)
```
     Mary    speaks            ← Step 1: combination of speak
               |                 with its first argument        time line
            speaks  French     ← Step 2: combination of speak
                                 with its second argument
```

The "time line" here runs from top to bottom, with each constituent consisting of a functor-argument pair (i.e., *Mary* + *speaks*, then *speaks* + *French*) on which the computational system has operated at a particular point in time.

19.2.2 Referential Dependencies

This brings us to the phenomenon of binding, which has long occupied a central place in theorizing about the computational system for language. The centerpiece of traditional UG-based theories of binding is Principle A, which requires—simplifying slightly—that reflexive pronouns be bound (i.e., have a c-commanding antecedent) in the same minimal clause.[2] Thus, (7a) is acceptable, but not (7b), in which the antecedent does not c-command the pronoun, or (7c), in which the antecedent is in a higher clause.

(7) a. The reflexive pronoun has a c-commanding antecedent in the same clause:
   Mary$_i$ overestimates herself$_i$.
  b. The reflexive pronoun has a non-c-commanding antecedent in the same clause:
   *[Mary's$_i$ brother] overestimates herself$_i$.
  c. The reflexive pronoun has a c-commanding antecedent, but not in the same clause:
   *Mary$_i$ thinks [$_S$ John overestimates herself$_i$].

In the computational system that I propose, Principle A effects follow from the Efficiency Requirement. The key assumption is simply that reflexive pronouns introduce a referential dependency—that is, they require that their reference be determined by another element. To see how this works, let us assume that referential dependencies are represented by "variable indices" drawn from the latter part of the roman alphabet (i.e., x, y, z). Thus, the reflexive pronoun *himself* has the syntactic representation depicted in (8), with the index x representing the referential dependency.

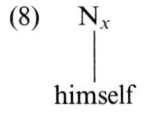

(8) N$_x$
     |
     himself

Like other dependencies, referential dependencies must be resolved at the first opportunity. As we will see directly, an opportunity to resolve a pronoun's referential dependency arises as soon as the computational system encounters the index of another nominal.

The first step in the formation of a sentence such as (7a) involves combining the subject nominal *Mary* with the verb and copying its index into the verb's argument grid, yielding the structure depicted in (9).

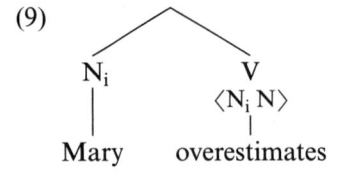

(9)
   N$_i$ V
    | ⟨N$_i$ N⟩
    | |
   Mary   overestimates

Deficits in Pronoun Interpretation 439

Next comes combination of the verb with its second argument, the reflexive pronoun *herself*, as shown in (10).

(10)

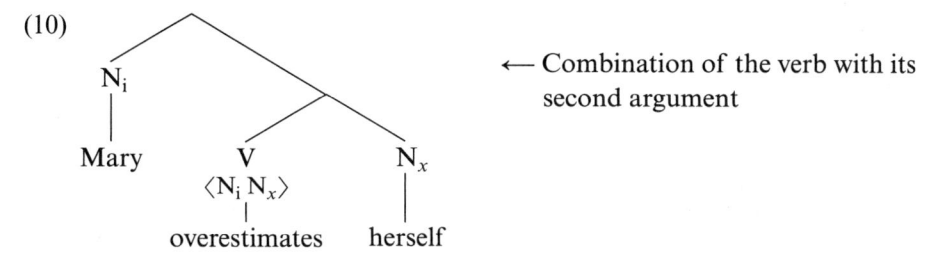

```
          N_i
          |
       Mary        V              N_x
                ⟨N_i N_x⟩          |
                   |            herself
              overestimates
```

← Combination of the verb with its second argument

As illustrated in (11), combination of *herself* with the verb, whose grid contains the index of *Mary*, creates an opportunity to resolve the pronoun's referential dependency, which the computational system must take advantage of.

(11)

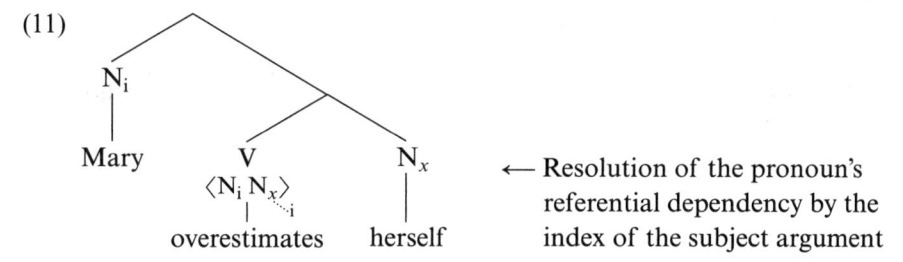

```
          N_i
          |
       Mary        V              N_x
                ⟨N_i N_x⟩          |
                   |            herself
              overestimates
```

← Resolution of the pronoun's referential dependency by the index of the subject argument

Given the Efficiency Requirement, no other result is possible: there is an opportunity to resolve a dependency, and it must be pursued. Anything else would be inefficient.

The unacceptability of sentences (7b) and (7c) now follows automatically. Consider first (7b), whose formation begins by combining the verb with its (previously formed) subject argument, yielding the representation in (12).

(12)

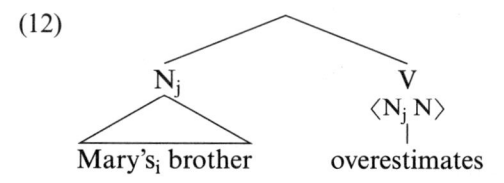

```
              N_j                    V
                                  ⟨N_j N⟩
                                     |
        Mary's_i brother        overestimates
```

At this point, the only index in the verb's grid is that of the subject argument *Mary's brother*. This in turn creates an irresolvable dilemma for the computational system when the verb combines with the reflexive pronoun, as depicted in (13).

(13)

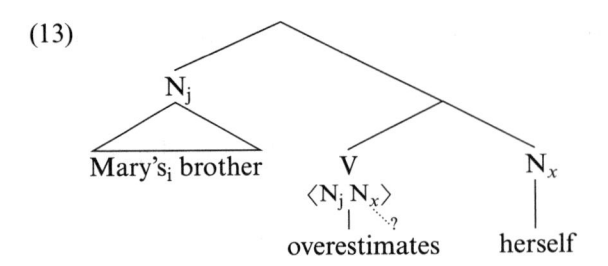

```
         N_j
        /   \
Mary's_i brother    V           N_x
              ⟨N_j N_x⟩          |
                | ...?        herself
           overestimates
```

If the pronoun's referential dependency is not resolved by the index in the verb's grid, the Efficiency Requirement is violated. And if it is resolved in this way, the sentence is semantically anomalous because of the gender mismatch between *herself* and *Mary's brother*. In either case, the sentence is unacceptable.

A similar problem arises in the case of (7c), repeated here.

(7) c. *Mary_i thinks [John overestimates herself_i].

Here, the first opportunity to resolve the referential dependency associated with the reflexive pronoun arises when *herself* combines with the verb *overestimate*, whose argument grid contains only the index of its subject argument *John*.

(14) a.

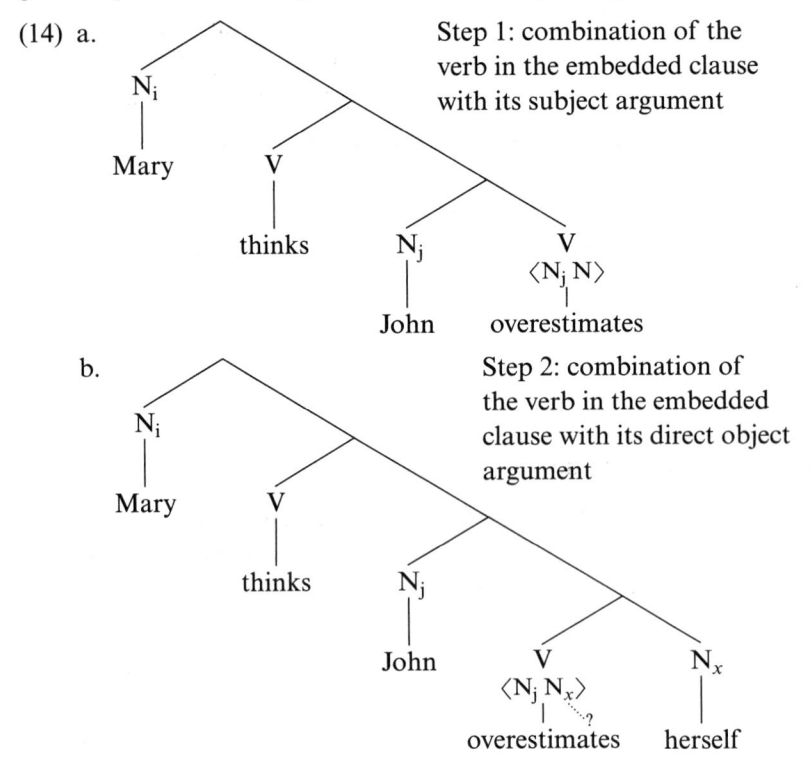

```
         N_i
          |
         Mary    V
                 |
               thinks    N_j         V
                          |       ⟨N_j N⟩
                        John          |
                                overestimates
```

Step 1: combination of the verb in the embedded clause with its subject argument

b.

```
         N_i
          |
         Mary    V
                 |
               thinks    N_j                  V                N_x
                          |               ⟨N_j N_x⟩              |
                        John                 | ...?           herself
                                       overestimates
```

Step 2: combination of the verb in the embedded clause with its direct object argument

If the index of *John* is used to resolve the referential dependency introduced by *herself*, a gender anomaly arises. If the index of *John* is not used, there is a violation of the Efficiency Requirement. Either way, the sentence is unacceptable.

In this manner, it is possible to derive both the c-command and locality requirements on anaphor interpretation from a simple processing property, efficiency, without reference to grammatical principles per se. See O'Grady, forthcoming, for much additional discussion, including an extension of the analysis to many other cases.

As the preceding examples of structure building and anaphor interpretation help illustrate, facts that must be stipulated by principles of grammar in the traditional UG-based approach, including the architecture of phrase structure and the interpretation of reflexive pronouns, follow from the manner in which an efficiency-driven linear processor works. If this sort of approach can be extended in a general way, as argued in detail in O'Grady 2002, forthcoming, then it may be necessary to fundamentally rethink established views concerning the nature of the language faculty.

In describing the computational system that I propose, I have been careful not to use words like *knowledge* or *principles*. As I see it, the computational system is not a body of information at all, contrary to what the traditional Chomskyan view holds (e.g., Fodor 1983, 4). Rather, it is an operating system that is built into the structure of the brain itself. (Derek Bickerton's aphorism "The brain just does it" comes to mind here; see also Searle 2002.) If this is right, then it makes no sense to say that speakers of a language know (or learn) that syntactic structure is binary-branching, that subjects are structurally more prominent than direct objects, or that reflexive pronouns require a more prominent local antecedent—any more than it makes sense to say that people know (or learn) that their heart should pump blood or that their pancreas should produce insulin. Language is the way it is because the brain requires efficiency for practical reasons; efficiency limits the burden on working memory.

If the key properties of the computational system for language do indeed reflect a neurophysiologically motivated drive for efficiency, then, on a strong version of the theory I propose, these properties should be discernable from the earliest stages of development, they should remain stable throughout life, and they should be extremely resistant to damage. This in turn brings us to the questions of why children initially have trouble with certain types of morphological and syntactic patterns, of why it is so difficult for adults to acquire a second language, and of why language is compromised in the way that it is following a stroke or other type of damage to the left frontal cortex. There is relatively little room to maneuver in answering these questions if the processing theory is right—no chance to say that a particular module of UG has not yet matured, is inaccessible, or has been damaged, for instance. The particular proposal I wish to put forward is simply this: language deficits reflect the operation of an intact but underpowered computational system.

A metaphor may help clarify the idea I am proposing: trying to use language with an underpowered computational system is like trying to drive an electric car with a weak battery—the system is intact, but there are certain types of adjustments that need to be made. You'll go more slowly, you'll be forced to take short trips, you'll avoid hills, you'll have to follow the most direct route, and so forth.

Is any of this right, or even on the right track? If it is, then we would expect to find in language acquisition and in language loss signs of computational limitations of a very particular type. Specifically, and following the metaphor I have just outlined, we would expect to see evidence that language learners and agrammatics avoid unnecessary computations, that they prefer short, quick computations, and that they have difficulty with computations that are complicated by external factors.

Ideas along these lines are commonly put forward in the literature on agrammatism (e.g., Linebarger, Schwartz, and Saffran 1983a,b; Caplan and Hildebrandt 1988; Kolk and Weijts 1996), although not with respect to the particular view of the language faculty that I have outlined. Rather, it is assumed that a processor exists alongside of and interacts with a grammar of a conventional sort—which is the standard view in the literature on processing, too (e.g., Fodor 1989, 177ff.; Frazier and Clifton 1996, 9, 25; Frazier 1998, 126). Claims about possible similarities between agrammatism and first language acquisition have a long and somewhat controversial history, dating back to early work by Jakobson (1941), to which I return below.

19.3 Consequences of Underpowered Computation

As explained above, the interpretation of reflexive pronouns is a prototypical case of computational efficiency: the referential dependency is resolved not just at the first opportunity, but *immediately*, by an index present in the grid of the verb with which the reflexive pronoun combines. As we have seen, the c-command and locality constraints that are traditionally stipulated as part of UG (Principle A) follow automatically.

But what of plain pronouns such as *him* and *her*? As is well known, they can take a nonlocal antecedent, as in (15).

(15) Dave$_i$ believes [that John$_j$ admires him$_i$/*himself$_i$].

Moreover, they routinely have antecedents that are external to the sentence, and they may even be used deictically to refer to a previously unnamed individual or entity.

(16) a. Antecedent in a preceding sentence:
Mary arrived yesterday. I saw *her* at the library this morning.
b. Deictic use (pointing):
Hey, look at *him*.

Deficits in Pronoun Interpretation

Figure 19.1
Sample pictures from the study in Chien and Wexler 1990

These facts suggest that the interpretation of plain pronouns somehow falls outside the domain of the Efficiency Requirement[3] and must therefore place extra strain on working memory.

Now, if I am right that the computational system is underpowered, at least initially, in the case of first and second language acquisition and agrammatism, there should be a tendency to misinterpret definite pronouns by resolving the referential dependency they introduce at the earliest opportunity, giving them the interpretation of reflexive pronouns. In fact, there is good evidence that this does happen.

19.3.1 First Language Acquisition

There is ample reason to believe that the interpretation of definite pronouns is initially difficult for first language learners, who mistakenly take the pronoun in patterns such as (17) to refer to the nearer antecedent about 50% of the time. In contrast, they correctly interpret a reflexive pronoun in the same position more than 90% of the time (Jakubowicz 1984; Solan 1987; Read and Hare 1979; Otsu 1981; Kaufman 1994; Chien and Wexler 1990).

(17) Dave believes [that John admires him/himself].

In Chien and Wexler's study, for instance, 177 children aged $2\frac{1}{2}$ to 7 participated in a truth value judgment task, in which they had to respond to queries such as the following with regard to pictures such as the ones in figure 19.1:

(18) This is Mama Bear; this is Goldilocks.
   Is Mama Bear touching her?

Chien and Wexler reported that children younger than 6 did poorly on this task, responding "yes" to the query "Is Mama Bear touching her?" more than half the time on average for the picture on the right, interpreting the plain pronoun *her* as if it were the reflexive pronoun *herself*. This is just what we would expect if the computational system favors the immediate resolution of referential dependencies and is too underpowered to consistently pursue less efficient interpretive options.[4]

19.3.2 Second Language Acquisition

Although the interpretation of reflexive pronouns by second language learners has been investigated quite extensively (see Hamilton 1996 for a review), few studies have sought to compare the interpretation of reflexive and nonreflexive pronouns. Nonetheless, the results are suggestive. Finer and Broselow (1986) report on a pilot study that investigated the interpretation of sentences such as (19a–b) by six intermediate and advanced adult students of English at SUNY Stony Brook. (The study involved judging whether the test sentence correctly described an accompanying picture.)

(19) a. Pattern containing a reflexive pronoun:
   Mr. Fat thinks that [Mr. Thin will paint himself].
   b. Pattern containing a definite pronoun:
   Mr. Fat thinks that [Mr. Thin will paint him].

Participants correctly selected the subject of the embedded clause (Mr. Thin in the example above) as antecedent of the reflexive pronoun 91.7% of the time, but they incorrectly permitted it to serve as antecedent of the plain pronoun in the second pattern 45.9% of the time. Cook (1990, 582) reports that even very advanced students sometimes gave such responses on a timed comprehension task that he conducted. These results suggest that second language learners too seek to resolve referential dependencies with the help of an underpowered computational system that favors short, quick computations.

A problem for this conclusion comes from White's (1998) attempt to replicate Chien and Wexler's study with Japanese-speaking and French-speaking learners of English. She reports that participants in her study (all in the high intermediate range on the University of Michigan English Language Institute Test of English) "largely rejected" local antecedents for plain pronouns, although three of them (two Japanese speakers and one Francophone) did "consistently accept" them (White 1998, 432). Crucially, however, White's study differed from Chien and Wexler's in an important respect: it presented the test sentences in written rather than spoken form (White 1998, 430). This is a potentially serious flaw, since it raises the possibility that the second language learners were able to consider (and reconsider) the test sentences in a way not available to the child first language learners.

Particularly relevant in this regard is a study carried out by Kim (2001) with nine low-intermediate Korean-speaking and Japanese-speaking learners of English that used the same procedure employed by Chien and Wexler, including oral presentation of the test sentences. She reports that her subjects correctly chose a local antecedent for reflexive pronouns 86.1% of the time and incorrectly chose a local antecedent for a plain pronoun 47.2% of the time, a pattern strikingly similar to what has been reported for children learning English as a first language.

19.3.3 Agrammatism

Grodzinsky et al. (1993) report that the eight agrammatics they tested had no trouble interpreting the reflexive pronoun in patterns such as (20a), but that they performed at a chance level on the definite pronoun in (20b), often interpreting it as coreferential with the subject. (See also Grodzinsky 1990 and Caplan and Hildebrandt 1988, 199ff., where a similar result is reported for an act-out task conducted with three seriously impaired agrammatics.)

(20) a. Is Mama Bear touching herself?
    b. Is Mama Bear touching her?

As Grodzinsky et al. note (1993, 408–9), this is exactly the pattern of results observed by Chien and Wexler (1990) for children learning English as a first language. And, I propose, it has exactly the same explanation: in both cases, the participants are tempted to resolve the referential dependency introduced by the pronoun via the shortest and quickest computation, which (incorrectly) links it to the subject of the same clause.

19.4 Making the Metaphor More Concrete

To this point, I have been attempting to describe and explain the existence of a parallel class of deficits associated with language acquisition and language loss in metaphorical terms. In particular, I have suggested that the computational system used by young children, by adult second language learners, and by agrammatics is "underpowered," thereby rendering long or complicated computations difficult or even impossible. The idea can perhaps be made more concrete.

To begin, let us assign a literal interpretation to the particular computational system I have outlined—that is, let us assume that dependencies really are resolved one at a time and at the first opportunity in just the manner described in section 19.2. Let us further assume that the execution of the required operations requires a certain amount of "computational space," by which I simply mean working memory in the sense of Carpenter, Miyake, and Just (1994) and others—a pool of operational resources that not only holds representations (words, phrases, etc.), but also supports computations on those representations.

There is reason to believe that the amount of computational space required by the processor increases with the difficulty of the sentence it is working on. In fact, Just et al. (1996) report that increased sentential complexity actually results in the recruitment of more neural tissue in each of a network of cortical areas (see also Sakai, Hashimoto, and Homae 2001).

There is also reason to think that no part of the brain is set aside in advance specifically to provide computational space for sentence processing. The required space must be found in the course of development through competition with other types of cognitive functions. As noted by Deacon (1997, 218), "the relative sizes of the brain's functional divisions are determined in a systematic competition for space." The brain's wiring, Deacon suggests, "is determined by virtue of the interaction of information conveyed by its connections.... This is a competitive selection process, a sort of rapid local evolutionary process on a microscopic scale" (1997, 221).

If this is right, then the language function has to compete for space in the course of early development. The territory that it seeks to stake out is selected for good reason: as Deacon notes (1997, 315), the left hemisphere seems "more often adept at ultra-rapid analysis of sound changes and control of rapid, precise, skilled movement sequences."

In any case, it seems reasonable to suppose that computational space is initially at a premium and that until the competition for adequate working memory resources is successfully concluded, the computational system is significantly underpowered, accounting for the patterns of performance observed above for pronominal reference.

Turning now to second language acquisition, there is good reason to think that here too computational space is an issue. Functional magnetic resonance imaging has yielded a suggestive finding in this regard in speakers who have acquired a second language as adults: Kim et al. (1997) report that different activation sites within Broca's area are associated with the first and second languages in the case of late bilinguals, but not early bilinguals.[5] (The task involved describing an event to oneself in one or the other language.) This suggests that an initial shortage of computational space results in a developmental profile for adult second language learning that parallels the one observed for first language acquisition on phenomena that require a fully powered computational system.[6]

Matters are different again in the case of the agrammatism associated with Broca's aphasia. Under these circumstances, a particular part of the brain that is involved in linguistic computation becomes physically damaged. Recovery, to the extent that it occurs, involves recruiting a different area of the brain to carry out the tasks formerly assigned to the damaged region (Demeurisse and Capon 1987; Basso et al. 1989; Cappa et al. 1997; Heiss et al. 1999). Once again, the issue of limited computational space arises, at least initially, since it seems reasonable to suppose that the new area must be recruited competitively in much the same way as the regions that support computations in the course of first and second language acquisition are. The characteristic consequences of an underpowered computational system that we observe in agrammatism are therefore expected.

At first glance, it might appear that this view of language deficits is a version of Jakobson's (1941) Regression Hypothesis, according to which language loss is in some sense the mirror image of language acquisition, with the things acquired last being most susceptible to loss. This is not so, however. My point is simply that (certain of) the grammatical deficits associated with language loss and with the early stages of language acquisition are due to the same cause: a shortage of computational space. The precise extent of this shortage and the time needed to remedy it vary even from individual to individual. This is true not only for language loss, where every patient exhibits a unique pattern of cell damage and recovery (e.g., Caplan and Hildebrandt 1988, 299), but also presumably for language acquisition, where differences in rate of development are widely attested for both first language acquisition (e.g., Bates, Bretherton, and Snyder 1988) and second language learning (Larsen-Freeman and Long 1991, 167). There is no reason to think that the computational resources available to an agrammatic will be *identical* to those available to a child acquiring a first language or to an adult learning a second language. There is thus no reason to think that the precise degree to which particular linguistic deficits are manifested will be identical either.

Nonetheless, the net effects of shortages in computational space should have predictable consequences for language acquisition and language loss, resulting in the relative difficulty of certain phenomena with respect to others. As we have seen, one instance of this is the relative difficulty of interpreting plain pronouns, with their nonlocal antecedents, compared with locally bound reflexives.

19.5 Concluding Remarks

As observed by Gregg (1996), drawing on a distinction proposed by Cummins (1983), an adequate account of language acquisition must offer two sorts of explanations. On the one hand, it must include a "property theory" that explains the properties of human language and how they are acquired, given the familiar limitations on input and experience. On the other hand, it must also offer a "transition theory" that explains how language learners are able to move through the acquisition process, "escaping" from the errors that are characteristic of early development. As noted by McCawley (1980, 27), such a theory did not accompany the property theory associated with early work on UG.

The processing theory offers an answer to both of these challenges, at least with respect to "core" syntactic phenomena such as the architecture of phrase structure and constraints on coreference. In particular, it proposes that languages with the specific properties we observe (binary-branching syntactic representations, subjects structurally more prominent than direct objects, c-command and locality constraints on anaphora, etc.) exist and are acquired because of an (inborn) computational system that seeks to construct sentences in the most efficient manner possible, that is, by resolving dependencies at the first opportunity, thereby reducing the burden on working memory.

Moreover, it proposes that the errors characteristic of the early use of this system in the course of language acquisition (including mistakes in the interpretation of plain pronouns) stem from a shortage of computational space. The transition theory implied by this view does not posit "stages" of acquisition, at least not in the sense of discrete developmental periods in which particular modules of language are missing. Rather, it holds that the "grammar" is at heart nothing but an efficiency-driven processor that is available from the beginning of the language acquisition process. "Development" takes place as two sorts of (gradual) changes occur. First, as the computational system for language succeeds in its competition with other cognitive functions for processing space, it improves on its capacity to carry out more demanding computations, including those that do not permit immediate resolution of dependencies, as is the case with the interpretation of plain pronouns.

Second, as the computational system is used to form and interpret sentences of a particular language, it becomes accustomed to carrying out particular operations and sequences of operations on the symbols (words and morphemes) that it encounters—for example, looking to the right for the noun with which a determiner combines, resolving a verb's first argument dependency with the help of a nominal bearing compatible person and number features, immediately resolving the referential dependencies introduced by pronouns ending in *-self/selves*, and so on. As a result, the computational system not only develops a set of more or less automatic routines that speed up language processing, but becomes set in its ways to the point where it attempts nothing but these routines when operating on symbols from English. This in turn gives a result identical in its consequences to having a grammar that orders determiners before nouns, that has a subject agreement rule, that imposes locality and c-command requirements on reflexive pronouns, and so forth (see table 19.1).

Table 19.1
Effects of the automatization of particular computational routines

Routine	Apparent effect
Looking to the right for the noun associated with a determiner (e.g., *the house*)	NP → Det N
Combining a verb with a first argument bearing matching person and number features (e.g., **The car** *runs well*)	Subject-verb agreement
Resolving the referential dependency introduced by *X-self/selves* at the first opportunity (e.g., *Mary overestimated herself*)	A reflexive pronoun has a local c-commanding antecedent

A remarkable feature of this account is that it offers a way to unify the theory of language acquisition with the theory of language loss, with both seeking an explanation for their subject matter in terms of a simple and robust efficiency-driven computational system whose operation can be compromised only by a shortage of processing space.

Take agrammatism, for example. As outlined earlier, I have adopted the view that damage to the left frontal cortex can reduce computational space, which in turn favors short, quick, uncomplicated computations. This view is widely held in the literature on agrammatism. For instance, Dick et al. (2001, 12) suggest that syntactic deficits in aphasia arise from "a generalized 'stress' on processing resources." A similar proposal is put forward by Caplan and Waters (1999), who attribute these deficits to the loss of computational space for language, and by Just and Carpenter (1992) and Just, Carpenter, and Keller (1996), who likewise posit a problem with working memory (which they take to be non-syntax-specific, contra Caplan and Waters 1999). Indeed, it is frequently observed that the lesion sites associated with receptive agrammatism overlap with the regions supporting working memory (e.g., Hickock 2000; Stowe 2000; also see Smith and Jonides 1997 for a review).

If this is right, then we are all but compelled to offer a similar account as the null hypothesis in trying to explain the parallel phenomena that arise in the case of first and second language acquisition. True, we *could* say that a particular module of the language faculty matures late in the case of first language acquisition. And we *could* propose that that same module is mysteriously no longer accessible to adults learning a second language. But surely the first hypothesis that we should consider is the one that is independently required to account for the very similar facts that are manifested in the case of language loss, namely, that the observed deficits are due to limitations on working memory resources that affect the operation of the computational system, but leave its internal structure otherwise untouched.

In closing, I would like to return to a fundamental matter on which the proposal that I have been outlining rests, namely, the nature of the language faculty itself. As explained at the outset, I take the view that there is no grammar per se; the phenomena that it is traditionally assumed to account for—the design of syntactic structure, constraints on coreference, and so forth—follow from the operation of a very simple, efficiency-driven computational system that is indistinguishable from what traditionally would be called a processor. In this regard, my proposal is very different from other processing-based accounts of agrammatism (e.g., Linebarger, Schwartz, and Saffran 1983a,b; Caplan and Hildebrandt 1988; Kolk and Weijts 1996) and of language acquisition (e.g., Berwick 1985 for first language acquisition; Pienemann 1998 for second language acquisition), which posit a full-fledged autonomous grammar in addition to a processor.

The merits of the processing theory of the language faculty must ultimately be evaluated in part by asking how insightfully it accounts for the phenomena that lie at the heart of contemporary syntactic theory, phenomena such as binding, control, agreement, and extraction (see O'Grady 2002, forthcoming, for extensive discussion of these matters). At the same time, however, it is important to recognize that this approach has implications that extend beyond the study of these traditional questions. In particular, as we have seen here, it literally forces us to adopt an account of language acquisition and language loss that attributes deficits to shortages of computational space—there is simply no alternative, once we admit that there is no grammar per se.

Notes

1. I intend this characterization to be neutral between production and comprehension. That is not to say that there are no differences between the two processes, only that the differences do not involve the Efficiency Requirement.

2. I deliberately set aside discussion of so-called long-distance anaphora here (see, e.g., Kang 1988; Pollard and Xue 1998; O'Grady, forthcoming).

3. A comparable assumption is necessary in grammar-based approaches to pronominal reference: the binding theory does not stipulate where a plain pronoun is to find its antecedent; it indicates only where the antecedent cannot be.

4. For reasons of space, I deliberately set aside the question of what happens when the pronoun has a quantified antecedent such as *everyone*.

5. Presenting results from a listening task, Perani et al. (1998) report differences in cortical activity for different languages in low-proficiency learners, but not in high-proficiency learners. As they note, it is unclear whether this finding extends to production and whether the observed differences are the cause or the consequence of successful second language learning.

6. There is evidence, although not yet totally clear-cut, that success in second language acquisition correlates in some way with working memory capacity (e.g., Gathercole and Thorn 1998; Miyake and Friedman 1998; Ellis 2001; Robinson 2002).

References

Basso, A., M. Gardelli, M. Grassi, and M. Mariotti. 1989. The role of the right hemisphere in recovery from aphasia: Two case studies. *Cortex* 25, 555–56.

Bates, Elizabeth, Inge Bretherton, and Lynn Snyder. 1988. *From first words to grammar: Individual differences and dissociable mechanisms*. New York: Cambridge University Press.

Berwick, Robert. 1985. *The acquisition of syntactic knowledge*. Cambridge, MA: MIT Press.

Caplan, David, and Nancy Hildebrandt. 1988. *Disorders of syntactic comprehension*. Cambridge, MA: MIT Press.

Caplan, David, and Gloria Waters. 1999. Verbal working memory and sentence comprehension. *Behavioral and Brain Sciences* 22, 77–126.

Cappa, S., D. Perani, F. Grassi, F. Bressi, M. Alberoni, M. Franceschi, M. Bettinardi, M. Todde, and M. Fazio. 1997. A PET follow-up study of recovery after stroke in acute aphasics. *Brain and Language* 56, 55–67.

Carpenter, Patricia, Akira Miyake, and Marcel Just. 1994. Working memory constraints in comprehension: Evidence from individual differences, aphasia, and aging. In *Handbook of psycholinguistics*, ed. by Morton Ann Gernsbacher, 1075–1122. San Diego, CA: Academic Press.

Chien, Yu-Chin, and Kenneth Wexler. 1990. Children's knowledge of locality conditions in binding as evidence for the modularity of syntax and pragmatics. *Language Acquisition* 1, 225–95.

Cook, Vivian. 1990. Timed comprehension of binding in advanced L2 learners of English. *Language Learning* 40, 557–99.

Cummins, Robert. 1983. *The nature of psychological explanation*. Cambridge, MA: MIT Press.

Deacon, Terrence. 1997. *The symbolic species: The co-evolution of language and the brain*. New York: Norton.

Demeurisse, Guy, and A. Capon. 1987. Language recovery in aphasic stroke patients: Clinical, CT, and CBF studies. *Aphasiology* 1, 301–15.

Derwing, Bruce. 1973. *Transformational grammar as a theory of language acquisition: A study in the empirical, conceptual and methodological foundations of contemporary linguistics*. Cambridge: Cambridge University Press.

Dick, Frederic, Elizabeth Bates, Beverly Wulfeck, Morton Gernsbacher, Jennifer Utman, and Nina Dronkers. 2001. Language deficits, localization and grammar: Evidence for a distributive model of language breakdown in aphasics and normals. *Psychological Review* 108, 759–88.

Ellis, Nick. 2001. Memory for language. In *Cognition and second language instruction*, ed. by Peter Robinson, 33–68. New York: Cambridge University Press.

Finer, Dan, and Ellen Broselow. 1986. Second language acquisition of reflexive binding. In *Proceedings of NELS 16*, 154–68. Amherst: University of Massachusetts, GLSA.

Fodor, Jerry. 1983. *The modularity of mind*. Cambridge, MA: MIT Press.

Fodor, Janet Dean. 1989. Empty categories in sentence processing. *Language and Cognitive Processes* 4, 155–209.

Frazier, Lyn. 1998. Getting there (slowly). *Journal of Psycholinguistic Research* 27, 123–46.

Frazier, Lyn, and Charles Clifton, Jr. 1996. *Construal*. Cambridge, MA: MIT Press.

Gathercole, Susan, and A. S. C. Thorn. 1998. Phonological short term memory and foreign language learning. In *Foreign language learning: Psycholinguistic studies on training and retention*, ed. by Alice Healy and Lyle Bourne, 141–58. Mahwah, NJ: Lawrence Erlbaum.

Gregg, Kevin. 1996. The logical and developmental problems of second language acquisition. In *Handbook of second language acquisition*, ed. by William Ritchie and Tej Bhatia, 49–81. San Diego, CA: Academic Press.

Grodzinsky, Yosef. 1990. *Theoretical perspectives on language deficits*. Cambridge, MA: MIT Press.

Grodzinsky, Yosef, Kenneth Wexler, Yu-Chin Chien, Susan Marakovitz, and Julie Solomon. 1993. The breakdown of binding relations. *Brain and Language* 45, 396–422.

Hamilton, Robert. 1996. Against underdetermined reflexive binding. *Second Language Research* 12, 420–46.

Hawkins, John. 1999. Processing complexity and filler-gap dependencies across grammars. *Language* 75, 244–85.

Heiss, W. D., J. Kessler, A. Thiel, M. Ghaemi, and H. Karbe. 1999. Differential capacity of left and right hemispheric area for compensation of poststroke aphasia. *Annals of Neurology* 45, 430–38.

Hickock, Gregory. 2000. The left frontal convolution plays no special role in syntactic comprehension. *Behavioral and Brain Sciences* 23, 35–36.

Jakobson, Roman. 1941. *Kindersprache, Aphasie und allgemeine Lautgesetze*. Uppsala: Almquist and Wiksell. Translated into English and published as *Child language, aphasia and phonological universals*. The Hague: Mouton, 1968.

Jakubowicz, Celia. 1984. On markedness and binding principles. In *Proceedings of NELS 14*, ed. by Charles Jones and Peter Sells, 154–82. Amherst: University of Massachusetts, GLSA.

Just, Marcel, and Patricia Carpenter. 1992. A capacity theory of comprehension: Individual differences in working memory. *Psychological Review* 99, 122–49.

Just, Marcel, Patricia Carpenter, and Timothy Keller. 1996. The capacity theory of comprehension: New frontiers of evidence and arguments. *Psychological Review* 103, 773–80.

Just, Marcel, Patricia Carpenter, Timothy Keller, William Eddy, and Keith Turlborn. 1996. Brain activation modulated by sentence comprehension. *Science* 274, 114–16.

Kang, Beom-mo. 1988. Unbounded reflexives. *Linguistics and Philosophy* 11, 415–56.

Kaufman, Diana. 1994. Grammatical or pragmatic: Will the real Principle B please stand up? Syntactic theory and first language acquisition. In *Cross-linguistic perspectives*. Vol. 2, *Binding, dependencies and learnabililty*, ed. by Barbara Lust, Gabrielle Hermon, and Jaklin Kornfilt, 177–200. Hillsdale, NJ: Lawrence Erlbaum.

Kim, Jaeyeon. 2001. The interpretation of English pronouns by second language learners. Manuscript, University of Hawaii.

Kim, Karl, Norman Relkin, Kyoung-Min Lee, and Joy Hirsch. 1997. Distinct cortical areas associated with native and second languages. *Nature* 388, 171–74.

Kluender, Robert, and Marta Kutas. 1993. Subjacency as a processing phenomenon. *Language and Cognitive Processes* 8, 573–633.

Kolk, Herman, and Marion Weijts. 1996. Judgments of semantic anomaly in agrammatic patients: Argument movement, syntactic complexity, and the use of heuristics. *Brain and Language* 54, 86–135.

Larsen-Freeman, Diane, and Michael Long. 1991. *An introduction to second language acquisition research*. New York: Longman.

Levelt, Willem. 1989. *Speaking: From intention to articulation*. Cambridge, MA: MIT Press.

Linebarger, Marcia, Myrna Schwartz, and Eleanor Saffran. 1983a. Sensitivity to grammatical structure in so-called agrammatic aphasics. *Cognition* 13, 361–92.

Linebarger, Marcia, Myrna Schwartz, and Eleanor Saffran. 1983b. Syntactic processing in agrammatism: A reply to Zurif and Grodzinsky. *Cognition* 15, 207–13.

MacWhinney, Brian. 1987. Toward a psycholinguistically plausible parser. In *ESCOL '86: Proceedings of the Eastern States Conference on Linguistics*, ed. by Fred Marshall, Ann Miller, and Zheng-Sheng Zhang. Ithaca, NY: Cornell University, CLC Publications.

MacWhinney, Brian, ed. 1999. *The emergence of language.* Mahwah, NJ: Lawrence Erlbaum.

McCawley, James D. 1974. Review of Derwing 1973. *Canadian Journal of Linguistics* 19, 177–88.

McCawley, James D. 1980. ¡Tabula si, rasa no! *Behavioral and Brain Sciences* 3, 26–27.

McCawley, James D. 1992. A note on auxiliary verbs and language acquisition. *Journal of Linguistics* 28, 445–51.

Miyake, Akira, and Naomi P. Friedman. 1998. Individual differences in second language proficiency: Working memory as language aptitude. In *Foreign language learning: Psycholinguistic studies on training and retention*, ed. by Alice Healy and Lyle Bourne, 339–64. Mahwah, NJ: Lawrence Erlbaum.

Newmeyer, Frederick. 1998. *Language form and language function.* Cambridge, MA: MIT Press.

O'Grady, William. 2002. An emergentist approach to syntax. Manuscript, University of Hawaii at Manoa.

O'Grady, William. Forthcoming. *Syntactic carpentry: An emergentist approach to syntax.* Mahwah, NJ: Lawrence Erlbaum.

Otsu, Yukio. 1981. Universal Grammar and syntactic development in children: Toward a theory of syntactic development. Doctoral dissertation, MIT.

Perani, D., E. Paulesu, N. Galles, E. Dupoux, S. Dehaene, V. Bettinardi, S. Cappa, F. Fazio, and J. Mehler. 1998. The bilingual brain: Proficiency and age of acquisition of the second language. *Brain* 121, 1841–52.

Phillips, Colin. 1996. Order and structure. Doctoral dissertation, MIT.

Pienemann, Manfred. 1998. *Language processing and second language development: Processibility theory.* Philadelphia: John Benjamins.

Pollard, Carl, and Ping Xue. 1998. Chinese reflexive *ziji*: Syntactic reflexives vs. non-syntactic reflexives. *Journal of East Asian Linguistics* 7, 287–318.

Read, Charles, and Victoria Hare. 1979. Children's interpretation of reflexive pronouns in English. In *Studies in first and second language acquisition*, ed. by Fred R. Eckman and Ashley J. Hastings, 98–116. Rowley, MA: Newbury House.

Robinson, Peter. 2002. Effects of individual differences in intelligence, aptitude and working memory on incidental SLA. In *Individual differences and instructed language learning*, ed. by Peter Robinson, 211–51. Philadelphia: John Benjamins.

Sakai, Kuniyoshi, Ryuishiro Hashimoto, and Fumitaka Homae. 2001. Sentence processing in the cerebral cortex. *Neuroscience Research* 39, 1–10.

Searle, John. 2002. End of the revolution. *New York Review*, 28 February 2002, 33–36.

Smith, Edward, and John Jonides. 1997. Working memory: A view from neuroimaging. *Cognitive Psychology* 33, 5–42.

Solan, Lawrence. 1987. Parameter setting and development of pronouns and reflexives. In *Parameter setting*, ed. by Thomas Roeper and Edwin Williams, 189–210. Boston: Reidel.

Starosta, Stanley. 1988. *The case for lexicase*. London: Pinter.

Steedman, Mark. 1996. *Surface structure and interpretation*. Cambridge, MA: MIT Press.

Steedman, Mark. 2000. *The syntactic process*. Cambridge, MA: MIT Press.

Stowe, Laurie. 2000. Sentence comprehension and the left inferior frontal gyrus: Storage, not computation. *Behavioral and Brain Sciences* 23, 51.

Stowell, Tim. 1981. Origins of phrase structure. Doctoral dissertation, MIT.

White, Lydia. 1998. Second language acquisition and Binding Principle B: Child/adult differences. *Second Language Research* 14, 425–39.

Chapter 20

Why Verb Agreement Is Not the Poster Child for Any General Formal Principle

Jerry L. Morgan and Georgia M. Green

20.1 Introduction

Since the 1960s, agreement between subject and verb has been used to illustrate key principles of syntactic theories, beginning with transformational grammar and continuing to this day. The desire to account for the fact that the heads of verb phrases have morphological reflections of properties associated with their subject NPs (Keenan 1974) has been the basis for theoretical claims relating to the linear character of structural analyses (Chomsky 1957, 1965), extrinsic ordering of rules of grammar, and information-based character of rules of grammar (Pollard and Sag 1988, 1994). Working grammarians consider having an adequate account of agreement as one of the benchmarks that any grammatical theory must satisfy to be taken seriously. In 1988, the Chicago Linguistic Society devoted an entire parasession to the role of agreement in grammatical theory (Brentari, Larson, and MacLeod 1988). And yet, as evidenced by the papers in that volume, the principles regulating agreement of subject and verb in a language are typically taken, without discussion, to be a property of a language that is common to all variants. We show that in English at least (and probably in all languages which mark agreement, because the issues that contribute to problems of number resolution are semantic and logical rather than specific to a particular grammatical system; see Corbett 2000), solutions to these problems in the internal grammars of individuals appear to be idiosyncratic, highly varied, and possibly inconsistent. As a consequence, conclusions about Universal Grammar based on arguments which treat grammars as having a single neat, uniform, and coherent account of agreement are based on false premises. This is why verb agreement cannot be the poster child for *any* general formal principle.

Variation per se is not a problem for linguistic theory, of course. Chomsky (1965, 3–4) proposed concentrating on an "ideal speaker-listener" to abstract away from performance "noise" and dialect variation. But before all of the empirical work prompted by the articulation of principles of generative grammar, linguists never imagined covert idiolects of the sort we describe; we write (partial) grammars of

English, Hindi, Japanese, and so on, on the assumption that there are *langues* with those names. Technical work in linguistic theory, especially applying learnability theory, depends on the assumption that internal "competence" grammars are complete and consistent formal objects. Quite likely, the gross outlines of most grammatical phenomena are uniform within recognizable speech communities. But if verb agreement has rough edges where speakers are on their own and may follow different paths in the course of language acquisition, some even perhaps arriving at a stasis where the internal grammar (competence) is incomplete or even internally inconsistent, then other aspects of grammar may be similarly underdetermined within a speech community that is to all appearances homogeneous. If the unhindered competence of actual speakers does not have the properties of the formal objects used to model it, we consider that an interesting fact to be explained. The alternative, abandoning the assumption that speakers know the languages they speak, pretty much cuts the empirical rug out from under the ability not only to do research in linguistic theory, but also to describe more than the gross outlines of languages.

Despite the apparent simplicity of the appealing prosaic claim that "function symbols may present a morpheme whose form is determined by the noun class of the argument expression" (Keenan 1974, 302), corroborating an empirically vulnerable formulation of a "rule of verb agreement" has always been problematic. Morgan noted a number of theory-independent problems with the content of "the rule of verb agreement" in the early 1970s (Morgan 1972a,b). Chief among these is the problem of determining what the grammatically relevant number of a coordinate noun phrase is. In the "normal" case, grammatical conjunction corresponds to arithmetical addition, and a conjoined coordinate NP whose conjuncts are singular constitutes a plural NP, as in (1a), whereas the corresponding NP with *or* counts as singular, as in (1b).

(1) a. A clerk [SG] and a technician [SG] are [PL] using that room.
    b. A clerk [SG] or a technician [SG] is [SG] using that room.

In such cases, commonsense interpretation is consistent with the agreement facts, since if a clerk *and* a technician are involved, two persons are using the room; whereas if a clerk *or* a technician is involved, only one person is using the room, assuming exclusive disjunction as the foremost interpretation.

But there are quite a few cases that diverge from this pattern, as documented in Morgan 1972a,b, 1984, 1985. Sometimes grammatical conjunction corresponds to conceptualization as a unit, allowing sentences like (2a–b), as well as their plural counterparts, to be grammatically well formed.

(2) a. Hash browns [PL] and eggs [PL] is [SG] a favorite of Sam's.
    b. Hash browns [PL] and eggs [PL] is [SG] the cat's pajamas.

And sometimes logic has nothing to do with the grammatical number of an NP. As noted in Morgan 1985, decimal quantifiers make an NP plural even if it refers notionally to exactly one unit—or less than one.

(3) a. Out of every 10 voters, 1.0 were careless enough to leave a hanging chad.
    b. Out of every 10 voters, one was careless enough to leave a hanging chad.
    c. Out of every 10 voters, 0.75 were careless enough to leave a hanging chad.
    d. Of every 100 polled, 1.0 high school seniors were unwilling to answer questions about marijuana use. (*1.0 high school senior)
    e. Of every 100 polled, 0.75 high school seniors were unwilling to answer questions about marijuana use.

The problem of what element is required to agree with the verb (the selection problem of Morgan 1972b, 1984) complicates matters further. Principles of selection may be highly construction-specific. For example, in NPs with comparative quantifiers, it is the number marking on the phrase-final noun that determines the number marking on the verb, even when it contradicts the notional number of the subject.

(4) a. More than one item is/*are in that cell. (That is, at least two items are in that cell.)
    b. Fewer than two children were/*was admitted. (That is, either one child was admitted, or no child was admitted.)

In predicate nominative constructions like (5a–b), the predicate NP may compete with the subject as an agreement controller. A singular nondistributive predicate NP can require a singular verb, (as in (5)), even when both disjuncts of a coordinate subject are plural, as in (5b).

(5) a. Peppers is/are a great choice.
    b. Peppers or tomatoes is/?*are a difficult choice.

This chapter reports an approach to an issue at the juncture of the selection problem and the determination problem: what determines the agreement marking on a verb when the subject NP is a coordinate structure? The additive logic of *and*-conjunction would seem to make this question a no-brainer, but it turns out that when the subject NP does not immediately precede the verb, as for example in *there*-constructions, speakers' choices are not so straightforward. Indeed, far from illustrating great insights into the architecture of linguistic knowledge, the account of verb agreement in *there*-constructions requires contortions or ad hoc mechanisms in every familiar theory (Green 1985). And as the logic of disjunction does not determine the grammatical number of the coordinate NP as a function of the cardinality of the referents of the conjuncts, it provides no principle at all for determining the number of a disjunctive coordinate subject. Our approach elaborates on Morgan's conclusion that the determination problem appears to involve a complex of principles. "In simple cases these principles generally give the same result. In complex cases they can conflict, in which case there may not be conflict resolution principles" (Morgan 1985, 71). Lest there be any misunderstanding, the point of this chapter is that the range of variation exhibited in verb agreement choices suggests that individuals' internal grammars for this basic phenomenon of language not only vary idiosyncratically,[1] but may be incomplete or inconsistent. If this is correct, it has consequences for discussions of the architecture of the human language faculty that crucially assume that internal grammars are as complete and consistent as the mathematical models are supposed to be.

Our attention to this problem was inspired by Jim McCawley's example of regularly questioning the significance of unexpected facts for basic principles of the theory that provoked their discovery rather than simply adding bells and whistles to the theory to accommodate them. He demonstrated this approach in his essays on language acquisition (e.g., McCawley 1976) and his work on the grammar of English auxiliary verbs (McCawley 1971, 1979, 1985), among others. In class and in public, Jim questioned the match between an adequate and theoretically orthodox grammar of a language, and the form that knowledge of that language takes in an individual's mind.

It is commonly stated that in standard, generic, uncontroversial varieties of English, finite verbs agree with their subjects in person and number. This chapter starts from the observation that that statement is incomplete, in that it says nothing about cases where the person or number of the subject NP is syntactically or semantically nonstraightforward. Beyond the well-known problems posed by plural nouns with singular referents (*pants*, *glasses*) and vice versa (group nouns like *faculty*, *committee*, *team*),[2] it is simply not clear to speakers (or linguists) what the person or number of disjunctive NPs like *Jo or I* or *the governor or his handlers* is. On the basis of data we discuss below, we conjecture that some individuals develop extensions and auxiliary principles in their internal grammars to cover various classes of noncanonical cases. Some apparently prefer to avoid using the constructions that would require additional or amended principles and find certain cases impossible to judge, or judge all alternatives as ungrammatical. In some cases, some speakers find more than one alternative equally acceptable. And in a few cases, the inconsistent performance of speakers appears to be a consequence of the fact that the rules in their internal grammars have nothing to say about some classes of noncanonical cases.

The supporting evidence comes from responses to a 133-item forced-choice questionnaire, reproduced here as appendix A. Ultimately, there were as many response patterns as there were respondents. Although on analysis the patterns were factorable into a small number of principles, the way the patterns divided up the domain was still unique to each respondent, and respondents varied widely on which cases were

Verb Agreement 459

impossible to judge, which seemed to admit no acceptable alternative among those offered, and which evoked inconsistent responses in repeated trials.

It was not always clear from the data what the boundaries of a principle's domain were in an individual's grammar. Sometimes, as detailed in section 20.3, there was insufficient data to tell which of two or three competing principles determined the grammatical number of a coordinate NP in a particular construction, or whether for at least some speakers, multiple principles must be satisfied to determine a choice. We conclude that the internal grammars of individuals may be far from elegant and may contain lacunae which occasion a variety of behaviors which result in the apparent chaos of the elicited judgments.

20.2 The Problem

Sometimes speakers are unable to determine the number of an NP: there are compositionally simple sentences for which individuals' grammars do not seem to provide the basis for judging acceptability. For example, there is no obvious principle for computing the number of a coordinate NP consisting of disjuncts with dissimilar number,[3] so that some speakers are uncomfortable if challenged to select the best verb for sentences like those in (6).[4]

(6) a. Is/Are there an orchestra or two digital pianos in that room?
    b. Is/Are there two digital pianos or an orchestra in that room?

There are well-known order and adjacency effects that may be observed in such situations. Verbs that do not immediately follow the head noun of the subject NP sometimes agree with a nonhead NP that immediately precedes them (the "*Finian's Rainbow* phenomenon"[5]), as illustrated in the examples in (7).

(7) a. What group of fish live in coastal waters of Australian New Guinea?
    (British National Corpus, *Practical Fishkeeping*, 1991, sentence 1038)
    b. A group of us evolve towards the door.
    (British National Corpus, *Lucker and Tiffany Peel Out*)
    c. Businessmen have watched the emergence of distressing reports from Wall St., and the plunge in stock prices that have accompanied them.
    (National Public Radio, *All Things Considered*, 9 July 2002)[6]

The fact that prescriptive grammar handbooks for native speakers instruct readers to avoid this pattern indicates that it is a normal pattern for at least some speakers. Not so well recognized, but solidly established in the questionnaire data reported in section 20.3, are order effects: when the subject NP follows the verb, some speakers use a different agreement principle for nonobvious cases than they use when it precedes. For example, in inversion constructions, the verb may agree not with the subject that follows it, but with a preceding NP, or it may take a "default" third person singular form, as in *To the victor belongs the spoils!!* (Dik Browne, *Hagar the Horrible*, 7 July 2002).

There are various scenarios for what could happen when a speaker with an incomplete grammar encounters a situation for which that grammar does not determine a unique form.

1. The grammar could be revised. An existent rule could be broadened so that it covers the class of cases exemplified.[7] Becoming more general (less restricted) is the sort of broadening that may come to mind first, but in the sense of extending coverage, the addition of auxiliary principles (either disjunctive or intersecting) for special cases would also constitute broadening.
2. The grammar could remain incomplete, but the speaker could adopt a performance strategy amounting to "what is not expressly forbidden is allowed" and be comfortable with any solution that is consistent with (an extension of) some agreement principle.
3. The speaker could adopt a performance strategy amounting to "what is not expressly required is forbidden" and be uncomfortable with any solution if all applicable principles do not converge on a unique solution. Here too, the grammar would remain incomplete.

The first (patchwork) scenario would result in speakers' having an ability to make judgments on sentences in classes not covered by the shared, general rule; but if different speakers extended different rules, or extended them in different ways, speakers would exhibit distinct idiolects. Furthermore, an individual's grammar might be non-optimal, even internally inconsistent, if that individual extended different rules in such a way that they imposed conflicting requirements on classes of cases that had not been recognized. Or, the extensions might be ephemeral, called into existence only as needed, and never becoming a permanent part of the grammar ("disposable" solutions). An individual's grammar would appear internally inconsistent if different rules were extended (or the same rules extended in different ways on different occasions) to deal with different instances of the same situation.

In the second scenario, where the incomplete grammar remains unchanged, speakers may be content with singular verbs on one occasion and plural verbs on another for NPs whose number is not determined or not determinable, in accordance with extragrammatical principles or conditions (e.g., priming effects). Speakers' grammars may appear to have conflicting rules, (necessarily) inconsistently adhered to, but the reality would be that they had no rule for these cases.

In the third scenario, in contexts where no rule is available (either because there is no applicable extension to the incomplete shared rule, or because more than one extension is available and they determine inconsistent solutions), speakers should either

Verb Agreement

find all of the distinct choices unacceptable or at least feel unable to judge any as more acceptable than the others.

Evidence from the questionnaire study shows that all of these situations arise. Some aspects of the determination problem involve highly nuanced semantic issues such as distributivity, collectivity, and classification. This chapter will not discuss analysis of the data collected on measure phrases, combinations like *ham and eggs*, and collection nouns (e.g., *kind, group*). A brief survey of these issues may prove useful, however, to anyone interested in variation in number agreement. Questionnaire items are reproduced in appendix A to allow the reader to get a feel for the phenomena and the factors that may affect the determination of number in these cases. Measure phrases are illustrated by the questionnaire items in (8), where variable letters represent positions where a choice of verb forms (of *be*, unless otherwise specified) was offered. The order of the forms was not predictable.

(8) 5 X 35 bushels too much to sell?
     19 Ten acres X ready to plow.
     22 X those 35 bushels sold?
     24 Several bushels X found to contain insects.
     33 X 12 pounds enough concrete for the driveway?
     39 Xn't several bushels found to contain insects?
     53 X 10 acres ready to plow?
     57 These 35 bushels X sold to Kellogg.
     65 Thirty-five bushels X too much to sell.
     71 Several bushels X wasted in spillage.
     81 Fifty acres X being sold at auction.
     96 Xn't 50 tons too heavy for this floor?
     98 Those 10 acres X ready to plow.
    101 Fifty acres X a lot to plow.
    114 Twelve pounds X not enough for the driveway.
    123 Fifty tons X too heavy for this floor.

The choice of a singular or plural verb in examples like those in (8), whose subjects are NPs denoting quantified masses, is affected by whether the subject is interpreted as individuated (the only sensible reading of items 22, 57, and 98) or as a measure (as is forced in items 5, 33, 96, 114, and 123). Quite frequently, an NP of this sort can be understood either way and take a plural or singular verb accordingly, as in item 19, or in *Fifty bushels is/are for sale*.

Similarly, a conjoined NP as in (9) can denote a collection of objects over which the property denoted by a predicate is distributed, as in *Pickles and ice cream are delicious*, or a composed object (a compote, casserole, or stew, say), as in *Pickles and ice cream is surprisingly delicious*, where the property denoted by the predicate is not a property of each of the parts, but only of the whole.

(9) 35 Pickles or ice cream X a difficult choice.
     48 Both pickles and ice cream X good for you.
     70 X my pickles and ice cream on the table?
     75 Pickles and ice cream X delicious.
     80 Your pickles and ice cream X ready to eat.
     99 Pickles and ice cream X eaten by pregnant women.
    103 Pickles and ice cream X delicious together.
    106 X pickles or ice cream a good choice?
    120 X pickles or ice cream a difficult choice?
    128 X pickles and ice cream good for you?
    131 Xn't pickles and ice cream delicious?

But the universal preference for a plural verb in item 103 (*Pickles and ice cream X delicious together*) shows that there is more than that going on. This example allows only a plural verb, and it can be true if neither pickles nor ice cream is delicious alone, as long as the pickle-and-ice-cream compote is delicious.

In addition to the "together or separately" ambiguity of NPs like *pickles and ice cream*, in some contexts there is an inclusive-exclusive ambiguity of *pickles or ice cream* (e.g., in *X pickles or ice cream good for you?*), which could muddy the interpretation of questionnaire data; if respondents were reacting to different interpretations, we would not be able to tell. Even items 120 and 35, cited in (9), ended up not contributing information about the determination problem, because the nominal predicate seems to determine the agreement (a selection issue). For item 35, the most common preference was for a third person singular verb agreeing with the predicate NP that follows the subject (the single *are* response seems anomalous). However, the question form appears to admit an additional "exclusive" interpretation, according to which *pickles* represents a distinct choice from the choice represented by *ice cream*. This is even clearer for item 106, since the semantics of *a difficult choice* in items 35 and 120 inhibits the exclusive interpretation, but apparently it is still salient for some speakers.[8] These phenomena are symptomatic of larger issues which have been treated in the extensive semantic literature on plurality (e.g., Lasersohn 1995; Winter 2001). The questionnaire items in (10) evoke interaction with genericity as well as plurality.

(10) 10 The kind of dogs that X shaggy Y large.
      15 The set of dogs that X shaggy Y unusually large.

Here, our attention will be restricted to coordinate subjects in various positions relative to their verbs. The very interesting issue of agreement in relative and relative-

Verb Agreement

like clauses, and how it is affected by the case of the antecedent in examples like those in (11), deserves a paper of its own.

(11) 37 I, who X an anarchist, will probably be arrested.
      52 I, who the FBI thinks X an anarchist, will probably be arrested.
      60 I, who the attorney general says the FBI thinks X an anarchist, will probably be arrested.
    117 Is it me who X going to be your interpreter?
    122 John gave the Simenon book to me, who X an avid Maigret fan.
    130 Is it I who X to be your interpreter?
       8 It's me who X your interpreter.
     13 It's me, after all, not that incompetent Ralph Smudge, who X going to be your interpreter.
     25 It's I who X your interpreter.
     26 It's I, after all, not that incompetent Ralph Smudge, who X going to be your interpreter.
     32 It's me who speaks/speak/NJ French.
     45 It's I who speak/speaks/NJ French.
     68 It's me, as of course you already know, who speak/speaks/NJ French.

We will also save for another day the analysis of cleft and inverted cleft sentences like (12) and (13) because of the omnipresent opportunity for the verb to agree with either the focused phrase or the third person singular neuter *wh*-phrase (or quantified phrase).

(12) 79 John and Harry X all I can see in the window.

(13) 83 All I can see X two gloves and a bat.

Additional phenomena even less recognized as affecting determination of number or selection of agreement controller are outlined in appendix B.

20.3 The Procedures

The evidence for the conclusions reported here comes from questionnaire data. Speakers responded to a 133-item forced-choice questionnaire. Eighty-three distinct items involved agreement with conjoint or disjoint subjects. The data were collected and analyzed, and the gist of the main conclusions arrived at, in 1975. The search for a theory of grammar that would accommodate them has been ongoing.[9]

    The questionnaire design perhaps would not pass muster by the standards of today's psycholinguistic survey research: all of the items were relevant to the research issues, and the cover page with the instructions announced that the data were being collected for a paper on agreement. Although the order in which alternative responses were presented was varied, the "unable to judge" option (NJ) was always last, and the five pages of examples to judge contained no "filler" items. As it was, most respondents found the task extremely taxing and reported judgment failure if they attempted more than a page or so of items at a sitting. Three items appeared twice in the list,[10] as a rough gauge of respondent consistency.[11] There was exactly one inconsistent pair of responses to multiple instances of the same question, out of 54 possible; in several other instances there was inconsistency in which of two acceptable alternatives was better. (Note that, as inconsistent reactions is a prediction of one of our hypotheses, the existence of inconsistent pairs of responses does not reflect negatively on the validity of the questionnaire responses in general.)

Although the questionnaire cover sheet instructed respondents how to indicate when two forms seemed equally good, when two seemed OK but one was better, when no form seemed acceptable, and when no judgment could be made, it did not provide instructions on what to do when the acceptability of a form depended on the interpretation of the sentence (usually on the interpretation of the subject NP). Some respondents made notes about this where it was relevant, but others may have just indicated that either of two forms was equally acceptable. In fact, even if they marked one form as more acceptable than the other, this might actually be a judgment that one possible interpretation was considered more likely or more plausible (in the absence of supporting context) than the other.

Respondents were 18 native or near-native speakers of English, linguistics graduate students or junior faculty in the mid-1970s at the University of Illinois, from the Midwest or the northeastern United States (1 from Ontario, Canada, 1 from the western United States). A number of potential respondents experienced too much judgment fatigue to complete the questionnaire. Eight respondents were male, 7 were female; the gender of 3 respondents is unknown. Most were in their 20s or 30s. Completed questionnaires were also submitted by 13 nonnative speakers; they are not included in this analysis.

20.4 The Principles

On first examination, the response patterns appeared completely chaotic. On analysis, however, the patterns could be factored into five principles, listed in (14), the domain of each principle being idiosyncratic to the individual.

(14) a. *Logic of 'and' (LA)*
    Conjoined subjects always require a plural verb.
  b. *Closest Conjunct Principle (CCP)*
    With a coordinate subject, the verb agrees with the closest conjunct. (*There is a lawyer and two doctors in the room* but *There are two doctors and a lawyer in the room.*)

c. *As If Conjoined (AIC)*
   The grammatical person and number of a disjoint subject is computed as if it were conjoined ([1st PERSON] *and* [ANY OTHER PERSON] is [1st PERSON PLURAL], [2nd PERSON] *and* [3rd PERSON] is [3rd PERSON PLURAL], [3rd PERSON SINGULAR] *and* [3rd PERSON SINGULAR] is [3rd PERSON PLURAL]. AIC is the disjunctive counterpart of LA for *and*-conjunction. As it never seems to be a strategy in affirmative [3rd SINGULAR] *or* [3rd SINGULAR] cases, its apparent presence in other [3rd SINGULAR] *or* [3rd SINGULAR] cases may be related to De Morgan's Law and the possibility of an inclusive interpretation for *or*. (*Are John or I going to be admitted? Are either Harry's wife or his daughter at the party?*)
d. *Default (Def)*
   Subjects whose agreement properties are not transparent have an invariant ("default") third person singular verb. (The most common use of this principle appears to be in relative clauses modifying an accusative case pronoun and with coordinate NPs containing an accusative case conjunct: *It's I who am your interpreter*, but *It's me who is your interpreter*.)
e. *Plural If Either Is Plural (PIEP)*
   Coordinate subjects require a plural verb if either conjunct is plural. (*Is a fly or a bee in the soup? Are a fly or two bees in the soup? Are two bees or a fly in the soup?*)

LA, AIC, and PIEP are determination principles; the CCP is a selection principle and Def is an auxiliary agreement principle.[12] It is important to note that for third person data, frequently at least three data points are needed to identify which principle determines the agreement for a particular construction: judgments on (1) a third person singular NP conjoined with a third person plural NP (3SG CONJ 3PL), (2) 3PL CONJ 3SG, and (3) 3SG CONJ 3SG. This is because a judgment on just two of these cases might be consistent with several principles. For example, a plural verb form for cases 1 and 2 would be consistent with LA/AIC as well as PIEP, and a singular form for cases 3 and 2 if the word order is canonical—or 3 and 1 if inverted—could reflect either the CCP or PIEP.

It was expected that for at least some speakers, for at least some cases, internal grammars might require a candidate solution to satisfy all principles, while in similarly restricted, "difficult" contexts, other more "permissive" speakers might accept a candidate solution as long as it satisfied any of a (possibly idiosyncratic) selection of principles. When different principles in a speaker's internal grammar do not converge on the same solution, there should be some sentence types which "restrictive" speakers find hard to judge, or for which they reject all agreement choices, while "permissive" speakers will be predicted to prefer different solutions on different occasions, or to find more than one agreement possibility acceptable.

Some may see a resemblance between these principles and Optimality Theory (OT) constraints. Indeed, Sadock (1998) analyzes Sobin's (1997) questionnaire data in terms of a set of OT-like satisfaction conditions which correspond almost one to one with the constraints in (14).[13] Sadock's analyses and OT accounts we are familiar with are offered to explain degrees of acceptability, not the range of variation and within-subject variability that the principles in (14) are offered to account for. There would seem to be no obstacle to using OT constraints to account for variation and variability, as indeed has been suggested by Kayne (1996) and Kortmann (2002).

20.5 The Patterns

As already indicated, globally there were as many response patterns as there were respondents, but on analysis, the patterns factored into combinations of the five principles listed in (14), with domains varying by individual. Examination of these principles provides (indirect) evidence of distinct strategies for dealing with an incomplete grammar.

20.5.1 Conjunction

With conjoined subjects and canonical word order, respondents were, not surprisingly, unanimous in making unequivocal plural verb form choices that were consistent with the additive logic of *and*. Although there are apparently British and American dialects where the form of the verb does not vary with person or number of the subject even in transparent cases (e.g., with nominative pronouns), but is invariably third person singular as in (15) or plural as in (16), neither of these patterns was evident in the questionnaire data.

(15) a. Was you [SG] going to drink that coffee? (addressed to one author)
 b. We was worried about you. (British National Corpus, *Esquire*, 1991, sentence 2595)

(16) a. Mum were going on about it.
 b. That's what it were.
 c. I were on my way up.
 d. It were terrible daft.
 e. It don't look good.
 f. That were crap.

A search of the British National Corpus yielded hundreds of cases of *we was*, *you was*, and *they was* from a wide variety of categories of speakers (even disregarding the cases where the pronoun was not the subject of *was*). The examples in (16) are all from the film *The Full Monty*, whose characters speak a Yorkshire dialect (no

Verb Agreement 467

examples with *are* were noted). *Do* and *don't* with a third person singular subject are common in varieties of American English as well (e.g., from Bob Dylan's "Don't Think Twice": *It ain't no use to sit and wonder why, babe. It don't matter, anyhow*), but *were* and *weren't* as in (16) are not so common.

In noncanonical clauses, the picture is considerably more complicated. The following parameters were used to classify examples with a coordinate subject:

(17) a. whether the subject precedes or follows the verb,
 b. whether the verb is adjacent to the subject or not,
 c. whether the grammatical subject is the notional subject or an expletive,
 d. whether the coordination is conjunction or disjunction,
 e. whether the coordinated phrases are definite or indefinite.

When the inverted-order constructions of polar questions, *there*-statements, and *there*-questions are considered, even examining just *and*-conjunction, several distinct patterns emerged. Six respondents indicated that the best (or only) choice was the plural form consistent with the logic of *and*, regardless of whether the individual conjuncts were singular or plural. However, smaller numbers of respondents eschewed LA for *there*-statements or *there*-questions, or both; for them, the CCP determined the number marked on the verb. An even smaller number appeared to use PIEP for polar questions or *there*-questions, other cases being determined by the CCP. Only 1 speaker found any of these constructions impossible to judge, but 12 gave either inconsistent or permissive (multiple acceptable forms) responses to some questions.

20.5.2 *Or*-disjunction

There was even more patterned variation in the disjunction data. For simple *or*-disjunction with third person subjects, the pattern found most frequently (4 respondents) among the 12 patterns observed was that verbs agreed with preverbal subjects according to PIEP, and elsewhere according to the CCP. Some of the other respondents used one pattern (AIC or the CCP) with definite preverbal subjects, and another one (PIEP or the CCP) with indefinite subjects. Five respondents were unable to choose an agreeing form for at least one case.

With mixed-person subjects (e.g., *John or I, you or John*), there were 11 distinct patterns for polar questions,[14] as respondents used different strategies (principles) depending on the order of the conjuncts (third person first or last) and on whether the non–third person conjunct was first person or second person. No two respondents patterned the same for conjunction and disjunction.

20.5.3 *Either ... or*-disjunction

With *either ... or*-disjunction there were also items involving negative *there*-questions, where the subject NP is one mora/syllable/morpheme/word farther after the verb that is to agree with it. Unfortunately, there were not enough data points to determine patterns for some constructions with certainty. Still, there were 16 distinct response patterns among 18 respondents, and 5 of the respondents were inconsistent or very permissive about agreement for at least one phrase-order type. About the only across-the-board consistency was found with *there*-questions, which in 10 cases clearly followed the CCP. Strategies for canonical statements showed the most variation across respondents, followed by polar questions.

20.6 Discussion

In a world where knowledge of a language means being able to recognize and correctly parse and interpret every possible sentence of that language, and acquiring that ability is attributed to being genetically designed to acquire the same grammar as all other members of the speech community upon exposure to an unpredictable sampling of sentences of the language,

• all normal adult members of the community have the same grammar and make the same judgments about sentences (grammaticality, interpretation, ambiguity, etc.);[15]
• each individual makes the same judgment about a sentence on every presentation of that sentence (in the same context);
• individuals are always able to judge the grammaticality and interpretation of a sentence.

These statements may seem strong with universal quantifiers in them, but the day-to-day research of the ordinary working grammarian depends on them. In weaker versions, they do not support drawing conclusions about the correctness of the predictions of a hypothesis based on the judgments of a few random individuals. As linguists, we all make these assumptions until we are confronted with facts that cast doubt on them.

The work reported here indicates that they do not hold for number agreement on verbs. The critical result is that, among speakers who otherwise appear to speak the same variety of the language, there is a wide variety of *patterns* of variation in number marking in sentences with coordinate subjects, especially postverbally. Judging from the results reported in section 20.4, normal exposure to samples of a language is not sufficient to cause all learners to arrive at the same grammar—or even to necessarily arrive at a grammar that could be used to parse (or even recognize) every single sentence of that language. Some (linguistically sophisticated) speakers categorically reject sentences that other speakers find unobjectionable. Speakers differ extensively on what judgments they make, how consistent they are in making those judgments, and what sorts of judgments they feel unable to make at all. One might attempt to preserve the assumption that all speakers of a language have the same grammar by saying that some defect in the performance system that uses the grammar to respond to the questionnaire is responsible for the variation. In the absence of an empirically vulnerable hypothesis describing that putative defect, the cost of such a move is the ability to make inferences about grammars from linguistic behavior (performance) of any sort.

If the grammars that individuals acquire are not so determined by their inborn language-learning capacity that individuals exposed to the same language necessarily develop the same grammar, or if the grammars individuals acquire are not necessarily sufficiently complete to drive a parser that will allow them to recognize and correctly parse and interpret every possible sentence of that language, but are only sufficient (in conjunction with a pragmatics "engine" for interpreting social behavior, including language use) to enable enough of an illusion of mutual understanding to foster continued discourse with other members of the community, then it is to be expected that

• not all individuals in the speech community will have the same grammar, and consequently, they will not make all the same judgments about the same sentences;
• if individual grammars can be incomplete, and impose very few constraints, or none at all, on some aspects of some syntactic constructions, individuals may make different judgments about the same sentences containing those constructions on different occasions, even in equivalent situational circumstances;
• some individuals may find themselves unable to judge whether certain classes of sentences are grammatical.

This prompts a view of Universal Grammar that differs somewhat from the one familiar from introductory linguistics. It relies less on inborn principles specific to language and standards of mathematical certainty to guarantee that infants will learn the language of their environment from unpredictable exposure to it, and more on the human instinct to make associations, interpret events, and act on likelihoods. This was part of the thrust of McCawley's (1976) paper on four pernicious ideas about the relation of language to language acquisition: the "primary data" for language acquisition would not provide a child with the basis for recognizing grammatical sentences of the language, and even if it did, it's not clear that that would play a role in language acquisition. Those data underdetermine a grammar; many grammars, even many grammars consistent with a restrictive theory of Universal Grammar, will be consistent with them. Rather, children appear to perceive speech in terms of whatever incipient grammar has formed within them at the time they hear it; anything that doesn't get an analysis within that grammar is perceived as noise. Consequently, he argued, measures of complexity are irrelevant to language acquisition because actual grammars may be formally nonoptimal because they are acquired by means of accretion through developmental stages. One thing he stressed was that children do not learn principles of linguistic well-formedness in isolation; they learn to identify varieties of structural types, in the *course* of learning how to use language as a tool. Our investigation of verb agreement demonstrates that at least in that domain, normal exposure to a language does not guarantee that an individual's grammar will be complete, and it certainly does not guarantee that all individuals who learn the "same" language will have identical grammars. As McCawley described it, first-language learners build grammars incrementally, by patching whatever grammar they have developed, and as a consequence, "speakers of what are to minutest details 'the same dialect' often have acquired grammars that differ in far more respects than their speech differs in" (1976, 157). This is something that can only be discovered by getting judgments on hard cases, as was attempted with our rather taxing questionnaire.

20.7 The Challenge of Getting the Crucial Data

It would be desirable to be able to confirm that speakers' language use is consistent with the principles invoked here to characterize it. The problem is that the number of judgments that would have to be sought from each speaker is quite intimidating: making judgments of the sort that are crucial to this research induces judgment fatigue quite rapidly. At present, the most we can say is that the questionnaire results are inconsistent with the sort of theory of Universal Grammar that is familiar since *Aspects*; what normal human infants bring to the task of language learning is not so specific and fixed that normal exposure to a normal range of data results in them all learning a unique grammar. The results are consistent with a more developmental theory as outlined by Bates and MacWhinney (1979, 1982) and Green (1998, in press): using the same general cognitive tools to solve comparable sets of problems in making sense of their linguistic environment results in a class of solutions that yield the same values for certain salient issues (verbs agree in person and number with canonical subjects in canonical position), but may differ quite a bit in their consequences for issues that were not salient during acquisition, like number determination for *or*-disjunction. In Government-Binding Theory, a distinction was made between "core" grammatical phenomena, learned in accordance with the Universal Grammar principles of an innate language faculty, and "peripheral" phenomena learned some other way. However, verb agreement does not seem to have been widely considered to be part of "the periphery,"[16] and if it was, then our point here, that verb agreement is not a good candidate for illustrating the virtues of theories of Universal Grammar, is nothing new. Showing that speakers' internalized grammars actually do differ in the domains of the patterns sketched in section 20.4 will require a much more extensive study than the one reported here, which may be considered to have the status of a pilot study. Obtaining the data necessary to confirm these patterns will require a questionnaire or study instrument many times longer (many, many times longer if filler items are included). The challenge of keeping respondents fresh will be formidable. (A reviewer suggests administering survey instruments in a series of phases.) But it seems clear that there should be

- tokens of every type that occurs in the conceptual grid;
- more tokens of each type, to test consistency and elucidate other relevant factors;
- more repetitions of identical tokens, to determine the degree of random variation (Cowart 1997) and differentiate consistent from inconsistent judgments.

Ideally, instruments that control contexts better than a simple forced-choice questionnaire can be devised.

Appendix A: The Questionnaire

All of the questionnaire items had the alternative responses spelled out as they are in items 1 and 2. For convenience, we have substituted a variable letter for this list (almost always forms of *be*) in the remainder of the examples in this reproduction of the questionnaire; *NJ* stands for *no judgment*. Space prohibits reproducing the table of results here; anyone wishing a copy should write to the authors in care of the Department of Linguistics, University of Illinois at Champaign-Urbana.

1. Are/am/is/NJ either I or John going to be admitted?
2. Is/are/NJ anybody besides his own supporters in agreement with this?
3. X either John or I going to get the job?
4. X two women or a man in the room?
5. X 35 bushels too much to sell?
6. Either Harry's wife or his daughter X at the party.
7. There X either 2 flies or a bee in the soup.
8. It's me who X your interpreter.
9. All I can see X 2 magazines and a book.
10. The kind of dogs that X shaggy Y large.
11. X either Harry's parents or his wife at the party?
12. X John or you going to leave early?
13. It's me, after all, not that incompetent Ralph Smudge, who X going to be your interpreter.
14. X 1 in 10 doctors qualified?
15. The set of dogs that X shaggy Y unusually large.
16. All I can see X John and Harry.
17. X either John or you coming to the party?
18. Two books or a magazine X all I can see.
19. Ten acres X ready to plow.
20. Themselves X all they can see in the mirror.
21. X either you or John coming to the party?
22. X those 35 bushels sold?
23. Two gloves and a bat X all I can see.
24. Several bushels X found to contain insects.

25 It's I who X your interpreter.
26 It's I, after all, not that incompetent Ralph Smudge, who X going to be your interpreter.
27 X a man and a woman in the room?
28 There X either a bee or two flies in the soup.
29 A magazine or two books X all I can see.
30 X there two women and a man in the room?
31 Either Harry's parents or his wife X coming to the party.
32 It's me who speaks/speak/NJ French.
33 X 12 pounds enough concrete for the driveway?
34 Either you or John X going to have to leave.
35 Pickles or ice cream X a difficult choice.
36 X themselves all they can see in the mirror?
37 I, who X an anarchist, will probably be arrested.
38 Only 1 in 10 X willing to take the test.
39 Xn't several bushels found to contain insects?
40 Myself X all I can see in the mirror.
41 Nobody besides his own supporters X in agreement with him.
42 Either John or me X going to be promoted.
43 There X a doctor or a lawyer at the party.
44 John and no one else X able to lift the stone.
45 It's I who speak/speaks/NJ French.
46 A bat and two gloves X all I can see.
47 X there either a bee or two flies in the soup?
48 Both pickles and ice cream X good for you.
49 X either Harry's wife or his daughter at the party?
50 There X two men and a woman in the room.
51 All I can see X a book or two magazines.
52 I, who the FBI thinks X an anarchist, will probably be arrested.
53 X 10 acres ready to plow?
54 A magazine or a book X all I can see.
55 There X two doctors or a lawyer at the party.
56 X John or I going to be admitted?
57 These 35 bushels X sold to Kellogg.
58 X either you or John coming to the party? [= 21]
59 Harry's parents or his wife X coming to the party.
60 I, who the attorney general says the FBI thinks X an anarchist ..., will probably be arrested.
61 All I can see in the mirror X myself.
62 X pickles or ice cream likely to produce indigestion?
63 X either I or John going to be admitted? [= 1]
64 There X either a bee or a fly in the soup.
65 Thirty-five bushels X too much to sell.
66 X there a doctor or a lawyer at the party?
67 She doesn't know that John or Bill X going to win the award.
68 It's me, as of course you already know, who speak/speaks/NJ French.
69 X there either a fly or a bee in the soup?
70 X my pickles and ice cream on the table?

Verb Agreement

71 Several bushels X wasted in spillage.
72 All I can see X a handkerchief or a scarf.
73 X I or John going to get the job?
74 Harry's wife or his parents X coming to the party.
75 Pickles and ice cream X delicious.
76 Either I or John X going to get the job.
77 X there either two flies or a bee in the soup?
78 X a man or two women in the room?
79 John and Harry X all I can see in the window.
80 Your pickles and ice cream X ready to eat.
81 Fifty acres X being sold at auction.
82 X pickles or ice cream good for you?
83 All I can see X two gloves and a bat.
84 I don't think Peyton Place or Love Story X suitable for children.
85 There X a woman and two men in the room.
86 Either me or John X going to get the job.
87 A man and a woman X in the room.
88 X one doctor in 10 qualified?
89 So a bird lands on the windowsill, and stupid me opens/open/NJ the window and let/lets/NJ him in.
90 X you or John going to leave early?
91 X there two lawyers or a doctor at the party?
92 Only 1 in 10 doctors X qualified to operate.
93 Either John or I X going to be promoted.
94 A man or two women X in the room.
95 Neither John's daughter nor his parents X coming.
96 Xn't 50 tons too heavy for this floor?
97 There X a man and a woman in the room.
98 Those 10 acres X ready to plow.
99 Pickles and ice cream X eaten by pregnant women.
100 Neither John's parents nor his daughter X coming.
101 Fifty acres X a lot to plow.
102 X there a man and two women in the room?
103 Pickles and ice cream X delicious together.
104 The Sting or The Iceman X most likely to win the award.
105 Either Harry's wife or his parents X coming to the party.
106 X pickles or ice cream a good choice?
107 X there a doctor or two lawyers at the party?
108 A man and two women X in the room.
109 X either Harry's wife or his parents at the party?
110 There X a doctor or two lawyers at the party.
111 Neither John's wife nor his daughter X coming.
112 All I can see X John.
113 X there either two flies or a bee in the soup? [= 77]
114 Twelve pounds X not enough for the driveway.
115 Two women and a man X in the room.
116 Either John or you X going to have to leave.

117 Is it me who X going to be your interpreter?
118 X a man or a woman in the room?
119 Only 1 doctor in 10 X qualified to operate.
120 X pickles or ice cream a difficult choice?
121 Two women or a man X in the room.
122 John gave the Simenon book to me, who X an avid Maigret fan.
123 Fifty tons X too heavy for this floor.
124 How many acres X being sold today?
125 X two women and a man in the room?
126 Neither Ray nor Awtrey X playing well enough to win.
127 X there a man and a woman in the room?
128 X pickles and ice cream good for you?
129 A man or a woman X in the room.
130 Is it I who X to be your interpreter?
131 Xn't pickles and ice cream delicious?
132 All I can see X a bat and two gloves.
133 X a man and two women in the room?

Appendix B: A Partial Catalogue of Other Cans of Agreement Worms

B.1 Fractions, Decimals, and Proportions

Like NPs with decimal quantifiers, ones with proportional quantifiers are problematic for a simple verb agreement principle and deserve further study. Five questionnaire items addressed this issue:

119 Only 1 doctor in 10 X qualified to operate.
 92 Only 1 in 10 doctors X qualified to operate.
 38 Only 1 in 10 X willing to take the test.
 14 X 1 in 10 doctors qualified?
 88 X one doctor in 10 qualified?

Logically, both *1 doctor in 10* and *1 in 10 doctors* refer to a quantity greater than one, and both are headed by a singular noun, but one ends with a plural noun and the other with a cardinal adjective. With a canonical noun-headed subject, agreement was not problematic; respondents chose almost exclusively third person singular in items 119 (18/18) and 88 (17/18). Where there is no explicit nominal head for the cardinal determiner *one*, there is more variation. On items 14, 38, and 92, a third person singular verb was the exclusive preference of only 8 to 13 of the 18 respondents. Item 14 showed the most variation, with only 8 respondents having an exclusive preference for the third person singular verb and 5 actually preferring a plural verb.

B.2 "Classifiers"

The set of classifier (or container) nouns that can head generic or quantified NPs ranges from the semantically transparent and grammaticalized *lot* and *kind* to more syntactically independent and semantically compositional ones like *group* and *set* (see Yuasa and Francis 2003). But there is quite a bit of variation, and perhaps confusion, with a few speakers even claiming to prefer *The set of dogs that are shaggy are unusually large* and even *The set of dogs that is shaggy are unusually large*.

B.3 Informal Speech

Some respondents noted that their choice varied depending on whether the verb was cliticized (reduced to *'s* or *'re*). HD gave responses for the unreduced forms; KW for the reduced forms, which sounded better to her.

B.4 Determiner-verb Mismatch

It appears that team names, even in U.S. English, and even names which contain singular heads and determiner words, allow plural verbs with distributive predicates.

(1) a. The Orlando Magic are all over 6'4".
    b. The Magic are big.
    c. The Magic are all college graduates.

(2) a. Manchester United are all over sixteen stone.
    b. Manchester United are big.
    c. Manchester United are all university graduates.

However, indefinite descriptions of the same entities do not have this freedom of occurrence, nor do definite descriptions, although a possessive determiner seems to allow a plural verb if there is a nominal predicate containing a distributive quantifier.

(3) a. *One team are bigger than all the others.
    b. *That team are big.
    c. *Our team are bigger than any of the others.
    d. Our team is/are all college graduates.
    e. That team is/??are all college graduates.

Notes

1. Variation in number agreement is not a new phenomenon; see Bailey, Maynor, and Cukor-Avila 1989.

2. See Pollard and Sag 1994 for discussion.

3. If the disjoined NPs are both plural, then a principle based on the logic of *or* predicts that they should have a plural verb. If they are both singular, the logic of exclusive *or* predicts a singular verb. It is not clear that any prediction can be made from the logic of inclusive *or*.

4. As a practical matter, when asked to provide advice to writers on this issue, we always advise them to recast the sentence with a modal verb or past tense to avoid having to make this troublesome choice.

5. "If I'm not with the girl I love, I love the girl I'm near."

6. Here's a curiosity: the normative grammar built into Microsoft Word 97 thinks (7a)—but not (7b) or (7c)!—is grammatically incorrect.

7. The class of cases exemplified by one sentence is, of course, indeterminate. Any sentence exemplifies numerous classes, many of which are "natural classes."

8. For item 106, 8 of 18 respondents preferred a plural verb that agrees with the first conjunct, which immediately follows the inverted verb. Three more allowed it, either as an equal or a second choice, and 1 volunteered that the number of the verb depended on the interpretation. For item 120, only 2 preferred a plural verb, although 3 others allowed it as an equal or second choice, and 3 more were unable to form a judgment.

9. For some discussion, see Green, in press.

10. All three involved *either ... or* coordination of disjuncts with unlike person and/or number.

(i) 63 X either I or John going to be admitted? [= 1]
    58 X either you or John coming to the party? [= 21]
   113 X there either two flies or a bee in the soup? [= 77]

11. Strictly speaking, because any of a considerable number of factors might make a particular example problematic, conclusions about consistency might not extend farther than examples very similar to the questionnaire item.

12. Alternatively, Def could be construed as a codicil of the determination principle. The CCP, however, cannot be construed that way, as it references structural or linear distance from an agreeing element.

13. Sadock's SEMSUBJ (verb agrees with the semantic number of the subject) is similar to our LA, his NEARNUM is the CCP, and his PUNT is explicitly our Def. His HIGHNUM, while not explicitly articulated, appears to be a generalization (plural if any NP in the subject NP is plural) of our PIEP.

14. No other construction types were included in the questionnaire for mixed-person simple *or*-disjunction.

15. "Knowledge of language within a speech community is shared to a remarkably fine detail, in every aspect of language from pronunciation to interpretation" (Chomsky 1987, 61).

16. Sobin (1997) averaged the judgments collected on a subset of the sentence types that are central to our analysis to arrive at acceptability ratings which he explains in terms of "grammar-external rules called grammatical viruses" which can still "read grammatical structure and affect it" (p. 319) in an effort to rescue the Minimalist Program from its prediction that sentences like (i) and (ii) are ungrammatical.

(i) She and her brothers arrived in a town car.

(ii) There are books on the table.

Sobin associates less optimal derivations with prestige usages (offering no sociolinguistic support) and accounts for variation in acceptability judgments by claiming that "viruses must be explicitly learned because they are lexically specific," although, being grammar-external, they "are costly to employ" and so are "not employed consistently" (p. 338).

References

Bailey, Guy, Natalie Maynor, and Patricia Cukor-Avila. 1989. Variation in subject-verb concord in Early Modern English. *Language Variation and Change* 1, 285–300.

Bates, Elizabeth, and Brian MacWhinney. 1979. The functionalist approach to the acquisition of grammar. In *Developmental pragmatics*, ed. by Elinor Ochs and Bambi Schiefflin, 167–209. New York: Academic Press.

Bates, Elizabeth, and Brian MacWhinney. 1982. Functionalist approaches to grammar. In *Child language: The state of the art*, ed. by Eric Wanner and Lila Gleitman, 173–218. Cambridge, MA: MIT Press.

Brentari, Diane, Gary N. Larson, and Lynn A. MacLeod, eds. 1988. *CLS 24: Papers from the 24th Regional Meeting of the Chicago Linguistic Society*. Part Two, *Parasession on Agreement in Grammatical Theory*. Chicago: University of Chicago, Chicago Linguistic Society.

Chomsky, Noam. 1957. *Syntactic structures*. The Hague: Mouton.

Chomsky, Noam. 1965. *Aspects of the theory of syntax*. Cambridge, MA: MIT Press.

Chomsky, Noam. 1987. *Language in a psychological setting*. Sophia Linguistica 22. Tokyo: Sophia University, Graduate School of Languages and Linguistics.

Corbett, Greville. 2000. *Number*. Cambridge: Cambridge University Press.

Cowart, Wayne. 1997. *Experimental syntax: Applying objective methods to sentence judgments*. Thousand Oaks, CA: Sage Publications.

Green, Georgia M. 1985. Why agreement must be stipulated for *there*-insertion. In *Proceedings of the First Eastern States Conference on Linguistics*, ed. by Gloria Alvarez, Belinda Brodie, and Terry McCoy, 27–34. Columbus: Ohio State University, Department of Linguistics.

Green, Georgia M. 1998. Modelling grammar growth. In *Proceedings of the GALA '97 Conference on Language Acquisition*, ed. by Antonella Sorace, Caroline Heycock, and Richard Shillcock, 338–45. Edinburgh: University of Edinburgh, Human Communication Research Centre.

Green, Georgia M. In press. Modelling grammar growth: Universal Grammar without innate principles or parameters. In *Non-transformational syntax: A guide to current models*, ed. by Kersti Borjars and Robert Borsley. Oxford: Blackwell.

Kayne, Richard S. 1996. Microparametric syntax: Some introductory remarks. In *Microparametric syntax and dialect variation*, ed. by James R. Black and Virginia Motapanyane, ix–xviii. Amsterdam: John Benjamins.

Keenan, Edward. 1974. The Functional Principle: Generalizing the notion of subject. In *Papers from the 10th Regional Meeting, Chicago Linguistic Society*, ed. by Michael W. LaGaly, Robert A. Fox, and Anthony Bruck, 298–309. Chicago: University of Chicago, Chicago Linguistic Society.

Kortmann, Bernd. 2002. New prospects for the study of dialect syntax: Impetus from syntactic theory and language typology. In *Syntactic microvariation*, ed. by Sjef Barbiers, Leonie Cornips, and Susanne van der Kleij, 185–213. Amsterdam: Meertens Institute Electronic Publications in Linguistics.

Lasersohn, Peter. 1995. *Plurality, conjunction and events*. Dordrecht: Kluwer.

McCawley, James D. 1971. Tense and time reference in English. In *Studies in linguistic semantics*, ed. by Charles J. Fillmore and D. Terence Langendoen, 96–113. New York: Holt, Rinehart and Winston.

McCawley, James D. 1976. Some ideas not to live by. *Die neueren Sprachen* 75, 151–65. Reprinted in *Adverbs, vowels, and other objects of wonder*, 234–46. Chicago: University of Chicago Press, 1979.

McCawley, James D. 1979. Language universals in linguistic argumentation. *Studies in the Linguistic Sciences* 8, 205–19. Reprinted in *Thirty million theories of grammar*, 159–75. Chicago: University of Chicago Press, 1982.

McCawley, James D. 1985. Kuhnian paradigms as systems of markedness conventions. In *Linguistics and philosophy: Essays in honor of Rulon S. Wells*, ed. by Adam Makkai and Alan K. Melby, 23–43. Amsterdam: John Benjamins.

Morgan, Jerry L. 1972a. Some problems of verb agreement. *Studies in the Linguistic Sciences* 2, 84–90.

Morgan, Jerry L. 1972b. Verb agreement as a rule of English. In *Papers from the Eighth Regional Meeting, Chicago Linguistic Society*, ed. by Judith N. Levi, Paul M. Peranteau, and Gloria C. Phares, 278–86. Chicago: University of Chicago, Chicago Linguistic Society.

Morgan, Jerry L. 1984. Some problems of agreement in English and Albanian. In *Proceedings of the 10th Annual Meeting of the Berkeley Linguistics Society*, ed. by Claudia Brugman and Monica Macaulay, 233–47. Berkeley: University of California, Berkeley Linguistics Society.

Morgan, Jerry L. 1985. Some problems of determination in English number agreement. In *Proceedings of the First Eastern States Conference on Linguistics*, ed. by Gloria Alvarez, Belinda Brodie, and Terry McCoy, 69–78. Columbus: Ohio State University, Department of Linguistics.

Pollard, Carl, and Ivan Sag. 1988. An information-based theory of agreement. In *CLS 24: Papers from the 24th Regional Meeting of the Chicago Linguistic Society. Part Two, Parasession on Agreement in Grammatical Theory*, ed. by Diane Brentari, Gary N. Larson, and Lynn A. MacLeod, 236–57. Chicago: University of Chicago, Chicago Linguistic Society.

Pollard, Carl, and Ivan Sag. 1994. *Head-driven Phrase Structure Grammar*. Chicago: University of Chicago Press.

Sadock, Jerrold M. 1998. Grammatical tension. In *CLS 34: Papers from the 34th Regional Meeting of the Chicago Linguistic Society. Part Two, Papers from the panels*, ed. by M. Catherine Gruber, Derrick Higgins, Kenneth S. Olson, and Tamra Wysocki, 179–200. Chicago: University of Chicago, Chicago Linguistic Society.

Sobin, Nicholas. 1997. Agreement, default rules, and grammatical viruses. *Linguistic Inquiry* 28, 318–44.

Winter, Yoad. 2001. *Flexibility principles in Boolean semantics*. Cambridge, MA: MIT Press.

Yuasa, Etsuyo, and Elaine J. Francis. 2003. Categorial mismatch in a multi-modular theory of grammar. In *Mismatch: Form-function incongruity and the architecture of grammar*, ed. by Elaine J. Francis and Laura A. Michaelis, 179–227. Stanford, CA: CSLI Publications.

Chapter 21
A Cognitively Plausible Model of Linguistic Intuition
Barbara J. Luka

21.1 Introduction

Jim McCawley's respect for individual differences and intraindividual variability in acceptability judgments was evident in both his research and his teaching. He had carefully considered and strongly held convictions regarding the use of acceptability judgments in the development of linguistic theory (McCawley 1968a,b, 1972, 1976a,b, 1994, 1996). His cautiousness and integrity in addressing linguistic intuition inspired my interest in this topic.

Linguists, psycholinguists, and computational linguists have relied on their intuitions in the pursuit of their varied goals. The theory of linguistic intuition outlined here is a synthesis of research from their various disciplines, including topics in theoretical syntax, cognitive psychology, and psychophysiology. Each reader should find some familiar aspects in the content, but will likely be introduced to new domains of research as well.

The conscious awareness and description of linguistic knowledge depends fundamentally on linguistic intuition. Intuitions are a primary source of evidence by which syntactic theories are constructed and evaluated (Chomsky 1957, 113; Chomsky 1965; Chomsky and Katz 1990). Recently, there has been renewed interest in syntactic methodology with the purpose of reaffirming grammaticality judgments as an empirical base of linguistics (Cowart 1997; Schütze 1996). For these reasons, it is a pressing task to provide an explanation for the cognitive basis of linguistic intuition.

This chapter is also designed to demonstrate to an interdisciplinary audience that research on linguistic intuition can contribute to a variety of cognitive topics more

---

Special thanks to Lawrence W. Barsalou, John T. Cacioppo, David McNeill, Howard Nussbaum, Jerrold Sadock, and Cyma Van Petten for their patient mentorship. For comments on previous versions of this chapter, thanks to Salikoko S. Mufwene, Brad Reed, Cyma Van Petten, Nell Whitman, Etsuyo Yuasa, Elaine Francis, and two anonymous reviewers. Thanks to J. P. Ryan for advice to improve the MAPIL ("maple") acronym.

generally. One argument I make, for example, is that research on linguistic intuition contributes to the further integration of research in language processing and systems of memory. These two fields of cognitive psychology consistently benefit from regular interchange, but research on linguistic intuition provides a unique instance for synthesis. A second argument made here is that linguistic intuitions provide a fruitful experimental case in which to test hypotheses about the interaction between conscious and unconscious processing.

Linguistic intuition in a broad sense could apply to introspective self-report on any aspect of language, such as ratings of typicality for variant spellings, subjective estimates of word frequency, or inferences regarding the age at which one acquired a word. In the context of this chapter, however, *linguistic intuition* will be limited to intuitions regarding the acceptability or grammaticality of a sentence structure. Although Chomsky (1965, 21, 27) makes an important contrast between grammaticality and acceptability, the terms *grammaticality judgment*, *acceptability judgment*, and *linguistic judgment* have been used rather interchangeably in linguistics and psycholinguistics papers to refer to the act of rating the structure of a sentence according to some response scale. The terms are used here in free variation to designate the result of a decision-making process regarding an utterance. In this sense, linguistic judgments are best described as evaluative categorizations. I use the term *linguistic intuition* to describe the internal evaluative state toward a linguistic example.

The theory of linguistic intuition proposed here is based on the assumption that a decision regarding the grammaticality of a sentence depends on the interaction of at least two cognitive systems: implicit systems of learning that do not require conscious attention or control, and conscious metacognitive systems that provide a decision or judgment regarding the syntactic well-formedness of an utterance. Aspects of this proposal are intuitively obvious in the sense that speakers do not have conscious access to their own mechanisms of language comprehension, but do have the conscious ability to report their linguistic intuitions. The goal of the current proposal is to replace obvious but unexplained assumptions with more detailed and testable hypotheses drawn from research in psychology to address unconscious (*implicit*) processes and metalinguistic (*metacognitive*) processes as well as their interaction.

This chapter is organized as follows. Section 21.2 reviews systems of memory as applied to language processing with special focus on implicit processing, metacognitive processing, and their interaction. Section 21.3 uses this background to develop a theory of linguistic intuition called MAPIL (Metacognitive Attribution and Preferences in Implicit Learning). This section also provides empirical support for MAPIL. Section 21.4 summarizes research regarding some cognitive processes that interact with linguistic intuitions and explains how MAPIL addresses these processes. The experiments reviewed emphasize that linguistic intuitions are dependent on cognitive processes such as learning, memory, and decision making, and that linguistic judgments are not easily separable from more general (nonlinguistic) cognitive processes. Section 21.5 outlines how MAPIL could be integrated with various theories of grammatical representation. Special attention is devoted to the point that MAPIL is separable from detailed claims of grammatical representation. Instead, MAPIL is shown to be compatible with a wide variety of syntactic theories to the extent that these theories embed syntactic processing in the human cognitive system.

21.2 Implicit Processes, Metacognitive Processes, and Their Interaction

The explanatory value of the MAPIL account arises from a rich volume of research on implicit processes in cognition. In cognitive psychology and cognitive neuroscience, *implicit learning* and *implicit memory* are defined by a number of characteristics (Schacter 1987; Seger 1994). First, individuals cannot provide a verbal account of what they have learned. The acquisition of knowledge is evident from indirect measures, such as increased speed and accuracy in processing a stimulus that has been frequently or recently encountered. Such outcomes are usually referred to as *facilitation* (Wolters and Logan 1998). Second, information is acquired as an incidental consequence of processing. Recall strategies or attention paid to study materials may influence explicit memory performance, but not implicit processing. Performance on explicit tests of memory is often statistically independent from performance on implicit tests (Kunst-Wilson and Zajonc 1980). Third, implicit processes are preserved in cases of permanent anterograde amnesia caused by bilateral damage to structures in the medial temporal lobes, especially the hippocampus and parahippocampal areas, or to regions of the diencephalon. The fact that amnesics still benefit from prior exposure means that different brain circuits are engaged as compared to those in which explicit memory performance is severely impaired (Squire 1992b). Fourth, implicit processes are comparatively age independent and IQ independent, unlike conscious recall and recollection—and there is comparatively lower individual variability in implicit processing, compared with high variability in the population for explicit processes of learning and memory (Reber 1993, 97–102). The degree of cognitive or neural separability between implicit and explicit learning is still under evaluation. The dissociations between implicit and explicit processing, however, do refute the suggestion that implicit learning is simply explicit memory operating below the threshold of conscious observation (Squire 1992a). The function and the neurological substrates of implicit and explicit processes support a degree of separability, but in practice it is difficult to separate conscious and unconscious influences of processing.

Studies of implicit learning and implicit memory have been conducted using different experimental paradigms. Both lines of research influence the theory of linguistic intuitions proposed here, so the topics of learning and memory will be reviewed separately and then integrated with respect to their shared contributions to research on indirect measures of processing, especially the role of familiarity in metacognitive processing.

Research in implicit learning began with artificial grammar learning (Reber 1967). This paradigm of research was inspired in part by Miller and Chomsky's investigations of the properties of finite state grammars (Mathews and Cochran 1998). Reber and colleagues investigated whether individuals could learn the underlying rules of a finite state grammar simply by exposure to letter strings ("utterances") produced by that grammar. During the learning phase of an artificial grammar study, participants are shown meaningless letter sequences such as *XMVTRX*, which, unbeknownst to the participants, are constructed using a finite state grammar. Later in the experiment, participants are told that an underlying rule had been used to construct the letter strings, but are not told what the rule is. Instead, they are shown letter sequences created by the same finite state grammar (*grammatical* strings) as well as random sequences (*ungrammatical* strings) and are asked to classify each string. The typical outcome is that participants profess no conscious awareness of the underlying rule and feel that they were simply guessing on the classification task, but their categorization performance is better than chance. Participants not only are sensitive to identical letter strings (individual tokens) repeated during learning and testing, but also are able to generalize their knowledge to patterns instantiated by entirely different letters (sequence types). This general pattern of results has been replicated many times using a variety of properties for sequence construction, and a variety of learning and transfer tasks (Stadler and Frensch 1998). A relevant conclusion to draw from this research is that participants can acquire information about patterns of stimuli in the absence of conscious awareness, and they can perform categorization judgments on the basis of that implicit knowledge. Early research on artificial grammar learning examined the nature of representation in memory, but the conclusion of interest here is that this experimental paradigm provides an indirect measure of learning. Research with amnesics confirms that artificial grammar learning relies on implicit rather than explicit knowledge (Knowlton and Squire 1996).

Studies of implicit memory, in contrast, began with different motivations than those in implicit learning. Early studies of implicit memory examined the perceptual characteristics of experience that are retained in memory and can be indirectly accessed even in the absence of conscious recollection. Kolers (1976) used indirect tests of memory to demonstrate that participants had good memory for details of typography (such as transformed or inverted orientations of text) even over long retention intervals. Studies of implicit memory have since been related to studies of perceptual priming, skill learning, and implicit learning in amnesics (Graf and Masson 1993).

Decreased processing time and increased accuracy are two indirect ways to measure memory for a previously presented stimulus, but repeated exposure to an individual stimulus also indirectly produces another effect, namely, an increase in affect toward the stimulus. Zajonc (1968) demonstrated a correlation between frequency of occurrence and positive affect, noting that words with high affective connotation have higher frequency of usage than their converse terms. Zajonc (1968) also showed in laboratory settings that increased exposure to stimuli resulted in more positive attitudes toward those stimuli. The stimuli Zajonc used in his experiments included not only words, but also pronounceable seven-letter nonwords (that participants were told were "Turkish"), symbols similar to Chinese characters, and pictures of faces. The average rating of affective connotation for the frequently presented symbols and the average rating of attitude toward frequently presented faces was significantly higher than the respective ratings for infrequently presented and novel stimuli of the same type. These studies show that the *mere exposure* effect is a generalizable property of cognition and is not unique to language processing (Bornstein 1989).

The connection between artificial grammar learning and the mere exposure effect was consolidated in pivotal research by Gordon and Holyoak (1983), who demonstrated that letter strings that were judged to be more grammatical also received higher ratings of liking. These results established that the mere exposure effect generalized to new but structurally similar stimuli that had not been shown previously in the experiment. Therefore, the mere exposure effect could not be due to perceptual memory for individual stimuli. Studies by Manza and colleagues continued to integrate research on the implicit learning of artificial grammars with ratings of likability and positive affect (Manza, Zizak, and Reber 1998). The use of positive affect as an indirect measure of artificial grammar learning has also been extended to studies of language development. Using a head-turn preference procedure, Gomez and Gerken (1999) found that infants who listen to sequences of nonsense words, where the particular sequences are the product of a simple artificial grammar, prefer to listen to novel word strings created by the same grammar as compared to random sequences. Infants exposed to a subset of the strings produced by an artificial language also showed a preference to attend to novel strings produced by the same grammar with a minimum of exposure, just as had been found for adults.

The relationship between artificial grammar learning and the mere exposure effect is important to the MAPIL theory of linguistic intuition. In these paradigms, findings of more positive affect have been explained as the result of familiarity. MAPIL proposes that affective evaluations regarding ease of sentence comprehension are one of the mechanisms by which unconscious information about language enters conscious awareness and influences the report of linguistic judgments. The fulcrum of the MAPIL hypothesis, however, is not simply that familiarity plays a role in syntactic processing, but rather that familiarity plays a role in the affective evaluation of syntactic structures. That is, familiarity is both an incidental result of processing and a cue to evaluation.

There are a number of accounts explaining the metacognitive attribution of familiarity, most of which tend to focus on cases in which familiarity is *mis*attributed to some source other than recent experience. These studies provide information about the process of attribution that would otherwise be unobservable, because only in the case of an error is it obvious that attribution of familiarity is distinct from remembering an event. For example, Jacoby and colleagues demonstrated that 24 hours after exposure to a series of proper names in the laboratory, participants were likely to classify the familiar (but made-up) names as belonging to famous people; that is, participants misattributed the familiarity of the names to fame (Jacoby et al. 1989). Additional studies have shown that recently processed stimuli in a variety of modalities are erroneously reported by participants to be brighter, louder, or more likeable, whichever characteristic seems to be most salient in the context of the experiment (Jacoby, Kelley, and Dywan 1989). Whittlesea and Williams (2000) propose that such attributions must be derived from a discrepancy between what is experienced and what is expected, because only those stimuli for which processing is "surprisingly fluent" fall prey to the misattribution effect.

The conclusion to be drawn from these studies is that while familiarity is the cue that informs conscious metacognitive reports, familiarity itself is not always recognized as the source of the information. The influence of familiarity does not require conscious, metacognitive processes, although these evaluative processes are themselves influenced by familiarity. The MAPIL theory proposes that these findings can be extended to describe the evaluative categorization of sentence structures as they occur in natural language.

21.3 MAPIL (Metacognitive Attribution and Preferences in Implicit Learning)

The MAPIL theory of linguistic intuition adopts and extends the following assumptions drawn from research on implicit processing and metacognition: (1) increased positive affect is a valid indirect measure of facilitation from previous exposure; (2) changes in affective rating generalize to structurally related stimulus types, not just stimulus tokens; (3) affective evaluation reflects an interaction between implicit structural knowledge and metacognitive processes of verbal report. As noted above, these findings hold equally well for nonlinguistic stimuli such as faces, pseudowords, pseudographemes, and structurally defined letter strings as well as linguistic stimuli such as single words and made-up proper names. Evidence is reviewed here supporting the conclusion that these domain-general cognitive processes also extend to the evaluation of syntactic patterns in natural languages.

MAPIL proposes that the conscious decisions made during linguistic judgments are grounded in implicit memory for previously encountered syntactic patterns. Similarity of a given syntactic structure to previously encountered structures makes processing less effortful. Analogous to the discrepancy-attribution hypothesis of Whittlesea and Williams (2000), an estimation of fluency is derived through a comparison of *perceived* ease of processing with *expected* ease of processing. Conscious recognition of structural similarity between sentences is not a prerequisite. Surprisingly fluent processing of a given syntactic structure can be misattributed to linguistic acceptability rather than recent exposure. A strong test of these claims would be to demonstrate increased affective responses for syntactic patterns of a natural language such as English. Studies relating artificial grammar learning to the mere exposure effect make it possible to equate increased affect with increased ratings of grammatical acceptability, at least within the context of artificial grammar learning. Are comparable indirect measures of facilitation evident for the processing of natural grammars as well?

Luka (1999) and Luka and Barsalou (2004) report a series of experiments that investigate the relationship between exposure to various English sentence structures and ratings of grammatical acceptability. In a manner analogous to studies of artificial grammar learning, the studies in this series included both a study phase and a subsequent categorization task. During the study phase, participants were asked to read a number of sentences, including some with uncommon or novel syntactic structures. Participants were later asked to rate the grammatical acceptability of a large set of grammatical and ungrammatical utterances (where acceptability of the stimulus sentences had been determined according to previously collected norms). The rated utterances included subsets of sentences that were verbatim repetitions of sentences presented earlier as well as structurally similar sentences composed of substantially different open-class words than those read in the study phase. Participants were not informed of any relationship between the initial reading task (the study phase) and the subsequent rating task, and they performed a third filler task between the study and evaluative categorization phases. In order to provide sufficient variability and avoid ceiling effects in the rating task, sentences used as critical stimuli were normed by a different group of participants as grammatically acceptable but not perfect (e.g., *Sam asked that we leave and he'd give us $10*). The critical sentences were thus constructions that most speakers of English find somewhat less than ideal, but not entirely ungrammatical on initial reading.

The first experiment reported in Luka and Barsalou 2004 examined identical repetitions of sentences at study and test, analogous to the standard procedure in studies of implicit memory (i.e., standard mere exposure paradigms repeat identical stimulus tokens from study to test). The results showed an increased rating of grammatical acceptability for previously studied sentences as would be predicted by the mere exposure effect.[1]

Mere exposure effects, however, are found not only for identical tokens of the same stimulus, but also for novel stimuli of the same structural type (Gordon and

Holyoak 1983; Manza, Zizak, and Reber 1998). Another study of this series investigated whether participants generalized facilitation to structurally similar sentence types after multiple exposures to syntactically similar sentences in the study phase. Structural similarities were defined as having a common constituent structure; that is, sentences shared the same sequences of grammatical categories at a coarse-grained level (single-word proper nouns were acceptable substitutions for multiword noun phrases). Sentences of the same syntactic type (i.e., a sentence *frame*) included repetitions of closed-class words and repetitions of a main verb or verb phrase, but related sentences did not otherwise share open-class words. For example, during the first part of the experiment, participants might read the sentences *The government attributed the annual deficit to inflation and bipartisan disagreement* and *The biologists ascribed their discrepant results to unsterile lab materials and genetically damaged control groups*. Later, they would rate *Your mother attributed your low grades to laziness and lack of motivation*. Eighteen different sentence frames (constituent structure configurations) were tested across conditions. Two groups of participants read different sets of sentences during the study phase, and all participants later rated the same set of sentences. Half of the critical sentences at test were structural repetitions for some participants while for other participants these sentences were structurally novel (vice versa for the other half of the rated critical sentences). Higher ratings of grammatical acceptability were accorded to sentences that were structurally similar to those read earlier. That is, although all participants rated the same set of sentences, their ratings consistently differed on the basis of their exposure to structurally similar sentences in the study phase. These results demonstrate that the evaluative categorization of sentences is influenced by recent exposure to sentences sharing the same constituent structure configurations. This observation for meaningful sentences conforms to properties already observed in the mere exposure and implicit learning literatures.

Three additional experiments replicated and extended these findings using a variety of materials and types of repetition. For example, participants first read *In the west, wheat was cultivated as a dietary staple, but in the east, rice* and *In Hawaii, hibiscus flowers were exchanged at wedding ceremonies, and in Thailand, ginger flowers.* Later, they rated the structurally similar sentence *In China, wine is served in small cups, and in Turkey, coffee*. The results of these studies are analogous to the findings for increased ratings of grammatical acceptability in the artificial grammar learning paradigm where preferences generalize to new instantiations of previously studied structural patterns. MAPIL explains the increased ratings as a misattribution of conceptual fluency; that is, sentence structures that have been processed recently are understood more quickly and easily. Metalinguistic processes do not have direct access to the source of facilitation and thus misattribute the ease of processing to properties of English grammar. The effect observed in this paradigm (increased ratings of gram-

A Model of Linguistic Intuition

matical acceptability following exposure to a structurally similar sentence) can be called *structural facilitation*. Additional studies are now in progress investigating the role that conscious awareness of repetitions may have in modulating or eliminating the increase in perceived grammaticality. In studies of the false fame effect by Jacoby and colleagues, misattribution of fame to made-up names did not occur immediately after the study phase when participants were still able to consciously recall that the name had been presented previously (Jacoby et al. 1989). If the misattribution heuristic is used in an analogous way during the evaluative categorization of sentences, we would predict that the improved rating of repeated sentence structures will be attenuated if participants become well aware of the structural repetition manipulation.

Thus far, MAPIL has been described at the level of implicit processing for syntactic structure and at the metacognitive level regarding heuristics of attribution. A number of additional cognitive systems, however, are involved in providing linguistic judgments. Characteristics of these systems are addressed in the next section. The MAPIL theory is then elaborated to address these additional findings.

21.4 Linguistic and Nonlinguistic Cognitive Systems Involved in Providing Linguistic Judgments

At the coarsest level of analysis, a speaker's ability to report a judgment of grammatical acceptability is assumed to depend upon first, perception, second, linguistic comprehension (including lexical access and syntactic parsing), and third, executive functions that report the result of syntactic parsing. If a parse was successful, then the sentence is reported to be grammatical. Otherwise, additional executive systems may be recruited to report the details of the parse failure. This series of operations is, at least, an introspective description of what a speaker subjectively experiences as he provides a linguistic judgment. However, this level of description leaves many questions unanswered regarding the interaction between linguistic knowledge and the processes required to perform and report a linguistic judgment. For example, what is the nature of the interaction between sentence comprehension and sentence evaluation? Is evaluation of grammaticality an automatic result of parsing? Are processes of memory, including effects of recent processing such as those demonstrated in studies of structural facilitation as described above, necessarily related to linguistic knowledge or can they be described at the level of sentence evaluation? If there are individual differences, or even intraindividual variabilities, in providing a linguistic judgment, are these differences attributable to linguistic knowledge or to other cognitive processes required to report linguistic judgments? If linguistic judgments exhibit specific biases, is it possible to isolate the source of the bias to extralinguistic versus linguistic factors? In order to address these questions and to provide a testable hypothesis regarding the cognitive basis of linguistic judgments, much more detail is required regarding the cognitive systems involved.

There are empirical studies that shed light on the nature of the interaction between sentence comprehension and grammatical evaluation. Blackwell, Bates, and Fisher (1996) argue that the similarity of subjects' performance on word-by-word comprehension judgments, sentence completion tasks, and a Rapid Serial Visual Presentation (RSVP) reading paradigm suggests that grammaticality judgments are incremental evaluations, inextricably dependent on processes of language comprehension.

Although linguistic judgments are dependent on comprehension systems, there is evidence to argue that linguistic evaluation is not heavily dependent on production systems. Labov (1975) noted a dissociation between linguistic judgments and linguistic performance, showing that consultants who rate a given linguistic construction as grammatically unacceptable may still use the construction (without conscious awareness) in their own informal speech. Furthermore, the dissociation between the ability to produce grammatical sentences and the metalinguistic skill of providing linguistic judgments is reversed in some types of aphasia, where patients are unable to produce normal utterances but are able to provide reasonable linguistic judgments (Linebarger, Schwartz, and Saffran 1983). These studies indicate that the ability to provide linguistic judgments is more dependent on systems of language comprehension than on production.

Linguistic judgments are also dependent on cognitive systems such as working memory. An extensive range of studies have investigated individual differences in reading comprehension related to short term or working memory capacities, as measured for example by tests of digit span or reading span (Carpenter, Miyake, and Just 1994; see Caplan and Waters 1999 and commentaries for a variety of perspectives). The impact of an external load on working memory has also been investigated and found to influence linguistic judgments as well. In a study of normal native English speakers performing online auditory grammaticality judgments, Blackwell and Bates (1995) found that accuracy of detecting grammatical errors was impaired if the participants were asked to remember a small set of random numbers during the task. Their results demonstrate that the ability to provide linguistic judgments cannot be explained without incorporating memory in sentence processing: processes of evaluation are not an automatic result of comprehension or parsing, but rather require attention.

The ability to provide linguistic judgments is also dependent on metacognitive and analytic reasoning capacities of individual speakers. Children are able to both comprehend and produce fluent speech, yet there is some debate whether children younger than 9 years of age can make adultlike linguistic judgments on the basis of purely syntactic rather than semantic oddity (Gombert 1992). Analytic skills, in addition to specific metalinguistic skills, emerge late in development in comparison to fundamental linguistic skills (Piaget 1952). Sensitivity in linguistic judgments continues to develop over the lifespan of a speaker and varies systematically with degree of education (Gombert 1992, 177–81).

The type of judgments performed by syntacticians in the course of evaluating the adequacy of a given syntactic theory may also rely more heavily on analytic skills than linguistic intuition alone. Syntacticians often evaluate the grammaticality of a structure that includes trace and coindexation notations, such as in *All parents$_1$ don't seem to their$_1$ children t$_1$ to be ingenious.*[2] It is still unclear to what degree, or in what manner, linguistic intuitions interact with analytic reasoning in the formation of linguistic judgment. It is clear, however, that a theory of linguistic intuition alone would not be able to address the task of deciding grammaticality with respect to a given syntactic theory, a skill that requires years of professional training rather than mere conversational ability in a language.

The studies reviewed thus far have used behavioral measures such as rating, reading time, response time, and accuracy. Studies using electrophysiological measures, especially event-related potentials (ERPs), have also provided empirical data about the role of various cognitive processes in the detection of ungrammaticality; a cognitively plausible theory of linguistic intuition should be able to address the growing body of research using these methods.

ERPs are voltage changes observed in electroencephalographic activity recorded noninvasively from the surface of the scalp. Recordings of electroencephalographic activity are timelocked to stimulus presentation and averaged across stimulus events of the same type to derive the ERP waveforms. ERPs provide millisecond accuracy about the time course of comprehension, via quantitative differences in the amplitude of the waveforms and qualitative differences in scalp topography (Brown and Hagoort 1999; Kutas and Van Petten 1994).

ERPs are sensitive to a variety of syntactic violations. A characteristic waveform called the P600 (an electrically positive-going waveform that peaks approximately 600 milliseconds after stimulus onset, also called syntactic positive shift, SPS) is sensitive to grammatical violations in verb subcategorization, number and gender agreement, and subjacency constraints (Hagoort, Brown, and Osterhout 1999; Osterhout 1994). The amplitude of the P600 correlates with the rated severity of a linguistic violation (Osterhout, Holcomb, and Swinney 1994). It would be tempting to treat the P600 as a direct index of grammatical evaluation, but the P600 and related waveforms are known to be influenced by a number of nonsyntactic factors. A P600 is evoked to fully grammatical sentences. Osterhout, Bersick, and McLaughlin (1997), for example, found a P600 in response to violations of gender stereotypes. They compared reflexive pronouns in sentence contexts that agreed with gender stereotypes (e.g., *The careless butcher cut himself with a knife*) or disagreed with prevailing stereotypes (e.g., *The romance novelist cried himself to sleep*). They found that the ERP response to the reflexive pronouns violating pragmatic expectancies are similar to the standard P600 effects elicited by purely syntactic violations such as verb agreement errors. Because processes of comprehension and evaluation occur at the same timescale, grammatical acceptability and ease of comprehension are not easily dissociated.

ERP findings also shed light on the interaction of sentence comprehension, sentence evaluation, and processes of working memory. Vos et al. (2001) used ERPs and reaction times to investigate working memory constraints on sentence processing. The experiment manipulated sentence complexity, additional verbal memory load, and verbal working memory span of the participants. Stimuli were conjoined versus embedded Dutch sentences, half of which contained agreement errors. (For example, literal translations of grammatical Dutch conjoined versus embedded sentences were, respectively, as follows: *The tourists have a busy schedule and visit the theater that very famous is* versus *The tourists that a busy schedule have, visit the theater that very famous is*.) Sentences containing verb agreement errors elicited more positive ERPs between 500 and 800 milliseconds poststimulus onset (the characteristic P600 waveform that would be expected), but Vos et al. found that sensitivity to grammatical error (measured by the delay in onset of the P600) was reduced under higher cognitive load. The decline in sensitivity was more evident for participants with low working memory spans. These results show that the P600, which is correlated with degree of syntactic violation, is also influenced by working memory load.

Electrophysiological measures also provide detail regarding individual differences in processing syntactic violations that are not evident using standard behavioral measures. Osterhout (1997, experiment 2) found that syntactic violations elicited a different waveform (the N400 rather than the P600) in half of the experimental participants. The proportion of participants exhibiting qualitatively different electrophysiological responses varied by the type of syntactic violation. Osterhout proposes a number of explanations for the observed differences, including that "the specific processing strategies and linguistic competences that participants bring with them determine, in part, both the category [of violation] some particular event falls into and the brain response elicited by that event" (Osterhout 1997, 514). That is, structurally defined ungrammaticalities also affect semantic processing; Osterhout proposes that a substantial subset of participants are sensitive to constraints of comprehensibility (eliciting an N400) while others are sensitive to violations of syntactic constraints (eliciting a P600). Individual differences for strategies in sentence processing require further investigation.

Experiments using behavioral measures have found that factors such as age, measures of personality (state and trait), handedness, literacy and education, and degree of linguistic training significantly influence linguistic judgments (Schütze 1996, 98–128).[3] It would seem that many of these findings should be described with respect to extralinguistic factors, implying that a full account of variability in linguistic intuition will necessarily address individual differences in addition to the metalinguistic processing influences that have been addressed thus far.

21.5 Implications of MAPIL for Theories of Grammatical Representation

MAPIL makes two strong claims, both of which are falsifiable: (1) implicit memory for previously encountered syntactic patterns contributes to linguistic knowledge; (2) grammatical acceptability is determined, at least in part, by evaluating the familiarity of a syntactic structure, comparing actual versus expected ease of processing. These claims would be falsified if the acquisition of knowledge for the structure of language does not conform to the criteria defining implicit processing or if the heuristics for evaluating syntactic structures are demonstrably different from those established for familiarity and discrepancy attribution as determined by research in metacognition (Metcalfe 2000; Reder 1996). The claim regarding implicit memory of syntactic structures is more relevant to specialists in language processing interested in the cognitive representation of syntactic knowledge and so special attention is devoted to this proposal.

Luka and Barsalou (2004) argue that structural facilitation in sentence comprehension, as observed in their series of experiments, may be related to the phenomenon of syntactic priming in sentence production. Studies in syntactic priming (also called structural priming or syntactic persistence) have demonstrated that reading a sentence with a particular syntactic construction can affect the subsequent production of a sentence even though the sentences that are read and produced are about completely different topics (Bock 1986). For example, a participant in a syntactic priming experiment first heard and then repeated a sentence such as *The referee was punched by one of the fans*. Then the participant would be shown an unrelated picture and asked to describe it, responding, for example, *The church is being struck by lightning* or *Lightning is hitting the church*. Participants in syntactic priming experiments were more likely to describe a picture using a passive sentence structure if they had just read a passive sentence. The duration of the syntactic priming effect may, however, persist over 10 intervening sentences, suggesting that it is a form of implicit learning rather than a temporary activation phenomenon (Bock and Griffin 2000). Luka and Barsalou (2004) used experimental designs that parallel those used to investigate implicit processing and found analogous results, supporting the argument that structural facilitation is an index of implicit learning. The effects of structural facilitation extend over a minimum of 10 intervening sentences, with durations of at least half an hour. Current experiments investigate longer durations.

Experimental findings in syntactic priming do not necessarily apply directly to hypotheses regarding the nature of structural facilitation, however. The traditional syntactic priming paradigm used by Bock and colleagues is a production paradigm; that is, the mechanisms to which priming is attributed are systems of language production rather than comprehension. The syntactic facilitation paradigm used by Luka and Barsalou (2004), in contrast, is dependent upon language comprehension. The rating task does not necessarily require participants to produce sentence structures. Moreover, grammaticality judgments have been shown to be at least somewhat dissociated from language production (Linebarger, Schwartz, and Saffran 1983). Although recent studies have demonstrated that syntactic priming is not limited to production systems (Branigan, Pickering, and Cleland 2000), the use of different experimental tasks (written vs. spoken production) has shown that syntactic priming effects are rather limited in duration, lasting only across adjacent sentences (Branigan, Pickering, and Cleland 1999). These findings argue against claims of implicit learning as the source of *all* syntactic priming effects, because a defining criterion of implicit learning is that the effects are not transient. Further research is required to investigate the role of production and comprehension systems using both syntactic priming and structural facilitation paradigms.

Currently, however, empirical findings regarding syntactic priming and structural facilitation already provide decisive information regarding the representation of linguistic knowledge. Studies of syntactic priming motivate the need for an independent level of representation for syntactic structure because syntactic priming cannot be explained without appealing to an independent level of structural representation (Bock and Levelt 1994). Branigan et al. (1995) press the issue of linguistic representation further:

If two stimuli are related only along one particular dimension, and the processing of one stimulus affects the processing of the other for reasons attributable to that relationship (i.e., if priming occurs), then we can infer that the cognitive system is sensitive to that dimension, and that it treats the two stimuli as related within that dimension. (Branigan et al. 1995, 491)

Analogous arguments hold for the results of syntactic facilitation found by Luka and Barsalou (2004). Syntactic priming studies have addressed primarily two classes of syntactic structures, active versus passive sentences and prepositional datives versus double object datives (in addition to the ordering of conjoined constituents), arguing that cognitive representations of syntax are shared at least at this broad grain of structural description. Luka and Barsalou's rating studies demonstrate structural facilitation for a wide variety of syntactic types defined with respect to a much more fine-grained description of constituent structure configurations.

The results of syntactic priming and syntactic facilitation experiments also support the conclusion that syntactic representations in memory are continually modified in the course of language use. The effects of frequency and exposure, at the phonological, lexical, morphological, and syntactic levels, have been used to explain aspects of language acquisition (Brooks and Tomasello 1999), second language acquisition (Ellis 2002), syntactic parallelism in discourse (Pickering and Branigan 1999), adaptations of dialect when speakers move to different regions (Trudgill 1981), and the processes of grammaticalization and historical language change (Bybee 1985; Matthews 1989). These findings accentuate the dynamic representation of syntactic knowledge as well as the short term and long term modifications of grammatical representation.

What the MAPIL theory adds to these accounts is a method for describing the implicit learning of structural patterns. MAPIL proposes that, as a side effect of language comprehension, the serial structured learning system abstracts information across lexical items. Abstracted representations of lexical class arise because lexical items share similar distributions across sentence structures. Across numerous instances of language comprehension, the statistical probabilities for the co-occurrence of lexical classes provide the basis for structural patterns or sentence frames in memory. There are a number of theories of linguistic processing that incorporate such assumptions, including those of Harrington and Dennis (2002), Jurafsky (1996), and Tabor, Juliano, and Tanenhaus (1997). Additional support for this type of representation in memory is provided by recent theories of language acquisition that are sensitive to serial orders of word classes, morphemic co-occurrence relations, and probabilistic contingencies among associatively related words (Kuhl 2000; Seidenberg 1997). These theories differ regarding the degree of abstraction drawn from the lexical level to the structural level, but they all emphasize speakers' abilities to generalize from previously encountered structures to novel structures. Related processes apply to lemma representations such as those discussed by Levelt, Roelofs, and Meyer (1999).

The proposal that co-occurrence relations among linguistic units are learned in the absence of attention and conscious awareness does not imply that implicit memory simply stores faint traces of a verbatim record of all experiences. The criteria for implicit memory, the dissociations between implicit and explicit measures, and the different neurological substrates underlying implicit and explicit processes all argue that such an implication does not follow from the proposal that co-occurrence relations play a role in language processing. There is a pervasive accord in implicit memory research that implicit processes depend upon neurological systems and substrates that impose structure upon perceptual inputs and actively organize information. Implicit processes are not the passive accumulation of unfiltered perceptual input. The manner in which current input is processed is influenced not only by characteristics of the input itself and by stored knowledge of stimuli perceived to be similar along some relevant dimension as argued above, but also by cognitive skills and limitations, some of which may be innately specified or subject to maturational constraints (Durkin 1989).

The interaction of input, stored knowledge, and proposed crosslinguistic constraints can be exemplified in one fairly transparent and relevant example: structural memory for ungrammatical utterances. Ungrammatical sequences can be memorized, and for some types of ungrammaticality, an intended meaning can be recovered such that discourse participants are able to propose syntactically acceptable corrections. To the extent that it depends on implicit processes of memory, the MAPIL theory accommodates the fact that linguistic examples of violation and ungrammaticality are also memorable. One hypothesis implied by the MAPIL account is that degree of difficulty in memorizing types of grammatical errors should be limited by type of unacceptability. Errors that are lexically, structurally, or analogically related to typical forms in memory should be easier to memorize, while other types of ungrammaticality may be very difficult to learn to produce, perhaps because of linguistic or cognitive constraints. For example, MAPIL would predict that it would be easier to extend a 'remove' verb such as *dislodge* to a previously unacceptable use of a causative like *The stones dislodged from the foundation* than it would be to extend a word to encompass improbable constituent structures, such as McCawley's (1973) examples of *flimp* 'to kiss a girl who is allergic to' and *thork* 'to give to one's uncle and'. Memory performance for types of ungrammaticality is thus predicted to be graded and to correlate with the rating of similarity or typicality for lexical classes and constituent structures previously incorporated in a speaker's memory. Proportional uses of a given verb or class of verbs in a given constituent structure provide an additional baseline of lexical and structural similarity against which to test predictions of graded grammaticality. These properties of MAPIL account for some of the variability and graded acceptability judgments that McCawley addressed in his methods of teaching and doing syntax (1996). Further experiments are necessary, however, in order to clarify how memories of ungrammatical structure are stored and accessed in comparison to structures that are not recognized as deviant during the course of comprehension.

MAPIL is not the first theory to address the cognitive basis of linguistic intuitions. Two earlier proposals are provided by Gerken and Bever (1986) and Schütze (1996, 172–80). Both of these models assume that linguistic descriptions can be functionally isolated from characteristics of processing; that is, they preserve a distinction between linguistic *competence* (the principles of grammar) and linguistic *performance* (characteristics of language use) (Chomsky 1965, 4, 11, 18–27). Linguistic descriptions, such as the model of Universal Grammar incorporated by both Gerken and Bever (1986) and Schütze (1996), are models of competence. In contrast, cognitive limitations such as memory constraints, comprehension, parsing strategies, and other potential biases in linguistic judgments are aspects of performance. The models developed by Gerken and Bever (1986) and Schütze (1996) propose that linguistic judgments reflect characteristics of both competence (a module of Universal Grammar) and performance (extralinguistic properties of cognition), and so both of these models have the primary goal of explaining how Universal Grammar interfaces with the mind and thus with observed behavior.

MAPIL is quite different from both of these models because it does not have as its primary goal the distinction between competence and performance. MAPIL has as its core psycholinguistic models of language processing and models of memory that take into account the neurobiological specialization of brain structures. MAPIL incorporates an independent level of abstract syntactic representation because data from studies of sentence priming and structural facilitation require it, but MAPIL does not assume that such representations are necessarily encapsulated or modular. On the contrary, studies of structural facilitation such as those reviewed here imply that the heuristics on which metalinguistic judgments are based must have detailed information regarding language-specific aspects of representation, especially regarding, for example, the frequency with which specific lexical items and lexical classes occur in given constituent structures. Linguistic intuitions have been shown to be sensitive to effects of frequency and recency in contexts where structural similarity between sentence stimuli is defined at a fine-grained level of common constituent structures, across a wide variety of sentence types. These findings would tend to exclude the assumption that linguistic representations are fully representationally encapsulated (Fodor 1983) or that a psychologically plausible description of grammar could be adequately characterized as a distinct module isolated from other processes upon which linguistic intuitions depend.

At a very abstract level, MAPIL shares some characteristics with Lieberman's (2000) neurophysiological and neuroanatomical model of social intuition based on implicit learning. Lieberman's theory is intended to address the emotional appraisal, deliberative decision making, and script processing that lead to nonverbal communication and inferences in social interaction. Lieberman suggests that his model may extend to linguistic intuition, and, at a very general level, there are some apparent similarities between linguistic intuition and social intuition. Linguistic intuitions are like social intuitions in their rapidity, their evaluative nature (ungrammatical sentences are not merely ungrammatical, they are "bad"), and their reliance on largely unconscious processes. However, there are many reasons why intuitions in the context of conscious or unconscious social reasoning do not transparently extend to the evaluation of grammatical structure.

In interpersonal situations, the interaction of perception with rapid, unconscious inferencing provides a quick estimation of the social risks and benefits for approach or avoidance, based on a synthesis of data regarding the sex, race, age, attractiveness, and social status of the observed party. These are not the sorts of factors that play a role in grammatical evaluation. Furthermore, it has been proposed that social intuition, social reasoning, and social judgment are "special" to the extent that (1) they are highly dependent on emotional processing (LeDoux 1998); (2) they are somewhat neurologically dissociated from other types of cognitive processing, involving especially the amygdala, orbitofrontal cortex, and superior temporal sulcus (Allison, Puce, and McCarthy 2000); (3) they developed from specific evolutionary pressures (Buss and Schmitt 1993); (4) the rudiments of these social cognitive systems are not specific to humans (Adolphs 1999). For these reasons, theories of intuition as social inference cannot be directly adopted to explain linguistic intuitions. It is parsimonious to infer domain-general properties in metacognition, and much can be gained from interdisciplinary approaches, but the characteristics of linguistic intuitions must be pursued in their own right rather than directly imported from research in nonlinguistic domains.

MAPIL is a synthesis of current research in implicit memory, implicit learning, sentence priming, and metacognition. Many aspects of the theory remain to be tested, but one advantage of this approach is that MAPIL has the potential to address current topics in neuropsychology as well as current computational models of language processing and language acquisition. MAPIL can also benefit from an interchange with syntactic theories to the extent that these theories are concerned with the cognitive representation of syntactic structure in memory.

As a cognitive approach emphasizing the interaction of systems of memory and language, MAPIL has the potential to develop as we learn more about the cognitive representation of linguistic knowledge. Jim McCawley would undoubtedly have supported this closer relationship between linguistics and psychology. He agreed that the subject matter of linguistics is psychological in nature (McCawley 1979, 245–46). MAPIL also respects Jim's exhortation that psychological conclusions must be drawn from psychological premises (McCawley 1979, 246). This is why MAPIL is a cognitive model of linguistic performance, embedded in the context of language use. Linguists, psycholinguists, and computational linguists who have relied on their intuitions realize that their judgments are influenced by a number of cognitive factors. MAPIL is an approach dedicated to identifying and characterizing these factors—not to isolate these processes from an abstract, idealized syntactic system but to address the practical fact that linguistic cognition is inextricably dependent on a variety of cognitive systems.

Jim McCawley gave all of his students "the joy of syntax." He gave us many other gifts as well. Through his meticulous practice of documentation, citation, and footnoting, he taught us respect for colleagues, provided a sense of academic heritage, and impressed upon us the gravity of historical accountability. His impressive multilingualism and his international collaborations reminded us not to let our theories or practice be Anglocentric. His interests in music, philosophy, and history of science showed us that interdisciplinary interests are more gratifying than theoretic isolationism. He also taught us the joy of great food and the irreplaceable value of humor. Rather than mourn his loss, we celebrate the fact that he ever existed.

Notes

1. Since the early days of generative grammar, syntacticians have reported shifts or blunting of their linguistic intuitions due to repeated exposure, although not on all occasions and not to all types of sentences (see Schütze 1996, 114). Note, however, that Luka and Barsalou (2004) investigated changes in judgments due to incidental exposure, in contrast to experiments of repeated rating reported by Schütze (1996, 135–40). In a rate-rerate paradigm, the speaker-hearer or participant is explicitly evaluating a given utterance for linguistic acceptability the first time the utterance is encountered. In these cases, the roles of attention and explicit memory systems are necessarily recruited and subsequent evaluation involves potential decision traces at the metalinguistic level, as well as comparison procedures of conscious recall. Because different memory systems are implicated in these different experimental procedures, different results are expected.

2. The term *grammaticality* is used in this paragraph in a technical sense of the term as described by Chomsky (1957, 13), namely, that an utterance is grammatical if it conforms to the rules of a grammar. Chomsky contrasts this use of *grammaticality* with a technical sense of the term *acceptability*, which he defines with respect to language use: that is, an utterance is acceptable if it is natural and completely comprehensible (Chomsky 1965, 10). Under this strict Chomskyan distinction, grammaticality is an issue of linguistic *competence*, while acceptability judgments are a matter of linguistic *performance* (Chomsky 1965; Chomsky and Katz 1990).

3. As noted by Clark (1973), many early studies such as those reviewed by Schütze did not calculate statistical significance values using a *minF'*, which uses F values from separate subject and item analyses. While the need to calculate *minF'* depends on details of the experimental design, the importance of the *minF'* calculation in psycholinguistic studies has recently been reaffirmed (Raaijmakers, Schrijnemakers, and Gremmen 1999). This means that findings from the early studies reviewed by Schütze must therefore be considered suggestive rather than conclusive until each of these factors can be reevaluated on a case-by-case basis.

References

Adolphs, Ralph. 1999. Social cognition and the human brain. *Trends in Cognitive Sciences* 3, 469–79.

Allison, Truett, Aina Puce, and Gregory McCarthy. 2000. Social perception from visual cues: Role of the STS region. *Trends in Cognitive Sciences* 4, 269–78.

Blackwell, Arshavir, and Elizabeth Bates. 1995. Inducing agrammatic profiles in normals: Evidence for the selective vulnerability of morphology under cognitive resource limitation. *Journal of Cognitive Neuroscience* 7, 1228–57.

Blackwell, Arshavir, Elizabeth Bates, and Dan Fisher. 1996. The time course of grammaticality judgment. *Language and Cognitive Processes* 11, 337–406.

Bock, J. Kathryn. 1986. Syntactic persistence in language production. *Cognitive Psychology* 18, 355–87.

Bock, J. Kathryn, and Zenzi M. Griffin. 2000. The persistence of structural priming: Transient activation or implicit learning? *Journal of Experimental Psychology: General* 129, 177–92.

Bock, J. Kathryn, and Willem Levelt. 1994. Language production: Grammatical encoding. In *Handbook of psycholinguistics*, ed. by Morton Ann Gernsbacher, 945–84. San Diego, CA: Academic Press.

Bornstein, Robert F. 1989. Exposure and affect: Overview and meta-analysis of research, 1968–1987. *Psychological Bulletin* 106, 265–89.

Branigan, Holly P., Martin J. Pickering, and Alexandra A. Cleland. 1999. Syntactic priming in written production: Evidence for rapid decay. *Psychonomic Bulletin and Review* 6, 635–40.

Branigan, Holly P., Martin J. Pickering, and Alexandra A. Cleland. 2000. Syntactic co-ordination in dialogue. *Cognition* 75, 13–25.

Branigan, Holly P., Martin J. Pickering, Simon P. Liversedge, Andrew J. Stewart, and Thomas P. Urbach. 1995. Syntactic priming: Investigating the mental representation of language. *Journal of Psycholinguistic Research* 24, 489–506.

Brooks, Patricia J., and Michael Tomasello. 1999. Young children learn to produce passives with nonce verbs. *Developmental Psychology* 35, 29–44.

Brown, Colin M., and Peter Hagoort. 1999. *The neurocognition of language.* Oxford: Oxford University Press.

Buss, David M., and David P. Schmitt. 1993. Sexual strategies theory: An evolutionary perspective on human mating. *Psychological Review* 100, 204–32.

Bybee, Joan L. 1985. *Morphology: A study of the relation between meaning and form.* Philadelphia: John Benjamins.

Caplan, David, and Gloria S. Waters. 1999. Verbal working memory and sentence comprehension. *Behavioral and Brain Sciences* 22, 77–126.

Carpenter, Patricia A., Akira Miyake, and Marcel A. Just. 1994. Working memory constraints in comprehension: Evidence from individual differences, aphasia, and aging. In *Handbook of psycholinguistics*, ed. by Morton Ann Gernsbacher, 1075–1122. San Diego, CA: Academic Press.

Chomsky, Noam. 1957. *Syntactic structures.* The Hague: Mouton.

Chomsky, Noam. 1965. *Aspects of the theory of syntax.* Cambridge, MA: MIT Press.

Chomsky, Noam, and Jerrold Katz. 1990. What the linguist is talking about. In *Foundations of cognitive science: The essential readings*, ed. by Jay L. Garfield, 332–50. New York: Paragon House.

Clark, Herbert H. 1973. The language-as-fixed-effect fallacy: A critique of language statistics in psychological research. *Journal of Verbal Learning and Verbal Behavior* 12, 335–59.

Cowart, Wayne. 1997. *Experimental syntax: Applying objective methods to sentence judgments.* Thousand Oaks, CA: Sage Publications.

Durkin, Kevin. 1989. Implicit memory and language acquisition. In *Implicit memory: Theoretical issues*, ed. by Stephan Lewandowsky, John C. Dunn, and Kim Kirsner, 241–57. Hillsdale, NJ: Lawrence Erlbaum.

Ellis, Nick C. 2002. Frequency effects in language processing: A review with implications for theories of implicit and explicit language acquisition. In *Frequency effects in language process-*

ing: A review with commentaries, ed. by Albert Valdman, special issue, *Studies in Second Language Acquisition* 24, 143–88.

Fodor, Jerry A. 1983. *Modularity of mind: An essay on faculty psychology.* Cambridge, MA: MIT Press.

Gerken, LouAnn, and Thomas Bever. 1986. Linguistic intuitions are the result of interactions between perceptual processes and linguistic universals. *Cognitive Science* 10, 457–76.

Gombert, Jean Emile. 1992. *Metalinguistic development.* New York: Harvester Wheatsheaf.

Gomez, Rebecca L., and LouAnn Gerken. 1999. Artificial grammar learning by 1-year-olds leads to specific and abstract knowledge. *Cognition* 70, 1109–35.

Gordon, Peter C., and Keith Holyoak. 1983. Implicit learning and generalization of the "mere exposure" effect. *Journal of Personality and Social Psychology* 45, 492–500.

Graf, Peter, and M. E. J. Masson. 1993. *Implicit memory: New directions in cognition, development, and neuropsychology.* Hillsdale, NJ: Lawrence Erlbaum.

Hagoort, Peter, Colin Brown, and Lee Osterhout. 1999. The neurocognition of syntactic processing. In *The neurocognition of language*, ed. by Colin Brown and Peter Hagoort, 273–316. Oxford: Oxford University Press.

Harrington, Michael, and Simon Dennis. 2002. Input-driven language learning. In *Frequency effects in language processing: A review with commentaries*, ed. by Albert Valdman, special issue, *Studies in Second Language Acquisition* 24, 261–68.

Jacoby, Larry L., Colleen M. Kelley, Judith Brown, and Jennifer Jasechko. 1989. Becoming famous overnight: Limits on the ability to avoid unconscious influences of the past. *Journal of Personality and Social Psychology* 56, 326–38.

Jacoby, Larry L., Colleen M. Kelley, and Jane Dywan. 1989. Memory attributions. In *Varieties of memory and consciousness: Essays in honour of Endel Tulving*, ed. by Henry L. Roediger III and Fergus I. M. Craik, 391–422. Hillsdale, NJ: Lawrence Erlbaum.

Jurafsky, Daniel. 1996. A probabilistic model of lexical and syntactic access and disambiguation. *Cognitive Science* 20, 137–94.

Knowlton, Barbara J., and Larry R. Squire. 1996. Artificial grammar learning depends on implicit acquisition of both abstract and exemplar-specific information. *Journal of Experimental Psychology: Learning, Memory, and Cognition* 22, 169–81.

Kolers, Paul A. 1976. Reading a year later. *Journal of Experimental Psychology: Human Learning and Memory* 2, 554–65.

Kuhl, Patricia K. 2000. A new view of language acquisition. *Proceedings of the National Academy of Sciences* 97, 11850–57.

Kunst-Wilson, William R., and Robert B. Zajonc. 1980. Affective discrimination of stimuli that cannot be recognized. *Science* 207, 557–58.

Kutas, Marta, and Van Petten, Cyma K. 1994. Psycholinguistics electrified: Event-related brain potential investigations. In *Handbook of psycholinguistics*, ed. by Morton Ann Gernsbacher, 83–144. San Diego, CA: Academic Press.

Labov, William. 1975. What is a linguistic fact? In *The scope of American linguistics*, ed. by Robert Austerlitz, 77–113. Lisse: Peter de Ridder Press.

LeDoux, Joseph. 1998. *The emotional brain.* London: Weidenfeld and Nicolson.

Levelt, Willem J. M., Ardi Roelofs, and Antje S. Meyer. 1999. A theory of lexical access in speech production. *Behavioral and Brain Sciences* 22, 1–75.

Lieberman, Matthew D. 2000. Intuition: A social cognitive neuroscience approach. *Psychological Bulletin* 126, 109–37.

Linebarger, Marcia, Myrna F. Schwartz, and Eleanor Saffran. 1983. Sensitivity to grammatical structure in so-called agrammatic aphasics. *Cognition* 13, 361–92.

Luka, Barbara J. 1999. Familiarity breeds consent: Is structural facilitation evidence for the implicit knowledge of syntactic structures? Doctoral dissertation, University of Chicago.

Luka, Barbara J., and Lawrence W. Barsalou. 2004. Structural facilitation: Mere exposure effects for grammatical acceptability as evidence for syntactic priming in comprehension. Manuscript, Bard College and Emory University.

Manza, Louis, Diane Zizak, and Arthur S. Reber. 1998. Artificial grammar learning and the mere exposure effect. In *Handbook of implicit learning*, ed. by Michael A. Stadler and Peter A. Frensch, 201–22. Thousand Oaks, CA: Sage Publications.

Mathews, Robert C., and Barbara P. Cochran. 1998. Project Grammarama revisited. In *Handbook of implicit learning*, ed. by Michael A. Stadler and Peter A. Frensch, 223–59. Thousand Oaks, CA: Sage Publications.

Matthews, Stephen J. 1989. French in flux: Typological shift and sociolinguistic variation. In *Synchronic and diachronic approaches to linguistic variation and change*, ed. by Thomas J. Walsh, 188–203. Washington, DC: Georgetown University Press.

McCawley, James D. 1968a. Concerning the base component of a transformational grammar. *Foundations of Language* 4, 243–69. Reprinted in *Grammar and meaning*, 35–58. Tokyo: Taishukan, 1973.

McCawley, James D. 1968b. The role of semantics in a grammar. In *Universals in linguistic theory*, ed. by Emmon Bach and Robert T. Harms, 124–69. New York: Holt, Rinehart and Winston. Reprinted in *Grammar and meaning*, 59–98. Tokyo: Taishukan, 1973.

McCawley, James D. 1972. On interpreting the theme of this conference. In *Limiting the domain of linguistics*, ed. by David Cohen, vi–xi. Milwaukee: University of Wisconsin, Department of Linguistics. Reprinted in McCawley 1979, 217–22.

McCawley, James D. 1973. Syntactic and logical arguments for semantic structures. In *Three dimensions of linguistic theory*, ed. by Osamu Fujimura, 259–376. Tokyo: TEC.

McCawley, James D. 1976a. ¡Madison Avenue, si, Pennsylvania Avenue, no! In *The Second LACUS Forum*, ed. by Peter Reich, 17–28. Columbia, SC: Hornbeam. Reprinted in McCawley 1979, 223–33.

McCawley, James D. 1976b. Some ideas not to live by. *Die neueren Sprachen* 75, 151–65. Reprinted in McCawley 1979, 234–46.

McCawley, James D. 1979. *Adverbs, vowels, and other objects of wonder*. Chicago: University of Chicago Press.

McCawley, James D. 1994. Linguistics as biology, as psychology, and as linguistics. In *LACUS 20*, 134–50. Linguistic Association of Canada and the United States.

McCawley, James D. 1996. Acceptability judgments in the teaching and doing of syntax. In *CLS 32*. Part 2, *The Parasession on Theory and Data in Linguistics*, ed. by Lisa McNair,

Kora Singer, Lise M. Dobrin, and Michelle M. AuCoin, 119–32. Chicago: University of Chicago, Chicago Linguistic Society.

Metcalfe, Janet. 2000. Metamemory. In *The Oxford handbook of memory*, ed. by Endel Tulving and Fergus I. M. Craik, 197–211. New York: Oxford University Press.

Osterhout, Lee. 1994. Event-related brain potentials as tools for comprehending language comprehension. In *Perspectives on sentence processing*, ed. by Charles Clifton, Lyn Frazier, and Keith Rayner, 15–44. Hillsdale, NJ: Lawrence Erlbaum.

Osterhout, Lee. 1997. On the brain response to syntactic anomalies: Manipulations of word position and word class reveal individual differences. *Brain and Language* 59, 494–522.

Osterhout, Lee, Michael Bersick, and Judith McLaughlin. 1997. Brain potentials reflect violations of gender stereotypes. *Memory and Cognition* 25, 273–85.

Osterhout, Lee, Phillip J. Holcomb, and David A. Swinney. 1994. Brain potentials elicited by garden-path sentences: Evidence of the application of verb information during parsing. *Journal of Experimental Psychology: Learning, Memory, and Cognition* 20, 786–803.

Piaget, Jean. 1952. *The origins of intelligence in children*. New York: International University Press.

Pickering, Martin J., and Holly P. Branigan. 1999. Syntactic priming in language production. *Trends in Cognitive Sciences* 3, 136–41.

Raaijmakers, Jeroen G. W., Joseph M. C. Schrijnemakers, and Frans Gremmen. 1999. How to deal with "The language-as-fixed-effect fallacy": Common misconceptions and alternative solutions. *Journal of Memory and Language* 41, 416–26.

Reber, Arthur S. 1967. Implicit learning of artificial grammars. *Journal of Verbal Learning and Verbal Behavior* 6, 317–27.

Reber, Arthur S. 1993. *Implicit learning and tacit knowledge: An essay on the cognitive unconscious*. New York: Oxford University Press.

Reder, Lynne M. 1996. *Implicit memory and metacognition*. Mahwah, NJ: Lawrence Erlbaum.

Schacter, Daniel L. 1987. Implicit memory: History and current status. *Journal of Experimental Psychology: Learning, Memory, and Cognition* 13, 501–18.

Schütze, Carson T. 1996. *The empirical base of linguistics: Grammaticality judgments and linguistic methodology*. Chicago: University of Chicago Press.

Seger, Carol Augart. 1994. Implicit learning. *Psychological Bulletin* 115, 163–96.

Seidenberg, Mark S. 1997. Language acquisition and use: Learning and applying probabilistic constraints. *Science* 275, 1599–1603.

Squire, Larry R. 1992a. Declarative and nondeclarative memory: Multiple brain systems supporting learning and memory. *Journal of Cognitive Neuroscience* 4, 232–43.

Squire, Larry R. 1992b. Memory and the hippocampus: A synthesis from findings with rats, monkeys, and humans. *Psychological Review* 99, 195–231.

Stadler, Michael A., and Peter A. Frensch, eds. 1998. *Handbook of implicit learning*. Thousand Oaks, CA: Sage Publications.

Tabor, Whitney, Cornell Juliano, and Michael K. Tanenhaus. 1997. Parsing in a dynamical system: An attractor-based account of the interaction of lexical and structural constraints in sentence processing. *Language and Cognitive Processes* 12, 211–71.

Trudgill, Peter. 1981. Linguistic accommodation: Sociolinguistic observations on a sociopsychological theory. In *Papers from the Parasession on Language and Behavior*, ed. by Carrie S. Masek, Robert A. Hendrik, and Mary F. Miller, 218–37. Chicago: University of Chicago, Chicago Linguistic Society.

Vos, Sandra H., Thomas C. Gunter, Herman H. J. Kolk, and Gijsbertus Mulder. 2001. Working memory constraints on syntactic processing: An electrophysiological investigation. *Psychophysiology* 38, 2041–63.

Whittlesea, Bruce W. A., and Lisa D. Williams. 2000. The source of feelings of familiarity: The discrepancy-attribution hypothesis. *Journal of Experimental Psychology: Learning, Memory, and Cognition* 26, 547–65.

Wolters, Gezinus, and Gordon Logan, eds. 1998. Introduction: Fluency and remembering. Special issue, *Acta Psychologica* 98, 121–25.

Zajonc, Robert B. 1968. Attitudinal effects of mere exposure. *Journal of Personality and Social Psychology* 9, 1–27.

PART VI
Encyclopedia and Language

Chapter 22

Language and Languages in the Eleventh *Britannica*

Peter T. Daniels

22.1 Introduction

"Since 1910 there has been a remarkable revival of interest in linguistic science." So wrote Edward Sapir[1] in his little-known survey of **Philology** in the 1926 Thirteenth Edition (comprising three supplementary volumes) of the *Encyclopædia Britannica*.[2] Sapir's evidence includes the volumes entitled *Language*, by himself (1921), Otto Jespersen (1922), and J. Vendryes (1921);[3] he might equally have included the predecessor to the one by Leonard Bloomfield (1933), whose author, at least (if no one else; cf. Kess 1983), considered it merely a "revised version" (1933, vii) of *Introduction to the Study of Language* (Bloomfield 1914). In this chapter, reflecting Jim McCawley's desire to understand the antecedents and obscurities of any topic that captured his interest, I explore the context into which those works were introduced: the knowledge about language and languages that was available to the educated layperson in the second decade of the twentieth century.

"The best encyclopedia ever written" (www.1911encyclopedia.org)[4] is a common accolade for the Eleventh Edition of the *Encyclopædia Britannica* (1910–11), and in many respects it is richly deserved. From the recent anthologies of articles from the entire history of the *Britannica* and from the Eleventh specifically, though, one would hardly know that language is discussed at all: B. L. Felknor quotes only the preface to the original **Grammar** of 1768, claiming (incorrectly) that it was kept all the way through the Ninth Edition (Fadiman 1992, 219). Coleman and Simmons (1994, 209–48) choose to quote quaint, naïve, or frankly offensive descriptions of "peoples"

I am indebted to the editors' reviewers, Bernard Comrie and Eric Hamp, for valuable comments, and to Phil Baldi for help with Giles, Conway, and the reception of Saussure's "laryngeal" theory. A subsequent hour and a half with Hamp at the 2003 meeting of the American Oriental Society in Nashville, and a similarly extended telephone conversation a few days later, provided rich insight and anecdote concerning the history of Indo-European studies, and some of those observations are included in the notes to this chapter.

(often extracted from articles that also carry a sentence or paragraph characterizing their languages); they observe (p. 210) that

there are no attempts to "sum up" the national character, say, of France, Germany, Italy, or England itself. These centers of cultural authority were the standard by which the rest of the world was being measured ... and thus hardly needed detailed description or summation.

But precisely because they overlook the treatments of languages, they fail to note that of all the world's (then) colonial languages, only those of the British Empire are accorded any sort of "detailed description or summation." Even the highly critical Einbinder (1964) has nothing to say on the topic (besides ignorantly calling William Moulton's discussion of Grimm's Law from the Fourteenth "hopelessly pedantic" and "learned mumbo-jumbo" (p. 288)). Kogan 1958 represents the "official" history of the institution; the author must have had access to the corporate archives, and concentrates on the economics and politics of creating and maintaining an encyclopedia rather than on its intellectual content.

An innovation in the Eleventh Edition was the "classified list of articles" at the back of the index volume; the portion for "Language and Writing" (29, 926–27) lists 77 "General" items[5] and 60 "Languages."[6] **Aphasia** and **Name** appear to have been accidentally omitted from the first category, but any number of language treatments, some very extensive, are not listed because they are included under names of countries (e.g., **Spain**: *The Spanish Language*, **China**: *The Chinese Language*) and peoples (e.g., **Celt**: *Celtic Languages*, **Slavs**), making it difficult to be sure the reader has located all available information on the languages of the world. Of non-Roman scripts, only Greek (passim) and Chinese and Egyptian (s.vv.) are deployed generously; a few words in Hebrew, Arabic, and even Coptic make appearances here and there. Charts under **Alphabet** and **Slavs** show a variety of letterforms, but the few Cyrillic letters within the text of an article are in an inappropriate sans serif font, and the need to print phonetic characters (even—especially—in the Thirteenth) drove the typesetters to acts of desperation.

The "classified list" shows **Philology** and (mistakenly) **Language**[7] as the key entries for the topic; the brief third part of **Philology**—uniquely in the *Encyclopædia*—is a guide to the treatment of the field, according to which the other main article is **Alphabet**, superordinate to **Phonetics**. Entirely unmentioned are **Grammar**, fourth in length but first in importance from the modern point of view, as well as a significant section of **Anthropology**.

22.2 From the Ninth to the Eleventh Edition

It is the Eleventh Edition of the *Encyclopædia Britannica* that has the reputation of containing "all there is to know," but that laurel rightly belongs to the Ninth Edition

(1875–89)—unsigned entries in the Eleventh are often abridgments of signed articles in the Ninth.[8] In the area of language and languages, some treatments are carried over verbatim or nearly so, notably the central **Philology:** *I.—The Science of Language in General* (1885) and **Grammar** (1880), as well as **Anthropology**, **Mongols:** *Language*, **Pahlavi**, **Provençal Language**, **Sanskrit:** *Sanskrit Language*, and **Spain:** *Spanish Language*; some are given minor revisions, either by a second named author (**English Language**, **French Language**, **Latin Language**, and **Italian Language**, wherein Carlo Salvioni's additions to Graziadio Ascoli's original and celebrated text are explicitly marked) or presumably by the author himself (**Persia:** *Persian (Iranian) Languages*, **Scandinavian Languages**, **Semitic Languages**, **Tamils**, and **Ural-Altaic**). **Aphasia** is an entirely new article by the original writer. Abridgments of two articles in the Eleventh are credited to authors other than those named in the Ninth: **Hungary:** *Language* and **Malays:** *Malay Language and Literature*.

An article that needs to be considered out of turn is **Philology:** *II.—Comparative Philology of the Aryan Languages* (18 columns),[9] by Eduard Sievers, youngest and "probably the most brilliant" of the pioneering Indo-Europeanists gathered at Leipzig (Lehmann 1993, 6).[10] After 3.5 columns on the history of "Indo-Germanic"[11] philology and 2.5 columns on phonetic change versus analogical change, Sievers devotes 12.5 columns to the family itself, beginning with a discussion of the name for it; his preference for *Aryan* is based on the belief that it represents the "primitive forefathers'" own name for themselves. A discussion, with bibliography, of the branches and languages of the family (2.5) is followed by their accepted subgrouping, with criteria (3). Last comes the (small-type) description of the parent language, devoted mostly to phonology: a table of correspondences justifies the positing of both a palatal and a guttural series of stops; the vowel system is shown to include not the Sanskrit *a* only (as previously believed), but the Greek *a*, *e*, *o*. A footnote here provides the only mention in the Ninth through Thirteenth editions of Ferdinand de Saussure: "In his earlier publications Brugmann wrote a_1, a_2, a_3 for *e*, *o*, *a* respectively; *A* was then substituted for a_3 by De Saussure." Saussure's *Mémoire* (1879), published in Leipzig, was certainly known to Sievers, but seems to have been understood as offering no more than a notational variant. Its importance (explicated by Hjelmslev (1970, 123–27), ref. from Koerner 1975, 807; cf. Morpurgo Davies 1998, 243–44 with refs. 273–74n27) was not recognized until after Kuryłowicz (1927) had identified the "laryngeals" in the newly deciphered Hittite; even then, it was generations before "laryngeal theory" was fully integrated into Indo-European studies (Lehmann 1993, 295–96n9; Polomé 1965).[12] Sievers goes on to describe vowel gradation, stress, and pitch, and the categories (though not the details) of morphology. He thus provided a solid foundation for articles on the history of the Indo-European language families.

Several significant authors make their first appearance in the Tenth Edition, eight supplementary volumes (plus one of maps[13] and one of index) published in 1902: (1) Peter Giles, whose **Writing** (29) was subsequently divided into **Alphabet** (18) and the unsigned **Writing** (which perversely deals mostly with prewriting devices for visual communication (4)), while his **Philology** (10) is a brief review of recent progress and a presentation of new topics in Indo-European studies: he discusses "phonetic law," societal explanations for sound change, and at considerable length the topic of comparative syntax (digesting the fundamental monographs of Berthold Delbrück); (2) Francis Llewellyn Griffith, whose **Egyptology** and **Hieroglyphics** contrariwise were combined within **Egypt** in the Eleventh; and (3) the geographer/ethnographer (and anarchist; cf. Fadiman 1992, 472–77) Prince Peter A. Kropotkin, who prepared a number of essays on the Russian Empire's principal divisions.[14] Decidedly insignificant, and quotable in its entirety, is the discussion of the language of **Korea** (Isabella Bishop and O. J. R. Howarth) in the Tenth and Eleventh:

Race.—The origin of the Korean people is unknown. They are of the Mongol family; their language belongs to the so-called Turanian group, is polysyllabic, possesses an alphabet of 11 vowels and 14 consonants, and a script named *En-mun*. Literature of the higher class and official and upper class correspondence are exclusively in Chinese characters, but since 1895 official documents have contained an admixture of *En-mun*.[15]

The other articles new in the Tenth and repeated in the Eleventh are **America:** *Ethnology and Archaeology*, **Bulgaria:** *Language and Literature*, and **Japan:** *Language and Literature*.

22.3 The Eleventh Edition: Language

William Dwight Whitney[16] published **Philology I** (31) in the Ninth Edition, and it lies unchanged in the Eleventh. It is, moreover (as he says), a condensation of his earlier scholarly (1867) and popular (1875) books. From the modern point of view—or even from Sapir's point of view in the Thirteenth—it appears bewilderingly obsolete. The questions treated are, in order, the purpose of language; the origin of language; the modality of language; language and culture; change of language; type of language. At no point, as McCawley (1967) observes, does Whitney exhibit any interest in the description of language, even though his grammar of Sanskrit (1879) is universally regarded as one of the finest descriptive grammars ever compiled. The last part of Whitney's contribution is a survey of the world's languages under 13 heads (Indo-European, Semitic, Hamitic, Monosyllabic, Ural-Altaic, Dravidian, Malay-Polynesian, Other Oceanic [i.e., Australian and Papuan], Caucasian, Remnants of Families in Europe [i.e., Basque and Etruscan], Bantu, Central African, and American). The introduction to this section begins nobly:

That a classification of languages ... is not equivalent to a classification of races, and why this is so, is evident enough from the principles which have been brought out by our whole discussion of languages.... No language is a race-characteristic, determined by the special endowments of a race; all languages are of the nature of institutions, parallel products of powers common to all mankind—the powers, namely, involved in the application of the fittest available means to securing the common end of communication. Hence they are indefinitely transferable, like other institutions.... As an individual can learn any language, foreign as well as ancestral..., so also a community.... Accordingly, as individuals of very various race are often found in one community, speaking together one tongue, and utterly ignorant of any other, so there are found great communities of various descent, speaking the dialects of one common tongue, which at some period historical circumstances have imposed upon them.

But a few lines later:

In strictness, language is never a proof of race ...; it is only a probable indication of race ...; it is one evidence, to be combined with others, in the approach towards a solution of the confessedly insoluble problems of human history.... On the whole, the contributions of language to ethnology are practically far greater in amount and more distinct than those derived from any other source.

The genetical classification of languages, then, is to be taken for just what it attempts to be, and no more: primarily as a classification of languages only; but secondarily as casting light, in varying manner and degree, on movements of community, which in their turn depend more or less upon movements of races.

It is this sentiment, and not the earlier, that seems to have prevailed among the contributors to the *Encyclopædia*.[17] Again and again, linguistic affinity is called "racial" affinity, sometimes with simply erroneous results (even acknowledging that "race" was broadly used for what is now called "ethnicity")—see the mention of Fijian below in connection with **Papuans**. **Anthropology** (2; E. B. Tylor) makes the same points as **Philology** in fuller terms, less cloaked in lofty abstraction.

What a contrast is found in **Grammar** (8), by the biblical and Near Eastern scholar A. H. Sayce! It treats grammar, grammaticality, and grammatical categories—a strikingly McCawleyan text. It seems not irrelevant that Sayce's *Principles of Comparative Philology* (also 1875) was in its fourth edition by 1893, while Whitney 1875 was still being reprinted unchanged in 1901.

Whitney and Sayce are still remembered in their respective fields. But the single most prolific contributor on language to the Eleventh Edition, Peter Giles, is forgotten. From an adulatory obituary (Dawkins 1935), we learn of his Scottish origin (Aberdeen, rather than Jim's Glasgow), which suffused his scholarship. After graduating from King's College, Aberdeen, he came to Gonville and Caius College, Cambridge, as a classical scholar in 1882, studied with Brugmann at Freiburg and Leipzig in 1886–87, and took his master's degree in 1889. The next year he moved to Emmanuel College, where he remained for 45 years—Lecturer in Classics, University Reader in Comparative Philology. His only book followed in 1895 (he managed only one new edition).[18] His time was taken up with teaching and administration, but he composed many publications in the nature of review articles—for *The Year's Work in Classical Studies* (eight contributions between 1906 and 1928–29), the *Cambridge Ancient History* (1924a,b) and *History of India* (1921), and several other reference works; so he was an experienced and logical candidate to contribute to the *Britannica*.

Giles's **Alphabet** was a model article. It (or rather its predecessor **Writing** in the Tenth, which was trimmed a bit in its dissection in the Eleventh) is the most comprehensive account ever to grace an encyclopedia, with naught to trouble the specialist even after a century; it is refreshingly free of mysticism, of leaps of faith; while most detailed on the history of the Greek and Italic alphabets, it of course includes runes and ogham and Armenian and the Slavic scripts and does not shirk Persia and Central Asia and South Asia—only Korea and, curiously, Georgian are unknown.[19] He uses the articles **A** through **Z** (18 total) not just for further information on the history of the alphabet and spelling, but also for topics like nasalization (**N**) and details of phonetics.[20] Under **Accent** (3), he discusses pitch and stress, and their function in Indo-European.

Phonetics (17.5) is in the capable hands of Henry Sweet. He eases in via "sound-notation" and spelling reform, and takes the opportunity to introduce his own transcription scheme, Broad Romic and Narrow Romic (as A. J. Ellis did before him with Palaeotype in **Speech-Sounds** in the Ninth, and Jones would after him with Cardinal Vowels in the Thirteenth), with extensive instruction in articulatory phonetics. At the other end of the utterance, the question of meaning is turned over to Lady Welby ("formerly Maid of Honour to Queen Victoria") in **Significs** (5), one of a handful of hobbyhorse articles that mar, or adorn, the *Britannica*:[21] it is difficult to tell just what Significs is, but it intends to remedy "a prison of senseless formalism and therefore of barren controversy."

Etymology (1), **Slang** (6.5), and **Name** (5) could be taken as the lexicon portion of the study of language. The heart of the first is an extensive quotation from Skeat's *Etymological Dictionary*; the second, by Henry Bradley, takes its topic in a broad sense, encompassing argot, cant, and jargon as well as informal or nonstandard usage; the last requires three authors to deal with the question in general (Andrew Lang), in Greece and Rome (J. H. Freese), and in law (T. A. Ingram). **Aphasia** (2.5; J. B. Tuke) describes a number of syndromes, the cerebral lesions believed to be associated with each, and the general absence of hope for a cure.

22.4 The Eleventh Edition: Languages

Not surprisingly, Indo-European receives far more coverage in the Eleventh Edition than any other language phylum—bulking about two-thirds of all the language articles,[22] about half of all the materials in our purview.[23] **Philology II** (18), which in the Ninth was the principal treatment of Indo-European, still carries the signature of Eduard Sievers, but his presentation of the structure of Proto-Indo-European has been discarded and upon the introductory portions of his article (history, phonetic change) follows Giles's Tenth Edition discussion of phonetic law; Sievers's discussion of analogy is retained with considerable expansion to include a psychological classification of analogy. Into his own discussion of comparative syntax Giles interpolates a long speculation on the origin of gender. Into Sievers's history he interpolates a mention of Whitney as having originally "inspired" the Neogrammarians;[24] Sievers himself names him as the first to recognize the importance of analogy. (Koerner seems to have overlooked these credits in reporting (1975, 760) early lack of recognition of Whitney's contributions to general linguistics.)[25] Thus, aside from taking all its examples from Indo-European languages, **Philology II** is not, as the title claims, a *Comparative Philology of the Indo-European Languages.*

The slack might be expected to be taken up by Giles's **Indo-European Languages** (11). Here, however, we find (after the list of families) another history of philology and another discussion of the group's name. Then come useful considerations of the nature of a protolanguage and the meaning of *root*; but the bulk of the article is devoted to the homeland[26] and spread of the Indo-European languages, including a variety of *Wörter und Sachen* fields. There is, however, nothing at all on phonology or morphology, no tables of correspondences. As a result, the cross-references by several contributors, who presumably expected something like Sievers's recapitulation of the system as so far reconstructed to be available to the *Encyclopædia*'s readers, are fruitless.

Giles's exposition of the basics of Indo-European is, in fact, contained within **Greek Language** (10.5)—but only appears after two-thirds of the article has discussed the ancient dialects; thereafter, he presents the sound changes producing the classical language, and grammatical categories. The Italic languages are in the capable hands of R. S. Conway, whose *Italic Dialects* (1897) is still cited in the handbooks (e.g., Baldi 2002). His general overview is tucked inside **Italy:** *History: A. Ancient Languages and Peoples* (2.5). Here he adumbrates his theory of the division of the Italic peoples into a -NO- group and a -CO- group (referring to the respective suffixes on their ethnica)—explication is put off to **Sabini** (2.5) and **Volsci** (1.3),[27] which are among his seeming dozens of articles on Italic tribes, most of which mention the inscriptional evidence for them and any dialectal peculiarities. The best-known languages are described under **Falisci** (1), **Veneti** (3), **Osca Lingua** (2.3), and **Iguvium** (he objected to the name *Umbrian*; 2.2); Conway also provides extensive information on **Etruria:** *Language* (5). His major achievement is the historical sketch of the grammar of the **Latin Language** (27.5), which begins with its connections with Celtic and its relations with Greek; phonology, morphology, syntax, borrowing, and pronunciation are clearly presented. The second half of the article (retained from the Ninth) is A. S. Wilkins's author-by-author survey of the characteristics of the language over some six centuries. A note at the end sends the reader on to **Romance Languages** (12), another contribution by a master of his field: Wilhelm Meyer-Lübke. On the origin of the Romance languages, he refers to G. Gröber's observation that "the process of Romanizing the various districts took place at epochs far remote one from the other, and between the earliest and the latest of these epochs Latin itself was modified";[28] and he accounts for the differences among the modern Romance languages by describing their many substrata.

Study of the individual Romance languages may best begin with **Italian Language** (19.5), where Ascoli and then Salvioni provide great descriptive detail on a range of idioms considerably transcending the Italian peninsula, as seen in the article's outline:

A. Dialects which depend in a greater or less [*sic*] degree on Neo-Latin systems not peculiar to Italy.
   1. Franco-Provençal and Provençal Dialects.
   2. Ladin [i.e., Romansh] Dialects.
B. Dialects which are detached from the true and proper Italian system, but form no integral part of any foreign Neo-Latin system.
   1. Gallo-Italian (Ligurian, Piedmontese, Lombard, Emilian).
   2. Sardinian dialects.
   3. Vegliote [i.e., Dalmatian].
C. Dialects which diverge more or less from the genuine Italian or Tuscan type, but which at the same time can be conjoined with the Tuscan as forming part of a special system of Neo-Latin dialects.
   1. Venetian.
   2. Corsican.
   3. Dialects of Sicily and of the Neapolitan Provinces.
   4. Dialects of Umbria, the Marches and the Province of Rome.
D. Tuscan, and the Literary Language of the Italians.

At once we see that the great divide that set in around the turn of the century between the Neogrammarians and the Dialectologists is reflected in the pages of the *Britannica*. But with **French Language** (14.5; Henry Nicol, lightly revised by Paul Meyer), we find a strictly historical account of the language, accounting briefly for some dialect differentiation; the section on *Orthography* veers surprisingly but welcomely into English spelling. **Provençal Language** (8.7; Paul Meyer), not surprisingly, presents the historical development of the old literary language and its "modification" into the modern form. **Spain:** *The Spanish Language* (12; Alfred Morel-Fatio, barely revised by James Fitzmaurice-Kelly) is probably the worst-titled article we will encounter, since it covers (1) Catalan, (2) Castilian with its dialects, and (3) Portuguese, to which it claims Galician is assimilating. The treatment is historical, and

Catalan is compared with Provençal. Portions of the article **Rumania** (1.5) are signed or cosigned *X.*, including *Language*, and this siglum is nowhere explained; clearly, no philologist was involved, and we read mostly of the language's purity, its orthography, and its "interesting" features[29]—a preview, in fact, of the treatments of many less-known languages of the world.

Celt: *Celtic Languages* (20; E. C. Quiggin) is an extensive historicodescriptive account of the six modern languages, preceded by Gaulish and followed by an appendix on Pictish. It is an especially impressive achievement in that "no comprehensive handbook of the Celtic languages" was yet available.[30] **Teutonic (Germanic) Languages** (7), by H. M. Chadwick,[31] who also wrote briefly on **Goths:** *Gothic Language* (.5), lays out the developments from Indo-European to Germanic and the distinctions within the family. A. G. Noreen's **Scandinavian Languages** (15.5) is very like the Celtic article, treating both old and current forms of each language. **Runes, Runic Language and Inscriptions** (2; Edmund Gosse) does not in fact discuss the language; Noreen's article does. **English Language** (26) is by James A. H. Murray, revised with the assistance of his eldest daughter Hilda. He himself called it "the most succinct account yet presented to Englishmen of the changes through which their language has passed, the causes of these changes, and the temporary phases of the long continuous whole" (K. Murray 1977, 99). It is thus historical but not descriptive, with some attention to dialect; a cross-reference to "Scottish Language" is to a requested article he never wrote (ibid.), but the faulty reference was carried over to the Eleventh. **Dutch Language** (5; J. H. Gallee) manages not to say anything specific about Dutch (or Frisian), beyond a spelling-to-sound guide. **German Language** (11; Robert Priebsch—replacing, incidentally, an article by Sievers) is mostly historical but also includes dialect description.

Peter Giles returns once more for **Aryan** (2.5), which is in part a commentary on the article by Max Müller it replaces: by 1910, it was necessary to rebut the notion of an "Aryan race"—despite Müller's insistence, in a passage quoted by Giles, that he himself used the term to refer only to speakers of Aryan (i.e., Indo-European) languages—and Giles prefers to limit the linguistic term to what is now usually called Indo-Iranian. He is so up to date as to mention the Mitanni cuneiform texts naming Aryan deities and even the "Tocharish" materials (both first published in 1908). After describing the peculiarities of Aryan, he directs the reader to **Persia:** *Language* and **Indo-Aryan Languages**. None other than the historian Eduard Meyer devotes two paragraphs of the ancient history of Persia to the linguistic situation of the Achaemenid empire; but *Persian (Iranian) Languages* (4.5) is the province of K. F. Geldner. He contrasts Iranian with Indo-Aryan, briefly describes "Zend" (despite recognizing the inappropriateness of that name for what is now called Avestan), comparing it with Sanskrit; then come notes on Old Persian, "New" (i.e., Classical) Persian, and four modern languages (cf. **Pushtu**, paragraphs under **Baluchistan** and

Kurdistan, but no separate mention of Ossetic). The article's age is shown by a note that the affinity of Armenian is controversial.[32] **Pahlavī** (3) is about all that remains of Theodor Nöldeke's Iranian contributions to the Ninth—his history was replaced by Meyer's—describing that adaptation of Aramaic script by the pre-Islamic Persian chanceries. **Indo-Aryan Languages** (5.5) marks the entry point into George A. Grierson's extensive series of grammatical sketches (rendering him after Giles the second most prolific contributor). **Prakrit** (6.5), **Hindostani** (9.5), **Gujarati and Rajasthani** (6), **Pahari** (2.5), **Kashmiri** (7), **Sindhi and Lahnda** (5.2), **Marathi** (10), **Bengali with Oriya and Assamese** (5.5), and **Bihari** (6) are constructed on a uniform plan, all referenced to the first two in the sequence and to **Sanskrit:** *I.—Sanskrit Language* (7; Julius Eggeling) and to Grierson's treatments in the *Linguistic Survey of India*, even volumes that had not yet been published.[33] **Pali** (4; T. W. Rhys Davids) unfortunately has nothing to say about the language. Moses Gaster's **Gipsies:** *Origin and Language* (2.5) describes work on the languages of the Rom around the world, noting their affinity with Indo-Aryan, but gives no examples or grammatical details. **Armenian Language and Literature:** *Language* (1.7; F. C. Conybeare) stresses the Iranian components and notes the difficulties, after factoring them out, in determining the exact place of Armenian among the other families of Indo-European.

Lithuanians and Letts: *Language and Literature* (1.3; unsigned) mentions the close relation with Slavonic and what distinguishes them, as well as a few distinctive characteristics of Latvian and Lithuanian.[34] **Slavs** (12.5; E. H. Minns) acknowledges but also skips over the Balto-Slav stage, listing 13 changes from Indo-European to Old Church Slavonic; a sketch of Old Slavonic (the brief unsigned **Slavonic, Old** (.7) summarizes the literary tradition) precedes a contrastive presentation of the modern Slavic languages. **Russian Language** (4.2), embracing White Russian (Belarusian) and Little Russian (Ukrainian), which treats the development from Slavic and the dialects, is also by Minns, as are several articles on Slavic peoples, most of which include a few words on their language. Those that accord them separate sections are **Servia:** *Language* (1.5; Chedomille Mijatovich), **Croatia-Slavonia:** *Language and Literature* (1.2; K. G. Jayne), and **Bulgaria:** *Language and Literature* (3; J. D. Bourchier). **Albania:** *Language* (1; also Bourchier) rounds off the Indo-European languages with a brief but adequate presentation. Bourchier's articles show awareness of the features, and their distribution, that would later define the Balkan "linguistic area." An extensive presentation on the **Hittites** (4; D. G. Hogarth), whose cuneiform inscriptions had not yet been read and whose distinctive hieroglyphs had not yet been deciphered, notes the hints—nominative *s*, accusative *m* known from names in the former—of Indo-European connection. B. Hrozný's (1915) insight was just around the corner.[35]

It was Theodor Nöldeke's **Semitic Languages** (25) that suggested the Eleventh Edition is of more than antiquarian interest, for it has always been recommended to students as the best overview of the external history and the internal structure of that family (the German original was published separately as *Die semitischen Sprachen: Eine Skizze*); only now is a worthy alternative available (Huehnergard 1995).[36] One of the small differences between the Ninth and Eleventh Editions shows that Nöldeke kept the article up to date—but was not careful about revisions. The discussion of subdivisions reads as follows, with material added in the Eleventh italicized:

> One thing at least is certain, that Arabic (with Sabaean, *Mahri and Socotri*) and Ethiopic stand in a comparatively close relationship to one another, and compose a group by themselves, as contrasted with the other Semitic languages, Hebraeo-Phoenician, Aramaic and Assyrian, which constitute the northern group.... The division between the northern and the southern Semitic languages is a recognized fact. *It is perfectly certain, moreover, that Hebraeo-Phoenician and Aramaic are closely related with each other, and form a group of their own, distinct even from Assyrian. In fact, Assyrian seems to be so completely* sui generis *that we should be well advised to separate it from all the cognate languages, as an independent scion of proto-Semitic.*

Mahri and Socotri are two of the Modern South Arabian languages, which had meanwhile received competent descriptions; but the longer added portion reflects a new understanding, due to Hommel (1892), of the main break within Semitic as between East (Assyrian) and West (all the others). The two earlier references to the north-south division should have been corrected! R. W. Rogers's **Cuneiform** (7) is a lucid discussion of the nature and use of the two scripts written with a stylus on clay, with the most accurate account of their decipherments to be found in a reference work (cf. Daniels 1994). **Hebrew Language** (3.7; A. E. Cowley, who wrote on several Semitic topics) deals with the place of the language in ancient and contemporary Jewish culture. (Cowley's **Hebrew Literature** acknowledges the existence of Jewish writings in vernacular languages, but the sole mentions of Yiddish in the Eleventh are in **Slang** and in **Anthropology**, where "Jewish-German" serves to illustrate the fallacy of equating race and language.) **Syriac Language** (2; Norman McLean) briefly describes the classical Aramaic language and was probably added to complement McLean's condensation of the celebrated treatise on **Syriac Literature** by W. Wright in the Ninth. No articles on Semitic-speaking peoples, nations, or regions appear to contain accounts of the languages, though D. H. Müller's **Sabaeans** (4) discusses the alphabets and content of the South Arabian inscriptions.[37] The related **Hamitic Races and Languages:** *Hamitic Languages* is by the Egyptologist W. Max Müller of Philadelphia (Gordon 1986, 18–28, esp. 18–19, 22, 26–27). He describes Libyan (for him "Berber" is a misnomer), Cushitic (to which he is certain that Haus[s]a belongs, unlike the anonymous author of **Hausa** (.5), who compares "Arabic or Semitic," Berber, and Coptic), and Egyptian, putting the separation from Semitic at "4000 or 6000 B.C." Of these, **Berbers** (unsigned) includes a brief discussion of the dialects, and the aforementioned **Egypt:** *II. Ancient Egypt: D. Egyptian Language and Writing*

(16.5; F. Ll. Griffith) is another of the crown jewels of this encyclopedia. **Sumer and Sumerian** (4.5) marks another of the rare appearances of an American contributor, J. Dyneley Prince; this was certainly the most sophisticated treatment of this ultra-obscure language ever to be offered to the general public.

Our first step outside Europe and the Near East is to the "monosyllabic family." Not from **Philology III**, but from Whitney's survey of the phyla in **Philology I** do we discover that **Siam:** *Language and Literature* (3; W. A. Graham) is to be there considered. Indeed, Graham refers to the "Tai group of the Siamese-Chinese family," though he does not seem to know that the Tai group extends well into China—indeed, Southeast Asia seems to be the linguistically least known region of the globe. He describes the vocabulary and the alphabet, marvels at the tones, classifiers, and honorific diglossia, but finds the syntax reassuringly close to English and German. **Tibeto-Burman Languages** (2.2) is the first of three contributions by Sten Konow (he wrote on the same topics for the *Linguistic Survey of India*). He identifies six Tibetan groups, several intermediate ones, and Burmese, and traces them back to an original homeland, neighbor to those of Chinese and Tai, calling the family "Indo-Chinese": its unity is apparent "in the phonetical system, in vocabulary and in grammar." His explanation for uniform tonogenesis, however, is mistaken. **Tibet:** *Language* (5; L. A. Waddell and A. Terrien de Lacouperie) is an extended abstract of a number of specialist studies; **Burma:** *Language and Literature* (.5; J. G. Scott) has merely a list of language groups ("joint members of a vast Indo-Chinese immigration swarm"), a statement that some say Burmese has three tones and some say it doesn't, and a note of the Pali-derived alphabet. **China:** *The Chinese Language* (12.5; Herbert A. Giles and Lionel Giles: father and son (Honey 2001, 185); not related to Peter) first describes the dialects, then discusses the script at great length, bemoans the nonexistence of "grammar," but then demonstrates how "syntax" takes care of the expression of all necessary grammatical relations. This was a great improvement over the article in the Ninth, which, though similarly extended, attempted to describe Chinese in terms of Western grammatical categories. The opposite is unfortunately the case for **Japan:** *III.—Language and Literature* (2; Captain Frank Brinkley), where an utterly fanciful "explanation" of relations among the Chinese, Japanese, and Korean languages and scripts is followed by complaints that "the difficulties that confront an Occidental who attempts to learn Japanese are enormous." The article in the Ninth, by T. R. H. M'Clatchie, is far more accurate. (It even notes that virtually nothing is known of Ainu; Brinkley's (unsigned in the Eleventh) **Ainu** is one of its uglier ethnologies, but mercifully it has not one word on the language.)

From the "monosyllabic" languages, we pass to **Ural-Altaic** (3), one of the few surviving contributions of A. H. Keane—a professor of Hindostani—who seems to have been the "go-to guy" of the Ninth and Tenth Editions,[38] for which he variously wrote on **Africa:** *Ethnology*; **Georgia**; **Hottentots**; and **Indians, American** as well (but **Hindostani** is by someone else). He discusses agglutination and vowel harmony, but not phonetic or morphological correspondences, despite a long list of scholars after whose labors "their genetic affinity can no longer be seriously doubted." This does seem to be the only place where Tungusic languages are mentioned. Bernhard Julg's **Mongols:** *Language* (4) is a more than worthy companion to the following group, discussing script as well as dialects and grammatical features. **Turks:** *Language* (2.5), **Finno-Ugrian** (9.5), and **Hungary:** *Language* (1.2) are all credited to C. N. E. Eliot (whose **Asia:** *History*, as well, contains virtually the only mention of the Hyperborean or Paleo-Siberian languages), though the too-brief **Hungary** is condensed from E. D. Butler's article in the Ninth. All are serious and credible treatments, touching on both description and dialect variation.[39]

Sten Konow reappears to competently describe **Dravidian** (3); **Tamils** (5) is the only one of several articles on Asian peoples/languages by Reinhold Rost in the Ninth to survive in the Eleventh, and it is respectable. Konow's third appearance is for **Mundās** (2.5); he recognizes their closest connection to the Mon-Khmer languages[40] but goes on to connect them with "the numerous dialects of Austronesia" (not naming them "Malay-Polynesian" as in **Philology I, III**). There seems, however, to be no discussion of Mon-Khmer as a family at all—note that these languages existed in French Indo-China. **Cambodia** (condensed from a full paragraph by Henry Yule in the Ninth) informs us that

Cambodian idiom bears a likeness to some of the aboriginal dialects of south Indo-China; it is agglutinate in character and rich in vowel-sounds. The king's language and the royal writing, and also religious words are, however, apparently of Aryan origin and akin to Pali. Cambodian writing is syllabic and complicated.

What **Annam** has to say about Vietnamese (from C. Maunoir's **Cochin China** in the Ninth) is so bizarre as to merit quoting.[41] The only real treatment of anything Malayo-Polynesian[42] is under **Malays:** *Malay Language and Literature* (2; Hugh Clifford, condensed from R. Rost). It lists the sounds, describes derivation, and notes the absence of inflection and the presence of numeral classifiers (he calls them "class-words or coefficients with numerals") and many strata of borrowings. A few words under **Samoa** ("The Samoan language is soft and liquid in pronunciation, and has been called 'the Italian of the Pacific.' It is difficult to learn thoroughly, owing to its many inflexions and accents, and its being largely a language of idioms.") and **Hawaii**, none under **Fiji**, **Maori**, or **Tonga** (surprisingly, these three being the main British-controlled groups; all five unsigned), are all there is; cross-references to **Polynesia** perhaps refer to the longer article in the Ninth, from which only a paragraph on languages survives under **Papuans**. Unfortunately, the allocation of materials was according to "race," so a few notes on Fijian appear there.

We skip back to Europe for the abridgment of Keane's **Georgia:** *Ethnology* (2.5), which takes linguistic divisions to be racial and describes "Karthli" (i.e., Kartvelian), with its two alphabets. J. T. Bealby's **Caucasia** (.5) includes a list of all the languages of that governor-generalship ("Although the Ingushes speak a Chechen dialect, they have recently been proved to be, anthropologically, quite a distinct race"). Both articles admit of the currently recognized tripartition into Northwest, Northeast, and South Caucasian or Kartvelian, but both also insist on an ultimate Caucasian unity, contrary to the current understanding. Last comes **Basques:** *Language* (2) by Wentworth Webster and Julien Vinson, a sober list of features with no speculations about genetic connections.

The next stop on **Philology III**'s tour of the world's languages is Africa, and it is here that the British bias is most obvious:

> The principal languages of southern and central Africa are treated fully under BANTU LANGUAGES. There is a brief account of the Bushman language under BUSHMEN and of the Hottentot languages under HOTTENTOTS.
>
> *Intermediate African Languages.*—Among the numerous languages spoken by the people of the great central belt of the African continent, the most important is the Hausa, described under that heading.

(Hausa is properly listed with Hamitic s.vv.) Even at the time of Whitney's writing, the languages (to a great extent spoken in French Africa) now grouped as Nilo-Saharan and Niger-Congo other than Bantu were not exactly unknown. There are a few notes under such ethnological entries as **Masai**, **Nubia**, **Songhoi**; **Ewe**, **Fula**, **Tshi**, **Wolof**, and **Yoruba** (all unsigned), but they rarely note more than the existence and perhaps extent of the language(s), and nowhere can a treatment be found of problems in African linguistic classification, or even a list of languages (let alone of articles mentioning them). **Bantu Languages** (13.5), on the other hand, is an extensive treatment by H. H. Johnston, in effect a preview of his major work that was to appear in 1919 (the second volume is an English index to the vocabularies).[43] It enumerates 44 groups of Bantu languages and goes into great detail on the prefix system. Johnston is also responsible for a rare signed African article, **Mandingo**, but it says nothing about the language beyond listing three dialect groups. **Hottentots:** *Language* (1; condensed from John Noble in the Ninth, ignoring Keane in the Tenth) gets beyond the clicks to discuss grammatical categories, morphology, and "dialects," adding the left-handed compliment "The vocabulary is not limited merely to the expression of the rude conceptions that are characteristic of primitive races." The account in **Bushmen** might be taken as an early instance of contrastive analysis:

> Their language, which exists in several dialects, has in common with Hottentot, but to a greater degree, the peculiar sounds known as "clicks." The Hottentot language is more agglutinative, the Bushman more monosyllabic; the former recognizes gender in names, the latter

does not; the Hottentots form the plural by a suffix, the Bushmen by repetition of the name; the former count up to twenty, the latter can only number two, all above that being "many."

Or not.

The native languages of North America fare considerably better. **Indians, North American** (13), by A. F. Chamberlain, slightly modifies J. W. Powell's classification to tabulate 55 linguistic stocks, stating for each its observed range, its postulated "earliest home," the number of "tribes &c.," and the population. Already in 1910, the number of extinct and "nearly extinct" languages is sobering. Chamberlain cites contemporary authorities like Boas, Dixon, and Kroeber to dispel widespread myths about these languages, and also makes astute typological observations. Of Chamberlain's 55 groups, only a handful have corresponding encyclopedia entries; among these, only three mention language at all. **Eskimo** (condensed from Robert Brown in the Ninth) includes an entire paragraph:

As regards language, the idiom spoken from Greenland to north-eastern Siberia is, with a few exceptions, the same; any difference is only that of dialect. It differs from the whole group of European languages, not merely in the sound of the words, but more especially, according to Rink, in the construction. Its most remarkable feature is that a sentence of a European language is expressed in Eskimo by a single word constructed out of certain elements, each of which corresponds in some degree to one of our words. One specimen commonly given to visitors to Greenland may suffice: *Savigiksiniariartokasuaromaryotittogog*, which is equivalent to "He says that you also will go away quickly in like manner and buy a pretty knife." Here is one word serving in the place of 17. It is made up as follows: *Savig* a knife, *ik* pretty, *sini* buy, *ariartok* go away, *asuar* hasten, *omar* wilt, *y* in like manner, *otit* thou, *tog* also, *og* he says.

(**Aleutian Islands** adds the sentence "[The natives] are a branch of the Esquimauan family, but differ greatly from the Eskimo of the mainland in language, habits, disposition and mental ability"); **Chinook** states, "'Chinook jargon' ... has been analysed as composed of two-fifths Chinook, two-fifths other Indian tongues, and the rest English and Canadian French; but the proportion of English has tended to increase. The Chinookan linguistic family includes a number of separate tribes"; and, uniquely, **Salishan** comprises a list of languages.

Mexico includes language counts (A. J. Lamoureux) as well as *Ancient History* by E. B. Tylor and *Ancient Civilization* by Tylor and Walter Lehmann, with notes on Aztec and Maya writing, respectively, the latter found again in Lehmann's **Central America**. For bibliography, Chamberlain refers to **America: III. Ethnology and Archaeology** (1; O. T. Mason), where a list of language families contains the only mention of any of South America: not Quechua, not Aymara, not Guaraní finds anything but a passing reference in **Peru** or **Bolivia**, and Brazil's natives are virtually invisible (and unnamed).[44]

In order to save the unmentioned for last, we look for a moment at three articles by Henry Sweet: **Universal Languages** (4.3), **Volapük** (1), and **Esperanto** (2). He is hostile to the concept but familiar with and not unfair to the languages themselves.

From **Philology III**, one would have no idea that the languages of Australia are mentioned anywhere in the Eleventh Edition. Whitney in **Philology I**, however, has this to say:

8. *Other Oceanic Families.*—... The continental island of Australia, with its dependency Tasmania (where, however, the native tongue has now become extinct), has its own body of probably related dialects, as its own physical type. They have been but imperfectly investigated, their importance, except to the professed student of language, being nothing; but they are not destitute of a rude agglutinative structure of their own.

Channing Arnold, in **Australia:** *Aborigines*, claims this:

No word exists in their language for such general terms as tree, bird or fish; yet they have invented a name for every species of vegetable and animal they know. The grammatical structure of some north Australian languages has a considerable degree of refinement. The verb presents a variety of conjugations, expressing nearly all the moods and tenses of the Greek. There is a dual, as well as a plural form in the declension of verbs, nouns, pronouns and adjectives. The distinction of genders is not marked, except in proper names of men and women. All parts of speech, except adverbs, are declined by terminational inflections. There are words for the elementary numbers, one, two, three; but "four" is usually expressed by "two-two." They have no idea of decimals. The number and diversity of separate languages is bewildering.

Capell (1971) informs us that decent linguistic descriptions were available for at least a few Australian languages in the nineteenth century. But even the equivalent article in the Tenth (J. Milne Curran and T. A. Coughlin) provided this anecdote:

The study of the languages of the various tribes has so far yielded nothing of exceptional importance. As an instance of how a spoken tongue may vary in a short time the following is of interest:—In 1893 a wild tribe of natives was discovered in the Wentworth district of New South Wales. This tribe originated through a black-fellow hiding in some little-known country with a few gins [Australian equivalent of *squaws*] for some thirty years. In that time the tribe had grown to thirty—men, women, and children.... The remarkable fact is that the station [= U.S. *ranch*] blacks had considerable difficulty in making the wild tribe understand them, although thirty years before they must have spoken the same language.

Perhaps this story was told because it was believed to reflect "primitivity" in the instability of speech. Perhaps it was dropped as incredible. But given what is now known of the taboo process in Australian languages (Dixon 1980, 28), and of creolization processes, this might have been the single most interesting datum in the entire linguistic *Britannica*.

22.5 Moral

Let us turn again to the Thirteenth to see how the field had changed in just 15 years. Sapir's **Philology** (6) first considers, under the heading *Psychology*, two behaviorist approaches. Sapir cautiously approves that of J. R. Kantor[45] and rejects the "extreme" approach of J. B. Watson. He expects that Gestalt psychology "will prove of the greatest value to linguistic science." Also here, he adumbrates the notion of phoneme but cedes the discussion to Jones. Under *Philosophy*, he welcomes attention to meaning—no Significs for Sapir! Under *Forms of Speech*, he seems to reject the interpretation now generally called the Sapir-Whorf Hypothesis (properly Whorf's Linguistic Relativity Principle):

A language may be said to have no "word" or other element for the "idea" in question, from which, however, it need not in the least follow that it is incapable of satisfactorily conveying the total psychic sequence ("thought") or unit of communication in which the "idea," in another language, figures as an essential element.

Under *General Tendencies*, he makes the observation that Whitney and Tylor failed to take seriously:

There is a growing realisation that the life of language is similar in all parts of the world, regardless of the race or cultural development of the speakers of the language, and that the rate of linguistic change is not seriously dependent on the presence or absence of writing.

Sapir refers to "drift" (under *Consistency of Change*), to the importance of language contact and bilingualism in language change, and to his new proposed typology along three dimensions. Very interesting is the fact that—*if* this article was prepared in 1925—under *North and South American Languages* he recorded for publication for the first time his sixfold classification of Eskimo, Nadene, Hokan-Siouan, Algonquin-Wakashan, Penutian, and Aztek-Tanoan: that is, earlier than the squib in the 16 October 1925 *Science* Supplement in which an unnamed reporter communicated his suggestion. His article concludes with additional notes on discoveries relating to other languages.

Both important components of Jones's **Phonetics** (4) have been mentioned—the cardinal vowels and the phoneme; he also discusses studies of intonation and lists a number of languages that had received proper or improved phonetic investigations.

It seems safe to say that readers lucky enough to have, and clever enough to use, the supplementary volumes of the Thirteenth alongside the Eleventh Edition[46] could learn as much as Sapir and his contemporaries might wish them to know about language and about, at least, the languages of Europe and Southwest and South Asia. But it also seems safe to say that most readers never read—never had the opportunity to read—what was laid out for them in the Thirteenth.[47] Thus, the old myths about language and "race" remained—and remain—lodged in the public consciousness.

Jim McCawley did not himself contribute to encyclopedias or address the general public, except as informal consultant to the "language maven" William Safire and in the not conspicuously successful *Eater's Guide to Chinese Characters* (1984).[48] In his review of a popular work (1995), he addresses not how the linguists and others involved communicated to their audience, but the ideas themselves, suggesting to teachers how they might amplify or exemplify them for their classes. As Jim doubtless appreciated, the contributors to the *Encyclopædia Britannica* during the half century we have surveyed, and indeed down through the current Fifteenth Edition, made no concessions to their audience. They faithfully presented the fruits of their latest research, making "a broad selection of the ideas and subject matter of linguistics accessible to millions ... who might otherwise live their entire lives with no conception of what kinds of questions linguists ask and why linguists find answering these questions ... a source of excitement and satisfaction" (McCawley 1995, 629).

Notes

1. At the time Associate Professor of Anthropology, University of Chicago (though the article may have been written while he was still in Ottawa).

2. Article titles are mentioned here in bold type. **Phonetics** by Daniel Jones would seem to complete the coverage in the Thirteenth.

3. The focus of this chapter being on the *Encyclopædia Britannica* and its readers, I concentrate here on English-language materials. The 1925 translation of Vendryes's book by Sapir's Americanist colleague Paul Radin was presumably not yet known to him at the time of writing.

4. This study was possible because of the existence of this website, which makes freely available the text of (most of) the Eleventh *Britannica* as processed by OCR software. While the content is far from perfect (pages and sometimes entire articles have been skipped, and the system is frequently defeated by diacritics and non-English words), by proofing against the print version and applying my own formatting, I was able to create output much more convenient for the user than the dense type of the original.

5. Of these, 34 are "dictionary headings," such as **Ablative** and **Accidence**—and **Language** itself—providing just a definition of the term; 26 of the full articles represent letters of the alphabet; of the rest, several would not now be considered relevant: **Cryptography**, **Inscriptions**, **Palaeography**, **Shorthand**, and perhaps **Dictionary**, leaving just a dozen articles to be investigated.

6. Of these, 16 are "dictionary headings," 14 treat language families, and 30 cover individual languages.

7. A far cry from the 33,000-word essay by Thomas Young reported to be found in the Fourth Edition (Einbinder 1964, 34).

8. Published at the rate of about two volumes per year between 1875 and 1889. I cite the "R. S. Peale Reprint" (Chicago, 1890), which claims to contain new maps and specially written articles on American topics, though I have found no differences from the standard edition.

9. The length in columns is appended for each article, or portion dealing with language, as it is discussed (.2 stands for $\frac{1}{4}$, .3 for $\frac{1}{3}$, .5 for $\frac{1}{2}$, .6 for $\frac{2}{3}$, and .7 for $\frac{3}{4}$). These figures are not fully comparable as they do not take into account the use of both regular (ca. 9/9.5 pt.) and small (ca. 8/8 pt.) type in the texts of the articles (25% smaller in the "handy volume issue").

10. Lehmann refers to Leskien (1840–1916), Brugmann (1849–1919), Delbrück (1842–1922), Osthoff (1847–1909), and Sievers (1850–1927).

Language in the Eleventh *Britannica*

11. Indicative of the editors' casual approach to our subject matter is the indiscriminate use of names for this family—*Indo-Germanic, Indo-European,* and *Aryan* all occur according to the preference of the several authors, rather than a uniform nomenclature having been imposed.

12. Compare Polomé 1965, 12–15, for Holger Pedersen's increasing understanding of the potential of Saussure's formulation. Eric Hamp (pers. comm., 2003) insists on Pedersen's insightfulness, particularly in his 1909 work, pointing out that his 1931 history of linguistics is a superb discussion of the state of the art at the time the *Britannica* articles were being written (and that the 1925 Danish original is a very rare work, prepared for an academic anniversary, that might have gone unnoticed but for the translation by his student Spargo). It is worth noting that all the contributors to the 1959 *Evidence for Laryngeals* conference were scholars near the beginning of their careers in linguistics. The late Prof. Henry Hoenigswald, the senior member of the group, assured me (pers. comm., 30 January 2003) that he did not take offense at that characterization!

13. Apparently identical to the *Atlas* of Whitney's *Century Dictionary and Cyclopædia,* a volume published in 1897 and updated annually.

14. Ironically, the entry for **Kropotkin** himself was reprinted—like the history portions of his articles in the Tenth—from the Ninth in the Eleventh without update, giving the impression that between 1880 and 1910, while living in England, his sole occupation might have been preparing encyclopedia articles. The Thirteenth notes only that he returned to Russia in 1917, fell ill, and died in 1921.

15. Prof. Hamp urges me to note that one of Jim McCawley's last published papers was on the Korean script (1997), though Young-Key Kim-Renaud notes (pers. comm.) that the published version suffers from several crucial misprints, making the privately circulated preprint the definitive version. And, of course, Jim threw an annual party on Hangul Day, "the only national holiday devoted to a linguistic topic," which marked the promulgation of the world's finest writing system by King Sejong in 1443.

16. Whitney was one of the few American contributors to the Ninth according to Phelps 1930, one of a series of Master's Essays written at the Columbia University School of Library Service on the making of the successive editions of the *Encyclopædia Britannica.* Another, Reed 1931, would likely have been helpful, but the Columbia University Libraries have misplaced both the microfilm and the original.

17. For previous generations' understanding of the interrelation of language and "race," see Alter 1999, 31–32 and passim.

18. This lengthy volume has neither an author index nor a general bibliography, but Saussure and his *coéfficients sonantiques* appear not to be mentioned in the most likely places. Giles in noticing Saussure's death (1916, 30) says that "by the publication of his *Mémoire* ... in 1879, while still an undergraduate, he sprang at once into the front rank of comparative philologists," but his perceptive review (1917, 33–36) of Saussure's posthumous *Cours* does not analyze his earlier contributions to Indo-European studies.

19. The 1902 version included about 20,000 words; measure this against roughly 10,000 (excluding tables) in the not uncomparable Daniels 2001.

20. The unsigned articles on the letters of the alphabet in the Ninth were by John Peile of Christ's College, Cambridge (Giles 1913, 142).

21. For example, **Typography** is devoted primarily to demonstrating that Johannes Gutenberg did not invent printing from movable type.

22. Versus exactly half in the Fifteenth (1974/1985; cf. Daniels 1997, 201–2, 212–19). Eric Hamp (pers. comm.) observes, "Surely $\frac{2}{3}:\frac{1}{2}$ is about right to reflect the proportion of exact, responsible, principled, & innovative scholarship on phylum linguistics from the 11th to 15th."

23. This account hews as closely as possible to the order of presentation found in **Philology III**. Compare Daniels 1993 for language classification schemes of the era.

24. In his obituary of Leskien (1918, 49), he goes further: "The chief importance of [Leskien 1876] in the history of Comparative Philology is that in it were first laid down clearly the principles of the 'Neo-grammarians.' ... Leskien had caught the ideas from Whitney, whose book he had translated."

25. Peter Giles is not mentioned anywhere in the 14 volumes of *Current Trends in Linguistics*.

26. Here he is noncommittal, but in Giles 1921, which had been set in type by 1914, he opts for the Hungarian plain; the suggestion was published in Giles 1915, 77.

27. The theory appears to have been neglected into justifiable oblivion.

28. The details were worked out by G. Bonfante in the late 1940s and published in 1999.

29. Eric Hamp (pers. comm.) notes that an opportunity was missed—the solidest work in Romance linguistics in the twentieth century, he claims, was done on Rumanian.

30. Quiggin's (1875–1920; like Giles, a Fellow of Gonville and Caius College) account of a dialect of Irish (1906) is "renowned"; it set the standard for the field (Eric Hamp, pers. comm.).

31. Chadwick's main interest was universals in literature (Eric Hamp, pers. comm.).

32. Further evidence of editorial inattention is the variety of statements regarding the affinities of Armenian: Hübschmann's demonstration (1875) that it is not part of Indo-Iranian postdated the preparation of the Ninth's **Armenian**; Sievers's **Philology II** has the correct formulation, citing that article; but Geldner's mistaken footnote to Hübschmann 1879 (**Persia** and **Philology** are in the same volume of the Ninth), attached to the statement mentioned in the text, has been trimmed from the Eleventh. Hübschmann 1879 definitively characterizes Indo-Iranian, Indic, and Iranian, with extensive data from all the languages cited by Geldner except Balochi (especially Avestan), but does not mention Armenian. (The page mentioned by Geldner deals only with Ossetic.)

33. The history of this monumental undertaking to document all the languages of British India—whose publication alone, in 11 volumes in 19 massive parts, spanned nearly 30 years—has never been written (Rosane Rocher, pers. comm.). The only even slightly extensive account, addressing dialectological methodology, is in Pop 1950, 1121–29 (Eric Hamp, pers. comm.).

34. "In Lithuanian there is an active literary movement which, however, is perhaps more in evidence in Chicago than it is in its native country" (Giles 1924b, 33).

35. Giles's treatment of Hittite and Tocharian, gauged to the same readership as the *Britannica* articles, appears in Giles 1925, 119–26.

36. I am grateful to John Huehnergard for copies of the two editions of the German original of this article (Nöldeke 1887, 1899); neither is identical to the corresponding English version, and a study of the differences among the four would be quite revealing. Baasten (2003, 68n42), for instance, discusses another correction he made in light of current scholarship.

Language in the Eleventh *Britannica* 525

37. There seems to be no treatment whatsoever of what would now be called Islamic civilization and its arts—a fortiori, of its calligraphic tradition in Arabic, Persian, and Turkish manuscripts.

38. His books include *Man, Past and Present* (1899) and *The World's Peoples: A Popular Account of Their Bodily & Mental Characters, Beliefs, Traditions, Political and Social Institutions* (1908).

39. Eliot 1890 was for many years the standard English-language treatment of Finnish (Bernard Comrie, pers. comm.); Eliot was a career diplomat and lifelong amateur philologist (Sansom 1949).

40. Konow himself was among the scholars instrumental in identifying these two families as constituting a genetic unity, which was established and named "Austroasiatic" by W. Schmidt in 1908 (Parkin 1991, 3; Schmidt 1926, 136).

41. But it deserves only to be relegated to a note.

Evidently derived from the Chinese, of which it appears to be a very ancient dialect [this was not straightened out until Haudricourt 1954], the Annamese language is composed of monosyllables, of slightly varied articulation, expressing different ideas according to the tone in which they are pronounced. It is quite impossible to connect with our musical system the utterance of the sounds of which the Chinese and Annamese languages are composed. What is understood by a "tone" in this language is distinguished in reality, not by the number of sonorous vibrations which belong to it, but rather by a use of the vocal apparatus special to each. Thus, the sense will to a native be completely changed according as the sound is the result of an aspiration or of a simple utterance of the voice. Thence the difficulty of substituting our phonetic alphabet for the ideographic characters of the Chinese, as well as for the ideophonetic writing partly borrowed by the Annamese from the letters of the celestial empire. To the Jesuit missionaries is due the introduction of an ingenious though very complicated system, which has caused remarkable progress to be made in the employment of phonetic characters. By means of six accents, one bar and a crotchet it is possible to note with sufficient precision the indications of tone without which the Annamese words have no sense for the natives.

42. The name "Austronesian" had been suggested by Schmidt in 1899 but was slow in finding acceptance (Schmidt 1926, 147).

43. This work is still useful for its vocabularies, but the classification has been superseded by much work building on Guthrie 1948; there is a survey in Hinnebusch 1989. Tuchscherer (1999, 57–58) calls attention to Johnston's "perverse" "contempt" for the indigenous scripts of Cameroon; such are not mentioned s.vv. **Cameroon**, **Sierra Leone**, or Johnston's **Liberia**.

44. Nonetheless,

The Australian black-fellow or the forest Indian of Brazil, who may be taken as examples of the lowest modern savage, had, before contact with whites, attained to rudimentary stages in many of the characteristic functions of civilized life. His language, expressing thoughts by conventional articulate sounds, is the same in essential principle as the most cultivated philosophic dialect [would that the sentence had stopped there!], only less exact and copious. (E. B. Tylor, **Anthropology**)

A long list of characteristics follows, demonstrating that "the savage differs in degree but not in kind from the civilized man"; finally, "If, again, high savage or low barbaric types be selected, as among the North American Indians, Polynesians, and Kaffirs of South Africa, the same elements of culture appear, but at a more advanced stage, namely, a more full and accurate language."

45. In another Chicago connection, Kantor (1888–1984) was known to me from his regular visits to his daughter, a professor of archeology in the Oriental Institute, until about 1980, and I think I recall seeing him chatting with Jim McCawley once.

46. The 12th Edition (seen only moments before going to press) was an earlier set of supplementary volumes dedicated primarily to the history of the Great War (also important in the 13th, but in new articles); among its encyclopedic articles is no entry for *Philology* or *Language*.

47. Kogan 1958 does not provide overall sales figures for the two editions.

48. In this work, Jim does not make allowances for the rather steep "learning curve" involved in becoming familiar with Chinese characters. It could have done with many more examples (and a much larger Chinese typeface). A similar attitude prevailed when he accompanied amateur musicians at his annual St. Cecilia's Day parties—he did not slow down, or assist by doubling notes, even in so difficult a passage as Mathis der Maler's final aria from Hindemith's opera.

References

Alter, Stephen G. 1999. *Darwinism and the linguistic image: Language, race, and natural theology in the nineteenth century*. Baltimore: The Johns Hopkins University Press.

Baasten, Martin F. J. 2003. A note on the history of "Semitic." In *Hamlet on a hill: Semitic and Greek studies presented to Professor T. Muraoka on the occasion of his sixty-fifth birthday*, ed. by M. F. J. Baasten and W. Th. van Peursen, 57–72. Leuven: Peeters.

Baldi, Philip. 2002. *The foundations of Latin*. Later edition. Berlin: Mouton de Gruyter.

Bloomfield, Leonard. 1914. *Introduction to the study of language*. New York: Henry Holt. Repr., Amsterdam: John Benjamins, 1983.

Bloomfield, Leonard. 1933. *Language*. New York: Holt, Rinehart and Winston.

Bonfante, Giuliano. 1999. *The origin of the Romance languages: Stages in the development of Latin*. Ed. by Larissa Bonfante. Heidelberg: Winter.

Capell, A. 1971. History of research in Australian and Tasmanian languages. In *Current trends in linguistics*. Vol. 8/1, *Linguistics in Oceania*, ed. by Thomas A. Sebeok, 661–720. The Hague: Mouton.

Coleman, Alexander, and Charles Simmons. 1994. *All there is to know: Readings from the illustrious eleventh edition of the* Encyclopaedia Britannica. New York: Simon & Schuster.

Conway, R. S. 1897. *Italic dialects*. Cambridge: Cambridge University Press.

Daniels, Peter T. 1993. Linguistics in American library classification systems. In *20th LACUS Forum* (Chicago), 706–18. Linguistic Association of Canada and the United States.

Daniels, Peter T. 1994. Edward Hincks's decipherment of Mesopotamian cuneiform. In *The Edward Hincks bicentenary lectures*, ed. by Kevin J. Cathcart, 30–57. Dublin: University College, Department of Near Eastern Languages.

Daniels, Peter T. 1997. Surveys of languages of the world. In *The life of language: Papers in linguistics in honor of William Bright*, ed. by Jane H. Hill, P. J. Mistry, and Lyle Campbell, 193–219. Berlin: Mouton de Gruyter.

Daniels, Peter T. 2001. Writing systems. In *The handbook of linguistics*, ed. by Mark Aronoff and Janie Rees-Miller, 43–80. Oxford: Blackwell.

Dawkins, R. M. 1935. Peter Giles, 1860–1935. *Proceedings of the British Academy* 21, 406–32.

Dixon, R. M. W. 1980. *The languages of Australia*. Cambridge: Cambridge University Press.

Einbinder, Harvey. 1964. *The myth of the Britannica*. New York: Grove.

Eliot, C. N. E. 1890. *A Finnish grammar.* Oxford: Clarendon.

Fadiman, Clifton, general ed. 1992. *The treasury of the* Encyclopaedia Britannica. Contributing ed., Bruce L. Felknor and Robert McHenry. New York: Viking Penguin.

Giles, Peter. 1895. *Manual of comparative philology for the use of classical students.* London: Macmillan. 2d ed., 1901.

Giles, Peter. 1913. Comparative philology. In *The year's work in classical studies, 1912*, ed. by Leonard Whibley, 141–52. London: John Murray.

Giles, Peter. 1915. Comparative philology. In *The year's work in classical studies, 1914*, ed. by Cyril Bailey, 67–77. London: John Murray.

Giles, Peter. 1916. Comparative philology. In *The year's work in classical studies, 1915*, ed. by Cyril Bailey, 29–48. London: John Murray.

Giles, Peter. 1917. Comparative philology. In *The year's work in classical studies, 1916*, ed. by Stephen Gaselee, 31–51. London: John Murray.

Giles, Peter. 1918. Comparative philology. In *The year's work in classical studies, 1917*, ed. by Stephen Gaselee, 47–74. London: John Murray.

Giles, Peter. 1921. The Aryans. In *Cambridge history of India.* Vol. 1, *Ancient India*, ed. by E. J. Rapson, 58–68. Cambridge: Cambridge University Press.

Giles, Peter. 1924a. The peoples of Asia Minor. In *The Cambridge ancient history.* Vol. 2, *The Egyptian and Hittite empires to c. 1000 B.C.*, ed. by J. B. Bury, S. A. Cook, and F. E. Adcock, 1–19. Cambridge: Cambridge University Press.

Giles, Peter. 1924b. The peoples of Europe. In *The Cambridge ancient history.* Vol. 2, *The Egyptian and Hittite empires to c. 1000 B.C.*, ed. by J. B. Bury, S. A. Cook, and F. E. Adcock, 20–39. Cambridge: Cambridge University Press.

Giles, Peter. 1925. Comparative philology. In *The year's work in classical studies, 1924–25*, ed. by D. S. Robertson, 111–28. Bristol: Arrowsmith.

Gordon, Cyrus H. 1986. *The Pennsylvania tradition of Semitics: A century of Near Eastern and biblical studies at the University of Pennsylvania.* Society of Biblical Literature Centennial Publications: Biblical Scholarship in North America 13. Atlanta, GA: Scholars Press.

Guthrie, Malcolm. 1948. *The classification of the Bantu languages.* London: Oxford University Press for the Africa Institute.

Haudricourt, André-G. 1954. De l'origine des tons en vietnamien. *Journal Asiatique* 242, 69–82.

Hinnebusch, Thomas J. 1989. Bantu. In *The Niger-Congo languages*, ed. by John Bendor-Samuel, 450–73. Lanham, MD: University Press of America for Summer Institute of Linguistics.

Hjelmslev, Louis. 1970. *Language: An introduction.* Trans. by Francis J. Whitfield. Madison: University of Wisconsin Press. Danish original, 1963.

Hommel, Fritz. 1892. Zunächst lasse ich den Unveränderten Abdruck meiner 1885 geschrieben buchhändlerisch fast unzugängliche Aufsatzes "Die sprachgeschichtliche Stellung des Babylonisch-assyrisches [einer- und des westsemitischen andrerseits]" (*Études archéologiques, linguistiques et historiques dédiées à C. Leemans*, Leide 1885, 127–29) folgen, um dann daran ein Nachwort (nebst einigen Nachträgen) anzuschliessen. *Aufsätze und Abhandlungen* 1, 92–123.

Honey, David B. 2001. *Incense at the altar: Pioneering sinologists and the development of classical Chinese philology*. American Oriental Series 86. New Haven, CT: American Oriental Society.

Hrozný, Friedrich [Bedřich]. 1915. December. Die Lösung des hethitischen Problems: Ein vorläufiger Bericht. *Mitteilungen der Deutschen Orient-Gesellschaft* 56, 17–50.

Hübschmann, H. 1875. Ueber die Stellung des Armenischen im Kreise der indogermanischen Sprachen. *Zeitschrift für vergleichende Sprachforschung* 23, 5–49.

Hübschmann, H. 1879. Iranische Studien. *Zeitschrift für vergleichende Sprachforschung* 24, 323–415.

Huehnergard, John. 1995. Semitic languages. In *Civilizations of the ancient Near East*, ed. by Jack M. Sasson, in association with John Baines, Gary Beckman, and Karen S. Rubinson, 2117–34. New York: Scribners.

Jespersen, Otto. 1922. *Language: Its nature, development and origin*. Repr., New York: Norton, 1964.

Johnston, H. H. 1919–22. *A comparative study of the Bantu and Semi-Bantu languages*. 2 vols. Oxford: Clarendon.

Kess, Joseph S. 1983. Introduction to *Introduction to the study of language*, by Leonard Bloomfield, xvii–xxxviii. Amsterdam: John Benjamins.

Koerner, E. F. K. 1975. European structuralism: Early beginnings. In *Current trends in linguistics*. Vol. 13/2, *Historiography of linguistics*, ed. by Thomas A. Sebeok, 717–827. The Hague: Mouton.

Kogan, Herman. 1958. *The great EB: The story of the* Encyclopædia Britannica. Chicago: University of Chicago Press.

Kuryłowicz, Jerzy. 1927. Schwa indoeuropéen et *h* hittite. *Symbolae grammaticae in honorem Ioannis Rozwadowski* 1, 95–104. Cracow: Gebethner & Wolff.

Lehmann, Winfred P. 1993. *Theoretical bases of Indo-European linguistics*. London: Routledge.

Leskien, August. 1876. *Die declination im Slavo-Litauischen und Germanischen*. Leipzig: Hirtzel.

McCawley, James D. 1967. The phonological theory behind Whitney's *Sanskrit grammar*. In *Languages and areas: Studies presented to George V. Bobrinskoy on the occasion of his academic retirement*, ed. by Howard I. Aronson, 77–85. Chicago: University of Chicago, Division of the Humanities.

McCawley, James D. 1984. *The eater's guide to Chinese characters*. Chicago: University of Chicago Press.

McCawley, James D. 1995. Review of *The human language*, a film by Gene Searchinger. *Language* 71, 622–29.

McCawley, James. D. 1997. Han'gul and other writing systems. In *Literacy & Hangul: Proceedings of an international conference in memory of the 600th anniversary of King Sejong, Seoul, 8–9 September 1997*, 5–16. Seoul: Republic of Korea Ministry of Culture & Sports and the International Association for Korean Language Education.

Morpurgo Davies, Anna. 1998. *Nineteenth-century linguistics*. Vol. 4 of *History of linguistics*, ed. by Giulio Lepschy. London: Longman.

Murray, K. M. Elisabeth. 1977. *Caught in the web of words: James Murray and the* Oxford English Dictionary. New Haven, CT: Yale University Press. Repr., Oxford: Oxford University Press, 1979.

Nöldeke, Theodor. 1887. *Die semitischen Sprachen: Eine Skizze.* Leipzig: Weigel. Zweite verbesserte Auflage, Leipzig: Tauchnitz, 1899.

Parkin, Robert. 1991. *A guide to Austroasiatic speakers and their languages. Oceanic Linguistics* Special Publication 23. Honolulu: University of Hawaii Press.

Pedersen, Holger. 1931. *Linguistic science in the nineteenth century: Methods and results.* Trans. by John Webster Spargo. Cambridge, MA: Harvard University Press. Reprinted as *The discovery of language: Linguistic science in the nineteenth century.* Bloomington: Indiana University Press, 1962. Danish original, 1924.

Phelps, Rose Bernice. 1930. The *Encyclopaedia Britannica*, Ninth Edition: A critical and historical study. Master's thesis, Columbia University, School of Library Service.

Polomé, Edgar. 1965. The laryngeal theory so far: A bibliographical survey. In *Evidence for laryngeals*, ed. by Werner Winter, 9–78. The Hague: Mouton.

Pop, Sever. 1950. *La dialectologie: Aperçu historique et méthodes d'enquêtes linguistiques.* Louvain: Author.

Quiggin, E. C. 1906. *A dialect of Donegal, being the speech of Meenawannia in the Parish of Glenties: Phonology and texts.* Cambridge: Cambridge University Press.

Reed, Doris Mary. 1931. The *Encyclopaedia Britannica*: A critical and historical study of the eleventh edition and its relation to the ninth edition. Master's thesis, Columbia University, School of Library Service.

Sansom, G. H. 1949. Eliot, Sir Charles Norton Edgecumbe (1862–1931). In *The dictionary of national biography 1931–1940*, ed. by L. G. Wickham Legg, 254–55. London: Oxford University Press.

Sapir, Edward. 1921. *Language.* New York: Harcourt, Brace & World.

Saussure, Ferdinand de. 1879. *Mémoire sur le système primitif des voyelles dans les langues indo-européennes.* Leipzig: Vieweg.

Sayce, Archibald H. 1875. *Principles of comparative philology.* London: Kegan Paul. 4th ed., 1893.

Schmidt, W., S.V.D. 1926. *Die Sprachfamilien und Sprachenkreise der Erde.* Heidelberg: Winter.

Tuchscherer, Konrad. 1999. The lost script of the Bagam. *African Affairs* 98, 55–77.

Vendryes, J. 1921. *Le langage.* Paris. Trans. as *Language: A linguistic introduction to history* by Paul Radin. London: K. Paul, Trench, Trubner; New York: Knopf, 1925.

Whitney, William Dwight. 1867. *Language and the study of language.* New York: Scribner's.

Whitney, William Dwight. 1875. *The life and growth of language: An outline of linguistic science.* New York: Appleton.

Whitney, William Dwight. 1879. *Sanskrit grammar.* Cambridge, MA: Harvard University Press.

Abbreviations

ABS	absolutive
ACC	accusative
ADNZ	adnominalizer
ADV	adverbial
ADVZ	adverbializer
AJP	adjectival participle
AM	aspect marker
a-rel	aspectual relation
ARG	argument
ARG-ST	argument structure
ASP	aspectual (relation)
AUX-CON	auxiliary connector
AVP	adverbial participle
BENEF	benefactive
BKG	background
CAUS	causative
CHGOFST	change of state
C-INDS	contextual indices
CL	noun class prefix
CLS	classifier
COMP	complementizer
COMPL	completive
COMPS	complements
CON	connective

COND	conditional
CONJ	conjunctor
CONT	continuous
COP	copula
d-act	discourse act
DAT	dative
DAT/ACC	dative/accusative postposition
DEC	declarative
DF	discourse function
DIR	direct case
DL	discourse level
DUR	durative
ECHOREDUP	echo-word reduplication
EMP	emphatic
E-NEG	evaluatively/emotively negative
EPIC	epicene
E-POS	evaluatively/emotively positive
ERG	ergative
EXDEIX	exdeixis
F	feminine
FOC	focus
FUT	future
FUTUTIL	future utility
GEN	genitive
HAB	habitual aspect
HD-DTR	head daughter
HON	honorific
HR	hearer
IA	illocutionary act
i-act	illocutionary act
IMP	imperative
IMPAT	impatience
IMPF	imperfective

Abbreviations

IMPL	implicature
INCHOAT	inchoative
IND	indicative
INF	infinitive
INSTR	instrumental
INT	interrogative
INTJ	interjection
ITERAT	iterative
LOC	locative
M	masculine
MD	mode
MDL	modal relation
MOD	modifier
MORPH	morphology
m-rel	modal relation
NECESS	necessity
NEG	negative
NHD-DTRS	nonhead daughter
NOM	nominative
NOMZ	nominalizer
NTR	neuter
OBL	oblique
OM	object marker
PART	participle
PASS	passive
PAST	past tense
PERF	perfective
PHON	phonology
PL	plural
PNG	person-number-gender agreement
POL	politeness marker
POLIMP	polite imperative
PPM	prosody-phonology-morphology

PRA	pragmatics
PRES	present tense
PROG	progressive aspect
PROP	proper noun
PROS	prosody
PRP	propositive
PRSP	presupposition
PSMT	presumptive
PT	particle
Q	interrogative marker
QT	quotative
RC	relative clause
REFL	reflexive
REL	relative participle
RES	resultative
RESTR	restriction
RETRO	retrospective
SA	speech act
SE	sentence ending
SEM	semantics
SFP	sentence-final particle
SG	singular
SI	simple
SIT	situation
SM	subject marker
SOA	state of affairs
SP	speaker
SPR	specifier
SSP	syntax-semantics-pragmatics
STR	stress
SUBJUNCT	subjunctive
SYN	syntax
TAM	tense-aspect-mood

Abbreviations

TC	terminal contour
TEMP	temporal marker (Jacobsen); temporal relation (Chang)
TM	topic marker
TNS	tense
TOP	topic marker
t-rel	temporal relation
UT	utterance time
VAL	valence
VAM	verbal aspect marking
vform	verb form
VOL	volitional
VR	verbal reflexive
XPRESLT	expected result

Contributors

E. Annamalai received his PhD from the University of Chicago in 1969. He wrote his dissertation on Tamil syntax, under Jim's supervision. After returning to India, he joined the Central Institute of Indian Languages, where he became interested in the country's multilingualism, focusing on how it functions and can be maintained through language use in education. This interest is reflected in his book *Managing Multilingualism in India: Political and Linguistic Manifestations* (Sage, 2001). He continues to do research on grammar, his most recent publication in this area being "The Constituent Structure of Tamil" (in *The Yearbook of South Asian Languages and Linguistics*, ed. by Rajendra Singh, Mouton de Gruyter, 2004).

Tista Bagchi is Professor of Linguistics at the University of Delhi, India. She received her PhD in linguistics from the University of Chicago in 1993, where she had Jim as her major professor. She was the Robert F. & Margaret S. Goheen Fellow for the academic year 2001–2002 at the National Humanities Center at Research Triangle Park, North Carolina. Her publications include *Languages of India*, an annotated English translation of a Bangla text by the late linguist Gopal Haldar (National Book Trust, 2000), and a textbook-cum-manual entitled *English Syntax* for the Master's in English Language program of the Indira Gandhi National Open University in India (IGNOU Press, 2000). Her research interests also lie in the philosophy of language and of mind, and in the relationship between language and ethics.

Katharine Beals took or audited most of the classes Jim taught at the University of Chicago between 1991 and 1993, and he was one of her dissertation advisors. After receiving her PhD in 1995, she worked for five years in the Natural Language Group at Unisys Corporation. In 2001, she founded Autism Language Therapies, where she designs and programs linguistic software to teach syntactic phenomena of English to children with hyperlexia and language delays. She also reviews books on language and cognition for LinguistList and writes essays about autism for publications in developmental pediatrics.

Robert I. Binnick is Professor of Linguistics at the University of Toronto. He earned his PhD at the University of Chicago in 1969, having had Jim as his major professor. Under the pseudonym of Sir Lancelot of Benwick, he coauthored with Morgan Le Fay (aka Jerry L. Morgan) and The Green Knight (aka Georgia M. Green) a chapter titled "Camelot, 1968" in *Notes from the Linguistic Underground* (Syntax and Semantics 7, ed. by James D. McCawley, Academic Press, 1976), a collection of essays in defense of Generative Semantics. He was a coeditor of *Studies Out in Left Field: Defamatory Essays Presented to James D. McCawley on the Occasion of His 33rd or 34th Birthday* (1971; reprinted by John Benjamins, 1992). His other publications include *Modern Mongolian: A Transformational Syntax* (University of Toronto Press, 1979) and *Time and the Verb: A Guide to Tense and Aspect* (Oxford University Press, 1991).

Suk-Jin Chang is Professor Emeritus at Seoul National University and member of the National Academy of Sciences, in the Republic of Korea. While he pusued his PhD in linguistics at the University of Illinois at Urbana-Champaign, which he received in 1972, he took some classes with Jim at the University of Chicago. Jim was also on his dissertation committee. His research areas include pragmatics, syntax, and computational linguistics. Among his publications are "Information Unpackaging: A Constraint-based Grammar Approach to Topic Focus Articulation" (in *Japanese/Korean Linguistics 10*, CSLI Publications, 2002), *Korean* (John Benjamins, 1996), and *A Unified Grammar: Discourse and Pragmatics* [in Korean] (Seoul National University Press, 1994).

Peter T. Daniels studied with Jim at the University of Chicago in the 1970s. He is coeditor of and principal contributor to *The World's Writing Systems* (with William Bright, Oxford University Press, 1996) and section editor for "Writing Systems," *Encyclopedia of Language and Linguistics* (new edition, Elsevier, 2005). In addition to much work on writing systems, he has published several articles on language classifications and classification overviews.

Donka F. Farkas earned her PhD in linguistics at the University of Chicago in 1981. Her dissertation, "Intensionality and Romance: Subjunctive Relatives," written under Jim's supervision, was published by Garland in 1985 under the title *Intensional Descriptions and the Romance Subjunctive Mood*. Her other publications include "Restrictive If/When Clauses" (with Yoko Sugioka, *Linguistics and Philosophy*, 1983), "On Obligatory Control" (*Linguistics and Philosophy*, 1988), "On the Semantics of Subjunctive Complements" (in *Romance Languages and Modern Linguistic Theory*, ed. by Paul Hirschbühler, John Benjamins, 1992), "Evaluation Indices and Scope" (in *Ways of Scope Taking*, ed. by Anna Szabolcsi, Kluwer, 1997), "Varieties of Indefinites" (in *SALT 12*, 2002), "Specificity Distinctions" (*Journal of Semantics*, 2002), and *The Semantics of Incorporation* (with Henriëtte de Swart, CSLI Publications, 2003). She is Professor of Linguistics at the University of California at Santa Cruz.

Elaine J. Francis earned her PhD in linguistics in 1999 at the University of Chicago, where she took numerous courses from Jim; he was also a member of her dissertation committee. She is an assistant professor in the Department of English and in the Linguistics Program at Purdue University. Her research focuses on how syntactic, semantic, and processing factors interact to determine grammatical structure, and particularly on syntactic categorization and syntax-semantics mismatch. She is a coeditor of a special issue of *Language & Communication* (with Gail Brendel Viechnicki, 1997) and of *Mismatch: Form-Function Incongruity and the Architecture of Grammar* (with Laura A. Michaelis, CSLI Publications, 2003). Her articles include "Some Semantic Reasons Why Iconicity between Lexical Categories and Their Discourse Functions Isn't Perfect" (*Language Sciences*, 1998).

Laurence R. Horn took several courses from Jim when the latter was a visiting associate professor at the University of Michigan from January to April 1970. He earned his PhD from the University of California at Los Angeles in 1972. He has taught at the University of California at Berkeley, the University of Southern California, the University of Wisconsin, and Aix-Marseille, as well as at LSA institutes at Stanford University (1987), the University of California at Santa Cruz (1991), the University of Illinois at Urbana-Champaign (1999), and Michigan State University (2003). Since 1981, he has been at Yale University, where he is Professor of Linguistics. Among his publications are *A Natural History of Negation* (University of Chicago Press, 1989; CSLI Publications, 2001), *Negation and Polarity* (coedited with Yasuhiko Kato; Oxford University Press, 2000), and *The Handbook of Pragmatics* (coedited with Gregory Ward; Blackwell, 2004), and numerous articles on neo-Gricean pragmatics, traditional logic, lexical semantics, and negative polarity. Since 1995, he has been editor of the Outstanding Dissertations in Linguistics series for Garland and Routledge.

Geoffrey J. Huck earned his PhD in linguistics from the University of Chicago in 1984. He was a student of Jim's, under whose supervision he wrote a dissertation titled "Discontinuity and Word Order in Categorial Grammar." He was the commissioning editor for linguistics at the University of Chicago Press from 1983 to 2001. He is coauthor of *Ideology and Linguistic Theory: Noam Chomsky and the Deep Structure Debates* (with John A. Goldsmith, Routledge, 1995) and coeditor of *Discontinuous Constituency* (Syntax and Semantics 20, with Almerindo E. Ojeda, Academic Press, 1987).

Wesley M. Jacobsen is Professor of the Practice of the Japanese Language and Director of the Japanese Language Program in the Department of East Asian Languages and Civilizations at Harvard University. He had Jim as his major professor and earned his PhD in linguistics at the University of Chicago in 1981. His publications include *The Transitive Structure of Events in Japanese* (Kurosio, 1992), "Time, Reality, and Agentivity in Japanese Negation" (in *Japanese/Korean Linguistics 6*, CSLI Publications, 1996), "Agentivity and Aspect in Japanese: A Functional Perspective" (in *Directions in Functional Linguistics*, ed. by Akio Kamio, John Benjamins, 1997), and "On the Interaction of Temporal and Modal Meaning in Japanese Conditionals" (in *Japanese/Korean Linguistics 10*, CSLI Publications, 2002). He is a coeditor of *On Japanese and How to Teach It* (Japan Times, 1990).

Barbara J. Luka earned her PhD in linguistics and psychology from the University of Chicago in 1999. Jim was to have been one of her dissertation readers. Her research areas include electrophysiology of language processing using event-related potentials, as well as conceptual and grammatical influences in language comprehension and memory. She is a visiting assistant professor in the Department of Psychology at Bard College and a research associate at the Institute for Mind and Biology at the University of Chicago and in the Department of Psychology at the University of Arizona. Her publications include "When Metacognition and Linguistic Data Crash and Burn" (in *MIT Working Papers in Linguistics 37*, 2001) and "Frontal Brain Activity Predicts Individual Performance in an Associative Memory Exclusion Test" (with Cyma Van Petten, Susan R. Rubin, and John P. Ryan, *Cerebral Cortex*, 2002).

Jerry L. Morgan and **Georgia M. Green** are professors of linguistics at the University of Illinois. They both studied with Jim and received their PhDs from the University of Chicago in, respectively, 1973 and 1971. In addition to the chapter coauthored with Robert I. Binnick, they contributed an essay titled "More Evidence for a Cycle of Transformations" to Jim's *Notes from the Linguistic Underground* (Syntax and Semantics 7, Academic Press, 1976). They also coauthored the *Practical Guide for Syntactic Analysis* (CSLI Publications, 1996) and articles on syntax, pragmatics, and language comprehension. Morgan is also the author of several articles on verb agreement, and many more on natural language processing and the interrelations of syntax, semantics, and pragmatics. Green is the author of *Pragmatics and Natural Language Understanding* (Lawrence Erlbaum, 1989) and numerous articles on syntax and pragmatics, including "Ambiguity Resolution and Discourse Interpretation" (in *Semantic Ambiguity and Underrepresentation*, ed. by Kees Van Deemter and Stanley Peters, CSLI Publications, 1996).

Salikoko S. Mufwene is the Frank J. McLoraine Distinguished Service Professor of Linguistics and the College at the University of Chicago. He studied semantics and syntax under Jim at Chicago, where he received his PhD in 1979. He then began to study structures and development of creole vernaculars, and now language evolution, on all of which he has published extensively. He is the author of *The Ecology* *of Language Evolution* (Cambridge University Press, 2001), editor of *Africanisms in Afro-American Language Varieties* (University of Georgia Press, 1993), and coeditor of *African-American English* (with John R. Rickford et al., Routledge, 1998). He is also the series editor of Cambridge Approaches to Language Contact. He chaired the Department of Linguistics at the University of Chicago from 1995 to 2001.

Lynn Nichols is an assistant professor in the Department of Linguistics at the University of California, Berkeley. She studied with Jim while pursuing a 1992 MA degree at the University of Chicago and received her PhD in linguistics from Harvard University in 1998. Her research includes syntax and semantics as well as fieldwork on languages of the Pueblo Southwest and East and Southeast Asia. Her publications include "The Syntactic Basis of Referential Hierarchy Phenomena: Clues from Languages with and without Morphological Case" (*Lingua*, 2001), "Attitude Evaluation in Complex NPs" (in *Formal Approaches to Functional Forces in Grammar*, ed. by Andrew Carnie and Heidi Harley, John Benjamins, 2003), and "Reference to Contexts in Zuni Temporal and Modal Domains" (in *Semantics of Underrepresented Languages in the Americas 2*, University of Massachusetts at Amherst, Graduate Linguistics Student Association, 2003).

William O'Grady is Professor of Linguistics at the University of Hawaii at Honolulu. He received his PhD from the University of Chicago in 1978, where he wrote his dissertation under Jim's supervision. He has published extensively on syntactic theory, language acquisition, and Korean. His recent publications include *The Sounds of Korean* (with Miho Choo, University of Hawaii Press, 2003), *How Children Learn Language* (Cambridge University Press, 2005), and *Syntactic Carpentry: An Emergentist Approach to Syntax* (Lawrence Erlbaum, 2005).

Almerindo E. Ojeda studied under Jim at the University of Chicago, defending his PhD dissertation in 1982. He is now Professor of Linguistics at the University of California at Davis. He has worked on topics in Spanish linguistics and on theoretical issues in syntax and semantics, on which he has published extensively. He is a coeditor of *Discontinuous Constituency* (with Geoffrey J. Huck, Syntax and Semantics 20, Academic Press, 1987) and the author of *Linguistic Individuals* (CSLI Publications, 1993). He is currently working on the semantics of quantity as well as the structural theory of meaning.

Harold F. Schiffman was a student of Jim's and received his PhD from the University of Chicago in 1969. He is Professor of Dravidian Linguistics and Culture at the University of Pennsylvania. His research focuses on structures of Dravidian languages (especially Tamil, and to a lesser extent Kannada) and on multilingualism, diglossia, language policy, the politics of language, language standardization, and grammaticalization. He is also Pedagogical Materials Director of the National South Asia Language Resource Center at the University of Pennsylvania. His recent publications include *Linguistic Culture and Language Policy* (Routledge, 1996) and *A Reference Grammar of Spoken Tamil* (Cambridge University Press, 1999).

Michael C. Shapiro is a professor in the Department of Asian Languages and Literature at the University of Washington. He has published *Language and Society in South Asia* (with Harold F. Schiffman, Motilal Banarsidass, 1981), *A Primer of Modern Standard Hindi* (Motilal Banarsidass, 1989), and many studies of Hindi and other Indo-Aryan languages. He received his PhD from the University of Chicago in 1974, with Jim as a member of his dissertation committee.

Yoko Sugioka is Professor of English and Linguistics at Keio University, Tokyo, Japan. She was a student of Jim's at the University of Chicago, where she earned her PhD in 1984. Her research areas are morphology and the syntax-lexicon interface. Aside from the article co-authored with Donka F. Farkas in 1983, her publications include *Interaction of Derivational Morphology and Syntax in Japanese and English* (Garland, 1986), "Neurolinguistic Evidence for Rule-based Nominal Suffixation" (with Hiroko Hagiwara et al., *Language*, 1999), and "Incorporation vs. Modification in Japanese Deverbal Compounds" (in *Japanese/Korean Linguistics 10*, CSLI Publications, 2002).

Timothy J. Vance is a professor and currently chairs the Department of East Asian Studies at the University of Arizona. He taught previously at the University of Florida, the University of Hawaii, and Connecticut College. He is the author of *An Introduction to Japanese Phonology* (SUNY Press, 1987) and the coordinating editor of *Japanese Language and Literature* (the journal of the Association of Teachers of Japanese). He received his PhD in 1979 with Jim as his major professor.

Rebecca S. Wheeler earned her PhD in linguistics in 1989 from the University of Chicago, where she took courses with Jim in syntax and semantics. She is Associate Professor of English Education at Christopher Newport University, in Newport News, VA. Her research focuses on language development in urban areas and how insights from applied linguistics can help reduce the achievement gap in dialectally diverse classrooms. Her publications include "Codeswitching: Tools of Language and Culture Transform the Dialectally Diverse Classroom" (*Language Arts*, 2004). She is also coauthor of *Grammar Alive! A Guide for Teachers* (NCTE, 2003) and editor of *The Workings of Language: From Prescriptions to Perspectives* (Praeger, 1999) and of *Language Alive in the Classroom* (Praeger, 1999).

Etsuyo Yuasa earned her PhD in linguistics at Chicago in 1998, having taken a wide range of courses with Jim in Japanese and English syntax, in logic, and in semantics. Jim was also a member of her dissertation committee. Etsuyo is Assistant Professor of Japanese in the Department of East Asian Languages and Literatures at the Ohio

State University. Her current research interests are the syntax-semantics interface, multimodular approaches to grammar, and complex clauses in Japanese and English. Her recent publications include "Pseudo-subordination: A Mismatch between Syntax and Semantics" (with Jerrold M. Sadock, *Journal of Linguistics*, 2002), "Categorial Mismatch in a Multi-modular Theory of Grammar" (with Elaine J. Francis, in *Mismatch: Form-function Incongruity and the Architecture of Grammar*, ed. by Elaine J. Francis and Laura A. Michaelis, CSLI Publications, 2003), and *Modularity in Language: Constructional and Categorial Mismatch in Syntax and Semantics* (Mouton de Gruyter, in press).

Index

Accessibility Hierarchy, 194, 198n15
Adjacency effects, 459
Adjective
　adjectival noun, 7, 147, 162, 170–173, 207, 211–212, 221n2
　deverbal adjective, 184
Adverb
　speaker-oriented, 139
Affixation, 203–221, 332, 334
　deadjectival affixation/nominals, 13, 210, 218, 221
　-mi affixation, 207–215, 221n5
　nominal affixation, 207–215
　-sa affixation, 207–220
Agrammatism, 17, 434, 442–443, 445–449
Agreement
　object-verb, 70–71
　subject-verb, 70, 448
Akmajian, Adrian, 227, 230, 237
American Indian, 508, 517, 519, 521, 525n44
Analogy, 9–10, 204, 206, 211–214, 215–221, 511
And, subordinate interpretation, 173–177, 179n12
Annamalai, E., 3–5, 47–67, 83, 94, 103, 105
Antecedent-contained deletion, 135, 139–140, 154n7, 154n8
Argument
　obligatory, 197–198n8
　optional, 191, 197–198n8
Aristotle, 242n4, 329–331, 337, 339, 359–360, 361n10
Armenian, 510, 514, 524n32
Artificial grammar, 482–483, 485–486
Aryan languages, 74, 81, 507, 513–514, 517, 523n11. *See also* Indo-Iranian languages
Aspect
　aspectual constraint, 131n13, 301–302
　aspectual verb, 5, 83–107, 322n13
　completive aspect, 58–60, 96 (*see also* Completion)
Associative memory, 9, 205–207, 211, 214–215, 219, 221n6

Atomless, 398–400, 402, 405, 407–408
Attitude, 5–12, 84, 89, 284–286, 290, 292–293, 320, 483
　attitude evaluation, 12, 284, 286, 290, 292–293
Attribute-value matrix (AVM), 323n30
Austin, J. L., 321n7, 323n34
Australian languages, 238, 508,520, 525n44
Autolexical syntax, 6, 8, 131n6, 147–148, 151, 168, 195, 226
Auxiliary/auxiliaries
　auxiliary selection, 117–118
　auxiliary verb, 10–11, 50, 117–118, 136, 144–147, 156n16, 156n18, 225–244, 255, 279n13, 458

Background assumptions, 16, 285, 411–412, 414–421, 423, 425–427
Bach, Emmon, 185, 196n3, 227
Bach, Kent, 321n7, 323n34
Bangla, 5, 6, 109–133. *See also* Bengali
Bantu, 393, 396, 405, 408n2, 508, 518
Barbosa, Pilar, 320
Bar-Hillel, Yehoshua, 308
Be
　consuetudinal/invariant, 233, 241n2
　copular, 10, 225–244
　equative, 239, 241–242
　existential, 10, 225, 227, 230–238, 241–242
　identificational, 239, 241n1, 241n3
　modal, 226, 231, 233, 235, 236, 243n9, 243n10
　passive, 231, 233, 244n10
　progressive, 10, 231
Beals, Katharine, 16, 411–428
Belletti, Adriana, 116, 117
Benefaction, 67n8, 83, 86, 96
Bengali, 101, 109, 514. *See also* Bangla
Blocking, 59, 116, 218–219, 336–337, 361n4
Burmese, 12, 283–294, 516

Carlson, Greg, 376
Carroll, Lewis, 355

Categorization, 7, 162–164, 178, 178n2, 375, 480, 482, 484–487, 489
  evaluative categorization, 480, 484–487
  prototype category, 5
Caucasian languages, 508, 518
Causative alternation, 119
Celtic languages, 408n4, 506, 511, 513
Chang, Suk-Jin, 12–13, 295–324, 535
Change of state, 89, 93, 100, 105n3
Chatterji, Suniti Kumar, 130n2
Chinese (language), 10, 35, 221n2, 228, 238, 241, 278, 483, 506, 508, 516, 525n41, 526n48
Choe, Jae-Woong, 323n26
Chomsky, Noam, xi, xv, 18–19, 66n2, 122, 131n12, 165, 198n13, 434, 455, 476n15, 479–480, 482, 494, 497n2
Classical categories, 164
Clausemate condition, 50–51
Clones, 6, 352, 362n13
  lexical clones, 14
Coexistent systems, 240
Coindex(ing), 4, 47–67, 127, 138, 157n22, 190–191, 193, 195, 197, 198n8, 303, 313, 314, 489
Combinatorial operation, 17, 435, 437
Common ground, 284–287, 290, 342, 351, 358, 362n12, 417
Competence, 268–271, 273, 275, 278, 279n11
Completion, 83–84, 89, 93, 97, 289, 301
Compound
  adjunct compound, 218–220
  argument compound, 218–220, 222n8
  deverbal compound, 215, 217–220, 222n8
  novel compound, 216
  noun-noun compound, 196n5, 196n6
Computation, 205, 434–450
  computational space, 17, 445–450 (*see also* Working memory)
Comrie, Bernard, 194–195, 198, 199n15
Conceptual fluency (misattribution of), 486
Conditional clause, 54, 56
Conditional construction, 109–133
Conflict resolution principle, 18, 458
Conjunction, 18, 110, 127, 162, 168, 173–174, 177, 279n6, 395, 397, 415, 418–419, 456–457, 465–467
Conjunctive participle, 5–6, 109–133
Connectionist, 204–205
Containment, 85–87, 90, 98–100
Continuity, 83–85, 92, 100, 105n10
Contradictories, 330–337, 360, 411–427
Contraries, 330–332, 334–336, 360
Contrastive focus, 9, 188–189, 195, 196n6, 352
Control, 65, 119, 125, 196n3, 198n13, 435, 450, 457, 463, 471
Coordination, 136, 149–152, 154n7, 157n22, 179n12, 423, 467, 476n10
Copestake, Ann, 308, 320

Coplural, 15, 390–391, 401–402, 404–405, 408. *See also* Cosingular
Copula, 10, 71–72, 212, 221n2, 225–244, 278n2, 296, 301, 308–309. *See also* Be
  absence, 232, 239–241
  deletion, 239
  insertion, 239–240
Corbett, Greville, 455
Cosingular, 15–16, 390–391, 401–402, 404–405, 408. *See also* Coplural
Count nouns, 15, 167, 392, 403, 406, 408, 409n5
Counterfactual, 12, 126, 129, 132n17, 283–294
Creoles, 10, 228, 238–241
Croft, William, 8, 162, 166–167, 169–170, 177, 178n4, 178n5
CUG, 295–296, 303, 307–309, 311, 320, 320n3, 323n26, 324n38
Culicover, Peter, 149, 157n22, 162, 168, 173–174, 191

Dasgupta, Probal, 111, 116, 120
Davies, William D., 117–118
Davison, Alice, 110
Deacon, Terrence, 17, 446
Default rule, 206, 208, 215, 337
Deixis, 11, 85–86, 90, 99–100, 250–255
  addeixis, 100
  exdeixis, 93–94, 100
Derived nominal, 208–210, 215
Determination, 457–458, 461–463, 465, 470, 476n12
Dik, Simon, 10, 226, 227, 229, 231, 243n5
Discontinuous constituent structure, 135
Discourse context, 4, 47, 49–51, 54–55, 62–63, 131n11, 176, 210, 214, 412, 416–7, 420, 423, 425, 427
Discourse Representation Theory (DRT), 14, 457, 368–371, 374, 377–379
Discrepancy-attribution hypothesis, 485
Disjunction, 58, 456–457, 467–468, 470, 476n14
Dixon, R. W., 235, 238, 240, 241n1, 241n3, 242n4, 520
Dowty, David, 184, 191, 241n3, 250, 268, 322n18
Dual-mechanism, 205–207, 211, 215, 221n7

Efficiency, 17, 152–153 435–443, 448, 450n1
  driven processor, 17, 441, 448–449
  requirement, 17, 435–443, 450n1
Emotive, 13, 295–324, 334–335
  internal adjective, 313
  nonstative, 306–307
Epitomization, 349, 351–352, 361n12, 476n14
Equi-, 303–304, 314, 322n21
  speaker/subject constraint, 303
Ergativity, 6, 80, 109, 115–116, 122–124, 129, 131n7, 131nn12–13
  unergative verb, 117–122, 131n12
Eskimo, 519, 521

Index

E-type pronoun, 6, 135, 139, 141, 143
Event-related potentials (ERPs), 489–490

Facilitation, 479–497
Fairbanks, Gordon H., 130n4
Farkas, Donka, 14–15, 368–385
Fellbaum, C., 321n8
For-constructions, 186
Francis, Elaine J., 5, 7–8, 14, 157n20, 158n24, 161–179, 195, 196n6, 227, 235, 237, 474
Fraser, Bruce, 321n7
French (language), 85–86, 101, 116–118, 205, 231, 244n11, 253–254, 273, 295, 332, 389, 397, 444, 463, 472, 507, 512, 517, 518, 519
Future utility, 87, 89–90

Gapless relative clauses, 193–194
Gazdar, Gerald, 414
Generative semantics, xii–xiii, 7, 9, 226, 228, 243n7, 249
Georgian, 510, 517, 518
German, 116, 221n7, 273, 295, 332, 348, 352, 513, 515, 516, 524n36
Germanic languages, 205, 273, 507, 513, 523n11
Gerundive modifier, 8–9, 183–199
  postnominal, 186–187, 192, 196n3, 196n7
  pronominal, 196
Giles, Peter, 508–511, 513–514, 516, 523n18, 523n20, 524nn25–26, 524n30, 524n34, 534n35
Giorgi, Alessandra, 284, 285
Grammaticalization, 5, 83–106, 493
  grammaticalized, 5, 84–89, 103–104, 105n8, 106n22, 168, 227, 474
Greek, 235, 331, 506–507, 510, 511–512, 520
Green, Georgia, 18, 455–476
Green, Lisa, 233, 241n2
Greenlandic, 149
Grice, Paul, 16, 132n16, 411–422
Grierson, George A., 514
Guru, Kamta Prasad, 75–76, 78, 80–81, 131n4

Hagiwara, Hiroko, 203–222
Hale, Kenneth, 122
Hall-Partee, Barbara. *See* Partee, Barbara
Harnish, Robert M., 321n7, 323n34
Hendrick, Randall, 122
Hindi, 4–6, 69–82, 89, 109–133, 456
Hittite, 507, 514, 524n35
Hopper, Paul, 5, 8, 83, 87, 102, 106nn19–20, 162, 166, 167, 170
Horn, Laurence R., xiii, 1, 6, 13–14, 131n10, 329–362
HPSG (Head-Driven Phrase Structure Grammar), 168, 295, 311, 323n26, 434
Huck, Geoffrey, 8–9, 183–199
Humpty Dumpty, 329, 353–358
Hungarian, 373, 377–384, 524n26

Ideal of a model, 400
Idiom chunk, 211
Illocutionary act, 303, 312, 323n34
Implicature
  implicature of causation, 125, 132n16
  conventional, 124–125, 132n16
  conversational, 9, 203, 412–413, 417–426
  generalized conversational implicature, 419–421, 424–426
  manner implicature, 426
  particularized conversational implicature, 421–425
  scalar implicature, 418, 420
Implicit learning, memory, processes, 479–497
Inchoative, 89, 96, 99, 322n18
Independent clause, 6–7, 131n6, 135–158
Individuation, 15–16, 403–407, 409nn9–10
Indo-European, 10, 507–508, 510–514, 523n11, 523n18
Indo-Iranian, 513, 524n32. *See also* Aryan languages
Infinitive clause, 47–67
Inflection
  inflectional paradigm, 204, 221
  irregular, 204–208, 211, 218
  regular, 204–208, 215–216, 218
Intent, 89, 94, 101–102
Interlingual verb, 303
Inuit, 131n13
Irony, 16, 102, 349, 361n12, 411–428
  ironic implicature, 413–414, 423–424
  ironic omission, 426, 428
Italian, 116–118, 284, 293n1, 507, 512, 517
Italic languages, 510–511

Jackendoff, Ray, 22, 148, 149, 157n22, 162, 168, 173–174, 179n11, 184, 191, 195
Jagannathan, V. R., 76–77, 80–81
Jamaican Creole, 238, 239
Japanese, xi, xv, 2, 3, 6, 9, 11–12, 27–41, 135–158, 168, 203–222, 261–281, 295, 305, 320, 321n12, 322n23, 323n25, 444, 456, 516
  Old Japanese, 2, 3, 27–33, 35, 37–39, 40
Jespersen, Otto, xiii, 185, 332, 334–335, 360, 391–392, 505
Johnson, Marc, 89, 93, 100
Johnston, H. H., 518, 525n43
Jones, Daniel, 510, 521, 522n2
Judgment
  acceptability, 3, 4, 9, 19–20, 476n16, 479–480, 497n2
  grammaticality, 479, 480, 488, 492
  linguistic, 19, 479–497

Kachru, Yamuna, 131n4
Kageyama, Taro, 207, 219
Kamp, Hans, 183, 368–370

Kayne, Richard, 192, 466
Keenan, Edward, 147, 194–195, 198n15
Keyser, Samuel Jay, 122
Kikongo-Kituba, 241n1
Kim, Jaeyeon, 323n27
Kim, Jong-bok, 444, 446
Kindaichi, Haruhiko, 269, 280n17, 281n24
Klaiman, Miriam H., 110
Koenig, J., 308, 310, 320, 370
Konow, Sten, 516–517, 525n40
Korean, 8–9, 12–13, 41n20, 183–199, 295–324, 444–445, 508, 516, 523n15
Kortmann, Bernd, 466
Kratzer, A., 12, 283, 285–286, 291
Kuroda, S.-Y., 33–39, 41n24, 41n27

Labov, William, 18, 163, 232, 239–240, 244n13, 488
Lakoff, George, xii, 8–9, 89, 93, 100, 152, 162, 166, 167, 321n9
Language acquisition, 17–19, 152, 433–450, 456, 458, 469, 493, 496
  first, 17, 434, 442–444, 446, 447, 449
  second, 443–445, 446, 449, 450n6, 493
Language and race, 508–509, 513, 515, 517–519, 521, 523n17. *See also* Race and language
Language faculty, 17–19, 433–435, 441–442, 449–450, 458, 470
Lapointe, Stephen, 195n1
Lascarides, Alex, 308
Latin, 507, 511–512
Levin, Beth, 109, 116, 118–120, 131n8, 154, 329, 360, 361n8
Levinson, Stephen C., 66n2, 324n38, 360, 414–416, 418–425
Lexical decomposition, 303, 322n18
Lexical pragmatics, 14, 330, 358–360
Lexical verb, 5, 83–96, 100–102, 105n3, 131n14, 228
Lingala, 15–16, 391, 393–396, 400, 408n2, 408n3, 408n5
Linguistic Flea Circus, xiii, 19
Linguistic intuition, 19, 479–497
Link, Godehard, 376, 389, 398, 409n7
Lycan, William G., 129
Lyman's Law, 2–3, 27–41

Mahajan, Anoop K., 131n7, 131n12
Manning, Christopher D., 131n13
MAPIL (Metacognitive Attribution and Preferences in Implicit Learning), 479–497
Marked
  markedness, 167, 334, 358, 360, 391
  umarked, 16, 69, 88, 187, 196n2, 267, 333, 361n10, 380–382, 384, 391, 405
Martin, Samuel E., 27, 39n1, 40n9, 40n14, 41n24, 41n29, 320n1, 320nn3–4, 321n12, 322n14, 323n25, 323n34

Mass nouns, 15, 16, 380, 389–409
Maxim
  of manner, 426
  of quality, 411
  of quantity, 413, 418, 425–426
  of relation, 413, 421–425, 427
McCawley, James D., xi–xxx, 1–23, 28, 41n24, 65, 66n2, 69, 81, 109, 111, 127–130, 132n16, 133n19, 135–138, 140, 151, 153, 153nn1–2, 154n4, 158nn24–25, 161–162, 165–175, 177, 178n5, 178n10, 204, 221n5, 225–232, 235–238, 242–234, 249–258, 261, 280n19, 296, 300, 303, 321n7, 322nn18–19, 323n34, 329–330, 346, 359, 360n1, 360n4, 368–369, 374, 377, 380, 382, 389, 392–393, 406–407, 411–412, 428, 433, 435, 447, 458, 469–470, 479, 494, 496, 505, 508, 521–522, 523n15, 525n45
McGregor, R. S., 131nn4–5
Mental mechanisms, 204, 221n6
Metacognitive process, 480–484
Metaphor, 5, 84–91, 98–102, 106n20, 336–337
  metaphoric extension, 5, 84–85, 101–102, 336–337, 445–447
Metonymy, 85–86
Mimicry, syntactic, 7, 161–179, 221n5
Minimal element, 400–405, 409nn8–9
Minimal recursion semantics, 320
Mismatch, 6, 8, 10, 136, 147–153, 157n20, 157n22, 157n24, 168–178, 221n5, 226
  coordination-subordination, 149, 152, 157n22
  independence-subordination, 136, 150, 152, 157n22
  syntax-semantics, 136, 147–152, 168–178
Misra, Bal Govind, 130n4
Modifier
  absolute, 183
  deverbal, 8, 13, 184–185, 195n1, 215, 217–220, 222n8, 334, 361n11
  gerundive, 8, 9, 183–199, 321n12
  nominal/adnominal, 183, 188–189, 297
  nonabsolute, 185
  participial, 184–185, 188, 196n4
  relative, 8, 183, 185
Morphologization, 101, 106n25
Morphology
  derivational, 204, 207, 210, 220–221
  level-ordered, 206
Mufwene, Salikoko, 7, 10, 15, 17, 158n25, 178n6, 178n8, 196n4, 196n7, 227, 230, 237, 239–240, 390, 394–395, 408n3, 408n5
Multiple inheritance hierarchy, 308–309

Na, Younghee, 188, 190–191, 194–195, 197n8, 198nn12–13, 198n15
Negation, xiii, 13, 85–86, 111, 113, 122, 131n10, 138, 142, 151, 211, 275, 331–332, 337, 347, 355, 360, 360n2, 378

Index 549

affix, 211
 placement of, 111, 122, 131n10
 prefix, 334
Newmeyer, Frederick J., 8, 157n20, 162, 164–165, 169–171, 177, 178nn7–8, 435
Nichols, Lynn, 12, 283–294, 409n6
Nöldeke, Theodor, 514–515, 524n36
Nominal typology, 368
 implicit arguments, 385n3
 nonquantificational NPs, 374–375
 restricted quantification, 120, 256
 quantificational, 374–375, 377–378
 thematic arguments, 370–372, 382–384
Nonmonolithic grammar, 240
Noun class, 393, 408, 456
NP gap, 3–4, 47–67
Number
 neutral, 15
 semantics of, 368, 376

Obstruent, 3, 27–41
Of-insertion, 243n7
Onomatopoeic morpheme, 213
Opposition, 13, 15–16, 261, 278n2, 329–332, 335, 347, 359, 360, 380–381, 384, 390–391, 394, 404, 408, 413
 square of, 330, 408
 varieties of, 330–331
Optimality Theory, 320, 466
Ordering source, 12, 283–286, 291, 293n3

Parenthetical phrase, 297–298
Partitive relation, 16, 397–400
Performance, 75, 163, 435, 446, 455, 458, 460, 469, 481–482, 494–496, 497n2
Partee, Barbara, 10, 11, 131n8, 241n3, 249–255, 257
Perlmutter, David, 117, 131n8, 329
Phonological reduction, 92, 103–104, 105n7
Pianesi, Fabio, 284–285
Pinker, Steven, 164, 191, 198n14, 204–205
Prayoga, 4, 69–82
Predicate Phrase Deletion/PredP Deletion, 230, 240
Preposition stranding, 192, 194
Presupposition, xiii, 16, 285, 293n2, 411–428
Priming, 339, 460, 482, 491–493, 495–496
 sentence, 495–496
 syntactic, 491–493
Privation, 13–14, 329–331, 337–340, 342, 358, 360, 360n2, 361n6
Productivity, 9–10, 203–222, 340, 358
Property theory, 447–448
Proposition denial, 349, 351–352. *See also* Epitomization
Prototype, 5, 7–8, 14, 149, 161–179, 329, 337–340, 352, 362n13

Pronouns
 general, 47–67
 plain, 442–445, 447–448, 450n3
 reflexive, 47–48, 50, 52–53, 55–57, 60, 62–64, 65n1, 67nn6–7, 174, 438–448, 489–490
Pseudopassive constructions, 73
Public language, 18–19
Purpose clauses, 184–186, 192, 196n3

Race and language. *See* Language and race
Reanalysis, 192
Referential dependencies, 438–442, 444, 448
Regression Hypothesis, 447
Reichenbach, Hans, 11, 13, 133, 255–257, 272–273, 277, 280n20, 300
Reflexive verb, 96
Relative clause, 6, 9, 60–65, 135–158, 189–195, 197n8, 275, 278n3, 465
 nonrestrictive, 6, 135–158
 restrictive, 194
Rendaku, 2, 3, 27–41, 218, 221n1
Representational modularity, 168, 195
Resultative formation, 118
Retrospective, 12–13, 295–324
 adnominal clause, 297, 321n6
 deferential-declarative, 297
 deferential-interrogative, 297
 interrogative, 321n5
 intimate-declarative, 297
 intimate-interrogative, 297
 mood, 12–13, 295–324
 morpheme, 295–297, 303, 307
 plain-declarative, 296–297
 plain-interrogative, 296–297
 polite declarative, 297
Reyle, Uwe, 368–369
Romance languages, 273, 512, 524n29
Root transformation, 135, 154n8
Rosch, Eleanor, 163, 166, 329, 343
Rosen, Carol, 117–118
Ross, John Robert (aka *Haj Ross*), xi–xii, 157n22, 162, 165–167, 171, 178n5, 232
Rothstein, Susan, 226, 242–243n5

Sadock, Jerrold M./Jerry, xii, 128, 136, 147–148, 168–169, 177, 195, 225–226, 466, 476n13
Sag, Ivan A., 139, 308, 309, 318, 320, 323n26, 323n32, 455, 475n2
Sanskrit, 69, 75, 507, 508, 513–514
Sapir, Edward, 334, 335, 360, 505, 508, 520–521, 522n3
Sapir-Whorf hypothesis, 521
Saussure, Ferdinand de, 507, 523n12, 523n18
Sayce, Archibald H., 509
Scope, xii, 65, 66n5, 135, 138–139, 141–142, 151, 243n10, 257, 287, 347, 374–375, 378, 385n7
Searle, John R., 321n7, 323n34, 441

Selkirk, Elisabeth, 185, 188, 196n6
Semitic languages, 507, 508, 514–515
Sentential object, 66n5
Sequential voicing, 2, 27–41
Shibatani, Masayoshi, 40n9
Sievers, Eduard, 507, 511, 513, 522n10, 524n32
Singulative, 394–395, 405, 408n4
Sino-Japanese, 30, 41n17, 221n2
Slavic languages, 84, 510, 514
Sobin, Nicholas, 466, 476n16
Spatial relations, 5, 83–106
Speech act, 4, 12–13, 47–49, 54, 136–137, 141, 255, 268, 295–308, 311–312, 320, 321nn6–7, 323n28
Stalnaker, Robert C., 254, 285, 293n2
Structural facilitation, 487, 491–492, 495
Structure building, 228, 441
Subinterval property, 267–270
Subjectless sentence, 4
Subjunctive, 113–114, 126, 130n3, 284, 320n1
Subordinate clause, 5, 6, 53–56, 62, 65, 66n5, 109–133, 135–158, 170, 174, 263, 265, 284
Sugioka, Yoko, xiii, 9–10, 203–222
Surface combinatoric constraint, 15, 243n7
Syntactic category, 10, 161, 165–169, 170, 172, 173, 228, 367
Swart, Henriëtte de, 370–371, 373, 377–381, 385n5
Szabolcsi, Anna, 377–378, 385n8

Tagalog, 131n13
Tamil, 3–5, 47–67, 83–106, 507, 517
Temporal
  clause, 53–56, 263, 278n3
  ordering, 277, 280n23
  structure, 267, 277–278, 280n23
Tense
  absolute, 265, 279n6
  eventive tense–aspect, 11–12, 265–266, 276
  relative, 11, 265, 279nn–6, 280n20
Thematic domain, 190–191, 194
Thematic Well-formedness Condition, 190–195, 197n8, 198n15
There-construction, 169, 457
Thompson, Sandra A., 8, 139, 147, 162, 166–167, 213, 218, 221n4
Time
  observation, 13, 300–301
  reference, 13, 128, 133n19, 145, 156n15, 253, 256–257, 272, 300
  retrospective, 12–13, 295–324
  of speech/speech time, 12, 262–266, 268–269, 272–275, 279n6
Tivari, Bholanath, 75
Transition theory, 447–448
Traugott, Elizabeth C., 5, 83, 87, 102, 106nn19–20, 170, 360

Unaccusative verb, 110–111, 116–123, 125, 128, 131n10, 131n12
unaccusativity, 6, 109, 115, 116–122, 124, 129, 131n8, 131n10
Unger, J. Marshall, 28, 41n20
Universal Grammar (UG), 18, 434–435, 438, 441–442, 447, 455, 469–470, 494–495
Un-noun, 329–362
Ural-Altaic, 507, 508, 516

Vacya, 4, 69–82
Vendler, Zeno, 12, 269, 278, 279n11
Verbal reflex, 50–52, 59, 64, 67n8
Verbs of motion, 85, 96
Verb, less, 232, 234, 240
Vietnamese, 517n41
VP Deletion/VP-Deletion, 137, 140–142, 154n8, 155n10, 229. *See also* Predicate Phrase Deletion
Voice, 69, 74–76
  active, xii, 73, 492
  passive, xii, 4, 8, 10, 54, 62, 72–73, 76–77, 80–81, 82n3, 120, 166, 225, 226, 231–232, 233–234, 237–240, 244n10, 370, 384, 385n3, 491–493

Wasow, Thomas, 227, 230, 237, 308, 310, 318, 320, 323n32
Webelhuth, Gert, 109
Whitney, William Dwight, 69, 508–509, 511, 516, 518, 520–521, 523n13, 523n16, 524n24
Wilkins, Wendy, 191, 512
Working memory, 436, 441, 443, 445–446, 448–449, 450n6, 488, 490

Yiddish, 148, 515
Yoon, James, 195n1, 196n7
Yuasa, Etsuyo, 6, 135–158, 168, 474

Zimmer, Karl, 332, 334–336, 360, 361n4
Zuni, 15, 391, 396, 400, 409n6